HRM

Recruitment and Selection in Canada

FOURTH EDITION

VICTOR M. CATANO
SAINT MARY'S UNIVERSITY

WILLI H. WIESNER
MCMASTER UNIVERSITY

RICK D. HACKETT
MCMASTER UNIVERSITY

LAURA L. METHOT
SAINT MARY'S UNIVERSITY
METHOT ASSOCIATES

SERIES EDITOR:
MONICA BELCOURT
YORK UNIVERSITY

NELSON / EDUCATION

NELSON

EDUCATION

**Recruitment and Selection in Canada,
Fourth Edition**

by Victor M. Catano, Willi H. Wiesner, Rick D. Hackett,
and Laura L. Methot

**Vice President,
Editorial Director:**
Evelyn Veitch

**Editor-in-Chief,
Higher Education:**
Anne Williams

Acquisitions Editor:
Jackie Wood

Marketing Manager:
Kathaleen McCormick

Developmental Editors:
Jennifer O'Reilly, Tracy Yan

Permissions Coordinator:
Sandra Mark

**Senior Content Production
Manager:**
Imoinda Romain

Production Service:
Newgen North America

Copy Editor:
June Trusty

Proofreader:
Christine Gever

Indexer:
Jay Marchand

Manufacturing Manager:
Joanne McNeil

Design Director:
Ken Phipps

Managing Designer:
Franca Amore

Cover Design:
Wil Bache

Compositor:
Newgen

Printer:
Edwards Brothers

**Library and Archives Canada
Cataloguing in Publication**

Recruitment and selection in
Canada / Victor M. Catano ...
[et al.]. — 4th ed.

Includes bibliographical
references and index.
ISBN 978-0-17-650012-2

1. Employees—Recruiting—
Canada—Textbooks. 2. Employee
selection—Canada—Textbooks.
I. Catano, Victor M. (Victor
Michael), 1944–

HF5549.5.R44R417 2009
658.3'110971   C2008-907698-2

ISBN-13: 978-0-17-650012-2
ISBN-10: 0-17-650012-X

Brief Contents

Detailed Contents

About the Series

The management of human resources has become the most important source of innovation, competitive advantage, and productivity, more so than any other resource. More than ever, human resources management (HRM) professionals need the knowledge and skills to design HRM policies and practices that not only meet legal requirements but also are effective in supporting organizational strategy. Increasingly, these professionals turn to published research and books on best practices for assistance in the development of effective HR strategies. The books in the *Nelson Series in Human Resources Management* are the best source in Canada for reliable, valid, and current knowledge about practices in HRM.

The textbooks in this series include:

- *Managing Performance through Training and Development*
- *Management of Occupational Health and Safety*
- *Recruitment and Selection in Canada*
- *Strategic Compensation in Canada*
- *Strategic Human Resources Planning*
- *An Introduction to the Canadian Labour Market*
- *Research, Measurement, and Evaluation of Human Resources*
- *Industrial Relations in Canada*
- *International Human Resource Management: A Canadian Perspective*

The *Nelson Series in Human Resources Management* represents a significant development in the field of HRM for many reasons. Each book in the series is the first, best-selling text in the functional area. Furthermore, HR professionals in Canada must work with Canadian laws, statistics, policies, and values. This series serves their needs. It is the only opportunity that students and practitioners have to access a complete set of HRM books, standardized in presentation, that enables them to access information quickly across many HRM disciplines. The books are essential sources of information that meet the requirements for the Canadian Council of Human Resources Associations (CCHRA) National Knowledge Exam for the academic portion of the HR certification process. This one-stop resource will prove useful for anyone looking for solutions for the effective management of people.

The publication of this series signals that the field of human resources management has advanced to the stage where theory and applied research guide practice. The books in the series present the best and most current research in the functional areas of HRM. Research is supplemented with examples of the best practices used by Canadian companies that are leaders in HRM. Each text begins with a general model of the discipline and then describes the implementation of effective strategies. Thus, the books serve as an introduction to the functional area for the new student of HR and as a validation source for the more experienced HRM practitioner. Cases, exercises, and endnotes provide opportunities for further discussion and analysis.

As you read and consult the books in this series, I hope you share my excitement in being involved in and knowledgeable about a profession that has such a significant impact on the achievement of organizational goals and on employees' lives.

Monica Belcourt, Ph.D., CHRP
Series Editor
October 2008

About the Authors

Victor M. Catano

Dr. Catano is professor and chairperson of the Psychology Department at Saint Mary's University, Halifax, Nova Scotia. He obtained a B.Sc. in electrical engineering from Drexel University in Philadelphia and went on to complete both a master's degree and a Ph.D. in psychology at Lehigh University, Bethlehem, Pennsylvania. He is a registered psychologist in Nova Scotia and a member of the Human Resources Association of Nova Scotia.

After joining the Saint Mary's faculty following completion of his doctoral degree, Dr. Catano was instrumental in establishing Saint Mary's master's and doctoral programs in industrial–organizational psychology. He has also served as a special lecturer at the Technical University of Nova Scotia and as a Visiting Research Fellow at the Canadian Forces Personnel Applied Research Unit in Toronto; he also served as an Honorary Adjunct Professor in the Graduate Faculty at Dalhousie University.

Dr. Catano has served as president of the Association of Psychologists of Nova Scotia, a member of the Nova Scotia Board of Examiners in Psychology (the body responsible for regulating the profession within Nova Scotia), and president of the Canadian Society for Industrial and Organizational Psychology. He is a past editor of *Canadian Psychology* and a member of the editorial board for *Advances in Organizational Behavior*, and has acted as a reviewer for numerous scholarly journals and granting agencies. He has published over 200 scholarly articles, conference papers, and technical reports. Dr. Catano's current research interests include personnel psychology, the psychology of labour relations, organizational and environmental constraints on productivity, and the impact of psychological environments on the health, safety, and productivity of workers.

He served as the Chair of the Canadian Council of Human Resources Associations' Exams and Capabilities Task Force that helped to establish the new national criteria for the Certified Human Resources Professional (CHRP) designation and now chairs CCHRA's Independent Board of Examiners, the agency responsible for developing and running the examinations and assessments that lead to the CHRP designation.

Dr. Catano has extensive consulting experience in personnel selection and assessment, job analysis, and industrial relations. He has served as an expert witness on personnel selection issues before several administrative tribunals. His clients have included NAV CANADA, the Department of National Defence, the Royal Canadian Mounted Police, Asea Brown Boveri, Nova Scotia Government Employees Union, Canadian Union of Public Employees, and the Nova Scotia Nurses' Union, among others.

In recognition of his contributions to the science and practice of psychology in Canada, Dr. Catano was elected a Fellow by the Canadian Psychological Association and an honorary member by the Canadian Forces

Personnel Selection Officers Association. He was the 2003 recipient of the Canadian Psychological Association's Award for Distinguished Contributions to Education and Training and the Canadian Society for Industrial and Organizational Psychology's Distinguished Scientist Award. In 2008, the Human Resources Association of Nova Scotia awarded him an honorary membership in recognition of his distinguished contributions to human resources in Canada.

Willi H. Wiesner

Dr. Wiesner received an honours B.A. in psychology from Wilfrid Laurier University and an M.A.Sc. and Ph.D. in industrial/organizational psychology from the University of Waterloo. He has taught in the faculty of Commerce at Concordia University in Montreal and is currently associate professor of Human Resources and Management in the DeGroote School of Business at McMaster University. Dr. Wiesner is a member of the Canadian Psychological Association, the American Psychological Association, the Canadian Society for Industrial and Organizational Psychology, the Society for Industrial and Organizational Psychology (U.S.), the Administrative Sciences Association of Canada, and the Academy of Management. He has served as Institute Coordinator and president of the Canadian Society for Industrial and Organizational Psychology, and as chair of the Human Resources and Management Area of the DeGroote School of Business at McMaster University from 1997 until 2008.

Dr. Wiesner has extensive consulting experience in the areas of employee selection, performance appraisal, work team effectiveness, and other human resources activities. His clients have included Accelio Corporation (now part of Adobe Systems Inc.), AIC Corporation, Tires Only, AFG Glass, the McQuaig Institute, Canada Revenue Agency, the Royal Canadian Mounted Police, Halton Regional Police Services, the Department of National Defence, Critical Corporation, Hamilton Health Sciences, St. Joseph's Hospital in Hamilton, Grand River Hospital Corporation in Kitchener, and McMaster University.

Dr. Wiesner has also presented workshops on employee selection, performance appraisal, training and development, and team building through the Executive Development Office of the School of Business and the Centre for Continuing Education at McMaster University. His recent research and publication activities have focused on employment interviewing and selection, group decision making, and work team effectiveness.

Rick D. Hackett

Dr. Hackett is professor and Canada Research Chair of Organizational Behavior and Human Performance at the DeGroote School of Business, McMaster University. He is editor-in-chief of the *Canadian Journal of Administrative Sciences*, Fellow of the Canadian Psychological Association, and past-president of the Canadian Society for Industrial and Organizational Psychology. From 2001 to 2003, Dr. Hackett was Visiting Scholar at the Hong Kong

University of Science and Technology. As president of Hackett & Associates Human Resources Consultants Inc., he advises firms in both the public and private sector on HR assessment and selection.

Laura L. Methot

Dr. Methot is a senior consultant with Continuous Learning Group, Inc. (CLG). She specializes in designing and implementing performance and process management systems that assist client organizations in executing their strategic goals. She has extensive international experience working as a consultant and performance coach to private-sector business and industry, health-care organizations, and government agencies. Dr. Methot's projects have included designing and implementing large-scale leadership and organizational development systems, leading executive coaching and training, and facilitating cross-functional teams in redesigning process and implementing change in global organizations.

Dr. Methot holds a B.A. in psychology from Saint Mary's University in Halifax, Nova Scotia. She also holds an M.A. in industrial/organizational psychology and a Ph.D. in applied behaviour analysis from Western Michigan University. Dr. Methot is an adjunct professor of Industrial/Organizational Psychology at Saint Mary's University, where she teaches graduate courses in training and development.

Dr. Method co-authored *Fundamentals of Behavior Analytic Research* with Alan Poling and Mark LeSage and has presented her research at conferences of the Association for Behavior Analysis, the Atlantic Conference on Ergonomics, the Canadian Psychological Association, and the Canadian Society for Industrial and Organizational Psychology. She is a past member of the executive council of the Association for Behavior Analysis and the Canadian Society for Industrial and Organizational Psychology. Dr. Methot has also served as a reviewer for academic journals and has been invited to speak at various academic and professional meetings.

Preface

Recruitment and Selection in Canada, Fourth Edition, is designed to meet the needs of both students and practitioners working in human resources or personnel psychology. It provides an up-to-date review of the current issues and methodologies that are used in recruiting and selecting employees for Canadian organizations. Over the years, the field of personnel selection and staffing has become more quantitative and subject to both federal and provincial human rights legislation. This book provides an introduction to these more technical areas in an easy-to-read style. Each chapter includes examples, cases, and other materials that illustrate how the practices discussed in the text are carried out in both private- and public-sector organizations. Many of these illustrations are drawn from current events reported in the media and presented in boxes we call *Recruitment and Selection Today.*

Meeting Scientific and Legal Standards

The text provides an introduction to sound procedures in recruitment and selection that meet scientific, professional, and Canadian legal standards. It presents recruitment and selection as essential components of strategic human resources planning and emphasizes their role in enhancing productivity. Starting with a presentation of the key elements in a recruitment and selection system, the text emphasizes the need for a solid scientific and legal foundation on which to build that system. The text introduces job analyses and competency modelling as the keys to developing a recruitment and selection system and to understanding the relationship between improved selection systems and increased organizational productivity. Also included in this book are contemporary developments related to competencies, interviewing, cognitive ability testing, personality testing, and drug and honesty testing. Recognizing the constraints under which organizations operate, the text presents recruitment and selection within the context of a global market and competition.

Use of the Internet

One of the most remarkable developments since publication of the first edition of this book has been the rise of the Internet as a resource tool. We have included in this fourth edition even more references to relevant websites and interactive material throughout the text and as part of the end-of-chapter exercises and cases. Web icons appear in the margin throughout each chapter to indicate the provision of relevant website URLs in the Web Links section near the end of the chapter.

Many of the exercises, illustrations, and cases now require students to obtain additional information from the Web through the links we provide; in particular, each chapter includes at least one Web-based exercise. While we have tested every link during the editorial process, the URL for a link may have changed. We suggest a quick Google search to track down the new location.

A Canadian Reference on Recruitment and Selection

This fourth edition of *Recruitment and Selection in Canada* offers several advantages to both students and practitioners. First, it provides an up-to-date introduction to the current developments in recruiting and selecting employees within a Canadian context. The approach taken with this text has been to incorporate the Canadian material organically into the development of the text rather than "Canadianizing" a popular American text. This approach has allowed us to focus in greater detail on issues of concern to Canadian organizations and to Canadian human resources practitioners. Canadian examples and websites and links to both public and private organizations are featured wherever possible.

We have attempted to provide as complete coverage as possible of current issues in recruitment and selection by integrating the role of recruitment and selection in a context of strategic human resources planning. At all stages of the recruitment and selection process, the text emphasizes the necessity of satisfying both professional and legal requirements and offers guidelines on how this can be accomplished through a feature called *Recruitment and Selection Notebook*. Each chapter includes several of these authoritative boxes.

Increasingly, both students and practitioners must understand the scientific, technical, and legal aspects that form the basis of current recruitment and selection practices. Often, texts on recruitment and selection make little attempt to explain the statistical and technical underpinnings of these topics, or do so in a way that those new to the material cannot comprehend. Unlike these other texts, we have provided a complete and thorough introduction to this essential material in a readable, nontechnical style that minimizes scientific jargon and emphasizes understanding of the basic concepts in a context of application. To assist understanding, we have also included learning objectives at the start of each chapter, definitions of important concepts throughout each chapter, and both exercises and case material at the end of each chapter to illustrate important principles and concepts.

This text is designed for one-semester courses in human resources management, staffing, personnel psychology, and personnel selection. It is also ideal for short courses that form part of diploma, certificate, or professional upgrading programs. The previous three editions of *Recruitment and Selection in Canada* were adopted for courses taught as part of degree programs in colleges and universities; as well, they were used as a standard reference for graduate courses and still can be found on the bookshelves of many HR professionals.

Addressing the Needs of Students and Teachers

One of the strengths of this text is the systematic integration of the different aspects of recruitment and selection with current legal and technical practices. However, the needs of students and instructors may differ across the settings in which this text may be used. Some students may already have had a substantial introduction to measurement issues in other courses that form part of their program. In those cases, parts of Chapter 2 can be omitted. Later chapters in the text, however, do refer to material contained in Chapter 2 or to concepts introduced in it, but the student can easily read the relevant sections of this chapter in conjunction with the later reference. We have not placed Chapter 2 in an appendix because it is our strong view that any human resources practitioner must be familiar with the content of this chapter in order to practice recruitment and selection in a professionally acceptable manner.

Similarly, Chapter 5 includes a discussion of issues related to the measurement of performance. It is our firm belief that students must be conversant with all aspects of the recruitment and selection system, and measurement of performance is essential to evaluating the effectiveness of any selection system. Often the problem with poor selection systems is not the selection instruments used, but how performance is measured. Performance is the bottom line and we have integrated that into the text. Again, if performance measurement and evaluation have been covered elsewhere in a student's program, Chapter 5 can serve as a brief, useful review.

In developing both Chapters 2 and 5, we have tried to strike a balance by presenting only the information that any human resources practitioner is likely to need to know. A guiding rule has been, "Is this information essential for a human resources practitioner to meet both legal and professional standards in the conduct of their practice?" We feel that we have met this standard.

Changes in This Fourth Edition

What's changed in this new edition? We have retained the inclusion of a vignette at the start of each chapter, as introduced in the third edition. Feedback suggests that students have found these to be very relevant ways of becoming engaged with the chapter's content. We have drawn these, as far as possible, from real-life situations and have made some changes in vignettes from the third edition. The significant changes that we made to chapter order and content in the third edition have been retained, but all of the chapters have been updated with current thinking based on the most recent theorizing and research. We have also retained all of the features from the third edition that enhance learning opportunities and make the text more interactive, including the use of websites, expanded exercises, and case material. One notable feature is the use of colour to highlight tables and figures.

A feature we included in the third edition was the addition of relevant required professional capabilities (RPCs) that form the basis of the two National Exams that an applicant must pass before receiving the Certified Human Resources Professional (CHRP) designation. Recently, the Canadian Council of Human Resources Associations (CCHRA) updated the RPCs to reflect the current state of the HR profession. The revised set of 183 RPCs was adopted by the CCHRA in the fall of 2007. We have inserted RPC icons in the margin of the book to designate content that is related to these RPCs and, near the end of each chapter, the full RPC descriptions are provided. All of the RPCs can be viewed on the CCHRA website at http://www.cchra.ca.

A word needs to be said about how we have numbered the RPCs throughout the text. On the CCHRA website, the RPCs are grouped by functional area and are numbered sequentially from 1 through 183. The material in this text cuts across several functional areas. We felt it would be confusing to have higher-numbered RPCs appear before those lower in the sequence; therefore, we have retained the numbering system we used in the third edition. The first time we refer to an RPC, we will designate it by the chapter number and the order in which it appears in the chapter. For example, RPC 8.3 designates the third RPC presented in Chapter 8. The RPCs are then listed at the end of the chapter in the order in which they were referenced in the text. We hope that this linkage of our content to the RPCs will help students and practitioners in preparing for the CHRP assessments.

Acknowledgments

The production of any book is a collaborative effort. Many people, other than the authors whose names appear on the cover, play an important role. We would like to acknowledge their assistance and to thank them for their valuable contributions to this process. We have tried to present in this book the latest scientific foundation for human resources management. We could not have done that without the research compiled by our academic colleagues throughout North America and the experience of human resources practitioners in adapting that research to the workplace. This book would not exist if it were not for their work.

We are also indebted to our past and present students who have challenged our ideas and made us be clear in the exposition of our arguments. In particular, we owe a debt to our students at Saint Mary's and McMaster universities; their feedback on earlier editions of this text were invaluable. Over the years, the book has benefited immensely from the feedback of reviewers and users at various colleges and universities across Canada. We are grateful for their invaluable comments, which have helped to make this a better text. We hope that the fourth edition continues the improvement of the text.

Monica Belcourt, the editor for the series, deserves special praise. She was the glue that held everything together and kept the project on track. It is truly the case that without her efforts, this book would not have materialized. We must also acknowledge the patience and professionalism of the team at Nelson: Jackie Wood, Tracy Yan, Kathaleen McCormick, and Imoinda Romain. We would be remiss if we did not also acknowledge the contributions of June Trusty, who copyedited the manuscript, and Jay Harward, who supervised its production.

Finally, we are most grateful to our families and friends who provided us with support and understanding throughout the long nights. They inspired us to think and write clearly.

Victor M. Catano
Saint Mary's University

Willi H. Wiesner
McMaster University

Rick D. Hackett
McMaster University

Laura L. Methot
Methot Associates
Applied Performance Solutions

1

An Introduction to Recruitment and Selection

THE COMPUTER ATE MY RÉSUMÉ

The Public Service Commission received online applications for a position of senior analytical advisor, Aboriginal Statistics, Statistics Canada. Due to a computer error in the selection process, only four and one-half pages of one applicant's nine-page résumé were considered in the appointment process. The employer's computer system was the cause of the error and did not provide any warning to the applicant. The selection board was not aware that the résumé was incomplete. As a result, the board held that his experience did not meet the minimum qualifications and awarded the position to another candidate.

When the applicant discovered after the hiring decision had been made that his résumé had been truncated, he appealed the outcome to the Public Service Appeal Board. That appeal was denied, as the candidate had been given an opportunity to add information after he had been screened out. The applicant appealed this decision to the Federal Court, where Mr. Justice Michael Kelen ruled:

> "The failure to assess the applicant based on his actual résumé, rather than the incomplete résumé transmitted due to the computer error, constitutes a material defect in the appointment process. Upon discovery of the error, the selection board should have re-opened the competition and considered the applicant's full résumé.... Moreover, there was a reasonable legitimate expectation by the applicant that the selection board would read his résumé and notice that it was cut-off and incomplete. At a minimum, the selection board should have questioned the applicant as to why the résumé ended in mid-sentence, and omitted important basic information such as the applicant's education. The onus was on the selection board to notice the obvious, and bring it to the applicant's attention. Instead, the selection board invited the applicant to submit further information which was declined because the applicant assumed that the selection board already had all of the relevant information."

Justice Kelen upheld the candidate's appeal and directed that a new selection board be established to assess the merits of all of the candidates, including the complete résumé of the applicant.

Source: *Stewart v. Canada (Attorney General)*, 2002 FCT 423.

Why Recruitment and Selection Matter

Our purpose in writing this book is to lay out the "best practices" in finding and hiring people who will contribute to the overall success of an organization. Best practices are valid, reliable, and legally defensible. They must comply with relevant legislation. In the case described above, the Public Service Act specifies how employees are selected.

By definition, best practices are supported by empirical evidence that has been accumulated through accepted scientific procedures. Best practices do not involve "hunches," "guesses," or unproven practices. Best practices involve the ethical treatment of job applicants throughout the recruitment and hiring process. Best practices result from human resources professionals following the accepted standards and principles of professional associations. "The Computer Ate My Résumé" illustrates the important role that proper recruitment and selection practices may play in Canadian organizations. The inability to defend recruitment and selection practices before a judicial tribunal may have serious financial consequences for an organization.

Best practices do not have to be perfect practices. As we will see in later chapters, there are no selection procedures that are free from error and always lead to correct decisions. Employers must show that their procedures are fair and do not discriminate against protected groups covered by various laws. Recruitment and selection have moved far beyond the time when a manager could look over a few résumés, talk to one or two applicants (who were mostly friends of current employees), and make a hiring decision. If people are an organization's most important asset, then those responsible for recruiting and selecting personnel must be capable of finding the best person for each position in the organization. Using best practices in recruitment and selection adds value to an organization and contributes to the success—including positive financial outcomes—of a company.

Human resources is a very broad field. Figure 1.1 presents a simplified model of some of the major HR functions within an organization. By no means is the model complete; its purpose is to emphasize that recruitment and selection are but one component of the HR system. That component, however, is a very important one that helps an organization meet its goals and objectives by producing competent, committed, and effective personnel. We are going to examine only the recruitment and selection components of the human resources field (the other books in this series will introduce you to other human resources topics). Recruitment and selection are the means that organizations use, for better or for worse, to find and choose employees. Our intent in this book is to present those practices that will lead to the staffing of organizations with the best-qualified candidates.

Recruitment is the generation of an applicant pool for a position or job in order to provide the required number of candidates for a subsequent selection or promotion program. Recruitment is done to achieve management goals and objectives for the organization and must also meet current legal requirements (human rights, employment equity, labour law, and other legislation).

R P C 1.1

Recruitment

The generation of an applicant pool for a position or job in order to provide the required number of candidates for a subsequent selection or promotion program.

FIGURE 1.1

Example of a Human Resources System

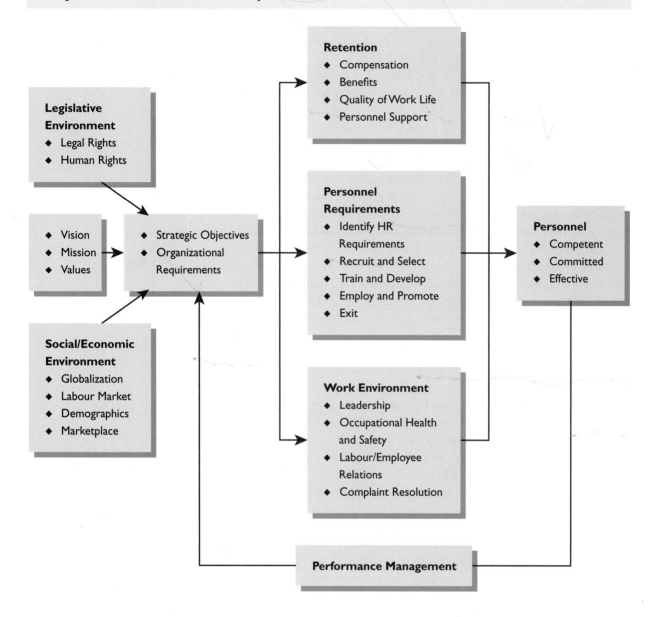

Selection

Selection
The choice of job candidates from a previously generated applicant pool in a way that will meet management goals and objectives as well as current legal requirements.

Selection is the choice of job candidates from a previously generated applicant pool in a way that will meet management goals and objectives as well as current legal requirements. Selection can involve any of the following functions: hiring at the entry level from applicants external to the organization, promotion or lateral transfer of people within the organization, and movement of current employees into training and development programs.

Effective recruitment and selection practices can mean the difference between an organization's success or failure. Differences in skills among job candidates translate into performance differences on the job that have economic consequences for an organization. Hiring people with the right skills or the highest levels of those skills leads to positive economic outcomes for the organization. Hiring a person with the wrong set of skills can lead to disaster for both the person and the organization. Effective recruitment and selection practices identify job applicants with the appropriate level of knowledge, skills, abilities, and other requirements needed for successful performance in a job or an organization.

Empirical studies demonstrate that organizations using effective recruitment and selection practices gain a competitive advantage in the marketplace. Best practices in recruitment and selection:

- Reduce employee turnover and increase productivity.[1] A one-standard-deviation increase in the use of sophisticated HR practices decreased turnover by 7 percent and increased sales by $27 000 per employee per year.[2]
- Are responsible for up to 15 percent of a firm's relative profit.[3]
- Correlate with an organization's long-term profitability and productivity ratios.[4]
- Help to establish employee trust.[5]
- Improve the knowledge, skills, and abilities of an organization's current and future employees, increase their motivation, and help to retain high-quality employees while encouraging poor performers to leave.[6]

Most importantly, a recently completed two-year study by The Work Foundation and the Institute for Employment Studies, both in England, established that businesses with good HR practices enjoyed higher profit margins and productivity than those without. The study concluded that if an organization increased its investment in HR by just 10 percent, it would generate gross profits of £1500 per employee.[7] In addition, progressive HR practices lead to greater organizational commitment on the part of employees and motivate them to exhibit proper role behaviour, resulting in lower compensation costs, higher quality, and greater productivity; as well, good HR practices reduce dysfunctional behaviours and lead to lower operating costs and higher profitability.[8]

Figure 1.1 presents two external factors that affect the HR system—legislative requirements and the social/economic environment. (We will take a comprehensive look at legal and human rights issues in Chapter 3.) Social/economic factors include, among others, global competition, rapid advances in information technology, changing work force demographics, a unionized work environment, the economic context, and an organization's type, size, and position in the marketplace. All of these social/economic factors have an impact on recruitment and selection procedures. Belcourt and McBey[9] present a detailed discussion of these topics in the context of strategic human resources planning. We will examine the relationship of many of these issues to recruitment and selection practices in later chapters.

To remain competitive, organizations must have in place human resource strategies for recruiting, identifying, and selecting employees who will contribute to the overall effectiveness of the organization. With respect to recruitment and selection, the old ways of hiring on the basis of a résumé and a brief interview, or on whom you know, do not work in the new economy. Those old practices may also lead an employer astray of new legal requirements, as well as to an underperforming organization.

The socioeconomic changes taking place in today's workplace have an impact on human resources recruitment and selection. Today, more than ever before, effective recruitment and selection matter. Figure 1.1 illustrates that recruitment and selection do not take place in isolation. They are influenced not only by the events occurring in broader society that affect the organization as a whole, but also by the somewhat narrower context of the organization itself. Recruitment and selection play an important role in the human resources management function. Effective human resources management contributes to organizational survival, success, and renewal.[10]

How do employers ensure that the people they hire will have the knowledge, skills, and abilities that are needed to perform the jobs for which they are being hired? How do employers decide that one candidate has "more" of the required abilities than another? More fundamentally, how do employers know that the knowledge, skills, and abilities that they are seeking in new hires are actually needed for a specific job? How do employers ensure that their hiring policies and procedures will treat candidates from different gender and ethnic groups fairly, as part of the recruitment and selection process? How do employers accommodate people with disabilities in both recruitment and selection? These are just a few of the questions that must be addressed by any HR manager or practitioner in setting up a recruitment and selection system. These are some of the questions we will seek to answer throughout this book.

A Systems View of HR

Two basic principles underlie the model presented in Figure 1.1:

1. **Principle 1:** Human resources management must carefully coordinate its activities with the other organizational units and people if the larger system is to function properly.
2. **Principle 2:** Human resources managers must think in systems terms and have the welfare of the whole organization in mind.

If HR managers fail to recognize the contributions of the others in the organization or if they fail to coordinate their efforts with other system components, senior management may begin to question the added value that human resources brings to the firm. Human resources must be in full touch with the needs of the larger organization and play a strategic role in the organization. As a staff unit, the role of human resources is to support line units pursuing the central mission of the organization. HR professionals must have an understanding and appreciation of their interdependencies with, and reliance on, other stakeholders throughout the organization. Recruitment and selection must be carried out in the context of the system, not simply as an isolated function divorced from other aspects of the organization.

Recruitment and selection set the stage for other human resources interventions. If recruitment and selection are done properly, the subsequent movement of the worker through the organizational system is made easier and the individual makes a long-term, positive contribution to organizational survival and success. When this happens, human resources management makes a positive contribution to the organizational system as a whole. Conversely, if the worker enters the organization on a flat trajectory because of poor recruitment and selection, then the entire system, including human resources, is adversely affected. The human resources management function becomes less of an organizational asset. In today's competitive, ever-changing, and unforgiving business environment, human resources must be seen as an effective change agent or else face a grim (but deserved) fate at the hands of results-oriented senior managers.

Recruitment and Selection and the HR Profession

We have emphasized the need for HR staff to be aware of both the external and the internal influences that affect the working environment in which organizations operate. We have also argued that HR staff must not become isolated within the organization. There is another aspect to isolation: HR staff are professionals who must keep abreast of developments in their field through continuous learning. HR staff are responsible for knowing the latest legal and scientific information with respect to recruitment and selection. They are responsible for implementing policies and procedures that are in accordance with accepted professional standards.

Recruitment and selection activities within human resources management are frequently carried out by in-house human resources staff, sometimes assisted by consultants from management consulting firms. These in-house staff and consultants come to human resources management from various educational backgrounds, which are augmented by practical experience in managing human resources (see Recruitment and Selection Today 1.1).

Many practitioners and consultants involved in human resources management hold membership in one or more professional associations and may be certified or registered with an association or professional licensing body in their area of specialization. Recruitment and Selection Today 1.2 gives some basic information on associations with an interest in recruitment and selection practices in Canada. These associations have professional involvement well beyond recruitment and selection. With membership in these associations come certain rights and obligations, including adherence to ethical codes or standards.

Only recently has the HR field gained recognition as an independent profession. Regardless of the educational and experiential routes taken into the HR profession, today there is an increasing emphasis on HR professionals holding the Certified Human Resources Professional (CHRP) designation.

Recruitment and Selection Today 1.1

Several Career Paths into Recruitment and Selection

Ms. L. became interested in human resources management while taking a business program at a community college. After obtaining her college degree, she took eight courses in order to earn a certificate in Human Resources Management. Since then, Ms. L. has worked as a human resources specialist in a large manufacturing plant, where she has run an assessment centre used by her employer to hire new workers. Ms. L. hopes to eventually move into a senior human resources management position with her present employer or with a similar company in the manufacturing sector.

Mr. R. moved into the field after completing his degree in sociology at university. He started work in the human resources department of an aircraft parts manufacturer, and over the following year, earned a Human Resources Certificate. Following completion of his human resources program, he accepted a more senior HR position with a new employer. Much of his time is spent in recruitment and selection activities, especially in monitoring the results of an employment equity program put in place by his current employer.

Ms. S. obtained a bachelor's degree in psychology and became interested in personnel psychology. She went on to complete a two-year graduate program in industrial and organizational psychology. Since receiving her master's degree, Ms. S. has worked in the human resources department of a major urban hospital, where her primary duties are testing and interviewing job applicants for various hospital positions. Her other duties focus on compensation and benefits.

Ms. M. also received a master's degree in industrial and organizational psychology, but continued her studies to obtain a Ph.D. She works for an internationally based consulting firm, where she designs and implements large-scale recruitment and selection systems for banks, insurance companies, and other financial institutions. She is now a partner with the consulting firm and takes regular overseas assignments to assist clients in Europe and Asia with installation and maintenance of their selection systems.

Recruitment and Selection Today 1.2

Links to Professional Associations Involved in Recruitment and Selection

Canadian Council of Human Resources Associations (CCHRA) (http://www.cchra.ca)

The CCHRA is a collaborative effort of nine provincial and specialist human resources associations. Its website provides links to each member organization. The mission of the CCHRA includes establishing national core standards for the human resources profession and being the recognized resource on equivalency for human resources qualifications across Canada.

Membership Qualifications

Practitioners and students join provincial associations, not the CCHRA. Membership requirements vary and can be found on each provincial association's website. Generally, provincial associations require completion of education and training as described under their professional certification requirements; student memberships are normally available for those taking approved courses in a postsecondary or degree program.

Professional Certification Offered

The Certified Human Resources Professional (CHRP) designation recognizes achievement within the human resources field and the holder's distinguished professionalism (see Recruitment and Selection Notebook 1.1 on page 10). To receive this designation, practitioners may have to complete accredited courses, have had supervised professional experience in HR, or other requirements as specified by their provincial human resources association (e.g., Human Resources Association of Nova Scotia: HRANS).

CCHRA National Code of Ethics: http://www.cchra .ca/Web/ethics/content.aspx?f=29756

Association of Canadian Search, Employment and Staffing Services (ACSESS) (http://www.acsess.org)

ACSESS resulted from the merger of the Association of Professional Placement Agencies & Consultants and the Employment & Staffing Services Association of Canada. Its mission is:

> providing services to, and communicating with, members of the employment, recruitment and staffing services industry; assuming a leadership role in industry licensing and regulation; coordinating educational programs and conferences; assisting in the development of required standards of professional performance; promoting best business practices, and adherence to both the spirit and letter of all applicable employment legislation and regulations; and developing pertinent statistics for the purpose of identifying economic and socioeconomic trends.

Membership Qualifications

ACSESS does not accept membership from individuals. Corporate membership in the association is open to any independent organization in Canada engaged in the business of providing staffing services to its customers.

Professional Certification Offered

ACSESS provides and administers the Certified Personnel Consultant (CPC) Program. Candidates who meet core requirements (which include postsecondary education, a specified length of service in the industry, compliance with the ACSESS Code of Ethics & Standards, and testing requirements) may use the designation CPC.

ACSESS Code of Ethics & Standards: http://www .acsess.org/ABOUT/ethics.asp

Canadian Psychological Association (including the Canadian Society for Industrial and Organizational Psychology) (http://www.cpa.ca)

The CPA is a national organization that represents all aspects of psychology, including industrial and organizational psychology and psychological testing and assessment. Psychologists, particularly practitioners, may also be members of provincial psychological associations. The CPA website contains links to provincial associations, provincial regulatory bodies, and psychology programs at Canadian universities.

The Canadian Society of Industrial and Organizational Psychology (CSIOP) is composed of CPA members and other professionals with a particular interest in personnel psychology and organizational behaviour. More information on CSIOP can be found at http://psychology .uwo.ca/csiop.

Membership Qualifications

Master's or Ph.D. degree in psychology.

Professional Certification Offered

Neither CPA nor CSIOP offers professional designations. Psychology is regulated at the provincial level through legislation. In order to use the designation "psychologist," an individual must be registered with a provincial regulatory body after meeting its educational, supervised practice, and other requirements.

CPA Canadian Code of Ethics for Psychologists: http://www.cpa.ca/cpasite/userfiles/Documents/Canad ian%20Code%20of%20Ethics%20for%20Psycho.pdf

Recruitment and Selection Notebook 1.1 gives an overview of the requirements for the new, national CHRP designation.

Maintaining memberships in professional associations keeps the HR professional from becoming isolated and provides assistance when the practitioner encounters ethical difficulties. Professional associations have

The CHRP Edge

There are six characteristics that define a profession:

1. a common body of knowledge;
2. agreed performance standards;
3. a representative professional organization;
4. external perception as a profession;
5. a code of ethics; and
6. agreed certification procedure.

All provincial HR associations have endorsed the CCHRA's national standards for granting the Certified Human Resources Professional (CHRP) designation. Applicants for the CHRP first have to join their provincial HR association and then pass a knowledge examination of eight major content areas in HR, including recruitment and selection. After gaining experience in the profession, CHRP candidates (a designation bestowed on those who pass the first examination) are required to pass a second examination developed from critical incidents encountered by practitioners. The candidates have to determine the most professional way of behaving in the given situations.

The "RPC" icons scattered through this book designate content that is related to the required professional capabilities (RPCs) that HR professionals are expected to perform; these form the basis of the two exams that an applicant must pass before receiving the CHRP designation. The RPCs presented in this fourth edition differ from those given in the third edition, reflecting an ongoing effort to refresh and update the RPCs as the field of HR evolves. The current RPCs were adopted and approved by the CCHRA board of directors in 2007.

Once granted the CHRP designation, HR professionals are required to keep abreast of current developments in their field through a recertification process based on continuous learning. More information on the CHRP designation process can be obtained from either your local HR association or from the national CCHRA website (http://www.cchra.ca).

Why bother going to this trouble to get a CHRP designation? A CHRP identifies you as possessing the required knowledge and skills and as someone who will behave ethically. A survey of employers by the Human Resources Professionals Association of Ontario shows that CHRPs have an edge in:

- getting jobs;
- keeping jobs;
- financial compensation; and
- stakeholders' perceptions of their achievement.

Increasingly, employers are requiring the CHRP for employment of HR professionals.

Source: M. Belcourt and A. Templar. 2002. "The CHRP Edge." *HR Professional* (April/May): 30–33, 36–39. Reprinted with permission.

developed well-thought-out codes of conduct and behaviour that are designed to protect both the HR professionals and their clients. These codes help the professional to act in a manner that will be accepted by others in the profession. Whenever possible, we will use these codes to guide our discussion on recruitment and selection practices, as should any HR professional.

Ethics

The determination of right and wrong; the standards of appropriate conduct or behaviour for members of a profession: what those members may or may not do.

An Introduction to Ethical Issues

Ethics are the means by which we distinguish what is right from what is wrong, what is moral from what is immoral, what may be done from what may not be done. Of course, the laws of our country also tell us what is or is not permissible by imposing penalties, such as fines or imprisonment,

Looking for Common Ground: Ethical Codes

The professional associations described in Recruitment and Selection Today 1.2 have ethical codes that apply to their members. In all of these codes, members are required to obey the laws of the country, avoid conflicts of interest, and remain current in their fields of expertise. In addition, these ethics codes outline other obligations that their members have to clients, management, and workers, as well as to the larger society. One of the principles in the National Code of Ethics of the Canadian Council of Human Resources Associations, which is binding on all holders of the CHRP designation, states that CHRPs shall "commit to the values of respect for human dignity and human rights, and promote human development in the workplace, within the profession and society as a whole."

The ACSESS Code of Ethics & Standards describes responsibilities that their members have to the public, the profession, other members, and the client. The code states, "We will ensure that our clients, candidates and employees are aware of our duty to abide by this Code of Ethics and will undertake to bring any potential infringements before the appropriate Association body." Finally, the CPA's Canadian Code of Ethics for Psychologists presents the following four ethical principles, which provide a guide for individual ethical decision making: respect for the dignity of persons, responsible caring, integrity in relationships, and responsibility to society.

All of these ethical codes place constraints on what their members may and may not do when practising human resources management, including recruitment and selection. However, ethical decision making is not always clear-cut; often decisions must be made in the grey areas of ethics where reasonable people differ in what they consider to be right and wrong. To complicate matters even more, an action that is considered ethical under one code might be deemed unethical under another. These inconsistencies can and do occur because the CCHRA, ACSESS, and CPA ethical codes differ in content, scope, and emphasis. The bottom line to this discussion is that ethics is a complex matter and has the potential to be the Achilles' heel of many a promising human resources career. Professionals practising recruitment and selection should read carefully the ethical codes that apply to them and their work, and then discuss the codes with colleagues.

The website URL for each association's code of ethics is listed in Recruitment and Selection Today 1.2 on pages 8 and 9.

on violators. Ethics is a difficult subject because it deals with the large grey area between those behaviours that society punishes as illegal and those that everyone readily agrees are noble and upright. A careful consideration of ethics is important because human resources management requires the balancing of the rights and interests of management with those of workers, as well as the rights and interests of the human resources professional with those of the larger society (see Recruitment and Selection Notebook 1.2).

 1.4

Three examples of ethical dilemmas in recruitment and selection will help to illustrate why ethics are so important and why a professional may need assistance in deciding how to behave. In the first ethical dilemma, put yourself in the position of a management consultant who is asked by a large employer to design and implement a system to select workers for a manufacturing plant. The plant is unionized, and there is a history of poor union-management relations. Management informs you that it intends to break the union and, as a part of this effort, you are to come up with a selection system that will screen out all new job applicants having pro-union attitudes. The

RPC 1.5

idea is to skew the work force toward management so that the union can be broken in a future decertification vote. What's more, you are to keep the purpose of the selection system a secret and are asked by management to sign a contract in which you promise not to reveal its intentions to the union, the labour board, or any other outsiders. Where do your loyalties lie? Whose interests should you serve? Is it wrong for you, as the management consultant, to accept a fee to do what management is asking?

For the second ethical dilemma, imagine that you are a human resources manager who is considering the use of a selection system. You know that it will do a good job at selecting the best workers, but it also screens out members of visible minorities at a rate much greater than that for the white majority. Should you use this system or try to find another that does not screen out so many members of visible-minority groups? What if the new system does not do as good a job at selecting the best workers? Should you favour societal goals of increasing visible-minority representation in the work force or the interests of your company?

For the third ethical dilemma, you have been directed by your manager to find a way to reduce employee theft. You believe that this can be accomplished by screening out people who fail a commercially available "honesty" test. You purchase the test and administer it to all current employees and new applicants and reject or dismiss those who fail the test. Should you be concerned that the test is screening out honest people? Should you be concerned about the reliability and validity of the test and whether it is appropriate to use in your situation? Should you be concerned about wrongful dismissal lawsuits on the part of employees, or human rights actions on the part of applicants? Can you defend your actions?

These ethical dilemmas raise difficult questions that cut to the very core of ethics. But such questions are unavoidable because ethics are central to any group representing itself as a professional association. Fortunately, professional human resources associations in Canada have written codes and standards to provide guidance on ethical matters to their members. Violations of these codes and standards result in professional censure, embarrassment, and, in the most serious cases, removal from the profession. Membership in the profession is based on adherence to its ethics and professional standards. Membership in the professional association is a public guarantee that the member operates in accordance with accepted principles. Naturally, these codes should factor heavily into the recruitment and selection work done by human resources professionals and described in this book.

Human Resources and the Internet

One of the most significant developments in recent years has been the growth of the Internet, which has made available to students and practitioners a vast array of resources and information related to every aspect of recruitment and selection. It is impossible to list every HR resource that is available on the Internet. Recruitment and Selection Notebook 1.3 lists some websites that we feel are very relevant to recruitment and selection. We have also listed throughout each chapter Web-related resources that provide more specific

Useful HR Web Sites

Human Resources–Related Organizations

Academy of Management	http://www.aomonline.org
Administrative Sciences Association of Canada	http://www.asac.ca
American Psychological Association	http://www.apa.org
BC Human Resources Management Association	http://www.bchrma.org
Canadian Psychological Association	http://www.cpa.ca
Canadian Society for Industrial and Organizational Psychology	http://psychology.uwo.ca/csiop
Council of Canadian Human Resources Associations	http://www.cchra.ca
Human Resources Association of New Brunswick	http://www.hranb.org
Human Resources Association of Nova Scotia	http://www.hrans.org
Human Resources and Social Development Canada	http://www.hrsdc.gc.ca
Human Resources Institute of Alberta	http://www.hria.ca
Human Resources Management Association of Manitoba	http://www.hrmam.org
Human Resources Professionals Association (Ontario +)	http://www.hrpa.ca
International Personnel Management Association Assessment Council	http://www.ipmaac.org
International Public Management Association for Human Resources	http://www.ipma-hr.org
Ordre des conseillers en ressources humaines et en relations industrielles agréés du Québec	http://www.rhri.org
Saskatchewan Association of Human Resource Professionals	http://www.sahrp.ca
Society for Human Resource Management	http://www.shrm.org
Society for Industrial and Organizational Psychology	http://www.siop.org

Human Resources Information Sources

Canadian Business Magazine	http://www.canadianbusiness.com
Canadian HR Reporter	http://www.hrreporter.com
Globe and Mail Report on Business	http://www.reportonbusiness.com
HR Focus	http://www.hrfocus.co.za
HR-Guide.com	http://www.hr-guide.com
HR Magazine	http://www.shrm.org/hrmagazine
HRN Management Group	http://www.hronline.com
Occupational Outlook Quarterly Online	http://www.bls.gov/opub/ooq/ooqhome.htm
People Management	http://www.peoplemanagement.co.uk
Statistics Canada	http://www.statcan.ca
Workforce Management	http://www.workforce.com

information on topics being discussed in the chapter. And, in Chapter 6, we provide extensive information on Internet-based recruitment and selection. The URLs provided were correct when this edition was printed, but URLs often change. If a URL produces an error message, use the name of the association for an Internet search.

A Preview of the Rest of This Book

The remaining chapters of this book present a detailed treatment of the science and practice of recruitment and selection in Canada. Chapter 2 provides a conceptual platform for a later discussion of the techniques and methods of recruitment and selection in Canada, presenting an overview of the basic recruitment and selection model. It also presents an introduction to basic psychometric measurement, which is at the heart of assessing individual differences among job candidates. This chapter is crucial: Human resources management, if it is to meet necessary legal requirements, must adhere to policies and practices that are supported by empirical evidence. A basic understanding of issues such as reliability and validity are necessary for any informed discussion of recruitment and selection.

In Chapter 3, we look at the legal and legislative context for Canadian recruitment and selection practices, which have been seriously affected by human rights and employment equity over the past 30 years. This chapter discusses important implications of these trends for the present and future practice of recruitment and selection.

Chapter 4 discusses job analysis and competency management frameworks, which are the means by which job and person variables are identified for the purpose of recruitment and selection. In fact, job and competency analyses provide the essential information for all of the recruitment and selection activities described in Chapters 5 through 10 of this book. Taken together, then, the material in Chapters 2, 3, and 4 provides a solid foundation of legal and scientific principles, as well as detailed job information, on which to build effective recruitment and selection systems.

Chapters 5 through 10 discuss how recruitment and selection are done. Chapter 5 deals with the job performance end of the recruitment and selection function, showing how the performance of individual workers can be measured as a criterion against which to evaluate the success of recruitment and selection efforts. We also present several methods that can be used to measure job performance.

Chapter 6 discusses recruitment strategies that can be used to attract a qualified applicant pool in preparation for selection; it includes information on how recent developments and the Internet are transforming recruiting. Chapters 7 and 8 examine different selection methods that can be used in screening the applicant pool to find the most qualified workers, including work samples, assessment centres, and psychological tests. Chapter 8 includes an expanded section on the use of cognitive ability and personality tests in selection, as well as recent topics such as emotional intelligence and integrity testing.

Chapter 9 discusses the employment interview, with an emphasis on structured interviews as highly effective selection tools. Chapter 10 concludes the text with a review of the strategies that are used to combine information from different selection methods as part of making selection decisions. It also discusses utility analysis as a means of evaluating the effectiveness of selection systems.

Summary

Effective recruitment and selection are important because they contribute to organizational productivity and worker growth. Recruitment and selection practices, which have found a place in organization practices for thousands of years, play an essential role in contemporary organizations. Effective human resource management, including recruitment and selection, must be carried out within the context of an organizational system, as well as that of the external environment. In both cases, the HR professional must not become isolated. In recognition of this, professional associations and groups exist to help HR professionals and their clients through ethical codes and standards of practice. Codes of ethics are important to HR as it continues to develop as a profession. This chapter also recognizes the increasing use of the Internet by HR professionals and provides Internet addresses for HR organizations and resources.

Key Terms

ethics, p. 10
recruitment, p. 3
selection, p. 4

Web Links

For more information on *Stewart v. Canada (Attorney General)*, visit **http://www.canlii.org/en/ca/fct/doc/2002/2002fct423/2002fct423.html**.

More information on the national standards for the CHRP designation can be found at **http://www.cchra.ca**.

To read the article on "Candidate Glut," visit **http://www.shrm.org/hrmagazine** and insert "Candidate Glut" in the search window.

Required Professional Capabilities (RPCs)

RPC 1.1 Contributes to the development of the organization's vision, goals, and strategies with a focus on human capabilities.
- Strategic business planning processes and principles
- The nature of the business environment, and the competitive position of the company within the industry
- Business operations
- The labour market specific to the industry
- Benchmarking and industry best practices
- Change management practices

- Human resources planning and forecasting, including importance/benefits of HRP and the process and techniques of HRP
- Organizational structures and management practices
- Labour market analysis, behaviour, data, and theory
- Trends in labour force characteristics (e.g., labour force growth, employment trends and rates, unemployment, participation rates, occupational distribution of the workforce, and compensation)

RPC 1.2 Provides leadership and ensures compliance with legislative requirements concerning conflict of interest and other technical issues.
- Applicable political, social, and cultural context and environment
- Professional standards and codes of ethics
- Industry practices
- Relevant legislation, regulations, and jurisprudence
- Theories and practices for protection of individuals and groups
- Investigative techniques
- Basic rules of evidence

RPC 1.3 Oversees the organization's recruitment and staffing policies and procedures (recruitment, selection, and orientation).
- Job markets
- Selection concepts and techniques
- Relevant legislation and regulations
- Recruiting sources and techniques (internal and external)
- Organization staffing needs
- Organization's internal HR inventory
- Assessment tools
- Orientation and career development needs of new employees
- Industry best practices
- The organization's strategic business plan and the goals of the business unit

RPC 1.4 Guides and advises the organization in the development and application of ethical practices.
- Standards of professional practice
- Codes of ethics and standards of the HR profession
- Conflict management/resolution techniques
- Industry best practices
- Organization's HR and business practices
- Concepts and processes of power and organization politics
- Issues related to privacy and the protection of information
- Influence tactics

RPC 1.5 Understands and adheres to the Canadian Council of Human Resources Association's code of ethics and applicable provincial/territorial HR association's codes.
- CCHRA code of ethics
- Organization values and culture
- Processes used to resolve ethical issues

Discussion Questions

1. How can HR professionals demonstrate that they add value to a company's bottom line?
2. What are possible consequences of using poor or outdated recruitment and selection practices?
3. What are the advantages of obtaining a professional designation such as CHRP?
4. What are some of the current socioeconomic changes taking place that may have an impact on recruitment and selection practices?

Using the Internet

1. Visit the CCHRA website and review the requirements for obtaining the CHRP designation. Also review information on the CHRP available on your provincial HR association's website. Are you qualified to begin the CHRP process? What will you have to do to become an HR professional?
2. Explore one of the websites listed in this chapter. Print a copy of the home page and present a description of the site to your classmates. Describe some of the information available on the site. Follow one of the links from that site and describe another site relevant to recruitment and selection.

Exercises

1. Visit the Statistics Canada website to determine the current socioeconomic and demographic composition of the Canadian work force. Identify how these factors may have an impact on human resources recruitment and selection. Illustrate with examples.
2. Think of a job you have held and write two brief profiles of that job. The first profile is to be that of a 95th-percentile job performer—that is, a person you have worked with who would be better than 95 out of a 100 of his or her co-workers. What was that person like? What skills and abilities did he or she have? Then write a second profile of a 5th-percentile job performer—a person who was only as good as the bottom 5 percent of his or her co-workers. Compare the profiles and discuss how use of recruitment and selection might be helpful in choosing the 95th- rather than 5th-percentile performer. How much difference would it make to have the 95th- rather than the 5th-percentile performer on the job? If you were the employer, would these differences be of sufficient value for you to invest the necessary money into recruitment and selection in order to get the 95th-percentile performer?

3. As a class or in small groups, discuss the three scenarios raised in the ethics section of this chapter. Decide what the human resources professional should do in each instance, and provide an ethical justification for your decision based on the CCHRA code of ethics.
4. Write a brief summary of your preferred career track in human resources management. What professional associations would you join and what activities would you engage in? Where do recruitment and selection fit in the mix of activities that you have planned for yourself?

Case

Note: Before you do this case, you might want to read "Candidate Glut,"[11] available at http://www.shrm.org/hrmagazine/articles/0803/0803frase-blunt.asp.

The Toyota (Cambridge, Ontario) plant exemplifies the changing workplace requirements described in this chapter and their impact on human resources practices. Toyota is a Japanese company that competes in the global marketplace. It has production facilities in many countries where labour costs are high, yet it strives to maintain a very efficient work force. One reason for Toyota's ability to be an effective producer is its use of empirically proven recruitment and selection practices.

Toyota's recruitment and selection practices are designed to find the best possible people to hire, whether the job being staffed is on the shop floor or at the executive level. In 1996, Toyota received thousands of applications for 1200 blue-collar positions. As part of its hiring procedure, Toyota took prospective employees through a rigorous, comprehensive, multi-stage assessment process. According to Sandie Halyk, assistant general manager for human resources, Toyota "wants people who take pride in their work and are able to work well with others. If you're not comfortable working for a team, you won't be comfortable working here."

The selection process involved realistic job previews, paper-and-pencil cognitive ability and personality assessments, tests of fine and gross motor coordination, work samples, and structured employment interviews. The work sample alone entailed a six-hour manufacturing assembly exercise that involved individual and group problem solving. Group leaders and first-line supervisors were active participants in the panel selection interview. For those "making the grade," references were checked, and health and fitness tests were undertaken by those given conditional offers of employment. The process was designed to "find out if you're able to identify problems and do something about them, and to ensure a good fit between the company and the new employee."

Source: G. Keenan. 1996. "Toyota's Hunt for 1,200 Team Players." *The Globe and Mail* (January 5): B7. Reprinted with permission from The Globe and Mail.

Discussion Questions

The intent of this exercise is not to have you develop detailed answers but to begin thinking about the many factors that affect recruitment and selection. We appreciate that the case does not contain detailed information, but in our opinion that information is not needed to meet our primary objective. We will review in detail many of the components of Toyota's selection procedures later in this text. For now, we would like you to discuss the following points, but first you may find it useful to review Figure 1.1 on page 4.

1. Is Toyota's elaborate selection system justified? What are appropriate criteria for assessing its effectiveness?
2. Toyota received over 40 000 applications for 1200 positions. Is this an effective approach? What are the costs, particularly human costs, associated with reviewing all of these applications? How do you reduce the number of applicants to a reasonable number that can be run through the selection system?
3. What are some of the cultural issues that might arise with a Japanese-managed auto plant located in Ontario?
4. Provide examples of how technology might be used to facilitate and improve the recruitment and selection used by Toyota.
5. What criteria should Toyota use in selecting "team players"?

Endnotes

1. Koch, M.J., and R. Gunter-McGrath. 1996. "Improving Labor Productivity: Human Resource Management Policies Do Matter." *Strategic Management Journal* 17: 335–54.
2. Huselid, M.A. 1995. "The Impact of Human Resource Management Practices on Turnover, Productivity, and Corporate Financial Performance." *Academy of Management Journal* 38: 635–72.
3. Huselid, M.A. 1995.
4. d'Arcimoles, C.-H. 1997. "Human Resource Policies and Company Performance: A Quantitative Approach Using Longitudinal Data." *Organizational Studies* 18: 857–74.
5. Whitener, E.M. 1997. "The Impact of Human Resource Activities on Employee Trust." *Human Resource Management Review* 7: 38–39.
6. Jones, G.R., and P.M. Wright. 1992. "An Economic Approach to Conceptualizing the Utility of Human Resource Management Practices." In K.R. Rowland and G. Ferris, eds., *Research in Personnel and Human Resources Management*, Vol. 10. Greenwich, CT: JAI Press.
7. Tamkin, P., M. Cowling, and W. Hunt. 2008. *People and the Bottom Line*. Report 448. London, UK: Institute for Employment Studies.
8. Wright, P.M., T.M. Gaedner, and L.M. Moynihan. 2003. "The Impact of HR Practices on the Performance of Business Units." *Human Resources Management Journal* 13: 21–36.
9. Belcourt, M.L., and K.J. McBey. 2003. *Strategic Human Resources Planning,* 2nd ed. Toronto: Nelson.
10. Tampkin, Cowling, and Hunt. 2008.
11. Frase-Blunt, M. 2003. "Candidate Glut." *HR Magazine* (August) 48(8): http://www.shrm .org/hrmagazine/ articles/0803/0803frase-blunt.asp.

Chapter 2

Foundations of Recruitment and Selection I: Measurement, Reliability, and Validity

Chapter Learning Objectives

This chapter develops the idea that personnel recruitment and selection strategies based on information obtained through scientific methods are more likely to benefit an organization than decisions based on impressions or intuition. The chapter starts with an introduction to scientific methodology and goes on to examine basic measurement concepts that underlie contemporary recruitment and selection practices. This chapter is an excellent review for those who have had previous courses on research methods and psychological measurement. For others, it is an overview of research terms and methods.

After reading this chapter you should:

- understand the basic components that make up a traditional personnel selection model;
- know what a correlation coefficient is, along with a few other basic statistical concepts used in personnel selection;
- have a good understanding of the concepts of reliability and validity;
- recognize the importance and necessity of establishing the reliability and validity of measurements used in personnel selection;
- identify common strategies that are used to provide evidence on the reliability and validity of measurements used in personnel selection; and
- appreciate the requirement for measurements used in personnel selection to evaluate applicants fairly and in an unbiased fashion.

THE *MEIORIN* CASE

The following is an extract from the Supreme Court decision in *British Columbia (Public Service Employee Relations Commission) v. BCGSEU (British Columbia Government Service Employees' Union)*, (1999) 3 S.C.R. 3.

Ms. Meiorin was employed for three years by the British Columbia Ministry of Forests as a member of a three-person Initial Attack Forest Firefighting Crew in the Golden Forest District. The crew's job was to attack and suppress forest fires while they were small and could be contained. Ms. Meiorin's supervisors found her work to be satisfactory.

Ms. Meiorin was not asked to take a physical fitness test until 1994, when she was required to pass the Government's "Bona Fide Occupational Fitness Tests and Standards for B.C. Forest Service Wildland Firefighters" (the "Tests"). The Tests required that the forest firefighters weigh less than 200 lbs. (with their equipment) and complete a shuttle run, an upright rowing exercise, and a pump carrying/hose dragging exercise within stipulated times. The running test was designed to test the forest firefighters' aerobic fitness and was based on the view that forest firefighters must have a minimum "VO2 max" of 50 ml.kg-1. min-1 (the "aerobic standard"). "VO2 max" measures "maximal oxygen uptake," or the rate at which the body can take in oxygen, transport it to the muscles, and use it to produce energy.

The Tests were developed in response to a 1991 Coroner's Inquest Report that recommended that only physically fit employees be assigned as front-line forest firefighters for safety reasons. The Government commissioned a team of researchers from the University of Victoria to undertake a review of its existing fitness standards with a view to protecting the safety of firefighters while meeting human rights norms. The researchers developed the Tests by identifying the essential components of forest firefighting, measuring the physiological demands of those components, selecting fitness tests to measure those demands and, finally, assessing the validity of those tests.

The researchers studied various sample groups. The specific tasks performed by forest firefighters were identified by reviewing amalgamated data collected by the British Columbia Forest Service. The physiological demands of those tasks were then measured by observing test subjects as they performed them in the field. One simulation involved 18 firefighters, another involved 10 firefighters, but it is unclear from the researchers' report whether the subjects at this stage were male or female. The researchers asked a pilot group of 10 university student volunteers (6 females and 4 males) to perform a series of proposed fitness tests and field exercises.

After refining the preferred tests, the researchers observed them being performed by a larger sample group composed of 31 forest firefighter trainees and 15 university student volunteers (31 males and 15 females), and correlated their results with the group's performance in the field. Having concluded that the preferred tests were accurate predictors of actual forest firefighting performance—including the running test designed to gauge whether the subject met the aerobic standard—the researchers presented their report to the Government in 1992.

A follow-up study in 1994 of 77 male forest firefighters and 2 female forest firefighters used the same methodology. However, the researchers this time recommended that the Government initiate another study to examine the impact of the Tests on women. There is no evidence before us that the Government has yet responded to this recommendation.

Two aspects of the researchers' methodology are critical to this case. First, it was primarily descriptive, based on measuring the average performance levels of the test subjects and converting this data into minimum performance standards. Second, it did not seem to distinguish between the male and female test subjects.

After four attempts, Ms. Meiorin failed to meet the aerobic standard, running the distance in 11 minutes and 49.4 seconds instead of the required 11 minutes. As a result, she was laid off. Her union subsequently brought a grievance on her behalf. The arbitrator designated to hear the grievance was required to determine whether she had been improperly dismissed.

Evidence accepted by the arbitrator demonstrated that, owing to physiological differences, most women have lower aerobic capacity than most men. Even with training, most women cannot increase their aerobic capacity to the level required by the aerobic standard, although training can allow most men to meet it. The arbitrator also heard evidence that 65% to 70% of male applicants pass the Tests on their initial attempts, while only 35% of female applicants have similar success. Of the 800 to 900 Initial Attack Crew members employed by the Government in 1995, only 100 to 150 were female.

There was no credible evidence showing that the prescribed aerobic capacity was necessary for either men or women to perform the work of a forest firefighter satisfactorily. On the contrary, Ms. Meiorin had in the past performed her work well, without apparent risk to herself, her colleagues or the public.

The Supreme Court of Canada decision in the *Meiorin* case set new legal standards for the use of tests in personnel selection. We will make reference to this case in other chapters when discussing specific issues that fall under that decision. For the moment, our interest in the case is with respect to what the Court said about research methodology and the need to validate selection procedures.

In the *Meiorin* case, the BC government undertook a job analysis of the position of firefighter to determine the essential components of firefighting and then to create a series of tests to measure those components among firefighters. In terms of a selection process as outlined in Figure 2.1, the

FIGURE 2.1

Job Analysis, Selection, and Criterion Measurements of Performance: A Systems Approach

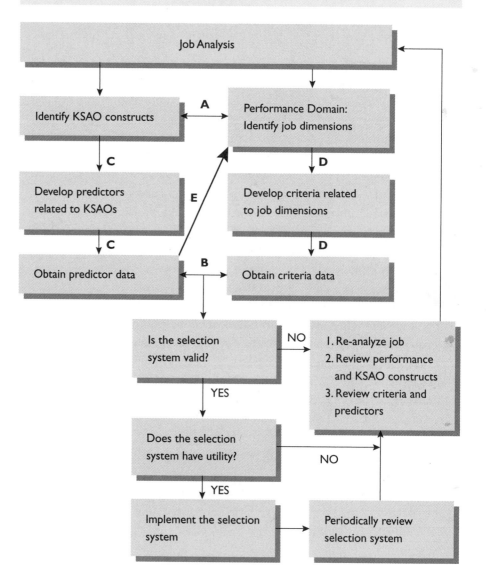

researchers followed all of the steps—except the most crucial one of showing that "the prescribed aerobic capacity was necessary for either men or women to perform the work of a forest firefighter satisfactorily." In the Court's opinion, the research failed to establish the linkage specified by line B in Figure 2.1, and also failed to take into account physiological differences between men and women.

In this chapter, we will develop a basic understanding of several of the measurement and **validity** issues that surfaced in this case and with which every human resources practitioner must be familiar. There are no guarantees that even when professionals attempt to follow accepted procedures, their work will meet standards set by courts or tribunals, as the *Meiorin* case illustrates, but at least HR professionals should know what standards they are expected to meet in order to defend their work.

The Recruitment and Selection Process

In most employment situations, there are many applicants for each available job. The employer's goal is to hire an applicant who possesses the knowledge, skills, abilities, or other attributes (KSAOs) required to successfully perform the job being filled. The employer makes a guess about which applicant will perform the job most effectively. This basic decision, which is made hundreds of times each day throughout Canada, is the end result of a complex process. Correct guesses by the employer have positive benefits for the organization and the employee; bad guesses not only affect the productivity and profitability of the company but may also have negative emotional consequences for the poorly performing employee.

As part of making a decision, the employer must have a good idea of both the duties that will be performed as part of the job and the level of performance required for job success. The employer must identify the knowledge, skills, abilities, or other attributes that are required for job success and measure or assess the KSAOs of all job applicants. In Chapter 3, we will discuss different techniques that provide this necessary information. Hiring someone through an assessment of job-related attributes is based on an assumption that higher levels of attributes are linked to higher levels of job performance. Recruitment and selection need not be based on guesses as to who is best suited to fill a position.

The Hiring Process

Recruitment and Selection Today 2.1 outlines the procedure used by the Winnipeg Police Department in selecting new recruits for the position of police officer. Candidates must meet a set of minimum requirements, including a job-related physical abilities test. Also, they must not have a criminal record for which a pardon has not been granted. If candidates meet the minimum requirements, they must provide evidence that they meet the vision standards needed to do the job. Next, only those candidates who pass a written examination are invited to a short screening interview, with

RPC 2.1

Validity

The degree to which accumulated evidence and theory support specific interpretations of test scores in the context of the test's proposed use.

RPC 2.2

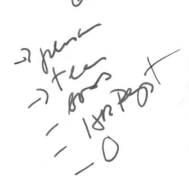

Recruitment and Selection Today

Selection Process for Winnipeg Police Service Constables

Minimum Qualifications

- Age (18 years or older)
- Education (Manitoba Grade 12 or equivalency—e.g., GED). Foreign credentials require assessment by Manitoba Labour and Immigration prior to application.
- Valid Full Class 5 driver's licence—no more than 4 demerits on Driver's Abstract as assessed by the Winnipeg Police Service
- Canadian citizen or landed immigrant/permanent resident status
- No involvement in any criminal activity within the last two years (including illegal drugs).
- No criminal record for which a pardon has not been granted
- Must meet current Winnipeg Police Service vision standards
- Successful completion of job-related physical test (Winnipeg Police Service–Physical Abilities Test: WPS–PAT) within 4 minutes and 15 seconds.

Selection Process

Each candidate must successfully complete each of the following steps:

1. **Completion of Application,** including submission of documents related to the minimum qualifications outlined above. The vision test must be certified by a qualified physician.
2. **Three-hour written exam** based on study guide material provided two weeks prior to written test. Pass mark is 65 percent and held for five years. Applicants who fail the exam must wait one year before reapplying. There are no restrictions on the number of failures.
3. **Screening interview**—This is a structured interview in which all applicants are asked the same straightforward questions, which are designed to allow interviewers to assess both the applicant's ability to communicate, as well as his or her potential suitability for policing. Each applicant reaching this stage will

be provided with an outline of the interview. Each candidate will be evaluated on his or her communication skills as well as his or her general demeanour and deportment. The interview is scored on a pass/fail basis. The pass result is held for three years; those who fail the interview must wait one year to reapply. There are no restrictions on the number of failures.

4. **Second interview**—This is a behaviour-based interview, which is also structured to ensure fairness to all applicants. The interview is approximately 30–45 minutes in length. The panel members will be two senior officers of the Winnipeg Police Service. The questions are structured and are based on essential qualities established as competency measurements that each applicant must satisfy. Each applicant will be evaluated on his or her communication skills as well as his or her general demeanour and deportment. The interview is scored on a pass/fail basis. The pass result is held for three years; those who fail the interview must wait one year to reapply. There are no restrictions on the number of failures.
5. **Background investigation**—This is a one-on-one interview with a background investigator assigned to the applicant. The interview is approximately three hours in length. This is not an interview that an applicant can prepare for. The investigator will delve into various facets of an applicant's personal and professional life. Given the nature of the job and the level of professionalism expected of police officers by the public, this interview is comprehensive and relevant. Upon completion of the interview, the background investigator will commence investigation into an applicant's suitability for employment with the Winnipeg Police Service.
6. **Selection Panel**—Recruits are selected from a pool of qualified candidates who have passed all previous hurdles, subject to Step 7. Applicants are compared to each other rather than to set standards in making the final selection. Applicants who fail to meet one or more of the competency measures (citizen and cus-

successful candidates given a second, more extensive selection interview. Background checks are carried out on applicants who have made it through all of the previous steps.

A selection panel compares all of the qualified candidates and must decide on whom to offer employment. At this stage, it is likely that there are more qualified candidates than positions, so the panel will compare candidates to each other to help it decide. Offers of employment as a police officer are then made to the selected candidates on the condition that they pass psychological and medical examinations.

The Winnipeg Police Service selection process illustrates the major components of a personnel selection process that we will be discussing throughout this book. These are the components that a candidate sees; however, there is much more to the process. How does an employer know which requirements are needed to carry out the job? Should the employer be concerned if the requirements discriminate against certain groups? Under what circumstances can requirements that do discriminate against groups be used in selection? What standards must be met by the tools used in the selection process in order for the employer to be sure that they are providing relevant and accurate information about the applicants? What procedures must an employer follow to ensure that its selection process is in compliance with legal and professional standards?

Every employer who makes a hiring decision follows a hiring process, even though it may not be as structured as that used by the Winnipeg Police Service. In many cases, the hiring process is informal, with little attention paid to the questions posed above. The hiring system used by many employers resembles, on the surface, the selection procedure used to hire police officers in Winnipeg, but there are important differences. When a position becomes vacant, or is newly created, the employer may have a general idea of the duties to be performed as part of the job, which are then included in an advertisement used to recruit candidates for the position. This job advertisement may also state broad educational or experiential requirements expected from the candidates. The important difference is whether the job duties and position requirements have been determined through some systematic

RPC 2.3

investigation or whether they represent a guess on the part of the employer's HR department.

Applicants submit résumés and, after a preliminary screening, a few may be interviewed. Based on review of the applicants' files, work references, and impressions formed during the interview, the employer makes a decision to hire one of the candidates. This decision may reflect the employer's experience, a gut feeling or intuition about a certain candidate, or simply personal preference. The employer has an *idea* of the type of person who will do well in the job or in the organization and looks for an applicant who matches this idealized employee. In any event, the employer is making a guess about which applicant will do well in the job based on information collected from the job applicant that may not, in fact, be related to the job or may be of questionable quality.

All too often, unfortunately, the employer's decision or guess reveals more about the biases of the employer than it does about either the requirements for the job or the qualifications and abilities of the applicants. In this type of selection procedure, there is little or no tracking of the performance of the people hired, and only those who happen to do well are recalled and used to reinforce the hiring process. Bad guesses may lead not only to lower productivity but also to legal difficulties.

Hiring decisions must be defensible; they must meet legal requirements and professional standards of reliability and validity. Defensible hiring decisions are not arbitrary; the measurements used to make hiring decisions must be stable and provide job-related information. The Winnipeg Police Service hiring procedure outlined in Recruitment and Selection Today 2.1 illustrates how selection ought to be done, but before it or any procedure can be considered to be a model selection system, it must satisfy certain standards. Figure 2.1 represents a model of a selection system, including the components that are not seen by job applicants. The model emphasizes the need for employment decisions to be valid and to meet legal requirements. Unfortunately, practice in human resources tends to lag behind the science. Far too many HR interventions, including those in selection, are based on intuition rather than empirical support.[1] Table 2.1 compares some of the differences between empirical evidence–based and practice-based selection processes.

A Selection Model

Figure 2.1 on page 24 presents an overview of the components and process of a traditional selection system. The components of this model are discussed in detail in later chapters. In this model, job analysis information (Chapter 4) is used to identify both the performance domain (i.e., the job tasks or duties; Chapter 5) and the KSAOs or competencies (Chapter 4) linked to job performance (Chapter 5). Job analysis information identifies the tasks and behaviours that make up a job and, through inference, the KSAOs that contribute to performance of these tasks and behaviours. These inferences are based on empirical evidence demonstrating validity between the job dimensions and KSAO **constructs** in other situations. This relationship between the

2.4

Construct

An idea or concept constructed or invoked to explain relationships between observations. For example, the construct "extroversion" has been invoked to explain the relationship between "social forthrightness" and sales; "learning" is a construct used to explain the change in behaviour that results from experience. Constructs are abstractions that we infer from observations and that we cannot directly observe. In the natural sciences, "gravity" is perhaps the most famous construct.

TABLE 2.1

Human Resources Management: Science versus Practice in Selection

	SCIENCE-BASED SELECTION	PRACTICE-BASED SELECTION
TYPE OF PROCESS	**Analytical** • Job analysis identifies KSAOs • Select valid measures of KSAOs • Validate predictors and assess utility • Retain valid and useful predictors	**Intuitive** • Untested approaches • "Fad"-based selection system • Lack of use of reliable and valid selection tools • Techniques and selection tools chosen on the basis of marketing • Selection procedures used are rarely validated
DECISION MAKING	• Rational	• "Gut-feel"
IMPLEMENTATION	• System-wide	• Case-by-case basis
EVALUATION OF PROCESS	• Empirical	• Subjective
WHY IS IT USED?	• Structured procedures • Consistent process • Maintains standards	• Comfort with the process • Flexibility and speed • Fits organizational culture
POTENTIAL OUTCOMES	• Defensibility of system • Increased productivity • Effective employees	• Human rights litigation • Lack of competitiveness • Marginal employees

Source: V.M. Catano. "Empirically Supported Interventions and HR Practice." *HRM Research Quarterly* 5, 2001, p. 1–5. International Alliance for Human Resources Research, York University. Reprinted with permission of V.M. Catano.

performance domains and the KSAO constructs is represented by line A in Figure 2.1.

The KSAOs and job dimensions linked by line A are abstractions—they cannot be measured directly. These constructs must be used to develop predictor and criteria data before they can be used to select job candidates. Chapter 5 discusses the process of defining the performance domain and developing related criterion measurements. Line D represents this process in Figure 2.1. In establishing a selection system, identifying and developing the performance domain and related criteria are just as important to the success of the system as properly developing the predictor side of the model. Unfortunately, in practice, insufficient attention is given to developing adequate performance measurements. Criterion measurements may be used because they are available and convenient rather than because they adequately represent the competencies or performance domain of interest.[2]

The human resources specialist must also translate the KSAO constructs into measurable predictors (Chapters 7, 8, and 9). The fact that a security dispatcher sends, receives, processes, and analyzes information suggests that an applicant for this position should demonstrate a fair degree of cognitive ability. Also, since a security dispatcher must be capable of operating a variety of electronic equipment, the applicant presumably should have experience operating such equipment. Similarly, if this same position requires the incumbent to remain calm under stressful conditions, applicants should demonstrate a stable emotional disposition (i.e., low neuroticism).

The human resources specialists must determine how each of these KSAOs will be assessed. With respect to cognitive ability, a general cognitive ability test may be most appropriate. Information about past work history and experience may come from an application form or the candidate's résumé, while information about the candidate's ability to deal with stressful situations may be assessed through a combination of a personality inventory and a situational interview. The predictors that are chosen must be valid measurements of the KSAO constructs that have been identified as related to job performance. This relationship is represented by line C in Figure 2.1. The validity of the predictor measurements is established through evidence based on test content—that is, either content or construct validity procedures. Either expert judgment or empirical evidence must support the use of a predictor measurement as representative of a KSAO construct.

Keep in mind that the goal of selection is to identify job candidates who have those attributes required for success on the job. On the basis of predictor data obtained through an assessment of job applicants, the human resources team predicts which applicants will be successful in the position. This prediction is represented by line E in Figure 2.1. In most organizations, this relationship is inferred through establishing a correlation at the measurement level between the predictor and criterion measurements—that is, evidence based on relationships to other variables. Line B in Figure 2.1 represents criterion-related validity. If the relationship in line E cannot be established through either criterion-related, content, or construct validity, the human resources team must begin the process again. This may include redoing the job analysis, but more often than not it involves only a review and refinement of the predictor and criterion measurements.

The work of the human resources team does not end once it establishes the validity of the selection system. The final step is to demonstrate that decisions based on the selection system have utility—that they result in higher levels of performance and overall productivity than would be the case without such a system. Several methods used in decision making and for assessing utility are described in Chapter 10. Finally, the selection system, once determined as providing utility, must be reviewed periodically as jobs and organizations change. We discuss the concept of validity presented as part of this model in greater detail later in this chapter.

The Legal Environment and Selection

Selection programs and practices must operate within the current legal context (Chapter 3). Ideally, they do not have an adverse impact on members of protected groups. Selection programs that intentionally or unintentionally exclude job applicants using characteristics or factors that are protected under human rights legislation (unless they are bona fide occupational requirements) run the risk of being declared unfairly discriminatory, and the organization may be subject to penalties and fines. Chapter 3 discusses in more detail the *Meiorin* decision and the standards that must be met for selection practices to withstand legal scrutiny. Recruitment, screening, and selection procedures should yield the best-qualified candidates within the context of agreed-upon **employment equity** programs.

Employment equity
A term coined in the 1986 federal Employment Equity Act referring to policies and initiatives to promote employment opportunities for members of designated minority groups.

 2.5

Building a Foundation

The chapters in this book explore in depth the topics that make up the typical recruitment and selection process. To move beyond a guess, a selection system must be built on a sound scientific foundation. In buying a house, you may not need to know how to lay a foundation, but you must be able to tell whether the house's foundation is solid. Often, human resources managers are asked to adopt selection systems; this chapter provides the tools needed to determine if a selection system or procedure rests on solid footings.

There are two major elements to building a sound foundation with respect to recruitment and selection. First, the system must be based on solid empirical support. Human resources personnel must be able to demonstrate the reliability and validity of their selection systems. Second, any selection system must operate within a legal context.

Correlation and Regression

Basic Statistics

If a human resources manager interviewed only a few job applicants, it is possible to directly compare the applicants on the basis of their assigned scores. What if there were a very large number of applicants? How would the manager keep track of all the scores? One way is to use statistical procedures to describe important information contained in the set of applicant scores.[3] The manager could compute the *mean* or average score. The mean represents the most typical or "average" score that might be expected within a group of scores; it is the one score that best represents the set of scores. When a professor tells you the class average grade, you have an idea of how the "typical" student performed on an exam. Not every applicant, or student, has a score that is similar to the mean score. It is also useful to know how different, on average, any one score is from the mean score and from any other score. The *variance* gives this information. The more the observed scores differ from each other and from the mean, the higher the variance; scores that are tightly clustered around a mean score will have a smaller variance.

W W W

 2.6

Often in reporting scores, the *standard deviation* is used rather than the variance. The standard deviation is the square root of the variance; it is more convenient to use since it presents information in terms of the actual measurement scale. Knowing both the mean and the variance allows the manager to know the score that an average applicant should attain, and how much variability to expect in applicant scores. If most applicant scores fall within one standard deviation from the mean, then someone with a score that exceeds three standard deviations might be considered an exceptional applicant. For example, if the mean was 65 and the size of the standard deviation was 5, most applicant scores normally would fall between 60 and 70. Scores greater than 80 would be exceptional and indicate that an applicant received a very high rating compared with the average applicant; on the other hand, scores less than 50 would indicate that the applicant fared poorly. In terms of performance on a test in college or university, a student scoring 80 or higher might receive a grade of "A," while those who fall below 50 would receive a grade of "F." Those students falling in the average range of 60 to 70 would receive a "C."

Correlation

Measurements of central tendency and variability are quite useful in summarizing a large set of observations. However, in many areas of personnel selection, the relationship between two variables is of considerable interest. The human resources manager is interested in the relationship between cognitive ability and job performance—that is, the degree to which the variation in cognitive ability is associated with the variation in job performance, or the degree to which the variation in job performance can be predicted from the variation in cognitive ability.

A *correlation coefficient* is a statistic that presents information on the extent of the relationship between two variables. To establish this correlation, the manager must have two scores for each applicant, one for cognitive ability and the other for job performance. In the case of job applicants, the manager could establish a know-how score based on the interview or through some other test that was administered to each applicant. But the manager would not have a job performance score, since this cannot be obtained until the applicants are hired. The manager has two options: (1) The applicants are hired and their job performance is evaluated after a period of time; the performance score of each new employee is then paired with the know-how score obtained at the time of application, or (2) a group of existing employees with known job performance scores could be put through the interview process to determine their degree of know-how, with both scores paired for each employee. These two approaches provide *predictive* and *concurrent* evidence, respectively, that may be used in establishing the validity of inferences about job performance made from the test scores. Validation strategies are reviewed later in this chapter.

Table 2.2 presents hypothetical data obtained from existing workers. Each pair of scores for each employee is graphed on a scatterplot where each

TABLE 2.2

Measuring a Relationship between Cognitive Ability and Job Performance

Employee	Cognitive Ability (X)	Job Performance (Y)	Predicted Job Performance (Y')
Mr. E	10	7	6.91
Ms. F	4	5	5.11
Mr. G	5	4	5.41
Mr. H	8	6	6.31
Mr. I	2	4	4.51
Ms. J	6	5	5.71
Mr. K	7	5	6.01
Mr. L	3	6	4.81
Ms. M	8	7	6.31
Mr. N	6	8	5.71

For the above data:

$r = 0.56$

$r^2 = 0.31$

$Y' = 0.30X + 3.91$

axis represents a variable. In Figure 2.2 these data points are enclosed within an ellipse to show the relationship between the two variables. In this case, the ellipse tends to tilt upward as both cognitive ability and job performance scores increase. This orientation of the ellipse suggests a linear, positive relationship between cognitive ability scores and job performance scores. High cognitive ability scores are associated with high job performance scores. If the ellipse had tilted downward at the high end of the job performance axis and upward at the low end, it would have suggested a linear, negative relationship—that high cognitive ability scores are associated with low job performance scores.

Correlation Coefficients

While the scatterplot gives a good visual indication of the relationship between the two variables, its usefulness becomes limited as the size of the data set increases. The information in a scatterplot is summarized through an index—r, the correlation coefficient. A correlation coefficient indicates both the *size* and *direction* of a linear relationship between two variables. For the data in Table 2.2, $r = 0.56$. Direction indicates the nature of the linear relationship between the two variables. A positive or direct relationship of the type presented in Table 2.2 is signified by a plus sign. Negative or indirect

FIGURE 2.2

Scatterplot of Cognitive Ability and Job Performance—I

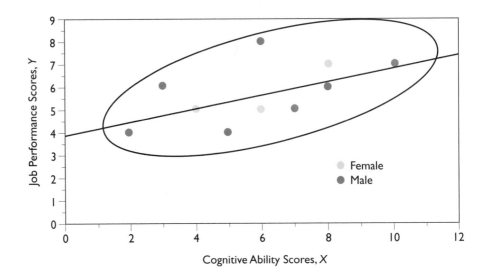

relationships are indicated by minus signs; for example, $r = -0.56$ indicates a situation in which high cognitive ability scores predicted low job performance scores.

The strength or size of the relationship is indicated by the value of the correlation coefficient. A correlation of $r = 1.00$ indicates a perfect positive linear relationship between two variables, while $r = -1.00$ indicates a perfect negative linear relationship. Correlations of $r = 0.00$ signify that there is no linear relationship between the two variables under study. With correlations approaching $r = 0.00$, one variable cannot be used to predict the score on the second variable; knowing the status of the first variable or characteristic does not help you to know anything about the status of the second. The more closely the correlation coefficient approaches a value of either $+1.00$ or -1.00, the more accurately one variable predicts the other.

Coefficient of Determination

Another index that gives an indication of the strength of a relationship between two variables is r^2, the *coefficient of determination*. This value represents the proportion of variability in one variable that is associated with variability in another. It is the proportion of variability that can be accounted for in one variable by knowing something about a different variable. For Table 2.2, about 31 percent (i.e., $r^2 = 0.56 \times 0.56 = 0.31$) of the variance in job performance ratings can be accounted for by knowing the applicants' cognitive ability scores. Looking at this from a different direction, about 69 percent of the variability in job performance ratings is not related to cognitive ability scores. Both r and r^2 give an indication of the size of a relationship.

Simple Regression

The relationship between two variables can also be expressed in terms of a straight line. Remember that a correlation expresses the degree and direction of a linear relationship between two variables. The correlation coefficient is used to derive an equation for a straight line that best fits the data points contained in the scatterplot. This is a *regression line*. The diagonal line in the scatterplot in Figure 2.2 is the regression line that provides the best fit to the data contained in the ellipse. In regression, one variable is used to predict another. The independent or *predictor variable* is plotted along the X-axis of the scatterplot, with the dependent or *criterion variable* plotted along the Y-axis. The equation used to generate the straight line is:

$$Y' = bX + c$$

This equation states that a predicted job performance score, Y', is equal to an individual's cognitive ability score, X, multiplied by b, the regression coefficient, plus c, a constant. The regression coefficient, b, represents the slope of the straight line, and the constant, c, represents the intercept, where the line crosses the Y-axis. For the hypothetical data in Table 2.2, $b = 0.30$, and $c = 3.91$; these values are used to generate a predicted job performance score, Y', for each applicant. These Y' values are also presented in Table 2.2. Notice that the predicted values differ from the actual values; for Mr. E, the difference is relatively small (6.91 vs. 7.00) but relatively large for Mr. N (5.71 vs. 8.00). The regression line produces the smallest error between predicted and actual values of the criterion variable.

Multiple Regression

Many practical situations involve more than two variables. The human resources manager may have not only information about cognitive ability and job performance but also other information obtained from letters of reference and the application form. Each one of these sources of information, on its own, may predict job performance scores to some degree. The set of predictors can be combined into one equation to indicate the extent to which the set, taken as a whole, is related to the criterion variable. The mathematical procedure to compute this equation, while more complicated than the case of two variables, follows the same logic as that for simple regression.

Both simple and multiple regression techniques are used to combine information to make valid human resources decisions. In Chapter 10, we will illustrate how both simple and multiple regression techniques are used to determine which job applicants are qualified to receive job offers.

Reliability

Hardly any human characteristic can be measured in an error-free manner. The act of measuring produces a score that measures both the true score and an error component. **Reliability** is the degree to which observed scores are

 2.4

Reliability
The degree to which observed scores are free from random measurement errors. Reliability is an indication of the stability or dependability of a set of measurements over repeated applications of the measurement procedure.

free from random measurement errors. Reliability is an indication of the stability or dependability of a set of measurements.[4] Reliability refers to the consistency of a set of measurements when a testing procedure is repeated on a population of individuals or groups.[5]

Think of an employer who requires each employee to punch a time clock upon arrival at work. Mr. X, Ms. Y, and Mr. Z, without fail, arrive at work each morning at 8:55 A.M., 8:56 A.M., and 8:57 A.M., respectively. If, on each day, the time clock stamped these same times, exactly, on each employee's time card, the time clock would be considered extremely reliable. The observed score—the time stamped on the time card—is the same as the true score, the time the employees arrived at work; no degree of error has been added to the measurement.

On the other hand, if the clock stamped times of 9:03 A.M., 9:00 A.M., and 9:00 A.M. for Mr. X, Ms. Y, and Mr. Z, the measurement would include an error component. Mr. X's time is off by eight minutes, Ms. Y's by four minutes, and Mr. Z's by three minutes. The time clock is not accurate, or reliable, in reporting the time people arrived for work. In this case, the error appears to be random or unsystematic; the occurrence or degree of the error does not appear to be predictable.

In terms of testing, we expect a test to provide approximately the same information each time it is given to that person. If you were given a multiple-choice test on the content of this chapter, we would expect that you would obtain approximately the same score if you were asked to retake the test. The smaller the differences between your two scores, the more reliable, or consistent, the test.

Errors may also be systematic; that is, the errors may be made in a consistent, or predictable, fashion. If the time clock was five minutes fast, it would report the three arrival times as 9:00 A.M., 9:01 A.M., and 9:02 A.M. The clock is still reliable in reporting the arrival times of the three employees, but it is systematically adding five minutes to each worker's time. The observed scores are reliable, but they do not represent the true arrival times. In other words, while the observed scores are accurate, they are not a valid indication of whether the employees started work on time.

Systematic errors do not affect the accuracy of the measurements but rather the meaning, or interpretation, of those measurements. In terms of testing, several test questions might be scored incorrectly both on the first occasion you took the test and on the subsequent administration. The incorrect scoring, which is systematic, does not affect the reliability of the test but it leads to the wrong conclusion about how well you know the material.

Interpreting Reliability Coefficients

Another way to think of reliability is in terms of the variability of a set of scores. The classical measurement model,[6] which has had a major impact on personnel research, assumes that any observed score, X, is a combination of a **true score**, T, and an **error score**, e, such that:

$$X = T + e$$

True score

The average score that an individual would earn on an infinite number of administrations of the same test or parallel versions of the same test.

Error score (or measurement error)

The hypothetical difference between an observed score and a true score.

This model assumes that the characteristic being measured is stable and that the only reason an observed score changes from one measurement to another is due to random error. Error scores are independent of the characteristic being measured; errors are attributable to the measurement process, not to the individual. That is, the magnitude of error scores is unrelated to the magnitude of the characteristic being measured. The error score for an applicant with a very high level of the critical characteristic could be very large or very small; that same situation would hold for any level of the characteristic. The model also assumes that true scores and error scores combine in a simple additive manner.

If the measuring instrument is not very accurate—that is, if it adds large random error components to true scores—then the variance of the measured scores should be much larger than the variance of the true scores. Reliability can be thought of as the ratio of true score variance, Var(T), to observed score variance, Var(X); this can be expressed as the following equation:[7]

$$r_{xx} = \frac{\text{Var}(T)}{\text{Var}(X)},$$

where r_{xx} is the reliability coefficient, the degree that observed scores, which are made on the same stable characteristic, correlate with one another. In this case, r^2 represents the proportion of variance in the observed scores that is attributed to true differences on the measured characteristic.

For the arrival times in our example, Var(T) = 1.0; for the reported times, Var(X) = 3.0, with r_{xx} = 0.33. Only 10 percent of the variability in the reported arrival times, $(r_{xx})^2$, is attributable to the true arrival time; the remaining 90 percent of the variability is attributable to the inaccuracy of the time clock. When the time clock is systematically fast by five minutes—Var(X) = 1.0, giving an r_{xx} = 1.00—the systematic error does not affect the reliability coefficient; the scores are very reliable, but they do not tell anything about the time people actually arrived at work.

Measurement Error

Measurement error can be thought of as the hypothetical difference between an individual's observed score on any particular measurement and the individual's true score. Measurement error, whether systematic or random, reduces the usefulness of any set of measurements or the results from any test. It reduces the confidence that we can place in the score the measurement assigns to any particular individual. Does the score accurately represent the individual's knowledge or ability, or is it so fraught with error that we cannot use it to make meaningful decisions?

Information on the degree of error present in any set of measurements must be considered when using the measurements to make employment decisions. In our example, the manager must consider the possible major sources of the error, the size of the error, and the degree to which the observed scores would reoccur in another setting or with other employees. The *standard error of measurement* is a statistical index that summarizes information related to measurement error. This index is estimated from observed scores obtained over a group of individuals. It reflects how an individual's score would vary, on average, over repeated observations that were made under identical conditions.

Factors Affecting Reliability

The factors that introduce error into any set of measurements can be organized into three broad categories: temporary individual characteristics, lack of standardization, and chance.

Temporary Individual Characteristics

Following his interview with the human resources manager, Mr. B is assigned a relatively low score for know-how, which is assumed to be stable over time. If Mr. B was sick on the day of the interview, or extremely anxious or tired, his know-how score might reflect a larger-than-normal error component. On another occasion, when Mr. B is in better shape, he is interviewed again and given a higher know-how score. The difference in the two scores is attributed to the difference in Mr. B's state of well-being, rather than to a change in know-how. Mr. B's ill health negatively affected his performance during the initial interview, leading to a lower score. Factors such as health, motivation, fatigue, and emotional state introduce temporary, unsystematic errors into the measurement process. In academic examinations, students are often heard to attribute lower-than-expected test performance to many of these same temporary factors.

Lack of Standardization

Changing the conditions under which measurements are made introduces error into the measurement process. Ms. A, Mr. B, Ms. C, and Mr. D are asked different questions during their interviews. Ms. A is interviewed over lunch in a very comfortable restaurant, while the other candidates are interviewed in a very austere conference room. Mr. B is given a few minutes to answer each question, but the others are given as long as they need. The manager displays a lack of interest in Mr. B during the interview, but reacts very positively to Ms. A. In school, most students write their exams in large, crowded, noisy rooms, while some others are allowed to write their exams in small, quiet, comfortable spaces. These are just a few of the ways that lack of standardization can enter into the measurement process.

Chance

Factors unique to a specific procedure introduce error into the set of measurements. Luck of the draw may have done in Mr. B during his interview. His know-how score is based on how he answered a specific set of questions. Mr. B did poorly on the questions he was asked, but he might have done extremely well on any others. Mr. D had no prior experience with interviews, while Ms. A knew what to expect, from previous experience. Ms. C was distracted and did not understand a critical question. In school, a student may "guess" correctly about what content will be covered on the exam and study only that material, while another student "guesses" incorrectly and studies material not on the test. The performance of the two students might be reversed if they had reversed their guesses about what to study.

Methods of Estimating Reliability

To measure reliability, we have to estimate the degree of variability in a set of scores that is caused by measurement error. We can obtain this estimate by using two different, but parallel, measurements of the characteristic or attribute. Over the same set of people, both measurements should report the same score for each individual. This score will represent the true score plus measurement error. Both measurements reflect the same true score; discrepancies between the two sets of scores suggest the presence of measurement error. The correlation coefficient based on the scores from both measurements gives an estimate of r_{xx}, the reliability coefficient. It is extremely difficult, if not impossible, to obtain two parallel measurements of the same characteristic; therefore, several strategies have been developed as approximations of parallel measurements.

Test and Retest

The identical measurement procedure is used to assess the same characteristic over the same group of people on two different occasions. The human resources manager invites the job applicants back for a second interview. They are asked the same questions in the same order. The correlation of their first and second interview scores estimates the reliability of the know-how scores. High correlations suggest high levels of reliability. Giving exactly the same test to students on two occasions is another example of estimating test–retest reliability.

Alternate Forms

Having a person take the same interview twice may lead to a false estimate of the reliability of the interview process. The candidates may recall their original answers to the interview questions; they may also have thought of better answers after the first interview and give the improved answers on the second opportunity. To prevent the intrusion of effects from the first interview, the manager asks the applicants alternate questions during the second interview. The correlation between both know-how scores again estimates reliability, with high correlations once more indicating strong reliability. Giving students two different forms of the same test is an example of estimating alternate forms reliability. The two tests cover exactly the same content but the questions are not the same on both occasions.

Internal Consistency

Both test–retest and alternate forms procedures require two sets of measurements made on different occasions. In the case of interviews, it is quite costly in time and money to put all of the candidates through a second interview procedure. Besides, isn't each question in the interview directed at measuring know-how? Why not consider any two questions in the interview to be an example of a test–retest situation, and determine the correlation between scores given to each item in that pair? This is the logic behind establishing reliability through internal consistency. Rather than select any particular pair of items, the correlations between the scores of all possible pairs of items are calculated and then averaged. This average estimates the internal consistency, the degree to which all of the questions in the set are measuring the same thing.

These estimates are sometimes called *alpha* coefficients, or *Cronbach's alpha*, after the formula used to produce the estimate. *Split-half reliability* is a special case of internal consistency, where all of the items are first divided into two arbitrary groups. For example, all of the even-numbered items may form one group, with the odd-numbered items placed into the second. The correlation over each person's average scores in the two groups is used as the reliability estimate.

Inter-Rater Reliability

Measurement in personnel selection is often based on the subjective assessment, or rating, of one individual by another. The human resources manager's assessment of know-how based on the interview is a subjective measurement. How likely would the rating assigned by one judge be assigned by other judges? The correlation between these two judgments estimates the reliability of their assessments. The manager and the assistant manager independently rate each applicant's interview; a high correlation between their two scores suggests that their scores are reliable measurements of know-how. Sometimes, this index is referred to as *classification consistency* or *inter-rater agreement*. This distinction is purely semantic. As part of group projects, professors may ask all of the members of the group to rate independently the contribution of all of the other members of the group. The more consistent the scores, the more reliable they are as measurements of a student's contribution to the group project.

Choosing an Index of Reliability

Measurements of test–retest reliability, alternate forms reliability, and internal consistency are special cases of a more general type of index called a *generalizability coefficient*. These three measurements, however, provide slightly different views of a measurement's reliability. Each is limited and does not convey all of the relevant information that might be needed. The specific requirements of a situation may dictate which index is chosen. As well, it remains within the professional judgment of the human resources specialist to choose an appropriate index of reliability and to determine the level of reliability that is acceptable for use of a specific measurement. Before using any measurement to make decisions about employees, the HR specialist must consider the consequences of the decisions based on the measurement. The need for accuracy increases with the seriousness of the consequences for the employee.[8]

Validity

It is important and necessary to demonstrate that a measurement is reliable; it is also necessary to show that the measurement captures the essence of the characteristic or attribute. Often, validity is incorrectly thought of as indicating the worth or goodness of a test or other measurement procedure. *Validity* simply refers to the legitimacy or correctness of the inferences that are drawn from a set of measurements or other specified procedures.[9] It is the degree to which accumulated evidence and theory support specific interpretations of test scores in the context of the test's proposed use.

Consider the following: During an employment interview, a human resources manager measures the height of each applicant with a metal measuring tape. These height measurements are likely to be very reliable. What if the manager assumes that taller applicants have more job-related cognitive ability and hires the tallest people? Are the inferences drawn from the physical height measurements valid statements of cognitive ability? In other words, can the manager make a legitimate inference about cognitive ability from the height data? What if your instructor in a course on recruitment and selection in Canada gave you a test based solely on Canadian history? Would the inferences made from that test be an accurate reflection of your knowledge of recruitment and selection?

Before using any set of measurements, it is essential to demonstrate that the measurements lead to valid inferences about the characteristic or construct under study. It is relatively easy to demonstrate that the metal tape provides valid measurements of physical height. The metal tape measure can be scaled to an actual physical standard that is used to define a unit of length. The standard exists apart from the measurement process. In the case of length, the standard is a bar of plutonium maintained under specific atmospheric conditions in government laboratories.

It is more difficult to demonstrate the validity of inferences made from many psychological measurements because they deal more with abstract constructs, such as cognitive ability or know-how. As discussed earlier in this chapter, the measurements may not represent important aspects of a construct (construct under-representation) or they may be influenced by aspects of the process that are unrelated to the construct (construct-irrelevant variance). In most of these cases, independent physical standards for the construct do not exist, making validation more difficult, but not impossible. Validation rests on evidence accumulated through a variety of sources and a theoretical foundation that supports specific interpretations of the measurements.

Validation Strategies

Validity is a unitary concept.[10,11] Content, construct, and criterion-related validity are different, but interrelated, strategies commonly used to assess the accuracy of inferences based on measurements or tests used in the workplace. Sometimes these different strategies are mistakenly viewed as representing different types of validity. To overcome this misinterpretation, the older terms of construct validity, content validity, and criterion-related validity are no longer used in the measurement literature, although they are still sometimes used in assessing selection systems.

Both construct and content validity are validation strategies that provide *evidence based on test content*, while criterion-related validity provides *evidence based on relationships to other variables*. Our presentation is based on *The Standards for Educational and Psychological Testing*,[12] but we will also use the more traditional terms, as we did in discussing Figure 2.1, when it is appropriate to do so. For example, one major document that HR specialists and personnel psychologists rely on is *Principles for the Validation and Use of Personnel Selection Procedures*.[13] The latest version of this document continues to use the traditional terms of content, construct, and criterion-related validity in its presentation of validation strategies, but within the context of evidence based on test content (content and construct validity) and evidence based on relationships to other variables (criterion-related validity).

Our presentation of validation strategies is not exhaustive; we will examine only those sources of evidence for validity that are likely to be encountered in employment situations. You may want to refer to both the *Standards* and the *Principles* for a more thorough discussion of validity issues. The *Principles* can be accessed online at http://www.siop.org/_Principles/principlesdefault.aspx.

Figure 2.3 illustrates different sources of evidence for validity using the cognitive ability data collected by the human resources manager. Figure 2.3 is, in fact, the part of the model presented in Figure 2.1 that is related to validity. The manager initially hypothesized that higher levels of cognitive ability were related to higher levels of job performance; this relationship is represented by line A. This relationship is based on theoretical and logical analyses of expert opinion and empirical data that show, in this case, that cognitive ability is linked to job performance. Both cognitive ability and job performance are abstract constructs, which we operationally defined, respectively, as a know-how score based on the employment interview and a job performance score derived from an assessment of an employee's work. Figure 2.3 presents the relationships between these two constructs and also their two measurements; these different relationships help to illustrate two different validation strategies.

Evidence Based on Test Content

This type of validity evidence comes from analyzing the relationship between a test's content and the construct the test is intended to measure. Each construct has a set of associated behaviours or events; these include not only

FIGURE 2.3

Validation Strategies

Construct Level

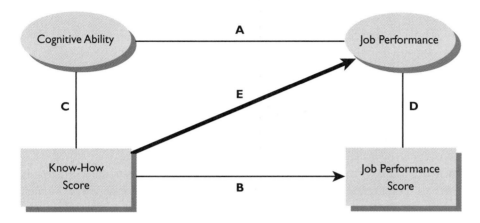

Measurement Level

test questions but also tasks, themes, and procedures for administering and scoring the test, among others. In any measurement situation, only a relatively small handful of these behaviours are measured.

Evidence of validity based on test content can consist of either empirical or logical analyses of how well the contents of the test, and the interpretation of the test scores, represent the construct. For example, suppose 10 questions are used to test your knowledge of the content of this chapter. Based on the number of correct answers, your instructor makes an inference about your *knowledge of measurement, reliability, and validity.* Is the inference justified? That is, do the 10 questions measure knowledge of measurement, reliability, and validity and does the score based on those questions represent your degree of knowledge of measurement, reliability, and validity?

Evidence for the validity of your instructor's test may be based on the consensus of a group of experts that the behaviours being measured (i.e., answers to the questions) do, in fact, fairly represent the behaviours associated with the construct (i.e., knowledge of measurement, reliability, and validity). It is a judgmental process. Evidence of the validity of the 10 questions used to measure knowledge of scientific methods could be established by a review of those questions by several experts on measurement. The agreement of these subject-matter experts (SMEs) that the questions fairly represented the information contained in this chapter constitutes evidence of validity based on the test contents. This type of validity is also known as *content validity.*

The job performance construct shown in Figure 2.3 may represent a large number of tasks that have been identified through one of the job analysis procedures that we will discuss in Chapter 4. SMEs next identify those tasks that are the most important, the most frequently performed, or the most critical to successful job performance. An HR specialist can take that information and turn it into a test that samples those job tasks. Chapter 9 provides examples of situational or patterned behaviour interviews that are linked to tasks performed on the job. In Figure 2.3, line D represents an inference based on a measurement of job performance about the job performance construct; line C illustrates an inference based on a score from the know-how or cognitive ability measurement to the cognitive ability construct.

The issue here is the degree to which valid inferences can be made about the cognitive ability and job performance constructs from their respective measurements. If Ms. C has a higher cognitive ability score than Mr. B, can we make the inference that Ms. C has more cognitive ability than Mr. B? If Mr. B has a higher job performance score than Ms. C, can we make the inference that Mr. B performs better on the job? In other words, do the two measurements—the know-how and job performance scores—measure the two constructs—cognitive ability and job performance—that they purport to measure? This is an issue of construct validity. Answers to these questions are based on logical analysis, expert opinion, and the convergence of the measurements with other accepted measurements of the construct, although this last type of evidence is really an example of evidence based on a relationship to another variable.

Evidence Based on Relationships to Other Variables

This type of evidence is based on an analysis of the relationship between test scores and other variables that are external to the test. For example, a relatively high correlation between the know-how test and the *Wonderlic Personnel Test* (a measurement of cognitive ability) and a relatively low correlation between the know-how test and the *16-PF* (a measurement of personality traits) would be evidence for its construct validity. In personnel selection, a test score is usually correlated with a score from a performance criterion rather than one from another test.

A criterion is an outcome measurement; it assesses the degree of success or failure associated with some decision. Job applicants are selected for employment; over time, some of the applicants perform at a higher level than do others. Measurements of job performance are criterion measurements. In selecting job applicants, one goal is to hire only those applicants who will perform at very high levels. But the applicants have to be hired before job performance can be measured. Is there another variable that is correlated with job performance that can be measured prior to hiring the applicant? Can we use information from this pre-employment measurement to make valid inferences about how an individual will perform once in the job? How accurately do test scores predict criterion performance?

The goal of establishing *test-criterion relationships* is to address questions like these. The usefulness of test-criterion relationship data rests on the reliability of the measurements of the test and the criterion and on the validity of the inferences drawn from those measurements about their respective constructs. In selection, correlations between predictor (scores on a selection test) and criterion (performance scores) measurements are examples of criterion-related validity.

In Figure 2.3, line B expresses a test-criterion relationship. Know-how scores, based on the pre-employment interview, are used to predict job performance scores. The arrow on the line indicates that a prediction is being made from one measurement to the other. Evidence for validity based on a test-criterion relationship involves establishing a correlation between two measurements. However, both of those measurements must validly represent their respective constructs. While test-criterion relationships focus on the observable measurements, the relationship that is of primary interest is represented in Figure 2.3 by line E. What the human resources manager really wants to do is predict, or make an inference about, the job performance construct from the know-how scores.

Similar to lines C and D, line E represents a relationship between a measurement and a construct. This relationship, like those of lines C and D, is established through validity evidence based on test content. If the test contains many aspects of the job performance construct, such as a work sample test, the test score itself may provide direct evidence for the relationship expressed in line E. For example, data entry clerks may be hired based on how well they perform on a keyboarding skill test, a sample of the performance they will be required to do on the job. The score on the test directly predicts job performance.

In most cases, the relationship of line E is established indirectly. In Figure 2.3, we want to make inferences from the know-how test scores to the job performance construct. We can establish that relationship only indirectly. First, we must show that both the predictor (the know-how scores) and the criterion (the job performance scores) are valid measurements of their respective constructs (line C and line D) *and* that a strong relationship exists between the predictor and criterion measurements (line D). We must also establish the theoretical or logical relationship between the two constructs (line A). Showing that these four relationships (lines A, B, C, and D) exist provides evidence for the existence of line E. Unfortunately, many test-criterion relationship studies suffer from a failure to demonstrate that the criterion measurement is a valid measure of the job performance construct.

Predictive Evidence for Test-Criterion Relationships

Predictive and *concurrent* strategies are popular methods used to provide evidence for test-criterion relationships. Predictive evidence is obtained through research designs that establish a correlation between predictor scores (know-how scores) obtained before an applicant is hired and criteria (performance scores) obtained at a later time, usually after an applicant is employed. If all of those who apply are hired, both variables can be measured, but at a substantial cost. Many applicants will be hired with the knowledge that they will likely fail on the job. This not only is expensive for the organization but also causes a great deal of emotional distress for those applicants who fail.

This procedure also raises serious legal and ethical considerations about the rights of job applicants and the obligations of people who make hiring decisions. To circumvent these problems, a variation on this procedure requires that hiring decisions be made without using information from the predictor measurement; the hiring decisions are made according to existing procedures, while the validity of the new predictor is established. The human resources manager interviews all of the applicants and collects know-how scores, but the hiring decision is based solely on information contained in the applicants' résumés and references. Job performance information is then collected from the group of hired applicants and correlated with their know-how scores. If the correlation is high, the know-how score may be used to select future job applicants. The high correlation is evidence in support of the position that accurate inferences can be made about job performance from the know-how scores.

But there is a problem with this strategy as well. Validity concerns the correctness of inferences made from a set of measurements. Does the validity coefficient, which is based on only those applicants who were hired, apply to all applicants? This will be the case only if the hired applicants fairly represent the total pool of applicants; the only way this can happen is if those hired were randomly selected from the larger pool. Therefore, those who are hired on the basis of the existing selection system will likely differ from those not hired on at least one characteristic, whether or not that characteristic is related to job success.

Concurrent Evidence for Test-Criterion Relationships

Concurrent evidence is obtained through research designs that establish a correlation between predictor and criteria scores from information that is collected at approximately the same time from a specific group of workers. The human resources manager interviews all current employees and assigns each a know-how score; at the same time, each worker is also assigned a job performance score. While concurrent evidence may be easier to collect, these strategies, too, are problematic. The group of existing workers used to develop the validity evidence are likely to be older, more experienced, and certainly more successful than those who apply for jobs. Unsuccessful or unproductive workers most likely are not part of the validation study as they probably were let go or transferred to other positions. The primary concern here is whether a validity coefficient based on only successful applicants can be used as evidence to validate decisions based on predictor scores from a pool of both successful and unsuccessful job candidates.

An additional concern is the same one expressed with predictive strategies: Does the validity coefficient computed on one group of workers apply to the pool of applicants? The current workers, who are asked to complete a battery of selection tests, may approach the whole exercise with a different attitude and level of motivation than job applicants. These differences may affect selection instruments, particularly those like personality and integrity tests that rely on the test-taker's cooperation in responding truthfully. Statistically, validity coefficients based on concurrent evidence will likely underestimate the true validity of using the predictor to make decisions within the pool of applicants. Recruitment and Selection Notebook 2.1 provides some guidance for assessing the validity of selection procedures in smaller organizations.

Validity Generalization

Suppose in attempting to establish the validity of the know-how interview as a predictor of specific job performance in the organization, the human resources manager discovered that there were many other studies that also

---

Validity

Validation studies require relatively large numbers of hires. This is a challenge for many Canadian organizations, particularly small businesses that do not hire many people. Several validation techniques are suited for use with small samples:

- Build a database by combining *similar* jobs *across* organizations or companies, with special care taken to ensure comparability of performance measurements.
- Accumulate selection scores and performance measurements *over time*, as workers leave and are replaced.
- Generalize to your particular case the mean (average) predictive validity for a test as found for jobs similar to the one to which you wish to generalize (i.e., *validity generalization*).
- Generalize to your case the *specific* validity of the test as previously established for a similar job in another setting (i.e., *validity transportability*).

Frequently, however, a *content sampling* strategy may be necessary. The steps for this process are:

1. Tasks (or activities) of the target position are identified by job experts.

2. Job experts infer, on a task-by-task basis, the required knowledge, skills, abilities, and other attributes (KSAOs).
3. Job experts independently rate the relevance of each KSAO for each task.
4. Assessment items (e.g., test questions, situational exercises, interview questions) are developed to measure the most relevant KSAOs.
5. Job experts provide independent ratings of the degree to which each assessment item is linked to the KSAOs.
6. Job experts evaluate the relationship between performance on each of the selection assessments and job success.
7. A scoring scheme is developed for the selection assessments.

The case for the validity of the selection system is then argued on the basis of an explicit systematic linking of the selection assessments (interview questions, test items, situational exercises) to the position requirements (KSAOs), as established by job experts.

Source: P.R. Sackett and R.D. Arvey. 1993. "Selection in Small N Settings." In N. Schmitt, W.C. Borman, and Associates, eds., *Personnel Selection in Organizations*. San Francisco: Jossey-Bass, 418–47. Reprinted with permission of Wiley-Blackwell.

investigated measurements of cognitive ability as predictors of similar job performance. Could the manager somehow combine all of the information provided by these other correlation coefficients to obtain an estimate of the true validity of cognitive ability as a predictor of job performance in the new employment setting? These other validity coefficients were obtained under vastly different measurement conditions and from employees who differ dramatically across these studies on a number of characteristics.

Most likely, the value of the individual validity coefficients will be very inconsistent across all of these other studies. In other words, can the manager estimate the validity of know-how scores as a predictor of job performance in the manager's work setting from the validity of inferences based on other measurements of cognitive ability found in other work settings with other groups of workers? **Validity generalization** procedures allow these types of predictions to be made.

Starting in the mid-1970s, Schmidt and Hunter,[14] in conjunction with several colleagues, challenged the idea that a validity coefficient was specific to the context or environment in which it was measured. They used a procedure known as *meta-analysis* to combine validity coefficients for similar predictor and criterion measurements reported by different validity studies. Schmidt and Hunter argued that the relative inconsistency in validity coefficients across studies could be attributed to statistical artifacts such as the range of scores in each study, the reliability of the criterion measurements, and sample size (i.e., the number of people in the validity study).

In combining the data, meta-analysis weights the results from each separate validity study according to its sample. On the whole, the smaller the study size, the less accurate the results. Validity studies usually involve relatively small study sizes since most organizations do not hire large numbers of people. Schmidt and Hunter demonstrated that, once the effects associated with study size and the other artifacts were removed, the validity between a predictor and a criterion remained relatively stable within similar occupations. For example, the human resources manager could use the know-how interview scores to make predictions about job performance if other validity studies had linked cognitive ability to job performance for similar jobs and if the know-how scores were a valid measurement of cognitive ability.

Should the HR specialist rely on validity generalization evidence or conduct a new validity study on-site? The answer is not straightforward. If the meta-analysis database is large and adequately represents the type of job to which it will be generalized in the local situation, there is a strong case for using the validity generalization data. On the other hand, if the database is small, the results inconsistent, and there is little in common between the specific job and those included in the meta-analysis, then a local validity study should be carried out. If conducted properly with an adequate sample size, the local study may provide more useful information than the validity generalization data. A study carried out on the specific job in the local environment will also provide a means of corroborating questionable validity generalization data.[15]

Validity generalization

The application of validity evidence, obtained through meta-analysis of data obtained from many situations, to other situations that are similar to those on which the meta-analysis is based.

Factors Affecting Validity Coefficients

Range Restriction

When measurements are made on a subgroup that is more homogeneous than the larger group from which it is selected, validity coefficients obtained on the subgroup are likely to be smaller than those obtained from the larger group. This reduction in the size of the validity coefficient due to the selection process is called *range restriction*. Selection results in a more homogeneous group. The applicant pool reviewed by the human resources manager contains a broad range of know-how. The people selected for employment are more likely to fall in the upper range of know-how; the existing workers are also more likely to have levels of know-how more similar to one another than to the applicant pool. The range of know-how scores for the hired workers is narrower or more restricted than the scores of all the applicants.

Statistically, the magnitude of correlation coefficients, including validity coefficients, decreases as the similarity or homogeneity of characteristics being measured increases. There are several statistical procedures that correct for range restriction and provide an estimate of what the validity coefficient is likely to be in the larger group. Range restriction is often encountered in selecting undergraduate students for graduate or professional programs. The students who apply for these positions are generally very similar with respect to their grade point averages and cognitive ability; this homogeneity generally leads to low correlation coefficients when their scores on standardized tests, such as the GRE, GMAT, LSAT, and others, are used to predict performance in graduate or professional school.

Measurement Error

The reliability of a measurement places an upper limit on validity. Mathematically, the size of a validity coefficient cannot exceed the reliability of the measurements used to obtain the data. Validity coefficients obtained from perfectly reliable measurements of the predictor and criterion will be higher than those obtained with less-than-perfect measurements. The decrease in magnitude of the validity coefficient associated with measurement error of the predictor, the criterion, or both, is called *attenuation*. As with range restriction, there are statistical procedures that provide an estimate of what the validity coefficient would be if it had been obtained by using measurements that were perfectly reliable (i.e., $r_{xx} = 1.00$).

Sampling Error

Criterion-related validity coefficients are obtained from people who have been hired and are used to assess the accuracy of inferences that are made about individual applicants. The validity coefficient based on a sample is an estimate of what the coefficient is in the entire population; usually, it is impractical or impossible to measure the validity coefficient directly in the population. Estimates of the validity within a population may vary considerably between samples; estimates from small samples are likely to be quite variable.

The statistical procedures that are used to compensate for range restriction, attenuation, and problems related to sampling will almost always produce higher estimates of validity than the uncorrected coefficients. When correction procedures are used, both the corrected and uncorrected validity coefficients should be reported, along with a justification for the use of the correction.

Bias and Fairness

Bias

In discussing reliability, we noted that measurement errors could be made in a consistent, or predictable, fashion. In the time clock example, five minutes were added to each worker's arrival time. What if the clock had added five minutes only to the arrival times of female employees? The observed scores are still reliable, but now they validly represent the true arrival times for male employees, but not for female employees. The clock is biased in measuring arrival times of female employees. **Bias** refers to systematic errors in measurement, or inferences made from measurements, that are related to different identifiable group membership characteristics such as age, sex, or race.[16] For example, suppose the human resources manager assigns higher know-how scores to females, when in fact there are no differences in cognitive ability between men and women. Inferences, or predictions, drawn from the biased measurements are themselves biased.

Figure 2.4 illustrates a hypothetical situation in which the cognitive ability scores of females are higher, on average, than those for the males, reflecting some type of systematic error. This is the same scatterplot given in Figure 2.2 (page 34), but with the data for Ms. F and Mr. E, and Ms. J and Mr. H, reversed. Therefore, it will have the same regression line as given in Table 2.2 on page 33. Now Ms. F's job performance score is predicted to be 6.91 versus 5.11 previously; Ms. J's is predicted to be 6.31 versus 5.71. The regression line, using the biased cognitive ability measurement as a predictor, overestimates the likely job performance of the female employees and underestimates that of males.

If this regression line was used to make hiring decisions (e.g., "We want employees who will obtain performance scores of 6 or better, so hire only applicants with cognitive ability scores of 8 or higher"), the predictions of successful job performance would be biased in favour of the female applicants. This type of bias is known as *differential prediction*; that is, the predicted, average performance score of a subgroup (in this case, males or females) is systematically higher or lower than the average score predicted for the group as a whole. This situation results in a larger proportion of the lower-scoring group being rejected on the basis of their test scores, even though they would have performed successfully had they been hired. This condition results from a less-than-perfect correlation between the predictor and criterion measurements.

Bias

Refers to systematic errors in measurement, or inferences made from those measurements, that are related to different identifiable group membership characteristics such as age, sex, or race.

FIGURE 2.4

Scatterplot of Cognitive Ability and Job Performance—II

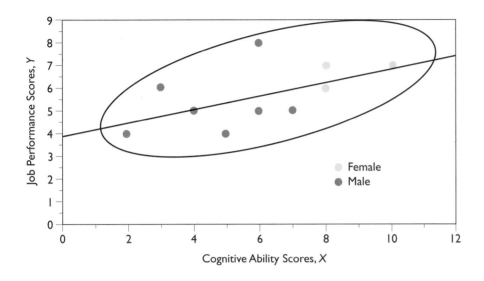

One way to overcome this type of bias is to generate separate regression lines (i.e., separate prediction formulas) for males and females.[17] In Canadian federal organizations, separate prediction formulas are often used in selecting job applicants from anglophone and francophone linguistic groups. In U.S. federal organizations, the use of different selection rules for different identifiable subgroups (often referred to as *subgroup norming*) is prohibited by U.S. federal law.

There are other, more complicated, types of bias that might occur in a set of measurements.[18] Items on a test may elicit a variety of responses other than what was intended, or some items on a test may have different meanings for members of different subgroups. For example, the *Bennett Mechanical Comprehension Test* contains pictures related to the use of different tools and machines that tend to be used mostly by males. Males are more likely to recognize these tools and their proper use and perform well on the test. On the other hand, females with good mechanical comprehension may not do as well on the test because of their lack of familiarity with specific tools pictured on the Bennett test. The result is that the test may underestimate the true mechanical ability of female job applicants. The statistical procedures needed to establish bias are often complicated and difficult to carry out. Nonetheless, the question of bias can be answered through empirical and objective procedures.

Fairness

The concept of **fairness** in measurement refers to the value judgments people make about the decisions or outcomes that are based on measurements. An unbiased measurement or test may still be viewed as being unfair either by society as a whole or by different groups within it. Canada is a bilingual

Fairness

The principle that every test-taker should be assessed in an equitable manner.

country composed of French- and English-language groups. Suppose that a completely unbiased cognitive ability test were used to select people for the Canadian civil service and that all the francophone applicants scored well above the highest-scoring anglophone. Such cognitive ability scores would predict that francophones would do better on the job than anglophones, so only francophones would be hired for the civil service. This outcome would very likely be judged as unfair by English-speaking Canadians, even though it would be the empirically correct decision. Canadians might expect their civil service to represent both official language groups. In fact, political considerations might require that the civil service be proportional to the two linguistic groups.

Issues of fairness cannot be determined statistically or empirically. Fairness involves perceptions. An organization may believe it is fair to select qualified females in place of higher-ranking males in order to increase the number of women in the organization; on the other hand, the higher-ranking males who were passed over might not agree. The *Principles for the Validation and Use of Personnel Selection Procedures*[19] states this about fairness: "Fairness is a social rather than a psychometric concept. Its definition depends on what one considers to be fair. Fairness has no single meaning and, therefore, no single statistical or psychometric definition."

Fairness is an even more complex topic than bias. Achieving fairness often requires compromise between conflicting interests.[20,21] This is particularly so in the case where, for whatever reason, there may be persistent differences in average test scores between different groups in the population but those differences do not necessarily indicate test bias. A test score predicts the same level of performance for members of all groups, but the average test score for one group is lower than another group's, leading to the exclusion of a larger proportion of the group with the lower average score. Lowering the selection standards to include more applicants from this group in order to make the work force more representative of the general population may come at the cost of hiring job applicants who, while they meet the minimum job qualifications, are not the most qualified candidates for the position. Presumably, the most qualified candidates bring the most return in productivity to the organization.

Does an organization have an obligation to make the enterprise as profitable as possible on behalf of its owners, or should it meet the objectives of society by providing equal employment opportunities for members of different population groups? There are no easy answers to this question. In cases such as this, one resolution is to compare the fairness of the test in question with the fairness of an alternative that might be used in place of the test.[22] Recruitment and Selection Today 2.2 presents some differing views on fairness.

In addition to the concerns about the impact of tests on different groups, fairness issues also include the reaction of applicants to testing and personnel selection decisions. It is important from business, ethical, and legal standpoints to have tests that are scientifically sound; it is also important to have procedures that are perceived as fair. From a business perspective, the

Different Views of Fairness

Any discussion of fairness quickly becomes complicated, as there are several ways of defining this concept. *The Standards for Educational and Psychological Testing* provides five definitions:

1. **Fairness as lack of bias.** A test or testing procedure is considered fair if it does not produce any systematic effects that are related to different identifiable group membership characteristics such as age, sex, or race.

2. **Fairness as equitable treatment in the testing process.** All examinees should be treated equitably throughout the testing process. They should experience the same or comparable procedures in the testing itself, in how the tests are scored, and in how the test scores are used.

3. **Fairness as opportunity to learn.** All examinees should have had an equal opportunity to learn the material covered in achievement tests. The opportunity to learn is relevant to some uses and interpretations of achievement tests.

[**Comment:** There is general consensus among professionals that these three conditions should be met in establishing the fairness of a test.]

4. **Fairness as equality in outcomes of testing.** This requires that the passing rates be comparable across identifiable group membership characteristics such as age, sex, or race. That is, the same percentage of applicants from each identifiable group should "pass" the test or score above the cut-off that might be used to make hiring decisions.

[**Comment:** This view of fairness is mostly rejected in the professional literature. Professionals would argue that examinees of equal standing with respect to the ability or skill being measured should, on average, earn the same test score regardless of group membership.]

5. **Fairness in selection and prediction.** This often requires a compromise between the perspective that equates fairness with lack of bias and the perspective that focuses on testing outcomes. A selection test might be considered fair if the same test score predicts the same performance level for members of all groups, but it might be considered unfair if average test scores differ across groups. The fairness of the test should, in this situation, be evaluated relative to fairness of other non-test alternatives that could be used in place of the test.

[**Comment:** This situation is the one most often encountered in personnel selection. It generally requires a compromise between the two perspectives to achieve a resolution.]

Source: *The Standards for Educational and Psychological Testing.* 1999. American Educational Research Association, American Psychological Association, and National Council on Measurement in Education. Washington, DC: American Educational Research Association.

adverse reactions to selection tests and procedures may impair the ability of an organization to recruit and hire the best applicants, thereby reducing the utility of the recruitment and selection process. In one example, the perceived fairness of selection procedures used by a major telecommunications company influenced the views of prospective employees on the attractiveness of the company as a place to work, their intentions to recommend the company to others, and their intentions to accept a job.[23]

From an ethical view, the perceived fairness of the testing procedures may negatively affect the unsuccessful candidates. From a legal perspective, the perception of unfairness may lead unsuccessful applicants to pursue discrimination charges against the prospective employer in various legal arenas.[24]

Serious consideration should be given to the perception of a test or selection procedure from the applicant's perspective prior to its adoption. This does not mean that an employer should discard scientifically valid procedures because they may be perceived as unfair; there is far more risk for an organization that makes employment decisions on the basis of unproven methods. In the final analysis, fairness is a question of balance.

Integrating Validity Evidence

An argument for the validity of interpretations from a selection test or procedure rests on the integration of scientific evidence obtained through a variety of sources. It includes information that is collected from the existing scientific literature as well as data newly collected as part of the validation effort. Both existing data and theory are used to support the proposition that test scores allow accurate inferences to be made about a candidate's future job performance.

The technical quality of the testing procedure (e.g., careful test development, test reliability, standardized test administration and scoring procedures, and test fairness) must also be considered along with other validity evidence. All of this evidence must support the proposed use of the information obtained through the testing procedure if that test is to be used as part of the selection process.

Summary

Science produces information that is based on accepting as true only objective information that can withstand continued attempts to cast doubt on its accuracy. The accuracy of scientific statements is examined empirically through methods that can be observed, critiqued, and used by others. Scientific information is dynamic and constantly evolving. One goal of personnel selection is to use scientifically derived information to predict which job applicants will do well on the job. As demonstrated by the *Meiorin* decision, courts and tribunals will review the methods used to develop selection procedures. The procedures used to select employees must meet acceptable professional standards. The best way of ensuring this is to be familiar with measurement, reliability, and validity issues, and to use only those procedures that will withstand legal scrutiny; that is the selection procedures used validly predict work performance in a nondiscriminatory manner.

Scientific procedures allow for the measurement of important human characteristics that may be related to job performance and are more likely than other procedures to produce results that meet legal requirements. The reliability and validity of the information used as part of personnel selection procedures must be established empirically, as noted in the *Meiorin* decision. The methods used to establish reliability and validity can be quite complex and require a good statistical background. As a scientific process, any personnel selection system must be able to withstand attempts to cast doubt on its ability to select the best people for the job in a fair and unbiased manner.

Key Terms

bias, p. 50
construct, p. 28
employment equity, p. 31
error score (or measurement error), p. 36
fairness, p. 51

reliability, p. 35
true score, p. 36
validity, p. 25
validity generalization, p. 48

Web Links

The complete *Meiorin* decision can be read at **http://csc.lexum.umontreal .ca/en/1999/1999rcs3-3/1999rcs3-3.html.**

For more information on basic statistical procedures, go to **http://wise.cgu .edu.**

Test reliability and validity information is provided at **http://www .socialresearchmethods.net/kb/relandval.php.**

Required Professional Capabilities (RPCs)

RPC 2.1 Audits existing HR programs to ensure they are aligned with business objectives.
- The organization's strategic business plan and the goals of the business unit
- Survey and data collection techniques
- Statistical analyses and evaluation including validity and reliability concepts and assessment techniques
- Benchmarking techniques and industry best practices
- HRIS/HRMS concepts
- Current HR programs and practices
- Research methods and designs
- Measurement and assessment tools and techniques (and their limitations)
- Techniques to evaluate effectiveness of HR programs (e.g., selection, training, and compensation, etc.)

RPC 2.2 Sets clear goals, objectives, evaluation standards, and measurements for HR programs and strategies.
- Goals of the organization
- Client requirements and work plans
- Work assignment/job design techniques
- Work flow analysis
- Measurement and assessment tools and techniques (and their limitations)
- Procedures for collection, manipulation, and analysis of information

- Techniques to evaluate effectiveness of HR programs (e.g., selection, training, and compensation, etc.)
- Key HR initiatives and considerations
- Strategic HR management
- Goal-setting processes and techniques

RPC 2.3 Ensures the HR information management function is fully capable of supporting the organization's strategic and operational needs.
- The organization's strategic business plan and the goals of the business unit
- HRMS and business software
- Evaluation techniques and issues
- Database concepts
- Work flow models
- Effective systems of managing HR information
- Collection, manipulation, and analysis of information
- Research methods and designs (including measurement of HR)
- Measurement and assessment tools and techniques (and their limitations)
- Importance, criteria, and techniques of program evaluation
- Cost–benefit analyses (including audits, utility analysis, ROI, and impact studies)
- Business operations

RPC 2.4 Evaluates the effectiveness of HR strategies, applying various measurement and assessment programs.
- The company's HR programs and culture of the organization
- Measurement and assessment tools and techniques (and their limitations)
- The organization's strategic business plan and the goals of the business unit
- Research methods and designs
- Statistical analyses and evaluation including validity and reliability concepts and assessment techniques
- Needs analysis
- Strategic HR management practices and techniques
- Techniques to evaluate effectiveness of HR programs (e.g., selection, training, and compensation, etc.)

RPC 2.5 Researches, analyzes, and reports on potential people issues affecting the organization.
- Use of business and HR management software
- Research methods and designs (including measurement of HR)
- Measurement and assessment tools and techniques (and their limitations)
- Statistical analyses and evaluation
- Needs analysis
- Organization culture, business environment, and objectives

RPC 2.6 Identifies the data required to support HR planning.
- HR planning concepts and techniques
- Use of business and HR software
- Research methods and designs (including measurement of HR)
- Trends in human resources planning

Discussion Questions

1. We presented a summary of the *Meiorin* case at the outset of this chapter. Can you think of procedures or changes that the consultants could have effected that would have allowed the test to meet the objections of the Supreme Court?
2. Discuss the reasons why it is better to base a selection system on science than on a "gut feeling."
3. Can an invalid selection test be reliable? Can an unreliable selection test be valid? (Hint: Consider finding Canadian history questions on your recruitment and selection exam.)
4. Does an organization have an obligation to make the enterprise as profitable as possible on behalf of its owners, or does it have an obligation to meet the objectives of society by providing equal employment opportunities for members from different population groups?

Using the Internet

1. **Note:** Class instructors might want to assign this exercise during the previous class and ask students to e-mail their data to them beforehand.

   A significant portion of this chapter has dealt with tests and testing procedures. In later chapters, we will explore the use of different types of employment tests that have good reputations for reliability and validity. Access to these tests is restricted for obvious reasons. They can be administered only by qualified examiners, unlike the types of "IQ" and "personality" tests that you may come across in newspapers or magazines. While these latter tests are fun to take, they may have questionable reliability and validity.

   Many sites on the Internet are devoted to tests, some serious and some for fun. One of the better sites is *Queendom Mind and Body* at http://www.queendom.com. This site offers an array of tests including IQ, personality, and emotional intelligence. All of the tests are free and can be taken online and are immediately scored. Unlike some of the other sites, it offers statistical information on the reliability of almost all of its tests and on the validity of some. Most of the reliability data are based on measurements of internal consistency.

As part of this exercise, take the Emotional Intelligence Test, the Classical IQ Test, and the Extroversion Test. Queendom.com will provide you with a report containing your scores and inferences from your scores about how you fare on the three constructs. Please download copies of each report as well as the statistical data provided for each test. Your instructor will arrange for you to anonymously record your scores from these tests so that data on the whole class can be accumulated for the following exercises. We will also ask you to record your sex and your cumulative grade point average or percentage (if you don't know this last item, an estimate will do).

a. *Test–Retest Reliability.* Wait at least one week after taking the three tests and then retake all three. Once all of the data from the class are compiled, your instructor will compute the correlation between the first and second administration of the three tests.

- Is each of the tests reliable? (Tests with reliability coefficients greater than 0.70 are generally considered to have acceptable reliability.)
- How does the test–retest reliability compare with the reliability values presented online?
- What reasons do you think there might be for any differences?
- What factors may have led you to perform differently on each of the two testing occasions?

b. *Validity.* Examine the content of each test; that is, examine the nature of the test questions (you are allowed to download a copy of each test).

- Do you think that the contents of each test reflect the essential nature of the construct it attempts to measure?
- Based on other empirical and theoretical evidence, we would not expect there to be a strong relationship between the results of the Classical IQ (a measurement of cognitive ability) and Extroversion/Introversion (a measurement of personality) tests. Emotional intelligence has been presented as a construct, which is different from both cognitive ability and personality. There should be very low correlations among the test scores from these three tests. A high correlation between the Emotional Intelligence and Extroversion/Introversion test results might suggest that both tests are measurements of the same construct. Your instructor will correlate the three test scores for the class using data from the first test administration. What is the relationship among the three test scores?
- Cognitive ability is associated with academic performance. The Classical IQ Test measures cognitive ability, and your cumulative grade point average (GPA) is an estimate of your academic performance. GPA is a criterion. What is the correlation between the Classical IQ Test results and GPA for your class, as reported

by your instructor? Does this correlation indicate that you may make accurate inferences about academic performance from your IQ test scores? Is there a strong correlation between the Emotional IQ Test result scores and GPA? Between the Extroversion/Introversion Test results and GPA? If so, what do you think these correlations suggest?

c. *Bias*. You or your instructor will have to analyze the class data separately for males and females. Compare the mean score for each group across the three tests. Compute the correlations among the three tests for men and women.

- Do you obtain similar results for males and females?
- Are any of the three tests biased?

d. *Fairness*. Do you believe that each of these three tests is fair? How would you react if you were given any of these three tests when you applied for your next job?

Exercises

1. A marketing company is evaluating a new employment test that measures the advertising aptitude of potential employees. You have used the new measurement on a trial basis over the past year, while you have continued to make selections using your established procedures. You have developed the following database, which includes information on gender, a score from the first administration of the test given during the selection process before the applicant was hired (Test 1), a score from a second administration of the test given at the end of

Employee	Gender	Test 1	Test 2	Performance
1	male	24	18	20
2	female	18	13	29
3	male	21	17	17
4	male	7	13	8
5	female	14	28	25
6	male	20	21	26
7	male	8	6	7
8	female	13	9	12
9	male	15	13	18
10	male	19	15	22
11	female	25	22	23
12	female	23	16	27
13	male	18	13	10
14	female	12	14	6
15	female	17	12	13
16	female	6	9	12

the first year on the job (Test 2), and a performance score assigned by the supervisor at the end of the employee's first year of employment (Performance). You have been asked to evaluate the reliability, validity, and any gender bias of the new test.

a. What is the reliability of the new test?
b. What is the predictive validity of the new test?
c. What is the concurrent validity of the job?
d. Is the test biased toward either males or females?
e. Would you recommend that the company adopt the new test as part of its hiring procedures?

2. Choose a specific job held by one of the people in your group. After discussing the job, choose one characteristic that you think is crucial to performing that job. How would you measure both the characteristic and job performance? Use Figures 2.1 and 2.3 (pages 24 and 43) to help you specify the conceptual and measurement levels. How would you establish the validity of your characteristic as a predictor of job performance?

3. *Group Project.* Each group is to choose two organizations and then interview the organizations' HR staff to identify the type of selection that is being used. Use the criteria in Table 2.1 (page 29) to determine if each organization's selection system is scientific or intuitive. Determine the validity of the selection procedures in use by each organization; that is, has the company conducted validation studies and, if so, what was the outcome? Collect any validation reports that the organizations might have produced and bring the reports back to the group for review and discussion. Each group could then present a report of its findings to the class.

Case

A story in the *Daily Commercial News*[25] reported that a growing number of Canadian companies are using measurements of emotional intelligence (EQ) as part of the screening devices administered to job applicants. These companies are looking for a measurement to tap into emotions. They are seeking candidates who have the ability to inspire colleagues, to handle customers, and to be a positive influence in the office. One of the more popular measurements of emotional intelligence is the *Bar-On Emotional Quotient Inventory* (EQ-i), which is distributed by Multi-Health Systems of Toronto. Steven Stein, president of Multi-Health Systems, is quoted in the article as saying that IQ has to do with solving math problems and that verbal ability has its place but emotional skills are much more valuable for success in the workplace.

Can a measurement of emotional intelligence predict job success? Lorne Sulsky, an industrial-organizational psychologist now at Wilfrid Laurier

University, is skeptical because the concept is too fuzzy and EQ tests are too imprecise to be reliable. Sulsky asks, "Why should there be a relationship between job performance and EQ?"

Discussion Questions

1. What do you think? Do the data that you collected in the Using the Internet exercise help you to answer this question? Should there be a relationship between job performance and EQ? Can you support your answer with any empirical data? How can the construct of EQ be improved? Is it too broad? Is EQ simply another aspect of personality?
2. If you were going to use EQ as part of your selection system, discuss the steps that you would take to ensure that you were able to make reliable and accurate inferences about job performance in your work situation. That is, what would you have to do to show that your measurement was reliable and valid?

Endnotes

1. Catano, V.M. 2001. "Empirically Supported Interventions and HR Practice." *HRM Research Quarterly* 5: 1–5.
2. Binning, J.F., and G.V. Barrett. 1989. "Validity of Personnel Decisions: A Conceptual Analysis of the Inferential and Evidential Bases." *Journal of Applied Psychology* 74: 478–94.
3. Kerlinger, F.N. 1986. *Foundations of Behavioural Research*, 3rd ed. New York: Holt, Rinehart and Winston.
4. Kerlinger, F.N. 1986.
5. American Educational Research Association (AERA), American Psychological Association, and National Council on Measurement in Education. 1999. *The Standards for Educational and Psychological Testing*. Washington, DC: American Educational Research Association.
6. Nunnally, J.C., and I.H. Bernstein. 1994. *Psychometric Theory*, 3rd ed. New York: McGraw-Hill.
7. AERA et al. 1999.
8. AERA et al. 1999.
9. Cronbach, L.J. 1971. "Test Validation." In R.L. Thorndike, ed., *Educational Measurement*, 2nd ed. Washington, DC: American Council of Education.
10. Binning, J.F., and G.V. Barrett. 1989.
11. AERA et al. 1999.
12. AERA et al. 1999.
13. Society for Industrial and Organizational Psychology, Inc. 2003. *Principles for the Validation and Use of Personnel Selection Procedures*, 4th ed. College Park, MD: Author.
14. Schmidt, F.L., and J.E. Hunter. 1977. "Development of a General Solution to the Problem of Validity Generalization." *Journal of Applied Psychology* 62: 529–40.
15. AERA et al. 1999.
16. AERA et al. 1999.
17. AERA et al. 1999.
18. Sackett, P.R., and S.L. Wilk. 1994. "Within-Group Norming and Other Forms of Score Adjustment in Pre-Employment Testing." *American Psychologist* 49: 929–54.

19. Society for Industrial and Organizational Psychology, Inc. 2003.
20. Gottfredson, L.S. 1994. "The Science and Politics of Race-Norming." *American Psychologist* 49: 955–63.
21. Sackett, P.R., and S.L. Wilk. 1994.
22. AERA et al. 1999.
23. Oliver, D.H. 1998. "Exploring Applicant Reactions to Selection Processes from an Organizational Justice Perspective." *Dissertation Abstracts International: Section B: The Sciences and Engineering* 59(2-B): 0902.
24. Gilliland, S.W. 1993. "The Perceived Fairness of Selection Systems: An Organizational Justice Perspective." *Academy of Management Review* 18: 694–734.
25. "Will EQ Gradually Replace IQ in Screening Candidates for Jobs?" 1998. *Daily Commercial News*, 71, S2, A14.

Foundations of Recruitment and Selection II: Legal Issues

Chapter Learning Objectives

This chapter presents an overview of the legal issues that affect the practice of recruitment and selection in Canada.

After reading this chapter you should:

- understand the major legal issues affecting recruitment and selection;
- know how relevant human rights and employment equity legislation and policies affect recruitment and selection in your organization;
- understand and be able to describe how legal concerns affect the practice of recruitment and selection;
- know, and be capable of explaining, the key legal concepts that have had an impact on recruitment and selection in this country; and
- be able to apply the basic concepts and principles discussed in the chapter to the development of recruitment and selection systems that meet legal requirements.

In Canada, Aboriginal peoples continue to encounter employment barriers and are under-represented in the federally regulated private-sector work force. The Nasittuq Corporation has been recognized by the federal government for its employment equity initiatives for Aboriginal peoples. The following was adapted from a Human Resources and Social Development Canada (HRSDC) annual report.

Nasittuq Corporation: Tapping into Aboriginal People's Talents

Nasittuq Corporation, headquartered in Ottawa, acts as the agent for a joint venture between ATCO Frontec Corporation and Pan Arctic Inuit Logistics Corporation. On behalf of the Department of Defence, the organization operates and maintains the North Warning System radar station network set up to detect airborne threats to North America. Nasittuq has 321 employees.

Reaching Out to Aboriginal Peoples

Partnerships

Nasittuq has benefited from partnerships with organizations in the communities in which it conducts business; by participating in community events, Nasittuq creates awareness of its operations and attracts individuals interested in employment. In 2006, it partnered with the Kitikmeot Economic Development Commission to attend a travelling trade show that visited five communities in five days throughout Nunavut's Kitikmeot region. Other organizations with which Nasittuq has created partnerships over the years include the Canadian Council for Aboriginal Business, Inuit Tapiriit Kanatami, the Chamber of Commerce of Inuvik, and the Baffin Regional Chamber of Commerce.

Job Postings

Nasittuq advertises career opportunities in several publications targeting Aboriginal peoples, including *Inuktitut Magazine, Native and Inuit Yearbook, Diversity Canada, Wind Speaker, Alberta Native News, Nunatsiaq News,* and *News North*.

Developing Potential

One of the keys to Nasittuq's success is its commitment to training existing and potential employees. Nasittuq believes that when employees are allowed to grow within the organization, they are more inclined to stay. Not only does Nasittuq attract and retain outstanding employees through its programs, but it also avoids expensive recruitment and retraining costs due to staff turnover. Nasittuq has implemented the following three programs to develop Aboriginal high-quality talent.

Training Program

Nasittuq has designed a unique on-the-job training program that is tailored to the individual needs of each trainee. On completion of the program, trainees can apply for vacancies within Nasittuq.

Development Program

Building on the success of its training program, Nasittuq implemented a development program that combines academic work and on-the-job training that, on successful completion, provides participants with an occupational designation or certification. The development program builds more senior technical skills and enhanced employment opportunities for Aboriginal peoples employed at Nasittuq. Since the creation of the development program in December 2001, 93 percent of participants have completed all required course work and on-the-job training.

Aboriginal Scholarship Program

Nasittuq has also established an annual Aboriginal Scholarship Program to encourage Aboriginal students to pursue advanced education in such areas as electronics, electrical engineering, computer science, environmental, business, and Aboriginal studies related to its activities.

Cost-Effective Initiatives

Nasittuq's cost-effective strategy commenced with the implementation and communication of employment equity–related policies throughout the organization. Training and development programs were established following the utilization of the Internet and the identification of organizations, designated group associations, and educational institutions. These activities were also supported by contacting and networking with other employment equity officers and human resources professionals, understanding the Employment Equity Act, and reviewing employment equity reports.

—Miria Visentin, staffing specialist, Nasittuq Corporation

Communicating Management's Commitment to Employment Equity

Nasittuq conveys commitment to employment equity through its website and internal application portal. Its internal portal contains information on employment equity policy, a copy of its self-identification survey, and various employment equity questions and answers. In addition, every year, Nasittuq requires that each employee sign a form indicating that he or she has read and understood the organization's employment equity policy. Having these documents readily available to its employees increases the response rates and accuracy of the work force survey, and awareness among its work force.

Embracing Work/Life Balance

When it comes to providing its employees with a good work/life balance, Nasittuq looks at individual needs. Programs that Nasittuq has implemented include job rotation, job sharing, family gym memberships, and various family events and activities. Nasittuq employees interviewed by HRSDC's Labour Program indicated that the ability to balance work, family, and their other responsibilities is the most influential factor as to why they stay with the organization.

Nasittuq's Commitment to Employment Equity

Every employee is made aware of the organization's support for employment equity and belief in equitable treatment of all employees. Is it just an initiative, or is it part of how we conduct our daily business? A good part of it starts with me as the manager, and how it trickles down throughout the organization.

—Ivan Warwyk, president, Nasittuq Corporation

Source: *Employment Equity Act Annual Report–2007*. http://www.hrsdc.gc.ca/en/labour/ publications/equality/annual_reports/2007/page10.shtml. Human Resources and Skills Development Canada, 2007. Reproduced with the permission of the Minister of Public Works and Government Services Canada, 2008.

Every Canadian organization falls under either federal or provincial legislation that has an impact on its recruitment and selection policies and practices. Many of the illustrations in this chapter focus on areas where an organization's practices have run afoul of the applicable law. We thought we would start by recognizing that the vast majority of companies comply with legislation in a positive way and use the legislation to improve their organizations. In the past, in addition to the *Nasittuq Corporation*, HRSDC has recognized the employment equity achievements of the Canadian Imperial Bank of Commerce, Arnold Bothers Transport Ltd., Husky Energy, Telsat Canada, IBM Canada, Pelmorex Media Inc., Shell Canada Ltd., Yanke Group of Companies, the University of British Columbia, and Manitoba Hydro

This chapter is organized into three parts. Part I describes the key legislation and legal requirements that affect recruitment and selection practices in Canada, including a review of existing legislation. Part II discusses the important legal concepts that have emerged from this existing legislation. These legal concepts require recruitment and selection programs to be nondiscriminatory with respect to hiring members of designated groups. Part III provides some practical guidance on what to do, and what not to do, in recruitment and selection to meet legal obligations. As well, the Recruitment and Selection Notebook boxes scattered throughout the chapter offer practical advice for HR practitioners with respect to these legal requirements.

We have taken many of the examples presented in this chapter from Canadian federal human rights, employment equity, employment standards, or labour laws for the following reasons. First, provincial and municipal jurisdictions often draw on federal law when drafting their own legislation and programs. Examining federal laws provides a common framework for understanding what is happening in these other jurisdictions. Second, the laws, policies, and practices vary across jurisdictions; for example, a human rights tribunal decision in British Columbia may have no applicability in any other province or territory, and vice versa. Although we present some illustrative cases from provincial rights tribunals, the rulings from these cases may not apply to your provincial situation unless those rulings have been upheld on appeal by federal courts such as the Supreme Court of Canada. Indeed, you may find two provincial human rights tribunals ruling in the opposite ways on the same issue or interpreting Supreme Court of Canada decisions differently.

This chapter is not intended to be a text on Canadian employment law or labour law. Our intent is to show the impact of legal requirements, as formulated through significant legislation and case law, on the practice of recruitment and selection in Canada. We encourage you to become familiar with the human rights, employment equity, employment standards, and labour laws that apply to your provincial, territorial, and municipal jurisdictions. Keep in mind that new legislation and decisions that are made following the publication of this book may change the presentation we make in this chapter.

Part I: A Basic Background in Legal Requirements for Nondiscriminatory Recruitment and Selection

 3.1

Four legal sources affect Canadian employment practices in recruitment and selection: (1) constitutional law; (2) human rights law; (3) employment equity legislation; and (4) labour law, employment standards, and related legislation. *Constitutional law* is the supreme law of Canada. It has a pervasive impact on employment practices, as it does on all spheres of Canadian society. *Human*

Discrimination

In employment, *discrimination* refers to any refusal to employ or to continue to employ any person, or to adversely affect any current employee, on the basis of that individual's membership in a protected group. All Canadian jurisdictions prohibit discrimination at least on the basis of race or colour, religion or creed, age, sex, marital status, and physical or mental disability.

rights legislation across Canada prohibits **discrimination** in both employment and the provision of goods and services (e.g., rental housing, service in restaurants). This legislation generally establishes human rights commissions or tribunals to deal with complaints, including those involving employment discrimination.

Employment equity programs are administrative mechanisms set up in many Canadian organizations in response to federal employment equity legislation initiatives and cover nearly 2 million working Canadians (see Recruitment and Selection Today 3.2 on page 76). Employment equity programs have a major impact on employment systems, including recruitment and selection. Employment equity programs are intended to promote the entry and retention of people from designated groups (including women, visible minorities, Aboriginal peoples, and people with disabilities).

Labour law, employment standards, and related legislation grant certain employment rights to both employers and employees, but also impose a wide range of employment responsibilities and obligations. Some of this legislation may have a direct impact on recruitment and selection practices in the jurisdiction where it is in force. Recruitment and Selection Notebook 3.1 illustrates some of the differences among these four types of legislation.

This chapter only hints at the complexity of the legal issues involved in recruitment and selection practices. For example, we do not discuss common law, the application of judicial precedents, or contract law, which may all have an impact on recruitment and selection decisions. As a starting point, human resources professionals must understand the origins, purpose, and stakeholders of each of the fundamental legal requirements if they are going to manage recruitment and selection activities in compliance with the law. They need to keep up with legislative changes on a continuing basis, as the law itself is always changing.

RPC 3.2

Constitutional Law

The Constitution of Canada consists of a series of Acts and orders passed since 1867 by the British and Canadian Parliaments.[1] These separate acts and orders begin with the British North America Act of 1867 and end with the Constitution Act of 1982. Sections 1 to 34 of Part 1 of the Constitution Act of 1982 are called the *Canadian Charter of Rights and Freedoms*. The Constitution, taken as a whole, serves as the supreme law of Canada, as stated in Subsection 52(1) of the Constitution Act of 1982:

> 52. (1) The Constitution of Canada is the supreme law of Canada and any law that is inconsistent with the provisions of the Constitution is, to the extent of the inconsistency, of no force or effect.

All laws in Canada that come into force in a dispute between a private person and a branch of government (whether legislative, executive, or administrative) fall under the Constitution.[2] The Constitution has precedence over all of the other legal means discussed in this chapter.

Not All Legal Requirements Are the Same

The four types of laws discussed in this chapter have varied historical roots and they address the needs of different stakeholder groups in society. *Constitutional law*, which has its origins in the British North America Act of 1867, spells out the division of powers between the federal and the provincial and territorial governments, as well as the rights and freedoms that Canadians enjoy under governments at all levels. All citizens are stakeholders under constitutional law, and its provisions directly or indirectly affect all of us.

Human rights legislation (federal and provincial/territorial) exists in Canada partly in response to international conventions declared by the United Nations and partly because of domestic pressure to eliminate discrimination in the workplace and in other areas such as housing and provision of services. Human rights Acts prohibit discrimination on protected grounds such as race or sex, and the legislation is restrictive in that its provisions have no force beyond the protected groups.

Employment equity legislation, policies, and programs have evolved in Canada as a response both to affirmative action programs in the United States and to pressures within our own country to increase work force diversity. Employment equity addresses the concerns of designated groups (visible minorities, women, Aboriginal peoples, and people with disabilities) and has no force or effect beyond these stakeholder groups.

Labour laws in the federal and provincial/territorial jurisdictions across Canada are a response to a long history of labour union activity undertaken to improve workers' job security, wages, hours, working conditions, and benefits. These laws provide mechanisms for collective bargaining and union certification and rules for a "fair fight" between management and unions, as well as protecting the public interest.* Of course, the stakeholders under this legislation are unionized workers covered by collective agreements and managers in unionized workplaces.

Employment standards, both federal and provincial, trace their origins back to the British North America Act and reflect societal norms about the respective rights and responsibilities of employers and their employees, whether these employees are unionized or not. Employment standards covered in legislation across Canada include statutory school-leaving age, minimum age for employment, minimum wages, vacations and leave, holidays with pay, and termination of employment. All workers in Canada, and their managers, are stakeholders in this legislation.

Other related legislation, including regulation of federal government workers, results from unique conditions in specific sectors and is restricted to addressing the needs of those stakeholders. As a general rule, human rights and employment equity address the problem of discrimination, whereas the remainder of the legal means (labour law, employment standards, and related legislation) provide mechanisms to resolve procedural or contractual disagreements between specific stakeholders named in the legislation. (Examples of the latter would be promotion based on the merit principle for federal government employees under the Public Service Employment Act passed by Parliament, seniority rights in collective agreements for employees of Crown corporations, and other types of contractual and legal obligations between employer and employee in either the private or public sector.) However, even this basic distinction between antidiscrimination legislation and procedural/contract enforcement legislation can blur in practice. For example, equal pay for men and women for work of equal value, which is a discrimination issue, comes under human rights Acts in some provinces and territories and employment standards legislation in others.

---

*D.D. Carter, G. England, D. Etherington, and G. Trudeau. 2002. *Labour Law in Canada*, 5th ed. Markham, ON: Butterworths.

A section of the Constitution often cited in employment law is Section 15 of the Canadian Charter of Rights and Freedoms, which lays out the principle of equality rights:

> 15. (1) Every individual is equal before and under the law and has the right to the equal protection and equal benefit of the law without discrimination and, in particular, without discrimination based on race, national or ethnic origin, colour, religion, sex, age or mental or physical disability.
>
> (2) Subsection (1) does not preclude any law, program or activity that has as its object the amelioration of conditions of disadvantaged individuals or groups, including those that are disadvantaged because of race, national or ethnic origin, colour, religion, sex, age or mental or physical disability.

The discrimination provision in Subsection (1) of the Charter resembles provisions found in human rights legislation across Canada. Subsection (2) makes it clear that programs such as employment equity, which may favour individuals or designated groups as a means to overcoming past disadvantages, are not, in themselves, discriminatory and barred by Subsection (1).

As a practical matter, constitutional law does not directly affect everyday recruitment and selection activities. Constitutional law becomes an issue only when recruitment or selection practices are challenged in a human rights tribunal or court. Nevertheless, constitutional law has a pervasive, indirect impact on employment practices by setting limits and conditions on what federal, provincial/territorial, and municipal governments and courts can legally do to alter employment policies and practices. The interpretation of constitutional law through legislation and jurisprudence has an indirect, but substantial, influence on all aspects of the practice of human resources management—from the development of an organization's human resources policy to the conduct of an employment interview.

 3.3

Human Rights Legislation

Each province and territory, as well as the federal government, has established a human rights Act or code that prohibits discrimination in employment and in the provision of goods and services. The federal or provincial/territorial Acts apply to organizations that fall under their respective jurisdictions. Normally, this means that organizations are governed by the laws of the political division in which they are chartered or incorporated. For example, a company incorporated in Ontario would fall under Ontario's human rights Act, while the Canadian Broadcasting Corporation, whose headquarters are in Ontario, would fall under the Canadian Human Rights Act, as it is a federally regulated organization. Federal legislation applies to all organizations in the transportation, broadcasting, and financial services sectors, as well as to any company that falls outside the exclusive legislative jurisdiction of a province or territory (e.g., a company operating in two provinces). HR directors must determine the legislative regime that applies to their organizations.

The Canadian Human Rights Act contains the following section:[3]

8. It is a discriminatory practice, directly or indirectly,

(a) to refuse to employ or continue to employ any individual, or

(b) in the course of employment, to differentiate adversely in relation to an employee, on a prohibited ground of discrimination.

The Canadian Human Rights Act applies to federal government departments, Crown corporations and agencies, and businesses under federal jurisdiction, including banks, airlines, railways, the CBC and other broadcasters, and Canada Post.[4]

Section 8 of the Canadian Human Rights Act refers to "a prohibited ground of discrimination." Under this act, the following are grounds on which discrimination is prohibited:[5]

- race
- national or ethnic origin
- colour
- religion
- age
- sex (including pregnancy and childbirth)
- marital status
- family status
- mental or physical disability (including previous or present drug or alcohol dependence)
- pardoned conviction
- sexual orientation

The prohibited grounds of discrimination vary somewhat among jurisdictions. Table 3.1 compares prohibited grounds of discrimination across federal, provincial, and territorial jurisdictions, listing 19 prohibited grounds of employment discrimination found across these jurisdictions. There are, however, only six prohibited grounds of employment discrimination on which all jurisdictions agree: race or colour, religion or creed, age, sex, marital status, and physical/mental handicap or disability. Recruitment and Selection Today 3.1 illustrates a case of potential sex discrimination that an HR person might have to solve.

3.4

Human rights legislation in all jurisdictions is enforced through human rights commissions or tribunals that have the legislated power to undertake actions that may be necessary to eliminate discrimination. The Canadian Human Rights Act empowers the Canadian Human Rights Commission (CHRC) to investigate complaints, develop and deliver public information programs, undertake or sponsor research programs, liaise with other human rights commissions, and review federal legislation for conformity with the

TABLE 3.1

Prohibited Grounds of Employment Discrimination in Canadian Jurisdictions

PROHIBITED GROUND	JURISDICTION	COMMENTS
Race or colour	All jurisdictions	
Religion	All jurisdictions	• Yukon's Act reads: "Religion or creed, or religious belief, religious association or religious activity"
Physical or mental disability	All jurisdictions	• Quebec uses the phrase "handicap or use of any means to palliate a handicap"
Age*	All jurisdictions	• BC: 19–65 • Alberta: 18+ • Saskatchewan: 18–64 • Ontario: 18–65 • Newfoundland/Labrador: 19–65 • Quebec: Except as provided for by law
Sex (includes pregnancy and childbirth)	All jurisdictions	• BC includes breast feeding • Alberta uses the term *gender* • Manitoba includes gender-determined characteristics • Ontario recognizes the protection of transgendered persons and accepts complaints related to "gender identity"; Ontario accepts complaints related to female genital mutilation • In Quebec, pregnancy as such is considered a ground of discrimination
Marital status	All jurisdictions	• Quebec uses the term *civil status*
Dependence on alcohol or drugs	All *except* Yukon and NWT	• Policy to accept complaints in BC, Alberta, Saskatchewan, Manitoba, Ontario, New Brunswick, and PEI • Quebec: Included in "handicap" ground • Previous dependence only in New Brunswick and Nova Scotia

continued

TABLE 3.1   *Continued from previous page*

Prohibited Grounds of Employment Discrimination in Canadian Jurisdictions

PROHIBITED GROUND	JURISDICTION	COMMENTS
Family status	All *except* New Brunswick and Newfoundland/ Labrador	• Saskatchewan defines as being in a parent–child relationship • Quebec uses the term *civil status*
Sexual orientation	All *except* NWT	• The Supreme Court of Canada read this ground into the Alberta Human Rights, Citizenship and Multiculturalism Act in 1998
National or ethnic origin (including linguistic background)	All *except* BC and Alberta	• Saskatchewan and NWT use the term *nationality* • Ontario's code includes both "ethnic origin" and "citizenship"
Ancestry or place of origin	Yukon, NWT, BC, Alberta, Saskatchewan, Manitoba, Ontario, and New Brunswick	
Language	Yukon, Ontario, and Quebec	• Ontario accepts complaints under the grounds of ancestry, ethnic origin, place of origin, and race • New Brunswick will accept language-related complaints filed on the basis of ancestry, although not an enumerated ground.
Social condition or origin	NWT, Quebec, New Brunswick, and Newfoundland/ Labrador	
Source of income	Alberta, Saskatchewan, Manitoba, Quebec, PEI, and Nova Scotia	• Defined as "receipt of public assistance" in Saskatchewan
Assignment, attachment or seizure of pay	Newfoundland/ Labrador	• Quebec: Included under social condition • Quebec: Included under social condition

continued

Chapter 3: Legal Issues

TABLE 3.1   *Continued from previous page*

Prohibited Grounds of Employment Discrimination in Canadian Jurisdictions

PROHIBITED GROUND	JURISDICTION	COMMENTS
Based on association	Yukon, Manitoba, Ontario, New Brunswick, Nova Scotia, NWT, and PEI	NWT has prohibition on basis of "political association"
Political belief	Yukon, BC, Manitoba, Quebec, Nova Scotia, PEI, New Brunswick, and Newfoundland/Labrador	Newfoundland/Labrador has prohibition on basis of "political opinion"
Record of criminal conviction	Yukon and Quebec	Yukon's Act reads: "Criminal charges or criminal record"
Pardoned conviction	Federal, Yukon, and NWT	

* All Canadian provinces and territories have or, as of 2009, will have legislation that prohibits employers from forcing mandatory retirement at age 65 or later. However, in some provinces, mandatory retirement is prohibited under the Act but a provision allows companies to enforce mandatory retirement under the terms or conditions of a retirement or pension plan. Also, some provinces have provisions to allow mandatory retirement for jobs where physical ability is a must, such as firefighting and police work.

Source: *Canadian Human Rights Commission Annual Report 2007*. http://www.chrc-ccdp.ca/publications/ar_2007_ra/page6-en.asp. Canadian Human Rights Commission. Reproduced with the permission of the Ministry of Public Works and Government Services, 2008.

Canadian Human Rights Act. The commission has a full-time, paid staff to carry out its mandate.

The Canadian Human Rights Commission spends much of its time investigating human rights complaints. Human rights protection is predicated on the idea that individuals who believe that they are victims of discriminatory practices bear the responsibility of filing complaints with the commission. In the case of workplace disputes, a complaint would be filed after discussions with the employer failed to resolve the matter. The commission's procedure for investigating complaints is shown in steps 4–8 in Recruitment and Selection Notebook 3.2. Applicants who believe that they have suffered discrimination in recruitment or selection can lodge a complaint with the human rights commission that has jurisdiction over the employer.

Tables 3.2 and 3.3 provide some data on the volume and nature of complaints received by the CHRC. In 2007, the commission received 840 complaints, with 36 percent of the complaints concerning discrimination related to disabilities and 13 percent related to sex. Table 3.3 shows that 73 percent of those complaints were employment-related, with 10 percent involving employment-related harassment and 2 percent involving trade union membership. Each signed complaint triggers a formal investigation and involves

No Babies Allowed

HR professionals may at times find themselves at odds with a manager who has responsibility for making the final hiring decision. Managers may not always be as knowledgeable of human rights issues as HR staff ought to be. The following incident was conveyed to us by an HR practitioner and illustrates potential problems faced by women trying to balance work and family obligations.

The manager and HR professional interviewed all of the short-listed candidates for a position. A female applicant interviewed exceptionally well and the HR professional felt that she was the strongest candidate. The manager, although agreeing that she was the best candidate, did not want to hire her. She had been previously employed by the company and was an excellent worker. When she became pregnant, she went on maternity leave; when that leave ended she resigned in order to stay home to raise her child, who was now school-aged. The manager felt that the individual was given the chance to work for the organization once and gave up that opportunity to raise her child. He felt that the opportunity to work for the company should now be given to someone else.

The applicant clearly met all of the requirements for the position, had previous working experience in the posi-

tion, interviewed well, and was the strongest candidate. A review of her previous employment record by the HR professional confirmed that the applicant was an excellent performer, had a spotless discipline record, and had indeed left the company to raise her child.

The HR professional advised the manager that not hiring this female applicant would likely constitute a human rights violation and lead to a complaint before the provincial human rights tribunal that the company would have to defend. The HR professional provided the hiring manager with a copy of the sections of the Human Rights Act that directly affect recruitment and employment. In addition, the HR professional pointed out to the manager that even if they were successful in defending a human rights charge, the company would be severely embarrassed by refusing to rehire an excellent former employee on the grounds that she took some time off to raise her child.

The outcome of the HR professional's intervention was that the manger changed his mind and agreed to rehire the former employee. The applicant successfully completed her training and probationary period with the company and remains a very productive employee.

considerable time and energy on the part of employees, an organization's HR staff, and the CHRC itself.

Employment Equity

Federal **employment equity** legislation requires organizations that come under its jurisdiction (see Recruitment and Selection Today 3.2) to set up and operate employment equity programs. Provincial/territorial and municipal governments may also enact legislation for employers that fall under their jurisdiction; however, only the province of British Columbia has done so. Seven provinces have established employment equity policies (see Table 3.4 on page 78). Employment equity policies provide general direction and give priority to the implementation of employment equity measures through various means, usually as directives to the provincial human rights agency. Provincial employment equity policies are mostly limited to government programs or public-sector workers. Quebec, however, extends employment equity policy to the private sector. Employment equity legislation, such as

Employment equity

Refers to the elimination of discriminatory practices that prevent the entry or retention of members from designated groups in the workplace, and to the elimination of unequal treatment in the workplace related to membership in a designated group.

Filing a Complaint under the Canadian Human Rights Act

1. First, the individual who believes he or she has been discriminated against should tell the people involved and attempt to resolve the problem on the spot.

2. If step 1 does not succeed, seek assistance from someone named under the organization's human rights policy.

3. File a company or union grievance against the practice believed to be discriminatory.

4. If steps 1–3 do not work, the individual may file a complaint with the Canadian Human Rights Commission.

5. If the complaint fulfills certain conditions (e.g., it is not trivial, frivolous, vexatious, or made in bad faith), the commission may assign an investigator to examine the complaint.

6. After the report from the investigator is filed, the commission may appoint a conciliator, who will attempt to bring about settlement of the complaint. The commission must then either approve or reject the settlement.

7. After the complaint is filed, the commission may refer the complaint to a human rights tribunal composed of not more than three members. The tribunal then investigates the complaint in a quasi-legal hearing. Both the complainant and the employer are permitted representation by legal counsel in this hearing. The tribunal will either dismiss the complaint or, if the employer is found to have discriminated, levy penalties (e.g., rehiring of the complainant, financial compensation).

8. A review tribunal may be set up to hear an appeal if one of the parties is not satisfied with the decision under step 7.

9. If either party is dissatisfied with the decision of the review tribunal, the complaint may go to the federal court system, in some instances ending at the Supreme Court of Canada.

Federal Employment Equity Programs

1. Federal Legislated Programs

- Apply to all federally regulated employers with 100 or more employees, including organizations in industries such as banking, communications, and international and interprovincial transportation. In 2007, there were approximately 536 such employers (private-sector employers and Crown corporations), representing approximately 843 522 employees.

- Apply to all federal departments, representing approximately 179 540 employees. As well, the Act has been extended by the federal Cabinet to cover parts of the public service, including the Canadian Forces and the Royal Canadian Mounted Police.

2. Federal Contractors Program

- Under the Federal Contractors Program, employers with 100 or more employees who have secured a federal goods or services contract of $200 000 or more are required to sign a certificate of commitment to fulfill their mandated goal of implementing employment equity in their workplaces. As of May 1, 2002 (the latest available data), there were approximately 891 federal contractors, representing approximately 1.08 million employees.

Sources: *Employment Equity Act Annual Report–2007*. http://www .hrsdc.gc.ca/eng/lp/lo/lswe/we/information/what.shtml. Human Resources and Skills Development Canada, 2007. Reproduced with the permission of the Minister of Public Works and Government Services Canada, 2008.

TABLE 3.2

Grounds of Discrimination Cited in Signed Complaints Made to the CHRC

GROUND	2006		2007	
	NUMBER	%	NUMBER	%
Disability	372	34	298	36
Sex	160	15	113	13
National or ethnic origin	68	6	99	12
Race	145	13	98	12
Age	112	10	79	9
Sexual orientation	82	8	52	6
Family status	56	5	37	4
Religion	39	4	31	4
Colour	36	3	18	2
Marital status	20	2	14	2
Pardon	0	0	1	0
Total	1090	100	840	100

Source: *Canadian Human Rights Commission Annual Report 2007*. http://www.chrc-ccdp.ca/publications/ar_2007_ra/page6-en.asp. Canadian Human Rights Commission. Reproduced with the permission of the Ministry of Public Works and Government Services, 2008.

TABLE 3.3

Types of Allegations Cited in Signed Complaints Made to the CHRC

ALLEGATION	2006		2007	
	NUMBER	%	NUMBER	%
Employment-related	925	72	774	73
Service-related	120	9	106	10
Harassment–employment	166	13	106	10
Retaliation	18	2	30	3
Union membership	5	0	17	2
Hate messages	20	2	16	2
Harassment services	18	1	5	0
Pay equity	9	1	2	0
Notices, signs, symbols	1	0	0	0
Total	1282	100	1056	100

Source: *Canadian Human Rights Commission Annual Report 2007*. http://www.chrc-ccdp.ca/publications/ar_2007_ra/page6-en.asp. Canadian Human Rights Commission. Reproduced with the permission of the Ministry of Public Works and Government Services, 2008.

TABLE 3.4

Employment Equity in the Provinces

PROVINCE	EMPLOYMENT EQUITY POLICY IN PLACE	EMPLOYMENT EQUITY LEGISLATION IN PLACE
Alberta	No	No
British Columbia	Yes, since 1991	Yes, since 1994
Manitoba	Yes, since 1983	No
New Brunswick	Yes, in development	No
Newfoundland/Labrador	No	No
Nova Scotia	Yes, since 1975 Affirmative Action Policy since 1997	No
Ontario	No	No, EE legislation repealed in 1995
Prince Edward Island	Yes	No
Quebec	Yes, Programme d'obligations contractuelles	No
Saskatchewan	Yes	No

Source: Her Majesty the Queen in Right of Canada. All rights reserved. *Employment Equity Policy in Canada: An Interprovincial Comparison,* ISBN 0-662-28160-8, Cat. no. SW21-46/1999E, Status of Women in Canada. Reproduced with the permission of the Minister of Public Works and Government Services Canada, 2008.

the federal government's Employment Equity Act, stands as the law of the land and generally includes mechanisms for enforcement and sanctions for violation.[6]

Employment equity programs involve any human resources activities introduced into an organization to ensure equality for all employees in all aspects of employment, including recruiting, hiring, compensation, and training.[7] Organizations may voluntarily adopt employment equity programs in the absence of employment equity legislation. The purpose of employment equity legislation is stated in the Employment Equity Act passed by the Canadian Parliament in 1986:

> 2. The purpose of this Act is to achieve equality in the workplace so that no person shall be denied employment opportunities or benefits for reasons unrelated to ability and, in the fulfilment of that goal, to correct the conditions of disadvantage in employment experienced by women, aboriginal peoples, persons with disabilities and persons who are, because of their race or colour, in a visible minority in Canada by giving effect to the principle that employment equity means more than treating persons in the same way but also requires special measures and the accommodation of differences.

The intent of the Employment Equity Act is to address past systemic discrimination in employment systems that have disadvantaged members of the designated groups. The intent of the Act is to ensure that all selection requirements are realistic and job-related. The Act provides for a review of practices that may constitute systemic barriers to the employment of members from designated groups and for establishing measures to eliminate any of the barriers. The federal Employment Equity Act of 1986 requires employers covered by the Act to implement equity, after consultation with employee representatives, by:

1. identifying and eliminating employment practices that act as barriers to the employment of persons in designated groups; and
2. instituting positive policies and practices and making reasonable accommodation to increase representation from designated groups among various positions in the organization to reflect the designated group's representation in either the work force or in those segments of the work force (identified by qualification, eligibility, or geography) from which the employer reasonably expects to hire or promote employees.

Recruitment and Selection Notebook 3.3 outlines the steps in implementing an employment equity plan.

An updated version of the Employment Equity Act came into effect on October 24, 1996. This revised Act extended coverage to all private employers who fell under federal regulation and to almost all employees of the federal government. The new Act gave power to the Canadian Human Rights Commission to audit all federally regulated employers' equity progress to determine if they are complying with the legislation and to require action when they fail to do so.

Employment equity programs often require an employer to undertake an extensive overhaul of the organization's recruitment and selection system. In comparison, a human rights commission may only require an employer to

---

Recruitment and Selection Notebook 3.3

Developing and Implementing an Employment Equity (EE) Plan

1. Obtain support of senior management for the EE effort.
2. Conduct a survey to determine the present representation of designated groups in the organization's internal work force.
3. Set future representation targets for designated groups based on availability of qualified workers in the labour market.
4. Remove systemic employment barriers to increase representation for designated groups in the internal work force.
5. Monitor the changing composition of the internal work force over time.
6. Make necessary changes to the EE intervention to bring designated group representation up to future targets.

take action to remedy a specific complaint. Both human rights and employment equity legislation have the same ultimate aim: to eliminate discrimination in the workplace against disadvantaged groups and to improve their positions in employment systems. Human rights commissions are more reactive in nature in that they respond to complaints about alleged discrimination in the workplace. Employment equity programs are proactive in that they require employers to take action to increase the number of protected group members in the workplace.

Employment equity legislation is often a contentious issue, subject to the political process. As times change, employment equity legislation may be delivered through different mechanisms, may be strengthened or weakened, or may even be discontinued altogether. For example, in 1995, the Ontario government repealed the Employment Equity Act passed by the previous NDP government and said that it would implement an "equal opportunity plan" together with business, labour, and community groups to replace the repealed legislation. The government claimed that the plan would better promote hiring and promotion policies based on merit.[8] Recruitment and Selection Notebook 3.4 provides "best practices" used by Canadian organizations to implement employment equity.

Recruitment and Selection Notebook **3.4**

Implementing Good Workplace Equity Practices

The following "best practices" are taken from the *2002–2007 Employment Equity Act Annual Reports* and endorsed by employer reports in subsequent annual reports. Under provisions of the Act, federally regulated employers must provide a statistical report on diversity issues along with a narrative report on actions they have taken to improve workplace equity. The following practices are those reported by employers in compliance with the Act.

Benefits of Implementing Employment Equity in the Workplace

- A work force representative of Canadian culture and diversity;
- An increase in global competitiveness and productivity;
- High employee morale and decreased absenteeism;
- Amicable relationships with customers and clients;
- Enhanced corporate reputation; and
- Increased profitability and a better bottom line.

Improving Workplace Communications on Diversity Issues

- Voluntary self-identification surveys that help identify the diversity present in the workplace;
- Focus groups and committees devoted to employment equity and responsible for conducting workshops, presentations, and sessions with employees;
- Dialogue with managers concerning their positions on employment equity;
- Internal and external newsletters and magazines with sections and/or articles on employment equity;
- Internal bulletin boards where job openings and recent employment equity news items are posted;
- Company Internet websites including information concerning employment equity plans;
- Internal employment equity memos and pamphlets; and
- Exit interviews.

Labour Law, Employment Standards, and Related Legislation

Federal and provincial labour laws stipulate the rights of employees to organize trade unions and to bargain collective agreements with employers. Provincial labour relations Acts and the Canada Labour Code establish labour relations boards to oversee union certifications and handle complaints about unfair labour practices. Collective agreements, which are legally binding and enforceable documents, cover unionized employees. Collective agreements set out the conditions under which job changes must occur and have a major impact on internal selection or internal movement of workers—for example, promotion, lateral transfer, and demotion.[9]

 3.5

Because closed-shop agreements, under which only union members may work for the organization, are legal in Canada, some unions have considerable control over external recruiting, even running their own hiring halls from which the employer must hire workers. While collective agreements do restrict the freedom of the employer, unions, on the whole, tend to be more cooperative than adversarial in terms of HR practices such as selection.[10]

Federal and provincial employment standards laws regulate minimum age of employment, hours of work, minimum wages, statutory holidays, vacations, work leaves, and termination of employment.[11] As well, common law, developed through judicial proceedings, may apply to individual contracts entered into by a person and an organization. These laws have little impact on recruitment and selection practices, with the possible exception of termination, which might be considered "deselection" of people already in the organization's work force.

Federal and provincial governments also have specialized legislation governing labour relations and setting employment standards for their own public service employees. Both the federal Public Service Employment Act and the Parliamentary Employment and Staff Relations Act illustrate the impact of this legislation on recruitment and selection. The Public Service Employment Act designates the Public Service Commission of Canada as the central staffing agency for the federal government. This Act gives candidates from the general public, as well as some public service employees, the right to request an investigation if they believe that their qualifications were not properly assessed as part of a hiring competition for a public service position.[12]

The Public Service Commission resolves complaints through mediation and conciliation or through the direct intervention of the commission or a deputy head.[13] Candidates may also lodge appeals against personnel selection processes used by the Public Service Commission. (An important appeal involving the use of psychological testing in the federal public service is summarized in Recruitment and Selection Today 3.3.)

The Parliamentary Employment and Staff Relations Act provides a mechanism for collective bargaining between the federal government as employer and the various unions certified to represent federal workers. This legislation

Recruitment and Selection Today 3.3

Psychological Testing in the Federal Government

In 1986, an appeal board of the Public Service Commission (PSC) heard the complaints of job applicants for the job of collections enforcement clerk with the federal taxation department (*Maloley et al.*).* Four individuals who were not hired alleged that the GIT-320 (a paper-and-pencil test of cognitive ability) in use at the time for screening job applicants was (1) not properly validated; (2) had an unjustifiably high cut-off score; and (3) was gender-biased. Expert witnesses, including several top personnel psychologists, testified on the technical merits of the test at the invitation of either the complainants or the commission. Based on this evidence, the appeal board concluded that the GIT-320 had been validated (using a method called *validity generalization*, which we discussed in Chapter 2). The two other allegations were dismissed because (1) the PSC had demonstrated the test cut-off score was reasonable and not excessively high under the circumstances and (2) the test was neither biased nor unfair to women. All three allegations about

the test were dismissed and the PSC continued to use the GIT-320 in its selection work.

The *Maloley* decision is especially informative because it involves allegations of two distinct types: (1) the first two allegations claimed that the GIT-320 violated procedural rules in the PSC selection system based on the merit principle and (2) the third allegation claimed the test was discriminatory against women. Here we see an internal appeal board, which normally would deal with procedural and technical matters only, ruling on discrimination issues customarily the prerogative of human rights commissions. This suggests that, in at least some instances, there is a blurring of the divisions separating the four legal sources discussed in this chapter. Legal issues in recruitment and selection are made even more complicated as a result.

---

* *Maloley et al. v. Department of National Revenue (Taxation),* 1986.

is administered by the Public Service Staff Relations Board (PSSRB), which is empowered to hear complaints under the Act and arbitrate collective bargaining disputes.[14] PSSRB decisions that address promotion practices covered in collective agreements between the federal government and public sector unions affect recruitment and selection practices in the public sector.

Part II: Key Legal Concepts in Recruitment and Selection

RPC 3.6

Direct Discrimination

In the 1985 Supreme Court of Canada decision *O'Malley v. Simpsons-Sears*,[15] Justice McIntyre defined direct discrimination in an employment setting as follows:

> Direct discrimination occurs in this connection where an employer adopts a practice or rule which on its face discriminates on a prohibited ground. For example, "No Catholics or no women or no blacks employed here." There is, of course, no disagreement in the case at bar that direct discrimination of that nature would contravene the Act.

The application of this definition to human resources practice is quite simple. If direct discrimination occurs, then the burden is on the employer to show that the rule is valid in application to all the members of the affected group. An employer who is hiring steelworkers for foundry work involving heavy lifting in a dirty environment may believe that this job is unsuited to women and specifies that no women will be hired. This is a clear instance of direct discrimination under the McIntyre ruling. If a female applicant complained about the blatant nature of this discrimination, the employer would have to prove to a human rights investigator that all women lack the ability to do the work—that is, that no woman could perform the work successfully. If even one woman can do the job, the employer's use of the "no women allowed" rule will be struck down by a human rights tribunal or court. In all but rare circumstances, it is impossible to justify direct discrimination.

As part of recruitment and selection, no statement may be made in advertising a job that would prohibit or restrict members of a protected group from seeking that job. A statement, for example, in any job advertisement or posting that the employer is seeking "single males" constitutes direct discrimination and is illegal. During the selection process itself, application forms and interviews are potential sources of direct discrimination. As a result, some human rights commissions have published guidelines for questions asked by employers on employment application forms and at employment interviews. An excerpt from these guidelines published by the Canadian Human Rights Commission is given in Table 3.5. These guidelines provide practical and detailed advice on how to avoid direct discrimination in many common selection situations and should be carefully heeded by employers. The complete guide is available on the Canadian Human Rights Commission's website at http://www.chrc-ccdp.ca/pdf/screen.pdf.

TABLE 3.5

Guidelines to Screening and Selection in Employment

Subject	Avoid Asking	Preferred	Comments
Name	—about name change; whether it was changed by court order, marriage, or other reason — maiden name		Ask after selection if needed to check on previously held jobs or educational credentials
Address	—for addresses outside Canada	Ask place and duration of current or recent address	
Age	—for birth certificates, baptismal records, or about age in general	Ask applicants if they are eligible to work under Canadian laws regarding age restrictions	If precise age is required for benefit plans or other legitimate purposes, it can be determined after selection
Sex	—males or females to fill in different applications —about pregnancy, child-bearing plans, or child-care arrangements	Can ask applicant if the attendance requirements can be met	During the interview or after selection, the applicant, for purposes of courtesy, may be asked which of Dr., Mr., Mrs., Miss, or Ms. is preferred
Marital Status	—whether applicant is single, married, divorced, engaged, separated, widowed, or living common-law	If transfer or travel is part of the job, the applicant can be asked if he or she can meet these requirements	Information on dependants can be determined after selection if necessary
Family Status	—number of children or dependants —about child-care arrangements	Can ask if the applicant would be able to work the required hours and, where applicable, overtime	Contacts for emergencies and/or details on dependants can be determined after selection
National or Ethnic Origin	—about birthplace, nationality of ancestors, spouse, or other relatives —whether born in Canada —for proof of citizenship	Since those who are entitled to work in Canada must be citizens, permanent residents, or holders of valid work permits, applicants can be asked if they are legally entitled to work in Canada	Documentation of eligibility to work (papers, visas, etc.) can be requested after selection
Military Service	—about military service in other countries	Can ask about Canadian military service where employment preference is given to veterans by law	
Language	—mother tongue —where language skills obtained	Ask if applicant understands, reads, writes, or speaks languages required for the job	Testing or scoring applicants for language proficiency is not permitted unless job-related

continued

Table 3.5   *Continued from previous page*

Guidelines to Screening and Selection in Employment

Subject	Avoid Asking	Preferred	Comments
Race or Colour	—any question about race or colour, including colour of eyes, skin, or hair		
Photographs	—for photo to be attached to application or sent to interviewer before interview		Photos for security passes or company files can be taken after selection
Religion	—about religious affiliation, church membership, frequency of church attendance —if applicant will work a specific religious holiday —for references from clergy or religious leader	Explain the required work shift, asking if such a schedule poses problems for the applicant	Reasonable accommodation of an employee's religious beliefs is the employer's duty
Height and Weight	—height and weight unless there is evidence they are genuine occupational requirements		
Disability	—for listing of all disabilities, limitations, or health problems —whether applicant drinks or uses drugs —whether applicant has ever received psychiatric care or been hospitalized for emotional problems —whether applicant has received Workers' Compensation		The employer should: • disclose any information on medically related requirements or standards early in the application process • then ask whether the applicant has any condition that could affect his or her ability to do the job, preferably during a pre-employment medical examination A disability is relevant to job ability only if it: • threatens the safety or property of others • prevents the applicant from safe and adequate job performance, even when reasonable efforts are made to accommodate the disability
Medical Information	—if currently under physician's care —name of family doctor —if receiving counselling or therapy		Medical exams should be conducted after selection and only if an employee's condition is related to job duties Offers of employment can be made conditional on successful completion of a medical exam

continued

TABLE 3.5   *Continued from previous page*

Guidelines to Screening and Selection in Employment

SUBJECT	AVOID ASKING	PREFERRED	COMMENTS
Pardoned Conviction	—whether an applicant has ever been convicted —if an applicant has ever been arrested —whether an applicant has a criminal record	If bonding is a job requirement, ask if applicant is eligible	Inquiries about criminal record or convictions are discouraged unless related to job duties
Sexual Orientation	—about the applicant's sexual orientation		Contacts for emergencies and/or details on dependants can be determined after selection
References			The same restrictions that apply to questions asked of applicants apply when asking for employment references

Source: *A Guide to Screening and Selection in Employment*. http://www.chrc-ccdp.ca/pdf/screen.pdf. Canadian Human Rights Commission. Reproduced with the permission of the Ministry of Public Works and Government Services, 2008.

Direct discrimination is much less frequent in Canadian workplaces than it once was. Discriminatory job advertising in major daily newspapers is now quite rare, as the media may also be held accountable for running such types of ads. Direct discrimination, however, does exist to some extent in selection practices, so continued vigilance is necessary. These instances generally occur in those occupations where gender-based stereotyping persists. Despite many efforts, people still think of certain occupations as being either "female" or "male"—for example, only women make good nurses, and only men make good construction workers. Direct discrimination occurs when this stereotyping carries over into the workplace and influences recruiting and selection practices. Hopefully, such gender-based stereotyping will occur much less often in the future than in the past.

Adverse Effect Discrimination

In Chapter 2, we outlined a commonly used selection model: A job analysis is used to identify the knowledge, skills, abilities, and other characteristics (KSAOs) that are related to job performance. A situation may arise where basing selection practices on a legitimately determined KSAO has an unintended negative impact on members of a protected group. This impact would constitute indirect discrimination and fall outside the law unless it could be shown that the selection practice was necessary to assure the efficient and economical performance of the job without endangering employees or the general public.

In the *O'Malley v. Simpsons-Sears* decision, Justice McIntyre also defined *adverse effect discrimination*—sometimes referred to as *indirect discrimination*. **Adverse effect discrimination** occurs in recruitment and selection when an employer, in good faith, adopts a policy or practice for sound economic or business reasons that is applied to all employees but has an unintended, negative impact on members of a protected group. In recruiting, for example, employers often ask current employees for the names of friends or relatives who might be suitable for a position. A human resources manager might solicit shop-floor employees for names of potential candidates to fill a welder's apprentice position. After receiving all the names, the HR manager chooses the best candidate according to a set of objective criteria.

How does this recruiting strategy lead to adverse effect discrimination? If the shop-floor employees were all white males, almost all of the candidates put forward by the current employees would be white males. This recruitment practice will likely lead to the outcome of hiring a white male, to the exclusion of women or visible minorities.

The HR manager may have believed that the strategy was a sound and effective business practice for identifying suitable candidates for the position (and as we will see in Chapter 6, referrals from family or friends constitute a very popular means of recruitment). The manager did not intend to exclude members of any protected group from consideration and asked all of the existing employees to nominate potential job candidates. Nevertheless, this recruitment strategy results in adverse effect discrimination by imposing penalties or restrictive conditions on women and visible minorities that are not imposed on white males; they are less likely to be nominated for the job, and less likely to be hired regardless of their qualifications. Women and visible minorities, two groups protected under human rights legislation, are negatively affected by the supposedly neutral recruiting practice. This is an example to illustrate a potential problem and it does not mean that all recruiting by referrals from family or friends represents indirect discrimination.

In selection, adverse effect discrimination often involves the use of a practice or use of an employment test. Suppose the HR manager in the above example corrected the flawed recruiting practice and subsequently obtained an applicant pool that included a proportion of women and visible minorities consistent with their representation in the general population. The HR manager decides to use a mechanical comprehension test to select applicants as a welder's apprentice. Performance on the mechanical comprehension test predicts success as a welder's apprentice and will identify those applicants who are most likely to contribute to the company's overall productivity.

Could this selection strategy lead to adverse effect discrimination? Women tend to score lower, on average, on mechanical comprehension tests than do men. If the same test cut-off score was used for men and women or if applicants were offered jobs in order of their test scores (from highest to lowest), proportionately fewer women than men would be hired for the job. The use of the mechanical comprehension test would impose on women, as a group protected under human rights legislation, a penalty not imposed on men. Even though the test is applied equally to women and men, the test affects

Adverse effect discrimination

Refers to a situation where an employer, in good faith, adopts a policy or practice that has an unintended, negative impact on members of a protected group.

women in a negative sense to a greater extent than men. Even though the test predicts performance for welder's apprentices and there was no intention to discriminate against women, a human rights complaint may be launched against the employer on the grounds that use of the test had an adverse effect on women as a group and, thus, discriminated against them on that basis. Any employment rule, practice, or policy that has a negative effect on a group protected under human rights legislation, no matter how well intentioned by the employer, constitutes adverse effect discrimination.

Adverse Impact

Adverse impact

Occurs when the selection rate for a protected group is lower than that for the relevant comparison group.

The concept of *adverse impact* is closely related to adverse effect discrimination. At times, *adverse impact* and *adverse effect* are used synonymously.[16] In terms of recruitment and selection, the concept of adverse impact has a narrower, more technical definition. **Adverse impact** occurs when the selection rate for a protected group is lower than that for the relevant comparison group (which has the higher selection rate). In our example of adverse effect discrimination, the mechanical comprehension test also had an adverse impact on women in that proportionately fewer women than men would be selected for the job (see Recruitment and Selection Today 3.4).

Adverse impact is based on statistical evidence showing that proportionately fewer members of the protected group are selected using a selection device (such as an employment test or interview) or that fewer of the protected group pass through the selection system taken as a whole. Establishing adverse impact in selection can be very complex.[17] One rough-and-ready rule

Recruitment and Selection Today 3.4

Cultural Bias in Selection Testing

Much of the legislation and policy discussed in this chapter draws heavily on examples from other countries, especially the United States. Nowhere is this truer than for human rights and employment equity, which are called *equal employment opportunity* and *affirmative action* in the United States. In fact, many Canadian tribunals and courts cite American cases as precedents when making their human rights decisions.

In addition, many of the same issues and concerns about recruitment and selection in this country are mirrored in the United States. For example, an article in the *U.S. News & World Report* described the political upheaval in Chicago over results of a promotional examination for city police officers.* Despite a cost of over $5 million paid to consultants to develop a bias-free promo-

tional system, the multiple-choice tests used in the promotion competition still had adverse impact against African Americans and Hispanics. As a result, fewer members of these groups were promoted than were whites, and city politicians were quick to line up on both sides of the controversy.

Chicago is a microcosm reflecting wider societal concerns in the United States and Canada over employment testing. The debate over adverse impact and cultural bias in selection testing continues to rage intensely on both sides of the border and is likely to do so for years to come.

* P. Glastris. 1994. "The Thin White Line: City Agencies Struggle to Mix Standardized Testing and Racial Balance." *U.S. News & World Report* (August 15): 53–54.

TABLE 3.6

Example of the Four-Fifths Rule in Determining Adverse Impact on Women: Selection Based on Mechanical Comprehension Test

	TOTAL APPLICANT POOL (A)	NUMBER OF PEOPLE MADE JOB OFFERS (B)	SELECTION RATE (RATIO OF B/A)
WOMEN	10	1	0.10
MEN	100	15	0.15

Minimum selection rate of women according to the four-fifths rule must be $4/5 \times 0.15 = 0.12$.

Because the selection rate of women (0.10) is less than the minimum selection rate under the four-fifths rule (0.12), we conclude that the mechanical comprehension test had adverse impact.

that is frequently used to establish adverse impact in selection is the *four-fifths* rule. According to this rule, adverse impact is established where the selection rate for the protected group is less than four-fifths that of the comparison group. Table 3.6 demonstrates a situation in which a mechanical comprehension test had an adverse impact on women according to the four-fifths rule. Despite its widespread adoption in Canada, the four-fifths rule has serious limitations on both rational and statistical grounds.[18]

Workplace Discrimination in the United States

In the United States, the primary federal legislation governing workplace discrimination is the Equal Employment Opportunity (EEO) Act of 1964, as amended in 1991. Along with the Equal Pay Act of 1963, the Age Discrimination Act of 1967, and the Americans with Disabilities Act of 1990, the EEO legislation and regulations made under it provide U.S. citizens with most of the protection against workplace discrimination afforded Canadians through the four legal sources we have discussed. In addition, significant rulings by U.S. courts have also had an impact on personnel selection standards, practices, and procedures.

Recruitment and Selection Today 3.5 provides a summary of the four most important U.S. Supreme Court cases that have had an impact on selection in the United States. While these cases do not hold any force in Canada, they do have influence in that they are used as part of legal briefs made to Canadian courts. The cases presented in Recruitment and Selection Today 3.5 have played a role in shaping the development of human rights and jurisprudence in Canada.

One of the most significant differences between Canadian and U.S. legislation is the incorporation of Section 15(2) into the Canadian Charter of Rights and Freedoms. Section 15(2) states that programs designed to ameliorate discrimination by favouring disadvantaged groups are not, themselves, discriminatory. In the United States, courts have often overturned programs on the grounds of "reverse discrimination." A second major difference is that

Landmark U.S. Supreme Court Cases Related to Selection

Griggs v. Duke Power (1971)

Thirteen black employees of Duke Power challenged the use of new selection requirements that included a high-school diploma, a mechanical aptitude test, and a general intelligence test on the grounds that they screened out a much higher proportion of black applicants than whites. Duke Power had no evidence to show that these requirements were job-related. The Supreme Court ruled any employment practice is prohibited if it discriminates against a minority group and it cannot be shown to be valid, that is, related to job performance.

Albemarle Paper Co. v. Moody (1975)

The U.S. government established *Uniform Guidelines on Employee Selection Procedures* for use in evaluating the validity of personnel selection programs. Black employees of the Albemarle Paper Company in North Carolina claimed that the use of a seniority system, requirement for a high school diploma, and application of two tests of general cognitive ability as part of a promotion process discriminated against blacks, who were employed mostly in unskilled positions and who historically had limited access to skilled jobs in the paper mill. The Court ruled that the research done to establish the validity of the tests did not meet the standards on validity set by the *Uniform Guidelines*. The Court ordered that the class of black workers were to be compensated for their discrimination, establishing the precedent for multimillion-dollar awards in subsequent cases of workplace discrimination.

Watson v. Fort Worth Bank & Trust (1988)

In reviewing candidates for promotion, Fort Worth Bank & Trust asked its supervisors to provide an assessment of each candidate in the context of the position's requirements. Clara Watson, who had been denied a promotion, challenged the system. The bank had argued that it did not have to establish that subjective evaluations such as those provided by the supervisors met the validity requirements established in previous case law for objective measures such as cognitive ability tests. The Court's ruling established that companies using subjective evaluations based on the judgment of supervisors or raters (including interviews) must show that those subjective evaluations are valid, using the same standards that the Court set for more objective assessments.

Wards Cove Packing v. Antonio (1988)

Unskilled, low-paying jobs in a salmon cannery were filled mostly by members of minority groups, while skilled and non-packing jobs were filled mostly by whites. The minority workers filed a class action suit alleging discrimination based on the racial imbalance between the two types of jobs. The Court ruled against the cannery workers. It held that the appropriate comparison for determining adverse impact was between *qualified* job applicants from the two different racial groups or between the proportions of those selected in different groups from the qualified pool of applicants. It further ruled that any racial imbalance must be attributable to an employment practice and not a result of statistical imbalances in the work force. The Court added that where an employment practice led to adverse impact, any alternative that led to less or no adverse impact must also be as effective as the practice it was replacing in meeting the organization's legitimate business purposes. The Court's ruling made it more difficult to establish an adverse impact case.

there is no ruling in Canada comparable to the *Wards Cove Packing* decision. In fact, the *Meiorin* decision (discussed at the beginning of Chapter 2 and later) has set a higher standard for employers to meet before allowing discriminatory work-related practices. Finally, as we will discuss in later chapters, human resources standards and practices that have developed in the United

States in response to legislation and court cases there tend to influence professional practice in Canada.

Discrimination Is Discrimination

Many people have had difficulty in differentiating direct discrimination from adverse effect discrimination since the outcomes in both cases are the same: Members of a protected group are subject to discrimination, although in one case, the discrimination is unintentional. In a Supreme Court of Canada decision—*British Columbia (Public Service Employee Relations Commission) v. BCGSEU*[19] (the *Meiorin* decision)—Justice McLachlin argued that, while one could differentiate between the two forms of discrimination, the distinction had little importance since the principal concern of the Court in human rights cases was the effect of an impugned law. According to Justice McLachlin, maintaining the distinction "ill serves the purpose of contemporary human rights legislation."

The *Meiorin* decision is a landmark ruling that has had a substantial impact on recruitment and selection policies and practices. The case originated as a complaint to the British Columbia Human Rights Commission but wound its way through the appeal process to the Supreme Court of Canada, which took up the case under the Charter of Rights. The Supreme Court ruling undermines use of the four-fifths rule as a defence to discrimination. Justice McLachlin wrote that leaving a "neutral" practice in place, even if its adverse effects were felt by only a small number of people, was questionable. The policy or practice is itself discriminatory because it treats some individuals differently from others on the basis of a prohibited ground; the size of the "affected group" is irrelevant. This suggests that the Court would not approve a selection practice that met the four-fifths rule.

In contrast to the *Wards Cove Packing v. Antonio* U.S. Supreme Court decision, the Canadian Supreme Court placed a higher onus on Canadian organizations to put in place nondiscriminatory selection procedures. The ruling laid out a unified approach for establishing whether performance standards for a job are discriminatory and reinforced the concept of individual accommodation in the workplace. Like the *Albemarle Paper Co. v. Moody* decision in the United States, this decision established new guidelines for research used in validating selection systems. These issues are addressed in greater detail in the following sections.

Bona Fide Occupational Requirement

Most human rights acts in Canada allow an employer to defend a discriminatory policy or practice as a **bona fide occupational requirement (BFOR)** if there is a good reason for it based on the employer's need to "engage and retain efficient employees."[20] The Canadian Human Rights Act[21] states that it is not a discriminatory practice if any refusal, exclusion, suspension, limitation, specification, or preference in relation to any employment is established by an employer to be based on a bona fide occupational requirement.

Bona fide occupational requirement (BFOR)

A procedure used to defend a discriminatory employment practice or policy on the grounds that the policy or practice was adopted in an honest and good-faith belief that it was reasonably necessary to assure the efficient and economical performance of the job without endangering employees or the general public.

In 1982, the Supreme Court of Canada[22] specified that a legitimate BFOR was imposed by an employer honestly in a good-faith belief that it was required for the adequate performance of the work involved in a safe, efficient, and economical manner. The BFOR had to be objectively related to job performance and reasonably necessary "to assure efficient and economical performance of the job without endangering the employee, his fellow employees and the general public." This definition of a BFOR guided selection policies and human resources practices until Justice McLachlin, in writing for the Supreme Court of Canada in *British Columbia (Public Service Employee Relations Comm.) v. BCGSEU*, set out a new "unified approach" to defining a BFOR for cases of both direct and adverse effect discrimination:

> Having considered the various alternatives, I propose the following three-step test for determining whether a prima facie discriminatory standard is a BFOR. An employer may justify the impugned standard by establishing on the balance of probabilities:
>
> (1) that the employer adopted the standard for a purpose rationally connected to the performance of the job;
>
> (2) that the employer adopted the particular standard in an honest and good faith belief that it was necessary to the fulfilment of that legitimate work-related purpose; and
>
> (3) that the standard is reasonably necessary to the accomplishment of that legitimate work-related purpose. To show that the standard is reasonably necessary, it must be demonstrated that it is impossible to accommodate individual employees sharing the characteristics of the claimant without imposing undue hardship upon the employer.

The "standard" referred to in this decision is the BC government's use of aerobics tests to assess forest firefighters against a minimum test score set for the "maximal oxygen uptake." This standard was believed to be necessary for firefighters to meet the physical demands required in fighting forest fires. All candidates had to meet the same minimum test score. The Supreme Court found that the standard had a prima facie discriminatory effect on women. Women have, on average, a lower aerobic capacity than men and had difficulty achieving the minimum test score that had been set for the test. Fewer women, therefore, would be hired under the standard.

The Court held that the BC government had met the first two steps of the unified approach by adopting the standard in an honest and good-faith belief that the standard was job-related and was linked to successful job performance. It failed, however, to demonstrate to the Court's satisfaction that the minimum performance standard set on the aerobics tests was reasonably necessary to the accomplishment of the legitimate work-related purpose for which it had been adopted. The employer had not demonstrated that women required the same minimum level of aerobic capacity as men to perform the job safely and efficiently, nor had the employer shown that it was impossible to accommodate women candidates without imposing undue hardship on itself. The employer failed to demonstrate that the aerobics standard was a BFOR under the new "unified" definition and so could not successfully defend the use of the test for assessing the fitness of forest firefighters. All selection practices that come under human rights scrutiny in the future will be asked to meet this new definition of a BFOR.

Reasonable Accommodation

The concept of reasonable **accommodation** is incorporated into the concept of a bona fide occupational requirement. Where discrimination has occurred, the employer is under a duty to accommodate the complainant, short of undue hardship. For example, an employer who administers a standardized employment test in selection may have to demonstrate that test instructions were appropriately modified to allow persons with mental or physical disabilities a fair chance to demonstrate their ability. The Supreme Court of Canada, in *O'Malley v. Simpsons-Sears* (1985), placed the employer under a burden to take reasonable steps to accommodate the complainant, with hardship occurring at the point where a policy or practice (such as modifying a selection procedure) causes undue interference in the operation of the business or unsupportable expense to the employer.

The Supreme Court of Canada, in *Central Alberta Dairy Pool v. Alberta (Human Rights Commission)* (1990), noted some factors that are relevant to assessing whether an employer has reasonably accommodated an individual or group protected under human rights legislation. Included among these factors that place the employer under a greater or lesser burden of accommodation are the following:

- the financial cost to the employer as a result of making the accommodation;
- disruption of an existing collective agreement;
- the impact of lowered morale on other employees;
- flexibility of work force and facilities; and
- the magnitude of risk for workers and the general public when safety is compromised.

Individual Accommodation

The concept of individual accommodation follows that of reasonable accommodation. In the *Bhinder v. CN Railway* (1985) decision, the Supreme Court of Canada found that once an employment policy or practice has been established as a BFOR, there is no need for the employer to accommodate to the special circumstances of the individual. For example, let us suppose that an individual with arthritis has asked for reasonable accommodation to this disability and wants to complete a realistic work sample in place of the usual standardized manual dexterity test required of job applicants. Under the *Bhinder* decision, the employer would not be under a burden to grant the applicant's request. As stated in that decision, the BFOR refers:

Accommodation
Refers to the duty of an employer to put in place modifications to discriminatory employment practices or procedures to meet the needs of members of a protected group being affected by the employment practice or procedure. As part of a BFOR defence, an employer must demonstrate that such accommodation is impossible to achieve without incurring undue hardship in terms of the organization's expense or operations.

to a requirement for the occupation, not a requirement limited to an individual. It must apply to all members of the employee group concerned because it is a requirement of general application concerning the safety of employees. The employee must meet the requirement in order to hold the employment. It is, by its nature, not susceptible to individual application.

The *Central Alberta Dairy Pool* decision, however, changed the basis of accommodation to an individual one. In the aftermath of the *Dairy Pool* decision, it is likely that an employer using the manual dexterity test will be required to accommodate the arthritic job candidate, even if that person is the only candidate with that disability applying for the job. The employer might accommodate such a candidate by using a realistic work sample or job tryout in place of the standardized test. As Recruitment and Selection Today 3.6 illustrates, failure to accommodate may be a costly proposition.

The decision of the Canadian Human Rights Tribunal in *Canada (Attorney General) v. Thwaites* (1993) clarified the application of the principles in the *Central Alberta Dairy Pool* case as follows (pp. 26–27):

> In respect of the BFOR defence provided for in Section 15(a) of the CHRA, the Supreme Court of Canada initially held in *Bhinder v. CN* in 1985 that consideration of a BFOR was to be without regard to the particular circumstances or abilities of the individual in question. In the short span of five years, the majority of the Court in *Alberta Human Rights Commission v. Central Alberta Dairy Pool* ([1990] 2 S.C.R. 489) reversed its position and held that in cases of adverse effect discrimination, the employer cannot resort to the BFOR defence at all. In such cases, there is now a positive duty on employers to accommodate the needs of employees disparately affected by a neutral rule unless to do so would create undue hardship for the employer. Put another way, the employer must establish that the application of the neutral rule or practice to the individual was reasonably necessary in that allowing for individual accommodation within the general application of the rule or practice would result in undue hardship. No longer, in such cases, can an employer justify its practice as a BFOR in relation to safety of employees in a general way and maintain that its discriminatory effect on certain groups of individuals is totally irrelevant.

Clearly, employers can no longer apply a BFOR as a general practice or policy and by so doing disproportionately exclude members of a protected group, especially in the case of mental or physical disability. To establish a BFOR, the employer must successfully argue that accommodating the needs of the adversely affected individual would produce undue economic or administrative hardship for the organization. Justice McLachlin raised the requirements for establishing the BFOR in the *British Columbia (Public Service Employee Relations Commission) v. BCGSEU* case. Employers must now demonstrate that it is *impossible* to accommodate individual employees who are

Accommodation May Be Expensive but Not Being Accommodating May Be Costlier

Accommodation on the job, while laudable, is not sufficient to accommodate those with a disability seeking employment or entry into a new position. At an individual level, accommodation also applies to the hiring process. Before an employer may rightfully conclude that an applicant's test score reflects a skill deficiency rather than the disability, the employer must accommodate the disability as part of the selection process.

Two decisions of the Canadian Human Rights Tribunal clearly state the need for accommodation with respect to tests used to hire employees with disabilities. In *Andrews v. Treasury Board and Department of Transport* (1994), which is discussed later in this chapter, the tribunal held that a hearing test administered to applicants to the Coast Guard College discriminated against a hearing-impaired applicant because "the test was flawed and the pass scores were established at unrealistic levels. Therefore, the test itself does not satisfy the requirements of the BFOR defence."

In *Green v. Public Service Commission* (1998), the Canadian Human Rights Tribunal held that the *Modern Language Aptitude Test*, a test of aptitude for learning a second language, discriminated against an applicant who had a learning disability. The disability, dyslexia (which affected auditory processing functioning), interfered with auditory discrimination and rote auditory memory and sequencing skills. The Public Service Commission took Green's test results as indicating a "negative prognosis" to acquire a new language.

The test requires a person to listen to obscure languages (e.g., Kurdish) and then answer questions based on relating sounds on the tapes to symbols, among other exercises. The intent of using obscure languages is to provide a level playing field for all candidates by not giving any one of the candidates an advantage by using a language that they might know. In this case, Green claimed to be at a severe disadvantage because she relied on contextual information to make sense out of auditory sounds.

An expert in the field of learning disabilities substantiated Green's claim. Green, on the basis of her test score, was denied access to a French-language training program and a promotion into a bilingual management position.

The Canadian Human Rights Tribunal ruled that Green must be given the management position without further testing. In coming to that conclusion, the tribunal had followed Supreme Court of Canada decisions, including *Andrews v. Treasury Board and Department of Transport*, which established the principle that an employer had to accommodate employees with disabilities to the point of undue hardship.

The Public Service Commission appealed the tribunal's decision to the Federal Court of Canada. The Appeal Court upheld the tribunal's decision. Justice François Lemieux, writing for the court, stated that the test dwelled on Green's disability and did not take into account evidence that showed she had a higher-than-average aptitude to learn French and that her skills, determination, and visual processing ability more than made up for her disability.

The Appeal Court awarded Green $170 000 plus interest, $5000 in special compensation, and compensation for the lost pension and benefits she would have received in the management position. It also ordered the government to admit her to a French-language training program, to give Green the promotion she should have received 13 years earlier (the complaint originated in 1987), and, upon her successful completion of a management training program, a further promotion to an executive-level position without holding a competition.

Sources: *Andrews v. Treasury Board and Department of Transport.* Canadian Human Rights Tribunal decision rendered September 1994 (T.D. 18/94); *Green v. PSAC, Treasury Board and Human Resources Development Canada.* Canadian Human Rights Tribunal decision rendered June 26, 1998 (T.D. 6/98); J. Tibbets and C. Grey. "Judge Slams PS Language Aptitude Testing." *Ottawa Citizen* (June 10, 2000): A1, A9.

members of the protected group without imposing undue hardship on the employer. As stated by Justice McLachlin:

> Employers designing workplace standards owe an obligation to be aware of both the differences between individuals, and differences that characterize groups of individuals. They must build conceptions of equality into workplace standards. By enacting human rights statutes and providing that they are applicable to the workplace, the legislatures have determined that the standards governing the performance of work should be designed to reflect all members of society, in so far as this is reasonably possible. Courts and tribunals must bear this in mind when confronted with a claim of employment-related discrimination. To the extent that a standard unnecessarily fails to reflect the differences among individuals, it runs afoul of the prohibitions contained in the various human rights statutes and must be replaced. The standard itself is required to provide for individual accommodation, if reasonably possible. A standard that allows for such accommodation may be only slightly different from the existing standard but it is a different standard nonetheless.

Reasonable Alternative

The concept of reasonable alternative is also closely related to the BFOR. Under the burden of reasonable alternative, the employer must show that no reasonable or practical substitute exists for the discriminatory practice. For example, where the employer uses a cognitive ability test that has adverse impact on members of visible minorities, a tribunal may require that employer to show that no other valid selection predictor (e.g., a different employment test or a structured interview) is available that has less adverse impact.

The concept of reasonable alternative can involve important elements of individual accommodation as well. As stated in the Canadian Human Rights Tribunal decision of *Andrews v. Treasury Board and Department of Transport* (1994), an employer, as part of a BFOR defence, must usually explain why it was not possible to assess individually the risk presented by an employee. For example, an employer who administers a manual dexterity test to all job applicants may have to show a tribunal why it was not possible to provide a practical work sample test as a reasonable alternative to assess the ability of one particular disabled applicant to do the job. Indeed, the *British Columbia (Public Service Employee Relations Commission) v. BCGSEU* decision placed more stringent obligations on employers to search for reasonable alternatives (see Recruitment and Selection Notebook 3.5).

Accommodating Physical and Mental Disability

The Supreme Court explicitly applied the *Meiorin* ruling to disability cases, such as *Grismer v. British Columbia (A.G).*[23] The Court emphasized that individualized, rather than standardized, testing must be used to accommodate individuals with disabilities. This case did not involve the workplace but

Search for Reasonable Alternatives

The *British Columbia (Public Service Employee Relations Commission) v. BCGSEU* decision requires an employer to address the following questions as part of establishing a defence that there were no reasonable alternatives to a practice that discriminated against individual workers. These questions are taken verbatim from the Supreme Court decision:

(a) Has the employer investigated alternative approaches that do not have a discriminatory effect, such as individual testing against a more individually sensitive standard?

(b) If alternative standards were investigated and found to be capable of fulfilling the employer's purpose, why were they not implemented?

(c) Is it necessary to have all employees meet the single standard for the employer to accomplish its legitimate purpose or could standards reflective of group or individual differences and capabilities be established?

(d) Is there a way to do the job that is less discriminatory while still accomplishing the employer's legitimate purpose?

(e) Is the standard properly designed to ensure that the desired qualification is met without placing an undue burden on those to whom the standard applies?

(f) Have other parties who are obliged to assist in the search for possible accommodation fulfilled their roles? As Sopinka J. noted in Renaud, supra, at pp. 992–96, the task of determining how to accommodate individual differences may also place burdens on the employee and, if there is a collective agreement, a union.

---

nonetheless has serious implications with respect to the accommodation of workplace disability.

The *Grismer* case revolved around the Superintendent of Motor Vehicles' refusal to issue a driver's licence on the basis of a visual disability. The Supreme Court ruled that the defendants in human rights cases, here the Superintendent of Motor Vehicles, have the burden of demonstrating that the standard they have adopted "incorporates every possible accommodation to the point of undue hardship, whether that hardship takes the form of impossibility, serious risk or excessive cost." The *Grismer* case suggests that an employer must accept some moderate risk in accommodating individuals with disabilities while maintaining reasonable safety standards.

In a subsequent ruling (*Québec [Commission des droits de la personne et des droits de la jeunesse] v. Montréal [City]*),[24] the Court broadened the definition of disability and directed employers to take into account the social context of the impairment. The Court ruled that a person with a disability must be assessed in terms of his or her own unique abilities; the person's disability must not be viewed through any prejudice or bias, stigma, or misunderstanding on the part of the employer about the disability.

Sufficient Risk

The notion of risk is important to the concepts of BFOR, reasonable and individual accommodation, and reasonable alternative. That is, the employer is obliged to accommodate workers, including job applicants, and provide reasonable alternatives up to, but not beyond, a certain level of risk. Tribunals and courts have restricted the application of the risk criterion to those situations in which workplace safety is at issue. After *Grismer*, however, each case will be judged on its own unique merits with respect to the degree of risk imposed by the disability. For example, an airline company may set a visual acuity standard for pilots, requiring that all candidates have uncorrected 20/20 full-colour vision, and defend this standard on the grounds that public safety would be compromised without it; however, a delivery company might not be able to defend not hiring a driver who was legally blind in one eye.

One of the key questions that tribunals and courts have dealt with lately is whether the criterion of risk should be defined as *acceptable risk, significant risk, sufficient risk,* or some other level. Although the issue is still being debated, one Federal Appeal Court decision, *Canada (Human Rights Commission) and Husband v. Canada (Armed Forces)* in 1994 established that the appropriate risk criterion applying to a BFOR is whether accommodating an employee with a particular characteristic would create "sufficient risk" to justify rejecting that individual for employment. **Sufficient risk** was defined in that decision as follows:[25]

> A BFOR will be established if there is a "sufficient risk of employee failure" to warrant the retention of an otherwise discriminatory employment qualification. Thus, whether or not an occupational requirement is "reasonably necessary" is dependent, at least in part, on whether members of the group alleging discrimination pose a sufficient risk of harm to themselves or others in the event of employee failure.

Justice Robertson, in this same decision, further defined sufficient risk as a "substantial" increase in safety risk within tolerable limits. Justice Robertson described some of the factors that have an impact on risk assessment for BFORs:

- the nature of the employment (e.g., teacher versus airline pilot in the case of visual impairment);
- the likelihood of employee failure, stated in empirical, rather than speculative, terms;
- whether risk of employee failure is restricted to health and safety considerations; and
- the seriousness of the harm arising from employee failure.

One area where direct discrimination might still happen with some regularity is in the area of physical or mental disability. For example, a hospital employer might screen out from the hiring process all people with the HIV virus or with AIDS. The concern of the employer would probably centre on the safety of patients during use of invasive techniques (such as injections by syringe). If the hospital did intentionally exclude all persons with HIV/AIDS during selection, then the employer would have to establish a BFOR and show through the use of objective data that (1) people with HIV/AIDS are a sufficient safety risk; (2) all persons with HIV/AIDS present a safety risk; (3) individual

Sufficient risk

As part of a BFOR defence, an employer may argue that an occupational requirement that discriminates against a protected group is reasonably necessary to ensure that work will be performed successfully and in a manner that will not pose harm or danger to employees or the public.

testing of applicants with HIV/AIDS is impossible or impractical; and (4) that these individuals cannot be accommodated without imposing undue hardship on the employer.

The sufficient risk criterion means that the risk must be well above a minimal or nominal risk. A minimal or nominal risk criterion would, for example, suggest that a person with muscular dystrophy should not be hired because that person might be injured in a fall (an organizational policy that many human rights authorities would argue reinforces a stereotype about the physically disabled, rather than being supportable by fact). On the other hand, a severe vision disability in an airline pilot would be well above minimal or nominal risk, because a plane crash caused or contributed to by that disability could kill hundreds of people. In that instance, risk resulting from the disability might well be sufficient to justify the otherwise discriminatory action of refusing to offer the disabled person a job.

In *Québec v. Montréal (City)* the Supreme Court was quite clear in stating that the limitations imposed by a disability must be considered individually within a particular context and that some risk is acceptable. Decisions about hiring someone with a disability cannot be made on the basis of prejudice or stereotypes held about the limitations imposed by the disability.

Legal Concepts Applied to Recruitment and Selection

Two human rights decisions illustrate the application of the above principles to employers' recruitment or selection systems. In both decisions, each employer's system was found wanting and the court or tribunal awarded damages or remedies to the complainant. Both decisions continue to have a significant impact on recruitment and selection in Canada.

The first decision is that of *Action Travail des Femmes v. Canadian National* (1984). Here a women's group in Quebec lodged a complaint with the Canadian Human Rights Commission aimed at CN's recruitment and selection practices in the St. Lawrence region. Action Travail des Femmes alleged that CN's practices disproportionately excluded women from nontraditional jobs, including those of trade apprentice, brakeman, and coach cleaner, all of which were male-dominated. Furthermore, they alleged that the employment practices in question were not bona fide occupational requirements.

One selection predictor that came under scrutiny by the tribunal was the *Bennett Mechanical Comprehension Test*, which was used to select people for entry-level positions. The *Bennett* is known to have adverse impact against women and, in addition, CN had not validated it for the jobs in question. As a result, the tribunal ordered CN to stop using the test. In addition, the tribunal ordered CN to cease a number of other discriminatory recruitment and selection practices. The tribunal also ordered CN to begin a special hiring program with the goal of increasing the representation of women in nontraditional jobs in that company. This decision was widely noted at the time and has since influenced recruitment and hiring practices in Canada.

The second decision is that of *Andrews v. Treasury Board and Department of Transport* (1994). In that decision, a Canadian Human Rights tribunal criticized a practical hearing test developed to assess a hearing-impaired applicant to the Canadian Coast Guard College. The test, which was administered in place of a maximum hearing loss standard for Canadian Coast Guard officers, was designed at a cost of over $100 000 and consisted of 14 different subtests administered to the applicant on the bridge of an operating Coast Guard ship. The subtest scenarios were administered by Coast Guard staff, who in turn supervised crew members of the ship serving as role players. The applicant's responses to the subtest scenarios were recorded and then compared against predetermined test standards.

Andrews subsequently failed the test, was declined admission to the college, and filed a complaint with the Canadian Human Rights Commission. When testifying about the test during the tribunal hearings, expert witnesses criticized it on various grounds, including incomplete technical development, lack of reliability and validity, administration under insufficiently standardized conditions, and absence of norm data against which to compare and interpret the applicant's scores. The tribunal concluded that the practical hearing test was discriminatory and granted monetary compensation to the complainant Andrews.

In the *Andrews v. Treasury Board and Department of Transport* decision, the tribunal cited all the legal principles previously discussed in this chapter. The complainant Andrews lodged his complaint against the Coast Guard on the grounds of physical disability (hearing impairment) and also alleged both direct discrimination and adverse effect discrimination. The application of the hearing loss standard had the effect of producing adverse impact against hearing-disabled persons.

The tribunal found that the Coast Guard had discriminated against Andrews by refusing him entry to the Coast Guard College and then considered whether the Coast Guard had successfully argued a BFOR defence. The tribunal accepted the subjective element of the BFOR (that the Coast Guard had set the limitation honestly, in good faith, and in sincerity that the limitation was necessary), but rejected the Coast Guard argument that it had established the objective element of the BFOR. Importantly, the tribunal found that the Coast Guard had not established the practical hearing test as a BFOR because of the numerous technical problems associated with it; that is, the Coast Guard had failed to validate the practical hearing test according to accepted, professional standards. What is more, the tribunal found that Andrews could have been reasonably and individually accommodated by use of a less expensive and simpler test, which would have been a reasonable alternative to the practical hearing test. Finally, the nature of Andrews's disability did not pose sufficient risk to the safe performance of a Coast Guard navigational officer to justify denying him entry to the college to train for the job.

A comparison between these two decisions, which were made 10 years apart, illustrates that at least four important legal concepts (those of reasonable accommodation, individual accommodation, reasonable alternative, and sufficient risk) assumed greater importance in the 1990s than in the 1980s. The *Meiorin* and *Grismer* decisions placed an even greater emphasis on these four legal concepts. Because of the rapidly evolving character of legal issues in Canadian human resources management, practitioners and HR specialists must continually upgrade their knowledge and skills in this area.

Part III: Some Practical Guidelines in Nondiscriminatory Recruitment and Selection

The first two parts of this chapter provided a historical and conceptual backdrop for legal issues in recruitment and selection in Canada. They reviewed important court and tribunal decisions that have affected the practice of recruitment and selection in Canada. This third part presents some practical guidelines for developing nondiscriminatory recruitment and selection practices and for reviewing and improving those practices already in place.

The guidelines presented here are exactly that—guidelines; they are not meant to be applied in a mechanical fashion. The guidelines point in the right direction and help to identify typical problem areas in recruitment and selection systems. The guidelines should stimulate critical discussion and appraisal of those systems with an eye to improvement. There are no easy answers to many of the problems discussed in this chapter; the issues are simply too complex. HR managers may need to draw on the expert help of legal and professional consultants in dealing with many of these complex issues, particularly when there is insufficient time or expertise to deal with them in-house.

Key Practical Considerations in Nondiscriminatory Recruitment

 3.4

Recruitment is a complex human resources activity. This can make it difficult to develop nondiscriminatory recruitment practices for protected group members (in the case of human rights legislation) or designated group members (in the case of employment equity). The scope of practices that must be considered is more manageable if the success or failure of recruitment is traced back to two main causes: (1) the effectiveness or ineffectiveness of the organization in contacting and communicating with target group members and (2) the positive or negative perceptions that target group members hold about the organization. (It is irrelevant whether those perceptions existed before the target group members were recruited or whether they developed during the recruiting process.)

People will not apply for a job if they are unaware that the job or organization exists or that the organization is recruiting. Getting the word out is not enough—job seekers must have a positive perception of the organization, as well as of their chances of getting the job, before they will apply. That perception is formed in at least two ways: (1) at the time the organization makes the initial contact through its **outreach recruiting** or (2) through knowledge gained about the organization and its practices via third parties (e.g., friends, family, or news media).

Outreach recruiting

A recruitment practice where the employing organization makes a determined and persistent effort to inform potential job applicants (including designated group members) of available positions within the organization.

Recruitment and Selection Notebooks 3.6 and 3.7 present a summary of effective and ineffective recruiting practices. They provide some practical guidance on what to do and what not to do when setting up and running recruitment programs that will meet legal requirements. As well, Recruitment and Selection Notebook 3.8 on page 104 presents a list of human rights resources available on the Internet.

Legal Requirements and HR Practice

An underlying assumption of recruitment and selection practices is that these practices are supported by empirical evidence, that they are reliable and valid procedures. Recruitment and selection practices that have an impact on careers or entry to occupations must be defensible with respect to legal requirements. That is, we expect practitioners to apply solutions that have a solid "scientific" grounding. Regrettably, HR practice too often runs ahead of research and leads to the adoption of interventions that do not have empirical support, or do not have support for the specific purposes for which they are used. Claims by a practitioner that a practice is "valid" because the practitioner "knows" it works or "it makes good business sense" will not meet legal scrutiny against the standards laid out in this chapter. Only those

---

Recruitment and Selection Notebook 3.6

Practices for Nondiscriminatory Recruiting

Effective Practices

- In employment offices, post in a conspicuous spot complete, objective, and specific information on all available jobs.
- Advertise job openings in media that are read, viewed, or listened to by protected or designated group members.
- Train employment clerical staff and recruitment officers in outreach recruiting.
- Use opportunities to visually present protected or designated group members in positive employment roles (e.g., in brochures and posters in employment office waiting areas, postings on company websites, and in profiles of board members).
- Establish networks with community groups from which protected or designated group members are drawn.
- Set and advertise objectively determined selection criteria for the job.

- Base selection criteria on bona fide occupational requirements.

Ineffective Practices

- Permit receptionists and recruiters in employment offices to "pre-screen" applicants on the basis of informal criteria (e.g., appearance, dress).
- Rely on word-of-mouth advertising.
- Post job advertisements only in-house.
- Rely solely on seniority when promoting employees without regard for meeting the qualifications needed for the position.
- Allow each recruiter to use and communicate idiosyncratic criteria for selecting among job applicants.
- Categorize and stream job applicants based on stereotyped assumptions about protected or designated group membership (e.g., that women are not physically strong enough for certain work).

Recruiting Perceptions

Practices That Promote Positive Recruiting Perceptions

- In job advertising, include role models from protected or designated groups, as well as equal opportunity statements.
- Implement management practices and policies that recognize and deal with special challenges or difficulties faced by protected or designated groups (e.g., wheelchair ramps for the physically disabled).
- Communicate and demonstrate the commitment of senior management to outreach recruiting.
- Actively challenge negative myths and stereotypes about protected or designated group members (e.g., through training programs).
- Bring organizational policies and procedures into line with human rights and employment equity legislation.
- Reward supervisors and managers with the pay and promotion system for success in advancing human rights and employment equity goals.
- Build outreach recruiting into departmental and organizational business plans.
- Set specific and measurable recruiting targets against which managers can work.
- Present protected and designated group members in positive roles within organization newspapers and magazines.
- Offer training and development programs to protected and designated group members to address their specific needs in adapting and progressing within the organization.
- Modify working conditions as needed to accommodate protected and designated group members.

Practices That Promote Negative Recruiting Perceptions

- Permit sexual, racial, or other forms of harassment in the organization.
- Show lack of interest by senior management in improving recruitment practices.
- Allow negative myths and stereotypes to persist regarding the capabilities of protected and designated group members.
- Leave outreach recruiting unrewarded by the pay and promotion system.
- Leave outreach recruiting outside of departmental and organizational business plans.
- Tell managers to "do your best" in recruiting protected and designated group members rather than providing them with specific numerical targets.

selection procedures that can be supported through empirical evidence will find acceptance with courts and human rights tribunals.

Adopting valid recruitment and selection practices is only part of the solution. Practitioners must ensure the proper implementation of the system and monitor it over time for any changes. It is not acceptable, for example, to show that a certain level of cognitive ability is a job requirement and then use an invalid test to measure it. Neither is it acceptable for the practitioner to use a valid test in an inappropriate manner or to lack the qualifications to use and interpret data from a valid test.

There is a need for better linkages between research and practice in human resources. Practitioners must understand the need to base recruitment and selection practices on empirical evidence. These linkages have become ever more important as the field of HR moves to establish itself as an inde-

Human Rights and the Internet

The following are Internet URLs for Canadian and provincial human rights tribunals and commissions, along with those for some other valuable human rights resources. On each site, you will find links to other related sites and to lists of decisions or publications that can be found on the site. For example, the "Publications" link on the Canadian Human Rights Commission site will provide you with access to a list of recent reports, guides, and other materials that you can read directly from the site, print, or download. By this means, you can obtain a copy of the *Guide to Screening and Selection in Employment*. HR managers and others who engage in recruitment and selection should make a habit of reviewing recent information, including new decisions posted on these sites.

Human Rights Boards/Tribunals

Canada	http://www.chrt-tcdp.gc.ca
British Columbia	http://www.bchrt.gov.bc.ca
Quebec (French)	http://www.cdpdj.qc.ca/fr/accueil.asp?noeud1=0&noeud2=0&cle=0
Quebec (English)	http://www.cdpdj.qc.ca/en/home.asp?noued=1&noeud2=0&cle=0

Human Rights Commissions

Canada	http://www.chrc-ccdp.ca
Alberta	http://www.albertahumanrights.ab.ca/default.asp
Manitoba	http://www.gov.mb.ca/hrc
New Brunswick	http://www.gnb.ca/hrc-cdp/index-e.asp
Newfoundland/Labrador	http://www.justice.gov.nl.ca/hrc
Northwest Territories	http://www.nwthumanrights.ca
Nova Scotia	http://www.gov.ns.ca/humanrights
Ontario	http://www.ohrc.on.ca
Prince Edward Island	http://www.gov.pe.ca/humanrights
Quebec	http://www.cdpdj.qc.ca
Saskatchewan	http://www.shrc.gov.sk.ca
Yukon	http://www.yhrc.yk.ca

Valuable Human Rights Resources on the Internet

Canadian Human Rights Reporter (CHRR)
http://cdn-hr-reporter.ca

Human Rights Research and Education Centre (Ottawa)
http://www.uottawa.ca/hrrec

Human Rights Information and Documentation Systems
http://www.hurisearch.org

LexUM (Law Library)
http://www.lexum.umontreal.ca/index_en.html

pendent profession. Regulatory and credentialing systems exist to ensure the protection of the welfare of the public and clients of the practitioner and to guarantee that the practitioner operates in accordance with accepted standards of professional ethics and practice guidelines.

Practitioners are expected to use procedures and practices that not only "do no harm" but actually provide benefits to the client. This is particularly important when invalid selection procedures bring the HR practitioner's organization in front of a court or tribunal and result in large-scale payouts to rectify wrongs done to employees. There are some questions that a practitioner can ask to determine if the recruitment and selection procedures they are using will meet with legal acceptance:

1. Do the procedures I am using result in direct or indirect discrimination?

2. If a selection procedure I am using results in direct or indirect discrimination, can I establish that it is a BFOR by showing that:
   - I am adopting the selection procedure in good faith?
   - the selection procedure cannot be replaced by one that is valid and has less or little adverse impact?
   - the selection procedure is related to job performance or safety?
   - *all* of those people in the class excluded by the selection procedure are incapable of performing the job or present a sufficient safety risk?
   - individual testing of class members affected by the rule is impossible or impractical?
   - there are no reasonable alternatives to that testing?
   - every attempt has been made to accommodate the unique capabilities and inherent worth and dignity of every individual, up to the point of undue hardship?
3. Is the selection procedure a valid predictor of job performance?

Finally, one last thing that the HR staff may need to do is to educate management about the legal requirements that must be met in recruitment and selection. More and more Canadian organizations understand the benefits of adapting their procedures to meet legislative requirements. The intent of human rights legislation is clear: Everyone should have the opportunity to compete for the jobs available on an equal footing and on the basis of objective qualifications, regardless of group membership or employer stereotyping about what members of particular groups can and can't do. If this message has not gotten through, then HR professionals have the primary responsibility for providing the necessary education within their organizations.

Selection systems must be as legally defensible as possible. HR specialists must have the knowledge and time to collect and interpret the technical data that are essential to establishing the legal defensibility of a selection system. The best defence is a system that meets the validity and reliability requirements outlined in Chapter 2; selection based on "gut feeling," intuition, or unproven techniques will lead to embarrassment before a legal tribunal. Managers and HR staff should question and challenge each other's assumptions about what constitutes a legally defensible selection system. Even then, the legal issues are complex enough that managers and HR staff may hold differing opinions about whether a selection system is legally defensible. In those cases, legal consultation should be obtained. Nevertheless, the discussion of practical selection problems should lead to more defensible selection systems over the long run.

Summary

The Canadian work force has always been ethnically heterogeneous, and now it is becoming increasingly diverse with regard to race, gender, and disabilities. Given that recruitment and selection are crucially important human resources activities for achieving diversity, human rights and employment equity are here to stay. As well, a large segment of the Canadian work force is unionized, which means that labour codes and related legislation will affect recruitment and selection practices in many Canadian organizations.

Legal issues in recruitment and selection are complex and take a great deal of time, study, and experience to master. What is more, the legal scene changes constantly and rapidly as new legislation, legislative amendments, human rights policies, and tribunal or court decisions are introduced. This requires practitioners in recruitment and selection to regularly update their knowledge and skills related to legal issues. The legal scene will continue to grow and develop in the future as members of protected groups seek fuller participation in the Canadian labour market and as employers and employees (unionized and nonunionized) renegotiate their relationships through labour law and employment standards.

In this chapter, we have presented an overview of the legal requirements that apply to recruitment and selection in Canada. We identified four main legal sources that influence the practice of HR in Canada: (1) constitutional law; (2) human rights legislation; (3) employment equity legislation and employment equity policies; and (4) labour law, employment standards, and related legislation.

The impact of these laws and policies mandates recruitment and selection practices that do not discriminate on the basis of specific characteristics. While there are differences across Canada, all human rights Acts prohibit discrimination in employment with respect to race or colour, religion or creed, age, sex, marital status, and physical/mental handicap or disability. Employment equity requires proactive recruitment and selection policies to increase the number of women, Aboriginals, visible minorities, and people with disabilities in the workplace by removing barriers to hiring them.

This chapter presents the most significant cases that have had a major impact on recruitment and selection. Over the past 25 years, a series of decisions by the Supreme Court of Canada and the Canadian Human Rights Commission have dealt with direct and indirect discrimination. These decisions have placed ever-increasing restrictions on an organization's ability to use a BFOR defence against charges of discrimination, with the *Meiorin* decision dramatically changing the definition of a BFOR. Now, an organization must show that it is impossible to accommodate an individual employee or job applicant with respect to selection procedures without undue hardship to the company. This requirement is more stringent than similar requirements in the United States. The chapter also presents the obligations placed on an employer to accommodate employees and job applicants with respect to selection procedures and factors such as risk that may mitigate that obligation.

The chapter concludes with a presentation of some practical guidelines that will assist HR practitioners in developing recruitment and selection procedures that will meet with legal acceptance, should they have to address a human rights complaint. In closing, we also emphasize the need for HR practitioners to educate management about the legal requirements that recruitment and selection systems must meet and that the best way of staying out of legal trouble is to use reliable and valid selection systems, as presented in Chapter 2.

Key Terms

accommodation, p. 93

adverse effect discrimination, p. 87

adverse impact, p. 88

bona fide occupational requirement (BFOR), p. 91

discrimination, p. 68

employment equity, p. 75

outreach recruiting, p. 101

sufficient risk, p. 98

Web Links

The HRSDC Workplace Equity website provides extensive information on laws, regulations, and compliance issues relating to employment equity. This information can be found at http://www.hrsdc.gc.ca.

The Human Rights Research and Education Centre's website provides links to full-text versions of the court and tribunal decisions referenced in this chapter. You can find these at http://www.uottawa.ca/hrrec.

The complete text of the *Meiorin* decision can be read at http://csc.lexum .umontreal.ca/en/1999/1999rcs3-3/1999rcs3-3.html.

Required Professional Capabilities (RPCs)

RPC 3.1 Identifies and masters legislation and jurisprudence relevant to HR functions.
- Relevant legislation, regulations, and jurisprudence
- The organization, its operations, and general business environment
- Applicable political, social, and cultural context and environment
- Common law as it relates to employment issues

RPC 3.2 Ensures the organization's HR policies and practices align with human rights legislation.
- Professional standards and codes of ethics
- Relevant legislation, regulations, and jurisprudence
- The organization, its operations, and environment
- Theories and practices for protection of individuals and groups
- Techniques in managing work force diversity
- Applicable political, social, and cultural context and environment

RPC 3.3 Leads an appropriate organizational response to formal or informal complaints or appeals related to alleged human rights, workplace, or employment violations.
- Relevant legislation, regulations, and jurisprudence
- Investigative techniques
- Professional standards and codes of ethics
- Applicable political, social, and cultural context and environment
- Basic rules of evidence
- Theories and practices for protection of individuals and groups

- Techniques in managing work force diversity
- Change management practices

RPC 3.4 Formulates organization development strategies in accordance with legislated and/or voluntary diversity and equity goals.
- Legal framework for equity and diversity (including reporting requirements)
- Principles and concepts of organizational development and intervention techniques
- Industry best practices
- Applicable political, social, and cultural context and environment
- Theories and practices for protection of individuals and groups
- Methods of accommodating employee needs (e.g., flexible hours, job sharing, child care)
- Techniques in managing workforce diversity

RPC 3.5 Establishes screening and assessment procedures.
- Selection concepts and assessment techniques (e.g., interviews, tests, and other widely used selection procedures)
- Human rights legislation
- Employment equity legislation
- Organization policies and procedures
- Validity and reliability (conceptual definitions and assessment techniques)
- Recruiting sources and techniques (both internal and external)

RPC 3.6 Analyzes and provides advice on employment rights and responsibilities.
- Relevant legislation and regulations
- Organization policies and procedures
- Information sources such as other organizations, publications, and associations
- Theories and practices for protection of individuals and groups
- Collective agreements
- Standards of professional practice

Discussion Questions

1. Would the Canadian Charter of Rights and Freedoms prohibit an employer from putting in place a selection system that favoured women over men in the hiring process? Could such discrimination ever be justified under the Charter?
2. What are the prohibited grounds of employment discrimination in your province's or territory's jurisdiction?
3. What grounds could a Canadian employer use to justify the adverse impact of a selection procedure, test, or other measure?
4. Is mandatory retirement allowed in your province or territory? If so, under what circumstances?

5. What does it mean to accommodate someone to the point of undue hardship?
6. Why is basing hiring practices on a "gut feeling" risky business?

Using the Internet

1. Recruitment and Selection Today 3.1 (page 75) presents a real-life case where a manager and an HR professional disagree on whom to hire, with the HR professional arguing that the manager's reasons for not hiring a female applicant would constitute a human rights violation and providing the manager with the relevant section of their province's or territory's human rights act. Recruitment and Selection Notebook 3.8 (page 104) lists the Internet URLs for most provincial and territorial human rights agencies. Download a copy of your province's or territory's human rights Act. (Note: The Nunavut government's Human Resources page provides policies in relation to a number of HR issues.)

   a. In the context of your provincial or territorial legislation, discuss whether the HR professional was correct in arguing that not hiring the female applicant would constitute a violation of your human rights Act. What is the basis of the alleged violation?
   b. Review the cases and annual reports that are available on your provincial or territorial human rights agency's website to locate a case that may be similar to the one described in Recruitment and Selection Today 3.1. What was the ruling in that case? Would the ruling in that case be applicable to the situation described in Recruitment and Selection Today 3.1?
   c. Would the manager ever be justified in not hiring the female applicant? If so, what would those circumstances be?

Exercises

1. In the *British Columbia (Public Service Employees Relations Commission) v. BCGSEU* case, a lower appeals court had suggested that accommodating women by permitting them to meet a lower aerobic standard than men would constitute "reverse discrimination." The Supreme Court of Canada disagreed and stated that

   > the essence of equality is to be treated according to one's own merit, capabilities and circumstances. True equality requires that differences be accommodated.... A different aerobic standard capable of identifying women who could perform the job safely and efficiently therefore does not necessarily

imply discrimination against men. "Reverse" discrimination would result only if, for example, an aerobic standard representing a minimum threshold for all forest firefighters was held to be inapplicable to men simply because they were men.

What are your views on reverse discrimination? Do you agree with the views expressed by the appeals court or the Supreme Court? Why or why not? Have you ever observed or been subjected to reverse discrimination? If so, what was the situation?

2. There is considerable evidence showing that smokers are less productive than nonsmokers. Costs to organizations, besides those related to medical care, health, and life insurance, include absenteeism and loss of on-the-job time. Estimates place time loss per day due to smoking at 35 minutes a day, or 18.2 lost days per year per employee who smokes. In addition, smokers are absent, on average, three more days per year than other employees. Estimates place the cost of smoking to an employer at around $4500 per smoker per year.[26] These data suggest that it is in an employer's best interests to hire only nonsmokers or to fire smokers who cannot overcome their addiction. Would such policies, hiring only nonsmokers and firing smokers, be acceptable under human rights legislation in your province or territory? Are smokers a "protected" group? How would you defend these policies to an investigator from a human rights commission?

3. You may recall hearing about females being fired from U.S. television news anchor positions because they were too old. Clearly, this practice would be contrary to all human rights codes in Canada. However, one area of discrimination that is less clear is "lookism," in which a person is chosen for a job on the basis of his or her looks rather than his or her other qualifications. Individuals, particularly females, who are overweight tend to receive fewer job offers than others, even in cases where their appearance has no possible bearing on their work performance or where they are not involved in dealing with clients or customers. Can an employer in Canada, or in your jurisdiction, choose not to hire someone on the basis of their looks or for being overweight? Do job applicants so denied have protection under your province's or territory's human rights provisions?

4. In the *Wards Cove Packing v. Antonio* decision, the U.S. Supreme Court stated that where an employment practice led to adverse impact, any alternative that led to less or no adverse impact must also be as effective as the practice it was replacing in meeting the organization's legitimate business purposes. The Court's ruling made it more difficult to establish an adverse impact case. In the *Meiorin* decision, the Canadian Supreme Court ruled that a policy or practice is itself discriminatory if it treats some individuals differently than others on the basis of a prohibited ground and that the size of the affected group was irrelevant. It also stated that an organization must accommo-

date individual employees to the point of imposing undue hardship upon the employer, unless it was impossible to do so. Discuss these two approaches to addressing selection practices that lead to adverse impact. Which approach do you support? Why?

Case

Marita Smith works as a data entry clerk in a government department that is undergoing downsizing. Smith, who is severely hearing-impaired, has been a productive employee in her department for the last five years. Her performance has always been above average.

Smith has received notice that her position is being eliminated as part of the downsizing. Under her union's contract, she must be given preference for any government job that becomes available and for which she is qualified. Smith has been invited to apply for a term position in another government department, which is converting archival data from paper to an electronic database. To qualify for the position, Smith will have to pass an interview, a timed typing test, an accuracy test that involves accuracy in transcribing information from a computer screen, and another accuracy test that involves following written instructions to enter written records into the computer database. These are the same tests that all candidates for the position have had to pass to become eligible for the job.

Smith was interviewed one week prior to being administered the three skill tests. The interview protocol followed a standardized form used by all government departments. The three skill tests were administered to groups of nine applicants each. The applicants were seated at desks with computers, which were arranged in three rows of three desks each. The instructions for the tests were given verbally by the test administrator. Smith was provided with the services of a sign language interpreter during the testing and interview sessions.

Smith passed the interview but failed the skill tests. Her scores are presented in Table 3.7, along with the minimum scores that had to be obtained on

TABLE 3.7

Smith's Scores Relative to Standards Needed to Pass Each Test

	STANDARDS	SMITH
INTERVIEW	30 out of 50 points	36
TYPING TEST	50 words per minute with 5 errors or less	36 wpm
		5 errors
ACCURACY—FOLLOWING INSTRUCTIONS	7 out of 10	5.5
ACCURACY—TRANSCRIBING	7 out of 10	5

each test to receive a job offer. Based on her performance on the tests, Smith did not receive an offer for the job and was laid off when her current job ended. Smith now believes that she was the victim of discrimination based on her physical disability; she claims that during the interview many references were made to her disability and that the interviewer always addressed questions to the sign language interpreter and never made eye contact with her. She feels that she was at a disadvantage in taking the skills tests.

Her prospective employer claims that had she passed the tests she would have been hired and her disability would have been accommodated. The employer argues that the testing standards were reasonably necessary for the efficient performance of the work. The standards in Table 3.7 are being justified as bona fide occupational requirements (BFORs). Smith has now filed a complaint with her provincial Human Rights Commission.

Discussion Questions

1. Should Smith have received a job offer? Why or why not? (In answering this and the following questions, base your arguments on the court cases presented in this chapter.)
2. Was Smith the victim of discrimination because of her disability?
3. Did she receive appropriate accommodation?
4. Are the employer's standards defensible as a BFOR?
5. Based on the material presented in this chapter, do you think the Human Rights Commission will support her claim of discrimination?
6. If you were the employer's legal counsel, how would you defend the employer at a human rights tribunal that is called to hear Smith's complaint? What would you advise your client to do with respect to the charge?

Endnotes

1. Simon, P.L.S. 1988. *Employment Law: The New Basics.* Don Mills, ON: CCH Canadian Limited.
2. Simon, P.L.S. 1988.
3. Canadian Human Rights Commission. 1989. *Office Consolidation: Canadian Human Rights Act.* Ottawa: Minister of Supply and Services Canada.
4. Canadian Human Rights Commission. 1994. *Filing a Complaint with the Canadian Human Rights Commission.* Ottawa: Minister of Supply and Services Canada.
5. Canadian Human Rights Commission. 1994.
6. Bakan, A.B., and A. Kobayashi. 2000. *Employment Equity Policy in Canada: An Interprovincial Comparison.* Ottawa: Status of Women Canada: http://www.swc-cfc.gc.ca.
7. Weiner, N. 1993. *Employment Equity: Making It Work.* Toronto: Butterworths.
8. Scotland, R. 1995. "Ontario Introduces Bill to Repeal 'Quotas': Aims to Restore 'Merit Principle.'" *The Financial Post* (October 12): 4.
9. Belcourt, M., and K.J. McBey. 2000. *Strategic Human Resources Planning.* Toronto: Nelson.

10. Jackson, S.E., and R.S. Schuler. 1995. "Understanding Human Resource Management in the Context of Organizations and Their Environments." *Annual Review of Psychology* 46: 237–64.

11. Human Resources and Social Development Canada. *Employment Standards Legislation in Canada*:http://www.hrsdc.gc.ca/en/lp/spila/clli/eslc/01Employment_Standards_Legislation_in_Canada.shtml.

12. Public Service Commission of Canada. Undated. *Investigations: An Overview*. Ottawa: Public Service Commission of Canada, Appeals and Investigations Branch.

13. Public Service Commission of Canada. 1994–95. *Annual Report*. Ottawa.

14. Public Service Staff Relations Board. 1994–95. *Parliamentary Employment and Staff Relations Act: Ninth Annual Report of the Public Service Staff Relations Board*. Ottawa.

15. *O'Malley v. Simpsons-Sears*. CCRR, D/3106, 24772.

16. Weiner, N. 1993.

17. Vining, A.R., D.C. McPhillips, and A.E. Boardman. 1986. "Use of Statistical Evidence in Employment Discrimination Litigation." *The Canadian Bar Review* 64: 660–702.

18. Vining, A.R., D.C. McPhillips, and A.E. Boardman. 1986.

19. *British Columbia (Public Service Employee Relations Comm.) v. BCGSEU*. CCHR, D/275, 54.

20. Canadian Human Rights Commission. 1988. *Bona Fide Requirement Policy*. Ottawa: Canadian Human Rights Commission.

21. Canadian Human Rights Commission. 1989.

22. *Ontario Human Rights Commission et al. v. the Borough of Etobicoke*. CCRR, D/783, 6894.

23. *Grismer v. British Columbia (A.G.)*. 1999, 3 S.C.R. 868.

24. *Québec (Commission des droits de la personne et droits de la jeunesse) v. Montréal (City)*. 2000, 1 S.C.R. 665.

25. *Husband v. Canada*. CCHR, D/301, 68.

26. Belcourt and McBey. 2000.

Chapter 4

Job Analysis and Competency Models

Chapter Learning Objectives

This chapter is divided into two parts. The first part begins with a discussion of job analysis and its relevance to human resources development and continues with a discussion of several job analysis techniques. Part II concludes the chapter with a presentation on competency models as an alternative procedure to job analysis.

After reading this chapter you should:

- understand the importance of job analysis and the role it plays in recruitment and selection;
- be able to describe guidelines for conducting analyses employing a variety of job analysis techniques;
- be able to use standard tools and techniques to conduct a job analysis;
- recognize processes for identifying job specifications to be used in recruitment and selection of human resources;
- understand what competencies are;
- understand the role competencies play in recruitment and selection;
- know how to identify competencies;
- understand the need to validate competency-based systems; and
- be able to distinguish competency-based human resources models from those based on job analysis.

Job Analysis: Time Well Spent

Job analysis is a process of identifying the critical skills, knowledge, and attitudes necessary to perform a job well in your particular environment. Any job—parts assembler, sales representative, executive officer—can be defined and measured. The key is to consider how much time is spent on each task, how complex it is, and how critical each task is to the organization's effectiveness.

Identifying a Job's "Success Factors"

A combination of job analysis methods yields the most accurate picture of what's required for success in a job. Start with the job description. Next, spend time with employees who have similar jobs. Observe. Let them know what you're doing so they won't alter their behaviour. Pay attention to any tasks not mentioned in the job description and the behaviours and personality traits involved.

A former DBM client, who went on to start a parking lot cleaning business, made a telling discovery: "I had been hiring people who did well in interviews and had good attitudes and people skills, but I was losing them quickly. So I drove around in the trucks with my employees at night. I discovered that it is a very solitary job, and the people who were the best at it enjoyed spending long hours alone. I never would've thought to look for this."

Also, don't limit yourself to only those you've observed; interview up, down and sideways. Then sort through what you've learned to define the essential and desired competencies.

Source: Jillian Taylor, "Selecting and Recruiting the Best Employees," DBM Canada. Reprinted with permission.

Chapter 1 showed why the Canadian Council of Human Resources Associations' Certified Human Resources Professional (CHRP) designation is an advantage (see Recruitment and Selection Notebook 1.1 on page 10). This designation is based on two assessments: one knowledge-related and the other more experiential. In both cases, the assessments are related to "required professional capabilities" (RPCs) that are deemed relevant to the occupation of human resources professional. Examples of these RPCs and related knowledge, skills, abilities, and other capabilities (KSAOs) are distributed throughout this book to illustrate the linkage of the chapter material to the RPCs.

Why these particular RPCs and related KSAOs? How were they established? The RPCs are based on the collective, real-world experience of Canadian HR professionals and their clients, gathered from across Canada. The National Competency Committee (NCC), a four-person steering committee of experienced HR professionals, directed the study and compiled the findings. They held focus group sessions across Canada to seek input from senior executives, including CEOs, HR practitioners, and representatives from educational sectors and provincial HR associations. Over the next year, the NCC synthesized and reviewed the data from the focus groups, resulting in a draft set of RPCs that were circulated to provincial HR associations for comments and changes. The final version of the RPCs was published in June 1998. The information obtained from the occupational focus groups was used by the Standards, Planning and Analysis Division of Human Resources Canada to develop an *Essential Skills Profile* for the RPCs.

The final step in the process was to have HR professionals from across Canada rate the 203 RPCs with respect to how frequently they performed each RPC, how important they believed each RPC to be to their work as an HR professional, how difficult they felt it was to become proficient in performing each RPC, and the level of proficiency needed to perform the RPC (i.e., whether it could be performed by someone with only a knowledge of HR but not experience in the field or whether it needed a degree of experience to be carried out successfully).

The information from this survey was used to categorize the RPCs into two groups that formed the basis for the *National Knowledge Assessment* for new entrants into the HR profession and the *National Professional Practice Assessment* designed as the last step before more experienced HR professionals are granted the CHRP designation.

Because jobs and occupations change over time, the Canadian Council of Human Resources Associations (CCHRA) board directed a review of the RPCs in 2005 to establish their currency. Again, groups of HR professionals throughout Canada reviewed the set of 203 RPCs with regard to determining whether each RPC was still valid, whether it should be refined, or whether there was a need for new RPCs that reflected the current work of HR professionals. The result was a new set of 187 RPCs. A nationwide survey was again conducted to link each RPC to either the *National Knowledge Assessment* or the *National Professional Practice Assessment*. The CCHRA board approved the new set of RPCs and their linkage to the two CHRP assessments in October 2007.

As you will see as you read through this chapter, what we have just briefly described is a job analysis of the HR occupation. More information on the development process can be found at the CCHRA website (http://www.cchra.ca).

Part I: Job Analysis

Job Analysis and Employment Law—A Reprise

Although there are no laws that specifically require a job analysis prior to implementing recruitment and selection programs, employment decisions must be based on job-related information.[1] Job analysis is a legally acceptable way of determining job-relatedness. In 1975, the United States Supreme Court made a precedent-setting decision when it criticized the Albemarle Paper Company for its failure to use a job analysis to demonstrate the job-relatedness of its selection procedures (see Recruitment and Selection Today 3.5 on page 90). According to Harvey, "Albemarle established job analysis as something that virtually must be done to defend challenged employment practices."[2]

We also saw in Chapter 3 the long list of precedent-setting cases in Canada that have established the need to determine that any job requirements that have the potential of discriminating against members of protected groups must meet the standards set in the Meiorin decision (*British Columbia [Public Service Employee Relations Commission] v. BCGSEU*) for being bona fide occupational requirements. In the *Meiorin* case, the Supreme Court of Canada found that new job requirements were not based on job-related information, and the job analysis in that case was seriously flawed. Conducting a job analysis, then, is also the first line of defence in protecting the organization if its selection procedures are challenged in court.[3,4]

RPC 4.1

A good job analysis ensures that accurate information on skill, effort, responsibility, and working conditions is specified, reducing the likelihood of impediments to equitable employment access for all Canadians. A job analysis provides objective evidence of the skills and abilities required for effective performance in the job, which can then be used to provide evidence of the relevance of the selection procedures measuring those abilities.

In *Albemarle Paper Co. v. Moody*, the U.S. Supreme Court relied heavily on the *Uniform Guidelines on Employee Selection*[5] in reaching its decision. The *Uniform Guidelines* represent a joint agreement between several U.S. government departments and agencies (the Equal Employment Opportunity Commission, Civil Service Commission, Department of Labor, and Department of Justice), outlining professional standards for employee selection procedures. Even though they are not law, the U.S. courts have granted them significant status in guiding administrative interpretations of the job analysis–job-relatedness link.[6,7]

Canadian human rights commissions and courts also recognize the *Uniform Guidelines on Employee Selection* as professional standards, unless it is established that Canadian legal precedent and professional practice deviate substantially from those set out in the *Guidelines*.[8] Furthermore, the Canadian Society of Industrial–Organizational Psychology has adopted the principles outlined in the *Guidelines* for developing equitable selection systems for use in Canada.[9] Latham explains that:

> Countries such as Australia, Canada and the United Kingdom have been strongly influenced by Title VII of the 1964 Civil Rights Act in the U.S. In each of these countries it is now illegal to make employment decisions regarding the hiring, firing, promoting, demoting, transferring or admitting someone into a training program on the basis of the person's age, sex, race, religion, colour, national origin, sexual orientation, or physical handicap.[10]

In practice, if not in law, the starting point for a defensible selection system is a job analysis.

Job Analysis and Job Evaluation

Job evaluation is the use of job analysis data to establish the worth of a job and to set compensation rates. While a discussion of job evaluation exceeds our interest in recruitment and selection, we feel it is useful to note it here as, after recruitment and selection, it is an application that is highly dependent on job analysis data. Job evaluation follows many of the same principles outlined in this chapter. The basis of job evaluation is to define a job in measurable terms that allow it to be compared with other jobs in the organization. Thus, it becomes possible to compare jobs in terms of "compensable" factors. There are many different methods that have been adapted for job evaluation uses. One common procedure is to assign points to each compensable factor to determine the worth of each job, but regardless of method, they all depend on a detailed analysis of the job.

 4.2

Job evaluation allows comparisons between jobs within an organization (i.e., internal equity) and to those outside of it (i.e., external equity) to determine the fairness of the company's compensation system. This can be a controversial exercise and is at the heart of pay equity exercises. Data consistently show that women's wages are between 70 percent and 90 percent of the wages paid to men. While there may be many reasons for this disparity, one that is often argued is that the difference is due to systemic discrimination, with women historically barred from higher-paying jobs.

Federal legislation requires organizations that fall under its authority to pay men and women the same for doing "work of equal value," using the compensable factors of skill, effort, responsibility, and working conditions. Using this type of analysis, the Canadian Human Rights Commission Tribunal ruled that 200 000 female federal public service employees deserved $5 billion in back pay for performing work of equal worth but not receiving equal pay. The decision was upheld by the Federal Court of Appeal in 1999.

Job Analysis and Organization Analysis

Recall our discussion of a human resources system in Chapter 1. (You may want to review Figure 1.1 on page 4.) HR functions are embedded within the context of an organization and are influenced by all of the factors that affect it. Organization analysis is an important step in the recruitment and selection process that can be used to anchor job analysis in the context of the organization's mission, goals, and strategy (see Figure 4.1).

 4.3

When designing and implementing recruitment and selection programs to fill jobs within their organization, human resources specialists must be aware of the overall organizational mission and goals. Losing sight of the organization level can result in less-than-optimal recruitment and selection policies and practices that are used to fill positions at the job level. Cronshaw proposes that job analysis methodologies for use in dynamic environments be prescriptive of how work should be organized, be interactionist and

FIGURE 4.1

Contribution of Individual Job Outputs to Organization Outputs

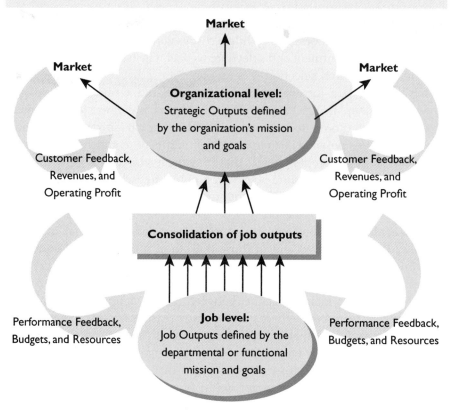

systems-based, and vividly portray "the unique skills, adaptations, and competencies each individual worker expresses in his/her specific work context, as a complement to the present methods emphasizing generalized person and work constructs."[11] In support of this position, Latham and Sue-Chan[12] predict that a major strategic focus in employee selection in the 21st century, one that will distinguish high-performing organizations from underperformers, is the linkage between organization goals and short-term organizational needs.

Although there are many ways to conduct an organization analysis, most methods share the common goals of describing and understanding the design and structure, functions and processes, and strategies and missions of organizations. Data obtained from an organization analysis can highlight areas of strength and weakness useful to human resources planning, such as:

- identifying expected changes in the external environment;
- aligning staffing and development plans to ensure appropriate succession planning;
- identifying expected structural changes in the organization; and
- understanding how expected changes will affect recruitment and selection practices.

The selection and placement process within an effective organization will link recruitment, hiring, placement, and promotion decisions within the context of the strategic goals of the organization. In fact, most modern organizations place the HR manager among the ranks of senior leadership, often reporting directly to a president, CEO, or senior business manager, thus enabling HR to directly contribute to and participate in strategic decision making. When the guiding principles of the organization are laid out as goals, and the environment in which the organization operates is defined, recruitment and selection processes can most effectively contribute to the overall success of the organization.

Job Analysis Procedures

Job analysis refers to the process of collecting information about jobs "by any method for any purpose."[13] In its simplest terms, a job analysis is a systematic process for gathering, documenting, and analyzing data about the work required for a job. Job analysis data includes a description of the context and principal duties of the job, including job responsibilities and working conditions, and information about the knowledge, skills, abilities, and other characteristics required in its performance. In short, it is a method that provides a description of the job and profiles the characteristics or competencies people need to have in order to be successful in the job. There are three key points to remember about job analysis:

1. A "job analysis" does not refer to a single methodology but rather to a range of techniques.
2. A job analysis is a formal, structured process carried out under a set of guidelines established in advance.
3. A job analysis breaks down a job into its constituent parts, rather than looking at the job as a whole

Job analysis data support several HR activities and can be used toward several ends (e.g., recruitment and selection, training and development, performance management and, as we've seen, job evaluation, among several others).[14] Many activities in an organization that focus on identifying a match between a person and a job rely on accurate information produced by job analysis. Job analysis helps to ensure that decisions made with respect to HR processes are good decisions (i.e., fair and accurate), and that those employee-related decisions can be defended in courts and tribunals, if necessary. All of these HR activities are concerned with matching people to jobs within a specific organizational context. Job analysis is a procedure to assess the goodness of this fit between people and jobs. It provides information about both the job requirements and the KSAOs needed to do the job.

Since job analysis data have the potential for many uses, it is important to know how the information will be used before deciding on an approach or method to use in collecting the data. As we will see after we review several different job analysis methods, each has its strengths and weaknesses, and the data from a particular method may be better suited to only one or some of the above uses. It is very unlikely that one method will produce information

Job description

A written description of
what job occupants are
required to do, how they
are supposed to do it,
and the rationale for any
required job procedures.

Job specification

The knowledge, skills, abilities, and other attributes
that are needed by a job
incumbent to perform well
on the job.

Job

A collection of positions
that are similar in their
significant duties.

Position

A collection of duties
assigned to individuals in
an organization at a given
time.

Job family

A set of different, but
related, jobs that rely on
the same set of KSAOs.

that can be used in all of the applications where we would want to use it. In
the context of employee recruitment and selection, the results of the job analysis should specify the requirements of the job that are subsequently used to
establish employee selection procedures.

In Chapter 2, we presented our selection model in which job analysis was
the first step in identifying job tasks and duties as well as the KSAOs needed
to carry out those duties. These are the two basic products of a job analysis.
The first is formally referred to as a **job description**, a written description of
what the persons in the job are required to do, how they are supposed to do
the job, and the rationale for any required job procedures. A job description
contains a summary of job analysis data. Recruitment and Selection Today 4.1
presents a job description for a CIBC customer service representative. The
second product is a **job specification**, which states the KSAOs that are
required to perform the job successfully. These may include the compensable
factors that are used in performing a job evaluation, such as analytical abilities,
physical exertion, accountability for budgets, and unpleasant working environments. A job description like that in Recruitment and Selection Today 4.1
is typically used to recruit employees.

Job versus Position

In understanding the key concepts in this chapter, keep in mind the difference between a **job** and a **position**. A job consists of a group of tasks; a job
may be held by one or more people. Many individuals perform the same job
in an organization: for example, secretary, architect, or electrician. A position,
on the other hand, consists of the group of tasks performed by one person in
an organization at a given time. Each person in the organization is assigned a
position. For example, one secretary may be assigned to the position of secretary to the HR director, while another is assigned to the position of secretary
to the vice-president of finance. Both secretaries would perform the same set
of general tasks, although each may be responsible for a small set of tasks
unique to his or her position.

Another way of distinguishing between jobs and positions is to consider a
job as a collection of positions that are similar in their significant duties and a
position as a collection of duties assigned to an individual in an organization
at a given time.[15] When the two sets of position-relevant tasks begin to diverge
considerably from the common set of job tasks or they begin to outweigh the
common job tasks, the two positions might then be considered to be different,
but related, jobs. **Job family** is a term used to refer to a set of different, but
related, jobs that rely on the same set of KSAOs. Jobs and positions are among
the basic building blocks of any organization, and selection of individuals to
fill these positions has a significant impact on the success of the organization.

Subject-Matter Experts

Job analysis data are collected from the people most knowledgeable about a
job and how it is currently performed. In practice, this means that data are
collected from job incumbents (those employees currently holding the position in question) and their immediate supervisors. Using these sources as

Job Description for a CIBC Customer Service Representative

Title: Customer Service Representative
Category: Customer Service/
Customer Associate

Key Accountabilities/Activities

As the primary point of contact and "face of CIBC" for many CIBC customers, the Customer Service Rep provides exemplary customer service by serving all customers quickly, professionally, and efficiently and recognizing the appropriate time to proactively position CIBC products and services. Improve customer loyalty by identifying opportunities to promote banking products and transaction services to better meet customer needs, fulfilling or referring the opportunity, as appropriate.

Creating a positive customer experience by understanding and meeting customers' service needs quickly, professionally, and accurately is the primary responsibility of the Customer Service Representative.

Major Activities Include:

1. Create a positive client experience by understanding and meeting service transaction needs quickly, professionally, and accurately.
2. Take initiative to promote banking products and transaction services that meet client needs.
3. Recognize client needs and make quality referrals to colleagues.
4. Take ownership when clients experience a problem and take the appropriate steps to resolve the problem.
5. Balance cash holdings. Act as joint custodian of cash and securities.

6. Protect client privacy.
7. Identify client needs and sales opportunities while processing transactions quickly and providing efficient service.

Requirements
Attributes

- Service-oriented.
- Thorough.
- Strong interpersonal understanding.
- Initiative.
- Results orientation.
- Teamwork and partnering.

Special Conditions

- Full time: 37.5 hrs./week.
- Days required to work: Monday to Saturday.
- Previous experience in customer service, retail environment an asset.
- An additional living allowance is available.

CIBC is an equal opportunity employer. It is the Company's policy to recruit and select applicants for employment solely on the basis of their qualifications, with emphasis on selecting the best-qualified person for the job. CIBC does not discriminate against applicants based on race, color, religion, sex, national origin, or disability, or any other status or condition protected by applicable federal, state or local law.

Source: From http://www.cibc.com/ca/inside-cibc/careers.html. Reprinted with permission.

---

subject-matter experts (SMEs) will generally result in the most accurate, and richest, information about the job. However, anyone with detailed knowledge about the job can serve as an SME. A good rule of thumb in choosing SMEs is that the closer the SME is to the job, the better the resultant information will be. However, Diedorff and Wilson[16] report data suggesting that trained professional job analysts provide more accurate information than job

Subject-matter experts (SMEs)

People who are most knowledgeable about a job and how it is currently performed; generally job incumbents and their supervisors.

incumbents when using self-report and survey instruments. They speculate that the trained professionals may be more objective in their assessment of what constitutes the job.

One question that must be answered is how many SMEs a particular job analysis method requires. This requirement will generally be stated in the procedures that have been established for each method. The lack of the requisite number of SMEs may argue against using a specific method. To ensure the defensibility of the job analysis results, SMEs should be representative of the target population for the job with respect to age, sex, ethnic background, and seniority in the position. Information from a diverse group of SMEs will produce job information that is likely to be more accurate, reliable, and valid.

Recall that one of the failures of the job analysis in the *Meiorin* case was lack of job information from female firefighters. If the job analysis is challenged in court, the analyst must be able to defend the procedure. A charge of unfair discrimination will be hard to defend if the analyst cannot demonstrate that the job analysis results were obtained from a sample representative of those who actually do the work.[17] Job information from a diverse group of SMEs is likely to produce a better picture of what the job is all about.

Work- and Worker-Oriented Job Analysis

There are several ways of classifying job analysis methods. One of the most complete classification schemes[18] is to categorize a job analysis technique as either work-oriented or worker-oriented.[19–22] Job analyses falling into either of these two categories are legally defensible. With one or two exceptions, all job analysis methods, including all of those presented here, fall into either of these two categories. In **work-oriented job analysis**, the emphasis is on work outcomes and description of the various tasks performed to accomplish those outcomes.

These methods produce "descriptions of job content that have a dominant association with, and typically characterize, the *technological* aspects of jobs and commonly reflect what is achieved by the worker."[23] The descriptions of tasks or job duties generated via work-oriented methods are typically characterized by their frequency of occurrence or the amount of time spent on them, the importance to the job outcome, and the difficulty inherent in executing them.[24,25] Because task inventories generated via work-oriented techniques are developed for specific jobs, or occupational areas, the results are highly specific and may have little or no relationship to the content of jobs in other fields.[26]

Alternatively, **worker-oriented job analysis** methods focus on general aspects of jobs, describing perceptual, interpersonal, sensory, cognitive, and physical activities. Worker-oriented methods generate descriptions "that tend more to characterize the generalized human behaviours involved; if not directly, then by strong inference."[27] These techniques are not limited to describing specific jobs; they are generic in nature and the results can be applied to a wide spectrum of task-dissimilar jobs.[28–31] Changes from a task- to

Work-oriented job analysis

Job analysis techniques that emphasize work outcomes and descriptions of the various tasks performed to accomplish those outcomes.

Worker-oriented job analysis

Job analysis techniques that emphasize general aspects of jobs, describing perceptual, interpersonal, sensory, cognitive, and physical activities.

process-based way of thinking highlight the usefulness of worker-oriented job analysis procedures in meeting the new demands placed on human resources specialists.

Whether work- or worker-oriented, Harvey[32] proposes three criteria that should characterize any job analysis method: First, the goal of job analysis should always be the description of observable work behaviours and analysis of their products. Second, the results of a job analysis should describe the work behaviour *"independent of the personal characteristics or attributes of the employees who perform the job."* [33] Positions in an organization exist independently of the incumbents who fill those positions; in job analysis, it is the job (i.e., the collection of positions) that is being analyzed, not the performance of the individual incumbents. Worker specifications (i.e., the knowledge, skills, abilities, and other attributes—or **KSAOs**) necessary to perform successfully on the job are inferred in a separate process using the results of a job analysis.

Finally, the analysis must be verifiable and replicable. That is, the organization must be able to produce evidence of both the validity and the reliability of each step in the job analysis process. Reliability and validity data for the job analysis method used are essential to determining the quality of the information produced by the analysis.[34] In many situations, assessing the validity of the method is redundant and an assumption is made that if reliability is acceptable, then the method is valid.[35]

Although the various existing job analysis techniques differ in the assumptions they make about work, they follow the same logical process when applied to the recruitment and selection of human resources. First, work activities are described in terms of the work processes or worker behaviours that characterize the job. Next, machines, tools, equipment, and work aids are defined in relation to the materials produced, services rendered, and worker knowledge applied to those ends. The job context is characterized in terms of physical working conditions, work schedules, social context and organizational culture, and financial and nonfinancial incentives for performance. Finally, job specifications are inferred by linking the job requirements identified in the analysis with the education, experience, skills, and personal attributes required for successful job performance.[36]

KSAOs

The knowledge, skills, abilities, and other attributes necessary for a new incumbent to do well on the job; also referred to as *job, employment,* or *worker specifications*.

Getting Started: Gathering Job-Related Information

In preparing for a job analysis, the first step should be to collect existing information describing the target job. The analyst mines information from organizational charts, legal requirements (e.g., the job *veterinarian* may be governed through legal statutes at the provincial level), job descriptions, union regulations, and previous data from related jobs. In addition, job-related information can be found in the National Occupational Classification (NOC) system.[37] The NOC systematically describes occupations in the Canadian labour market based on extensive occupational research and is available at the Human Resources and Social Development Canada website: http://www5.hrsdc.gc.ca/NOC-CNP/app/index.aspx.

Occupational Description for Veterinarians

Veterinarians prevent, diagnose, and treat diseases and disorders in animals and advise clients on the feeding, hygiene, housing, and general care of animals. Veterinarians work in private practice or may be employed by animal clinics and laboratories, government, or industry.

Examples of Titles Classified in This Group

Small-animal veterinary specialist

Veterinary inspector

Veterinary physiologist

Veterinarian

Veterinary pathologist

Zoo veterinarian

Main Duties

Veterinarians perform some or all of the following duties:

- Diagnose diseases or abnormal conditions in animals through physical examinations or laboratory tests
- Treat sick or injured animals by prescribing medication, setting bones, dressing wounds, or performing surgery
- Perform routine, emergency, and post-mortem examinations

- Inoculate animals to prevent diseases
- Provide obstetrical and dental services
- Advise clients on feeding, housing, breeding, hygiene, and general care of animals
- Provide euthanasia services

Employment Requirements

- Two to four years of pre-veterinary university studies or, in Quebec, completion of a college program in health science
- A four-year university degree in veterinary medicine
- Completion of national certification examinations is required
- Provincial licensure is required
- Entry into research positions may require postgraduate study

Source: "Occupational Description for Veterinarians." *National Occupational Classification.* http://www23.hrdc-drhc.gc.ca/92/e/groups/3114.shtml. Human Resources Development Canada. Reproduced with the permission of the Minister of Public Works and the Government Services Canada, 2009.

Recruitment and Selection Today 4.2 presents the NOC description for veterinarians. The NOC profile presents both a description and specification of the job or occupation. Each occupation or job is given a four-digit code that will provide the analyst with a more extensive description related to the KSAOs associated with the job.

Figure 4.2 presents a synopsis of the descriptors used in the NOC system, along with scales used to rate each job. For example, a rating of 3 on the "Vision" subscale in the "Physical Activities" section means that the job in question requires both near and far vision for successful completion. Full descriptions of all the scales can be found in the *Career Handbook* that is available on the NOC website. Such information, when gathered and studied in advance, will prove invaluable for organizing and conducting the ensuing analysis.

Alternative sources to the NOC have until recently included the *Canadian Classification Dictionary of Occupations* (CCDO)[38] and the *Dictionary of Occupational Titles* (DOT).[39] The CCDO, designed in 1971 by Employment and Immigration Canada, was widely used by human resources professionals in Canada. Although some found the CCDO easier to use than the NOC[40] (which

FIGURE 4.2

A Synopsis of Descriptors and Labels

APTITUDES

One of five levels assigned for each factor, with levels representing normal curve distribution of the labour force:

G	General Learning Ability	**Q**	Clerical Perception
V	Verbal Ability	**K**	Motor Coordination
N	Numerical Ability	**F**	Finger Dexterity
S	Spatial Perception	**M**	Manual Dexterity
P	Form Perception		

INTERESTS

Three of five descriptive factors, assigned in order of predominance and lower case rating indicating weaker representation:

D	Directive
I	Innovative
M	Methodical
O	Objective
S	Social

DATA/INFORMATION, PEOPLE, THINGS

D – Data/Information		**P – People**		**T – Things**	
0	Synthesizing	0	Mentoring	0	Setting up
1	Coordinating	1	Negotiating	1	Precision working
2	Analyzing	2	Instructing – Consulting	2	Controlling
3	Compiling	3	Supervising	3	Driving – Operating
4	Computing	4	Diverting	4	Operating – Manipulating
5	Copying	5	Persuading	5	Tending
6	Comparing	6	Speaking – Signalling	6	Feeding – Offbearing
7	—	7	Serving – Assisting	7	Handling
8	Not significant	8	Not significant	8	Not significant

PHYSICAL ACTIVITIES

One of several levels assigned for each factor:

Vision

1	Close visual acuity
2	Near vision
3	Near and far vision
4	Total visual field

Colour Discrimination

0	Not relevant
1	Relevant

Hearing

1	Limited
2	Verbal interaction
3	Other sound discrimination

Body Position

1	Sitting
2	Standing and/or walking
3	Sitting, standing, walking
4	Other body positions

Limb Coordination

0	Not relevant
1	Upper limb coordination
2	Multiple limb coordination

Strength

1	Limited
2	Light
3	Medium
4	Heavy

ENVIRONMENTAL CONDITIONS

Location

L1	Regulated inside climate
L2	Unregulated inside climate
L3	Outside
L4	In a vehicle or cab

Hazards

H1	Dangerous chemical substances
H2	Biological agents
H3	Equipment, machinery, tools
H4	Electricity
H5	Radiation
H6	Flying particles, falling objects
H7	Fire, steam, hot surfaces
H8	Dangerous locations

Discomforts

D1	Noise
D2	Vibration
D3	Odours
D4	Non-toxic dusts
D5	Wetness

EMPLOYMENT REQUIREMENTS

Education/Training Indicators

1	No formal education or training requirements	5	Apprenticeship, specialized training, vocational school training
2	Some high school education and/or on-the-job training or experience	6	College, technical school (certificate, diploma)
3	Completion of high school	7	Undergraduate degree
4	Completion of course work, training, workshops and/or experience related to the occupation	8	Postgraduate or professional degree

+	Indicating an additional requirement beyond education/training (e.g., extensive experience, demonstrated or creative ability, appointments, etc.)
R	Regulated requirements exist for this group

Source: "A Synopsis of Descriptors and Labels." *Career Handbook*, Second Edition. http://www23.hrdc-drhc.gc.ca/ch/e/docs/intro_pdf_synopsis.pdf. Human Resources & Social Development Canada. Reproduced with the permission of the Minister of Public Works and the Government Services Canada, 2009.

replaced it), the CCDO was abandoned in 1992 because its design was no longer able to accurately reflect the contemporary Canadian labour market.

Similarly, the DOT has been replaced by the O*NET system of gathering and disseminating job analysis data in the United States. O*NET, the Occupational Information Network, is an electronic database developed by the U.S. Department of Labor to replace the DOT. The occupational/skill descriptors "serve as a solid, but flexible foundation for vendors and others to develop sophisticated occupational and career information systems."[41] O*NET was first released for public use in the fall of 1998 and is available online at http://www.doleta.gov/programs/onet. The database grows as information becomes available on more occupations, and the U.S. Department of Labor encourages organizations to use the new database in place of the DOT, which was last updated in 1991.

Figure 4.3 presents the conceptual foundation of the O*NET model and "provides a framework that identifies the most important types of information about work and integrates them into a theoretically and empirically sound system."[42] Peterson et al.[43] present an excellent introduction to the O*NET model and the implications for researchers and practitioners.

In addition to occupational databases, attention should be given to determining which techniques will be employed for gathering job information. Gael[44] notes that, depending on the objective of the job analysis, some techniques are better suited than others for providing job information. Analyses typically involve a series of steps, often beginning with interviews or observations that provide the information to construct a task inventory or to complete a structured questionnaire. Ideally, the job analyst employs a combination of strategies to arrive at a comprehensive and accurate description of the job in question,[45,46] although analysts operating within the very real constraints of time and funding often use a single method. Each analysis method contributes slightly different information and, by using a combination of methods, potential gaps in the results are minimized.

Survey of Job Analysis Techniques

The following discussion is intended as an overview of common job analysis methods and their major strengths and weaknesses. We also include in each overview a brief description of the method that is normally used to derive employee specifications from the job analysis data. You should consult the references for each method for detailed descriptions of how to conduct job analyses before using the different techniques.

Interviews

The interview is perhaps the most commonly used technique for gathering job facts and establishing the tasks and behaviours that define a job. This method involves questioning individuals or small groups of employees and supervisors about the work that gets done. The interview may be structured or unstructured, although for job analysis purposes, a structured format is recommended. The results of a job analysis interview may stand on their own,

FIGURE 4.3

The O*NET® Content Model

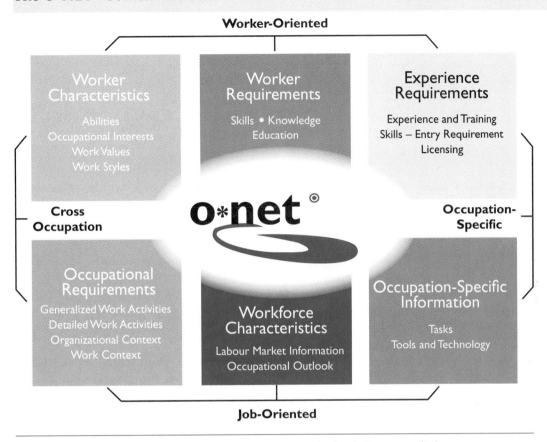

Worker-Oriented

Worker Characteristics	Worker Requirements	Experience Requirements
Abilities	Skills • Knowledge	Experience and Training
Occupational Interests	Education	Skills – Entry Requirement
Work Values		Licensing
Work Styles		

Cross Occupation

Occupation-Specific

Occupational Requirements	Workforce Characteristics	Occupation-Specific Information
Generalized Work Activities		Tasks
Detailed Work Activities	Labour Market Information	Tools and Technology
Organizational Context	Occupational Outlook	
Work Context		

Job-Oriented

Source: *The O*NET® Content Model.* http://www.onetcenter.org/content.html. U.S. Department of Labor.

as in a formal integrated report, when there are few incumbents working within a small geographical area. Or they may provide the necessary information for completing a task inventory, structured questionnaire, or other analytic technique.[47,48]

The structured interview method is designed so that all interviewees are asked the same job-related questions. Inter-observer reliability, that is, the agreement between the persons serving as interviewers, increases when interviews are structured because the individual biases of different interviewers are minimized. Whetzel et al.[49] demonstrated that a written, structured interview is a flexible and cost-effective alternative to a traditional oral structured interview. Their *Written Structured Interview* produced very reliable job analysis information across a number of jobs. Because it is such an important step in most job analyses, the interview should be well planned and carefully conducted. McCormick[50] and others[51–54] offer many valuable guidelines for conducting interviews. These are summarized in Recruitment and Selection Notebook 4.1.

Guidelines for a Job Analysis Interview

1. **Announce the job analysis well ahead of the interview date.** The impending job analysis and its purpose should be well known among employees and management. The job analysis process should be positioned as a collaborative effort, with all job incumbents and their supervisors holding valid information about the job and invited to contribute to the process.

2. **Participation in interviews should be voluntary, and job incumbents should be interviewed only with the permission of their supervisors.** The job analyst avoids creating friction within the organization and is sensitive to the use of coercion in obtaining information. In general, when analysis interviews are free from organizational politics, they can be completed in a timely manner with valid, uncontaminated results.

3. **Interviews should be conducted in a private location free from status earmarks.** It would be unwise, for example, to conduct interviews with hourly workers in the company president's office. The job analyst is a nonpartisan party whose primary objective is to accurately describe the content of jobs; interviewees should feel comfortable and able to provide truthful information about their work and the conditions under which it is done.

4. **Open the interview by establishing rapport with the employee and explaining the purpose of the interview.** Interviews are often associated with anxiety-provoking events such as job and promotion applica-

tions and even disciplinary action. The experienced interviewer takes time at the outset to create a non-threatening environment and alleviate any fears that interviewees might have.

5. **Ask open-ended questions, using language that is easy to understand, and allow ample time for the employee's responses.** Most people, given the opportunity, will talk in great detail about the work they do. The good analyst avoids rushing or intimidating people, does not talk down to them, and takes a genuine interest in the interviewee's responses.

6. **Guide the session without being authoritative or overbearing.** Keep the interview on topic and avoid discussions concerning worker–management relations and other unrelated topics. When discussions become tangential, the analyst can bring them back on track by summarizing relevant details and referring to the interview outline.

7. **Explain to the employees that records of the interviews will identify them only by confidential codes.** The names of interviewees and other personal information should be protected. When confidentiality is ensured, more accurate information will be obtained. The limits of confidentiality should be explained to all interviewees before they agree to participate. For example, data on age, sex, and ethnic background may have to be recorded in order to demonstrate in any subsequent court challenges that the data are based on a representative sample of the work force.

The job analyst should record the incumbent's or supervisor's responses by taking notes or by tape-recording the interview. Trying to remember what was said following the interview is difficult at best and likely to produce inaccurate information. Recall that the purpose of the interview is to obtain information about the work that the employee does; thus, questions should elicit information describing important job tasks, physical activities involved in the job, environmental conditions (physical and social) under which the work occurs, and typical work incidents.

An interview outline prompts the interviewer to ask all interviewees important questions about the job. The interviewer may start out asking:

"What are the main things that you do in your job?" Based on the response, and on the interviewer's previous knowledge of the job, the interviewer then probes for more detail.[55,56] The tasks that make up each job area are identified, and the result of the interview should be a clear description of critical job domains and their related elements. Interview outlines can vary from presenting a few informal prompts to listing very structured questions to be addressed in a specific order. In general, the more specific the interview outline is, the more reliable the information obtained from interviewees will be.

While there are no hard-and-fast rules concerning how many people should be interviewed, the job analyst is wise to demonstrate that the collection of incumbents interviewed is representative of the employees whose job the analysis reflects. For example, when conducting a job analysis for meeting planning consultants employed in a large travel company, the analyst may obtain a stratified sample that reflects the proportion of males and females in the position. Other demographic variables such as race and ethnicity, age, physical disabilities and abilities, and native language would also be considered in a representative sample of interviewees. Supervisors should always be included in the pool of interview respondents, as they have a unique perspective of how jobs are performed and the standards for acceptable performance.

Although interviews should be well structured, they also allow interviewees to contribute information that may be overlooked by other analysis techniques. There are, however, certain disadvantages to job analysis interviews. First, they can be expensive and time-consuming and may be impractical for jobs with a large number of incumbents. Interviews take a great deal of time to conduct and may require a substantial number of interviewees to be truly representative of the job incumbent pool. Whetzel and colleagues' written structured interview method,[57] however, may reduce both the time and cost of doing a structured interview.

Individual interviews are more time-consuming and more expensive to conduct than group interviews, but the benefits of individual interviews can outweigh the relative costs. Individual employees, free from immediate social controls, are likely to respond with greater openness than those interviewed in a group. Thus, the information obtained from the individual interview may be more accurate than that obtained from the same people interviewed together. A second disadvantage of this technique is that workers may be prone to distorting the information they provide about their jobs, particularly if they believe that the results will influence their pay.[58] This distortion can be overcome by making the purpose of the interview clear and by interviewing multiple incumbents and supervisors.

Direct Observation

Martinko makes the case that "the most effective way to determine what effective job incumbents do is to observe their behaviour."[59] In direct observation, the job analyst watches employees as they carry out their job activities. This procedure is sometimes called "job shadowing." This method allows the analyst to come into direct contact with the job; thus, the data are obtained firsthand, as contrasted with the "more remote types of information generated by questionnaires and surveys."[60]

Direct observation is most useful when the job analysis involves easily observable activities.[61] Analyzing the job of "poet" through direct observation would likely produce little of value, whereas the job of "landscaper" lends itself more readily to direct observation. Before conducting direct observations, the analyst will already have learned about the job by studying existing documents. Next, the job analyst determines the nature of the job by asking: "Does the job involve easily observable activities?" and "Is the work environment one in which unobtrusive observations can be made?" If the answer to both questions is "yes," then direct observation may be a viable analysis method.

In direct observation, systematic observations of employee activities can be recorded either in narrative format or using a customized checklist or worksheet.[62,63] Different jobs and environments will require different observation methods. A landscaper's job, one that does not occur within a complex social context, might best be observed and recorded by using a tally sheet such as that shown in Figure 4.4. The job of residential counsellor, in which the job tasks are heavily influenced by dynamic social conditions, will require a recording format that enables the observer to identify important activities and the conditions under which they occur.

An example of a recording sheet used in observing residential counsellors at work can be found in Figure 4.5. The form enables the observer to collect information about the job by defining the conditions under which a particular activity occurs and listing the tools and aids employed in the activity. Both recording formats permit the observer to record valuable qualitative and quantitative data.

FIGURE 4.4

Example of a Frequency Tally Sheet for Observing a Landscaper at Work

Date: 15-03-09   Start time: 10:30 a.m.   End time: 11:07 a.m.

         Observer: Leslie   Employee ID: 734

Tasks (planting trees)	Check if done	Time spent
1. Measure area & mark spot	X	5 min
2. Dig hole	X	16 min
3. Move shrubbery	—	—
4. Lift trees (manually)	X	<1 min
5. Lift trees (winched)	—	—
6. Fill hole	X	7 min
7. Rake area	X	5 min

Figure 4.5

Form for Recording Work Activities of Residential Counsellors in a Community Group Home

Observer: _Faiz_   Employee ID: _735_   Date: _15 Feb 2009_

Condition	Activity	Tools	Time
Resident arrives home from school	Counsellor helps resident remove snow clothes	No special tools	5 min
Physiotherapy program	Counsellor leads resident through exercises	Walker, leg splints, physiotherapy program instructions	20 min
After meal	Medication delivery to residents	Medication recording forms, medication instructions	15 min

In preparing for observations, the analyst might ask: "How many observations are enough?" or "How long should observations be?" These questions are addressed in planning the job analysis observations; once again, there is no rule book one can turn to for the answers. As with the individual and group interviews, a representative sample of workers is needed. If the organization or department is small (e.g., Modern Builders, with only three employees in the job "electrician"), samples from all workers should be obtained. If, however, the organization or department is large (e.g., New World Residential Centres, with 10 homes employing over 120 residential counsellors), a sample of workers consisting of at least 10 to 15 percent of the staff should be observed.[64]

Observation times should be stratified so that all shifts are covered and all work conditions are observed, ensuring that important patterns in worker activities are evident and extraneous information is eliminated. When observing at New World Residential Centres, for example, an analyst would want to observe morning, afternoon, and evening shifts during weekdays and weekends, as activities during these periods can change substantially. Similarly, when observing shift workers in a manufacturing plant, activities may change during peak and down times, and shift and day considerations will influence the observation schedule.

A variety of technological aids are available to the observer. Audio and video recording, for example, can facilitate the observation process. Each has its advantages and disadvantages. Digital audio recordings can augment observer notes with the important verbal behaviour of the worker, but they are rarely useful observation tools on their own. Important information may be lost because of poor recording quality and background noise, or because many of the behaviours of interest may be nonverbal.[65]

Video recording provides a permanent product of the verbal and non-verbal components of the observation session, which the analyst can review in private for later data collection. When the work area is small and a camera can be placed unobtrusively, videotaping is an option to consider. But, while it may be easier to make unobtrusive observations in some settings using a video recorder, the camera cannot follow workers around in large work areas without someone at the controls. As technology shrinks video recorders to increasingly smaller sizes, this becomes less of a disadvantage. Another disadvantage, reactivity to observation, may be greater during videotaped sessions than during observation sessions employing live observers.

Analysts conducting direct observation sessions should be aware that regardless of the observation technique employed, their presence may change the behaviour of the employees. Imagine yourself at work, and a strange individual with a clipboard begins to write down everything you do. Knowing you are being watched, you may respond by doing your work according to what you think the observer is looking for rather than doing it as you would in the normal day-to-day routine. This effect can be minimized when the analyst blends into the surroundings (e.g., by choosing an unobtrusive observation position) and when the employees have been informed of the purpose of the observations and are observed only with their explicit permission.

In addition to direct observation, the job analyst may ask incumbents to monitor their own work behaviour.[66,67] Martinko[68] describes several advantages that self-monitoring may have over other observation procedures. First, it is less time-consuming and less expensive because the job incumbents observe and record their own behaviour. Second, self-monitoring can be used when the conditions of work do not easily facilitate direct observation by another person, as in potentially dangerous or sensitive work. Finally, self-monitoring can provide information on otherwise unobservable cognitive and intellectual processes involved in the job. The potential shortcomings of self-monitoring are that incumbents may not be reliable observers of their own behaviour, the self-monitoring task is an additional duty to be completed in addition to the normal workload, and some amount of training may be required in order to generate valid and reliable results from self-generated data.

After interview, observational, or self-monitoring data are collected, the analyst uses the resulting notes and tally sheets to identify critical task statements, which are used to generate employee specifications. The analyst objectively describes the critical components of the job in terms of (1) the actions performed, (2) the person, data, or things affected by the actions, (3) the intended outcome or product of the action, and (4) the materials, tools, and procedures used in performing the action. Once the task statements are identified, they are further described in terms of the KSAOs required to perform the job successfully. Gatewood, Feild, and Barrick[69] proposed these definitions of knowledge, skills, and abilities in order to make inferences concerning employee specifications for a job:

> *Knowledge:* A body of information, usually of a factual or procedural nature, that makes for successful performance of a task.

Skill: An individual's level of proficiency or competency in performing a specific task. Level of competency is typically expressed in numerical terms.

Ability: A more general, enduring trait or capability an individual possesses at the time he or she first begins to perform a task.

The "O" in KSAO stands for "other attributes" and includes personality traits and other individual characteristics that are integral to job performance. For example, some jobs may require people to work in teams and specify "cooperativeness" as a necessary characteristic, to hold a valid driver's licence, or to be fluently bilingual. Sometimes, a job description will specify physical requirements or other attributes that may be related to a person's age, sex, or race, which may bring about a legal challenge on the basis of discrimination. The job analyst must ensure that any characteristics of this type will pass legal scrutiny should they be challenged.

Rating Task Statements and KSAOs

It is good practice to have the incumbents or other subject-matter experts (SMEs) rate the importance of the identified task statements and the KSAOs associated with each task after the final inventory is generated. All tasks are not equal: Some are performed more frequently than others, some are more important, and some require a degree of difficulty to perform. A task may be performed frequently but have little importance and not require a great deal of skill, while another may be performed rarely but have extreme importance attached to it. Table 4.1 presents an example of one task statement for the job of "meeting planner." The SMEs would rate this task, and all of the others, with respect to frequency, importance, and difficulty. Evaluation of the ratings obtained from all the SMEs helps the job analyst to fully understand what goes on in the job.

The KSAOs, as well, must be rated, as these will ultimately be sampled by the selection measures used in choosing new employees or assigning current employees to new positions. Each of the KSAOs must be rated by the SMEs with respect to at least its importance in performing the specific task and its proficiency (i.e., whether it is required upon entry to the job). Table 4.1 presents KSAOs for the sample task statement for the meeting planner job. Keep in mind that the SME would perform the KSAO ratings for every identified task statement. Reviewing the proficiency information helps to set the selection standards for entry into the job. They are also useful in establishing training standards for the new hires to show what the person must be capable of doing after a period of learning either through courses or on-the-job training.

The job analyst finally integrates the information by compiling a Task × KSAO matrix. Several tasks may require the same KSAOs. Table 4.2 illustrates a Task × KSAO matrix.[70] The rows represent task statements and all of the KSAOs that the job analysis has identified for the target job. Each cell in the matrix states whether the KSAO applies to a task. In Table 4.2, we can see that K3 (knowledge of reference guides) applies to all eight tasks that have been identified for the meeting planner, while S2 (keyboard skills) applies to five of the eight tasks, A1 (information processing) applies to all eight, and O2

TABLE 4.1

Task Statement and Associated KSAOs with Rating Scales

TASK STATEMENT	FREQUENCY	IMPORTANCE	DIFFICULTY
Summarizes information in report form from potential hotel, air-, and ground-transportation vendors in order to convey information to clients and facilitate comparisons between vendor offers and bids for service using meeting and travel reference guides.	0 – Never 1 – A few times a year 2 – Once a month 3 – Once a week 4 – Once a day 5 – Several times a day 0 1 2 3 4 5	0 – None 1 – Little importance 2 – Some importance 3 – Moderate importance 4 – Very important 5 – Extremely important 0 1 2 3 4 5	0 – Never perform 1 – Very easy 2 – Easy 3 – Average difficulty 4 – Very difficult 5 – Extremely difficult 0 1 2 3 4 5

		IMPORTANCE	PROFICIENCY
		0 – None 1 – Little importance 2 – Some importance 3 – Moderate importance 4 – Very important 5 – Extremely important	0 – Not needed 1 – Needed upon entry to job 2 – Can be learned through training 3 – Needed at end of training
Knowledge			
K1. Knowledge of service offers from vendors.		0 1 2 3 4 5	0 1 2 3
K2. Knowledge of negotiated goods and services agreements from vendors.		0 1 2 3 4 5	0 1 2 3
K3. Knowledge of facility and travel reference guides.		0 1 2 3 4 5	0 1 2 3
K4. Knowledge of vendor pricing structures and policies.		0 1 2 3 4 5	0 1 2 3
Skills			
S1. Skill in typing 40 words per minute without error.		0 1 2 3 4 5	0 1 2 3
S2. Keyboard skills.		0 1 2 3 4 5	0 1 2 3
S3. Skill in using computer software.		0 1 2 3 4 5	0 1 2 3
Abilities			
A1. Ability to use *Meeting Facilities Guide*.		0 1 2 3 4 5	0 1 2 3
A2. Ability to use *Official Airlines Guide*.		0 1 2 3 4 5	0 1 2 3
A3. Ability to use SABRE and Apollo airline reservation systems.		0 1 2 3 4 5	0 1 2 3
A4. Ability to compile information from several sources.		0 1 2 3 4 5	0 1 2 3
Other			
O1. Emotional Intelligence		0 1 2 3 4 5	0 1 2 3
O2. Conscientiousness		0 1 2 3 4 5	0 1 2 3
O3. Honesty		0 1 2 3 4 5	0 1 2 3

TABLE 4.2

Task Statement by KSAO Matrix

		KNOWLEDGE				SKILLS			ABILITY				OTHER		
		K1	K2	K3	K4	S1	S2	S3	A1	A2	A3	A4	O1	O2	O3
Task Statement	T1	Y	N	Y	N	Y	Y	N	Y	N	N	Y	Y	N	N
	T2	N	N	Y	N	N	Y	N	Y	N	Y	Y	N	Y	N
	T3	Y	Y	Y	N	N	Y	N	Y	Y	Y	N	N	Y	N
	T4	N	Y	Y	N	Y	Y	N	Y	Y	Y	Y	N	Y	Y
	T5	Y	Y	Y	N	Y	N	N	Y	N	N	Y	N	Y	N
	T6	N	Y	Y	N	N	N	Y	Y	Y	N	Y	Y	N	N
	T7	N	Y	Y	Y	N	Y	N	Y	N	N	Y	N	N	N
	T8	N	N	Y	Y	N	N	N	Y	N	N	Y	N	N	N

"Y" in a cell means that the KSAO in the column applies to the task statement listed in the row. "N" means that the KSAO does not apply to the specified task.

(conscientiousness) applies to four of the eight tasks. In developing selection instruments, the HR staff might wish to concentrate on the KSAOs that apply to the most tasks in the matrix. In the case of Table 4.2, these would be K2, K3, S2, A1, A4, and O2. The Task × KSAO matrix provides a linkage between the KSAOs that are needed to perform tasks effectively.

The rating methods illustrated in Tables 4.1 and 4.2 do not apply only to data collected through interviews, observation, and self-report techniques. They can be used with any procedure that generates task statements that are used to derive KSAOs. A limitation of this approach is that it may be very time-consuming when there are large numbers of task statements and KSAOs.

Structured Job Analysis Questionnaires and Inventories

Structured job analysis questionnaires and inventories require workers and other subject-matter experts to respond to written questions about their jobs. Respondents are asked to make judgments about activities and tasks, tools and equipment, and working conditions involved in the job. These can be off-the-shelf questionnaires and inventories that can be used for a variety of jobs, such as the worker-oriented *Position Analysis Questionnaire* (PAQ),[71] or they can be developed by the analyst for the specific job and organization in question using the critical incident technique,[72] functional job analysis,[73,74] or other inventory methods.

POSITION ANALYSIS QUESTIONNAIRE (PAQ)   The PAQ is a structured job analysis questionnaire that focuses on the general behaviours that make up a job. It assumes that all jobs can be characterized in terms of a limited number of human abilities. The PAQ includes 195 items, called *job elements;* the first 187 describe general work activities and the remaining items relate to compensation. The job elements are organized into six dimensions:

1. *Information input* assesses the sources of information a worker uses on the job.

Chapter 4: Job Analysis and Competency Models

2. *Mental processes* statements refer to the types of reasoning, decision-making, planning, and information-processing behaviours used by the employee.
3. *Work output* items relate to the physical activities engaged in and the tools used by the worker.
4. *Relationships* with other persons measure the types of interpersonal relationships inherent in the job.
5. *Job context* elements measure the physical and social environment in which the work takes place.
6. *Other job characteristics* measure other conditions of work not falling into the other five categories.[75]

Each of the six dimensions is subdivided into sections made up of items related to particular job facets (i.e., components of job dimensions). Facets of information input, for example, include visual sources of job information, nonvisual sources of job information, sensory and perceptual processes, and estimation activities. Items used to assess visual sources of job information ask respondents to rate the extent to which they use written, quantitative, and pictorial materials, visual displays, mechanical devices, and so on. With this method, the job analyst reviews background job information, conducts extensive interviews with incumbents, observes the job, and rates the extent to which each item of the questionnaire applies to the target job.[76] Each item is rated using a specified response scale. For example, the response scale accompanying the facet "visual sources of job information" is:

Extent of Use
0 Does not apply
1 Nominal/very infrequent
2 Occasional
3 Moderate
4 Considerable
5 Very substantial[77]

"Extent of use" measures the degree to which an item is used by the worker. The five other scales employed are importance to this job, amount of time (spent doing something), possibility of occurrence (of physical hazards on the job), applicability (of an item to the job), and other special codes used for a small number of job elements.[78]

The PAQ can be completed by trained job analysts, HR practitioners, or job incumbents and supervisors, although trained job analysts produce the most accurate and reliable results in the least amount of time.[79] Researchers have concluded that the quality of job information obtained via the PAQ is partially dependent on the readability of the instrument. Ash and Edgell[80] assessed the readability of the PAQ using four indexes. These authors concluded that the PAQ requires at least a college-level reading ability for both the directions and the questionnaire items, and that "the questionnaire as presently constituted probably should not be routinely given to job incumbents and supervisors except in those areas requiring much higher levels of education than 10–12 years." The authors of the *Position Analysis Ques-*

tionnaire: Job Analysis Manual[81] recognize that although some organizations have obtained useful job information from having incumbents and supervisors complete the questionnaire, some of the items have unique definitions that may not be readily apparent to those employees.

The job analyst begins the PAQ process by reviewing available information about the job and by observing the work, the work environment, and the equipment used on the job. Job description questionnaires administered to a large sample of employees may also be used to gather information. Finally, interviews with a sample of incumbents and supervisors provide the detailed information required to accurately complete the PAQ. An interview guide can be found in the PAQ manual[82] and is recommended for use by novice job analysts.

The authors warn that the interview should not be conducted "as an oral administration of the PAQ. The analyst's goal in the interview is to gain enough information about the job to enable him or her to respond to all of the PAQ items at some later time."[83] When complete information about the job is obtained, the job analyst assigns ratings to each of the PAQ items; one PAQ answer sheet is completed for each individual interviewed.

Because the PAQ is a standardized job analysis tool, data from single or multiple positions may be used.[84,85] Ratings from the 195 PAQ items are sent to PAQ Services, Inc., for computer processing, where job dimension scores and estimates of required aptitudes to perform the job are derived based on statistically determined relationships. Attribute profiles were generated during the development of the PAQ using a sample of industrial psychologists who rated the relevance of 76 human attributes (e.g., verbal comprehension, movement detection) to each of the job elements assessed by the instrument.[86] For employee selection purposes, the final analysis of PAQ data identifies individual attributes that serve as employee specifications, which can subsequently be used for selecting new employees.

There are several advantages to using the PAQ. First, it can be used with a small number of incumbents yet generates valid results, and it is standardized, thereby permitting easy comparisons between jobs. Second, it is a straightforward process to get from PAQ results to selection procedures. Finally, the PAQ has been rated as one of the most cost-efficient job analysis methods.[87] The primary disadvantages are that (1) because it is a worker-oriented technique, the PAQ does not quantify what work actually gets done on the job,[88,89] and (2) the reading level of the PAQ is too difficult for many lower-level workers. Considering the change in the world of work, from task- to process-based modes of thinking, this first disadvantage may well be an advantage. However, because the required reading level is high and the content of the PAQ is best suited to blue-collar-type jobs, the people occupying those jobs are unlikely to be able to understand the questions.[90] Furthermore, important task differences between jobs may not be picked up because of the PAQ's focus on behaviours and the emphasis on overlooking the context within which the work occurs (hence the homemaker job ends up looking similar to that of a police officer).

The interview, direct observation, and self-monitoring methods define task statements. The PAQ does not generate task statements; instead, SMEs rate the criticality to the job of those PAQ items that received the highest ratings for the "extent of use" category. In particular, the SMEs note whether the PAQ attribute is essential for new hires to possess at the time of their hiring. If so, the attribute is included as a KSAO to be used in employee selection. More information on the PAQ can be found on the PAQ website at http://www.paq.com.

TWO ALTERNATIVES TO THE PAQ   Two recently available alternatives to the PAQ are Harvey's *Common-Metric Questionnaire* (CMQ)[91,92] and Saville and Holdsworth's *Work Profiling System.* The CMQ is a structured, off-the-shelf job analysis questionnaire that captures important context variables. It promises up-to-date job analysis information corresponding to what people actually do at work and a database describing jobs in terms of observable aspects of the work rather than subjective ratings systems.[93] The reading level is appropriate for lower-level jobs and the content appears to be appropriate for both lower- and higher-level jobs. The CMQ asks questions in five sections pertaining to background information, contacts with people, decision making, physical and mechanical activities, and work setting:

1. *Background:* 41 questions about work requirements such as travel, seasonality, and licensure requirements.
2. *Contacts with people:* 62 questions regarding level of supervision, degree of internal and external contacts, and meeting requirements.
3. *Decision making:* 80 questions focusing on relevant occupational knowledge and skill, language and sensory requirements, and managerial and business decision making.
4. *Physical and mechanical activities:* 53 items about physical activities and equipment, machinery, and tools.
5. *Work setting:* 47 items that focus on environmental conditions and other job characteristics.[94]

The CMQ has been field-tested on 4552 positions representing over 900 occupations. Job descriptions produced by the CMQ correlate strongly with descriptions found in the DOT ($0.80 < r < 0.90$).[95] More information on the CMQ can be found at http://cmqonline.com.

The *Work Profiling System* (WPS) is a job analysis method that consists of three versions applicable to managerial, service, and technical occupations. The WPS is a computer-administered structured questionnaire that can be completed and scored online in the workplace. It measures ability and personality attributes, including hearing skills, sight, taste, smell, touch, body coordination, verbal skills, number skills, complex management skills, personality, and team role.[96] WPS defines the KSAOs required for effective performance and generates employment specifications based on the highest-ranking survey items across respondents. Another advantage to using the WPS is that it "builds an organizational map of related jobs and job families, providing critical information for selecting jobs for rotation, cross-training and teams."[97]

Task Inventories

Task inventories
Work-oriented surveys that break down jobs into their component tasks.

Task inventories are work-oriented surveys that break down jobs into their component tasks. A well-constructed survey permits workers to define their jobs in relation to a subset of tasks appearing on the inventory.[98] Drauden[99] indicates that certain task inventory methods were developed in response to the *Uniform Guidelines* criteria for job analysis. According to these criteria, job analysis should assess (1) the duties performed, (2) the level of difficulty of job duties, (3) the job context, and (4) the criticality of duties to the job. An inventory comprises task statements that are objectively based descriptions of what gets done on a job. Tasks are worker activities that result in an outcome that serves some specified purpose.[100,101] These inventories are typically developed for specific jobs or occupations, in contrast to worker-oriented methods that permit application of instruments to a wide variety of unrelated jobs.

FUNCTIONAL JOB ANALYSIS   Fine and his colleagues[102,103] distinguish between what a worker does and what is accomplished in the functional job analysis (FJA) method. They define task statements as "verbal formulations of activities that make it possible to describe what workers do *and* what gets done, so that recruitment, selection and payment can be efficiently and equitably carried out."[104]

In FJA, well-written task statements clearly describe what an employee does so that an individual unfamiliar with the job should be able to read and understand each task statement. Task statements contain four elements: (1) a verb describing the action that is performed; (2) an object of the verb that describes to whom or what the action is done; (3) a description of tools, equipment, work aids, and processes required for successful completion of the task; and (4) an expected output describing the result of the action.[105,106] Taken together, task statements describe all of the essential components of the job.

Although recommendations vary for the optimal number of task statements that define a job—from as few as 6 to 12[107] to as many as 30 to 100[108]—one is well advised to keep in mind the purpose of generating task statements: When conducting a job analysis to support a human resources selection program, the task statements should be specific enough to be useful in pinpointing employment specifications, but not so specific as to be cumbersome. Generally, 20 to 30 task statements are sufficient for this purpose.

Task statements should be carefully edited for inclusion in the task inventory. As part of this process, a group of analysts should compare their understanding of the tasks and reach an agreement on their meaning. The group of analysts that edits the task statements should have a broad range of experience to increase the likelihood that the task statements are complete, accurate, and clearly stated, and that it is less likely that their information is dismissed as simply the opinion of the analyst. Group editing helps to increase the objectivity of task analysis and the reliability of task statements.[109]

Once the inventory is made (consider Table 4.1 on page 136 without the rating scales as an example of an FJA task statement), it is distributed to a sample of job incumbents and other experts, who are asked to rate the tasks on several scales, including (1) data, people, and things, which describe the way in which the worker interacts with sources of information, other people, and the physical environment; (2) worker function orientation, which describes the extent of the worker's involvement with data, people, and things; (3) scale of worker instructions, which describes the amount of control a worker has over the specific methods of task performance; and (4) general educational development scales, which assess the abilities required in the areas of reasoning, mathematics, and language.[110-112] Workers are then asked to rate tasks on the inventory according to whether or not they perform the task and, if desired, to indicate the frequency, criticality (i.e., the consequences of errors), and importance of the task to the job.

Fine[113] notes that the usefulness of the latter three ratings is dubious: "The critical issue is really whether the task needs to be performed to get the work done. If it is necessary, then it is important and critical, and frequency does not matter." A worker in a nuclear power facility may, for example, be required to enter and conduct rescues in radiologically contaminated confined spaces. While such a rescue operation is rarely, if ever, necessary in the life of a job, it is essential that certain workers be able to perform to stringent standards at any given time, so this is a critical component in employee selection.

Once a task inventory is completed by the incumbent sample, the results can be summarized according to the mean rating each item received. McCormick[114] points out that there is no easy formula for determining job requirements from task inventories. Gatewood, Feild, and Barrick[115] suggest that the analyst set a cut-off point for mean ratings (e.g., 3 on a 5-point scale) and for standard deviations (e.g., 1), which are computed for each item scored by the respondents. Items with a mean rating of >3 and a standard deviation of <1 would, according to this rule, be included in the list of job requirements.

Finally, they suggest that at least 75 percent of employees indicate that they perform the task. Thus, any task statements receiving a score of 3 or higher, a standard deviation of 1.0 or less (lower standard deviations are associated with more agreement among raters), and that indicate that at least 75 percent of employees engage in the task are included in the final task inventory that describes the job. The final inventory determines the content of the measurements to be used in the new selection program.

These guidelines can also be used to evaluate task ratings developed through interview, observation, and self-report techniques. As well, it is good practice to have the incumbents rate the KSAOs associated with each task after the final inventory is generated, and then for the analyst to generate a Task $\times$ KSAO matrix to assist in identifying the KSAOs that will ultimately be sampled with the subsequent selection measurements.

Task inventories are advantageous in that they are efficient to use with large numbers of employees and are easily translated into quantifiable measurements. On the other hand, they can be time-consuming to develop and thus can be expensive.[116] Motivating incumbents to participate in the rating process may also be a problem with long inventories. When the task inventory procedure and analysis are well planned, the results can be extremely valuable in developing human resources selection programs.

CRITICAL INCIDENT TECHNIQUE   Critical incidents are examples of effective and ineffective work behaviours that are related to superior or inferior performance. The critical incident technique, which generates behaviourally focused descriptions of work activities, was originally developed as a training needs assessment and performance appraisal tool.[117] The critical incident technique provides important, contextually rich examples of job behaviours that are particularly useful in developing behaviourally anchored rating scales (BARS; see Chapter 5) and behavioural interviews (see Chapter 9), as well as being the basis for situational judgment tests and assessment centre exercises such as role-plays and in-basket exercises (see Chapter 8).[118]

The first step in this method is to assemble a panel of job experts, usually consisting of people with several years' experience who have had the opportunity to observe both poor and exemplary workers on the job. The job of the panel is to gather critical incidents. Flanagan[119] defined an incident as an observable human activity that is sufficiently complete to facilitate inferences and predictions about the person performing the act. Panel members describe incidents, including the antecedents to the activity, a complete description of the behaviour, the results of the behaviour, and whether the results were within the control of the worker. Incidents are also rated in terms of whether they represent effective or ineffective behaviour on the part of the employee. After the incidents are gathered, they are edited and translated into performance dimensions that are then used to derive KSAOs and to help identify appropriate selection methods. The rated incidents help to develop the anchors for the BARS instruments and structured interviews as shown in later chapters.

Worker Traits Inventories

Worker traits inventories are not job analysis techniques according to strict criteria.[120] Harvey[121,122] takes the position that the term *job analysis* should be used in describing only those procedures that provide information on verifiable job behaviours and activities, and not for those procedures that make inferences about the KSAOs needed for a job. Not everyone shares Harvey's position on this matter.[123] Worker trait inventory methods would not satisfy Harvey's definition of a job analysis procedure as they do not provide information on the job as a whole, but only certain requirements needed to carry out the job. These methods are, however, widely used to infer employee specifications from job analysis data, and are commonly included in the job analysis literature and accepted by most practitioners as legitimate job analysis methods.

Worker traits inventories Methods used to infer employee specifications from job analysis data; commonly included in the job analysis literature.

THRESHOLD TRAITS ANALYSIS SYSTEM   The threshold traits analysis system[124] is designed to identify worker traits that are relevant to the target job. This method assumes that work behaviours encompass the position functions, the worker traits, and the resulting job performance. According to Lopez, a trait is "a set of observable characteristics that distinguishes one person from another."[125] Supervisors, incumbents, and other subject-matter experts rate the job according to the relevancy of 33 worker traits (e.g., stamina, perception, oral expression, adaptability to pressure, and tolerance). Traits are also rated with respect to the level of trait possession necessary to perform the job, and the practicality of expecting potential incumbents to possess the traits upon hiring.

FLEISHMAN JOB ANALYSIS SURVEY (F-JAS)   The *Fleishman Job Analysis Survey* (F-JAS),[126] formerly known as the *ability requirements scale* (ARS), was developed as a system for identifying employee characteristics that influence job performance. It assumes that job tasks differ with respect to the abilities required to perform them successfully, and that all jobs can be classified according to ability requirements. Fleishman and his colleagues[127,128] used factor analysis to identify a collection of 52 ability categories. Categories range from oral comprehension to multi-limb coordination to night vision.

Administration of the F-JAS requires that 20 or more subject-matter experts, including job incumbents, supervisors, and others, be presented with a job description or task list. The experts are asked to rate the extent to which each ability is required for the job. Ratings on the ability scales are then averaged to identify the overall ability requirements essential to the job.[129]

The F-JAS is relatively simple to administer and cost-efficient, but its biggest limitation is that it provides information only on the 52 abilities. Fleishman and Reilly[130] have produced a companion handbook that provides examples of tasks and jobs that require the specific ability, as well as listing examples of tests designed to measure the ability. The F-JAS, however, does not identify knowledge, skills, or other attributes that may also be required to perform a job.

JOB ELEMENT METHOD   A third worker trait technique is the job element method (JEM), which attempts to distinguish between superior and inferior workers on the basis of job-related abilities. Elements describe the range of employee specifications in terms of KSAOs.[131] The JEM procedure requires supervisors and other subject-matter experts to generate a list of elements required for job performance. Elements (e.g., accuracy for a grocery store cashier) are broken down into sub-elements (e.g., ability to determine cost of items, press register keys, and make change) that exhaustively describe the job.[132] The expert panel is subsequently asked to rate the elements and sub-elements on four scales: (1) *barely acceptable* measures whether or not minimally acceptable employees possess the ability; (2) *superior* asks whether the ability distinguishes superior workers from others; (3) *trouble likely if not considered* asks whether or not the ability can be safely ignored in selecting employees; and (4) *practical* asks whether or not workers can be expected to have an ability.

One advantage of worker trait inventories is that they are designed to identify traits or KSAOs that are predictive of job success. The identification of these KSAOs is made by SMEs, who are the individuals most familiar with the job or occupation. The F-JAS in particular stands out as a standardized approach, based on a solid theoretical foundation, for rating the KSAOs critical to performance on the job. In many ways, worker trait procedures are first cousins to the competency-based approaches we will discuss shortly in Part II of this chapter.

Rating Job Analysis Methods

Much research has considered the efficacy of various job and worker trait analysis techniques for generating employee specifications. Levine and his colleagues[133] assessed seven job analysis methods for a variety of organizational purposes and for their practicality (see Recruitment and Selection Notebook 4.2). Job analysis experts were asked to rate the threshold traits analysis, ability requirements scales (F-JAS), position analysis questionnaire, critical

Criteria for Choosing a Job Analysis Method

The following criteria were developed by Levine and his colleagues to evaluate seven job analysis techniques. They remain a useful set of questions for any HR practitioner to use in deciding among various procedures.

- **Operational status:** Has the method been tested and refined sufficiently?
- **Availability:** Is it available off the shelf?
- **Occupational versatility:** Is it suitable for analyzing a variety of jobs?
- **Standardization:** Is it possible to compare your results with others that have been found elsewhere?
- **User acceptability:** Is the method acceptable to the client and the employees who will have to provide the information?
- **Training requirements:** How much training is needed and available to use the method; must one receive special certification in the procedure to use it? Can it be done "in-house"?
- **Sample size:** From how many employees must data be collected for the method to provide reliable results?
- **Reliability:** Will the method give results that are replicable?
- **Cost:** What are the costs of the method in materials, consultant fees, training, and person-hours?
- **Quality of outcome:** Will the method yield high-quality results (e.g., legally defensible)?
- **Time to completion:** How many calendar days will the data collection and analysis take?

Source: E.L. Levine, R.A. Ash, H. Hall, and F. Sistrunk. 1983. "Evaluation of Job Analysis Methods by Experienced Job Analysts." *Academy of Management Journal* 26: 339–48. Copyright © 1983 Academy of Management, NY. Reprinted with permission of the Copyright Clearance Center (CCC).

incident technique, functional job analysis, and the job element method, all of which have been discussed in this chapter. Additionally, they assessed a task inventory method, the *Task Inventory/Comprehensive Occupational Data Analysis Program* (TI/CODAP).

For purposes of identifying personnel requirements and specifications, the seven methods were rated in the following order: (1) threshold traits analysis, (2) job elements method, (3) functional job analysis, (4) ability requirements scales, (5) position analysis questionnaire, (6) TI/CODAP, and (7) critical incident technique (see Table 4.3). The first five ratings were not significantly different from each other, meaning that they were rated as equally acceptable for identifying personnel requirements. All five were rated significantly higher than the TI/CODAP and the critical incident technique.

Since job analyses must meet legal requirements if challenged in court, respondents were asked to rate each of the job analysis methods in terms of how well they stand up to legal and quasi-legal requirements. TI/CODAP and functional job analysis ranked highest (see Table 4.3), followed closely by the PAQ. The job elements method, critical incident technique, threshold traits analysis, and ability requirements scales ranked fourth through seventh, respectively. Hence, the highest-ranking method for meeting legal requirements scored as one of the least-preferred methods for identifying personnel requirements and specifications. Functional job analysis was highly ranked by job analysis experts on both of these important aspects of use.

Regarding practicality, Levine and his colleagues[134] assessed the versatility, standardization, user acceptability, amount of training required for use,

TABLE 4.3

Rank Order of Job Analysis Methods According to Effectiveness and Practicality versus Ability to Meet Legal Requirements

Job Analysis Method	Effectiveness and Practicality	Legal Requirements
Threshold traits analysis	1	6
Job elements method	2	4
Functional job analysis	3	2
Ability requirements scales (F-JAS)	4	7
Position analysis questionnaire	5	3
TI/CODAP	6	1
Critical incident technique	7	5

There is essentially no difference between the first five methods ranked on effectiveness and practicality. 1 = Highest-ranked method; 7 = Lowest-ranked method.

Source: Based on E.L. Levine, R.A. Ash, H. Hall, and F. Sistrunk. 1983. "Evaluation of Job Analysis Methods by Experienced Job Analysts." *Academy of Management Journal* 26: 339–48. Copyright © 1983 Academy of Management, NY. Reprinted with permission of the Copyright Clearance Center (CCC).

operational practicality, sample size requirements, off-the-shelf usability, reliability, cost of use, quality of outcome, and amount of time required for completion for each of seven job analysis methods. The PAQ received consistently high ratings (i.e., above 3 on a 5-point scale) on all items except the amount of training required. Functional job analysis was next, with high ratings on all scales except for training, cost, and time to completion. In terms of overall practicality scores, these methods were followed by the JEM, the threshold traits analysis, ability requirements scales, and TI/CODAP. The critical incident technique received the overall lowest ratings on practicality measures. The TI/CODAP and PAQ rated highest for reliability, followed by functional job analysis.

Other researchers have assessed job analysis techniques to determine whether or not different results are produced when different subject-matter experts are used. Mullins and Kimbrough[135] found that different groups of SMEs produced different job analysis outcomes using the critical incident technique. They also determined that performance levels of SMEs influenced analysis outcomes. These results are inconsistent with previous studies that found no difference in job analysis outcomes relative to performance levels. The authors suggest that the complexity of the job may mediate the performance level–analysis outcome relationship.

In a similar study, Schmitt and Cohen[136] found that when using a task inventory, people with different occupational experience produced different outcomes, as did males and females. No difference was found for experts of different races. Finally, a meta-analysis of 38 articles including inter-rater reliability data found that experienced job analysis professionals produced significantly higher reliability coefficients compared to nonprofessional raters.[137]

Job analysis researchers have also questioned the relationship between the amount of information analysts are given about a job and the quality of analysis outcomes.[138] They concluded that differential accuracy of analysis results is a function of the amount of information provided for the analysts. Specifically, analysts who knew the job title and job description were more accurate in their analyses than those who knew only the job title. The authors make an important conclusion that should be considered when preparing for a job analysis:

> Our results indicate that the amount of job descriptive information available to raters has a significant effect on job analysis accuracy. Raters with more detailed job information are consistently more accurate than those given only a job title.[139]

An important issue that must be addressed as part of selecting a job analysis method is the accuracy of the information that the method will provide. Dierdorff and Wilson[140] used a meta-analysis of 299 reliability estimates that were from different job analyses involving a variety of occupations. They concluded that methods that gathered specific task data (e.g., "replaces ink cartridges in desktop printers") did so with greater accuracy than methods that assessed generalized work activity (e.g., "supervises work of office staff"). These results support Harvey and Lozada-Larsen's position[141] presented above. They also reported that professional job analysts made more accurate assessments than did job incumbents who made self-reports or surveys. Finally, their analysis showed that SMEs made the most reliable estimates when using "importance" and "frequency" scales rather than other types of measurements.

This information should be of value to practitioners in designing job analysis projects. "For instance, when only a certain amount of financial resources are procurable to conduct a job analysis, one could use the information presented herein to provide an estimate of how much reliability could be expected from using 25 incumbents versus five trained analysts rating tasks as opposed to [generalized work activity]."[142] Dierdorff and Wilson's findings do not imply that only task-oriented job analysis methods should be used. The value of a job analysis lies in how the information from the analysis will be used. For some uses, such as training and development, task data may be necessary, while for some other uses, such as designing a performance management system, a more holistic method may be acceptable. The practitioner must take the intended use into consideration when choosing a method.

Recently, job analysis proponents have debated on the best way to assess the reliability and validity of different job analysis methods. Sanchez and Levine[143] have taken the position that traditional methods of assessing reliability are inappropriate for assessing job analysis data in that they are of little practical value. They propose that job analysis data be evaluated in terms of its consequences: "Thus, the evaluation of [job analysis] data should focus on (1) the inferences derived from such data; and (2) the rules governing the making of such inferences." They note that Levine et al.[144] showed that four very different job analysis methods, which likely had very different degrees of accuracy, led HR professionals to develop very similar selection strategies.

Morgeson and Campion[145] echo these arguments by endorsing an inferential approach to validation, similar to our presentation in Chapter 2 (see Recruitment and Selection Notebook 2.1 on page 47). In their model at the conceptual or construct level, the analyst identifies job performance and job-related psychological constructs. SMEs produce a job description outlining tasks and duties that is made by inference from the job performance construct. Similarly, job specifications, in terms of KSAOs, are inferred from the job-related psychological constructs. An operational linkage is assumed to tie the KSAOs to the tasks and duties. Validation rests on verifying the different inferences.

Harvey and Wilson[146] take issue with these approaches; they maintain the position that a procedure that focuses only on job specifications or the consequences of those specifications is not a true job analysis procedure. They argue that holistic ratings, or direct inferences of KSAOs from psychological constructs rather than from job tasks, will always produce inferior data.

There is little empirical evidence at this time on which to judge the merits of these two competing positions to provide guidance to an HR practitioner. The best advice that we can give is to be aware of these two differing views toward assessing reliability and validity of job analysis systems and the implications for legal defensibility.

Recruitment and Selection Notebook 4.3 presents guidelines developed by Thompson and Thompson[147] to determine whether a job analysis procedure would meet legal standards. The guidelines are based on U.S. court decisions but represent what HR professionals could expect from Canadian courts and tribunals when they evaluate the information produced by a job analysis. Although the guidelines are a bit dated, they are still relevant, but they may change with the adoption of new laws or standards or what is considered to be acceptable professional practice.

There is no guarantee that any job analysis method will find acceptance before the courts. The best that can be said is that having done a formal job analysis, regardless of method, is better than not having done one, and having carried it out properly will increase the probability that the courts will accept its results. Given the limitations of different methods and their suitability to different HR management functions, it is not unusual for an organization to use several job analysis techniques. Often, such multi-method approaches are needed to understand the complexity of today's jobs where the dividing lines between job, worker, and job-related behaviours become blurred.

Using a variety of approaches is a form of "triangulation" and provides different perspectives on the job that when synthesized produce the best information for matching people to jobs. Ultimately, what the HR practitioner must decide is: (1) Which job analysis method best serves the intended purpose of the job analysis (i.e., Will the data be used for selection, performance appraisal, job evaluation, etc.?)? (2) Can the job analysis be carried out reliably given the number of positions to be assessed, the availability of SMEs, the time allowed to complete the project, and the cooperation of job incumbents? (3) Which job analysis method has the best track record with respect to technical adequacy and legal defensibility?[148]

Assessing the Legal Defensibility of a Job Analysis

Based on U.S. court and tribunal decisions, Thompson and Thompson identified the following factors that influence the defensibility of job analysis data used as evidence in legal proceedings:

- A job analysis must be performed according to a set of formal procedures. It is not acceptable to rely on what "everyone" knows about a job since that knowledge may be based on inaccurate stereotyped notions of the job demands.
- The job analysis must be well documented; it is not enough to simply carry around job information in the analyst's head.
- The job analysis should collect data from several up-to-date sources. This suggests using several different methods of job analysis.
- The sample of people interviewed should be sufficient in number to capture accurately the job information.

The sample should also represent the full diversity of job incumbents (e.g., ethnic and gender groups, people with and without formal qualifications) to ensure the validity of the data.

- The job analysts should be properly trained in the different techniques to ensure that they collect objective information and are as free from bias as possible.
- The job analysis should determine the most important and critical aspects of the job, and it is on these that the key attributes and selection and evaluation for the job should be based.

Source: D.E. Thompson and T.A. Thompson. 1982. "Court Standards for Job Analysis in Test Validation." *Personnel Psychology* 35: 872–73.

Part II: The Role of Competencies in Recruitment and Selection

Today's workplace is in the midst of unprecedented change as it struggles to adapt to increasing global competition, rapid advances in information technology, multitasking, and changing work force demographics. Emerging from this turbulence are worker requirements unlike any we have seen in the past. With many of the routine aspects of work now done by machines, jobs have been redefined, with greater emphasis given to the management of technology.

In this post-industrial information era, workers are required to apply a wider range of skills to an ever-changing series of tasks. Individuals just entering the work force will face at least three to four career changes in their lifetime. Workers will be expected to possess the skills and knowledge of two or three traditional employees.[149] On the factory floor, jobs change rapidly, and workers constantly rotate among positions, acquiring multiple and generic skills. Today's workplace poses special challenges when trying to match people to jobs.

For many workers, these changes mean that the tasks performed today may be radically different from those required a few months from today. Skill requirements for employees may be increased or decreased, depending on the type of technology employed.[150] Task and job instability create a growing need for hiring people with an already-learned set of skills and the ability to make decisions and adapt to changing organizational demands. The results of a job analysis may hold for only as long as the job remains configured as it was at the time of the job analysis.[151] For example, today there is a greater emphasis on the strategic role played by HR professionals than there was 10 years ago. This new role must be taken into account in current job profiles. With decreasing specialization and shifting of shared work assignments typical of today's work, traditional methods of job analysis may not be appropriate. That is, they are simply inconsistent with the new management practices of cross-training assignments, self-managed teams, and increased responsibility at all organizational levels.

The evolution toward rapidly changing jobs and organizations that demand flexibility of their workers has led some HR practitioners to search for alternatives to traditional job analysis techniques. In order to recruit, select, and promote flexible workers who are able to make their own rules and adjust to the changing demands of work, human resources specialists are faced with the ever-increasing need to adjust their methods to ensure that people are hired based on the needs of the organization, while remaining within legal boundaries. One approach that HR practitioners are using in a rapidly changing environment is to select employees through work-related **competencies** that are thought to be related to successful job performance. A growing number of Canadian organizations have implemented competency-based management strategies.

Competencies
Groups of related behaviours that are needed for successful job performance in an organization.

What Is a "Competency"?

Boyatzis[152] popularized the term *competency* in *The Competent Manager* and defined it as a combination of a motive, trait, skill, aspect of one's self-image or social role, or a body of relevant knowledge. This definition left much room for debate and has been followed since by a plethora of definitions that tend to reflect either individual or specific organizational concerns. While various definitions of competency may differ, they generally contain three elements. First, most suggest that competencies are the KSAOs that underlie effective and successful job performance; second, the KSAOs must be observable or measurable; and third, the KSAOs must distinguish between superior and other performers.[153] Competencies, then, are measurable attributes that distinguish outstanding performers from others in a defined job context.

Competencies have also been defined as groups of related behaviours, rather than the KSAOs, that are needed for successful job performance in an organization. Similarly, they have been defined as the behaviours that superior performers in an organization exhibit more consistently than others do. In practice, competencies at times have been based on "average" performance; nonetheless, we will base our discussion on the original intent: to distinguish competencies that identify superior performance, while recognizing that organizations may have to modify the definition of a competency to meet their own needs.

Competencies are then used to identify the KSAOs that distinguish superior performers from others. All of these definitions require the identification of KSAOs from behaviours displayed by superior employees. In one case, the KSAOs are labelled "competencies," and in the other, the term is applied to the behaviours. In both cases, we are concerned with identifying and measuring the KSAOs that underlie what the organization considers to be successful job performance, whether that performance is recognized as average or superior.

Competency-based selection systems take the view that employees must be capable of moving between jobs and carrying out the associated tasks for different positions.[154] In the competency-based approach, the human resources specialist attempts to identify those KSAOs that distinguish superior performers from others and that will allow an organization to achieve its strategic goals. By selecting people who possess KSAOs that lead to superior performance, organizations are attempting to establish a closer connection between organizational success and individual performance. Recall that worker trait systems identify KSAOs for specific jobs; competency-based approaches initially sought to identify KSAOs *regardless* of job. However, this has changed and many competency-based systems now identify job-level KSAOs as well as those that apply at the organizational level.

Competency Framework or "Architecture"

Many of the early competency models identified a single, target job in the organization to describe the key job requirements and KSAOs. The information obtained from this approach could not be applied to other jobs in the organization. In other cases, a common set of competencies was identified for a broad range of jobs and became the basis for recruitment and selection.[155] This common set of competencies did not describe any one job because it had to be sufficiently generic to describe a broad range of jobs. In effect, the KSAOs for a specific job are de-emphasized. Both of these approaches had limited value in selection. Would you want to fly in an airplane where an airline selected both pilots and flight attendants using only the competencies of leadership, motivation, trust, problem solving, interpersonal skills, and communication and ignored the specific skills required for either position?

More recently, organizations that use competency models have recognized that they must include the competencies required at the specific job level. Today, organizations that use competency models mostly develop a three-tiered framework or architecture. They identify competencies that apply across all jobs in the organization (core competencies), those that apply to a group of similar jobs (functional competencies), and those that apply to a single class of jobs (job-specific competencies).

Competency Categories

Core competencies are those characteristics that apply to every member of the organization regardless of position, function, or level of responsibility within the organization. Core competencies support the organization's mission, vision, and values. They are organizational KSAOs that are required for organizational success.[156] Core competencies are what an organization or individual does or should do best; they are key strengths that organizations and individuals posses and demonstrate.[157] An airline could require that all

Core competencies

Characteristics that every member of an organization, regardless of position, function, job, or level of responsibility within the organization, is expected to possess.

employees from the chief executive officer down to pilots and flight attendants and on to the lowest-level employee exhibit the common core competencies of leadership, motivation, trust, problem solving, interpersonal skills, and communication.

Functional competencies are characteristics shared by different positions within an organization that belong to a common job group or occupational family or by employees performing a common function. They are the common characteristics shared by different positions within the job group. They describe the KSAOs that are required for any job within the job group. For example, pilots and navigators may share the same KSAOs of map reading and developing flight plans, while flight attendants and ticket agents must both exhibit courtesy and a service orientation.

Job-specific competencies are characteristics that apply only to specific positions within the organization. These are competencies that are associated with a position in addition to core and role competencies. A pilot needs a wide range of skills to fly a plane; a navigator does not have to have those skills even though they may be part of the same occupational family. Similarly, a ticket agent needs to operate the computerized reservation system; the flight attendant does not need those skills. Employees need to know the competencies that are required for them to do their own jobs successfully.

Core, functional, and job-specific competencies comprise the architecture of a company's competency model. Core competencies are the foundation on which to build functional competencies, which in turn serve as the base for job-specific competencies (see Figure 4.6). In practice, the architecture may vary across organizations, with some companies increasing or decreasing the number of layers. As well, organizations may choose to use different names for the layers in the competency model; for example, referring to "organizational" competencies in place of "core" competencies, "group" in place of "functional," and "task" in place of "job-specific."

Competency Dictionaries

A **competency dictionary** lists all of the competencies that are required by an organization to achieve its mandate. It includes the core and all functional and job-specific competencies identified throughout the organization and defines each competency in terms of the behaviours and KSAOs related to it. As part of developing a competency framework, an organization must develop a competency dictionary. The HR specialist and subject-matter experts, using an accepted procedure, identify the competencies they believe are most relevant to the organization's success.

In some cases, the HR specialist will start with a generic list of competencies[158] that has not been tailored to any particular company or position and then adapt those generic competencies to its own needs. This shortcut procedure saves time and money but may not be as valid as initially identifying competencies specific to the organization. Simply selecting competencies from a generic competency dictionary may fail to capture those that are not in the dictionary but are critical for successful job performance.

Functional competencies

Characteristics shared by different positions within an organization (i.e., a group of related or similar jobs). Only those members of an organization in these positions are expected to possess these competencies.

Job-specific competencies

Characteristics that apply only to specific positions within the organization. Only those people in the position are expected to possess these competencies.

Competency dictionary

A listing of all of the competencies required by an organization to achieve its mandate, along with the proficiency level required to perform successfully in different functional groups or positions.

FIGURE 4.6

A Common Architecture for Competency Models

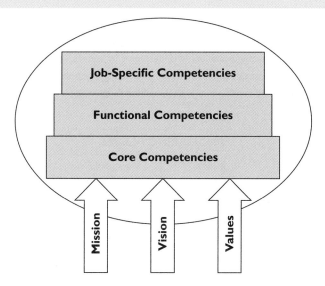

A competency dictionary also includes information on the **proficiency level** needed to successfully perform each competency for each position in the organization. All organization members are expected to exhibit all of the core competencies; however, they are not expected to do so to the same degree. Similarly, individuals may need the same functional and job-specific competencies, but each competency may require a different level of proficiency, depending on the organizational level of the individual.[159] As employees take on more responsibility in an organization, they may be required to become more proficient with respect to any competency if they are to perform effectively.

For example, communication might be identified as a core competency; however, the behavioural expectations for communication may vary across positions in the organization (see Figure 4.7). The level of proficiency increases with organizational level. A corporate vice-president would be expected to have a greater proficiency in communication than a sales representative. Those at the higher levels are expected to be capable of expressing the behavioural demands at one level before moving on to a higher-ranking position. Organizations using a competency model identify the proficiency levels on the required competencies for each position in the organization. The organization assesses each employee or potential employee with respect to the required proficiency levels and then uses these for selection, development and training, and promotion purposes.

Proficiency scales, like that represented in Figure 4.7, are included as part of a competency dictionary. The proficiency scale is independent of any position. The levels in a proficiency scale reflect real, observable differences from one organizational level to another. The proficiency scale is not a tool to assess employees; it presents a series of behaviours that are expected at specific levels of a competency. Figure 4.7 presents a competency dictionary entry

Proficiency level
The level at which competency must be performed to ensure success in a given functional group or position.

Proficiency scale
A series of behavioural indicators expected at specific levels of a competency.

FIGURE 4.7

A Sample Competency Dictionary Entry and Its Associated Proficiency Scale

Communication involves communicating ideas and information orally and/or in writing in a way that ensures the messages are easily understood by others; listening to and understanding the comments and questions of others; marketing key points effectively to a target audience; and speaking and writing in a logical, well-ordered way.

PROFICIENCY LEVEL			
Basic 1	Proficient 2	Very proficient 3	Mastery 4
Using basic communication skills • writes and speaks meaningful language • comprehends written and verbal instructions	*Using effective communication skills* • delivers information in a timely manner to ensure that others have needed facts • communicates effectively with other work units	*Using communication skills to make effective presentations* • structures communication to meet the needs of the audience • presents complex information in a clear, concise, and credible manner	*Using strategic communication skills* • represents the organization with tact and diplomacy both internally and externally • articulates and promotes the interests of the organization

Communication proficiency levels required for different positions within a company

Level 1: Data entry clerk

Level 2: Sales associate

Level 3: General manager

Level 4: Corporate vice-president

for a "communication" competency, along with its associated proficiency scale. The behavioural indicators listed on the scale in Figure 4.7 are there simply to illustrate the concept. An actual scale might have considerably more indicators at each proficiency level as well as having more rating levels. The proficiency scale would be developed to meet the needs of the organization.

Competency Profiles

Competency profile

A set of proficiency ratings related to a function, job, or employee.

A **competency profile** is a set of proficiency ratings related to a function, job, or employee. Since core competencies apply to all functions and jobs, they are included as part of functional and job-specific profiles. The proficiency level required on the core competencies, however, would vary across functions and positions. A functional competency profile would include the proficiency levels for all of the core and functional competencies related to the occupational family that form the functional group. A job-specific profile adds the proficiency levels required for a specific position within the functional group. Figure 4.8 presents a competency profile developed by Human Resources and Social Development Canada (HRSDC) for its citizen service agents.[160] The number in parentheses following each competency represents the proficiency level required for that competency for successful job performance.

An employee profile represents the proficiency level demonstrated by an employee on each competency that is included in the competency dictionary. A match between an employee profile and a job-specific or functional profile suggests that the employee is suitable for holding the specific position or a position in the functional group. Employees, once they know their own profile, can match it to other jobs in the organization and determine the positions or functional areas for which they meet the minimum proficiency level on the required competencies. In cases where they are deficient, comparing their profile to that of a position of interest suggests where they need to undertake developmental activities.

FIGURE 4.8

A Competency Profile for an HRSDC Citizen Service Agent

A Competency Profile for an **HRSDC** Citizen Service Agent

competency profile

Citizen Service Agent (PM–01)

Group Competencies (Primary)
- Applying Principles and Procedures (4)
- Diagnostic Information Gathering (4)
- Verification and Accuracy (4)
- Interpersonal Awareness (4)

Task Competencies
- Knowledge of Service Canada Programs and Services (3)

Core Competencies
- Communication (4)
- Thinking Skills (4)
- Using Technology (3)
- Changing and Learning (3)
- Client Focus (4)
- Initiative (3)
- Positive Attitude (4)
- Working with Others (3)
- Knowing Our Business (3)

Source: Arieh Bonder. 2008. *A Blueprint for the Future: Competency-Based Management in Human Resources and Skills Development Canada* (HRSDC). Unpublished presentation, HRSDC. Used with permission of the author.

An organization that decides to use competency models must have the capability to identify the required competencies and then to assess accurately the competency level of each employee with respect to the competency. It must also have in place an information management system that is capable of storing all of the required competency information for each position and for each employee. It must also allow accessibility to managers and employees to track the competency profiles for positions and for themselves.

Identifying Competencies and Profiles

There is no agreed-upon methodology for identifying competencies or proficiency levels. This lack of standardization has given rise to several different procedures for identifying competencies. These methods generally start with the identification of target groups of workers that include both high and low performers for each job included in the group. The HR specialist observes the workers doing their jobs and interviews the workers and/or their supervisors to obtain as much information as possible on how the workers actually perform their jobs.

The HR specialist reviews all of the data to identify patterns of behaviour that separate superior performers from others. Finally, the HR specialist, assisted by subject-matter experts, identifies those competencies and related KSAOs that are linked to superior performance for the organization, the functional group, and/or the position. This is essentially the methodology suggested by Dubois[161] that is based on David McClelland's[162] original theory that led to the development of competency-based models.

In some ways, these methods are similar to job analysis procedures; however, the lack of an agreed-upon methodology leads to a lack of methodological rigour. Courts and tribunals in both Canada and the United States have ruled that human resources systems must be supported by empirical evidence that there is a link between selection measures and the essential duties of a job. Whether a competency-based system is deemed to meet legal standards may well depend on the methodology chosen to develop the competency dictionary, the resultant competency profiles, and their links to jobs. Recruitment and Selection Notebook 4.4 presents a methodology that should meet those standards.

Assessing Employee Competencies

Developing reliable and valid ways of measuring employee competencies is crucial to the success of the competency model. At some point, a human resources manager must determine whether a job applicant possesses the required competencies or whether an internal candidate is qualified to hold or be promoted into a position. An organization must adopt an assessment strategy for assessing employee proficiency levels. A variety of assessment methods may be used to assess employee competencies. The choice of method depends on how the results will be used. For example, assessment of competencies for selection and promotion decisions must be carried out with methods that are fair, reliable, and valid. Chapters 7, 8, and 9 examine the

Steps in Developing a Competency-Based Management Framework

1. Obtain executive level support, including sufficient human and financial resources, to develop a competency model.
2. Review the organization's mission, vision, and values statements.
3. Adopt a competency definition that meets the needs of the organization (e.g., average versus superior performance issue; KSAOs versus behaviour).
4. Determine the HR functions for which competencies will be used (e.g. selection, training, compensation).
5. Determine the architecture of the competency model (core, functional, job-specific layers?) that best meets the intended functions for which it will be used.
6. Develop the competency dictionary.
7. Define the profiling methodology.
   a. Advance planning and preparation.
      • Review jobs and data collection techniques most appropriate for use.
   b. Consult key stakeholders in the organization.
   c. Identify subject-matter experts (SMEs) for each level in the competency model.
      • Specify the competencies and proficiency levels.
   d. Validate the draft competency profiles.
      • Use focus groups or surveys to ensure that profiles accurately reflect the critical competencies required for the function and/or job.
   e. Confirm compatibility of draft competency profile and human resources management information system.
   f. Revise and finalize competency profiles based on feedback from key stakeholders.
8. Identify reliable and valid assessment strategies to determine employee competency profiles.
9. Document all steps in the development and implementation of the system and the rationale for key decisions, in case these are needed as evidence before tribunals or courts.
10. Evaluate the system on an ongoing basis to ensure that the competency profiles continue to predict successful job performance.

different techniques that have been developed over the years to make assessments that meet these criteria.

Validating Competency-Based Selection Systems

A substantial number of professional and business articles have been written on competency-based models; however, most of these articles offer only theoretical or anecdotal descriptions of competencies. These articles are short on details describing the process used to establish the competencies or how they were assessed as part of a selection process. Rarely do any of these articles present data showing the impact of competency-based selection on job or organizational performance. Research is needed to compare the bottom-line effectiveness of traditional selection systems based on job analysis with that of competency-based systems. There is a need to validate competency–job performance relationships and not to accept their validity and superiority without benefit of research. Klein[163] called for empirical research on the reliability and validity of competency-based systems to avoid litigation. Only recently have empirical studies[164] surfaced that have a bearing on the validity of competency models.

Competency Modelling versus Job Analysis

Concern over the increasing use of competency models led the Professional Practice Committee and the Scientific Affairs Committee of the Society for Industrial and Organizational Psychology to form the Job Analysis and Competency Modeling Task Force. The task force, which was composed of advocates of both traditional job analysis and competency-based procedures, identified 10 technical criteria on which it evaluated both approaches. Job analysis was judged superior on 9 of the 10 criteria. The only criterion where competency modelling was seen to have an edge was with respect to a more transparent linkage between business goals or strategies and the information provided by the competency-based approach. In all other instances, both proponents of job analysis and competency modelling rated the traditional job analysis methods as more rigorous, particularly in providing more reliable information.[165]

The task force also identified other, less technical criteria and concluded that competency approaches were more likely to focus on generic personal characteristics that are common across a broad range of jobs. It viewed competency approaches as being closely aligned with worker-oriented job analyses. The emphasis on these types of characteristics gave competency modelling higher levels of "face validity" with organizational decision makers. Executives typically commented that competencies provided them with a common language. As organizations continue to "de-complicate" business processes, the increased face validity of competency modelling procedures and their focus on core competencies holds wide appeal. However, these factors have resulted in decreased quality of the technical information needed for legal defensibility purposes.[166]

Pearlman[167] suggests that there are both good and bad approaches to competency modelling. He refers to good approaches as "Trojan Horse" work in that traditional job analysis procedures are altered slightly and delivered under the guise of competency modelling. Characteristics of bad approaches include ill-defined competencies, a lack of methodological rigour, inappropriate applications of competency profiles, lack of legal defensibility, and a lack of attention to validating the competency models. In other words, good competency modelling applies the techniques and approaches that have been used for years by worker-trait procedures to identify job specifications. Keep in mind, however, the criticisms of Harvey[168,169] that without knowing something about the tasks associated with a position, the inferences of competencies, or KSAOs, in a holistic fashion will produce less reliable data.

A Generic Competency Framework

Recently, Bartram[170] analysed 29 competency studies through a meta-analysis. He presented a model of performance that was based on eight broad competency factors. The eight factors were based on analyses of self-ratings and manager ratings of workplace performance. The "Great Eight" factors aggregate 112 sub-competencies. These eight generic factors and their definitions are presented in Table 4.4, along with likely predictors of those competencies.

TABLE 4.4

Great Eight Competencies and Their Definitions and Likely Predictors

Factor	Competency	Competency Definition	Predictor
1	Leading and deciding	• Takes control and exercises leadership • Initiates action, gives direction, and takes responsibility	Need for power and control, extraversion
2	Supporting and cooperating	• Supports others and shows respect and positive regard for them in social situations • Puts people first, working effectively with individuals and teams, clients, and staff • Behaves consistently with clear personal values that complement those of the organization	Agreeableness
3	Interacting and presenting	• Communicates and networks effectively • Successfully persuades and influences others • Relates to others in a confident, relaxed manner	Extraversion, general mental ability
4	Analyzing and interpreting	• Shows evidence of clear analytical thinking • Gets to the heart of complex problems and issues • Applies own expertise effectively • Quickly takes on new technology • Communicates well in writing	General mental ability, openness to new experiences
5	Creating and conceptualizing	• Works well in situations requiring openness to new ideas and experiences • Seeks out learning opportunities • Handles situations and problems with innovation and creativity • Thinks broadly and strategically • Supports and drives organizational change	Openness to new experiences, general mental ability
6	Organizing and executing	• Plans ahead and works in a systematic and organized way • Follows directions and procedures • Focuses on customer satisfaction and delivers a quality service or product to the agreed standards	Conscientiousness, general mental ability
7	Adapting and coping	• Adapts and responds well to change • Manages pressure effectively and copes well with setbacks	Emotional stability
8	Enterprising and performing	• Focuses on results and achieving personal work objectives • Works best when work is related closely to results and the impact of personal efforts is obvious • Shows an understanding of business, commerce, and finance • Seeks opportunities for self-development and career advancement	Need for achievement, negative agreeableness

Source: D. Bartram. 2005. "The Great Eight Competencies: A Criterion-Centric Approach to Validation," Table 1. *Journal of Applied Psychology* 90, 1185–1203. American Psychological Association. Reprinted with permission.

Much more work must be done toward specifying the predictors of these eight competencies. It is most likely that there will be several different predictors for each competency. Practitioners must be prepared to use a variety of selection tools to capture the essence of work-related behaviours. Bartram[171] argues that practitioners need to remember why we measure different characteristics: performance at work and the outcomes of that performance. In the next chapter, we will examine different models of performance and ways of measuring performance.

Summary

This chapter began with a discussion of job analysis and its relevance to employee recruitment and selection, continued with a discussion of several job analysis methodologies, and ended with an introduction to competency-based models as alternatives to job analysis. As the workplace rapidly changes with the introduction of new technologies and global competition, human resources practitioners will need to combine organizational and job analysis techniques to develop employee selection programs that lead to the selection and hiring of the best job candidates. At the organizational level, objectives for success are defined relative to delivery of products or services to paying customers. At the job level, the analyst describes collections of positions that are similar in their significant duties, which when taken together contribute to process outputs. Job analysts must link job requirements to organization functioning to optimize recruitment and selection systems.

Job analysis is a process of collecting information about jobs and encompasses many methods, which fall into two broad categories: work-oriented and worker-oriented methods. Work-oriented methods result in specific descriptions of work outcomes and tasks performed to accomplish them. Worker-oriented methods produce descriptions of worker traits and characteristics necessary for successful performance. There is no one right way of conducting a job analysis; all methods follow a logical process for defining employment or worker specifications (KSAOs). While job analysis is not a legal requirement for determining KSAOs and selecting employees, the employer must demonstrate job-relatedness of selection criteria if challenged in court.

Regardless of the method used, a good job analysis begins with collection of background information. Gathering job descriptions defined in the NOC or O*NET is a recommended first step. It is also good practice for the analyst to employ a combination of methods, typically beginning with interviews or observations of employees on the job. The resulting information can then be used to construct a task inventory or provide a backdrop for completing structured questionnaires. Employment specifications are generated by identifying the most frequently occurring activities or requirements in interviews and observations or by identifying those items in an inventory or questionnaire receiving the highest ratings of criticality.

A wide variety of techniques are available for analyzing jobs. While some focus primarily on the work that gets done, others focus on generic human behaviours that are relevant to all work. Deciding which of these techniques to use is based on the goal of the analysis, the resources available to the analyst, and the needs of the organization. No one method will be completely acceptable for all selection needs in an organization. Job analysts must themselves be adaptable in the methods they apply. Recruitment and Selection Notebook 4.5 presents a list of job analysis resources available on the Internet.

Organizations that compete in a global environment that is often unpredictable and unstable have to change quickly in order to survive. To meet these demands, some organizations are placing more emphasis on the competencies of individual workers rather than on the specific tasks that those workers will perform. They expect all employees to possess core competencies that are related to the organization's mission or goals, as well as functional and job-specific competencies, which are related to successful performance in a position or job. This emphasis on competencies has taken place in the absence of an agreed-upon definition of what constitutes a "competency" and of an agreed-upon methodology for identifying competencies. In several respects, competency-based systems are similar to worker-trait job analysis methods in providing information about the KSAOs and behaviours needed for successful job performance, but without identifying the tasks that workers are required to do in their jobs.

Competency-based systems must provide information that is valid and meets legal requirements, just as more traditional job analysis methods must. The chapter provides several guidelines that should help in choosing job analysis or competency-based methods to identify KSAOs. In deciding between the two approaches, competency-based models may "speak the language of business" but they provide technically inferior information. HR practitioners must decide which of these factors is most relevant to their situation.

Key Terms

competencies, p. 150

competency dictionary, p. 152

competency profile, p. 154

core competencies, p. 151

functional competencies, p. 152

job, p. 122

job description, p. 122

job family, p. 122

job specification, p. 122

job-specific competencies, p. 152

KSAOs, p. 125

position, p. 122

proficiency level, p. 153

proficiency scale, p. 153

subject-matter experts (SMEs), p. 123

task inventories, p. 140

worker-oriented job analysis, p. 124

worker traits inventories, p. 143

work-oriented job analysis, p. 124

Web Links

The CCHRA website is at **http://www.cchra.ca.**

The National Occupational Classification (NOC) system can be accessed at **http://www5.hrsdc.gc.ca/NOC-CNP/app/index.aspx.**

The DOT is available at **http://www.oalj.dol.gov/libdot.htm.**

O*NET can be accessed at **http://online.onetcenter.org.**

Additional PAQ information can be found at **http://www.paq.com.**

For more information about the CMQ, go to **http://cmqonline.com.**

More information about the WPS can be found at **http://www.shl.com.**

Required Professional Capabilities (RPCs)

RPC 4.1 Provides advice to governing bodies on design and implementation of HR-related issues.
- Trends in HR
- Communication theories, tools, techniques, and processes

- Influence techniques
- Strategic HR management
- Organizational issues and challenges

RPC 4.2 Develops and implements effective job evaluation procedures.
- Principles and methods of job analysis, documentation, and evaluation
- Industry best practices
- The organization's strategy and financial capabilities
- HR policies, procedures, and processes
- Relevant legislation and regulations including collective agreements
- Legal and regulatory environment and reporting requirements regarding all aspects of compensation (including employment and pay equity, federal contractors program)
- Various methods and techniques for determining relative job worth and maintaining internal equity (qualitative and quantitative)
- Methods and procedures to prepare job descriptions
- Methods to identify job requirements and specifications
- Compensation goals

RPC 4.3 Develops an organization or unit design to align with business objectives and environmental factors.
- Concepts of work flow analysis
- Methods of job analysis and job design
- Principles of organizational structure and design
- Principles of re-engineering
- Applicable political, social, and cultural context and environment

RPC 4.4 Contributes to improvements in the organization's structures and work processes.
- Benchmarking and industry best practices
- Existing organization structures and work processes
- Principles of organizational structure and design
- Relationship between task, technology, strategy, environment, and structure
- Understanding how organization structure and work process affect employee motivation and behaviour
- Job and organizational design
- Techniques in managing organizational change

RPC 4.5 Develops people plans that support the organization's strategic directions.
- HR planning concepts and techniques
- Research methods
- Use of business and HR software
- HR functions and activities
- The organization's strategic business plan and the goals of the business unit

RPC 4.6 Analyzes position and competency requirements to establish selection criteria.

- Human Rights legislation
- Employment Equity legislation
- Methods of job analysis
- Recruiting sources and techniques (both internal and external)
- Selection concepts, and assessment techniques (e.g., interviews, tests, and other widely used selection procedures)
- Current and future business plans

Discussion Questions

1. Why is a job analysis essential to the defence of any selection process or selection system?
2. What is the difference between a job analysis and a job evaluation? Can different jobs be equated? Are the "compensable" factors the best way of equating jobs?
3. What is the relationship of a "position" to a "job" and a "job" to a "job family"?
4. Why do some researchers argue that worker trait inventories are not job analysis techniques?
5. What are the major differences between a competency-based selection system and one developed through job analysis?
6. What is a competency? Defend your answer.
7. Discuss why you might not wish to fly in an airplane if the pilot was selected on the basis of only core competencies.
8. What is the difference, or similarity, between a proficiency level and a skill?

Using the Internet

1. Using the NOC and O*NET websites, compare the occupational descriptions, main duties or tasks, and employment requirements listed for human resources managers.

   a. Provide a one-page summary describing the similarities and differences you found between the information contained in the two databases for these jobs.

   b. Provide a brief critique regarding the ease or difficulty of retrieving information from each system.

2. Job analysis is useful for describing many job types, even those that you know well and can describe objectively.

   a. Identify a job that you are familiar with and list the tasks associated with it. Now, using the O*NET website, search the job title and compare the task inventory listed there to the one that you wrote down.

b. How does O*NET function as an SME?

c. What are the benefits to using the O*NET database as opposed to conducting a full-scale job analysis? What are the costs?

Exercises

1. Develop a questionnaire using the online *Position Description Questionnaire Program* located at http://www.hr-guide.com/cgi-local/pdq .html. Use the questionnaire you develop to interview a job incumbent or supervisor. You may choose to interview a parent or sibling about his or her work, a co-worker or supervisor from your workplace, or a classmate. Make careful notes during the interview in the spaces provided. Submit your completed questionnaire for review. (Note: You must identify the position you will be analyzing before using the *Position Description Questionnaire Program*.)

2. Develop an interview that can be used to conduct a job analysis. Select a job for which you can find three or more incumbents willing to provide job analysis data. These may be jobs held by family, friends, or classmates. Conduct the analysis and provide a summary report that includes a list of task statements and describes the requisite abilities for your chosen job.

3. In groups of five, determine the competencies related to teaching. Act as your own subject-matter experts. Keep in mind that you are focusing on teaching only, and not other aspects of a professor's or instructor's duties, such as research or administration activities. Compare the competencies your group has identified with those of the other groups. (Note: This exercise can be carried out for any occupation, but teaching is used since it is an occupation with which all students will have some familiarity. Other occupations, such as doctor or dentist, may be substituted.)

   a. Are the groups using different labels for the same set of behaviours?

   b. Specify the KSAOs that are critical to successful teaching performance.

   c. Develop a competency profile for a superior teacher.

Case

Root of the Problem Landscaping is a small yard-maintenance company that got its start in 2006. The company specializes in small-scale operations, including installing and maintaining flower beds, ponds, hedges, and lawns.

The company employs five site supervisors and approximately 30 grounds-keepers. The owner, Daniel Black, is himself involved in the work performed at most sites and is the sole negotiator of terms with clients.

Originally serving only Halifax, Nova Scotia, the company has grown to accommodate clients as far away as the Moncton, New Brunswick, area. Now in its third season of operation, however, Black has noticed a decline in his company's rate of growth because the gains associated with opportunities afforded by new clients have been offset by the loss of older ones and also because he is having difficulty maintaining lasting employer–employee relationships.

You have been hired on a consulting contract by Root of the Problem Landscaping to investigate why business growth has stalled. You begin by interviewing Black and his site supervisors to establish what, if any, customer feedback they have received, to find out what qualifications both Black and the supervisors have, and to investigate the state of employment satisfaction.

Some negative customer feedback is associated with lack of knowledge and skills on the part of both the supervisors and the groundskeepers. Clients have noted that there have been instances where flowers have been removed that should not have been and weeds have gone unnoticed. In addition, there have been some instances where trees and shrubs were not properly planted and cared for. There has been a lack of attention paid to sun/shade and/or depth considerations, so some plants did not survive the winter. Most negative feedback that has resulted in a lack of repeat business is associated with job sites where Black had little or no involvement in the actual landscaping.

You notice a tendency for Black to attribute customer dissatisfaction to their own personality flaws as opposed to anything his company may be doing wrong. The supervisors can provide little or no additional information because, as instructed by Black, they rarely communicate with clients.

Your interview with Black has revealed that he has extensive knowledge and skills associated with landscaping as a result of a lifetime of hands-on experience. He is also very passionate about his work. You also notice that he doesn't know where his knowledge came from and sometimes thinks specialized knowledge that he has should be common sense to others.

Black's employees have gained limited knowledge of landscaping compared to Black's knowledge, and what they have seems to have been gained by learning on the job with Root of the Problem Landscaping. You have noticed that many of the employees seem to be dissatisfied with their workplace environment, and some report that they find Black to be unprofessional and inconsiderate as an employer. Jobs are often interrupted or delayed because of a lack of proper inventory procedures, resulting in frequent trips to hardware stores, etc.

You notice some employees having difficulty with lifting tasks and the operating of machinery. Some employees are working with two gloves and others with only one or none. Some employees seem to be suffering from aches and pains and you can see bad sunburns on their bodies because of a lack of sunscreen use. Some older and less agile employees seem to be attempting physically demanding tasks while the younger, fitter employees are engaged in less strenuous activity.

You have been observing Root of the Problem Landscaping both when Black is there and when he is not. When Black is present, the job seems to get done, but you notice he often has to go back and work on tasks that were not completed properly by his employees. When fixing a problem, he tends to complain to the employees but does not instruct them on how to do it properly in the future. You observe instances where Black is unduly harsh in his criticisms of the employees and seems to lack some people skills. There is evidence that the employees do not have respect for Black and his business when you observe them "cutting corners" on the job when he is absent.

Discussion Questions

1. If Black had conducted a job analysis prior to employee selection, how might his company have benefited? Include considerations of employer, employees, and clients.

2. Using the O*NET website, if you type "landscaper" into the space provided for the occupational quick search, a list of job titles appears. Select the "first-line supervisors/managers of landscaping" job title and review the knowledge, skills, and abilities listed. Which of these does Black currently possess? Which of these is he lacking? What about the employees?

Endnotes

1. Sparks, C.P. 1988. "Legal Basis for Job Analysis." In S. Gael, ed., *The Job Analysis Handbook for Business, Industry and Government*, Vol. I (pp. 37–47). New York: John Wiley and Sons.

2. Harvey, R.J. 1991. "Job Analysis." In M.D. Dunnette and L.M. Hough, eds., *Handbook of Industrial and Organizational Psychology*, Vol. I (pp. 71–163). Palo Alto, CA: Consulting Psychologists Press, Inc.

3. Ash, R.A. 1988. "Job Analysis in the World of Work." In S. Gael, ed., *The Job Analysis Handbook for Business, Industry and Government*, Vol. I (pp. 3–13). New York: John Wiley and Sons.

4. Levine, E.L., J.N. Thomas, and F. Sistrunk. 1988. "Selecting a Job Analysis Approach." In S. Gael, ed., *The Job Analysis Handbook for Business, Industry and Government*, Vol. I (pp. 339–52). New York: John Wiley and Sons.

5. Uniform Guidelines on Employee Selection Procedures. 1978. *Federal Register* 43: 38290–315.

6. Levine, E.L. 1983. *Everything You Always Wanted to Know About Job Analysis*. Tampa, FL: Mariner Publishing Company, Inc.

7. Sparks, C.P. 1988.

8. Cronshaw, S.F. 1988. "Future Directions for Industrial Psychology in Canada." *Canadian Psychology* 29: 30–43.

9. Latham, G.P., and C. Sue-Chan. 1998. "Selecting Employees in the 21st Century: Predicting the Contribution of I-O Psychology to Canada." *Canadian Psychology* 39: 14–22.

10. Latham. G.P. 2001. "Minimizing Legal Challenges to Hiring and Promotion Decisions": http://www.hrpao.org/ knowledge%5Fcentre/kc%5Fs01210302.asp.

11. Cronshaw, S. F. 1998. "Job Analysis: Changing Nature of Work." *Canadian Psychology* 39: 5–13.
12. Latham, G.P., and C. Sue-Chan. 1998.
13. Ash, R.A. 1988.
14. Levine, E.L., R.A. Ash, and N. Bennett. 1980. "Exploratory Comparative Study of Four Job Analysis Methods." *Journal of Applied Psychology* 65: 524–35.
15. Harvey, R.J. 1991.
16. Dierdorff, E.C., and M.A. Wilson. 2003. "A Meta-Analysis of Job Analysis Reliability." *Journal of Applied Psychology* 88: 635–46.
17. Thompson, D.E., and T.A. Thompson. 1982. "Court Standards for Job Analysis in Test Validation." *Personnel Psychology* 35: 872–73.
18. Peterson, N.G., and P.R. Jeanneret. 2007. "Job Analysis: An Overview and Description of Deductive Methods." In D.L. Whetzel and G.R. Wheaton, eds., *Applied Measurement: Industrial Psychology in Human Resources Management* (pp. 13–56). Mahwah, NJ: Lawrence Erlbaum Associates.
19. Harvey, R.J. 1991.
20. McCormick, E.J. 1979. *Job Analysis: Methods and Applications*. New York: AMACOM.
21. McCormick, E.J., P.R. Jeanneret, and R.C. Mecham. 1972. "A Study of Job Characteristics and Job Dimensions as Based on the Position Analysis Questionnaire (PAQ)." *Journal of Applied Psychology* 56: 347–67.
22. McCormick, E.J., P.R. Jeanneret, and R.C. Mecham. 1972.
23. McCormick, E.J., P.R. Jeanneret, and R.C. Mecham. 1972.
24. Gael, S. 1983. *Job Analysis: A Guide to Assessing Work Activities*. San Francisco, CA: Jossey-Bass Limited.
25. Ghorpade, J.V. 1988. *Job Analysis: A Handbook for the Human Resource Director*. Englewood Cliffs, NJ: Prentice Hall.
26. McCormick, E.J., and P.R. Jeanneret. 1991. "Position Analysis Questionnaire (PAQ)." In S. Gael, ed., *The Job Analysis Handbook for Business, Industry and Government*, Vol. II (pp. 825–42). New York: John Wiley and Sons.
27. McCormick, E.J., P.R. Jeanneret, and R.C. Mecham. 1972.
28. Harvey, R.J. 1991.
29. McCormick, E.J. 1979.
30. McCormick, E.J., and P.R. Jeanneret. 1991.
31. McCormick, E.J., P.R. Jeanneret, and R.C. Mecham. 1972.
32. Harvey, R.J. 1991.
33. Harvey, R.J. 1991.
34. Peterson, N.G., and P.R. Jeanneret. 2007.
35. Peterson, N.G., and P.R. Jeanneret. 2007.
36. McCormick, E.J. 1979.
37. Human Resources and Social Development Canada. *About the NOC:* http://www5.hrsdc.gc.ca/NOC-CNP/app/index.aspx.
38. Employment and Immigration Canada. 1989. *Canadian Classification and Dictionary of Occupations Guide*. Ottawa: Canadian Government Publishing.
39. *Dictionary of Occupational Titles (DOT)*. Washington, DC: U.S. Department of Commerce: http://www.oalj.dol.gov/libdot.htm.
40. Human Resources and Social Development Canada. *About the NOC:* http://www5.hrsdc.gc.ca/NOC-CNP/app/index.aspx.
41. DOL Office of Policy and Research. 2000. *O*NET Project:* http://www.doleta.gov/programs/onet.
42. O*NET Resource Centre. *The O*NET Content Model:* http://www.onetcenter.org/content.html.

43. Peterson, N.G., M.D. Mumford, W.C. Borman, P.R. Jeanneret, E.A. Fleishman, K.Y. Levin, M.A. Campion, M.S. Mayfield, F.P. Morgeson, K. Pearlman, M.K. Kowing, A.R. Lancaster, M.B. Silver, and D.M. Dye. 2001. "Understanding Work Using the Occupational Information Network (O*NET): Implications for practice and research." *Personnel Psychology* 54: 451–91.

44. Gael, S. 1988. "Interviews, Questionnaires, and Checklists." In S. Gael, ed., *The Job Analysis Handbook for Business, Industry and Government*, Vol. I (pp. 391–418). New York: John Wiley and Sons.

45. Cascio, W.F. 1998. *Applied Psychology in Human Resources Management*. 5th ed. Toronto: Prentice Hall Canada.

46. Harvey, R.J. 1991.

47. Gael, S. 1983.

48. Gael, S. 1988.

49. Whetzel, D.L., L.E. Baranowski, J.M. Petro, P.J. Curtin, and J.L. Fisher. 2003. "A Written Structured Interview by Any Other Name Is Still a Selection Instrument." *Applied HRM. Research* 8: 1–16.

50. McCormick, 1979.

51. Fine, S.A., and S.F. Cronshaw. 1999. *Functional Job Analysis: A Foundation for Human Resources Management*. Mahwah, NJ: Lawrence Erlbaum and Associates.

52. Gael, S. 1988.

53. Gatewood, R.D., H.S. Feild, and M. Barrick. 2008. *Human Resources Selection*. Mason, OH: Thomson/South-Western.

54. Levine, E.L. 1983.

55. Gael, S. 1988.

56. Ghorpade, J.V. 1988.

57. Whetzel, D.L., L.E. Baranowski, J.M. Petro, P.J. Curtin, and J.L. Fisher. 2003.

58. Cascio, W.F. 1998.

59. Martinko, M.J. 1988. "Observing the Work." In S. Gael, ed., *The Job Analysis Handbook for Business, Industry and Government*, Vol. I (pp. 419–31). New York: John Wiley and Sons.

60. Martinko, M.J. 1988.

61. Cascio, W.F. 1998.

62. Cascio, W.F. 1998.

63. Martinko, M.J. 1988.

64. McPhail, S.M., P.R. Jeanneret, E.J. McCormick, and R.C. Mecham. 1991. *Position Analysis Questionnaire: Job Analysis Manual*. Rev. ed. Palo Alto, CA: Consulting Psychologists Press, Inc.

65. Martinko, M.J. 1988.

66. Harvey, R.J. 1991.

67. Martinko, M.J. 1988.

68. Martinko, M.J. 1988.

69. Gatewood, R.D., H.S. Feild, and M. Barrick. 2008.

70. Tenopyr, M.L. 1977. "Content-Construct Confusion." *Personnel Psychology* 30: 47–54.

71. McCormick, E.J., P.R. Jeanneret, and R.C. Mecham. 1989. *Position Analysis Questionnaire*. Palo Alto, CA: Consulting Psychologists Press, Inc.

72. Harvey, J.L., L.E. Anderson, L.E Baranowski, and R. Morath. 2007. "Job Analysis: Gathering Job-Specific Information." In D.L. Whetzel and G.R. Wheaton, eds., *Applied Measurement: Industrial Psychology in Human Resources Management* (pp. 57–96). Mahwah, NJ: Lawrence Erlbaum Associates.

73. Fine, S.A., and S.F. Cronshaw. 1999.

74. Fine, S.A., and S.F. Cronshaw. 1999.

75. McCormick, E.J., P.R. Jeanneret, and R.C. Mecham. 1989.

76. McPhail, S.M., P.R. Jeanneret, E.J. McCormick, and R.C. Mecham. 1991.

77. McCormick, E.J., P.R. Jeanneret, and R.C. Mecham. 1989.

78. McCormick, E.J., P.R. Jeanneret, and R.C. Mecham. 1989.

79. McPhail, S.M., P.R. Jeanneret, E.J. McCormick, and R.C. Mecham. 1991.

80. Ash, R.A., and S.L. Edgell. 1975. "A Note on the Readability of the Position Analysis Questionnaire (PAQ)." *Journal of Applied Psychology* 60: 765–66.

81. McPhail, S.M., P.R. Jeanneret, E.J. McCormick, and R.C. Mecham. 1991.

82. McPhail, S.M., P.R. Jeanneret, E.J. McCormick, and R.C. Mecham. 1991.

83. McPhail, S.M., P.R. Jeanneret, E.J. McCormick, and R.C. Mecham. 1991.

84. McCormick, E.J., R.C. Mecham, and P.R. Jeanneret. 1977. *Technical Manual for the Position Analysis Questionnaire (PAQ) (System II)*. Logan, UT: PAQ Services, Inc.

85. Mecham, R.C., E.J. McCormick, and P.R. Jeanneret. 1977. *User's Manual for the Position Analysis Questionnaire (PAQ) (System II)*. Logan, UT: PAQ Services, Inc.

86. McCormick, E.J. 1979.

87. Levine, E.L., R.A. Ash, and N. Bennett. 1980.

88. Gatewood, R.D., H.S. Feild, and M. Barrick. 2008.

89. McCormick, E.J. 1979.

90. Cascio, W.F. 1998.

91. Personnel Systems and Technologies Corporation. 2000. T*he Common-Metric System:* http://cmqonline.com.

92. Harvey, R.J. 1993. *Research Monograph: The Development of the CMQ*. Monograph describing the development and field-testing of the Common-Metric Questionnaire (CMQ): http://www.pstc.com/documents/monograph.pdf.

93. Personnel Systems and Technologies Corporation. 2000.

94. HR-Guide.Com. 2000. *Classification Systems Used as Basis for or Resulting from Job Analyses:* http://www.hr-guide.com/data/ G012.htm.

95. Harvey, R.J. 1993.

96. Harvey, R.J. 1993.

97. SHL Group: http://www.shl.com/SHL/americas/Products/Access_Competencies/Competency _Questionnaires/Competency_Questionnaires_List/WorkProfilingSystem.htm.

98. Christal, R.E., and J.J. Weissmuller. 1988. "Job-Task Inventory Analysis." In S. Gael, ed., *The Job Analysis Handbook for Business, Industry and Government*, Vol. II (pp. 1036–50). New York: John Wiley and Sons.

99. Drauden, G.M. 1988. "Task Inventory Analysis in Industry and the Public Sector." In S. Gael, ed., *The Job Analysis Handbook for Business, Industry and Government*, Vol. II (pp. 1051–71). New York: John Wiley and Sons.

100. Levine, E.L., R.A. Ash, H. Hall, and F. Sistrunk. 1983. "Evaluation of Job Analysis Methods by Experienced Job Analysts." *Academy of Management Journal* 26: 339–48.

101. McCormick, E.J., and P.R. Jeanneret. 1991.

102. Fine, S.A., and S.F. Cronshaw. 1999.

103. Fine, S.A., and S.F. Cronshaw. 1999.

104. Fine, S.A., and S.F. Cronshaw. 1999.

105. Fine, S.A., and S.F. Cronshaw. 1999.

106. Levine, E.L. 1983.

107. Gatewood, R.D., H.S. Feild, and M. Barrick. 2008.

108. Levine, E.L. 1983.

109. Fine, S.A., and S.F. Cronshaw. 1999.

110. Fine, S.A. 1989. *Functional Job Analysis Scales: A Desk Aid*. Milwaukee, WI: Sidney A. Fine Associates.

111. Fine, S.A. and S.F. Cronshaw. 1999.

112. Gatewood, R.D., H.S. Feild, and M. Barrick. 2008.

113. Fine, S.A. 1988. "Functional Job Analysis." In S. Gael, ed., *The Job Analysis Handbook for Business, Industry and Government*, Vol. II (pp. 1019–35). New York: John Wiley and Sons.

114. McCormick, E.J. 1979.

115. Gatewood, R.D., H.S. Feild, and M. Barrick. 2008.

116. Cascio, W.F. 1998.

117. Bownas, D.A., and H.J. Bernardin. 1988. "Critical Incident Technique." In S. Gael, ed., *The Job Analysis Handbook for Business, Industry and Government*, Vol. II (pp. 1120–37). New York: John Wiley and Sons.

118. Harvey, J.L., L.E. Anderson, L.E Baranowski, and R. Morath. 2007.

119. Flanagan, J.C. 1954. "The Critical Incident Technique." *Psychological Bulletin* 51: 327–58.

120. Harvey, R.J. 1991.

121. Harvey, R.J. 1991.

122. Harvey, R.J., and M.A. Wilson. 2000. "Yes Virginia, There Is Objective Reality in Job Analysis." *Journal of Organizational Behavior* 21: 829–54.

123. Sanchez, J.I., and Levine, E.L. 2000. "Accuracy or Consequential Validity: Which Is the Better Standard for Job Analysis Data?" *Journal of Organizational Behavior* 21: 809–18.

124. Lopez, F.M. 1988. "Threshold Traits Analysis System." In S. Gael, ed., *The Job Analysis Handbook for Business, Industry and Government*, Vol. I (pp. 880–901). New York: John Wiley and Sons.

125. Lopez, F.M. 1988.

126. Fleishman, E.A. 1992. *The Fleishman Job Analysis System*. Palo Alto, CA: Consulting Psychologists Press.

127. Fleishman, E.A., and M.D. Mumford. 1988. "Ability Requirement Scales." In S. Gael, ed., *The Job Analysis Handbook for Business, Industry and Government*, Vol. I (pp. 917–35). New York: John Wiley and Sons.

128. Fleishman, E.A., and M.K. Quaintance. 1984. *Taxonomies of Human Performance: The Description of Human Tasks*. Orlando, FL: Academic Press.

129. Fleishman, E.A., and M.D. Mumford. 1988.

130. Fleishman, E.I., and M.E. Reilly. 1992. *Handbook of Human Abilities*. Palo Alto, CA: Consulting Psychologists Press.

131. Primoff, E.S., and L.D. Eyde. 1988. "Job Element Analysis." In S. Gael, ed., *The Job Analysis Handbook for Business, Industry and Government*, Vol. I (pp. 807–24). New York: John Wiley and Sons.

132. Primoff, E.S., and L.D. Eyde. 1988.

133. Levine, E.L., R.A. Ash, H. Hall, and F. Sistrunk. 1983.

134. Levine, E.L., R.A. Ash, H. Hall, and F. Sistrunk. 1983.

135. Mullins, W.C., and W.W. Kimborough. 1988. "Group Composition as a Determinant of Job Analysis Outcomes." *Journal of Applied Psychology* 73: 657–64.

136. Schmitt, N., and S.A. Cohen. 1989. "Internal Analyses of Task Ratings by Job Incumbents." *Journal of Applied Psychology* 74: 96–104.

137. Voskuijl, O.F., and T. van Sliedregt. 2002. "Determinants of Interrater Reliability of Job Analysis: A Meta-Analysis." *European Journal of Psychological Assessment* 18: 52–62.

138. Harvey, R.J., and S.R. Lozada-Larsen. 1988. "Influence of Amount of Job Descriptive Information on Job Analysis Rating Accuracy." *Journal of Applied Psychology* 73: 457–61.

139. Harvey, R.J., and S.R. Lozada-Larsen. 1988.

140. Dierdorff, E.C., and M.A. Wilson. 2003.

141. Harvey, R.J., and S.R. Lozada-Larsen. 1988.

142. Dierdorff, E.C., and M.A. Wilson. 2003.

143. Sanchez, J.I., and Levine, E.L. 2000.

144. Levine, E.L., R.A. Ash, and N. Bennett. 1980.

145. Morgeson, F.P., and M.A. Campion. 2003. "Work design." In W.C. Borman, C. Walter, D.R. Ilgen, and R.J. Klimoski, eds., *Handbook of Psychology: Industrial and Organizational Psychology*, Vol. 12 (pp. 423–52). Hoboken, NJ: John Wiley & Sons Inc.

146. Harvey, R.J., and M.A. Wilson. 2000.

147. Thompson, D.E., and T.A. Thompson. 1982.

148. Peterson, N.G., and Jeanneret, P.R. 2007.

149. Greenbaum, P.J. 1996. "Canada's Hiring Trends: Where Will Canadian Jobs Come From in the Next Millennium?" *HR Today* (July). Ottawa: Canadian Institute of Professional Management.

150. Methot, L.L., and K. Phillips-Grant. 1998. "Technological Advances in the Canadian Workplace: An I-O Perspective." *Canadian Psychology* 39: 133–41.

151. Cascio, W.F. 1998.

152. Boyatzis, R.E. 1982. *The Competent Manager: A Model of Effective Performance*. New York: John Wiley & Sons.

153. Catano, V.M. 2002. "Competency-Based Selection and Performance Systems: Are They Defensible?" Summary. *Canadian Psychology* 43(2a): 145.

154. Reitsma, S.J. 1993. *The Canadian Corporate Response to Globalization*. Report No. 10693. Ottawa: Conference Board of Canada.

155. Mansfield, R.S. 1996. "Building Competency Models." *Human Resource Management* 35: 7–18.

156. Prahalad, C., and G. Hamel. 1990. "The Core Competence of the Corporation." *Harvard Business Review* (May–June): 79–91.

157. Lahti, R.K. 1999. "Identifying and Integrating Individual Level and Organizational Level Core Competencies." *Journal of Business and Psychology* 14: 59–75.

158. Slivinski, L., E. Donoghue, M. Chadwick, F.A. Ducharme, D.W. Gavin, A. Lorimer, R. McSheffrey, J. Miles, and G. Morry. 1996. *The Holistic Competency Profile: A Model*. Ottawa: Staffing Policy and Program Development Directorate, Public Service Commission of Canada.

159. Trainor, N.L. 1997. "Five Levels of Competency." *Canadian HR Reporter* 10: 12–13.

160. Bonder, A. 2003. *A Blueprint for the Future: Competency-Based Management in HRDC*. Unpublished presentation, HRDC Canada.

161. Dubois, D. 1993. *Competency-Based Performance: A Strategy for Organizational Change*. Boston, MA: HRD Press.

162. McClelland, D.C. 1973. "Testing for Competence Rather Than for 'Intelligence.'" *American Psychologist* 28: 1–14.

163. Klein, A.L. 1996. "Validity and Reliability for Competency-Based Systems: Reducing Litigation Risks." *Compensation and Benefits Review* 28: 31–37.

164. Russell, C.J. 2001. "A Longitudinal Study of Top-Level Executive Performance." *Journal of Applied Psychology* 86: 560–73.

165. Shippmann, J.S., R.A. Ash, M. Battista, L. Carr, L.D. Eyde, B. Hesketh, J. Kehoe, K. Pearlman, and E.P. Prien. 2000. "The Practice of Competency Modeling." *Personnel Psychology* 53: 703–40.

166. Shippmann et al. 2000.

167. Pearlman, K. 2002. *Competency Modeling: Mirror into the 21st Century Workplace or Just Smoke?* Paper presented at the 26th Annual IPMAAC Conference on Personnel Assessment, New Orleans.

168. Harvey, R.J. 1991.

169. Harvey, R.J., and M.A. Wilson. 2000.

170. Bartram, D. 2005. "The Great Eight Competencies: A Criterion-Centric Approach to Validation." *Journal of Applied Psychology* 90: 1185–1203.

171. Bartram, D. 2005.

Chapter 5

Recruitment, Selection, and Job Performance

This chapter provides the foundation for the measurement of job-related performance as an integral part of the recruitment and selection process. Job performance is presented as a multidimensional construct that is composed of task, contextual, and counterproductive behaviours. Each of these three job-related behaviours is linked to factors that should be considered during recruitment and selection.

The last part of the chapter discusses measurements of job performance that may be used as criteria in validating selection systems as well as a means of evaluating employees. Although job performance and appraisal may be taught in other courses, we feel that it is important to address these issues in a recruitment and selection context to emphasize that valid performance and appraisal measurements play an essential role in developing a defensible selection system.

After reading this chapter you should:

- appreciate the important role played by job performance in selection and assessment;
- know and be able to discuss how organizational goals influence both individual and group performance;
- be able to define the difference between task, contextual, and counterproductive work behaviours;
- be able to describe the importance of developing and using scientifically sound measurements of job performance in selection and assessment;
- understand the relationship between individual performance measurements, criteria, and performance dimensions related to a job;
- appreciate the technical aspects of measuring job performance;
- be able to discuss the strengths and weaknesses of different types of performance rating systems; and
- be able to define the characteristics that a performance appraisal system should have in place to satisfy human rights concerns.

WHO IS THE BEST PERSON FOR THE JOB?

Psychologists Frank Schmidt and John Hunter debunked the belief that it was not possible to use generalizable links to predict individual success in more than one job or workplace. Details are provided in the following American Psychological Association article about their research.

Findings

Psychological tests and assessments have been used in personnel selection since World War I, but until the 1980s, it was assumed that the determinants of success varied extensively from job to job and from organization to organization. In particular, it was widely believed that tests that were highly effective predictors of success in one job or one organization might turn out to be useless as predictors of success in other similar jobs or organizations, and that it would be necessary to build selection tests one job and one organization at a time. Several decades of research by psychologists Frank Schmidt, Ph.D., and John Hunter, Ph.D., showed that this assumption was incorrect, and that it was possible to establish clear, simple, and generalizable links between broad individual difference variables, such as general cognitive ability or personality traits, and success in a wide range of jobs.

Significance

Two broad individual difference variables, general cognitive ability and conscientiousness, appear to be relevant to performance in virtually every job studied. Measuring these two variables alone, it is often possible to account for 20–30 percent of the variance in job performance, with even higher predictability in more complex jobs. It is often possible to improve prediction somewhat by adding job-specific predictors, but the most important predictors of performance are often the most universal (psychologist Malcolm Ree and colleagues* suggest that the influence of general cognitive abilities is so broad and so strong that there is little to be gained by studying specific abilities that would seem relevant on the basis of an examination of job content). As a result of this research, our understanding of how individual differences influence job performance has moved from a model in which every job and every organization was thought to be unique (meaning that whatever you learned from studying performance in one job would have little relevance to understanding performance in other jobs) towards a model in which broad theoretical statements about the relationships between characteristics of people and characteristics of jobs interacting can be proposed and tested.

For example, Schmidt and Hunter's research suggests that general cognitive ability influences job performance largely through its role in the acquisition and use of information about how to do one's job. Individuals with higher levels of cognitive ability acquire new information more easily and more quickly, and are able to use that information more effectively. Drawing from this literature, psychologist Kevin Murphy, Ph.D., suggested that cognitive ability should be more important in complex jobs, when individuals are new to the job, and when there are changes in the workplace that require workers to learn new ways of performing their jobs. All of these predictions have been tested and supported.

Practical Application

Research linking broad concepts such as cognitive ability and conscientiousness to performance in a wide range of jobs has transformed the practice of personnel selection. At one time, personnel selection seemed to require custom test development for every new job, organization, etc., and it often appeared that these tests did a relatively poor job predicting job performance. Psychological research has led to better approaches to selection that provide an excellent starting point for predicting future success (applicants who are high on cognitive ability and conscientiousness are likely to be relatively successful in a wide array of jobs).

Cognitive ability tests are widely used in both military and civilian sectors, but their use is often controversial because of ethnic group differences in ability test scores. Personality inventories typically do not show these ethnic group differences, and the combination of cognitive tests and measurements of broad personality factors can serve to both increase the validity of selection decisions and reduce, somewhat, the group differences in selection outcomes that would be produced using cognitive tests alone.

* For the sources of references cited in this article, go to the American Psychological Association website at http://www.psychologymatters.org/personnelselect.html.

Source: American Psychological Association. http://psychologymatters.apa.org/personnelselect.html. Reprinted with permission.

Selection and job performance are inextricably linked to one another. We started out this book by presenting an overview of a human resources system in Figure 1.1 (see page 4). We presented recruitment and selection as influenced by several variables, including the mission, vision, and values of the organization. Recruitment and selection carried out properly, in conjunction with other organizational factors, leads to personnel who are competent, committed, and effective. We presented performance management as a feedback loop that allowed the organization to monitor the quality of employees who were being recruited and selected.

We continued this discussion in Chapter 2 by showing the necessity of evaluating performance as part of validating a selection system and the specific KSAOs that will be used to select employees. All HR staff personnel must have an understanding of the role that performance plays in developing recruitment and selection strategies, unless they are unconcerned about a total systems failure. Job performance and performance management are complex topics in and of themselves.

Our goal in this chapter is to introduce the current thinking on performance measurement so that those working in HR may appreciate the need to measure performance as part of a recruitment and selection system. Selection is not simply interviewing and testing employees. The HR person must know that the tools being used are appropriate and valid. This means the HR staff must be aware of any inadequacies in the methods they are using to assess employee performance. Performance measurement goes beyond providing employees with an evaluation of their performance.

To manage performance, organizations and companies must take job performance and its measurement seriously. Performance measurement is a means to emphasize and reinforce an organization's core values in addition to identifying performance differences between employees. Performance measurement is used to transform companies into results-oriented organizations. It provides a means of identifying employees who need improvement and development.[1] Measuring performance is easier said than done. The organization, or its human resources manager, must decide what performance to measure and the level of performance needed to attain organizational excellence.

Job performance is behaviour—the observable things people do—that is relevant to accomplishing the goals of an organization. As we saw in Chapter 4, rarely if ever do jobs involve the performance of only one specific behaviour. Also, individuals may perform at different levels of proficiency across job-related tasks or competencies (see Chapter 4). Measurements of job performance that attempt to capture these differences are called **criteria**.[2] They are the performance standards for judging success or failure on the job. Criteria also provide guidance on the standards that must be met by someone placed into a job. A lack of standards may lead to the selection of inappropriate job candidates.

Choosing a criterion or performance measure may be rather complex. Suppose you are a personnel selection officer in the Canadian Forces and are placed in charge of selecting military engineering officers. You are responsible for recruiting and selecting men and women who will perform successfully in places such as Afghanistan, Rwanda, Bosnia, and Somalia. Do you recruit and select people on the basis of their job-related technical skills, or

 5.1

Job performance
Behaviour (the observable things people do) that is relevant to accomplishing the goals of an organization.

Criteria
Measurements of job performance that attempt to capture individual differences among employees with respect to job-related behaviours.

do you also consider core competencies such as leadership, courage, loyalty, selflessness, and self-discipline? What, then, constitutes successful performance by a military engineer? What if someone is judged to be a success as a leader but a failure in the technical aspects of engineering, or vice versa? Are any of the competencies on which we select people more important than others? And what about self-discipline—how does that enter into the equation?

Job performance is a complex, multidimensional construct.[3,4] We can break job behaviour into three subcategories: task performance, contextual performance, and counterproductive performance.[5] Task performance includes the direct production of goods and services and direct contribution to the efficient functioning of the organization and is, perhaps, closest to traditional definitions of *job performance*.[6] Task performance behaviours contribute to the core activities of an organization and include producing goods, selling merchandise, acquiring inventory, and managing and administering the enterprise.[7] Contextual performance is closely related to the notion of organizational citizenship behaviour.[8] Generally, contextual performance has included both interpersonal job performance and job dedication.[9,10] Contextual performance contributes to the culture and climate of the organization; it is the context in which the organization's core activities take place.[11]

Counterproductive behaviour is in some sense the opposite of organizational citizenship, although the two are clearly distinct constructs.[12,13] **Counterproductive behaviours** include both deviance and aggression.[14] The fundamental issue that an organization must address when it develops an integrated recruitment and selection system is which aspect or aspects of performance should drive recruitment and selection. How an organization answers this question determines whom the organization will recruit and hire. We will consider each of these three types of job behaviours with respect to how they are measured and how they influence recruitment and selection.

Counterproductive behaviours

Voluntary behaviours that violate significant organizational norms and in so doing threaten the well-being of an organization, its members, or both.

Job Performance as a Multidimensional Concept

In the early part of the 20th century, job performance meant the performance of a set of tasks that were specifically related to a job. Job performance was synonymous with task performance. Over the past 30 years, definitions of job performance have broadened to include all activities or behaviours that may affect, positively or negatively, organizational effectiveness.[15,16] Not only should we consider individual outputs for a specific set of job tasks, but also the contributions of those outputs to meeting the goals of the organization. Job performance depends on the specific job requirements as they relate to the goals of the organization and the value that the organization places on contextual factors such as teamwork and cooperation.[17,18]

Recently, a number of job performance models have argued for a multidimensional conceptualization of job performance that includes nontask behaviours that may be important to job success. Figure 5.1 presents an

FIGURE 5.1

A Job Performance Domain for an Airplane Pilot

Performance Domain—Air Pilot					
Job Task Behaviours			Contextual Behaviours		Counterproductive Behaviours
Take-off and Landing	Navigation	Managing Air Crew	Mentors Junior Pilots	Promotes Safety Procedures	Self-Discipline

Job performance domain

The set of job performance dimensions (i.e., behaviours) that is relevant to the goals of the organization, or the unit, in which a person works.

example of a possible **job performance domain** for an airplane pilot that is composed of task, contextual, and counterproductive behaviours. Job performance is behaviour (i.e., the observable things people do) that is related to accomplishing the goals of the organization, or the unit, in which a person works. The goals pursued by an organization are value judgments on the part of those empowered to make them. Goals are defined for employees who hold specific positions within the organization. Individual performance must contribute to achieving the organizational goals. The activities or behaviours needed to accomplish goals may vary considerably from job to job, or across levels in organizations. It becomes a matter of expert judgment whether particular actions or behaviours are relevant for particular goals. Performance is not the consequence or result of action; it is the action itself.[19]

Performance Dimensions

Performance dimensions

Sets of related behaviours that are derived from an organization's goals and linked to successful job performance.

Job behaviours can be grouped into categories, called **performance dimensions**. Performance dimensions are sets of related behaviours that are derived from an organization's goals and linked to successful job performance. In Figure 5.1, a pilot must be capable of performing many job task behaviours. Some of these behaviours are related to taking off and landing an aircraft, another set of task behaviours might be related to navigating the plane from one location to another, while a third set of task behaviours are needed to manage and direct the flight crew under the pilot's command.

The pilot performs all of these task behaviours within a specific organizational context that emphasizes senior pilots serving as mentors for their juniors and promoting safety rules and regulations. All of the pilot's behaviours directed at these last two dimensions may not be strictly necessary to flying an airplane, but they are valued job behaviours. The performance domain also contains negative, counterproductive behaviours that interfere with job performance. Successful employees are expected not to exhibit counterproductive behaviours. The pilot is expected to maintain self-discipline by showing up for work on time and not drinking alcohol while on flight duty.

A Multidimensional Model of Job Performance

One of the most significant developments has been the attempt by John Campbell and his associates to specify a theory of work performance.[20] Campbell proposes that the behaviours that people are expected to exhibit as part of their jobs appear to fall into eight job performance dimensions, which together specify the job performance domain. These eight performance dimensions, as identified by Campbell,[21] are as follows:

1. *Job-specific task proficiency* reflects the degree to which an individual can perform technical tasks that make up the content of the job. A petroleum engineer and an accountant must perform different behaviours as part of their specific jobs. Within jobs, individuals may vary in their level of competence. One engineer may be more technically proficient than another, just as one accountant may be more technically proficient than some other accountants.

2. *Non-job-specific task proficiency* reflects the degree to which individuals can perform tasks or behaviours that are not specific to any one job. Both the engineer and accountant may have to have a good understanding of the business environment in which their company operates.

3. *Written and oral communication task proficiency* is the degree to which an individual can write or speak, independent of the correctness of the subject matter. Both the engineer and accountant make oral reports to people they deal with on the job; both also make written reports on the work they perform.

4. *Demonstrating effort* reflects the degree to which individuals are committed to performing all job tasks, to working at a high level of intensity, and to working under adverse conditions. How willing is the engineer or accountant to work overtime to complete a project? Do they begin their workdays earlier than expected? Can they be relied on to give the same level of effort day in and day out? Do they show initiative?

5. *Maintaining personal discipline* characterizes the extent to which negative behaviours are avoided. Does the engineer or accountant drink on the job? Do they follow the appropriate laws, regulations, or codes that govern their professions? Do they show up for scheduled assignments?

6. *Facilitating peer and team performance* is the degree to which an individual supports co-workers, helps them with job problems, and keeps them working as a team to achieve their goals. Is the engineer or accountant available to give the others a helping hand? Does either

offer new trainees the benefit of their experience? Do they keep their colleagues focused on completing the work team's goals?

7. *Supervision/leadership* includes behaviours that are directed at influencing the performance of subordinates through interpersonal means. Do the engineer and accountant set goals and performance standards for people they direct? Do they use whatever influence is at their disposal, including the authority to reward and punish, to shape the behaviour of subordinates?

8. *Management/administration* includes all other performance behaviours involved in management that are distinct from supervision. Do the engineer and accountant contact clients and arrange appointments? Do they schedule work in the most efficient manner? Do they complete all of the paperwork related to a project?

Job-specific task proficiency, demonstrating effort, and maintaining personal discipline are major performance components of every job;[22] however, not all eight dimensions have to be present in every job. Few, if any, management skills are required by an assembly-line worker in an auto plant; on the other hand, the requirements and attributes of the CIBC's customer service representative (see Chapter 4, Recruitment and Selection Today 4.1, on page 123) fit nicely into this framework. The pattern of differences in these eight dimensions can be used to classify jobs and is consistent with the job classification schemes used by the U.S. *Dictionary of Occupational Titles*, the *Canadian Classification Dictionary of Occupations*, and the *National Occupational Classification* system.

In Table 5.1, we map Campbell's eight job dimensions onto the three types of job behaviour we have presented here. Note that the three components that

TABLE 5.1

The Relationship of Campbell's Eight Job Dimensions to Task, Contextual, and Counterproductive Behaviour

JOB TASK BEHAVIOURS

- Job-specific behaviours
- Non-job-specific behaviours
- Leadership/supervision
- Management/administration

CONTEXTUAL BEHAVIOURS

- Communication proficiency
- Demonstrating effort
- Facilitating peer and team performance

COUNTERPRODUCTIVE BEHAVIOURS

- Maintaining personal discipline

Campbell states are present in each job—job task proficiency, demonstrating effort, and maintaining discipline—correspond respectively to task, contextual, and counterproductive behaviours. Arguably, each of these three types of job behaviours is present in every job. It remains for each employer to determine which of the three is most important in terms of recruitment and selection and other organizational outcomes.

What determines individual differences on these eight job performance components? That is, why does one pilot perform more efficiently than another? Campbell and his associates[23] showed that these job dimensions are influenced by three factors: declarative knowledge, procedural knowledge and skill, and motivation. *Declarative knowledge* is knowledge about facts and things including knowledge of rules, regulations, and goals. It is the technical knowledge necessary to do a job properly. *Procedural knowledge and skill* are attained when declarative knowledge, knowing what to do, is combined with knowing how to do it. One pilot knows all about landing procedures but lacks the appropriate skills to perform a smooth landing every time. Procedural knowledge and skill include cognitive, psychomotor, physical, perceptual, interpersonal, and self-management skills. *Motivation* is defined in terms of choice to perform, level of effort, and persistence of effort.

Job performance is some combination of these three factors; performance cannot occur unless there is both a choice to perform at some level and at least a minimal amount of knowledge and skill. In later chapters on selection, we will see how different selection tools are related to the most important dimensions in an effort to predict those job applicants who will be the most effective job performers.

Contextual Performance

Campbell's job dimensions specify what people do as part of their jobs. Borman and Motowidlo[24] make the point that work performance extends beyond performing tasks that are related to their jobs. Employees are called on to perform activities that are not part of their formal job duties; they are, however, part of the context in which those job tasks are performed. **Contextual performance** involves activities or behaviours that are not part of a worker's formal job description but that remain important for organizational effectiveness.

While job performance is closely related to underlying knowledge, skills, and abilities, contextual performance supports the organizational, social, and psychological environment in which the job is performed. Contextual activities are not related to a specific job or role but extend to all jobs in an organization. Contextual performance often reflects organizational values. For example, many Canadian companies actively support worthwhile causes as part of their desire to be good corporate citizens and may expect their employees to contribute time or money to these projects. The United Way campaign is one fund-raising activity that enjoys strong corporate support. Volunteer fund-raising activities on the part of employees are not related to specific jobs but may advance the goals of the organization.

Contextual performance

The activities or behaviours that are not part of a worker's formal job description but that remain important for organizational effectiveness.

Contextual performance appears to fall into five major categories:[25]

1. Persisting with enthusiasm and extra effort as necessary to complete one's own task activities successfully.
2. Volunteering to carry out task activities that are not formally part of one's own job.
3. Helping and cooperating with others.
4. Following organizational rules and procedures.
5. Endorsing, supporting, and defending organizational objectives.

Contextual performance is closely related to organizational citizenship behaviour (OCB).[26,27] OCB is individual behaviour that is discretionary, that is not directly recognized by a formal reward system, and that, overall, promotes the effective functioning of the organization. The difference between contextual performance and OCB is that OCB is considered to be beyond the role requirements of a job and, thus, not rewarded. Contextual performance, on the other hand, is not required to perform specific job tasks, but it is behaviour, much like core competencies, that an organization wishes all of its employees to exhibit. Contextual performance is regarded as part of an employee's role in an organization and is often rewarded through pay increases or promotion.[28]

In many ways, the contextual performance dimensions appear to be extensions of the eight job performance dimensions included in Campbell's model.[29] As we showed in Table 5.1, several of Campbell's job dimensions can be deemed to be aspects of contextual performance. For example, "persisting with enthusiasm and extra effort" appears to be related to "demonstrating effort"; "volunteering to carry out tasks not part of one's job" and "helping and cooperating with others" to "facilitating peer and team performance"; "following organizational rules and procedures" to "maintaining personal discipline"; and "endorsing, supporting, and defending organizational objectives" to "supervision/leadership."

The primary difference is that Campbell's job dimensions relate to specific jobs, while contextual performance may relate to broader organizational roles taken on by an employee without reference to specific job-related tasks. However, this distinction is becoming increasingly blurred. Recently, Hoffman and his colleagues[30] did an extensive review of the relationship of organizational citizenship behaviour in relation to job task behaviour. They concluded that the various components of OCB could be mapped onto a single dimension that was distinct from, but strongly related to, task performance. They also concluded that because the OCB factor correlated with several job attitudes, such as job satisfaction and commitment, OCBs should be considered when assessing job performance.

Contextual performance activities may represent important criteria for jobs in many organizations because of their relationship to organizational effectiveness. Contextual performance dimensions may not all have the same degree of relevance or importance across organizations. Organizations are likely to emphasize those that are most compatible with their values and goals. Contextual performance is not a substitute for job performance; it represents *additional* factors that may be considered in developing personnel selection criteria.

Contextual performance by itself does not get the job done; in evaluating staff, managers place more emphasis on task performance than on contextual performance.[31] In fact, Rotundo and Sackett[32] found that managers placed the least weight on contextual or citizenship behaviours. Managers from 15 different organizations that were geographically dispersed across the United States fell into one of three categories when asked to rate the three types of job behaviour. The first group rated task performance the highest over the other two, the second group felt that counterproductive behaviours were the most important, and the third group of managers rated task and counterproductive behaviours higher than citizenship (contextual) behaviours. The managers were a diverse group that came from five different occupational groups.

An increasing number of North American companies, such as Apple Computer, GE, Honeywell, and 3M, assess how well employees fit the organization in addition to how well they can do the job.[33] Organizational fit between an employee's organizational culture and the desired environment predicts an employee's contextual performance.[34] In Chapter 6, we will review person–organization fit in the context of recruitment.

Counterproductive Work Behaviours

A complete conception of the performance domain must include behaviours that have both positive and negative impacts on organizational effectiveness. Robinson and Bennett define *counterproductive work behaviours* as "voluntary behaviours that violate significant organizational norms and in so doing threaten the well-being of an organization, its members or both."[35] Examples of these behaviours include lying, theft, property damage, violence, engaging in risky behaviours, harassment of co-workers, and sabotage, among others.[36] The causes for these different types of counterproductive behaviours vary. Abuse and sabotage appear to be most strongly related to anger and stress, while withdrawal appears to be associated with boredom and being upset.[37] Withdrawal is discussed below.

Counterproductive work behaviours (CWBs) are intentional acts by employees intended to harm their organization or the people in it. CWBs included acts of both physical and psychological violence.[38] Estimates of the prevalence of physical and psychological violence in the workplace vary dramatically. A survey of 2508 representative wage and salary workers in the U.S. work force found that 6 percent (nearly 7 million) workers in the United States had experienced nonfatal, physical violence in the workplace, with 41 percent reporting that they had experienced psychological harassment.[39] Bureau of Labor Statistics data showed that U.S. workplace homicides accounted for 631 deaths in 2003.[40] Counterproductive behaviours lead, ultimately, to decreases in productivity through loss of efficiency and effectiveness. In the United States, the Workplace Violence Research Institute estimates that workplace violence costs around US$35 billion per year (http://www.workviolence.com).

Perhaps the most negative work behaviour is withdrawal from the job. This may take the form of complete withdrawal through resignation but also includes partial withdrawal through tardiness, absenteeism, leaving work early, and taking extended breaks. Hanisch[41,42] proposed that frustrated employees who cannot engage in withdrawal behaviours may lash out at their employer through counterproductive behaviours such as theft, sabotage, or violence.

Predicting Task, Contextual, and Counterproductive Job Performance

Figure 5.2 uses Campbell's model to integrate task, contextual, and counterproductive behaviours. Declarative knowledge influences all three behaviours, as do motivation, procedural knowledge, and skill. Their influences may not be the same, however, on each type of performance. We might expect

FIGURE 5.2

The Antecedents and Outcomes of Task, Contextual, and Counterproductive Job Behaviours

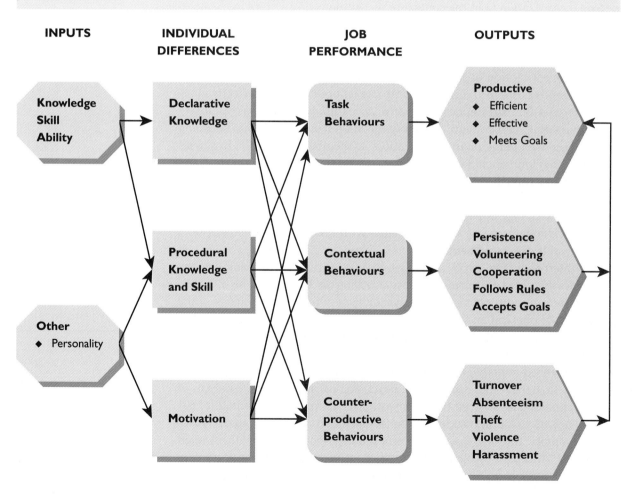

that technical knowledge and skill would have more of an impact on task performance while procedural knowledge and skills, for example, with respect to interpersonal behaviour, would have more of an influence on the contextual factors of facilitating peer and team performance.

The likelihood that productivity is the end result of an interaction of all three factors poses a challenge for selection. In fact, the relationship may be very complex; for example, contextual behaviour may be moderated by the nature of the task being performed.[43] In highly technical and complex occupations (e.g., air traffic controller), the role of contextual performance in organizational effectiveness may be less critical than task performance, but counterproductive behaviours on the part of the controller could have devastating consequences.

In most cases, contextual behaviours should lead to increases in productivity that are primarily influenced by task behaviour, while counterproductive behaviours detract from it. How individuals differ in terms of declarative knowledge, procedural knowledge and skill, and motivation may determine how they ultimately perform in the workplace. These individual differences reflect differences in knowledge, skills, abilities, and other factors (e.g., personality). This suggests that any selection system should consider measuring all three of these determinants of performance and finding KSAOs that are related to each performance dimension.

In Chapter 4, we saw that many job analysis methods produced a list of job-related behaviours or tasks that comprise a job. For each task, the job analyst can infer, with the help of SMEs, the KSAOs associated with successful performance of the given task or competency. In later chapters, we will discuss various procedures, including employment tests and interviews, that are used to predict performance on tasks or competencies. Predicting task or competency behaviour is a fairly well-established procedure that makes use of accepted assessment techniques. One position we will explore is the role of cognitive ability in predicting task performance. Cognitive ability appears to be the best predictor of task performance across all job situations,[44,45] although it may carry with it some adverse impact on protected groups.[46]

The expansion of the job performance domain to include contextual performance and counterproductive behaviours has important implications for personnel selection. Contextual performance, counterproductive behaviours, and task performance may have different sets of predictors. Contextual performance appears to be linked to different aspects of personality and motivation. When opportunities for advancement within an organization are limited, employees may perform contextual acts because they are conscientious; however, when there are opportunities for advancement, employees may engage in contextual acts because they are ambitious.[47]

Assessment of personality improves the ability to predict contextual performance among sales and service representatives.[48] The increasing emphasis on organizational citizenship behaviour and contextual performance as performance dimensions may require the addition of personality measures as part of the selection process. We also saw in Chapter 4, Table 4.4, that several predictors of the eight great competencies were personality factors. We will return to the use of personality in selection in Chapter 8. You may want to read that chapter now to gain a better understanding of some of the issues related to these types of measurements.

Counterproductive behaviours are often taken into account by managers when assessing job performance.[49–51] Regrettably, our understanding of the causes of deviant organizational behaviour is very limited even though these behaviours may have significant costs for individuals, the organization, and society. One theory argues that counterproductive behaviours are caused by work stress and can be triggered by negative emotions such as boredom, frustration, anxiety, and lack of self-control; others propose that differences in personality may be linked to counterproductive behaviours.[52]

In particular, different aspects of personality appear to predict violence and aggression and drug and alcohol use, along with honesty or integrity.[53] In Chapter 8, we will review integrity and honesty tests that have been developed to predict whether a job applicant or employee is likely to engage in specific types of counterproductive behaviour, including those based on personality. When such tests are used, the employer tends to value elimination of the counterproductive behaviour over task performance on the part of the applicant and will screen out the applicant on the basis of the honesty test, regardless of how proficient the applicant might be with respect to task performance. Honesty testing is a very controversial procedure.

Measuring Performance

The usefulness of selection measures is assessed by how well they predict performance. Typically, a supervisor's rating of the employee's performance is used for this purpose. Hard measurements of performance, such as dollar sales, units produced, and absenteeism data, are less frequently available. Performance measurements need to capture the contributions workers make as they move from one assignment to another, and from team to team. Frequently, these measurements will have to come from multiple sources (e.g., peers, customers, supervisors).

In validating selection measurements, we will need to decide whether we want to predict one or more performance dimensions or some overall composite measure of performance. Are we interested in task, contextual, or counterproductive job behaviours? If we assess several competency or performance dimensions, then we need to determine which aspects of performance contribute most to the success of the organization and what weights should be given to the different dimensions.[54,55] If we want an overall performance measure, then we must find a method for combining the performance data that we obtain from different sources.

Most efforts directed at improving selection systems have focused on the measurement of job-related KSAOs or competencies. Until recently, relatively less thought has been given to improving the measurement of job performance. Most organizations rely on criterion-related validity studies to defend the appropriateness of their selection systems before human rights and other tribunals. No matter how accurately the organization measures KSAOs or competencies, the criterion-related validity will still be low without improvement in performance measurement. There remains a need to use valid criterion measures and to develop a better understanding of what constitutes job performance.[56] Fortunately, more companies and human resources managers are beginning to appreciate the linkage between selection and performance measurement.[57] Performance measurements, however, are still too often chosen because the pressure of getting things done leads to choosing the most convenient measurement at hand and hoping it will turn out all right.

The performance measurement or criterion problem is really one of defining what is meant by performance and choosing a measurement or set of measurements that best capture the essence of that complex job-related performance. Without a clear understanding of what constitutes job performance in a specific organizational position (i.e., task, contextual, or counterproductive behaviour), the best measurement systems will never be able to effectively measure performance at work. We need first to define job performance before we can attempt to assess it.[58] One implication of a multidimensional conception of job performance is that any performance management system should include measures of task, contextual, and counterproductive behaviours.

Performance measurement plays an important role in developing strategies for effective recruitment and selection. Rather than simply choosing a measure and hoping it works, the first step is to specify job performance in terms of measurable behaviours; the next step is to find valid measures of those behaviours. The criterion or performance measure must be a valid indicator of job performance as determined by job and organizational analysis. There is an important difference in contemporary approaches to establishing criteria. Desired job-related behaviours and outcomes are those that secure organizational goals. Increasingly, companies are looking for a fit between the person and the organization; this search for a person–organization fit often drives the company's recruitment process. (We will discuss the person–organization fit in more detail in Chapter 6.)

We discussed the need to validate selection measures to establish that they are meeting legal requirements. We also need to establish validity to assure ourselves that the people we are hiring will be the "best" or most "productive." Improvements in selection procedures can lead to substantial increases in productivity. For example, in sales occupations, replacement of invalid selection procedures with valid procedures produces an average increase in sales of $60 000 per employee for each year that the employee stays on the job.[59] To evaluate the effectiveness of selection systems, we must find a way to measure those task, contextual, and counterproductive job behaviours we identify as important for job success. Criterion measurement plays an essential part in recruitment and selection. Measuring performance is easier said than done; criterion measurement is a complex and technical process.

Effective Performance Measures

 5.2

Once job analysis has identified the major performance dimensions, the next step is to measure employee performance on those dimensions. How will we measure job task proficiency, supervision, or helping and cooperating with others? We can think of these job dimensions as labels that are constructed to describe different aspects of job performance. Before we can measure any job dimension, we have to define that dimension in terms of specific, measurable activities or behaviours. For example, supervision includes giving orders to subordinates, accomplishing organizational goals, and teaching employees the proper way to do a job, among many other things. One person may be better at "giving orders to subordinates" than "teaching subordinates"; our view on that person's supervisory performance will depend on which of these behaviours we include in our measure of supervisory performance. Smith[60] established general guidelines to help identify effective and appropriate performance measurements, based on relevancy, reliability, and practicality.

Relevancy

Relevancy requires that a criterion measure be a valid measure of the performance dimension in question. Suppose we develop a measure of a sales associate's performance based on an overall rating assigned by a supervisor. This measure might be relevant to sales performance in that it captures behaviours related to service orientation, communication, and interpersonal relations. The measure may be deficient in not measuring competencies such as achievement, business orientation, self-discipline, and organizing, which may also be related to success in sales. Additionally, the measure may be influenced by problem solving, learning, and management competencies that are not critical for success in this particular job. As a criterion measure, a supervisor's rating may be contaminated in that it is measuring things other than the sales associate's performance. **Criterion relevance** is the degree to which the criterion measure captures behaviours or competencies that constitute job performance. **Criterion deficiency** refers to those job performance behaviours or competencies that are not measured by the criterion. **Criterion contamination** is the degree to which the criterion measure is influenced by, or measures, behaviours or competencies that are not part of job performance. These three aspects of criterion measurement are illustrated in Table 5.2.

Reliability

Reliability involves agreement between different evaluations, at different periods of time, and with different, although apparently similar, measures; that is, the criterion measure must meet scientific and professional standards of reliability. Reliability is the degree to which observed scores are free from random measurement errors (i.e., the dependability or stability of the measurement). Criterion or performance measures are subject to the same errors as any other kind of measurement. There is no such thing as error-free criterion measurement; some criteria, however, are more reliable than others. Reliable criterion measures will tend to produce similar scores when the same behaviour is measured on more than one occasion. The reliability of any cri-

Criterion relevance

The degree to which the criterion measure captures behaviours or competencies that constitute job performance.

Criterion deficiency

Refers to those job performance behaviours or competencies that are not measured by the criterion.

Criterion contamination

The degree to which the criterion measure is influenced by, or measures, behaviours or competencies that are not part of job performance.

TABLE 5.2

Illustration of Criterion Relevancy for Performance in a Sales Associate Position

Unmeasured Competencies	Relevant to Sales Performance	**CRITERION DEFICIENCY** Achievement Business Orientation Self-Management Organizing
Measured Competencies	Relevant to Sales Performance	**CRITERION RELEVANCE** Service Orientation Communication Interpersonal Relations
	Not Related to Sales Performance	**CRITERION CONTAMINATION** Problem Solving Learning Management

terion measure must be established, as part of its use in a personnel selection system, through the procedures discussed in Chapter 2.

Practicality

Practicality means that the criterion measure must be available, plausible, and acceptable to organizational decision makers. The supervisor's rating of the sales associate's performance must mean something to those responsible for evaluating the sales associate. It must also be a number that can readily be obtained from the supervisor with little cost in time or money. It should also be a plausible indicator of individual performance. That is, the criterion measure must have meaning and credibility for those who will use the measurement in making decisions.

There is a danger of being seduced by practicality and choosing criteria that, while readily available, do not meet standards of validity and reliability. These two requirements cannot be traded off in favour of practicality. For example, the supervisor may be tempted to use the number of units sold in a month to evaluate the sales associate's performance. This is a very practical measure; however, it may be neither reliable nor valid. The sales volume may be affected by a number of factors outside of the sales associate's control, such as the state of the economy, sales campaigns by the competition, and so forth. As well, the records of the number of sales attributed to the associate may not be accurate or entered consistently into a database. That is, while the

Practicality

The degree to which a criterion measure is available, plausible, and acceptable to organizational decision makers.

monthly sales volume may be an easy-to-use, practical measure, it may not meet acceptable standards for reliability and validity. Criteria must be practical as well as being reliable and valid measures of job performance.

Developing Criterion Measures

Several issues must be considered as part of the process of developing a criterion or a set of criterion measures. Criteria are "dynamic, multidimensional, situation-specific, and serve multiple functions."[61] Although progress has been made on these issues over the last 10 years, there are still gaps between research and practice when it comes to designing a selection system.[62] The resolution of these issues influences which measures are selected as criteria and when measurements are made.

Multiple, Global, or Composite Criteria

The Ultimate Criterion

The first issue is one that has generated a great deal of controversy over the years—namely, how criteria should be measured. In large part, this controversy arises through misunderstanding of the job performance domain. At one time, criterion research was dominated by a concern to find the ultimate criterion for a given job. The **ultimate criterion** is the concept of a single criterion measure that could reflect overall job success. The idea of an ultimate criterion implies that job performance is a unitary concept, that one measure could be found that assessed a person's overall job performance.

Even Thorndike,[63] who developed the idea, recognized that an ultimate criterion would rarely, if ever, be found in practice: "A really complete ultimate criterion is multiple and complex in almost every case. Such a criterion is ultimate in the sense that we cannot look beyond it for any higher or further standard in terms of which to judge the outcomes of a particular personnel program." Unfortunately, many who followed Thorndike did not heed his advice and wasted considerable time trying to find ultimate measures of job performance. It is unlikely that you will ever find one measure that will tell you everything about performance in a specific job, considering the complexity of measuring task, contextual, and counterproductive behaviours.

Global versus Multiple Criteria

Job analysis procedures used by most organizations are inductive: The job analyst infers the dimensions that make up the overall job performance domain from specific empirical data. Other approaches deduce performance dimensions from organizational goals with or without the help of job analysis data.[64] As we saw in Chapter 4, many organizations are turning directly to deriving competencies without going through a traditional job analysis procedure and building competency profiles. If there is a need, then, to compare the relative performance of employees in the same occupational group, is it appropriate to

Ultimate criterion

The concept that a single criterion measure reflects overall job success.

combine the scores on each dimension into an overall composite score, or should a new criterion be developed to measure overall, global performance?

Many practitioners, heavily influenced by the controversy surrounding the search for the ultimate criterion, would answer "no." They would emphasize that the multidimensionality of job performance requires the use of multiple, independent criteria to measure performance. They would say that independent criteria, reflecting independent performance dimensions, should not be combined into an overall composite measurement of job performance. Combining *navigational skills, managing air crew,* and *self-discipline* to understand a pilot's performance would be, to use Smith's[65] analogy, like adding toothpicks to olives to understand a martini. Furthermore, they would not believe it was appropriate to obtain a separate, overall measure of performance because such a global criterion measure would lose the rich information contained in the multiple performance dimensions.

Our discussion of task, contextual, and counterproductive job performance supports this position. Nonetheless, there is still support for use of a global criterion measure, particularly if there is a need to make a global, overall assessment: "If you need to solve a very specific problem (e.g., too many customer complaints about product quality), then a more specific criterion is needed. If there is more than one specific problem, then more than one specific criterion is called for. But in most situations, a global measure will serve quite well."[66]

The difficulty is in identifying those situations where the global measure is best suited. In practice, the best strategy will be to collect multiple criteria data to measure important, diverse dimensions. In Chapter 10, we will review different methods of decision making—how to make use of the data we collect from our personnel selection system. As part of decision making, we can require that job candidates meet minimum requirements on each of the multiple criteria that we used in the selection process. Multiple data can always be combined into a composite measurement.

Composite versus Multiple Criteria

We have emphasized the multidimensionality of job performance and the requirement of assessing those different dimensions through multiple criterion measures. Nonetheless, there may be times when a single, all-inclusive criterion measure is needed in making employment decisions and no global criterion measure is available. Not everyone agrees that it is inappropriate to combine individual criterion measures into a single composite.[67] There seems to be general agreement on how to proceed. Since performance measurements will be used for a variety of purposes, it makes sense to collect each criterion measurement separately or in its multiple, uncollapsed form. That information can be combined to compute a composite criterion as needed for different administrative decisions.

The weights assigned to the separate performance measures in creating a composite measure should reflect the priority of the different performance dimensions as set by the organization's goals. Implicit in this position is a recognition that the priority of organizational goals may change over time. If separate performance measures have been maintained, it is a relatively straightforward exercise to recompute the composite to reflect the new organizational, and economic, realities. Caution should be taken; creating a composite averages performance across all of the performance dimensions. Performance on one dimension may be so critical that deficiencies cannot be made up by excellent performance on other dimensions. In this case, a composite criterion is inappropriate.

Consistency of Job Performance

In discussing reliability as a requirement for criterion measurement, we assumed that the employee's behaviour was more or less consistent at the time the observations were made. Of course, people's job performance may change over time. This is a substantially different issue from the random, daily fluctuations in performance. Changing performance levels may affect criterion measurements.

Training versus Job Proficiency Criteria

Do you obtain the same criterion results if you measure performance very soon after a person is placed in a job as opposed to several months or years later? Generally, early performance in a job involves informal learning or systematic training. Workers are continually evaluated during training or probationary periods. Performance measurements taken during early training will be very different from those taken later when workers are more proficient. Criterion measurements taken during training periods may produce validity coefficients that overestimate the selection system's ability to predict later job proficiency.[68] Nonetheless, the convenience of short-term performance measures, rather than their relevance to long-term performance, dictates their use in many situations as criteria. Training criteria remain very popular performance measures.

Typical versus Maximum Job Performance

Maximum performance occurs in situations where individuals are aware that they are being observed or evaluated, or where they are under instructions to do their best. Their performance is measured over a short time period when their attention remains focused on performing at their highest level. Typical performance is the opposite of maximum performance, in which individuals are not aware that their performance is being observed and evaluated, in which they are not consciously attempting to perform to the best of their ability, and in which performance is monitored over an extended period of time.

There is very little relationship between performance under typical and maximum performance situations, for either inexperienced or experienced workers. Performance measurements taken during training are measurements of maximum performance and may be inappropriate if a selection system is to predict long-term typical performance. Motivational factors play a larger role in typical, everyday performance. In maximum performance, motivation is probably at high levels for everyone; in typical performance situations in the actual work setting, motivation is likely to differ among individuals.[69,70]

The use of typical or maximal criteria has important implications for selection decisions. First, each of these types of criteria seemed to have different relationships with predictors. Marcus and colleagues,[71] using supervisory ratings as data for typical performance and assessment centre evaluations for maximal data, found that cognitive abilities were more strongly correlated with maximal performance than with typical performance, while personality variables were more closely related to typical performance. The obvious implication is that predictors based on cognitive ability will have a greater degree of validity when used with maximal criteria, while personality measurements may be more useful in predicting typical criteria.

Dynamic versus Stable Criteria

Employee performance appears to decrease over time, regardless of the employee's experience or ability. These changes may reflect the effects of many personal, situational, and temporal factors. Early job performance may be limited only by ability and experience, since every new employee is motivated to do well, while later job performance may be influenced more by motivation.[72,73]

Developing Criterion Measures: Summary

Early job performance, which may occur under more rigorous scrutiny than later performance, is ability-driven and is a better estimate of what individuals can maximally achieve, rather than how they will typically perform on the job. Performance will decrease over time, generally reflecting changes in motivation. Training criteria are acceptable performance measures for estimating maximum performance, but will overestimate typical performance. To be safe, several performance measures should be taken at different times when validating selection systems.

Job Performance Criteria and Performance Appraisal

It is very unlikely that any two workers doing the same job will perform at exactly the same level. Factors such as knowledge, skill, and motivation are likely to cause variation in job performance within and between workers. As we saw in our discussion of competencies in Chapter 4, the essence of a competency profile is the specification of the proficiency level required on each competency to successfully perform a job, and then being able to assess those employee proficiencies in a reliable and valid manner. Two employees doing exactly the same job, although they meet the minimum proficiency required

R P C 5.3

for a job, may not perform at the same level. Most likely, any two pilots would not perform exactly at the same level on all critical job dimensions; nor is it likely that any one engineer would perform at the same level on all dimensions that applied to the engineer's work. Every employee has strengths and weaknesses.

How do we actually measure these differences in performance between employees on the relevant job dimensions? How do we determine that they meet the performance requirements for a position? How do we determine areas in which an employee needs training and development? What do we actually use as the criterion data necessary for validating selection systems? The remainder of this chapter reviews some of the more common ways of measuring job-related performance.

Performance Appraisal

 5.4

If you have previously studied performance appraisal, or performance management, you will recognize many of the methods presented in the following sections. Performance appraisals or evaluations often provide the answers to the above questions. Despite their importance, performance appraisals tend to be resisted by both employees and their supervisors. Many managers responsible for completing annual performance evaluations express considerable discomfort with the process and as a result may give uniformly high ratings to all employees that they are evaluating.[74] Employees, who are on the receiving end of the appraisal, express dissatisfaction with both the decisions made as a result of performance assessment and the process of performance assessment.[75]

Bowman[76] offered the somewhat tongue-in-cheek definition of performance appraisal as something "given by someone who does not want to give it to someone who does not want to get it." One reason that performance evaluation is stressful for both employees and their supervisors is that most performance measures are based on a judgmental process subject to many sources of error and bias. Some performance measures are better than others and have a better chance of being accepted by workers and their supervisors, as well as by legal tribunals. Performance appraisals, and the perceived fairness of performance appraisal systems, are playing a greater role in legal challenges to human resources decisions.[77] Performance evaluations are more likely to be challenged if they and the evaluation process are perceived to be unfair.

In an attempt to produce a more favourable attitude toward the use of performance appraisals, many organizations limit the use of appraisals to developmental or formative uses and prevent their use in administrative situations such as promotions or pay increases. That is, they are intended to help the employee grow as an employee. The reasoning behind this is that raters, when they know that the appraisals will be used only for feedback to the employee, will be more honest in their evaluations. Research, however, shows otherwise. The different uses of performance appraisals do not improve rating accuracy. In fact, limiting their use may lead the rater to believe that the organization does not take the appraisal system seriously and so may not be motivated to take the appraisal process seriously.[78]

Types of Performance Measures

There are several different ways of grouping criteria that have been used to measure job performance. The broad categories used in the following presentation are based on traditional grouping methods.[79]

Objective Measures: Production, Sales, and Personnel Data

Objective production, sales, and personnel data, also known as *hard criteria* or *ancillary measures,* are often used as performance measurements. These data are produced by the workers in doing their jobs, or are related to observable characteristics or behaviours of the workers. They are called **objective performance measures** because they represent the actual number of things produced or number of sales made. The assigned number does not depend on the subjective judgment of another person. The number of audits completed by an accountant is known for any given period; the quality of those audits may be reflected in the number of errors detected by a higher-level review. In this case, both the quantity and quality (the number that are error-free) of audits are objective measurements related to the actual job performance of the accountant. If the quality of the audit rested on the judgment or perception of the accountant's supervisor that the audits met acceptable, professional standards, quality would then constitute a subjective measure. Production or sales measurements generally involve quantity, quality, and trainability (which is the amount of time needed to reach a specific performance level). Recruitment and Selection Today 5.1 lists examples of production and sales criteria.

Objective performance measures

Production, sales, and personnel data used in assessing individual job performance.

Personnel Data

Using personnel data as criteria involves the use of objective measures that are not directly related to actual production or sales but that convey information about workplace behaviour. Criteria derived from personnel data tend to be global in nature and may tell more about contextual performance than the worker's actual performance on specific job dimensions. Personnel data may be better measures of organizational behaviours than of job performance. Absence data are routinely collected and stored in each worker's file and are often used as criteria. Absence measures likely tell more about employee rule-following behaviour than how well they perform their jobs (i.e., when they do show up for work); but, as a form of counterproductive behaviour, absence or tardiness data may be criteria that managers value highly.

In addition to absence data, information on job tenure, rate of advancement or promotion within the organization, salary history, and accident

Examples of Objective Measures of Job Performance*

Production or Sales Measures

Quantity

- Number of items produced
- Volume of sales
- Time to completion
- Number of calls processed each day
- Average size of sales orders
- Words typed per minute
- Speed of production

Quality

- Number of errors
- Dollar cost of errors
- Number of customer complaints
- Number of spelling and grammatical mistakes
- Degree of deviation from a standard
- Number of cancelled contracts

Trainability

- Time to reach standard
- Rate of increase in production
- Rate of sales growth

Personnel Data

Absenteeism

- Number of sick days used
- Number of unscheduled days off work
- Number of times late for work

Tenure

- Length of time in job
- Voluntary turnover rate
- Involuntary turnover rate

Rate of Advancement

- Number of promotions
- Percentage increase in salary
- Length of time to first promotion

Accidents

- Number of accidents
- Cost of accidents
- Number of days lost to accidents
- Number of safety violations

*These are measures that have been used over time; inclusion in this list does not necessarily mean that these are the best objective measurements of individual or group performance.

history have been used as criteria. Recruitment and Selection Today 5.1 also presents examples of personnel data used as criteria. Criteria should be selected because they are reliable, relevant, and practical. While most objective measures may meet the test of practicality, they may not necessarily be reliable or relevant. While quantity may be measured with a fair degree of accuracy, the consistency of the information may depend on the time of the measurement or the duration over which it was taken.

Contamination and Deficiency of Objective Measures

Objective measures may be influenced by factors beyond a worker's control. Recruitment and Selection Today 5.2 presents some of the constraints on individual performance. Insurance companies use the total dollar value of insurance sold in a month to measure an agent's performance. One agent may sell more insurance in a month than another because one's territory includes a

Some Potential Constraints on Individual Performance

Lack of supplies/materials	High stress levels in workplace
Lack of needed staff	Change in policies, procedures, and/or regulations
Absenteeism of critical personnel	Peer pressure to limit production
Failure to receive material/assemblies from other units	Poor communication of goals and objectives
Poor working conditions	Lack of necessary equipment
Inadequate physical facilities	Inadequate training of new hires
Poor leadership	Too many inexperienced staff in unit
Excessive bureaucracy	Lack of support staff
Unpredictable workloads	Budget restrictions/cost-saving measures
Overextended staff	

compact city district populated by upper-income professionals, while the other's includes a sparsely populated rural county of low-income farm workers. Both the opportunity to make sales and the amount of insurance sold may have more to do with the sales territory than the sales ability of either of the agents. The total dollar value of insurance sold may not measure how safely the agents drove to their territories, the oral communication skills needed to explain the complex insurance policies, or how accurately they completed the necessary paperwork to initiate the policy and to bill for its premiums.

Successful performance of these other job dimensions may have as much to do with the long-term success of the insurance company as the dollar sales volume. Using personnel data, such as absenteeism, turnover, rate of advancement, salary history, and accidents, as criteria leaves an organization open to criticism of criterion deficiency or contamination with respect to task performance. Some of these measures, such as those of absenteeism, turnover, and accidents, however, may be good indicators of counterproductive behaviours. It is important for HR professionals to understand what job behaviour they intend a criterion to measure. The practicality and convenience of objective data do not justify their use. Before these types of data can be used as criteria, their reliability and validity as measures of job performance dimensions must be established.

Subjective Measures: Rating Systems

It is relatively easier to find objective measures for jobs that involve people in the actual production of goods and services. As a person's job becomes removed from actual production or sales work, it becomes more difficult to associate objective measures to the employee's performance. Upper-level jobs in an organization may involve more administration, leadership, team building, and decision making—dimensions that are not easily measured in objective terms. The issues of criterion relevance, deficiency, and contamination become even more serious. How should an organization evaluate the performance of an accountant's supervisor? Most likely, the supervisor's own manager, peers, and perhaps even subordinates will be asked to rate, or judge, the supervisor's performance on relevant job dimensions. Without a doubt, performance ratings are the most frequently used criterion measure.

Evidence suggests that, when used as performance criteria, subjective performance measures may provide better estimates of a selection system's validity than objective measures. Farrell and Hakstian[80] compared the effectiveness of typical selection measures (cognitive ability, interviews, personality, etc.) in predicting either objective or subjective criteria that had been used to evaluate performance in sales occupations. They used meta-analytic procedures to integrate results across 59 empirical performance appraisal studies. On average, a combination of predictors (e.g., a cognitive ability test and a biographical inventory, or a job knowledge test and a personality test) led to higher validity coefficients when subjective criteria ($r = 0.65$) were used as performance measures compared with objective criteria ($r = 0.51$). The choice of criteria may lead an HR manager to come to different conclusions about the effectiveness of a selection system.

Rating Errors

A rating system is simply a procedure that is used to quantify an opinion or judgment. A rating system must satisfy all the measurement requirements we discussed in Chapter 2. As with any measurement system, ratings are open to error. Leniency, severity, and central tendency errors are types of errors made by judges who restrict their ratings to only one part of the rating scale. Some raters may assign only extreme ratings; some may give only very positive ratings (leniency errors), while others give only very negative ones (severity errors); others may judge all performance to be average and not assign extreme ratings in either direction (central tendency errors).

Most students can identify teachers who have a reputation for giving mostly A or F grades (extreme ratings) or those who pass everyone with a C. Leniency errors are common in performance appraisal, as many supervisors try to keep on good terms with their employees or think that a higher-than-deserved rating might motivate them to do better. If the employee's compensation is linked to the performance appraisal, the supervisor may not wish to be the person responsible for denying the raise. Supervisors may also believe that high ratings for everyone in their work group will reflect positively on their managerial skills.[81]

Halo errors occur when the rating a judge first assigned to a particularly important dimension influences the judge's ratings over several job dimensions. For example, after assigning a very high rating on "leadership," a rater may feel that the same score is warranted for "effort," particularly since the judge may have little experience with the employee on this dimension. Halo errors are often the result of the following type of thinking: "If I rated her excellent on leadership, she must be excellent on effort as well. Besides, if I give her a low rating on effort, or say I have no basis for judging her effort, my boss, who will review this assessment, may think I'm not doing my job. So, I

Subjective performance measures

Ratings or rankings made by supervisors, peers, or others that are used in assessing individual job performance.

Leniency errors

Rating errors in which a rater tends to assign only positive ratings, regardless of the true level of performance.

Severity errors

Rating errors in which a rater tends to assign only negative ratings, regardless of the true level of performance.

Central tendency errors

Rating errors in which a rater tends to assign only average ratings, regardless of the true level of performance.

Halo errors

Occur when a rater uses a rating assigned to one job dimension to rate several other dimensions, regardless of the true level of performance on those dimensions.

know she's excellent on leadership; she's probably excellent on effort. I'll give her an excellent rating on effort." A similar effect can occur when a manager's negative perception or observation of the employee on one job dimension or competency spills over to another dimension. That is, the "black mark" on one dimension colours the whole appraisal. These types of rating errors introduce the personal biases of the raters into the measurement process and reduce the likelihood that the assigned ratings are appropriate measures of the performance under review.

What impact do rating errors have on the accuracy of a performance rating? Surprisingly, the answer may be "not much." Rating errors are largely unrelated to direct measures of the accuracy of the ratings. Using a meta-analysis approach, Murphy and Balzer[82] computed accuracy scores and measurements of the three common types of error discussed above. There was little, if any, correlation between the two sets of measurements. The relationships that did emerge, particularly for halo errors, were paradoxical in that rater errors appeared to contribute to rating accuracy! Along these lines, Nathan and Tippins[83] demonstrated that the validity of selection tests increased when more halo errors seemed to be present in performance ratings; this was contrary to common assumptions that the presence of rating error would lead to decreases in validity.

Murphy and Cleveland[84] suggest that this "paradox" is not really a paradox but rather a reflection of the inadequate ways in which rating errors have been operationalized. As well, they make the point that raters may have goals that influence the ratings they assign to employees. More recent work suggests that the rater's attitudes about both the organization and the performance appraisal system, along with their own personality, are related to their rating behaviour. These factors may influence tendencies to give inappropriately high or low ratings.[85]

Reducing Rating Errors

Over the years, many different aspects of both raters and rating systems have been examined in an attempt to reduce rating errors. While rating errors can never be eliminated, they can be reduced by (1) defining the performance domain; (2) adopting a well-constructed rating system; and (3) training the raters in using the rating system. Reducing rating errors may have unintended effects. The procedures used to reduce rating errors may also reduce rating accuracy. Trained raters appear to be so focused on avoiding rating errors that they stop using whatever strategy they were using before training. Rather than devising strategies to reduce rating errors, a better approach may be to develop programs to increase rating accuracy.[86] Frame-of-reference training is one method of improving rating accuracy, but before discussing rater training programs, we will briefly review different types of rating systems.

Relative Rating Systems

Relative rating systems, also known as *comparative rating systems*, for obvious reasons, compare the overall performance of one employee with that of others

Relative rating systems
Compare the overall performance of one employee with that of others to establish a rank order of employee performance.

to establish a rank order of performance. With the exception of the relative percentile method, these techniques provide global assessments, as the rater compares overall performance rather than performance on each job dimension. The use of a single overall rating avoids the problems with rating errors over the set of dimensions. The tradeoff for avoiding these errors is the loss of performance information on specific job dimensions. As we discussed previously, global criteria may not always be the most appropriate to use.

There are three traditional relative rating systems—rank order, paired comparison, and forced distribution methods—as well as the more recent relative percentile method.

Rank Order

In rank ordering, the rater arranges the employees in order of their perceived overall performance level. For a group of 10 workers, the best performer would be assigned rank 1 and the worst, rank 10. There are two problems with this procedure. Raters may have a good idea of who are the best and worst performers but often have difficulty discriminating—that is, assigning ranks—among the remaining employees. Second, because the system is relative, it does not tell whether any or all of the workers are performing above or below acceptable levels. In other words, an employee may be rated the third-best accountant but, in absolute terms, may not meet acceptable performance standards.

Paired Comparisons

In paired comparisons, the rater compares the overall performance of each worker with that of every other worker who must be evaluated. In rating four employees, their supervisor compares every possible pair of workers: Employee 1 versus Employee 2, Employee 1 versus Employee 3, and so on. The workers are then ranked on the basis of the number of times they were selected as the top-rated performer over all of the comparisons.

One problem with the procedure is the large number of comparisons that often have to be made. With four workers, a supervisor must make six comparisons; for 10 workers, the number of paired comparisons increases to 45. Making a large number of paired comparisons becomes tedious, leading some raters to rush through the procedure. While this technique does guarantee that all employees being rated are given due consideration, it still does not provide information on absolute performance levels.

Forced Distribution

The forced distribution system attempts to provide absolute information within a relative rating context. Rather than rank workers from top to bottom, the system sets up a limited number of categories that are tied to performance standards. For example, the rater may be given a scale with the categories excellent, above average, average, below average, and poor to evaluate each worker overall or on specific job dimensions. So far, this procedure resembles that used by an absolute graphic rating scale procedure; the difference is that the rater is forced to place a predetermined number or percentage of workers into each of the rating categories.

Generally, raters assign workers to categories on the basis of a normal frequency distribution, which assumes most workers to be average with only a few judged excellent or poor. This technique is quite good at controlling leniency, central tendency, and severity errors; however, it does not reduce halo effects. Often raters oppose systems like this, which require them to label a given percentage of their subordinates into extreme categories, on the grounds that this distorts the true state of affairs. They may feel that the number of poor or excellent performers working for them does not match the quota the system has allocated to those categories. Forced systems work best when only gross discriminations are required among workers.

Relative Percentile Method

The relative percentile method (RPM) is a new and improved comparative rating system.[87] This system overcomes one of the major shortcomings of other comparative rating systems by allowing raters to compare individuals on job performance dimensions that have been derived through job analytic procedures. The system can also be used to make overall performance ratings. The RPM requires raters to use a 101-point scale (0 to 100), with a score of 50 representing *average* performance. For each performance dimension, or for the global comparison, a rater uses the 101-point scale to assess each ratee relative to one another. The rating scale anchors each rater's comparisons to an absolute standard and, thus, allows meaningful comparisons among ratings obtained from different raters. The RPM appears to be a very promising relative rating procedure. It appears to produce validity estimates and levels of accuracy that surpass those obtained with some absolute rating scales.[88,89]

Absolute Rating Systems

Absolute rating systems compare the performance of one worker with an absolute standard of performance. These methods provide either an overall assessment of performance or assessments on specific job dimensions. A rating scale is developed for each dimension that is to be evaluated. Over the years, a variety of formats have been developed to assess performance in absolute terms. While these rating scales may have important qualitative differences, they usually lead to the same administrative decisions. One rating system may provide more effective feedback, while supervisors are more likely to favour another and support its use. The ratings assigned to employees by either rating system are likely to be highly correlated, once measurement errors are taken into account. The particular ratings scale format may not make much difference in the relative order of scores derived for each employee. However, different rating formats may not have the same degree of validity or meet relevant legal requirements.[90] A review of several of the more popular rating formats follows.

Absolute rating systems

Compare the performance of one worker with an absolute standard of performance; can be used to assess performance on one dimension or to provide an overall assessment.

Graphic Rating Scales

Graphic rating scales can be produced to assess an employee on any job dimension. The scale usually consists of the name of the job component or dimension, a brief definition of the dimension, a scale with equal intervals between the numbers placed on the scale, verbal labels or anchors attached to the numerical scale, and instructions for making a response. Figure 5.3 presents samples of graphic rating scales that have been designed to rate effort. The presence or absence of elements such as a definition, instructions on how to make a response, and the subjectivity of labels attached to different numerical values on the scale help to distinguish between the relative goodness of the scales. The poor rating scale presented in Figure 5.3(a) does not provide the rater with a definition of effort. Each rater may define this term in a different way or have a different understanding of the characteristic, leaving open the possibility that different raters are not assessing the same thing. The better example in Figure 5.3(b) provides a definition of the performance dimension and instructions on how to make a response.

FIGURE 5.3

Examples of Graphic Rating Scales

a)   A Poor Rating Scale: The scale does not provide a definition of the trait or characteristic being measured, and it provides little if any instruction on how to make a response. The labels for values "1" and "5" are subjective and open to interpretation by different raters. Does the "X" represent a value of "2," "3," or somewhere in between?

Effort

Low   High

| 1 | 2 | X | 3 | 4 | 5 |

b)   A Better Rating Scale: The scale offers a definition of "Effort" and provides instructions on how to rate, but the value labels are still subjective and open to different interpretations by different raters.

EFFORT – Consider the amount of energy brought to the job. Personal convenience is secondary to completing work in a professional manner. Circle the number that best reflects the employee's effort on the job.				
1	2	③	4	5
Poor	Below Average	Average	Above Average	Excellent

There is no guarantee that the raters will not use other interpretations of effort in making their ratings (or that this is the best way to define effort), but at least they have had to consider the standardized definition. The poor example contains very general anchors at each end of the scale but provides no information on what constitutes high or low effort. Again each rater may use a different reference point to characterize the effort of the person being rated. The anchors in the better example provide benchmarks to help the rater to understand the differences between various degrees of effort; however, different raters may still have a different understanding of what constitutes "average" behaviour or any of the other types specified on the scale. Finally, the poor example allows the rater such latitude in making a response that the person in charge of reviewing the completed assessments may have difficulty knowing what rating was given. In the poor example, does the X indicate a rating of 2 or 3? In the better example, there is no doubt about which response was intended.

Trait-Based Rating Scales

Trait-based rating scales are graphic rating scales that ask the rater to focus on specific characteristics of the person being reviewed. The rater judges the extent to which a worker possesses traits such as dependability, leadership, friendliness, and so on. In most cases, the traits are either very poorly defined or extremely vague. Furthermore, the traits under assessment are rarely chosen because they are job-related. The failure to demonstrate the relevance of the chosen traits to job dimensions is a fatal flaw, which makes such appraisal systems next to worthless. Nonetheless, trait-based performance measurement systems continue to be used. Partly, this is due to the ease with which such a scale can be concocted and the apparent cost savings of using one general performance measure across all jobs that are being evaluated. Organizations that use such systems in decision making run the risk of justifying the validity of such performance ratings in costly litigation before various tribunals.

Checklists

Checklists present the rater with a list of statements that may describe either work behaviours or personality traits. Sometimes the list is restricted to behavioural statements only. The rater goes through the list and identifies those statements that apply to the employee being evaluated. With behavioural checklists, the rater is describing what the worker does. Since some behaviours may be more valuable to an organization, weights can be assigned to the different statements. Generally, the weights are developed through a job analysis or by people who are very familiar with the job. The rating for an individual is obtained by adding the weights of those statements that have been identified for that person. This approach is known as the *method of summated ratings*.

A second checklist method is the forced-choice procedure, in which a rater is given several statements and is asked to select one that most or least typifies the employee. By forcing the rater to choose from among a group of all positive or all negative statements, the format tends to reduce leniency, central tendency, and severity errors. On the whole, raters detest using the forced-choice procedure, particularly when they believe that several statements apply equally well to the worker.

A further limitation of the forced-choice procedure is its failure to provide an easily understood performance measurement that can be interpreted in terms of job dimensions. One purpose of any evaluation is to provide workers with feedback on their performance, to identify strengths and weaknesses. This is difficult to do if either the rater or the person being measured does not readily understand the performance measurement.

Critical Incident Methods

Critical incident methods require raters to observe the job behaviour of an employee and to record those behaviours displayed by the worker that are critical to effective or ineffective performance. The technique forces the rater to concentrate on the behaviour, not traits or characteristics, of the worker. The critical incidents are identified through interviews with people knowledgeable about the specific job. The critical incidents are then given to an observer who checks off those that are displayed by the worker while performing the job. This method is essentially the same as a summated checklist method.

Recruitment and Selection Today 5.3 contains a series of critical incidents for a security dispatcher related to the job dimensions of job-specific task proficiency, demonstration of effort, and personal discipline. These critical incidents were collected as part of a job analysis for the security dispatcher position at a Canadian university. The dispatcher's supervisor would mark off those behaviours present in the dispatcher's job performance.

One drawback of this type of system is its very nature of focusing on specific behaviours. Workers may perform those activities that can be easily recorded or documented. It may also lead to supervisors micromanaging

Recruitment and Selection Today 5.3

Critical Incidents for a Security Dispatcher

Job-Specific Task Proficiency

- Properly secures lost and found articles
- Controls visitor access to buildings
- Monitors multiple surveillance devices

Demonstration of Effort

- Reports early for shift to hear debriefing from preceding shift

- Remains at post until relieved
- Volunteers for overtime when needed

Personal Discipline

- Follows safety procedures
- Does not take unauthorized breaks
- Maintains proper demeanour during stressful situations

employees by looking for employee mistakes rather than accomplishments, since employees are assumed to be competent.[91] This is like a parent noticing only a child's mistakes and never complimenting good behaviour.

Mixed Standard Rating Scales

Mixed standard rating scales are variations on critical incident checklists. Three critical incidents, similar to those presented in Recruitment and Selection Today 5.3, are selected for each job dimension being reviewed. The items represent excellent, average, and poor performance, respectively. The items are randomly presented on a checklist without labelling the job dimensions, and raters are asked to indicate whether the employee's behaviour is better, worse, or the same as the behaviour presented in the statement. A score is assigned to each job dimension on the basis of the pattern of ratings for each dimension. For example, if a security dispatcher was judged to perform better than that given in the statement, he or she would be given a score of 7, while a dispatcher judged to perform worse on all three statements would be given a score of 1. Other weights would be assigned to the remaining possible patterns.

While the mixed standard rating scale does reduce rating errors, it tends to introduce another: Many raters make logically inconsistent responses to the set of three statements within each dimension. The time needed to construct mixed standard rating scales, coupled with the inconsistent responding of those who use it, argues against its wide-scale use. It can be very useful, however, in those organizations willing to spend time and money improving the scales to eliminate the inconsistent responding.

Behaviourally Anchored Rating Scales

Behaviourally anchored rating scales (BARS) use empirically derived critical incident job behaviours to anchor the values placed on a rating scale. Although this procedure sounds simple, it is actually quite complex and time-consuming. To construct a BARS scale, a group of workers most familiar with the job use a critical incident procedure to identify specific job dimensions. A second, independent group generates behavioural examples of excellent, average, and poor performance on each dimension identified by the first group. A third group is given the dimensions identified by the first group and the behavioural items generated by the second and asked to match items to dimensions. This step is called *retranslation* and represents an attempt to establish the content validity of the items. A fourth group then takes the valid items and assigns each a value from the measurement scale that represents its level of performance. Items with low variability in assigned scale values are retained for the scale. The resultant scale is tested and refined before being adopted for general use.[92]

Figure 5.4 shows the resulting behaviourally anchored rating scale developed for the competency of communication. The definition for communication is identical to the one given in Chapter 4, Figure 4.7, on page 154. Since the competency has already been identified, the first step in the procedure

FIGURE 5.4

Behavioural Anchors Used to Assess Communication Competency

Communication involves communicating ideas and information orally and/or in writing in a way that ensures the messages are easily understood by others; listening to and understanding the comments and questions of others; marketing key points effectively to a target audience; and speaking and writing in a logical, well-ordered way. Circle the rating that best represents the degree of communication exhibited by the employee you are rating.

5 — Excellent

Makes interesting and informative presentations; explains complicated points in different ways to ensure understanding; written reports are concise, understandable, and lead to defendable and convincing conclusions; uses e-mail effectively and replies in a timely fashion; actively listens to others to ensure understanding of what they said; uses humour to capture and maintain attention of audience; makes effective use of nonverbal communication; provides feedback to ensure comprehension of messages that are received.

4 — Above Average

Written and oral communication exhibit excellent grammar and vocabulary; maintains eye contact with audience during oral presentations; speaks with confidence and authority; written and oral presentations are well organized; gets to the point in oral presentations; accurately summarizes positions taken during group discussions; listens carefully to opinions and concerns of others.

③ — Average

Performs well in a structured setting; actively participates in group discussions; presents unpopular positions in a nonthreatening manner and acknowledges opposing points of view; asks for feedback from audience; makes presentations in a clear and concise manner.

2 — Below Average

Oral presentations are factual and accurate but lose the attention of the audience; presentations are overly long; leaves out important points in both oral and written reports; e-mail messages are confusing; performs other tasks while listening to people and does not hear what was said; needs to repeat points to get them across to an audience; does not make an effort to obtain feedback from audience.

1 — Unsatisfactory

Has difficulty establishing a relationship with the audience; uses inappropriate grammar and vocabulary; responds inappropriately to what has been said; does not make an effort to ensure that presentation was understood; ideas are presented in a disorganized manner; written communication and e-mails are brief and incomplete.

may be skipped. This definition is presented to subject-matter experts (SMEs), who are asked to generate behavioural examples for each competency under review. The behavioural examples are matched to a competency, retranslated, and rated. Behavioural examples with similar ratings are grouped together, edited, and refined to form the anchors for a competency. In Figure 5.4, statements such as "Makes interesting and informative presentations," "Uses e-mail effectively and replies in a timely fashion," and "Explains complicated points in different ways to ensure understanding" would have been assigned similarly high ratings by SMEs. A rating scale like this could then be used to evaluate an employee's level of proficiency with respect to communication.

Compare the richness of information provided by the scale in Figure 5.4 to those in Figure 5.3. The behavioural anchors provide greater guidance to raters and help to ensure greater consistency in ratings by providing raters with detailed behavioural descriptions of what is meant by "average" or "excellent" behaviour. Scales like this could be constructed for all competencies that were related to successful job performance. A procedure very similar to this one was used to develop scales for eight core competencies that were then used in evaluating the performance of RCMP members who applied for promotion.[93]

BARS is the Rolls-Royce of rating scales (and perhaps as costly). It has the advantage of being, arguably, the best rating procedure in use today. It integrates job analytic information directly with the performance appraisal measure. It also involves a large number of people in the development of the measure. Generally, these people—supervisors and workers—support the process and become committed to its success.

Behaviour Observation Scales

Behaviour observation scales (BOS) are very similar to BARS in that the starting point is an analysis of critical job incidents by those knowledgeable about the job to establish performance dimensions.[94] Once the list of behaviours that represent different job dimensions is constructed, supervisors are asked to monitor the frequency with which employees exhibit each behaviour over a standardized time period. Next, the frequency data are reviewed through an *item analysis*, where the response to each item is correlated to a performance score for a dimension. This performance score is obtained by summing all of the items that belong to a particular dimension. Only those items that attain high correlations with the total score are retained for the performance appraisal measure. This procedure assures a high degree of internal consistency for each dimension.

An example of a BOS scale used in evaluating the performance of a security dispatcher is presented in Table 5.3. Several differences are apparent in comparison to a BARS designed to measure the same dimension. First, there is no attempt to integrate the critical incidents into one overall scale. Second, there are no behavioural anchors attached to the scale; rather, the rater judges the frequency with which each employee displays the critical behaviours.

TABLE 5.3

Behavioural Observation Scale Used to Evaluate a Security Dispatcher

Job-Specific Task Proficiency

Properly secures lost and found articles	Almost Never	1 2 3 4 5	Almost Always
Controls visitor access to buildings	Almost Never	1 2 3 4 5	Almost Always
Monitors multiple surveillance devices	Almost Never	1 2 3 4 5	Almost Always
Ensures confidentiality and security of information	Almost Never	1 2 3 4 5	Almost Always
Activates appropriate emergency response teams as needed	Almost Never	1 2 3 4 5	Almost Always

Total Score _____

6–16	17–19	20–21	22–23	24–25*
Very Poor	Unsatisfactory	Satisfactory	Excellent	Superior

*Management sets performance standards.

Latham and Wexley[95] recommend using a five-point scale, where the numbers are defined in terms of frequencies; for example, they would assign the value 1 if the worker displayed the critical behaviour 0–64 percent of the time, 2 for 65–74 percent, 3 for 75–84 percent, 4 for 85–94 percent, and 5 for 95–100 percent. In this way, the rater assesses the frequency of engaging in actual critical behaviours as opposed to rating the employee in terms of a behavioural expectation that the worker might not have had an opportunity to perform.

BOS generally take less time and money to develop than BARS. The BOS development procedure requires the participation of supervisors and workers, leading to their greater acceptance of the system. Nonetheless, there are some weaknesses in this procedure. One major problem lies with the rating scale. A rating of 1 suggests poor performance since the critical behaviour is displayed less than 65 percent of the time. Consider using this scale to rate the hitting and fielding performance of a major league baseball player. A ballplayer who hits the ball 30 percent of the time is called a *millionaire;* the BOS would classify him as a failure. A major leaguer who successfully fielded the ball 85 percent of the time would soon be out of a job; the BOS would classify his performance as excellent.

The frequency with which a behaviour occurs may have different interpretations depending on the behaviour. Frequency measurements also do not capture the importance or criticality of the behaviour. The captain of the

Titanic almost always missed hitting icebergs. Another very serious problem with the BOS is that the demands it makes on human memory may exceed the available capacity. Raters may not be able to remember accurately the specific behavioural information required by the BOS and may end up making global judgments.[96]

Management by Objectives

Management by objectives (MBO) is a performance measurement system that emphasizes completion of goals that are defined in terms of objective criteria such as quantity produced or savings realized. It is a results-based system. MBO starts with the identification of organizational goals or objectives and uses these to specify goals for each employee's job performance. Before any goals can be set, the job-related behaviours must first be identified through a job analysis. The employee plays an important role in this process. Once both the employee and supervisor understand the job, both meet to develop a mutually agreeable set of goals that are outputs of the employee's job. Once the goals are established, the supervisor uses them to evaluate the employee's performance. Over the review period, there are several meetings between employee and supervisor to review progress. At the end of the review period, there is a final meeting to assess whether the employee met the established goals and to set the goals for the next review period.

Strengths of this system involve the linkage between organizational and individual goals, frequent analysis and discussion of employees' progress toward meeting the goals, and immediate feedback about performance. The employees know, from the objective criteria, whether they are performing up to expectations. Because the system is based on objective or hard criteria, the system suffers from all the problems inherent in the use of that type of performance measure. The emphasis on task performance through hard criteria mostly ignores contextual performance that may be as critical to the organization's success. In addition, the process can be as time-consuming as a BARS procedure to develop, with managers at different levels in the organization having conflicting views on what constitutes appropriate goals. The process may stifle creativity because of its emphasis on short-term results. It leads to an emphasis on personal goals, which may impede the development of teamwork.[97]

Balanced Scorecard

A balanced scorecard approach, like MBO, links higher-level strategic goals to individual performance. It provides feedback around both the internal business processes and external outcomes in order to continuously improve strategic performance and results. The balanced scorecard approach is an approach to describing and communicating strategy and selecting performance measurements linked to strategic outcomes.[98] The balanced scorecard approach provides a measurement system for evaluating organizational effectiveness as well as providing a management framework for aligning activities with an organization's mission, vision, and strategy. The basic premise of the balanced scorecard system is that organizational effectiveness is a multidimensional concept and that the major elements of the system, including individual performance, must be in alignment with accepted organizational objectives.

The balanced scorecard incorporates performance feedback around internal business process *outputs* and the *outcomes* of business strategies. Measurement is key to improvement and the success of the system. Measures and indicators are developed for the strategic plan's priorities. The selected measures and indicators provide the necessary information on the organization's progress toward meeting its strategic objectives. Processes are then designed to collect information relevant to these metrics and reduce it to numerical form for storage, display, and analysis. Decision makers examine the outcomes of various measured processes and strategies and track the results.

The balanced scorecard approach is a useful method for clarifying the multiple performance dimensions of a job that should be the basis of evaluation. It also establishes the linkages of any one job or position to other components of the organization. For example, a human resources professional's job may involve contact with specific employees, service to other organizational units, interaction with budgeting and finance, working with the training department to establish development plans for employees or groups, and so forth.

 In the case of teams, the balanced scorecard can be used to track team performance with respect to key objectives or activities. Actions or processes that are under the control of individual team members can be tracked and can help the team to take corrective action in support of individual members. The approach can help the team to identify ongoing problems and to address those issues to avoid further complications.[99] More information on the balanced scorecard approach can be found at http://www.balancedscorecard.org.

Perceived Fairness and Satisfaction of Rating Systems

An important consideration in the choice of a rating system is not only the validity and reliability of the system, but also its acceptance by those it will be used to evaluate. This is critical to the system's successful implementation and continued use.[100] The perceived fairness and perceived justice of the performance appraisal process play a central role in determining employee reactions. Rating systems that are perceived to be fair and those that produce a high degree of satisfaction among the ratees are more likely to find acceptance.[101]

Both the BOS and BARS produce greater degrees of satisfaction and perceived fairness than trait scales. The BOS also reflects a greater degree of procedural justice. Managers do not view trait scales as an acceptable measurement instrument, particularly when these scales are used to assess their own performance by other managers.[102] Most importantly, organizations are more likely to win cases involving performance evaluation when they can show a court or tribunal that the performance appraisals were fair and carried out with due process.[103]

What influences perceptions of fairness? Participation in the performance appraisal process is strongly correlated with positive reactions on the part of employees, particularly if the employees have an opportunity to express their opinions as part of the process.[104] Fairness perceptions also increase when both managers and employees have an opportunity to participate in the development of performance standards and the rating forms that will be used to assess performance on those standards.[105] Also, following the work of Rotundo and Sackett,[106] rating forms that address all relevant aspects of job performance are more likely to receive both managerial and employee support.

Improving Ratings through Training and Accountability

Rater Training

Training raters in the use of the rating system helps to reduce rating errors and to increase the reliability of the measurements.[107] A training program for raters ensures that all the raters are operating from a common frame of reference. One criticism of performance appraisal systems is that they often measure the wrong things.[108] **Frame-of-reference (FOR) training** seeks to ensure that raters have the same understanding of the rating system's instructions, that they have the same interpretation of the performance dimensions that are to be evaluated, and that they know how to use the rating system's measurement scale.

Uggerslev and Sulsky[109] provided insight into raters' use of performance dimensions. They had undergraduate students rate instructors based on videotaped lectures and identify the performance dimensions the students were using as part of those ratings. Before FOR training, the researchers measured the degree of rater idiosyncrasy, that is, the degree to which the raters used different performance dimensions from those specified by the researchers to rate the instructors videotaped performance. In comparison to a group that had just been given the appraisal forms, those raters who had been given the FOR training showed increased accuracy in their ratings, with those who were more idiosyncratic showing the largest increases in accuracy. Uggerslev and Sulsky make the point that all raters are idiosyncratic to some degree and that FOR training therefore improves the accuracy of all raters.[110]

Training programs can also include information on the types of rating errors that occur and how to avoid them. Some programs include information on how to improve observation of work behaviour. Although training programs can become quite elaborate, involving role-playing and use of demonstration videotapes, many rater training sessions consist of workshops built around explanation of the rating system, accompanied by practice rating sessions.

Rater Accountability

Apart from training, the factor that has the most impact on rating accuracy is rater accountability. Feelings of accountability on the part of a rater have an impact on the ratings they assign to those being evaluated.[111] Rating accuracy increases when raters are called on to explain or to justify the ratings they make. Accountability can be built into a system by requiring the rater to provide the employee who is being rated with feedback from the appraisal. Many

5.5

Frame-of-reference (FOR) training

A procedure used to "calibrate" raters by ensuring that they have the same understanding of a rating system's instructions, that they have the same interpretation of the performance dimensions that are to be evaluated, and that they know how to use the rating system's measurement scale.

supervisors are uncomfortable doing this, particularly when the feedback is negative. However, if feedback is not given, the employee can neither benefit from the appraisal by improving performance nor challenge evaluations that are suspect.

In 1996, the Alberta Court of Queen's Bench ordered Purolator Courier Ltd. to pay a former employee $100 000 in a wrongful dismissal suit that centred on the appropriateness of the employee's performance evaluation.[112] The trial judge in this case was most concerned that the employee had not been given assistance to meet increased expectations.

Most organizations that undertake performance appraisals require both the rater and the employee to review, and to sign, the completed rating form. Employees, however, cannot be forced to sign rating forms with which they disagree. Accountability is also established by building into the rating system a mechanism for the formal review of all performance appraisals. When raters are required to account for their ratings in person as opposed to in writing, their ratings become more accurate, particularly when they have to account for those ratings to those with higher status.[113]

By monitoring all evaluations, a review panel can assess whether any one rater's assessments appear to significantly deviate from those obtained from the other raters. Knowing that their ratings will be reviewed can lead raters to play it safe by giving everyone an acceptable evaluation (i.e., making a central tendency error). On the other hand, raters under this type of system can usually justify any extreme ratings they give to employees. Organizations that cannot justify their performance evaluations may suffer both public and financial embarrassment.

Who Does the Rating?

Supervisor Ratings

Most workplace assessments are traditionally carried out by an immediate supervisor or manager. In recent years, organizations have started to recognize that this may not be the best practice. They have started to obtain ratings from other co-workers and subordinates. Some organizations also ask workers to perform an appraisal of their own performance. Each of these groups provides information about the employee's performance from a different perspective and some may not see the total scope of the employee's job performance.[114]

Peer Ratings

Co-workers tend to provide more lenient reviews than supervisors. As part of a class project, suppose the professor requires the members of the group to evaluate each other with respect to certain criteria related to the project. Would you assign a very lenient grade in the expectation that the other students will evaluate you similarly, or would you assign a grade that reflects your honest judgment of how others contributed to the project? If you knew your grade was based on this peer evaluation, would group performance be enhanced or hindered? Self-comparisons with other members of a work group do have an impact on peer performance evaluations and may lead to tensions within the work group and ultimately affect both individual and group performance.[115]

Most organizations avoid involving co-workers in the assessment process out of the fear that doing so will lead to hostility between co-workers, increased competitiveness among co-workers, and a breakdown in team functioning. Nonetheless, evaluations from co-workers or peers can be quite reliable and valid sources of information about an employee's job performance.[116] In fact, peer feedback is among the best predictors of job performance, since peers may have access to relevant job performance data that is not available to other raters. This information may be related to peers placing more consideration on aspects of contextual performance that may have been overlooked by other raters.[117]

Subordinate Ratings

Ratings by subordinates of their supervisor are relatively rare, although some large companies, such as Ford Motor Company,[118] do obtain such ratings as part of reviewing managerial performance. Subordinate ratings, however, are very common in universities, where a professor's teaching performance is evaluated through student evaluations, and where faculty routinely evaluate the performance of their supervisors (department heads, deans, presidents). Student evaluations of teaching performance are used by a professor's peers in evaluating that professor for promotion or tenure. While the students would be in a good position to observe teaching effectiveness, they might not be the best persons to evaluate the professor's research productivity or administrative work on committees.

There are two related concerns about subordinate ratings: either the subordinates will give lenient ratings to influence their own treatment ("If I rate my professor highly, I'm more likely to get a good grade") or the supervisor will attempt to manipulate the subordinate ratings through altering performance expectations ("I'll give them an easy test so they all pass, and perhaps they'll remember this gift when they evaluate my teaching").

Self-Ratings

What if your professor asked you to evaluate your own performance on the group project? How would your evaluation compare with those of other students in your group and of your professor? Generally, self-appraisals are the most lenient of all. That is, while people tend to give ratings that accurately reflect differences in their performance on different job dimensions, the ratings they give themselves tend to be higher than ratings given to them by others. More and more companies, including most of the Fortune 500 firms, are including self-assessments as part of their performance appraisal systems. These self-ratings are typically used along with ratings obtained from other sources as part of a 360-degree feedback process. Self-ratings, however, have the least agreement with ratings from other sources. They also are not very good predictors of actual job performance.[119]

Self-ratings and those made by an employee's manager will disagree substantially. The extent of the disagreement does not extend only to the appropriate rating that should be applied, but also to fundamental differences in how the employee and supervisor view the job dimensions underlying the rating scales.[120] That is, if both were evaluating the competency of communication, the employee and supervisor would most likely have different views of what that competency included. Employees and managers have different perceptions of whether job factors are under the control of the employee. When employees perform less than their best, they tend to attribute this to external factors beyond their control. On the other hand, their supervisor tends to attribute the less-than-stellar performance to internal factors under the employee's control. These differences in perception are another factor in the discrepancy between self- and supervisory ratings.[121]

Client or Customer Ratings

An increasing number of organizations ask customers or clients to rate the performance of employees with whom they have interacted. For example, Sun Life of Canada asks customers to rate the performance of salespeople in terms of the service they provided to the customer. Other companies, such as Ford and Honda's Acura division, also obtain information from an employee's internal clients. Internal clients include anyone who is dependent on the employee's work output. For example, the manager of an engineering division might be asked to evaluate the human resources manager in charge of recruiting engineers for the division.

Both internal and external customers can provide very useful information about the effectiveness of an employee or a team of employees.[122] This information provides a unique view of the employee's performance from individuals who are directly involved with the employee, but who at the same time are neither subordinate nor superior to the employee.

360-Degree Feedback or Multisource Feedback

360-degree or multisource feedback

The use of information obtained from supervisors, peers, subordinates, self-ratings, and clients or customers to provide the employee with feedback for development and training purposes.

 5.6

The **360-degree feedback or multisource feedback** procedure uses information obtained from supervisors, peers, subordinates, self-ratings, and clients or customers to provide the employee with feedback for development and training purposes. To a lesser extent, such feedback has also been used for administrative purposes such as promotion or pay increases. The intent of the process is to provide employees with feedback about their performance from numerous independent sources to give the employees as complete a picture as possible about their performance.[123]

This method of multi-source feedback is a an increasingly popular performance appraisal process.[124] Brutus and Derayeh[125] reported that 43 percent of their sample of Canadian organizations obtained appraisals from multiple sources, and that the use of multisource feedback was more likely in larger organizations. Originally, this procedure focused on management and leadership development, and, although adopted by almost all major corporations, it is still largely limited to managerial-level employees.[126] The majority of companies that use multisource feedback do so solely for the purposes of employee development.[127]

As noted above, the information provided by these different sources is likely to disagree to some extent. Self-ratings tend to be higher than those provided by others and show less congruence with others' ratings. There is a relatively high correlation between peer and supervisor ratings but only modest correlations between self–peer and self–supervisor ratings.[128,129] That is, supervisors and peers are more likely to agree on a rating they apply to someone else than that person is likely to agree with either of them.[130] Over time, however, some ratings may converge. Bailey and Fletcher[131] found this happening with respect to a subordinate's rating of a manager and the manager's self-rating.

The difference in information from different sources may suggest that no one evaluation is the right one. Given conflicting feedback from the different sources, which ones should the ratee follow? Darr and Catano linked feedback on eight competencies used to develop police officers for promotion to executive-level positions. A critical aspect of the promotion was performance on a structured interview that was based on the same eight dimensions that were used as part of the 360-degree evaluation. Supervisor and peer ratings predicted performance on the interview. As well, peer, subordinate, and self-ratings did not improve on the supervisors' predictions.[132]

There is no clear evidence why the assessments from different sources disagree. Harris and Schaubroeck[133] have suggested that ego-defensiveness and attributional differences produce the discrepancies. Sulsky and Keown[134] note some other possibilities for these differences:

- quality differences in the ratings across sources;
- individual performance variability across different contexts (e.g., being friendlier to customers than to peers); and
- different conceptions of work performance across rating sources.

A recent study by Whiting, Podsakoff, and Pierce[135] may offer another reason for these differences. They had undergraduate business students evaluate the performance of a university department secretary based on written critical incidents related to the secretary. Students read vignettes that varied in descriptions of both task and contextual performance. Both task and organizational citizenship behaviours were significantly related to performance appraisals. Organizational citizenship behaviours such as helping, voice behaviors that promote constructive change rather than convey criticism, and loyalty all made significant contributions to the appraisal of the secretary's performance. It stands to reason that of all the sources, a supervisor may be more attuned to performance of OCBs than peers, subordinates, or clients, and that the OCBs are more likely to affect a supervisor's feedback while the other sources focus more on job tasks.

During the mid-1990s, many companies embraced 360-degree feedback and saw it as an essential tool in developing managers. Many organizations that adopted this procedure had no clear idea of what they wanted to achieve through its use or which competencies they wished to evaluate. Experience over the years since suggests that the success of this procedure depends on

Integrating Individual and Organizational Performance

Individual performance appraisals should be based on the following principles:

- The appraisal process should focus on long-term employee development.
- Appraisal needs to focus on the behaviours that will produce desired outcomes.
- Performance management should be ongoing, not an annual event.
- Performance appraisal needs to be from multiple perspectives (not just supervisor/manager).
- Performance management should encompass employee development opportunities.
- The performance appraisal instrument should be related to those job behaviours that are most relevant to organizational effectiveness.

- The performance appraisal instrument should be developed according to best practices and should include assessments of task, contextual, and counterproductive behaviours.
- All persons involved in the performance appraisal process should be trained in the use of the performance appraisal instrument.
- The performance appraisal system must emphasize principles of fairness and procedural justice.
- Performance appraisal must be fully integrated into a performance management system.
- Performance appraisal should emphasize continuous performance.

the organizational culture in which it is embedded. It does not do well in a "command and control" environment.[136] Because 360-degree feedback includes peer appraisals, it is also prone to all the disadvantages associated with peer ratings.

Performance Appraisal—Differing Views

Although there are many serious problems with the use of performance appraisals, most organizations are loath to abandon them, even if the information collected from them is often ignored. While many technological improvements can be made with respect to performance appraisal instruments, they will continue to be problematic unless they are placed into the broader context of an organizational performance management system. Performance appraisals must be used to integrate and to align individual and organizational objectives. The procedure we outline in Recruitment and Selection Notebook 5.1 may be helpful to HR practitioners in accomplishing this alignment.

Nontraditional Methods for Measuring Performance

Following a decline in use during the 1970s, ratings have regained popularity with the development of rating systems that focus on behaviours related to the job's performance domain. Ratings remain the most popular method of performance appraisal. Performance measurement systems developed over the past several years, however, offer alternative methods for obtaining criteria data. In most cases, these procedures are adapted from techniques used in personnel selection. We briefly discuss some of these alternative measurements.

Job Knowledge/Skill Testing

Job knowledge or **skill testing** procedures include paper-and-pencil tests as well as "walk-through" procedures, which require an individual to demonstrate knowledge or general skills such as manipulating controls or equipment to achieve a desired outcome. These types of measures reflect a worker's requisite skill or knowledge to perform a task; they do not indicate the worker's proficiency or what the worker will or can do. Since these measures are "tests," the same issues arise as when they are used as predictors; particularly, they must not lead to adverse impact against subgroups. These procedures and issues will be discussed in later chapters.

Job knowledge/skill testing

In performance appraisal, a procedure that is based on an assessment of an employee's knowledge or skills required to achieve a desired outcome.

Hands-On Testing and Simulation

There are two categories containing related techniques but differing in the degree to which they attempt to reproduce actual critical work behaviours: hands-on testing and simulations. In **hands-on testing**, workers perform one or more tasks associated with their job. The testing may take place either through formal observation of normal job tasks or off-site, where the worker is asked to perform using normal job equipment and techniques. This latter case is really a type of work samples test, where the employee is asked to produce a sample of job-related behaviour. Similarly, a **simulation** attempts to duplicate salient features of the work site and to measure job proficiency under realistic conditions.[137]

Hands-on testing

In performance appraisal, a procedure in which raters assess workers as they perform one or more tasks associated with their job.

Simulation

In performance appraisal, a procedure in which raters assess workers as they perform one or more tasks associated with their job in a setting that emulates salient features of the job and the work environment.

As part of the RCMP's promotion procedures, constables must successfully complete a paper-and-pencil job-situation exercise that simulates conditions they encounter on the job.[138] So do candidates for the Certified Human Resources Professional (CHRP) designation. The professional practice assessment that is the final step toward attaining the CHRP designation is a paper-and-pencil job-situation exercise designed to simulate critical work situations experienced by human resources professionals. This is called the *National Professional Practice Assessment* (NPPA).

Work samples testing and simulation have been used primarily as predictor measures rather than criteria or, in the case of simulation, as a training method (e.g., flight simulators). When used to measure performance, hands-on methods appear to produce reliable scores on critical job-related tasks. These new evaluation procedures are generally complex, expensive to develop, and demanding to administer, raising the issue of their practicality in most situations. Nonetheless, they may have immense potential for use in validation research.

Human Rights and Performance Appraisal

Ever since *Griggs v. Duke Power Co.*,[139] which we discussed in Chapter 3, personnel practices in the United States and Canada have been increasingly subject to review by judiciary or human rights tribunals. Although the Canadian legal precedents have occurred more recently, they have been influenced by U.S. case law.[140,141] Reviews of U.S. decisions related to criterion-related validity studies and performance measurement systems emphasize that the defensibility of performance measurements rests on the ability to demonstrate that they are job-related.[142] This point was emphasized in the Supreme Court of Canada's *Meiorin* decision.[143] The court ruled that a standard—that is, a criterion—must be reasonably related to the accomplishment of work-related purposes (see Chapter 3, pages: 91–92).

The absence of a job or work analysis as part of criterion development will likely cast suspicion on any performance measurement system subject to judicial review.[144] In *B.L. Mears v. Ontario Hydro,*[145] a tribunal under the Ontario Human Rights Commission decided that black employees were unfairly ranked for layoffs, compared with white employees, through the use of vague and undefined criteria (e.g., productivity, safety, quality of work, attendance, and seniority). Additionally, the ranking system was informal, as no written records of productivity or quality of work were kept. In reviewing U.S. court decisions involving performance appraisal systems, Barrett and Kernan[146] also note the requirement for written documentation regarding performance measurements. They go on to advise employers to maintain a review mechanism through which employees can appeal performance assessments they believe to be unfair or discriminatory.

There is evidence that performance appraisals, regrettably, are subject to both gender and racial bias. In North American studies that have reviewed race, whites tend to receive consistently higher ratings than blacks, although the overall difference is small.[147] This is not necessarily a consequence of whites rating minorities lower; Lefkowitz and Battista[148] found that both black and white supervisors gave lower performance ratings to black employees, suggesting that the raters may hold racial stereotypes about employees. Dewberry[149] found similar effects for ethnic minority versus white comparisons in the United Kingdom.

With respect to gender, the effect of bias is more complex. There appear to be no overall differences between ratings assigned to male and female employees; however, if all the raters are male, the ratings assigned to females are lower. If the rating instrument makes reference to gender in any way, then the performance ratings assigned to females will be lower.[150] For example, Pazy and Oron[151] found that women in the Israeli army received consistently lower performance evaluations than men when women constituted token representation in a unit. Conversely, when the proportion of women in a unit increased, the gender difference in performance ratings vanished. There was no relationship between the ratings assigned to men and the degree of their representation in the group. HR staff should be aware of these effects when conducting performance evaluations or implementing a performance measurement system.

Increased critical examination of performance measurement practices by Canadian human rights commissions and courts will mean strict adherence to accepted professional standards of criterion development.[152] These standards will include those that apply in the United States unless it can be shown that professional standards in Canada seriously deviate from those in the United States, or that Canadian legislation or case law has established practices that vary from U.S. standards. At present neither of these conditions hold. The most explicit statement on criteria is contained in the "Uniform Guidelines on Employee Selection Procedures,"[153] which were jointly developed by the U.S. Equal Employment Opportunity Commission, Civil Service Commission, Department of Labor, and Department of Justice.[154]

> Whatever criteria are used should represent important or crucial work behaviors or work outcomes ... The bases for the selection of the criterion measures should be provided, together with references to the evidence considered in making the selection of criterion measures. A full description of all criteria on which data were collected and means by which they were observed, recorded, evaluated, and quantified should be provided. If rating techniques are used as criterion measures, the appraisal form(s) and instructions to the raters should be provided as part of the validation evidence or should be explicitly described and available. All steps taken to insure that criterion measures are free from factors which would unfairly alter the scores of members of any group should be described.

The research presented in this chapter suggests that a performance measurement system must meet both legal and professional practice standards to satisfy human rights requirements. Reviews of legal decisions and research suggest that the steps outlined in Recruitment and Selection Notebook 5.2 must be included in a performance measurement system to meet those requirements.

Recruitment and Selection Notebook 5.2

Designing a Performance Measurement System to Meet Legal and Professional Standards

1. Conduct a job and organization analysis to describe the job performance domain and competencies that are necessary for successful completion of the organization's goals.

2. Select criteria that are valid, reliable, and practical measurements of the job performance dimensions or competencies. Document the development of the criteria and measurement scales as well as their validity.

3. Identify the performance standards and goals or expected results that will be used to evaluate employees on the selected criteria. These standards should be made known to employees in understandable terms at the beginning of the review period. These standards must be work-related and bona fide occupational requirements.

4. Train people in the use of the performance measurement system, particularly when they will be called on to make judgments about employee performance. This training should include a review of the criteria, the measurement scales, and the standards.

5. Provide written instructions to all assessors on the proper use of the measurement system, particularly if the system involves the use of rating procedures.

6. Provide feedback from the performance evaluation to the employees. Assist those employees who receive poor evaluations to improve their performance. Raters should be trained in the effective use of feedback.

7. Establish a formal review mechanism, which has responsibility for the appraisal system and for any appeals arising from the evaluation process.

8. Document all steps in the development of the appraisal system and its use, as well as all decisions affecting employees that result from using the performance measurement data.

Summary

This chapter illustrates the important role that job performance plays in recruitment and selection. The premise of the chapter is that a solid understanding of job performance and its measurement is an integral part of building a selection system that will meet professional and legal standards. A key to validating selection systems, whether competency-based or the more traditional type, is to understand the nature of the job performance that is being predicted by the competencies or KSAOs. Job performance is linked to an organization's mission, values, and goals. One useful approach to understanding job performance is to recognize that job performance is a multidimensional construct composed of task, contextual, and counterproductive behaviours.

The chapter uses the performance model developed by Campbell[155] that categorizes jobs in terms of their performance requirements into eight performance dimensions to illustrate the role that contextual and counterproductive behaviours play in any job. Understanding the factors that underlie job performance is necessary to its measurement. The Campbell model emphasizes that declarative knowledge, procedural knowledge, and motivation underlie job performance. The chapter uses these concepts to illustrate likely predictors of different aspects of job behaviour, particularly contextual and counterproductive behaviours.

The usefulness of any selection system is determined by how well it predicts job performance as measured by job-related criteria. Any criteria chosen as a measure of job performance must be valid, reliable, practical, and capable of withstanding legal challenge. A construct validation strategy such as that outlined by Campbell[156] will help to satisfy legal requirements. Once job-related performance dimensions or competencies have been identified, the type of criterion measurement that most validly represents each performance dimension or competency should be selected. Most likely there will be different measurements for different performance dimensions or competencies.

The chapter reviews different factors that affect criteria and the pros and cons of combining different criterion measures to form composites. It also assesses the stability of performance measures over time. Current research suggests that training criteria are acceptable performance measures for estimating maximum performance. However, to obtain a better understanding of possible changes in validities over time, repeated measurements of performance should be taken over time. Data from the various criterion measures should be collected in an uncollapsed form and formed into composites when necessary. The weighting of composites should reflect the priority assigned by the organization to the different goal-related behaviours. All of the procedures used in establishing the performance dimensions or competencies, their measures, and data collection and analysis should be documented.

There are many ways to measure performance; these fall into two main groups: objective and subjective measures. Objective measures are constrained by other employee and organizational constraints but some types (e.g., absenteeism measures) may serve as indicators of counterproductive behaviour. Subjective measures, mostly performance appraisals carried out by employee supervisors, are the predominant method of evaluation. There are many different types of performance appraisal/rating systems. All rating systems are subject to rating errors; however, these can be reduced through appropriate training of the raters.

While there is no evidence to suggest that any one type of measure is inherently more sound than any other, BARS and BOS systems appear to produce better rater and ratee satisfaction. The perceived fairness of an appraisal system is key to its acceptance as well as its legal defensibility. Performance appraisal systems, if properly developed, will provide data that are as reliable as systems based on objective measurements.

Recently, 360-degree feedback systems that acquire performance information from an employee's peers, subordinates, supervisors, and clients have become very popular. The 360-degree process illustrates the different views that these sources have on someone's performance. Mostly, these views reflect concern with different aspects of performance that are not normally seen by only a supervisor. Peers are more likely to attend to contextual performance than task performance. Supervisors are more likely to focus on task behaviour.

Although performance appraisals may be problematic, most organizations will continue to use them to assess employee job behaviours. More consideration is being given to performance measurement that is not based on performance ratings but on direct observation of the employee in actual or simulated work environments. While many technological improvements can be made with respect to performance appraisal instruments, they will continue to be problematic unless they are placed into the broader context of an organizational performance management system. Performance appraisals must be used to integrate and to align individual and organizational objectives.

Key Terms

absolute rating systems, p. 201

central tendency errors, p. 198

contextual performance, p. 181

counterproductive behaviours, p. 177

criteria, p. 176

criterion contamination, p. 188

criterion deficiency, p. 188

criterion relevance, p. 188

frame-of-reference (FOR) training, p. 211

halo errors, p. 198

hands-on testing, p. 217

job knowledge/skill testing, p. 217

job performance, p. 176

job performance domain, p. 178

leniency errors, p. 198

objective performance measures, p. 195

performance dimensions, p. 178

practicality, p. 189

relative rating systems, p. 199

severity errors, p. 198

simulation, p. 217

subjective performance measures, p. 198

360-degree or multisource
    feedback, p. 214

ultimate criterion, p. 190

Web Links

The National Occupational Classification (NOC) systm is available online at **http://www5.hrsdc.gc.ca/NOC-CNP/app/index.aspx.**

More information on the balanced scorecard approach can be found at **http://www.balancedscorecard.org.**

More information on the CCHRA's NPPA outcome assessment can be found at **http://www.cchra.ca/Web/exam/content.aspx?f=29881.**

Information on workplace violence from the Workplace Violence Research Institute can be found at **http://www.workviolence.com.**

Required Professional Capabilities (RPCs)

RPC 5.1 Provides performance feedback, coaching, and career development to teams and individuals to maximize their probability of success.
- Principles of performance management
- Organization culture, business environment, and objectives
- Principles of learning and development
- Performance appraisal policies and procedures
- Issues regarding team-based work
- Methods of creating interpersonal effectiveness
- Career development policies and procedures

RPC 5.2 Ensures performance feedback is an integral part of the organization's business process.
- Feedback systems and methodology
- Industry best practices
- Organization culture, business environment, and objectives
- Performance appraisal policies and procedures
- Methods of discipline

RPC 5.3 Provides development information, support activities, and procedures for learners, supervisors, and managers to assist in achieving performance improvement.
- Performance improvement process
- Training, coaching, feedback, and goal-setting techniques
- Performance appraisal policies and procedures
- The behaviour of individuals, groups, and organizational units
- Motivation theories and applications
- Employee recognition and reward systems
- Training and development needs analysis techniques
- Performance measurement issues
- Concepts of work flow analysis
- Methods of job analysis and job design

RPC 5.4 **Identifies, evaluates, and implements measurement systems for current and future job/team performance.**
- Systems for measurement of both objective and subjective productivity and job performance
- Issues regarding team-based work
- Employee competencies, training, and development
- Importance, criteria, and techniques of program evaluation
- Principles of performance management
- Organization culture, business environment, and objectives

RPC 5.5 **Measures the effectiveness of the performance feedback systems.**
- Organization culture, business environment, and objectives
- Feedback systems and methodology
- Performance appraisal policies and procedures
- The identification, assessment, development, implementation, and maintenance of effective systems of managing HR information
- Procedures for collection, manipulation, and analysis of information
- Techniques to evaluate effectiveness of HR programs (e.g., selection, training, and compensation, etc.)
- Performance measurement issues

RPC 5.6 **Ensures performance feedback is an integral part of the organization's HR information system.**
- HRMS concepts
- Feedback systems and methodology
- Performance appraisal policies and procedures
- The identification, assessment, development, implementation, and maintenance of effective systems of managing HR information
- HRMS and business software

Discussion Questions

1. Why is it important to understand performance as part of the recruitment and selection process?
2. In this chapter, we discuss task performance, contextual performance, and counterproductive behaviour. Discuss the role that each of these plays in developing a recruitment and selection system.
3. If you were limited to selecting employees on the basis of only one of the three types of performance discussed in this chapter, which one would you choose? Why?
4. Discuss Campbell's performance taxonomy. Can you think of a job that does not fit that model?
5. Compare Campbell's model to the "Eight Great Competencies" presented in Chapter 4. What are the differences/similarities?
6. Discuss the problems in using "objective" measures of performance to assess job performance.
7. Discuss the distinction among criterion relevance, criterion contamination, and criterion deficiency.

8. What are the characteristics of a good criterion measure?
9. Do you think that rating errors can be reduced? How?
10. Discuss the characteristics of a good rating scale.

Using the Internet

1. Many online consulting companies offer services in the area of performance appraisal and 360-degree feedback, usually in the form of software packages that assist in both types of appraisals. Three companies that do so are Cognology at http://www.cognology.com.au, Halogen Software at http://www.halogensoftware.com, and SumTotal at http://www.sumtotalsystems.com. All of these companies offer free demonstrations of their software. Choose any two of these companies and evaluate their 360-degree software packages against the standards we have discussed in this chapter. First, you may want to review their mission statements, hiring policies, and procedures if these are available online.

   a. Does the software allow assessment of task, contextual, and counterproductive behaviours?
   b. Does the software allow appraisals from the self, peers, subordinates, supervisors, and clients?
   c. Is the software interactive?
   d. Can the software be modified to suit the needs of a client?
   e. Which of the approaches are likely to be perceived as fair?
   f. Which of the two do you prefer? Why?

Exercises

Many of the forms used by colleges and universities to assess teaching performance suffer from all the defects of graphic rating scales. For this exercise:

1. Obtain a copy of the teaching assessment form used by your institution and critique it using the information presented in this chapter. If a teacher was dismissed solely on information obtained from this instrument that indicated the person was a poor teacher, would the decision stand up before a court or labour arbitration board?
2. Assume that teaching involves the following major activities: lecture preparation and organization; communication skills; use of examples and exercises; use of audio-visual materials/PowerPoint/Internet; grading; course-related advising and feedback; interaction with students; and maintaining class and office hours.

   a. Place these activities into the job performance dimensions developed by Campbell as well as the Eight Great Competencies. More than one activity may be placed in a dimension.
   b. Identify the major behaviours and/or KSAOs for each dimension.

3. (May be done as a group exercise.) For each job dimension or competency, construct a behaviourally anchored rating scale of the type shown in Figure 5.4 on page 206. You do not have to follow all the steps required to construct a BARS. Act as your own SME and then have a classmate rate the different behaviours for their importance. Shaw, Schneier, and Beatty[157] present useful information for constructing a BARS.
4. Compare your scale with the one used in your institution. Which one would you prefer to use? Which does your professor prefer? Why?
5. What are your views on performance appraisal? Do you believe that individual performance feedback has an impact on improving team or organizational performance?

Case

As part of restructuring, a television network decided to close one of its local stations in Cape Breton. Several different unions represented the employees at the station. Employees were given severance packages or opportunities to transfer to the network's Halifax station if they were qualified for any available positions. Two electronic news-gathering (ENG) camera operators received layoff notices and requested transfer to Halifax, where two ENG positions were open. Two ENG operators—two ENG positions to fill. No problem? Not quite. A recent hire at the Halifax station also applied for one of the two positions. Under the terms of the ENG operators' collective agreement, during any restructuring the employer had the right to fill positions with employees deemed to be the best performers.

The network had never used any type of performance assessments with its unionized employees and was at a loss as to how to determine which two of the three were the best, other than through their supervisors' opinions. The collective agreement, however, called for an "objective" assessment. The network's HR director recalled that a few years previously its Toronto station had to prepare for compliance with pay equity legislation and had developed a rating system to evaluate all their Toronto employees, from secretaries to on-air news anchors. The survey was a graphic rating scale very similar to the type shown in Figure 5.3(b) on page 202. It listed 12 traits or characteristics, including "effort," as shown in Figure 5.3(b). The 12 traits were very general characteristics such as "knowledge," "willingness to learn," and so on. The HR director asked two different managers who had worked with the three employees to use the form to rate the employees' performance. The new hire received the highest rating and was offered a position. The two potential transfers received low ratings and neither was offered a position.

Under the terms of the collective agreement, the two laid-off employees had the right to grieve the decision, and their union carried the case to arbitration. The arbitration panel was composed of a neutral chairperson, who was mutually selected by the other two members of the panel, one of whom was appointed by the employer and the other by the union. In presenting its case to the arbitration panel, the union's lawyer decided to call an expert in human resources to comment on the performance measure that had been used to assess the employees. After hearing the expert's opinion, which was not challenged by the employer, the arbitration panel threw out the decision based on the performance measure and declared that the two laid-off employees must be offered the two vacant positions.

Discussion Questions

1. What did the expert most likely tell the arbitration panel?
2. If you were that expert, what would you tell the arbitration panel? Be as detailed as possible and call on all the material that has been covered in previous chapters.
3. Do you think an "off-the-shelf" measure that was designed for one purpose can be used to assess performance in another context?
4. After rejecting the performance measure, the arbitration panel itself was charged with assessing which two of the three employees were the best performers. What would you advise the panel to do in this situation? How should they evaluate the employees' performance?

Endnotes

1. "Best Practices in Performance Appraisals." 2000. *HR Focus* 2: 8.
2. Austin, J.T., and P. Villanova. 1992. "The Criterion Problem: 1917–1992." *Journal of Applied Psychology* 77: 836–74.
3. Borman, W.C., and S.J. Motowidlo. 1993. "Expanding the Criterion Domain to Include Elements of Contextual Performance." In N. Schmitt and W.C. Borman, eds., *Personnel Selection in Organizations* (pp. 71–98). San Francisco: Jossey-Bass.
4. Campbell, J.P., M.B. Gasser, and F.L. Oswald. 1996. "The Substantive Nature of Job Performance Variability." In K.R. Murphy, ed., *Individual Differences and Behavior in Organizations* (pp. 258–99). San Francisco: Jossey-Bass.
5. Rotundo, M., and P.R. Sackett. 2002. "The Relative Importance of Task, Citizenship and Counter Productive Performance to Global Ratings of Job Performance: A Policy-Capturing Approach." *Journal of Applied Psychology* 87: 66–80.
6. Motowidlo, S.J., W.C. Borman, and M.J. Schmit. 1997. "A Theory of Individual Differences in Task and Contextual Performance." *Human Performance* 10: 71–83.
7. Motowidlo, S.J., and M.J. Schmit. 1999. "Performance Assessment in Unique Jobs." In D.R. Ilgen and E.D. Pulakos, eds., *The Changing Nature of Performance* (pp. 56–86). San Francisco: Jossey-Bass.
8. Coleman, V.I., and W.C. Borman. 2000. "Investigating the Underlying Structure of the Citizenship Performance Domain." *Human Resource Management Review* 10: 25–44.
9. Conway, J.M. 1999. "Distinguishing Contextual Performance from Task Performance for Managerial Jobs." *Journal of Applied Psychology* 84: 3–13.
10. VanScotter, J.R., and S.J. Motowidlo. 1996. "Interpersonal Facilitation and Job Dedication as Separate Facets of Contextual Performance." *Journal of Applied Psychology* 81: 525–31.
11. Motowidlo, S.J., and M.J. Schmit. 1999.
12. Kelloway, E.K., C. Loughlin, J. Barling, and A. Nault. 2002. "Self-Reported Counterproductive Behaviors and Organizational Citizenship Behaviors: Separate but Related Constructs." *International Journal of Assessment and Selection* 10: 143–51.

13. Sackett, P.R., C.M. Berry, S.A. Wiemann, and R.M. Laczo. 2006. "Citizenship and Counterproductive Behavior: Clarifying the Relationship between Them." *Human Performance* 19: 441–64.

14. Robinson, S.L., and R.J. Bennett. 1995. "A Typology of Deviant-Workplace Behaviors: A Multidimensional Scaling Study." *Academy of Management Journal* 38: 555–72.

15. Organ, D.W., and J.B. Paine. 1999. "A New Kind of Performance for Industrial and Organizational Psychology: Recent Contributions to the Study of Organizational Citizenship Behavior." *International Review of Industrial and Organizational Psychology* 14: 337–68.

16. Borman, W.C. 1991. "Job Behavior, Performance, and Effectiveness." In M.D. Dunnette and L.M. Hough, eds. *Handbook of Industrial and Organizational Psychology,* Vol. 2 (pp. 271–326). 2nd ed. Palo Alto, CA: Consulting Psychologists Press.

17. Motowidlo, S.J., and M.J. Schmit. 1999.

18. Murphy, K.R., and A.H. Shiarella. 1997. "Implications of the Multidimensional Nature of Job Performance for the Validity of Selection Tests: Multivariate Frameworks for Studying Test Validity." *Personnel Psychology* 50: 823–54.

19. Campbell, J.P. 1990. "Modelling the Performance Prediction Problem in Industrial and Organizational Psychology." In M.D. Dunnette and L.M. Hough, eds., *The Handbook of Industrial and Organizational Psychology,* Vol. 1 (pp. 687–732). 2nd ed. San Diego: Consulting Psychologists Press.

20. Campbell, J.P., R.A. McCloy, S.H. Oppler, and C.E. Sager. 1993. "A Theory of Performance." In N. Schmitt, W.C. Borman, and Associates, *Personnel Selection in Organizations*. San Francisco: Jossey-Bass.

21. Campbell, J.P. 1990.

22. Campbell, J.P. 1990.

23. McCloy, R.A., J.P. Campbell, and R. Cudeck. 1994. "Confirmatory Test of a Model of Performance Determinants." *Journal of Applied Psychology* 79: 493–505.

24. Borman, W.C., and S.J. Motowidlo. 1993.

25. Borman, W.C., and S.J. Motowidlo. 1993.

26. Coleman, V.I., and W.C. Borman. 2000.

27. Organ, D.W. 1997. "Organizational Citizenship Behavior: It's Construct Clean-Up Time." *Human Performance* 10: 85–97.

28. Organ, D.W. 1997.

29. Campbell, J.P., M.B. Gasser, and F.L. Oswald. 1996.

30. Hoffman, B., C. Blair, J. Meriac, and D. Woehr. 2007. "Expanding the Criterion Domain? A Quantitative Review of the OCB Literature." *Journal of Applied Psychology* 92: 555–66.

31. Conway, J.M. 1999.

32. Rotundo, M., and P.R. Sackett. 2002.

33. Bowen, D.E., G.E. Ledford, Jr., and B.R. Nathan. 1991. "Hiring for the Organization, Not the Job." *Academy of Management Executive* 5: 35–51.

34. Goodman, S.A., and D.J. Svyantek. 1999. "Person-Organization Fit and Contextual Performance: Do Shared Values Matter?" *Journal of Vocational Behavior* 55: 254–75.

35. Robinson, S.L., and R.J. Bennett. 1995.

36. Gialacone, R.A., and J. Greenberg. 1997. *Antisocial Behavior in Organizations*. Thousand Oaks, CA: Sage.

37. Spector, P.E., S. Fox, L.M. Penney, K. Bruursema, A. Goh, and S. Kessler. 2006. "The Dimensionality of Counterproductivity: Are All Counterproductive Behaviors Created Equal?" *Journal of Vocational Behavior* 68: 446–60.

38. Spector, P., S. Fox, and T. Domagalski. 2006. "Emotions, Violence, and Counterproductive Work Behaviors." In E.K. Kelloway, J.Barling, and J.J. Hurrell, Jr., eds., *Handbook of Workplace Violence* (pp. 29–46). Thousand Oaks, CA: Sage.

39. Schat, A.C.H., M.R. Frone, and E.K. Kelloway. 2006. "Prevalence of Workplace Aggression in the U.S. Workforce." In E.K. Kelloway, J.Barling, and J.J. Hurrell, Jr., eds., *Handbook of Workplace Violence* (pp. 47–89). Thousand Oaks, CA: Sage.

40. Schat, A.C.H., M.R. Frone, and E.K. Kelloway. 2006.

41. Hanisch, K.A. 1995. "Behavioral Families and Multiple Causes: Matching the Complexity of Responses to the Complexity of Antecedents." *Current Directions in Psychological Science* 4: 156–62.

42. Hanisch, K.A., C.L. Hulin, and M. Roznowski. 1998. "The Importance of Individuals' Repertoires of Behaviors: The Scientific Appropriateness of Studying Multiple Behaviors and General Attitudes." *Journal of Organizational Behavior* 19: 463–80.

43. Griffin, M.A., A. Neal, and M. Neal. 2000. "The Contribution of Task Performance and Contextual Performance to Effectiveness: Investigating the Role of Situational Constraints." *Applied Psychology: An International Review* 49: 517–33.

44. Schmidt, F.L., and J.E. Hunter. 1998. "The Validity and Utility of Selection Methods in Personnel Psychology: Practical and Theoretical Implications of 85 Years of Research Findings." *Psychological Bulletin* 124: 262–74.

45. Schmidt, F.L. 2002. "The Role of General Cognitive Ability and Job Performance: Why There Cannot Be a Debate." *Human Performance* 15: 187–210.

46. Outz, J.L. 2002. "The Role of Cognitive Ability Tests in Employment Selection." *Human Performance* 15: 161–71.

47. Hogan, J., S.L. Rybicki, S.J. Motowidlo, and W.C. Borman. 1998. "Relations between Contextual Performance, Personality, and Occupational Advancement." *Human Performance* 11: 189–207.

48. McManus, M.A., and M.L. Kelly. 1999. "Personality Measures and Biodata: Evidence Regarding Their Incremental Predictive Value in the Life Insurance Industry." *Personnel Psychology* 52: 137–48.

49. Orr, J.M., P.R. Sackett, and M. Mercer. 1989. "The Role of Prescribed and Nonprescribed Behaviors in Estimating the Dollar Value of Performance." *Journal of Applied Psychology* 74: 34–40.

50. Rotundo, M., and P.R. Sackett. 2002.

51. Viswesvaran, C., and D.S. Ones. 2000. "Perspectives on Models of Job Performance." *International Journal of Selection and Assessment* 8: 216–26.

52. Daw, J. 2001.

53. Ones, D.S., C. Viswesvaran, and S. Dilchert. 2005. "Personality at Work: Raising Awareness and Correcting Misconceptions." *Human Performance* 18: 389–404.

54. Murphy, K.R., and A.H. Shiarella. 1997.

55. Rotundo, M., and P.R. Sackett. 2002.

56. Austin, J.T., and P. Villanova. 1992.

57. "Best Practices in Performance Appraisals." 2000.

58. Sulsky, L.M., and J.L. Keown. 1998. "Performance Appraisal in the Changing World of Work: Implications for the Meaning and Measurement of Work Performance." *Canadian Psychology* 39: 52–59.

59. Farrell, S., and R. Hakstian. June 2000. *A Meta-Analytic Review of the Effectiveness of Personnel Selection Procedures and Training Interventions in Sales Occupations.* Paper presented at the annual meeting of the Canadian Psychological Association, Ottawa.

60. Smith, P.C. 1976. "Behaviours, Results, and Organizational Effectiveness: The Problem of Criteria." In M.D. Dunnette, ed., *Handbook of Industrial and Organizational Psychology* (pp. 745–76). Chicago: Rand McNally.

61. Austin, J., and P. Villanova. 1992. "The Criterion Problem: 1917–1992." *Journal of Applied Psychology* 77: 836–74.

62. Austin, J., and T. Crespin. 2006. "Problems of Criteria in Industrial and Organizational Psychology: Progress, Pitfalls, and Prospects." In W. Bennett, Jr., C.E. Lance, and D.H. Woehr, eds., *Performance Measurement: Current Perspectives and Future Challenges* (pp. 9–48). Mahwah, NJ: Lawrence Erlbaum Associates.

63. Thorndike, R.L. 1949. *Personnel Selection: Test and Measurement Technique* (p. 121). New York: Wiley.

64. Austin, J., and P. Villanova. 1992.

65. Smith, P.C. 1976.

66. Guion, R.M. 1987. "Changing Views for Personnel Selection Research." *Personnel Psychology* 40: 199–213.

67. Landy, F.L. 1989. *Psychology of Work Behavior,* 4th ed. Pacific Grove, CA: Brooks/Cole.

68. Ghiselli, E.E. 1966. *The Validity of Occupational Aptitude Tests.* New York: Wiley.

69. Sackett, P.R., S. Zedeck, and L. Fogli. 1988. "Relations between Measures of Typical and Maximum Job Performance." *Journal of Applied Psychology* 73: 482–86.

70. Sackett, P. 2007. "Revisiting the Origins of the Typical-Maximum Performance Distinction." *Human Performance* 20: 179–85.

71. Marcus, B., R. Goffin, N. Johnston, and M. Rothstein. 2007. "Personality and Cognitive Ability as Predictors of Typical and Maximum Managerial Performance." *Human Performance* 20(3): 275–85.

72. Deadrick, D.L., and R.M. Madigan. 1990. "Dynamic Criteria Revisited: A Longitudinal Study of Performance Stability and Predictive Validity." *Personnel Psychology* 43: 717–44.

73. Austin, J., and P. Villanova. 1992.

74. Bowman, J.S. 1999. "Performance Appraisal: Verisimilitude Trumps Veracity." *Public Personnel Management* 28: 557–76.

75. Milliman, J., S. Nason, C. Zhu, and H. DeCieri. 2002. "An Exploratory Assessment of the Purposes of Performance Appraisals in North and Central America and the Pacific Rim." *Human Resource Management* 41: 87–102.

76. Bowman, J.S. 1999.

77. Martin, D.C., K.M. Bartol, and P.E. Kehoe. 2000. "The Legal Ramifications of Performance Appraisal: The Growing Significance." *Public Personnel Management* 29: 379–406.

78. Tziner, A., K.R. Murphy, and J.N. Cleveland. 2005. "Contextual and Rater Factors Affecting Rating Behavior." *Group & Organizational Management* 30: 89–98.

79. Austin, J., and P. Villanova. 1992.

80. Farrell, S., and R. Hakstian. 2000.

81. Bowman, J.S. 1999.

82. Murphy, K.R., and W.K. Balzer. 1989. "Rater Errors and Rating Accuracy." *Journal of Applied Psychology* 74: 619–24.

83. Nathan, B.R., and N. Tippins. 1990. "The Consequences of Halo 'Error' in Performance Ratings: A Field Study of the Moderating Effects of Halo on Test Validation Results." *Journal of Applied Psychology* 75: 290–96.

84. Murphy, K.R., and J.N. Cleveland. 1995. *Understanding Performance Appraisal: Social, Organizational, and Goal-Based Perspectives.* Thousand Oaks, CA: Sage.

85. Tziner, A., K.R. Murphy, and J.N. Cleveland. 2005.

86. Murphy, K.R., and J.N. Cleveland. 1995.

87. Goffin, R.D., I.R. Gellatly, S.V. Paunonen, D.N. Jackson, and J.P. Meyer. 1996. "Criterion Validation of Two Approaches to Performance Appraisal: The Behavioral Observation Scale and the Relative Percentile Method." *Journal of Business and Psychology* 11: 23–33.

88. Goffin, R.D., I.R. Gellatly, S.V. Paunonen, D.N. Jackson, and J.P. Meyer. 1996.

89. Wagner, S.H., and R.D. Goffin. 1997. "Differences in Accuracy of Individual and Comparative Performance Appraisal Methods." *Organizational Behavior and Human Decision Processes* 70: 95–103.

90. Greene, L., H.J. Bernardin, and J. Abbott. 1985. "A Comparison of Rating Formats after Correction for Attenuation." *Educational and Psychological Measurement* 45: 503–15.

91. Bowman, J.S. 1999.

92. Smith, P.C., and L.M. Kendall. 1963. "Retranslation of Expectations: An Approach to the Construction of Unambiguous Anchors for Rating Scales." *Journal of Applied Psychology* 47: 149–55.

93. Catano, V.M., W. Darr, and C.A. Campbell. 2007. "Performance Appraisal of Behavior-Based Competencies—A Reliable and Valid Procedure." *Personnel Psychology* 60: 201–30.

94. Latham, G.P., and K.N. Wexley. 1981. *Increasing Productivity through Performance Appraisal.* Reading, MA: Addison-Wesley.

95. Latham, G.P., and K.N. Wexley. 1981.

96. Murphy, K.R., and J.N. Cleveland. 1995.

97. Bowman, J.S. 1999.

98. Kaplan, R.S., and D.P. Norton. 1996. *The Balanced Scorecard: Translating Strategy into Action.* Boston: The Harvard Business School Press.

99. Meyer, C. 1998. "How the Right Measures Help Teams Excel." In *Harvard Business Review on Measuring Performance* (pp. 99–122). Boston: HBS Publishing.

100. Hedge, J.W., and M.S. Teachout. 2000. "Exploring the Concept of Acceptability as a Criterion for Evaluating Performance Measures." *Group & Organizational Management* 25: 22–44.

101. Smither, J.W. 1998. "Lessons Learned: Research Implications for Performance Appraisal and Management Practice." In J.W. Smither, ed., *Performance Appraisal: State of the Art in Practice.* San Francisco: Jossey Bass.

102. Latham, G.P., and G.H. Seijts. 1997. "The Effect of Appraisal Instrument on Managerial Perceptions of Fairness and Satisfaction with Appraisals from Peers." *Canadian Journal of Behavioural Science* 29: 278–82.

103. Werner, J.M., and M.C. Bolino. 1997. "Explaining U.S. Courts of Appeals Decisions Involving Performance Appraisal: Accuracy, Fairness, and Validation." *Personnel Psychology* 50: 1–24.

104. Cawley, B.D., L.M. Keeping, and P.E. Levy. 1998. "Participation in the Performance Appraisal Process and Employee Reactions: A Meta-Analytic Review of Field Investigations." *Journal of Applied Psychology* 83: 615–33.

105. Roberts, G. 2002. "Employee Performance Appraisal System Participation: A Technique That Works." *Public Personnel Management* 31: 333–42.

106. Rotundo, M., and P.R. Sackett. 2002.

107. Day, D.V., and L.M. Sulsky. 1995. "Effects of Frame-of-Reference Training and Ratee Information Configuration on Memory Organization and Rater Accuracy." *Journal of Applied Psychology* 80: 156–67.

108. Latham, G.P., and S. Mann. 2006. "Advances in the Science of Performance Appraisal: Implications for Practice." *International Review of Industrial and Organizational Psychology* 21: 295–337.

109. Uggerslev, K., and Sulsky, L. 2008. "Using Frame-of-Reference Training to Understand the Implications of Rater Idiosyncrasy for Rating Accuracy." *Journal of Applied Psychology* 93(3): 711–19.

110. Uggerslev, K., & Sulsky, L. 2008.

111. Roch, S.G., and L.A. McNall. 2007. "An Investigation of Factors Influencing Accountability and Performance Ratings." *The Journal of Psychology* 141: 499–523.

112. Gibb-Clark, M. 1996. "Court Orders Purolator to Pay Fired Employee." *The Globe and Mail* (May 4): B3.

113. Mero, N.P., R.M. Guidice, and A.L. Brownie. 2007. "Accountability in a Performance Appraisal Context: The Effect of Audience and Form of Accountability on Rater Response and Behavior." *Journal of Management* 33: 223–52.

114. Murphy, K.R., and J.N. Cleveland. 1995.

115. Saavedra, R., and S. Kwin. 1993. "Peer Evaluation in Self-Managing Work Groups." *Journal of Applied Psychology* 78: 450–62.

116. Borman, W.C. 1991.

117. Zazanis, M.M., S.J. Zaccaro, and R.N. Kilcullen. 2001. "Identifying Motivation and Interpersonal Performance Using Peer Evaluations." *Military Psychology* 13: 73–88.

118. Bernardin, H.J., and R. Beatty. 1984. *Performance Appraisal: Assessing Human Behavior at Work*. Boston: Kent-PWS.

119. Beehr, T.A., L. Ivanitskaya, C.P. Hansen, D. Erofeev, and D.M. Gudanowski. 2000. "Evaluation of 360 Degree Feedback Ratings: Relationships with Each Other and with Performance and Selection Procedures." *Journal of Organizational Behavior* 22: 755–88.

120. Cheung, G.W. 1999. "Multifaceted Conceptions of Self-Other Ratings Disagreement." *Personnel Psychology* 52: 1–36.

121. Bernardin, H.J. 1992. "An 'Analytic' Framework for Customer-Based Performance Content Development and Appraisal." *Human Resources Management Review* 2: 81–102.

122. Belcourt, M., A.W. Sherman, Jr., G.W. Bohlander, and S.A. Snell. 1996. *Managing Human Resources*. Toronto: Nelson Canada.

123. Sulsky, L.M., and J.L. Keown. 1998.

124. Ghorpade, J. 2000. "Managing Five Paradoxes of 360-Degree Feedback." *Academy of Management Executive* 14: 140–50.

125. Brutus, S., and M. Derayeh. 2002. "Multisource Assessment Programs in Organizations: An Insider's Perspective." *Human Resource Development Quarterly* 13: 187–202.

126. Ghorpade, J. 2000.

127. Brutus, S., and M. Derayeh. 2002.

128. Beehr, T.A., L. Ivanitskaya, C.P. Hansen, D. Erofeev, and D.M. Gudanowski. 2000.

129. Harris, M.M., and J. Schaubroeck. 1988. "A Meta-Analysis of Self-Supervisor, Self-Peer, and Peer-Supervisor Ratings." *Personnel Psychology* 41: 43–62.

130. Furnham, A., and P. Stringfield. 1998. "Congruence in Job-Performance Ratings: A Study of 360-Degree Feedback Examining Self, Manager, Peers, and Consultant Ratings." *Human Relations* 51: 517–30.

131. Bailey, C., and Fletcher, C. 2002. "The Impact of Multiple Source Feedback on Management Development: Findings from a Longitudinal Study." *Journal of Organizational Behavior* 23: 853–67.

132. Darr, W., and V.M. Catano. 2008. "Multisource Assessments of Behavioral Competencies and Selection Interview Performance." *International Journal of Selection and Assessment* 16: 68–72.

133. Harris, M.M., and J. Schaubroeck. 1988.

134. Sulsky, L.M., and J.L. Keown. 1998.

135. Whiting, S., P. Podsakoff, and J. Pierce. 2008. "Effects of Task Performance, Helping, Voice, and Organizational Loyalty on Performance Appraisal Ratings." *Journal of Applied Psychology* 93: 125–39.

136. McCurry, P. 1999. "New Angle on 360-Degree Feedback." *Director* 53: 36.

137. Murphy, K.R. 1989. "Dimensions of Job Performance." In R.F. Dillon and J.W. Pelligrino, eds., *Testing: Theoretical and Applied Perspectives* (pp. 218–47). New York: Praeger.

138. Catano, V.M., W. Darr, and C.A. Campbell. 2007.

139. *Griggs v. Duke Power*. 1971. 401 U.S. 424.

140. Cronshaw, S.F. 1986. "The Status of Employment Testing in Canada: A Review and Evaluation of Theory and Professional Practice." *Canadian Psychology* 27: 183–95.

141. Cronshaw, S.F. 1988. "Future Directions for Industrial Psychology in Canada." *Canadian Psychology* 29: 30–43.

142. Barrett, G.V., and M.C. Kernan. 1987. "Performance Appraisal and Terminations: A Review of Court Decisions since *Brito v. Zia* with Implications for Personnel Practices." *Personnel Psychology* 40: 489–503.

143. *British Columbia (Public Service Employee Relations Commission) v. BCGSEU.* Supreme Court of Canada decision rendered September 9, 1999.
144. Landy, F.L. 1989.
145. *B.L. Mears, Gifford Walker, George Wills, Hollis Trotman, Thomas Atherly, Hubert Telphia and Leon Francis v. Ontario Hydro and Jack Watson, A. Watkiss, T. Ouelette and Mossis Loveness.* 1984. *Canadian Human Rights Reporter* 5: D/3433. Ontario Human Rights Commission Board of Inquiry, December 1983.
146. Barrett, G.V., and M.C. Kernan. 1987.
147. Dewberry, C. 2001. "Performance Disparities between Whites and Ethnic Minorities: Real Differences or Assessment Bias?" *Journal of Occupational and Organizational Psychology* 74: 659–73.
148. Lefkowitz, J., and M. Battista. 1995. "Potential Sources of Criterion Bias in Supervisor Ratings Used for Test Validation." *Journal of Business and Psychology* 9: 389–414.
149. Dewberry, C. 2001.
150. Bowen, C.C., J.K. Swim, and R.R. Jacobs. 2000. "Evaluating Gender Biases on Actual Job Performance of Real People: A Meta-Analysis." *Journal of Applied Social Psychology* 30: 2194–215.
151. Pazy, A., and I. Oron. 2001. "Sex Proportion and Performance Evaluation among High-Ranking Military Officers." *Journal of Organizational Behavior* 22: 689–702.
152. Cronshaw, S.F. 1988. "Future Directions for Industrial Psychology in Canada." *Canadian Psychology* 29: 30–43.
153. "Uniform Guidelines on Employee Selection Procedures." 1978. *Federal Register* 43: 38290–315.
154. "Uniform Guidelines on Employee Selection Procedures." 1978.
155. Campbell, J.P. 1990.
156. Campbell, J.P. 1990.
157. Shaw, D.G., C.E. Schneier, and R.W. Beatty. 1991. "Managing Performance with a Behaviorally Based Appraisal System." In J. Jones, B.D. Steffy, and D.W Bray, eds., *Applying Psychology in Business: The Handbook for Managers and Human Resource Professionals* (pp. 314–25). New York: Lexington Books.

Chapter

6

Recruitment: The First Step in the Selection Process

Chapter Learning Objectives

This chapter reviews the role played by recruitment in human resources planning. We present this topic from the perspective of recruitment as the first step in selection. The first part of the chapter reviews factors that may attract job applicants and influence them to apply for jobs with an organization. The second part reviews different recruitment methods and their overall effectiveness.

After reading this chapter you should:

- understand the link between recruitment and selection;
- appreciate how the characteristics of the job and organization are influential in attracting job applicants;
- know the role that accurate expectations play in developing a fit between a person and an organization;
- be able to discuss why a realistic job preview may benefit both the job seeker and the organization;
- be aware of the internal and external factors that influence an organization's recruitment strategy;
- be able to design and implement a recruitment action plan;
- be aware of the different methods that can be used to recruit internal and external job applicants;
- understand the increasingly important role played by the Internet in recruiting; and
- appreciate the need to evaluate the effectiveness of different recruitment methods.

On January 30, 1997, major newspapers in North America featured a news item in their sports pages that a former heavyweight boxing champion, Riddick Bowe, had joined the United States Marine Corps Reserve and would soon be headed for 12 weeks of basic training at Paris Island, South Carolina. Bowe, who was 29 years old with a wife and five children plus an estimated US$100 million in the bank, was quoted as saying that joining the Marines was a lifelong dream and something he wanted to do before he got too old. He also wanted to make his mother proud of him and to prove everyone wrong who said he wouldn't make it. These motives differed considerably from those of most people who join the U.S. military: service to country, education, training, adventure, and money. The Marines accepted Bowe's enthusiasm in place of the specific motivators it looks for in new recruits.*

On February 22, 1997, the newspapers were once again filled with a story about Riddick Bowe. "Bowe finds Marine life hits too hard," said the headline in the *Toronto Star*. "What did he imagine he was getting into?"† Bowe left the Marines after 11 days of basic training. The Marines had, in fact, waived several of their selection criteria to enroll a high-profile celebrity in the belief that his prowess and physical conditioning as a boxer would compensate for his deficiencies on the waived criteria. They believed his physical conditioning and training were a match for the physical conditioning requirements of boot camp.*

The Marines did not appreciate the difference between the training regimen of a heavyweight boxer, where an entourage is at hand to cater to the fighter's every need, and boot camp, where a no-nonsense drill instructor makes a trainee repeat exercises until the drill instructor is satisfied. They also failed to realize that one of the criteria they waived, not to enroll people with more than one dependant, was there for a very valid reason: Bowe severely missed his kids and extended family.*

On the whole, Bowe had developed a very unrealistic perception of life as a Marine, based on watching movies like *Full Metal Jacket*. He did not understand that boot camp was a process that was important in socializing new recruits into the Marine Corps values and traditions. For its part, the Marines never gave Bowe a realistic preview of what life would be like at boot camp. Bowe suffered culture shock in going from being a multimillionaire who had complete control over his life to someone who had to take orders from a drill instructor 24 hours a day.*

Riddick Bowe failed, in part, because the Marines deviated from a very successful recruitment and selection program that gave recruits a realistic expectation of what was in store for them and an introduction to the culture of the Marine Corps. By waiving selection criteria, they created a mismatch between Bowe and the Marines. A fit between a person and an organization is vital to establishing a long-term relationship between both. The answer to the question posed by the *Toronto Star* was that Riddick Bowe had no idea what he was getting into until he arrived at boot camp. He had based his decision on the myth of the Marine Corps, reflected in the handsome dress uniform, rather than the reality of someone continuously in his face as part of being socialized into the values and culture of the Marines.

For their part, the Marines, in their desire to enroll a high-profile celebrity, did not make their usual effort to provide Bowe with a realistic and accurate preview of either the job or the organization. They ignored the fact that they had established the selection criteria, which they waived, precisely to prevent this type of situation from occurring. The end result was a high-profile failure for both Riddick Bowe and the U.S. Marine Corps.

Sources: * H.E. Baker, III, and K.M. Jennings. 2000. "Limitations in 'Realistic Recruiting' and Subsequent Socialization Efforts: The Case of Riddick Bowe and the United States Marine Corps." *Public Personnel Management* 29: 367–77. † G. Woolsey. 1997. "Bowe Finds Marine Life Hits Too Hard." *Toronto Star* (February 22): B3.

The Riddick Bowe case is not an isolated example. Failures of this type occur every day in business and industry; we just don't hear about them. In the first part of this chapter, we review those organizational factors that attract job candidates and procedures that can be used to ensure job candidates are provided with accurate information about the job and organization. Accurate information and expectations help to prevent recruitment failures and promote the staffing of organizations with people who are not only qualified for the job but also have a good understanding of the organization in which the job takes place. In the last half of the chapter, we discuss factors that affect an organization's recruitment strategy, including the media that an organization uses as part of its recruitment strategy, and provide an assessment of the different recruitment strategies.

Attracting Job Applicants

Recruitment is the first step in the selection process. People apply for jobs in organizations on the basis of their interest in the job and their belief that they have the required knowledge, skills, abilities, and other talents needed to do the job well. They also hope that the organization will provide a hospitable environment in which to spend their working hours. Obviously, this is an idealized view of the world; in bad economic times, when jobs are at a premium, people may change their perceptions of jobs and organizations, as well as their willingness to work in either. In hard economic times, people may value the security of having a job and the income it provides above everything else. However, security and income, although important considerations, are not always the most influential factors in attracting applicants to jobs or organizations.

Figure 6.1 presents a simplified view of the human resources management system, which serves as the framework for our discussion of recruitment issues in this chapter. In this model, recruitment is an outcome of human resources planning. The decision to recruit candidates for jobs in an organization is based on (1) an assessment of the internal and external factors affecting the organization, (2) an organization analysis based on those factors, and (3) a job analysis that identifies worker behaviours and characteristics to aid in selecting candidates who are qualified for the position.

The ultimate goal of a job-related selection system is to bring people into the organization who will perform at above-average levels and who will increase the productivity of the organization. The goal of **recruitment** is to attract a large pool of qualified candidates (an **applicant pool**) from whom the organization can select the best-qualified people for the position. Recruitment is done to meet management goals and objectives for the organization and must also meet current legal requirements (human rights, employment equity, labour law, and other legislation).

Only within the last 25 years has recruitment received serious attention for the important role it plays in the selection process. Previously, recruitment was simply a means of attracting a large enough pool of candidates from which the organization could select the best-qualified people, without much thought as to how that was done or what factors influenced applicants to become part of that pool of candidates.[1] The availability of a job and the need for money were assumed to be motivation enough to attract candidates. Hardly any consideration was given to the possibility that candidates were using the recruiting process to select the organization. Job applicants are not passive organisms. During the recruitment and selection process, they form opinions about the organization, the selection process, the people they meet, and the desirability of working in the organization.

In effect, recruiting has become a two-way street. Breaugh and Starke[2] present a model of how the formation of job expectations on the part of an applicant influences their attitudes and behaviours toward an organization and a job (see Figure 6.2). We will examine several components of this model throughout this chapter.

Because of their experience, many candidates conclude that they do not want to work in a particular organization, or that they will not fit in; they may also form other attitudes, which last through their early work experience.[3] A study of over 3500 police applicants showed that those who self-selected out of the process and those who stayed differed in their perceptions of the organization, expectations about the job, and the opinions of family and friends about joining the police.[4]

 6.1

Recruitment

The generation of an applicant pool for a position or job in order to provide the required number of qualified candidates for a subsequent selection or promotion process.

Applicant pool

The set of potential candidates who may be interested in, and who are likely to apply for, a specific job.

Recruitment and Selection in Canada

FIGURE 6.1

Recruitment as Part of the HR Planning Process

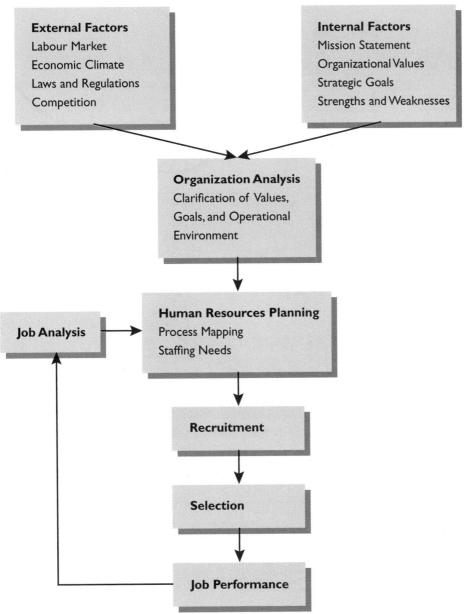

In the long run, such **self-selecting out** may be in the best interests of both the applicant and the organization, if that decision is based on accurate information and a realistic perception of the job and the organization. It certainly would have been in the case of Riddick Bowe and the U.S. Marines. On the other hand, if these early decisions are based on inaccurate information,

Self-selecting out

Occurs during the recruitment and selection process when candidates form the opinion that they do not want to work in the organization for which they are being recruited.

FIGURE 6.2

The Formation of Job Expectations and Their Influence on Job Applicant Attitudes and Behaviours

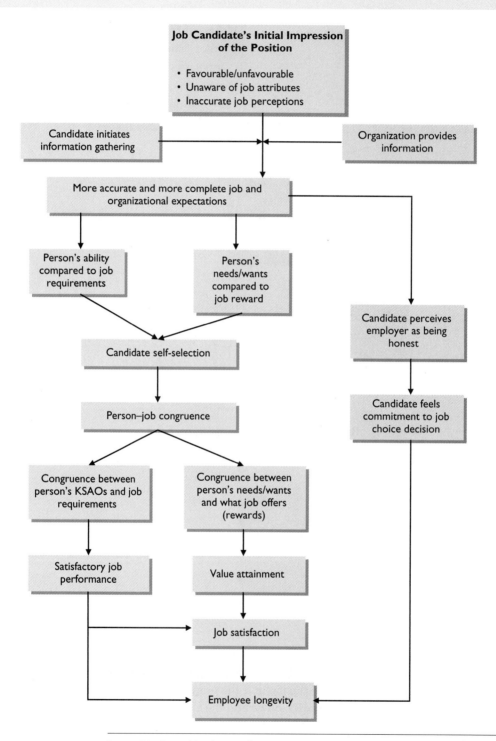

Source: J.A. Breaugh and M. Starke. 2000. "Research on Employee Recruitment: So Many Studies, So Many Questions," Figure 2. *Journal of Management* 26: 405–34. Copyright © 2000 Sage Publications, Inc. Reprinted with permission of the Copyright Clearance Center (CCC).

both the candidate and the organization may be worse off. Ryan and colleagues[5] found that the perceptions of women and blacks who withdrew from the police application process differed from the majority group, posing difficulties for organizations trying to increase their diversity.

The Organizational Context

Individuals become job applicants after forming an opinion on the desirability of working in a particular job within a specific organization.[6] Organizational characteristics such as location, size of the enterprise, and type of industry may steer individuals away from applying for jobs no matter how attractive the job or how qualified they are to do it.[7] For example, a physician is unlikely to apply for a position in the Yukon if she is concerned about her aging parents living in Nova Scotia, regardless of pay or career opportunities. Location may be the main factor in deciding whether to apply for the position.

In today's rapidly changing workplace with a highly educated work force, jobs providing autonomy, decision-making authority, and opportunities for self-development win out over those that lack these attributes. Moreover, with the increase in dual-career couples, single-parent families, and female representation in the work force, organizations that offer special accommodations and flexible work arrangements gain competitive advantages in recruiting. For positions requiring geographical relocation of candidates, employers that assist working spouses to secure local employment gain further advantage.

Ultimately, the interests and values of the job applicant influence the relative importance of different organizational attributes and whether an individual will apply for a specific job. Interests and values do not indicate whether a person is qualified for a job; they only suggest the type of work a person may find satisfying. Potential job applicants must also have the knowledge, skills, abilities, and other attributes (KSAOs) or competencies that are required for the job. Nonetheless, the degree of satisfaction with a job is one of the many factors that influence job turnover, especially in good economic times when jobs are plentiful.[8]

The Department of National Defence actively recruits members for both civilian and military jobs in the Canadian Forces through its website (http://www.forces.ca/Default.aspx?bhcp=1), which includes a "Jobs" menu that provides information on specific jobs and occupations in the Canadian Forces. The site also includes information on the working environment and requirements for entry and training for the different positions. Many professional associations also provide information on careers in their professions and the KSAOs and credentials needed for entry. These sites also list positions that are available. A good example, which deals with chartered accountants, is http://www.casource.com.

The size of an organization influences its attractiveness to prospective employees, as well as the organization's recruitment strategies. A study of 119 small-business employers and 184 large employers showed that job seekers have distinct preferences regarding firm size that influence their job search behaviours to such an extent that one might argue that large and small

Interests and values

An individual's likes and dislikes and the importance or priorities attached to those likes and dislikes.

Job search

The strategies, techniques, and practices an individual uses in looking for a job.

firms comprise separate labour markets.[9] Job seekers appear to tailor their **job search** to match the recruiting strategies used by large or small organizations. Large firms, particularly when recruiting college or university graduates, tend to have more formal and bureaucratic recruiting practices, while smaller firms rely on more informal methods.

Large firms tend to start recruiting earlier and to use trained recruiters and campus placement offices. They also are more likely to base their decisions on a candidate's objective qualifications and the results of employment tests. Smaller firms tend to rely more on traditional sources such as advertising and internal referrals to fill their positions and to base their decisions on an interview. Students who prefer a large firm start their job search earlier and make use of recruiting sources, such as the campus placement office, that are used by larger firms. Students who prefer smaller firms are less intense in their search efforts and rely on traditional sources of information about jobs.[10]

The strategies and information that people use in forming preferences and opinions about organizations are by no means clear. In some cases, such as Riddick Bowe and the U.S. Marines, information is based on preconceived stereotypes or information obtained from inaccurate sources. In other cases, people may undertake extensive job searches before applying for employment with an organization. They may consult a variety of published documents for information about the organization, including annual reports and stories about the company and its employees in newspapers and business periodicals. Also, they might check companies' Internet sites for job opportunities.

Internet employment-related websites offer profiles on the various companies that use their sites. For example, Monster.ca (http://www.monster.ca) provides information on who the company is, its major products or services, the number of people it employs, its location, and current employment opportunities. The Government of Canada now uses the Internet extensively to recruit people for different positions throughout Canada. Job listings can be found at http://jobs-emplois.gc.ca/index-eng.htm. Selecting a specific job posting provides a wealth of information about the job and its organizational environment. Also, job applicants sometimes seek out employees of an organization or friends or acquaintances who have worked for a company to obtain personal views on what it is like to work there and what the employees are like as co-workers. Recruitment and Selection Today 6.1 provides more information on Internet job searches.

Corporate Image

Often, the reputation of an organization is an important concern to job applicants. Corporate image predicts the likelihood of interest on the part of a job seeker: The better the image, the more attractive the organization is.[11] Again, consider the case of Riddick Bowe—his attraction to the U.S. Marines was based on romanticized portrayals in movies. Job seekers may not even consider applying for jobs in organizations that have a negative image. This lack of attractiveness may be particularly troublesome in tight labour markets, when there is a scarcity of qualified job applicants.

Government-Sponsored Internet Job Site

One of the most useful tools in conducting a job search is the Internet, where there are hundreds of sites related to work and occupations. One of the best is the Job Bank site operated by Service Canada at http://www.servicecanada .gc.ca/en/sc/jobs/jobbank.shtml on behalf of Human Resources and Social Development Canada (HRSDC). The Job Bank provides a wealth of information not only about jobs available across Canada, but also about effective job search strategies, including information on preparing a résumé. Available jobs are listed by province and territory, and there are also links to numerous other public- and private-sector employment sites.

Service Canada also has a "Training, Career, and Worker Information" site at https://www.emploisetc.ca/ home.jsp. This site has an interactive feature that takes the user through a series of quizzes to help identify possible career choices (choose "Career Exploration" and then

"Identify your career options"). By choosing a resulting identified occupation, the Career Navigator will provide you with information (wages, number of jobs available, and employment prospects, etc.) to help you make an informed career decision. The quizzes relate to:

- Abilities
- Data, people, things
- Work preference
- Work values
- Multiple intelligence
- Seeing, hearing, doing

The variety and depth of the information provided, plus the links to many excellent relevant sites, means that spending time at the Service Canada website before beginning a job search will be time well invested.

What influences organizational attractiveness? One of the most prominent factors that influence perceptions of an organization's image is the job applicant's degree of familiarity with the organization. The more familiar the applicants are with the company, the more likely they will hold a positive image of it.[12,13] The profitability of a company and its pay level positively influence attractiveness and reputation,[14] with pay strongly predicting whether a job applicant will pursue a job with an organization.[15] Job applicants rate vacant positions as less attractive when the company's help-wanted advertisements contain minimal information about both the attributes of the position and the pay associated with it.[16]

Organizations often initiate activities designed to enhance their image and reputation. Providing job applicants with more information about an organization appears to influence job applicant behaviour; organizational familiarity, and thus attractiveness, seems to increase when an applicant receives more information about a company through employment advertisements and other recruitment materials.[17] A company's recruitment image is also affected by the advertisements it places for products or services.[18] Many companies undertake **image advertising** to raise the profile of their organizations in a positive manner to attract interest from job seekers, as well as increasing interest in its services and products.[19] A good example of image advertising is the sponsorship of the many summer jazz festivals and other cultural events by Canadian companies. The hope is that associating their

Image advertising

Advertising designed to raise an organization's profile in a positive manner in order to attract job seekers' interest.

names with high-profile events will improve the corporate image and result in greater interest in the company.[20] Presumably, working for companies with positive images raises the self-esteem of employees, and this prospect is attractive to potential employees.[21]

Similar to image advertising, another strategy that corporations use to enhance their identity in the marketplace and to sell the organization is "branding." Companies use branding to establish certain perceptions about the corporation in the public's mind through associating the organization with high-profile celebrities or being known as one of the best 100 employers in Canada. Again, these strategies may backfire. Many retail companies used Martha Stewart, who had a reputation for sensible style and elegance, as a means of enhancing their own identity through associating her with many of their own products. After Stewart was indicted on charges of securities fraud and obstruction of justice, these same companies scrambled to disassociate themselves from her.

An organization that is having trouble attracting qualified candidates should investigate how it is perceived by job candidates and take corrective action, if necessary. One of the difficulties here is identifying the components that influence an organization's image, as different individuals may have different perceptions of the same company. Job seekers and company executives may hold very different perceptions of the organization's image. Image advertising must present an accurate and consistent picture of the organization. Image advertising that creates misperceptions will lead to mismatches in the fit between person and organization and lead to more Riddick Bowe cases. Image advertising should be designed to improve the attractiveness of the organization on the basis of an accurate representation of its characteristics. Recruitment and Selection Notebook 6.1 provides a few guidelines for organizational recruiting.

Recruitment and Selection Notebook 6.1

Guidelines for Effective Recruiting

- Ensure that candidates receive consistent and non-contradictory information about important features of the job and its environment from all people involved in the recruiting process.
- Recognize that the behaviour of recruiters and other representatives gives an impression of the organization's climate, efficiency, and attitude toward employees.
- Ensure that all recruiting information and materials given to job applicants present accurate and consistent information, whether positive or negative.

- Present important information to job candidates by several different, reliable, and credible sources.
- Give serious consideration not only to the content of information presented to candidates but also to the context in which it is presented.

Take extreme care in preparing recruiting materials and selecting advertising media, and also in choosing the recruiters who will interact with job applicants.

The Person–Organization Fit

No matter how desirable or compatible a job and organization appear to the candidate, it is all for naught unless the candidate receives an offer of employment. During the recruitment process, the organization, through its representatives, is seeking to learn as much as it can about the candidate. Recruiters assess potential employees in terms of their fit with both the job and the organization. **Person–job fit** concerns whether the job applicant has the knowledge, skills, abilities, or competencies required by the job, while **person–organization fit** is the recruiter's belief that the candidate fits with the organization's values and culture; that is, the candidate has the contextual attributes that company is looking for.

Recruiters distinguish between these two types of "fit" and tend to make decisions early in their interview with a candidate on whether the candidate matches what the organization is looking for.[22] The recruiter's perception that the applicant fits the job appears to be based mainly on an assessment of the candidate's skills and experience, derived from information gathered during the recruiting process. These sources are likely to include a review of the candidate's résumé and a brief screening interview. In some cases, candidates may also be asked to take employment tests at this stage. These screening and selection procedures are the focus of Chapters 7, 8, and 9. The recruiter's perception of a person–organization fit is mostly based on an assessment of the candidate's personality and values.

Both the perception of person–job fit and of person–organization fit predict whether the company will make a job offer. The perception of a poor person–organization fit, however, will reduce the likelihood that a person with a good job fit will receive a job offer. Recruiters form and use perceptions of a candidate's organizational fit as part of the hiring process.[23]

The assessment of fit and the decision of the company to make an offer and the candidate to accept it are based on the exchange of information that takes place over the recruitment process. If the job candidate does not make an adequate investigation of the job or organization, or if the organization does not represent itself accurately through the people involved in recruiting and selection, the probability of a person–organization mismatch increases. Mismatches can be quite costly in terms of absenteeism, low productivity, and turnover. A major goal of any recruitment campaign should be to improve the chance of making a good fit between candidates and the organization.

Communication and Perception

Based on information that was available or obtained during the recruitment process, the candidate and the organization form a perception of each other. If the perceptions of both are positive ("This is the right candidate," "This is the right job for me"), a job offer is made and accepted. If the perceptions of one do not match those of the other, a job offer is either not made, or if made, not accepted. Figure 6.3 presents the possible outcomes from this process. In all cases, there is a possibility that the perceptions formed by the candidate

Person–job fit
This is the case when a job candidate has the knowledge, skills, abilities, or competencies required by the job in question.

Person–organization fit
This is the case when a job candidate fits the organization's values and culture and has the contextual attributes desired by the organization.

FIGURE 6.3

Matching the Candidate's and Organization's Perceptions: Job Offer Outcomes

		Candidate's Perception of the Organization	
		Positive	Negative
Organization's Perception of the Candidate	Positive	Job offer made by organization and accepted by candidate.	Job offer made by organization and rejected by candidate.
	Negative	Job offer not made by organization but would have been accepted by candidate.	Job offer not made by organization and would not have been accepted by candidate.

and/or the organization are wrong. Candidates, particularly, may develop overly positive perceptions of the organization.[24]

Perceptions are based on communication. During the recruiting process both the candidate and the organization try to control the flow of information from one to the other. One party may not wish to share some information with the other. An organization may fear losing top-quality candidates by revealing that it is not the perfect workplace; candidates may fear losing a job offer by admitting they do not plan to stay with the organization for a long period of time. Both may misrepresent their attributes or characteristics. An organization may exaggerate the chances for promotion to attract a candidate; candidates may exaggerate their experience. Both the organization and the candidate evaluate each other during the recruitment process.[25]

Inaccurate, incomplete, or distorted information leads to misperceptions and inaccurate decisions. A primary goal of recruitment should be to increase the accuracy of the perceptions that each party holds about the other.

Accurate Expectations

By developing a systematic job search strategy, job candidates will come into contact with information on jobs and organizations. Many of the initial expectations that candidates develop are based on the accuracy of this preliminary information, as well as the more extensive information that accumulates during the recruiting process. For example, accuracy of information received from the recruiting source and the organization directly influenced the length of time that Canadian students stayed in seasonal jobs, as well as their commitment to the organization and their job satisfaction.[26] Candidates actively evaluate the merits of any message they receive.[27] Organizations, however, have no control over whether candidates search for any information, or which information they select and use in forming an opinion about the job or organization.

Newcomers in an organization often develop overly high expectations about the job and organization. These initial expectations may substantially influence the long-term relationship between the candidate and the organization.[28] Organizations do, however, have control over the accuracy and the completeness of the information they present when recruiting job candidates (see Recruitment and Selection Notebook 6.2). During the United States' first war with Iraq, many military personnel who were recruited into the U.S. Reserve Forces were shocked and outraged to learn that they were liable for combat duty; they claimed that they had never been made aware of such a possibility before signing on.[29] Unmet expectations on the part of new hires leads to lack of job satisfaction and organizational commitment.[30]

Courts in both Canada and the United States have held employers accountable for the accuracy of information they present to job candidates as part of the recruiting process. False promises and misrepresentations

---

Recruitment and Selection Notebook 6.2

Creating Accurate Expectations

Four factors play an influential role in creating accurate expectations that candidates hold about prospective jobs:

1. **Source of Information.** In describing a job or position, the organization should present information to job candidates that accurately describes the job and its context.
2. **Communication Media.** Recruitment media differ in their effectiveness. Organizations should use as many different types of communication media as it can afford, including newer technologies such as job postings on their websites or on Internet employment sites.
3. **Content of Information.** The content of information provided throughout the recruitment process is the most important factor in creating accurate job expectations and should be:
   - Accurate—Job candidates should be given both positive and negative information about the job and the organization.
   - Specific—Job candidates should be given detailed information that will allow them to make an informed decision.

   - Broad—Job candidates should be given information about a wide range of job and organizational attributes, not only information related to a narrow range of topics.
   - Credible—Job candidates must believe that the information they receive is reliable and accurate.
   - Important—Job candidates should be given information that is important to their decision making which they are unlikely to receive through other means.
4. **Nature of the Job Candidates.** The organization must know something about the audience that it wants to respond to the information. This includes knowledge of the social and demographic characteristics of the target group. The content of the message should be compatible with its intended audience and address their needs and interests. It should be placed in media most likely to be used by the target group.

made in recruiting candidates to work for a company may result in a damage award. Employees who believe that they were misled about the nature of their working conditions or their working environment are likely to take legal action against their employers to the extent that they are injured through reliance on the false or misleading statements.[31] As part of orienting newcomers into an organization, a company may wish to initiate a set of procedures that are designed to lower the expectations of the new hire to more realistic and accurate perceptions of the organization, apart from that individual's specific job.[32]

Realistic Job Previews

Recruitment programs can be designed to increase the accuracy of the expectations that job candidates hold about the job and the organization. One such program, **realistic job previews** (RJPs), is intended to improve the possibility of identifying a fit between the job candidate and the organization. The primary goal of RJPs is to reduce turnover among newcomers to an organization by providing job candidates with accurate information about the job and the organization.[33] Other hoped-for outcomes of the RJP are (1) that the job candidates will develop realistic perceptions of what it is like to work in the organization, (2) that they will view the organization in a more credible light, and (3) that, if they accept the job offer, they will be more satisfied with their job and committed to the organization. Extensive research shows that while RJPs accomplish their goals, they do so at a modest level.[34]

Rather than have a candidate accept a job on the basis of unrealistic expectations, only to quit after discovering a mismatch with the organization, RJPs give the candidate an accurate preview of the job before the job offer is accepted (e.g., weekend work, limited promotional opportunities). In this way, candidates who discover a mismatch self-select out, or remove themselves from the competition, saving themselves the aggravation of having made a bad decision and the organization the cost of hiring and training them. There are some concerns, however, that the realism also discourages very qualified candidates from accepting job offers from the organization;[35] however, the number of withdrawals from the applicant pool after an RJP is not great.[36]

The more exposure a job applicant has to a job, the more likely it is that the applicant may overemphasize the negative aspects of the job and refuse a job offer; this aspect of RJPs may prove problematic in extremely competitive job markets.[37] The negative information in the RJP appears to influence the job applicant's decision and may have a greater adverse impact on the best-qualified applicants,[38] requiring greater compensation to attract them to the position.[39]

On the other hand, presenting negative information as part of the RJP may have positive effects. In addition to lowering job candidates' expectations and attraction to the organization, RJPs may increase perceptions of the trustworthiness of the organization and facilitate a person–organization match more so than a traditional job preview.[40] Similarly, RJPs enhance a job candidate's perception that the organization is a caring one that is concerned

Realistic Job Previews in the Canadian Forces

The Canadian Forces (CF) use RJPs as part of their recruitment program. The program was designed to reduce early attrition of new recruits by improving identification of both the person–job fit and person–organization fit. RJPs are carried out throughout the Canadian Forces as a matter of policy. They are embedded in a comprehensive counselling system designed to match the goals, interests, and abilities of applicants to the characteristics and conditions of service associated with specific trades in the CF.

By using advertising media and recruiting visits to schools and public places such as shopping malls, the Canadian Forces raise the interest of potential applicants in the military as a career and attract them to recruiting centres. The applicant is met by a recruiting officer, who presents the candidate with brochures and information on the CF and determines initial suitability of the candidate for a CF career. Applicants who pass this first screening then view an orientation video, which depicts the careers of two actual candidates from recruitment through basic and trades training, and on to their first job postings. The video provides a realistic preview of life in the forces in general and includes information on both the positive and negative aspects of military life. For example, it may portray the personal and social support offered to CF members and their families as well as the hazards and physical demands of military duty.

Following the orientation video, the candidate meets with a military career counsellor and has an opportunity to raise any questions or concerns stimulated by the video. At this point, the candidate must make a decision about whether to continue the process by completing an application form and a series of ability and aptitude tests. Candidates are next shown up to five trade/lifestyle videos for entry-level positions for which they qualified through ability and aptitude testing. These videos are based on interviews with personnel from each trade they represent; they contain both verbal descriptions and live-action footage of what it is like to work in that trade in a military environment. The speakers not only provide a description of what the trade is like but also express their views about their work.

Following these videos, the candidate meets once again with a military career counsellor to review all aspects of the different trades and the military lifestyle. If the candidate remains interested in one of the selected trades, if there is an appropriate vacancy in that specialty, and if the candidate has passed a series of employment tests and interviews, the candidate is given an offer to enroll in the Canadian Forces. This offer is made conditional on the candidate's meeting appropriate medical and physical requirements.

Internet versions of some of the initial RJP material can be found on the Canadian Forces website at http://www.forces.ca/Default.aspx?bhcp51#en81-81. Clicking on "Jobs Explorer" and then on the "Hot Jobs" button produces a list of available CF jobs. If you select "Personnel Selection Officer," a function similar to many HR positions, a written description of the job is provided, along with photos and a video that illustrate the working environment.

As illustrated by this example, RJPs, when done right, require an extensive array of resources during their development and implementation. The cost to produce an RJP may place it beyond the reach of many small- to medium-sized organizations.

for its employees.[41] There is some evidence that RJPs lead to increased commitment and reduced turnover through perceptions of employer concern and honesty.[42] Recruitment and Selection Today 6.2 outlines the use of RJPs in the Canadian Forces.

RJPs remain one of the most intriguing aspects of the recruiting process. Notwithstanding the methodological flaws in RJP research,[43] RJPs lead to accurate expectations on the part of job candidates, to reductions in turnover, and to improvements in job satisfaction;[44] however, the magnitudes of these significant effects are small, raising questions about whether the costs and time needed to develop an RJP are balanced or offset by its benefits. Rynes and Cable[45] do not expect RJPs to remain a major priority for recruitment research, given the modest effects found by Phillips.[46]

Nonetheless, when prospective employees know more about an organization, whether through an RJP or other means, there appear to be more positive outcomes for the employees with respect to their job satisfaction and organizational commitment. Moser[47] found that job applicants who were recruited by an organization through referrals from family and friends, internships, or in-house notices had fewer unmet expectations about the job and expressed more job satisfaction and organizational commitment. Moser argued that the internal recruitment sources provided the applicants with more and better information about the organization and the jobs, much like an RJP.

Expectation-Lowering Procedures

Today's increasingly educated workers have higher expectations about their workplaces and their jobs. They expect greater opportunities for skill development and empowerment (i.e., input into decision making). Many of these expectations may be unrealistic. Realistic job previews may be a valuable tool in helping to lower these expectations to more reasonable levels and to improve communications and trust. There is another step an organization can take to ensure accurate expectations once job applicants become new hires. Many companies have new hires go through an orientation procedure to learn about the policies and practices of the company. The inclusion of material designed to lower expectations as part of this orientation will also lead to a reduction in some of the negative outcomes experienced by new hires. These expectancy-lowering procedures (ELPs) focus on the expectations of the new hires rather than on specific aspects of the job or organization, which are typically included in an RJP.

An ELP workshop would present information showing (1) how important it is to have realistic expectations at the start of a job and how expectations are formed, (2) how unrealistically high expectations are related to negative organizational outcomes, and (3) how unrealistically high expectations that remain unfulfilled lead to dissatisfaction with work and turnover. Buckley and his colleagues[48] demonstrated that an ELP such as this led to less dissatisfaction and turnover and recommended that organizations use it as a complement to RJPs.

Subsequently, Buckley and another team of researchers[49] assessed the effectiveness of an ELP, RJP, or both together in predicting the number of days worked by applicants for telemarketing jobs, which are notorious for high turnover rates. The combination of RJP and ELP given to all job applicants resulted in the largest number of days worked by candidates who were hired, compared to applicants who were given only one of the procedures or no preview at all. The RJP by itself did not increase the number of days worked beyond that of the group not given any preview.

Decision-Making Training

Decision-making training (DMT) operates on the assumption that any actions that improve the decision-making process on the part of job candidates, either by providing accurate information or enhancing decision-making skills, will lead to the party delivering the actions being seen as helpful.[50] In DMT, candidates are taught how to identify and weigh positive and negative outcomes from a set of alternatives. The message is similar to that conveyed by RJPs except that the message need not include negative information; the intention is to establish that the organization wants candidates to make decisions that are good for them even if those decisions are at the expense of the organization in losing the candidate.

DMT may be a viable, less costly alternative to RJP that produces longer-lasting benefits. Because the DMT does not contain information about the company, let alone negative information, it avoids the negative spinoffs of RJP. DMT may prove to be a good means for determining person–organization fit but, because it does not convey job information, it may be less appropriate for determining person–job fit. DMT is a relatively new concept and much more research is needed.

Recruitment Strategy

Understanding what attracts candidates is only the first part of the recruitment process. To be successful in recruiting, an organization must understand factors that influence the process. Recruitment takes place in a human resources context, which is influenced by both internal and external factors, as well as by the more immediate needs of the job and the organization. Figure 6.1 (see page 237) illustrates the role that these factors play in recruiting. These factors raise a number of issues that must be addressed when developing a recruitment strategy in the context of an organization's strategic planning. A sustainable competitive advantage is achieved through people, starting with recruiting the best. Increasingly, recruiting is seen as part of a staffing system where internal decisions influence how staffing occurs.[51]

 6.3

External Factors

All recruitment is influenced by two factors over which the organization has little control: (1) the labour market, and (2) the legal environment.[52]

Labour Markets and Recruiting

Organizations must develop a recruiting campaign that makes sense in the context of a specific labour market. Labour markets and economic conditions impose different constraints. The overall nature of the economy may influence an organization's decision to hire or not to hire, but once a decision to hire is made, the nature of the labour market determines how extensively the organization will have to search to fill the job with a qualified candidate. In 1996, Toyota Canada was in the enviable position of having more than 50 000 people apply for 1200 positions that were being created as part of an expansion at its Cambridge, Ontario, plant. The jobs paid $20 per hour plus benefits in a geographic area that had an 8.3 percent rate of unemployment. Toyota had 11 000 applications on file before it had run a single advertisement or posted the jobs with Human Resources Canada Centres.[53]

When qualified labour is scarce, the organization must broaden its recruiting beyond its normal target population. This includes going beyond normal recruiting channels to attract applicants it might not seek in more favourable times. For example, if there is a shortage of chartered accountants, the organization may take a look at hiring finance majors with a background in accounting who they believe will develop into the position with some additional training. The organization may also recruit outside its normal territory, emphasizing those geographic regions with high unemployment rates or low economic growth.

In favourable labour markets, the organization may advertise the accounting position only in one or two professional journals. In a poor market, it may decide to use a variety of media to attract as many qualified applicants as possible. With poor labour markets, the organization may make the job more attractive by improving salary and benefits, training and educational opportunities, and working conditions. In poor markets, the organization may spend additional resources to overcome the shortage of qualified applicants and to increase the attractiveness of the organization and the job. These considerations become even more important when the organization must compete with its rivals for scarce human resources. Recruiting when the labour market is poor is an expensive proposition.

PART-TIME LABOUR MARKETS AND RECRUITING In response to today's global economy, more and more companies are employing low-wage, entry-level workers on a part-time basis. Temporary or contingent jobs have shown tremendous growth over the last decade. Nearly 2 million people go to work each day in North America on a part-time basis. North American retailing giants such as Sears, Wal-Mart, and K-Mart have made part-time work their industry norm.

Recruiting and retaining the best part-time workers present unique problems to companies choosing to go this route. Workers who receive lower pay and benefits are less likely to feel committed to their organization or to go out of their way to get the job done. Many part-time workers are unskilled and poorly educated. Companies such as Whirlpool have responded to the need to recruit part-time workers by restructuring their pay and benefits, as well as by providing training and educational opportunities for them. Others, such as Taco Bell, have attempted to restructure the work environment to meet the needs of their part-time employees.[54]

Increasingly, temporary work is serving as a training ground for more permanent positions. A recent survey found that over two-thirds of temporary workers reported that they gained new skills while in their temporary positions. On the other hand, ever-greater numbers of skilled professionals and retired workers are taking jobs on a part-time or contract basis.[55] Organizations that depend on part-time workers will need to develop recruiting methods to attract and retain contingent employees. Indeed, some workers prefer part-time status, and when these employees are placed in part-time positions, they tend to be satisfied and committed to the organization. They also tend to remain longer.

On the other hand, placing them into full-time positions leads to less satisfaction and more turnover. The opposite effects occur when workers who desire full-time jobs are placed into part-time positions: less satisfaction and commitment and higher turnover.[56] The contingent or part-time status of jobs should be clearly indicated in all recruiting materials.

OUTSOURCING Outsourcing is the practice of contracting with an outside agent to take over specified human resources functions, specifically, recruitment. Companies that need workers on a temporary or short-term basis often turn to temporary help agencies to provide them with contingent workers. In these cases, the workers are employees of the temporary help firm, not of the organization in which they do their work. The employee is actually "leased" from the outside firm. The individual is employed by the outside agency but assigned to a position with the client organization.

The outside firm assumes all payroll responsibilities (pay and benefits), but charges the client administration and placement costs, usually prorated to salary. If the client chooses to hire the individual for a full-time permanent position, then additional fees are paid to the employment agency. Some Canadian banks now meet part of their staffing needs through these arrangements. Client organizations benefit from increased work force flexibility and savings in administrative costs. They also get to see the worker on the job over a period of time before any decisions to hire directly are made.

Investigations in both Canada and the United States suggest that some temporary help agencies may be willing to accommodate their client organizations' requests that the agency not send blacks, people with accents, or unattractive women.[57,58] Often, the client organizations have the mistaken notion that since they are not the legal employer, they are immune to charges of discrimination and free from any employment equity obligations. By allowing temporary workers on their premises and directing their work, the client organization can be subject to discrimination claims, unless it can show that the assignment based on group membership was a bona fide occupational requirement.[59]

Current information on the state of the Canadian labour market and the availability of different skill sets can be found at http://www.labour marketinformation.ca/standard.asp?pcode=lmiv_main&lcode=e.

Outsourcing

Contracting with an outside agent to take over specified human resources functions.

 6.4

The Legal Environment

Any organizational recruitment program must comply with the legal and regulatory requirements that apply to its operation. Chapter 3 presented some of the landmark cases and legislation that govern employment in Canada. In the United States, employment laws and regulations are assumed to affect both recruitment practices and outcomes.[60] It is likely that Canadian employment

Systemic discrimination

In employment, the intentional or unintentional exclusion of members of groups that are protected under human rights legislation through recruiting, selection, or other personnel practices or policies.

legislation has similar effects on recruitment in Canadian organizations. The most important considerations are employment equity and pay equity legislation. Any recruitment campaign that intentionally or unintentionally excludes members of groups that are protected under human rights legislation runs the risk of being declared discriminatory, with the organization subject to penalties and fines. The best defence against charges of systemic discrimination is to document that every attempt has been made to attract members from the protected groups.

In Canada, employment equity legislation seeks to eliminate discrimination in the workplace for women, people with disabilities, Aboriginal people, and visible minorities. Organizations may be called on, particularly if they wish to do business with the federal government, to demonstrate that they have actively sought to recruit members from these four groups. Good-faith recruitment efforts mean that the organization must use a variety of communication channels to get its message to members of different groups and to present its recruiting message in a way that interests different audiences. The recruitment effort must make members from these groups feel welcome in the organization, even when they are working there on a temporary basis. Organizations perceived as hostile to workplace diversity will see the effectiveness of their recruitment efforts significantly compromised, and the quality of their overall applicant pool adversely affected.

Many Canadian communities have made an effort to recruit women and visible minorities for employment as police officers. Most of these efforts have been relatively unsuccessful. In this regard, black police applicants often perceive a lack of fit between their attitudes and the demands of modern policing that is related to racial prejudice on the part of serving police officers and the community.[61] To help overcome these types of barriers, women, visible minorities, Aboriginal people, and people with physical challenges should participate as front-line recruiters to help send a clear message that equal employment opportunities and a welcoming environment will be provided.

Organizations must think very carefully about the messages they convey to job applicants when they seek to increase workplace diversity. While members of minority groups react favourably to recruiting efforts, white males tend to react negatively.[62] All job candidates, however, react negatively to questions about their age, marital status, gender, or ethnicity.[63] Efforts to recruit minorities may lead to reduced self-esteem on the part of the minority hires and reduced perceptions of their competence (i.e., perceptions that they were hired because they were from a minority group and not because of their fit to the job and organization).

White males often see a process that emphasizes group membership as a factor in hiring as unfair where unqualified people are hired in place of those more qualified. These negative issues, for members of both minority and majority groups, seem to decrease when merit is central to the decision-making process.[64] When organizations seek to recruit members from minority groups, they should emphasize that hiring decisions are merit-based.

The sources used to recruit minorities may also be very important to the success of attracting them to apply for jobs with an organization. Ryan,

Horvath, and Kriska[65] demonstrated that the informativeness of the source was related to whether individuals who were interested chose to apply for a firefighter's job. Applicants who received more and better information about a job were more likely to apply for the job and saw themselves as a good fit with the job and organization. Often minorities do not choose to apply for positions as they see themselves as a poor fit with the organization, no matter how well-qualified they are. One strategy to improve diversity would be to ensure the use of highly informative recruitment sources when recruiting minorities.

Internal Factors

While it is clear that different organizations take different approaches to recruiting new employees, very little is known about how organizational characteristics produce differences in recruiting practices, processes, or outcomes. Partly, this is the result of most research focusing on job seekers rather than on the employing organizations.[66] As we discussed in the beginning of this chapter, there are many possible organizational characteristics that could influence a job seeker's perception of the organization during the job search phase (e.g., the type of industry, size of the organization, profitability, growth, and financial trends). These characteristics may influence both the number and the quality of applicants who apply for a position with the organization. They may also influence how the organization recruits candidates and how competitive the organization is in making offers to the best applicants.[67]

Business Plan

A company's business plan has a major impact on its recruiting strategy. An organization's business plan includes a statement of its mission and philosophy, a recognition of its strengths and weaknesses, and a statement of its goals and objectives for competing in its economic environment. A business plan addresses those aspects of the external environment that affect how the organization does business. An organization's business plan also influences the degree to which the organization fills vacancies with internal or external applicants.[68] Rarely do organizations fill entry-level positions with internal candidates; however, it is quite common to bring someone in from the outside to fill a vacant position.

Organizations differ in their approach to staffing vacant positions. Some insist, as a matter of organizational policy, that internal candidates be given preference as a means of motivating employees (recall that advancement is a recruiting factor) and ensuring that the successful candidate knows and shares the organization's philosophy, values, goals, and attitude toward achieving a return on investment in both human and material resources. In some cases, collective agreements with employees may require that internal applicants be given first consideration for positions for which they are qualified. Other organizations insist that external candidates be given preference for jobs in order to expose the company to new ideas and to new ways of doing business. Still other organizations may insist that the best candidate be given the job offer, regardless of whether that person is an internal or external applicant.

Job Level and Type

Both the type of occupation and the nature of the industry in which it is involved may influence an organization's recruiting strategy.[69] In some industries or occupations, people are recruited in a particular way, not so much because that method is very effective, but because it is the norm. It is how recruiting is done for that type of work, and how it is expected to be done. For certain executive-level positions, vacancies are never advertised but given to a consulting company to carry out an executive search. Such "head-hunting" firms generally have a list of potential executive candidates that they have developed over time through contacts in many different organizations. The search firm knows the organization and works to find a match with one of its candidates. Rarely, if ever, are such firms used to recruit production or service workers; vacancies for those types of positions are filled from candidates who respond to local newspaper advertisements or job postings with HRSDC Service Canada's Job Bank or who are referred by other employees, as was the case with the 50 000 applicants for the production jobs at Toyota Canada.[70]

Recruiting Strategy and Organizational Goals

Organizations often tie their recruiting initiatives to achieving organizational goals. Different organizational goals lead to different recruitment strategies. Similarly, an organization's philosophy and values influence whether it actively seeks to recruit women and members of minorities, or whether its approach to employment equity is one of minimal compliance. Organization analysis helps to clarify these issues. In developing recruiting strategies, one must decide whether to concentrate recruiting efforts on internal or external candidates. Organization analysis reveals the likelihood of finding suitable internal candidates, and the extent to which qualified internal candidates can fill the job openings, by providing an inventory of skills and abilities that exist within the company as well as indicating the potential for advancement among current employees. In conjunction with job analysis, this information gives a good indication of the likelihood of finding the right internal people for the job and the need for external recruiting. Unfortunately, relatively few companies inventory their employees' skills and abilities; such inventories are expensive to develop and to maintain.

Describing the Job

One of the most important pieces of information candidates rely on throughout the recruiting process is a description of the job and worker requirements. Recruiting information should give applicants a clear idea of the duties and tasks that form part of the job and the resources that they will need to do the job. It is very difficult to recruit job applicants without knowing the essential characteristics of the position or the worker requirements. Job descriptions that are up to date and based on a job analysis lead to accurate expectations on the part of the job candidate. Both applicants and recruiters should have a clear idea of the qualifications needed by people in the position. Often recruiters are told to seek the "best person" for the job, instead of being told to find the "best-qualified person" for the job. Recruitment and Selection Today 4.1 (see Chapter 4, page 123) presented a job description for a CIBC customer service representative. This description, used in recruiting, is sufficiently detailed to provide both the job candidate and the recruiter with a clear idea of what the position entails and how it fits into the organization. It also suggests the type of person who will best fit with the values and culture of CIBC.

Human Resources Planning

Human resources planning "is a process of developing and implementing plans and programs to ensure that the right number and type of individuals are available at the right time and place to fill organizational needs."[71] This planning process is based on analysis of the organization's business plan, resulting in a forecast of the number and type of employees required to meet the plan's objectives. Through organization and job analyses, the planning process identifies the human resources needed to carry out the business plan, both those resources that exist within the organization and those that must be secured through a recruiting program. Human resources planning develops an action plan (see Recruitment and Selection Notebook 6.3) to eliminate any discrepancy between the supply of and demand for human resources.

 6.5

Recruitment and Selection Notebook 6.3

Developing a Recruitment Strategy

With respect to the recruitment process, human resources planning must provide answers to the following questions:

- Based on our business plan, how many positions will we need to staff?
- Based on the job analysis, what is the nature of the position that must be filled?
- Based on the job analysis, what qualifications (knowledge, skills, abilities, experience) must job candidates possess to do the job successfully?
- Based on organization analysis, what percentage of the positions can, or should, be staffed with internal candidates?
- Based on the labour market, is there an available supply of qualified external candidates?

- Based on the labour market, how extensively will we have to search for qualified applicants? Will we have to search beyond our normal geographic boundaries? Will we have to take special measures to locate our target applicant population? What sources or methods should we use to reach the potential applicants?
- Based on legal considerations, what are our goals with respect to employment equity?
- Based on the business plan, organization analysis, and job analysis, what information and materials will we present to job candidates?

Answers to these questions form the organization's recruiting strategy (i.e., its plan for staffing the organization). The human resources management team must also have a plan for implementing the strategy.

Recruitment Action Plan

Timing of Recruitment Initiatives

In many organizations, recruiting occurs in response to need. An employee leaves for one reason or another and, if the position is retained, must be replaced either through internal or external hiring. In cases like this, there is little organizational control over timing. Delays in hiring may lead to delays in production, with unrealistic demands placed on the remaining employees. The recruitment goal is to hire someone qualified to do the work as soon as possible, even if hiring at a later date may have led to finding someone who was better qualified for the position. In other organizations, where there is a systematic turnover of employees, recruiting may follow a well-defined pattern.

This pattern occurs most often in large organizations, which recruit heavily from among college and university graduates.[72] The availability of such graduates in the spring of each year often determines when organizations implement their recruiting strategy; it influences when they send information to campus employment centres, place advertisements in campus newspapers, visit the schools, meet with the potential applicants, extend invitations to visit the organization, and make their job offers. If an organization is late in recruiting, top candidates may have already accepted offers from the competition. To remain competitive, the organization must synchronize its recruiting to when the best candidates are likely to be available. This means that the human resources team must have a good working knowledge of the labour market and an effective recruitment and staffing plan (see Recruitment and Selection Notebook 6.4).

In competing for qualified candidates, particularly when supply is weak, organizations are starting to incorporate in their recruiting strategies knowledge of how job candidates evaluate jobs and make choices. There is evidence to suggest that job seekers prefer early job offers as a way of reducing anxiety and uncertainty about other offers; there is also evidence to suggest that more-qualified candidates generate offers earlier and more easily than less-qualified candidates.[73] If this is so, then organizations may have to begin recruiting as early as possible if they want to hire the most-qualified candidates. Instead of waiting until the spring to recruit college and university graduates, a company may begin the process earlier in order to make job offers before the end of the fall semester.

Some organizations are also beginning to pursue college and university students before they enter the job market. Companies often use summer job placements, internships, or cooperative education as early-recruitment programs.[74] These strategies are designed to have candidates accept an early job offer that meets their minimum standards rather than waiting to make a choice between competing offers.

The timing of events within a recruiting program is important. The recruiting process can extend over a considerable period of time, with several candidates evaluated for each vacancy. Job candidates do not stop their job search activities while waiting for a decision. An organization that does

Elements of a Recruitment and Staffing Action Plan

1. **Develop Recruitment Strategy**
   - Establish selection committee.
   - Review organization's goals and objectives.
   - Establish budget for the recruitment process.
   - Establish timelines for recruitment and selection activities.
   - Review job description for position.
   - Develop selection criteria.
   - Develop profile of "ideal" applicant.
   - Develop job advertisement/recruiting materials.

2. **Develop the Applicant Pool**
   - Review state of the labour market.
   - Consider employment equity issues.
   - Determine if recruitment will be internal or external.
   - Identify target applicant pool.
   - Identify recruitment methods to be used.
   - Place ad/recruiting materials in agreed-on media.

3. **Screen the Applicant Pool**
   - Determine whether applicant pool is large enough; if not, renew recruitment efforts.
   - Screen job candidates' application forms and résumés.
   - Conduct short screening interviews.
   - Select "long list" of candidates for further review.

4. **Conduct Review of Job Applicants**
   - Selection committee develops shortlist of candidates.
   - Arrange visits of short-listed candidates to company.
   - Conduct realistic job preview for candidates.
   - Conduct employment tests.
   - Conduct selection interview.
   - Identify leading candidate(s) for position.
   - Complete reference and background checks on leading candidates.
   - Make hiring recommendation.
   - Contingent on offer of employment, arrange for any required medical or physical examinations.

5. **Evaluate the Recruiting Effort**
   - Review the recruiting process: What went right? What went wrong?
   - Review the outcome of the recruiting process.
   - Review the performance of people who were hired.

not provide candidates with timely feedback about their progress through the recruitment and selection process may risk losing top candidates. Job seekers may take lack of contact as a lack of interest and accept an early offer from a less-preferred company. Job candidates may not stop their job search activities even after accepting an early offer from an organization. They may continue to receive interest from other companies that were late off the mark in recruiting, and if they receive an attractive offer, they may change their minds about accepting the first offer. Maintaining contact with the candidate after an offer is accepted helps to forestall such reversals.

Locating and Targeting the Applicant Pool

In an ideal world, an organization could search as broadly as possible until it found the most suitable applicant. However, extensive recruiting is an expensive proposition that few organizations can afford. It is also questionable whether the benefits of extensive recruiting surpass its associated costs.

A more effective plan is to target recruiting efforts on a specific pool of job applicants who have the appropriate knowledge, skills, abilities, competencies, and other talents needed to perform the job. This applicant pool may be concentrated in one geographic area or spread widely throughout the country. The human resources team must know where to find the appropriate applicant pool.

If a company wants to hire electronics technicians, it makes more sense to concentrate on recruiting graduates from electronics training programs or from areas where there is a concentration of electronics technicians rather than search broadly throughout the country. The human resources team must know which colleges or institutes offer training in electronics; they must know where electronics industries are concentrated. If a company was recruiting experienced miners, it would be more appropriate to target Cape Breton as a source for this applicant pool rather than Metropolitan Toronto. On the other hand, recruiting upper-level executives might require a nationwide search to find the best candidate.

Targeting a specific applicant pool allows the organization to tailor its message to that group, to understand where that applicant pool is likely to be located, and to attract applications from that pool. In limiting its recruiting to a target applicant pool, however, an organization must be careful not to systematically exclude members of protected groups.

Recruitment Sources

Once the target applicant pool has been identified and located, the human resources team must choose the most appropriate recruitment methods or sources for reaching all members of internal and external applicant pools, including members of protected groups. The following sections describe some of the more popular recruiting methods that have been used to contact members of different applicant pools.

Internal Candidates

Internal candidates provide the organization with a known source of labour. Many of the activities carried out as part of human resources planning provide the organization with information about the best-qualified internal applicants. As Moser[75] showed, internal applicants are likely to have fewer unrealistic expectations about the job or organization and have more job satisfaction and organizational commitment, but there is a risk that internal sources may lead to a work force that is less diversified with respect to minority applicants.

Internal Job Postings

Internal job postings can be notices posted on bulletin boards, ads placed in company newsletters, announcements made at staff meetings, or notices circulated through departments. The intent of the posting is to make internal employees aware of the vacancy and to allow them an opportunity to apply for the position. As a matter of policy, some organizations seek to fill positions through internal sources before going to the external market. Other organizations may have agreed, through a collective agreement with employees, to give first consideration to internal candidates for any vacant position that falls under the collective agreement. In these cases, the jobs are posted for a period of time in specified locations. Internal postings generally provide information on the job, its requirements, and the compensation associated with the position.

Internal job postings provide an excellent means of discovering talented people in the organization and providing them with an opportunity for advancement within the organization. Knowing that good performance will be awarded through advancement has a positive effect on employee motivation. Internal job postings make the vacancy known to all employees, which is an important consideration when implementing employment equity programs throughout different levels of the organization.

There are, however, disadvantages to internal job postings. Internal postings lengthen the time needed to fill the position, as external searches generally do not begin until after all internal candidates are first evaluated. Internal candidates who are unsuccessful may become less motivated, or may initiate a job search outside the organization. Placing an internal candidate in a vacant position sets off a sequence of events that brings with it a degree of instability and change: The position the employee leaves must itself be posted and filled. The effects of filling the first position with an internal candidate reverberate through several layers of the organization before the process comes to an end.

Replacement Charts

Organizations expect that vacancies will occur through death, illness, retirement, resignation, or termination and, as part of the human resources planning function, develop a succession plan for filling vacancies with existing employees. Organizations have a good idea of the talent in other positions that can step in to fill a vacancy, either on a short- or long-term basis. Replacement charts, like organizational charts, list each job with respect to its position in the organizational structure, particularly its relationship to positions above and below it. The replacement chart lists the incumbent for the position and the likely internal replacements for the incumbent. The chart includes information on the present job performance of each potential successor (e.g., "excellent performer"), an assessment of his or her readiness to step into the position (e.g., "needs more experience in present position"), and a rank-ordering of each as the incumbent's replacement.

Replacement charts provide a quick, visual presentation of an organization's human resources, but they give little information beyond that of a candidate's performance and promotability. These charts are limited by the constraints imposed by the organizational chart. Employees are evaluated for positions one level above theirs in the chain of command. They are not evaluated for positions that are horizontal or lateral to theirs, although in contemporary organizations, employees are expected to have skills and competencies that are transferable to jobs that are related to their position.

Human Resources Information Systems

Human resources planning often involves the creation of a comprehensive computerized database that contains the job analysis information on each position, including information on the required KSAOs. This computerized inventory also contains information on employee competencies and KSAOs, along with employee work histories, experiences, and results of performance evaluations. Internal candidates for a vacant position may be found through a computer match of the person's characteristics with those required by the job. The match does not give any indication of employee interest in the position or motivation to take on the new job. It is simply a first cut of employees who qualify for the position.

Nominations

Nominations are the least systematic internal recruitment method. They occur when someone who knows about a vacancy nominates another employee to fill it. In most cases, supervisors nominate one or more of their employees for a vacant position. Presumably, the supervisor nominates those employees whose KSAOs or competencies match those needed by the job. This process often results in very good employees not being nominated for a position. Supervisors or managers may use the nominating process to rid themselves of a problem employee or someone with whom they have poor interpersonal relations.

Nominations also leave the organization open to charges of discriminatory promotion practices. For example, in replacing a manager, the other senior managers who are male may fail to nominate any women for the position. The women employees who were passed over may ask whether the failure to nominate women was due to a lack of qualified female employees or to male bias against female managers.

External Candidates

Organizations usually do not have a dependable supply of external applicants. The sources they use to attract external applicants have to be more creative and varied than those for internal candidates. The following section reviews some of the more common means used to reach external candidates.

Job Advertisements

Organizations spend a considerable part of their recruiting budgets on advertising vacant positions, and the "help-wanted" ad is one of the most commonly used methods of recruiting job candidates.[76] Help-wanted ads come in various forms and use different media. The advertisements identify who the employer is and include basic information on the job and compensation, the job requirements, and how to apply (including closing dates for applications). The ad may also contain information on the organization's employment equity program. The ad should not include any statements that could lead to charges of discrimination (e.g., "The ideal applicant will be between 25 and 30 years old"), unless those statements can be supported as bona fide occupational requirements.

Organizations also use job advertisements to enhance their image with potential candidates. Image concerns may dictate the size of the advertisement, where it is placed, and the content of the ad as much as the information needed to attract qualified candidates. Effective ads are generally based on the AIDA formula:

A—**Attention.** Grab the reader's attention with the use of headlines, white space, graphics, and changes in type fonts.

I—**Interest.** Make the copy interesting and emphasize how the product or service (or job) is better than others that are being offered.

D—**Desire.** Make sure the ad copy answers the basic question of "What's in it for me?" Show how the product or service (or job) will benefit the reader.

A—**Action.** The ad should urge the reader to take some action and should make it easy to do so.

Job advertisement campaigns should also be designed with the target applicant pool in mind:

- Who are we trying to reach? Who is in our target applicant pool?
- How large is the target applicant pool and what portion of it do we need to reach to obtain a reasonable number of applicants?
- How many applicants do we need to fill the position with qualified people?
- What type of ad content will attract the target applicant pool's attention?
- What advertising media are likely to reach the target applicant pool?

The answers to most of these questions are very complex and depend on consideration of many factors, including the nature of the organization, the job, and the target applicant pool. One of the most important decisions is choosing the media for the advertising campaign.

Newspapers are perhaps the most common media for job advertisements. They offer a quick and flexible means of contacting potential applicants. Newspapers need only two or three days of lead time before an ad is published. The ad can be placed in the classified ads section listing employment opportunities or prominently displayed in another section of the paper. Often managerial and professional positions are advertised in a newspaper's business section.

Newspapers have specific geographic distribution areas. An organization can choose to advertise locally in a paper that serves the immediate area of the organization, or it can advertise in papers such as *The Globe and Mail*, which have a national distribution but also publish regional editions. Of course, the increased distribution comes at an increase in cost. Blue-collar positions tend to be advertised locally, with managerial and professional positions advertised nationally.

Newspaper ads run for a very short period of time; they attract the interest of people who are actively searching for a job and who happen to see the advertisement before it disappears. There is some evidence that newspaper ads are not a very effective means of attracting very qualified applicants,[77] particularly scientific and technical personnel.[78] Newspaper ads tend to be less effective in attracting candidates than other recruiting methods.[79]

Professional periodicals and trade journals allow the organization to reach very specialized groups of applicants. Many professional and trade associations publish newsletters or magazines that are distributed to each member. These publications carry job advertisements. The association, and the distribution of its publication, may be international, national, or regional. Publications of this type are the best means of reaching people with specific skills or qualifications.

Ads in these types of publications can be quite expensive and often require a long lead time before the ad appears. For example, an advertisement appearing in the March issue of a newsletter may have had an early January deadline for ad copy. With the recent growth of the World Wide Web, many professional and trade associations have reduced the publication lag by posting job ads in their online publications as the ads are received; the ads are also published in the print edition later. For example, the Canadian Association of University Teachers (CAUT) places ads for college and university teachers in its monthly hard-copy *CAUT Bulletin* and its online job service, *Academic Work*, at http://www.academicwork.ca.

Radio and television job advertising, in comparison to print media, has not been used extensively. These media offer the potential to reach large numbers of the target applicant pool. Radio and television advertising directors have detailed demographic information on the audience for specific shows and can place the advertisement during shows likely to be watched or listened to by the target applicant pool. Nonetheless, organizations appear reluctant to use these methods for job advertisements and limit their use to image advertising. The cost of radio and television advertising, particularly on a national scale, may be quite high even for a 15- or 30-second commercial. The short duration of most commercials prevents the inclusion of essential job information.

When radio and television advertising is used, the focus of the ads is to stimulate interest in the organization and to motivate the potential applicant to seek additional information from another recruiting source. This approach is used in the radio and television advertising of the Canadian Forces. While much of the ad content is devoted to image advertising, the ads always end with a phone number or address where interested people can obtain more detailed information. Recent Canadian Forces ads can be viewed at http://www.forces.ca.

As well, many organizations now place ads on the Internet, including YouTube.com, with the expectation that they will reach a wider audience at little cost. In fact some organizations rely solely on the Internet rather than running ads on broadcast outlets.

Public displays attempt to bring job vacancies to the attention of the target applicant pool through the use of advertisements that range from help-wanted notices to display ads placed in buses, trains, and subway stations. Service and retail employers rely on help-wanted signs posted in their windows or near service counters to attract job applicants. Most positions advertised through these types of notices are at the entry level and do not require extensive skills or abilities on the part of the applicant. These ads are directed at recruiting employees from among the employer's normal range of customers.

Display ads in public transportation stations and vehicles attempt to reach a broader population than service and retail help-wanted ads, but like those notices, they are also directed at attracting people for low-skill or limited-ability entry-level positions. These ads simply advertise the availability of jobs with an organization and provide those who are interested with a means of contacting the organization to obtain more specific information. Public display ads tend to be low in cost relative to the number of people that they reach. For example, one ad inside a bus may be seen by several thousand commuters over a month's display.

Direct mail advertising attempts to bring the organization's recruiting message directly to members of the target applicant pool. The potential employer sends each person on the mailing list recruiting information about the organization and the job, reaching both those who are actively seeking jobs and those who may become interested through reading the materials. The keys to this type of advertising are the acquisition or development of a mailing list consisting of names and addresses of the target applicant population, the attractiveness of the recruiting materials, and the ease with which follow-up contacts can take place. Often, mailing lists can be obtained from various professional associations.

In Canada, many rural communities have had trouble in recruiting medical practitioners. In response to this need, several communities have started active recruitment campaigns involving direct contact with potential graduates of medical schools, where the target applicant population is easy to identify and locate.[80]

Special recruiting events involve bringing a large number of potential job candidates into contact with an organization that is seeking to fill positions. Two well-established events used successfully to attract job seekers are open houses and job fairs. In an *open house*, an organization invites potential job applicants in its community to visit the company facilities to view demonstrations or videos about the company and its products, and to meet the organization's employees informally over refreshments. Sometimes, the organization may choose to hold the affair at a non-company facility such as a trade centre or hotel because of security or other concerns.

Open houses work best when an organization has several jobs to fill and when there are tight labour markets. Figure 6.4 presents a flyer used by the Halton Regional Police Service to attract potential candidates for the position of police constable to an open house.

At a *job fair*, several organizations seeking to hire from the same target applicant pool arrange to recruit in conjunction with an ongoing event. For example, a trade or professional association may invite employers to hold a job fair as part of its annual convention. The employers, who pay a fee to

FIGURE 6.4

Flyer Inviting Potential Police Constable Candidates to an Open House

**Recruiting
Information Session**

Halton Regional Police Service
is actively seeking candidates for the position of

Police Constable

Join us for our Recruiting Information Night.
The evening will include:

• Explanation of the Constable Selection Process

• Videos about the O.A.C.P. Constable Selection
Process

• How to prepare for testing and interviews

• Opportunity to ask questions of police officers

Seating is on a first come first served basis.
No registration needed to attend.

*Applications will be available only to those who provide
a resume and current O.A.C.P. Certificate of Results.
Please call our Recruiting Information Line 905-825-4747ext 5116.*

www.hrps.on.ca/

Wednesday March 31, 2004
7:00 p.m. to 9: 00 p.m.
Georgetown District High School
70 Guelph Street,
Halton Hills, Georgetown

Source: Reprinted with permission of the Halton Regional Police Service.

participate, have access to all of the convention delegates, both those who are actively seeking jobs and those who may become interested through meeting an organization's representative. The convention delegates represent the ideal target applicant pool. The job seekers make contact with organizations, while the employers meet many prospective employees in a short period of time at a relatively low cost. The disadvantage is information overload, where the candidate is bombarded with too much information from too many organizations.

Employee referral is word-of-mouth advertising that relies on current employees telling their friends and relatives about job vacancies in their company. This is a low- or no-cost method of advertising. It assumes that the employees know other people with skills and abilities similar to their own, that the employees refer people with good work habits and attitudes similar to their own, and that current employees are the best representatives of the organization. In some companies, employees are paid a bonus for each successful referral.

Advocates of realistic job previews or information regard referrals as an effective means of recruiting, since the candidate is likely to have been given an accurate representation of the job and organization by the friend or relative.[81,82] There is some evidence that employees recruited by referral remain with the organization longer than employees recruited through other means and have more positive organizational outcomes.[83,84] The greatest concern with using referrals as a recruiting method is the probability that it may produce charges of discriminatory hiring practices. In referring friends and relatives, employees are likely to refer individuals from their own ethnic, racial, or gender groups; this could work against meeting employment equity goals. Referrals, however, are a very popular means of attracting job applicants.[85,86]

Networking is a cross between a recruiting method (such as referrals and nominations) and a job search technique. For professionals, networking is deemed to be vital to career advancement and is promoted by career transition experts as the best way for a professional to find a job. Job seekers are encouraged to join industry groups and professional organizations, to join study groups, read journals, and attend conferences. Networking also involves joining college or university alumni associations; keeping in touch with family, friends, professors, advisors, coaches, and tutors; and joining social clubs or volunteer groups. It also includes activities such as meeting an old friend for coffee to obtain information on career opportunities or asking a friend's father to put in a good word for you at his company.

Networking contacts can keep the job seeker informed about what life is like in a company from the perspective of an insider. At the same time, the networking contact is aware that the job seeker is looking for employment or for a new position and can forward that information to appropriate people in the company. Monster.ca (http://content.monster.ca/section1967 .asp) and CareerKey.com (http://www.careerkey.com) are examples of two Internet recruiting sources that have established websites that provide advice on networking.

Walk-Ins

In the external sources described above, the organization makes every attempt to contact members of the target applicant pool. The recruitment is initiated by the employer. Walk-in recruitment is initiated by the job seeker, who visits an organization's personnel office and requests to fill out an application for employment, even though the company may not have any job vacancies. The *write-in* method is a variation of this approach; rather than visiting the company, job seekers send their résumés to the company. The company usually holds the applications and résumés for a period of time (e.g., three months), in case vacancies do occur. Walk-in and write-in methods are inexpensive ways to fill entry-level positions, although they are less effective than referrals.[87] In the past, these methods were rarely used to recruit professionals or managers, but with the prevalence of corporate downsizing, where supply exceeds demand, more professional and technical positions are being filled by walk-ins.

Employment Agencies

Employment agencies are independent organizations that attempt to find a match between a person and a job. Their success depends on the willingness of both the job seeker and the organization to use their services. We will look at the major types of employment agencies: HRSDC Service Canada's Job Bank, private employment agencies, executive search firms, in-house recruiters, and temporary help agencies.

Service Canada Centres throughout the country provide no-charge access to the online Job Bank for both job seekers and employers. As soon as employers post a job vacancy, the position is listed in the Job Bank at http://www .jobbank.gc.ca. Available jobs across the country are listed by province to facilitate the job search for workers who want to remain in their home provinces or who want to relocate. The job seeker selects a job category, and all of the available jobs in that category are displayed, along with the salary (if specified) and location of each job. Clicking on one of the job titles produces a detailed description of the job, including a list of the skills, education, and credentials required. The manner in which a job application is to be made is specified (e.g., in person, mail, e-mail, fax, or website).

As noted in Recruitment and Selection Today 6.1 (see page 241), the Service Canada site also offers information about effective job search strategies and even a "Job Match" feature, for which applicants have to register to gain access. The effectiveness of Service Canada's Job Bank is somewhat mixed; most of the job placements are in sales, clerical, and service industries, with very few in managerial and professional occupations.

The primary function of *private employment agencies* is to bring together job seekers and organizations who are seeking to hire. These agencies charge a fee for their services. Most provinces regulate employment agency fees and prohibit the agency from charging job seekers for placing them with employers. The agency fees are paid by the employing organization, usually in the form of a commission tied to a percentage of the job candidate's starting salary. Employment agencies may use any of the recruiting methods we've discussed, but they tend to rely on walk-ins, newspaper advertising, and lists of potential job seekers compiled over time. Employment agencies tend to have a fair degree of success in finding both skilled and managerial workers.

Executive search firms are private employment agencies that specialize in finding executive talent. These firms charge the organization for their services, whether or not they are successful in filling a position. The major difference between search firms and employment agencies is that search

Executive Search Firms

Why Use an Executive Search Firm?

- To obtain suitable candidates who otherwise might not have applied.
- To maintain objectivity.
- To avoid conflicts of interest between parties involved in the search.
- To eliminate administrative burdens related to the search.
- To maintain confidentiality related to organizational strategic plans (i.e., expansions, mergers, terminations, restructuring, etc.)

What Does an Executive Search Firm Do?

- Anything, within reason, that the client wants.
- Obtains description from the client of the type of person being sought.
- Develops a profile of suitable applicants.
- Develops and places advertisements, if necessary.
- Contacts potential candidates directly.
- Searches résumé banks.
- Facilitates the interview process.
- Conducts reference checks.
- Conducts hiring negotiations.

What Does an Executive Search Cost?

- Fees: As a rule of thumb, 30 percent of the candidate's gross starting salary.
- Expenses: As high as 15 percent of gross starting salary.
- Fees and expenses are generally negotiable.
- Hiring is guaranteed: If the new employee does not work out by the end of the first year, a replacement is found without cost.

How Long Does an Executive Search Take to Complete?

- Three to four months.

---

firms rarely advertise positions, although they will do so if requested by their clients. Rather, they seek out candidates who are not actively searching for jobs through an extensive list of contacts that they have developed over time. Their main supply of talent comes from executives who are already employed by other organizations; consequently, these search firms are known as "headhunters." More recently, search firms have started to use online recruiting websites as a source for their referrals. The major disadvantages of using search firms are their cost and the likelihood that some firms develop specific recruiting philosophies that lead them to look for the same type of executive to fill all positions. Recruitment and Selection Notebook 6.5 offers more information on executive search firms.

Hiring a search firm does not absolve the company of all responsibilities for the hiring process. A successful search depends on the company working with the search firm and doing its homework about the nature of the position to be filled and the required KSAOs and competencies before the search firm is called on to begin the search. Recruitment and Selection Today 6.3 presents the views of a headhunter on the common mistakes companies make when recruiting executives.

In-house recruiters are usually executive-level employees or highly respected professionals who hold an executive title such as vice-president or director.

A Headhunter's View of Company Mistakes in Executive Recruiting

Carlos Fernandez-Aroaz, a partner with Egon Zehnder International of Switzerland, discussed with *The Globe and Mail* some common mistakes that companies make when recruiting executives. According to Fernandez-Aroaz, these missteps include:

- **Reactive approach:** Companies seek someone with the same qualities as the person they are replacing but without that person's defects.
- **Unrealistic expectations:** Asking for a candidate who can do it all.
- **Evaluating people in absolute terms:** A person may be a "good manager" but under what terms?
- **Accepting people at face value:** Readily believing the information provided by candidates either on résumés or in interviews.
- **Believing references:** Accepting references at their word.

- **The "just-like-me" bias:** Favouring candidates with the same experience and education as current employees.
- **Delegation gaffes:** Letting others do the groundwork, such as writing job descriptions.
- **Unstructured interviews:** Basing decisions on loose conversations that cover subjects such as mutual acquaintances and sports events.
- **Ignoring emotional intelligence:** Looking only at hard data such as education, cognitive ability, and job history.
- **Political pressures:** Hiring for reasons other than the candidate's qualifications.

Source: E. Church. 1999. "Headhunter Warns of Matchmaking Missteps." *The Globe and Mail* (October 29): M1. Reprinted with permission from The Globe and Mail.

They are similar to headhunters in that they seek to recruit upper-level executives and professionals, except that they work only for their own company and do not recruit for any other company. In-house recruiters know the opportunities that exist in their organization; as well, they know the strengths of the local community and the social environment in which the new recruits are likely to live. Relying on networking to identify potential candidates, in-house recruiters are typically used to recruit professionals who are in high demand and in short supply. In the health-care industry, many hospitals use nurses and physicians as in-house recruiters who travel across the country seeking to recruit other health-care professionals for their hospitals.

In-house recruiters do have some disadvantages. Most companies use them to reduce the costs associated with an executive search firm. Unless in-house recruiters take time to become familiar with different recruiting methods, they may limit their work to posting notices on different Internet sites. In-house recruiters may also suffer from "tunnel vision" in looking only for certain types of candidates and ignoring a broader range of qualified job seekers.

Temporary help agencies are similar to private employment agencies except that they specialize in providing organizations with short-term help. In most cases, the worker remains employed by the temporary help firm, but carries out duties under the direction and control of the temporary help firm's client organization. These agencies provide clients with temporary help, contract workers, and seasonal and overload help in certain specialized occupations, such as secretaries, computer experts, labourers, and executives, among others. Temporary help agencies are an example of outsourcing, which we discussed earlier in this chapter. These agencies rely on inventories of talent pools they have developed over the years and are capable of filling their clients' needs within a reasonable amount of time. However, as discussed previously, the client organizations may be liable for any discrimination claims incurred through the control and direction of the temporary employee.

Recruiting at Educational Institutions

Technical schools, colleges, and universities are common sources of recruits for organizations seeking entry-level technical, professional, and managerial employees. Many schools provide their students with placement services, which assist the recruiting efforts of visiting organizations. Recognizing educational institutions as a good source of target applicants, organizations have well-established campus recruiting programs that involve both campus advertising and campus visits by company recruiters. Campus recruiting is one of the most popular ways in which graduates find their first job. It is also an expensive proposition in terms of both time and money. It becomes even more expensive considering that, on average, about 50 percent of recruits may leave the organization within the first few years of employment.[88]

Many research studies have tried to identify factors that produce successful recruiting campaigns at educational institutions. At one time, the characteristics of the recruiter were thought to be of utmost importance, but reviews of recent studies on this topic suggest there is little, if any, relationship between recruiter characteristics and the success of a recruiting program.[89] A more likely determinant is the choice of campuses an organization decides to visit. In a recent meta-analysis, Chapman and his associates found that while job-organization characteristics, recruiter behaviours, perceptions of the recruiting process, perceived fit, and hiring expectancies predicted applicant attraction to an organization, the recruiter demographics, such as age, gender, and race, did not.[90] Rynes and Cable[91] reviewed the post-1991 research on recruiter effects and came to much the same conclusion: that "recruiters probably do not have a large impact on actual job choices."[92]

The Internet/World Wide Web

In a few short years, the Internet has transformed recruiting. Traditionally, a company used one of the means we just described to reach potential job applicants. The company may have placed an advertisement in the print media, made use of referrals and nominations from current employees, or participated in job fairs. Applicants who happened to become aware of the vacancy submitted their résumés by mail or fax, or dropped them off in person. Staff in the HR department reviewed the applications. Candidates whom the staff judged to be qualified on the basis of that review were invited for an interview and possible further review through employment tests. Eventually, one of these applicants might be offered a position. The remaining applications were likely discarded, with perhaps a few kept on file. This process could take weeks or months from the initial announcement of the position to an offer.

Internet recruiting

The use of the Internet and World Wide Web to match candidates to jobs through electronic databases that store information on jobs and job candidates.

The Internet has changed everything. With **Internet recruiting**, a company can place notice of a vacancy on its website or list it with one of the online job or career websites (see Recruitment and Selection Today 6.4). The job or career site does a keyword search of résumés in its database and forwards those that match the position requirements to the company. For example, the Government of Canada conducts external recruitment almost exclusively online and provides online application blanks on the Public Service Commission's website (http://jobs.gc.ca). Some sites alert job seekers who are listed with it by e-mail when a job is posted that exactly matches their qualifications. Some HR practitioners argue that someday online recruiting will be the only job hunting source[93] and that it is driving the integration of other HR functions.[94]

Once a company receives résumés or applications from a posting on its own website or from an Internet job site, it begins its review. It may decide to continue its search or to invite a few of the applicants for interviews, after which it may make job offers. The interviews may take place on-site at the company or through videoconferencing if the candidate is outside the company's geographic area. Any employment testing that the company wishes to do may also be carried out online with a human resources consultant. Videoconferencing and online testing are becoming increasingly popular since the Internet has no geographical boundaries. A company may receive applica-

Recruitment and Selection Today 6.4

Canadian Job and Career Internet Websites

General Job and Career Sites

CanadianCareers.com	http://www.canadiancareers.com
CareerBuilder	http://www.careerbuilder.ca/CA/Default.aspx
CareerPath.com	http://www.careerpath.com
CareerXchange.com	http://www.careerexchange.com
Monster.ca	http://www.monster.ca
Service Canada Job Bank	http://www.jobbank.gc.ca/Intro_en.aspx
Service Canada Training, Career, and Worker Information	http://www.jobsetc.ca

Workopolis.com	http://www.workopolis.com

Sites Designed for High School, College, and University Students

College Grad Job Hunter	http://collegegrad.com
Public Service Commission	http://jobs-emplois.gc.ca/stud-etud/jobs-postes-eng.htm
Youth Resources Network of Canada	http://www.youth.gc.ca

tions from far outside its normal territory. The whole process may take just a few days from placing the notice of the vacancy to making an offer.

Corporations can combine their job listings with a wealth of information about the company, making it easier for candidates to develop an impression of the company's culture and values. Most job search sites also provide job-hunting advice to applicants listed in their databases.

Large national or international Internet sites (e.g., Service Canada's Job Bank) may list tens of thousands of jobs. The job seeker usually has the option of limiting the search to specific geographic areas or types of work, occupations, or industries. Some sites are limited to specific regions of the country. Certain sites are specific to an industry or profession; for example, prospective university professors can find out about job postings by checking the Canadian Association of University Teachers' website at http://www.academicwork.ca. Job seekers interested in working in the not-for-profit sector can go to http://www.charityvillage.com; those interested in working in the arts can review the postings at http://www.workinculture.ca. Increasingly, newspapers and professional journals are placing copies of classified ads for job openings on their websites to run either before or at the same time as print ads.

Internet recruiting has several advantages for both the employer and the job seeker. The biggest advantage to the company is that it can reach a potentially limitless talent pool at minimal cost and beyond its normal geographic location. It allows the company to provide more information about the position to job seekers than does a typical print ad. New jobs can be posted on a daily basis rather than being at the mercy of a newspaper's or journal's publication schedule. Most of all, it speeds up the process of finding good prospective employees by facilitating searches of thousands of résumés stored in data banks.

From the job seeker's perspective, Internet recruiting allows them to apply for many jobs quickly at no cost other than that of an Internet connection. Also, résumés posted on a job search website can be accessed by an unlimited number of potential employers. Their résumés remain in the database for a specified length of time, and résumés can usually be modified at any time. In addition, job seekers registered with some Internet job sites receive information about new job openings as they become available. Internet recruiting does not appear to affect job seekers' perceptions of the realistic nature of the information they find on the Internet; they perceive it to be as realistic as information provided by other means.[95]

Internet recruiting is not without its disadvantages. The ease of submitting résumés coupled with the sheer number of websites devoted to jobs and careers means that a company may be flooded with applications. According to the Internet Business Network,[96] there are now more than 100 000 career websites on the Internet. Whatever savings a company makes through Internet recruiting may be eroded by the costs of dealing with the large volume of applications.

The disadvantages of Internet recruiting for job seekers take a different form. First of all, given a choice, some job seekers prefer to read job postings in traditional paper formats, as opposed to Web-based postings. Job seekers are also turned off by low-quality websites.[97] Next, Internet recruiting and job searching are available only to job seekers who have access to the Internet and the expertise to use computers and related software. This restriction may impede an organization's ability to attract candidates from different population subgroups and meet employment equity goals.

In addition, most, if not all, job and career sites require candidates to complete a standardized online résumé, which limits the type of information that can be included and requires the job seeker to specify keywords under which the résumé is filed in the database. When job seekers send their résumés directly to employers, they often include it as an attachment, which may make the file unreadable when it is received. Most companies expect the file to be sent as either an ASCII file (text only with no formatting) or a Microsoft Word file, which is more or less the business standard.

Perhaps the major concern of job seekers is related to privacy. When a résumé is included in a database, or when it is circulated, it becomes more or less a public document. Often, job seekers who are employed do not want their current employer to know they are looking for other work; they should first assure themselves of the privacy policy of the website before submitting an application through the site. Some employers now routinely have staff or agencies comb through job and career sites to find out if any of their employees are on the job market. Corporate recruiters routinely "mine" job sites using sophisticated technology to gather lists of prospects. They also mine news articles and corporate websites for candidates, even though those individuals may not be seeking employment elsewhere.[98]

Although managerial and professional jobs appear to be particularly well suited to Internet recruiting, people in these types of positions have concerns about their résumés appearing in databases and having others know that they are "shopping around." Except for a few high-tech firms, most companies have not abandoned more traditional forms of recruiting. Internet recruiting is used as part of a mix of methods to obtain the "best" candidates. With the phenomenal growth of the Internet, this may change very rapidly as more companies start to rely solely on Internet recruiting.

Internal versus External Recruitment

Table 6.1 summarizes the advantages and disadvantages of different recruitment methods. Internal recruitment has the advantage of dealing with known quantities. Internal job applicants already have realistic expectations of life in the organization. They are, or should be, aware of the organizational goals and values. Likewise, the organization is familiar with the internal applicant's work history and performance record. Internal recruitment is also relatively inexpensive. Most middle-level jobs in an organization are filled through this means. External recruitment, on the other hand, is used mostly to staff jobs at either the entry or executive levels. External recruitment brings needed skills and competencies to an organization and prevents organizations from becoming "inbred." It exposes companies to new people, new ideas, and new ways of doing things. External recruitment may be the only means through

TABLE 6.1

Comparison of Internal and External Recruitment Methods

METHODS	ADVANTAGES	DISADVANTAGES
Internal Recruitment		
Job Postings	Inexpensive. Rewards performance. Discovers talent.	Time-consuming. Produces instability. Demoralizing process.
Replacement Charts	Based on known human resources.	Limited by organizational chart and structure.
Information Systems	Known KSAO database linked to job.	Expensive. Rarely used by companies.
Nominations	Based on known human resources.	Random process. May lead to discrimination.
External Recruitment		
Newspaper Ads	Quick and flexible. Specific market.	Expensive. Short lifespan for ads.
Periodicals/Journals	Targets specific groups or skills.	Long lead time for ads. Expensive.
Radio and TV	Mass audience. Targets specific groups. Image advertising.	Very expensive. Short ad duration. Provides little information.
Public Displays	Inexpensive.	Provides little information.
Direct Mail	Targets specific groups and skills. Can provide much information.	Expensive and inefficient. Requires mailing list. Often not read.
Special Events	Useful for filling multiple jobs. Relatively inexpensive. Targets job pool.	Shares job pool with competition. Information overload/ stress.
Employee Referrals	Inexpensive.	May lead to discrimination and inbreeding.
Networking	Inexpensive	May lead to discrimination and inbreeding.
Walk-Ins	Inexpensive.	Random process. Inefficient.
Canada Employment Centres	Inexpensive. Job–KSAO fit.	Success limited to certain occupational categories.

continued

Table 6.1 *Continued from previous page*

Comparison of Internal and External Recruitment Methods

Methods	Advantages	Disadvantages
Private Employment Agency	Person–job fit.	Expensive.
Executive Search Firm	Known talent pool.	Very expensive.
In-House Recruiter	Knows company.	Limited knowledge of recruiting methods.
Temporary Help Agency	Access to short-term labour pool. Few recruiting demands.	Exposure to risk of discrimination claims. Mostly unskilled and poorly educated talent pool.
Recruiting at Schools	Known talent pool. Pretrained applicants.	Time-consuming. Very expensive.
Internet	Mass audience. Inexpensive. Specific audience.	Random process. Unknown audience.

which employment equity programs succeed. External recruitment can be very time-consuming and expensive.

Recruiting and International Assignments

With the spread of globalization, Canadian organizations increasingly need to staff foreign operations. Recruiting someone to head a project in another country is very important if a company is to expand its business into foreign markets. Typically, Canadian organizations have recruited internally or domestically for foreign assignments and have paid the recruits up to three times their normal salaries for accepting foreign postings.[99] Use of North American expatriates to staff the operations of North American firms overseas, however, has not been successful in many cases. Problems associated with family adjustment to new cultures and the manager's lack of personal adjustment to the foreign business environment often lead to failure.[100]

Canadian firms must do a much better job of identifying, recruiting, and selecting individuals based on those competencies related to success abroad. With the development of the borderless job-search websites and résumé data banks, companies may have an easier time finding job applicants from around the world who have the requisite knowledge of the laws and culture of the host country.

Effectiveness of Recruiting Methods

Some publications assert that recruiting online is becoming increasingly popular with employers and potential employees, that Internet recruiting can give organizations a competitive advantage, that it is faster and cheaper than many other recruiting techniques, and that recruiting online is a good way to pre-screen and pre-test candidates.[101-103] Regrettably, there is hardly any evidence to back up these claims except anecdotes. The effectiveness of Internet postings in assisting matches between potential employees and employers is yet to be determined. Compared to other recruitment methods, the Internet is still in its infancy.

Table 6.2 presents data from Statistics Canada's *Workplace and Employee Survey* that were gathered in 1999, 2001 and 2003, the last available data set. The data were obtained in each cycle from approximately 5400 organizations and 25 000 employees that were considered to be a representative sample of Canadian businesses and industries and their employees. Bissonnette and Catano[104] found that informal recruitment sources (i.e., family and friends) remained the most frequently used recruitment source in each of the three cycles, being used about twice as often as the second most frequently used source, personal initiative (e.g., walk-ins).

While only a small proportion of the sample (0.2 percent) found a job through the Internet in 1999, that percentage had grown to 2.2 percent in 2003. When the data were reviewed for employees with job tenure of one year or less, the percentage use of the Internet as a recruiting device increased. The values were 0.6, 2.5, and 5.1 percent, respectively, for the three data-gathering cycles. That is, use of the Internet to hire new employees increased by 850 percent from 1999 to 2003![105]

TABLE 6.2

Percentage of Canadian Employees Finding Jobs through Different Recruitment Methods: Change over Time			
TYPE OF SOURCE USED	1999 (%)	2001 (%)	2003(%)
Family or Friend	37.7	40.6	39.0
Personal Initiative	21.6	17.8	20.3
Help-Wanted Ad	17.7	16.1	15.3
Directly Recruited by Employer	10.7	9.3	11.3
Other	8.7	8.8	8.7
Canada Employment Centre	3.0	2.9	2.6
Recruitment Agency (Headhunter)	2.2	2.9	3.2
On-Campus Recruitment	2.0	2.4	2.0
Union Posting	0.5	0.5	0.7
Internet	0.2	1.0	2.2
News Story	0.2	0.4	0.3
Job Fair	0.2	0.4	0.3
Using More Than One Recruitment Source	4.0	2.9	5.4
Not Using Any Recruitment Source	8.0	8.9	7.7

Source: A. Bissonnette and V.M. Catano. 2007. *Recruitment Source over Time: Correlations, Perceptions, Interpretations and Future Directions.* Paper presented at the annual meeting of the Administrative Association of Canada, Ottawa. Reprinted with permission of V.M. Catano.

Bissonnette and Catano's Canadian data reflect findings from previous American research. Zottoli and Wanous[106] reviewed over 50 years of research on recruiting source effectiveness, as measured through job turnover/survival and job performance. Referrals by family and friends and current employees, in-house job postings, and rehiring of former employees were the most effective methods in filling positions. Walk-ins were slightly less effective, with the least effective sources consisting of newspaper ads, placement services, and employment agencies, whether private or government-run. As the most popular recruiting methods also have the potential to produce systemic discrimination, HR practitioners must be particularly alert to this undesirable outcome.

ⓡⓟⓒ 6.7   Evaluating Recruiting Efforts

We started this chapter with the proposition that recruitment is the first step in the selection process through which an organization finds the best-qualified people to fill job vacancies. It is quite obvious that recruiting can be very expensive and time-consuming. While it is important to know the effectiveness of different recruiting methods, organizations that engage in recruiting should also be concerned that their money and time are well spent. They should not only want to know whether the job advertisements paid off in more applications, but also whether better-qualified candidates were hired, what it cost to recruit the new employees, whether the new recruits are more productive or have a more positive attitude about the organization, and whether they stay with the organization for a longer period of time.

Unfortunately, many companies do not bother to ask these questions or evaluate the effectiveness of their recruiting efforts, the quality of the people they recruited, or the recruits' success on the job. Their primary criteria for judging the success of recruiting appears to be the number of applications received and whether the vacant jobs were filled. Very few organizations track the performance and behavioural outcomes of people recruited into the organization or the costs associated with the recruiting campaign, including advertising costs.[107] Without doubt, recruiters will increasingly be required to demonstrate the effectiveness of their programs. It is essential that HR practitioners demonstrate the effectiveness, and worth, of recruiting.[108]

Recruiting should not be taken at face value but should be evaluated on the basis of specific criteria. Recruiting efforts should be evaluated separately from the selection system. The criterion measures that an organization uses to evaluate its recruiting program should be consistent with the goals that were set for that effort. If the organization wanted to recruit the best possible candidates available, it would be unfair to evaluate the recruiting program on the cost involved in finding those candidates. The appropriate measure would be whether the best possible candidates were hired. If the organization used recruiting to generate a large applicant pool, then an appropriate criterion measure might be the number of applications that were received rather than the quality of the people hired.

There are many different criterion measures that can be used to evaluate recruiting efforts, some of which are shown in Recruitment and

Recruitment and Selection Today 6.5

Examples of Criteria Used to Evaluate Recruiting Methods

Behavioural Measures

- Turnover
  - within 6 months
  - within 12 months
  - within 24 months
- Absenteeism

Performance Measures

- Performance ratings
- Sales quotas
- Performance potential

Attitudinal Measures

- Job satisfaction
- Job involvement
- Satisfaction with supervisor
- Commitment to organization
- Perceived accuracy of job descriptions

Sources: S.L. Rynes. 1991. "Recruitment, Job Choice, and Post-Hire Consequences." In M.D. Dunnette and L.M. Hough, eds., *Handbook of Industrial and Organizational Psychology*, Vol. 2 (pp. 399–444). 2nd ed. Palo Alto, CA: Consulting Psychologists Press; J.P. Wanous and A. Colella. 1989. "Organizational Entry Research: Current Status and Future Directions." In K.M. Rowland and G.R. Ferris, eds., *Research in Personnel and Human Resource Management*, Vol. 7 (pp. 59–120). Greenwich, CT: JAI Press.

Selection Today 6.5.[109],[110] These criteria can be grouped into three broad categories: behavioural measures, performance measures, and attitudinal measures.

Noticeably absent from Recruitment and Selection Today 6.5 are any measures that are based on cost or an integration of cost and benefits. Human resources professionals will be called on to link their activities to their company's bottom line. Utility analysis, which will be discussed in Chapter 10, provides a mechanism for applying cost–benefit analysis to human resources decisions. Boudreau and Rynes[111] adapted utility analysis to incorporate the effects of recruitment, including financial and economic factors, and the effects associated with changes in the size and quality of the applicant pool, the number of applicants processed, and the average qualification level of those hired.

Improved recruitment altered the benefits that could be expected from improved selection procedures because recruitment produced a more qualified and less diverse applicant pool. Boudreau and Rynes concluded that the most effective procedure was an integrated recruitment–selection strategy. Boudreau[112] demonstrated the use of utility analysis to evaluate the effectiveness of different recruiting approaches in conjunction with selection models.

More recently, Carlson, Connerley, and Mecham[113] showed how utility analysis, along with other procedures, could be used to assess the quality of recruited applicants in terms of a cost–benefit analysis and to provide a comparison of outcomes from different recruitment events. They showed that the value of different recruitment methods can be substantial when assessing applicant quality. Carlson and his colleagues concluded that assessing recruitment outcomes is critical to systematic improvement of recruitment effectiveness.

Employment equity

Policies and practices designed to increase the presence of qualified women, visible minorities, Aboriginal people, and people with disabilities in the work force.

One final criterion, **employment equity**, should be considered as part of evaluating any recruitment efforts. The organization must review whether its recruiting campaign has produced an increased presence of qualified women, visible minorities, Aboriginal people, and people with disabilities in its work force. In the context of Canadian employment equity legislation, as discussed in Chapter 3, recruiting efforts must be judged on this basis as well as the more traditional outcome measures.

Recruitment Audit

Ryan and Tippens[114] developed an audit of recruitment practices to help HR managers determine if their recruitment practices reflected best practices based on research. The questions that form that audit are presented in Recruitment and Selection Today 6.6. Review of the audit questions can assist HR professionals in identifying gaps in their recruitment practices.

Recruitment and Selection Today 6.6

An Audit of Recruitment Practices

- Have we determined which applicant groups to target?
- Are efforts being made to recruit a diverse applicant pool?
- Are efforts being made to have a low selection ratio (i.e., a low number of people selected relative to the total number of applicants)?
- Are we considering combinations of tools to achieve the highest validity and lowest adverse impact?
- Have we considered how our ordering of tools affects validity and adverse impact?
- Are we considering all aspects of job performance in choosing tools?
- Have we determined which recruiting sources provide the best yield?
- Are we providing applicants with the specific information they desire?
- Have we selected recruiters who are warm and friendly?
- Is appropriate attention being given to early recruitment activities?

- Are applicants being processed quickly?
- Do we solicit feedback from applicants on satisfaction with the staffing process?
- Are applicants being provided with information about the job-relatedness of the selection process?
- Are applicants provided with accurate information on which to judge their fit with the position?
- Do we have evidence that selection procedures are job-related?
- Are applicants treated with respect?
- Is the selection process consistently administered?
- Does the process allow for some two-way communication?
- Is feedback provided to applicants in an informative and timely manner?

Source: A.M. Ryan and N.T. Tippens. 2004. "Attracting and Selecting: What Psychological Research Tells Us." *Human Resource Management* 43:4 305–18. Reprinted with permission of Wiley-Blackwell.

Summary

Recruitment is the first step in the hiring or staffing process, but, unlike other aspects of this process, the actions and decisions of the job seeker play a major role. A recruitment process, no matter how brilliantly conceived, is a failure if it does not attract qualified job applicants. Recruitment campaigns are a success when they understand what organizational characteristics attract job seekers. The recruitment process must take into account the strategies that job seekers use to investigate jobs and organizations. The process should provide job candidates with information they need to make appropriate job choices. Job candidates should receive information about the job, the organization, and the organization's approach to compensation. For example, job candidates will want to know whether the company will meet market pay rates, if compensation is related to performance, and what reward systems are in place, among other issues.

Recruitment campaigns should be based on the principle of improving the fit between job candidates and the organization. Organizations can help to achieve this by presenting an accurate image of both the job and the organization to job seekers. The organization should use communications in a way that develops accurate expectations and perceptions on the part of job applicants. One method that appears capable of doing this is a realistic job preview.

In developing a recruitment strategy, human resources planners must consider both the internal and external constraints on the organization. All recruitment is influenced by external factors over which the organization has little control (e.g., the labour market and the legal environment), as well as internal factors that it can influence (e.g., its compensation strategy, business plan, and values). Recruitment strategies and materials, which are grounded in organization and job analysis, establish both realistic expectations among job applicants and the availability of qualified internal and external job candidates.

Every recruitment strategy must contain an action plan, which schedules recruiting initiatives and provides a means of identifying and locating the target applicant pool. The action plan must also identify the appropriate methods for contacting the target applicant pool. The action plan should also include a method for evaluating the effectiveness of the recruitment campaign.

HR professionals must know the effectiveness of different recruiting methods and build into their recruitment strategy plans for evaluating the recruiting outcomes. They also must know the appropriate recruitment source for the target pool of applicants. In cases where informal methods such as referrals and job postings are used, care must be taken to avoid systemic discrimination. In evaluating outcomes, the quantity of applicants should not be the only criterion, as the quality of the applicants attracted to the organization is an even more important factor.

Key Terms

applicant pool, p. 236
employment equity, p. 278
image advertising, p. 241

interests and values, p. 239
Internet recruiting, p. 270
job search, p. 240

Web Links

For information on careers in the military, check out the Canadian Forces site at http://www.forces.gc.ca.

Job postings can be found at http://www.monster.ca, http://www.engineeringjobs.com, and http://www.casource.com.

Check out government-sponsored job posting and job search information sites at http://www.jobbank.gc.ca, http://jobs-emplois.gc.ca/index-eng.htm, and http://www.labourmarketinformation.ca/standard.asp?pcode=lmiv_main&lcode=e.

Networking resources can be found at http://content.monster.ca/section1967.asp and http://www.careerkey.com.

Required Professional Capabilities (RPCs)

RPC 6.1 Develops people plans that support the organization's strategic directions.
- HR planning concepts and techniques
- Research methods
- Use of business and HR software
- HR functions and activities
- The organization's strategic business plan and the goals of the business unit

RPC 6.2 Oversees the organization's recruitment and staffing policies and procedures (recruitment, selection, and orientation).
- Job markets
- Selection concepts and techniques
- Relevant legislation and regulations
- Recruiting sources and techniques (internal and external)
- Organization staffing needs
- Organization's internal HR inventory
- Assessment tools
- Orientation and career development needs of new employees
- Industry best practices
- The organization's strategic business plan and the goals of the business unit

RPC 6.3 Identifies the organization's staffing needs.
- Data collection techniques
- Research methods and designs (including measurement of HR)

- Business and HR software
- HR planning concepts and techniques
- Organization's internal HR inventory
- The organization's strategic business plan and the goals of the business unit

RPC 6.4 Identifies the potential source of internal and external qualified candidates.
- Job markets
- Organization's internal HR inventory
- Relevant legislation and regulations
- Recruiting sources and techniques (both internal and external)
- Organization policies and procedures

RPC 6.5 Evaluates the relevance of alternatives to recruitment (developing, outsourcing, contingent workers, agencies, etc.).
- Organization staffing needs
- Current and future business plans
- Availability of internal and external developmental programs
- Training and development needs analysis techniques (i.e., skill assessment strategies and levels of training needs analysis)
- Stakeholders and their respective interests
- Cost–benefit analysis (including the direct and indirect costs and benefits associated with conducting training and development programs and the costs and benefits of the alternatives
- Research methods and designs (including measurement of HR)
- Measurement and assessment tools and techniques (and their limitations)
- Organization's internal HR inventory
- Preparation and presentation of business cases.

RPC 6.6 Develops, implements, and monitors processes for attracting qualified candidates.
- Job markets
- Recruitment ethics and professional practices
- Relevant legislation and regulations
- Communication theories, tools, techniques, and processes
- Recruiting sources and techniques (both internal and external)
- Fundamentals of marketing communications
- Organization policies and procedures

RPC 6.7 Evaluates effectiveness of recruitment process.
- Benchmarking techniques
- Organization staffing needs
- Statistical analyses and evaluation
- Recruiting sources and techniques (both internal and external)
- Measurement and assessment tools and techniques (and their limitations)
- Validation of selection and training decisions and measurements

Discussion Questions

1. Discuss the relationship between recruitment and selection.
2. Discuss how the characteristics of the job and organization influence job seekers.
3. Why is it important that job seekers develop accurate expectations of what their position/role will be in an organization before accepting employment there?
4. Why does a realistic job preview benefit both the job seeker and the organization?
5. What are the internal and external factors that influence an organization's recruitment strategy?
6. What are the elements of an effective recruitment and staffing action plan?
7. What are the different methods that can be used to recruit internal and external job applicants?
8. Is the Internet an effective recruiting method? Why or why not?

Using the Internet

1. Recruitment and Selection Today 6.1 (page 241) presents information on the interactive Government of Canada site (https://www .emploisetc.ca/home.jsp) that contains quizzes to help you identify a career that would fit with your abilities, interests, and preferences. Visit the site and complete the interactive exercises. Print out your summaries from these quizzes. Do they provide an accurate picture of you? What do they suggest in terms of your "fit" to a career or job? Is this an accurate picture of your abilities and interests? Visit another job search site listed in Recruitment and Selection Today 6.4 (page 270) that offers career advice based on your abilities, interests, and preferences. Complete any exercises on its site as well. How does the feedback from the two sites compare?

Exercises

1. Choose an organization in your community and schedule a meeting with its human resources manager (or designate). Using the material in this chapter as a guide, interview the HR representative on the organization's recruiting efforts (e.g., determine the role that job and organization analysis played in developing the strategy). Ask whether the organization considers how potential applicants would react to the recruiting materials. Prepare a report on the organization's recruiting strategy and its effectiveness.

2. Examine the organization's recruiting program (the one chosen for Exercise 1) from a job candidate's perspective. With the assistance of the human resources representative, interview a recently hired employee who was an external applicant. Ask the employee about his or her job search strategy, perceptions of the organization, the recruiting process, requirements for pay and benefits, what influenced that person's decision to take the job, and whether his or her views have changed after being in the organization for a period of time. Prepare a report summarizing this interview.

3. Using the information presented in this chapter and the information obtained from your interviews in Exercises 1 and 2, develop a comprehensive recruitment strategy for the organization based on the job of the new employee whom you interviewed.

4. How did the organization advertise the position? Identify the best ways for reaching the target applicant pool for this job.

5. Prepare an advertisement for the position of the person you interviewed using the AIDA formula discussed in this chapter. Compare the costs of running this advertisement in some of the commonly used media discussed in this chapter.

6. Obtain advertisements for several positions that have run in newspapers, professional journals, or trade magazines. Analyze the ads using the AIDA formula discussed in this chapter.

7. Find a job description for a position that is of interest to you. Write an effective job advertisement for that position.

Case

When qualified applicants are scarce, recruiting becomes extremely competitive, particularly when two companies go after the same candidate, as often happens in the case of searching for professionals. This case was recently the subject of an Internet discussion.

After interviewing three short-listed candidates, a high-tech company, Company X, made an offer to one and advised the other two candidates that they were unsuccessful. The successful candidate was given one week to consider the offer. The candidate asked for a week's extension to consider the offer but was granted only an additional three days.

At the end of the time period, the candidate verbally accepted the offer and was sent a contract to sign. Rather than returning the signed contract, the candidate informed Company X that he had accepted a position at Company Y. He had received the second offer after verbally accepting the first position at Company X. The second company knew that the candidate had verbally accepted Company X's offer.

Before accepting Company Y's offer, the candidate had consulted a respected mentor who advised him to ignore his verbal commitment to

Company X and to accept Company Y's offer. There were no substantial differences in the salaries being offered by each company or in the work that each would expect the candidate to perform. The candidate simply saw Company Y as the more prestigious of the two employers.

Discussion Questions

1. Did the candidate act in an appropriate manner?
2. What should the candidate have done?
3. What would you have done if you had been in the candidate's position?
4. Did Company Y act ethically, knowing that the candidate had verbally accepted another offer?
5. Does a verbal acceptance constitute a legal and binding contract?
6. What should the candidate's mentor have advised him to do?
7. Should Company X take any action to enforce the verbal commitment? Should it take any legal action against the candidate or Company Y? Why or why not?
8. How can situations like this be avoided?

Endnotes

1. Guion, R.M. 1976. "Recruiting, Selection, and Job Placement." In M. Dunnette, ed., *Handbook of Industrial and Organizational Psychology* (pp. 777–828). Chicago: Rand-McNally.
2. Breaugh, J.A., and M. Starke. 2000. "Research on Employee Recruitment: So Many Studies, So Many Questions." *Journal of Management* 26: 405–34.
3. Rynes, S.L. 1993. "Who's Selecting Whom? Effects of Selection Practices on Applicant Attitudes and Behaviour." In N. Schmitt, W.C. Borman et al., eds., *Personnel Selection in Organizations* (pp. 240–74). San Francisco, CA: Jossey-Bass.
4. Ryan, A.M., J.M. Sacco, L.A. McFarland, and S.D. Kriska. 2000. "Applicant Self-Selection: Correlates of Withdrawal from a Multiple Hurdle Process." *Journal of Applied Psychology* 85: 163–79.
5. Ryan, A.M., J.M. Sacco, L.A. McFarland, and S.D. Kriska. 2000.
6. Schwab, D.P., S.L. Rynes, and R.J. Aldag. 1987. "Theories and Research on Job Search and Choice." In K.M. Rowland and G.R. Ferris, eds., *Research in Personnel and Human Resource Management*, Vol. 5 (pp. 129–66). Greenwich, CT: JAI Press.
7. Turban, D.B., J.E. Campion, and A.R. Eyrung. 1995. "Factors Related to Job Acceptance Decisions of College Recruits." *Journal of Vocational Behavior* 47: 193–213.
8. Carsten, J.M., and P.E. Spector. 1987. "Unemployment, Job Satisfaction, and Employee Turnover: A Meta-Analytic Test of the Muchinsky Model." *Journal of Applied Psychology* 72: 374–81.
9. Barber, A.E., M.J. Wesson, Q.M. Roberson, and M.S. Taylor. 1999. "A Tale of Two Job Markets: Organizational Size and Its Effects on Hiring Practices and Job Search Behavior." *Personnel Psychology* 52: 841–68.
10. Barber, A.E., et al. 1999.
11. Lemmink, J., A. Schuif, and S. Streukens. 2003. "The Role of Corporate Image and Company Employment Image in Explaining Application Intentions." *Journal of Economic Psychology* 24: 1–15.

12. Turban, D.B. 2001. "Organizational Attractiveness as an Employer on College Campuses: An Examination of the Applicant Population." *Journal of Vocational Behavior* 56: 293–312.

13. Cable, D.M., and M.E. Graham. 2000. "The Determinants of Organizational Reputation: A Job Search Perspective." *Journal of Organizational Behavior* 21: 929–47.

14. Cable, D.M., and M.E. Graham. 2000.

15. Aiman-Smith, L., T.N. Bauer, and D.M. Cable. 2001. "Are You Attracted? Do You Intend to Pursue? A Recruiting Policy-Capturing Study." *Journal of Business and Psychology* 16: 219–37.

16. Yeuse, P., and S. Highhouse. 1998. "Effects of Attribute Set Size and Pay Ambiguity on Reactions to 'Help Wanted' Advertisements." *Journal of Organizational Behavior* 19: 337–52.

17. Cable, D.M., L. Aiman-Smith, P.W. Mulvey, and J.R. Edwards. 2000. "The Sources and Accuracy of Job Applicants' Beliefs about Organizational Culture." *Academy of Management Journal* 43: 1076–85.

18. Gatewood, R.D., M.A. Gowan, and G.J. Lautenschlager. 1993. "Corporate Image, Recruitment Image, and Initial Job Choices." *Academy of Management Journal* 36: 414–27.

19. Magnus, M. 1985. "Recruitment Ads at Work." *Personnel Journal* 64: 4–63.

20. Gil, A. 2003. "It's Party Time at Film Festival." Report on du Maurier's sponsorship of a Toronto Film Festival event. *The Globe and Mail* (September 23): A13.

21. Ashforth, E., and G. Kreiner. 1999. "'How Can You Do It?' Dirty Work and the Challenge of Constructing a Positive Identity." *Academy of Management Review* 24: 413–34.

22. Kristof-Brown, A.L. 2000. "Perceived Applicant Fit: Distinguishing between Recruiters' Perceptions of Person–Job Fit and Person–Organization Fit." *Personnel Psychology* 53: 643–71.

23. Kristof-Brown, A.L. 1998. "The Goldilocks Pursuit in Organizational Selection: How Recruiters Form and Use Judgments of Person–Organization Fit." *Dissertation Abstracts International Section A: Humanities and Social Sciences* 58(11-A): 4345.

24. Wanous, J.P., and A. Colella. 1989. "Organizational Entry Research: Current Status and Future Directions." In K.M. Rowland and G.R. Ferris, eds., *Research in Personnel and Human Resource Management*, Vol. 7 (pp. 59–120). Greenwich, CT: JAI Press.

25. Rynes, S.L. 1993.

26. Saks, A.M. 1994. "A Psychological Process Investigation for the Effects of Recruitment Source and Organization Information on Job Survival." *Journal of Organizational Behavior* 15: 225–44.

27. Wanous, J.P., and A. Colella. 1989.

28. Buckley, M.R., D.B. Fedor, D.S. Marvin, J.G. Veres, D.S. Wise, and S.M. Carraher. 1998. "Investigating Newcomer Expectations and Job-Related Outcomes." *Journal of Applied Psychology* 83: 452–61.

29. Buckley, M.R., D.B. Fedor, and D.S. Marvin. 1994. "Ethical Considerations in the Recruiting Process: A Preliminary Investigation and Identification of Research Opportunities." *Human Resource Management Review* 4: 35–50.

30. Moser, K. 2005. "Recruitment Sources and Post-Hire Outcomes: The Mediating Role of Unmet Expectations." *International Journal of Selection and Assessment* 13: 188–97.

31. Buckley, M.R., D.B. Fedor, and D.S. Marvin. 1994.

32. Buckley, M.R., et al. 1998.

33. Wanous, J.P. 1980. *Organizational Entry: Recruitment, Selection, and Socialization of Newcomers*. Reading, MA: Addison-Wesley.

34. Phillips, J.M. 1998. "Effects of Realistic Job Previews on Multiple Organizational Outcomes: A Meta-Analysis." *Academy of Management Journal* 41: 673–90.

35. Rynes, S.L. 1991. "Recruitment, Job Choice, and Post-Hire Consequences." In M.D. Dunnette and L.M. Hough, eds., *Handbook of Industrial and Organizational Psychology*, Vol. 2 (pp. 399–444). 2nd ed. Palo Alto, CA: Consulting Psychologists Press.

36. Phillips, J.M. 1998.

37. Meglino, B.M., E.C. Ravlin, and A.S. DeNisi. 1997. "When Does It Hurt to Tell the Truth? The Effect of Realistic Job Reviews on Employee Recruiting." *Public Personnel Management* 26: 413–22.

38. Bretz, R.D., Jr., and T.A. Judge. 1998. "Realistic Job Previews: A Test of the Adverse Self-Selection Hypothesis." *Journal of Applied Psychology* 83: 330–37.

39. Saks, A.M., W.H. Wiesner, and R.J. Summers. 1996. "Effects of Job Previews and Compensation Policy on Applicant Attraction and Job Choice." *Journal of Vocational Behavior* 49: 68–85.

40. Travagline, A.M. 2002. "Online Recruiting: Implementing Internet-Based Realistic Job Previews." *Dissertation Abstracts International: Section B: The Sciences and Engineering* 63 (1-b): 579.

41. Meglino, B.M., A.S. DeNisi, and E.C. Ravlin. 1993. "Effects of Previous Job Exposure and Subsequent Job Status on the Functioning of a Realistic Job Preview." *Personnel Psychology* 46: 803–22.

42. Hom, P.W., R.W. Griffeth, L.E. Palich, and J.S. Bracker. 1999. "Revisiting Met Expectations as a Reason Why Realistic Job Previews Work." *Personnel Psychology* 52: 97–112.

43. Rynes, S.L. 1991.

44. Phillips, J.M. 1998.

45. Rynes, S.L., and D.M. Cable. 2003. "Recruitment Research in the Twenty-First Century." In W.C Borman, D.R. Ilgen, and R. Klimoski, eds., *Handbook of Psychology: Industrial and Organizational Psychology*, Vol. 12 (pp. 55–76). New York: John Wiley and Sons.

46. Phillips, J.M. 1998.

47. Moser, K. 2005.

48. Buckley, M.R., et al. 1998.

49. Buckley, M.R., T.A. Mobbs, J.L. Mendoza, M.M. Novicevic, S.M. Carrahar, and D.S. Beu. 2002. "Implementing Realistic Job Previews and Expectation-Lowering Procedures: A Field Experiment." *Journal of Vocational Behavior* 61: 263–78.

50. Ganzach, Y., A. Pazy, Y. Ohayun, and E. Brainin. 2002. "Social Exchange and Organizational Commitment: Decision-Making Training for Job Choice as an Alternative to the Realistic Job Preview." *Personnel Psychology* 55: 613–37.

51. Carlson, K.D., and M.L. Connerley. 2003. "The Staffing Cycles Framework: Viewing Staffing as a System of Decision Events." *Journal of Management* 29: 51–78.

52. Rynes, S.L. 1991.

53. Keenan, G. 1996. "Toyota Swamped in Rush for Jobs." *The Globe and Mail* (February 21): A1, A7.

54. Greengard, S. 1995. "Leveraging a Low-Wage Work Force." *Personnel Journal* 74 (January): 90–102.

55. Flynn, G. 1995. "Contingent Staffing Requires Serious Strategy." *Personnel Journal* 74 (April): 50–58.

56. Holton, B.C., T.W. Lee, and S.T. Tidd. 2002. "The Relationship between Work Status Congruence and Work-Related Attitudes." *Journal of Applied Psychology* 87: 903–15.

57. Galt, V. 1992. "Agencies Still Refer Whites Only." *The Globe and Mail* (September 8): B1.

58. Castro, J. 1993. "Disposable Workers." *Time* (March 29): 43–47.

59. Ryan, A.M., and M.J. Schmit. 1996. "Calculating EEO Statistics in the Temporary Help Industry." *Personnel Psychology* 49: 167–80.

60. Rynes, S.L. 1991.

61. Perrott, S.B. 1999. "Visible Minority Applicant Concerns and Assessment of Occupational Role in the Era of Community-Based Policing." *Journal of Community and Applied Social Psychology* 9: 339–53.

62. Kravitz, D.A., and S.L. Klineberg. 2000. "Reactions to Two Versions of Affirmative Action among Whites, Blacks, and Hispanics." *Journal of Applied Psychology* 85: 597–611.

63. Saks, A.M., J.D. Leck, and D.M. Saunders. 1995. "Effects of Application Blanks and Employment Equity on Applicant Reactions and Job Pursuit Intentions." *Journal of Organizational Behavior* 16: 415–30.

64. Heilman, M.E., W.S. Battle, C.E. Keller, and R.A. Lee. 1998. "Type of Affirmative Action Policy: A Determinant of Reactions to Sex-Based Preferential Selection?" *Journal of Applied Psychology* 83: 190–205.

65. Ryan, A.M., M. Horvath, and S.D. Kriska. 2005. "The Role of Recruiting Source Informativeness and Organizational Perceptions in Decisions to Apply." *International Journal of Selection and Assessment* 13: 235–49.

66. Rynes, S.L. 1991.

67. Rynes, S.L. 1991.

68. Rynes, S.L. 1991.

69. Rynes, S.L. 1991.

70. Keenan, G. 1996.

71. Dolan, S.L., and R.S. Schuler. 1994. *Human Resource Management: The Canadian Dynamic*. Toronto: Nelson Canada.

72. Barber, A.E., and M.J. Wesson. 1999.

73. Rynes, S.L. 1991.

74. Rynes, S.L. 1991.

75. Moser, K. 2005.

76. Arthur, D. 2001. *The Employee Recruitment and Retention Handbook*. New York: AMACOM.

77. Decker, P.J., and E.T. Cornelius. 1979. "A Note on Recruiting Sources and Job Survival Rates." *Journal of Applied Psychology* 64: 463–64.

78. Breaugh, J.A. 1981. "Relationships between Recruiting Sources and Employee Performance, Absenteeism and Work Attitudes." *Academy of Management Journal* 24: 142, 147–48.

79. Zottoli, M.A., and J.P. Wanous. 2000. "Recruitment Source Research: Current Status and Future Directions." *Human Resource Management Review* 10: 353–82.

80. LeBlanc, S. 1996. "Guarantee of Extra Cash Not Luring Doctors to Rural Areas." *The Halifax Mail-Star* (March 1): A1, A2.

81. Taylor, S.G. 1994. "The Relationship between Sources of New Employees and Attitudes toward the Job." *Journal of Social Psychology* 134: 99–111.

82. Wanous, J.P., and A. Colella. 1989.

83. Taylor, S.G. 1994.

84. Moser, K. 2005.

85. Zottoli, M.A., and J.P. Wanous. 2000.

86. Bissonnette, A., and V.M. Catano. 2003. *Revisiting the Efficacy of Recruiting Methods*. Paper presented at the 11th Congress of the European Association of Work and Organization Psychology, Lisbon, Portugal.

87. Zottoli, M.A., and J.P. Wanous. 2000.

88. Dolan, S.L., and R.S. Schuler. 1994.

89. Rynes, S.L. 1991.

90. Chapman, D.S., K.L. Uggerslev, S.A. Carroll, K.A. Piasentin, and D. A. Jones. 2005. "Applicant Attraction to Organizations and Job Choice: A Meta-Analytic Review of the Correlates of Recruiting Outcomes." *Journal of Applied Psychology* 90: 928–44.

91. Rynes, S.L., and D.M. Cable. 2003.

92. Rynes, S.L. 1991.

93. Capelli, P. 2002. "Making the Most of On-Line Recruiting." *Harvard Business Review* (March): 139–46.

94. Cullen, B. 2001. "E-Recruiting Is Driving HR Systems Integration." *Strategic Finance* 83: 22–26.

95. Rozelle, A.L., and R.S. Landis. 2002. "An Examination of the Relationship between Use of the Internet as a Recruitment Source and Student Attitudes." *Computers in Human Behavior* 18: 593–604.

96. Pearsall, K. 1998. "Web Recruiting Complicated by Sheer Numbers." *Computing Canada* 24: 11, 14.

97. Zusman, R.R., and R.S. Landis. 2002. "Applicant Preferences of Web-Based versus Traditional Job Postings." *Computers in Human Behavior* 18: 285–96.

98. Piturro, M. 2000. "The Power Of E-cruiting." *Management Review* 89: 33–37.

99. Ondrack, D. 1996. "Global Warning." *Human Resources Professional* (May): 27–29.

100. Ondrack, D. 1996.

101. Zall, M. 2000. "Internet Recruiting." *Strategic Finance* 81: 66–72.

102. Arthur, D. 2001.

103. Bingham, B., S. Ilg, and N. Davidson. 2002. "Great Candidates Fast: Online Job Application and Electronic Processing." *Public Personnel Management* 31: 53–64.

104. Bissonnette, A., and V.M. Catano. 2007. *Recruitment Source over Time: Correlations, Perceptions, Interpretations and Future Directions*. Paper presented at the annual meeting of the Administrative Association of Canada, Ottawa.

105. Bissonnette, A., and V.M. Catano. 2008. *Recruitment Sources: Correlates and Temporal Changes*. Unpublished manuscript.

106. Zottoli, M.A., and J.P. Wanous. 2000.

107. Rynes, S.L., and J.L. Boudreau. 1986. "College Recruiting in Large Organizations: Practice, Evaluation, and Research Implications." *Personnel Psychology* 39: 729–57.

108. Grossman, R.J. 2000. "Measuring Up, Appropriate Metric Help: HR Proves Its Worth." *HR Magazine* 45: 28–35.

109. Rynes, S.L. 1991.

110. Wanous, J.P., and A. Colella. 1989.

111. Boudreau, J.W., and S.L. Rynes. 1985. "The Role of Recruitment in Staffing Utility Analysis." *Journal of Applied Psychology* 70: 354–66.

112. Boudreau, J.W. 1991. "Utility Analysis for Decisions in Human Resource Management." In M.D. Dunnette and L.M. Hough, eds., *Handbook of Industrial and Organizational Psychology*, Vol. 2 (pp. 399–444). 2nd ed. Palo Alto, CA: Consulting Psychologists Press.

113. Carlson K.D., M.L. Connerley, and R.L. Mecham, III. 2002. "Recruitment Evaluation: The Case for Assessing the Quality of Applicants Attracted." *Personnel Psychology* 55: 461–90.

114. Ryan, A.M., and N.T. Tippens. 2004. "Attracting and Selecting: What Psychological Research Tells Us." *Human Resource Management* 43: 305–18.

Chapter 7

Selection I: Applicant Screening

Chapter Learning Objectives

This chapter introduces procedures that are commonly used in applicant screening. Generally speaking, *screening* refers to the early stages of a sequential selection process in which applicants meeting critical minimal qualifications or selection criteria are selected for further consideration involving more resource-intensive assessments, while those without these requirements are "screened out." *Screening* might also refer to any rough and quick selection process even when not followed by further selection assessments.[1] Screening takes on increasing importance the larger the ratio of applicants to positions (or conversely, the fewer selected for hire as a percentage of the total applicant pool—the *selection ratio*).

As the more resource-intensive assessments are reserved for the most promising candidates, well-developed and well-implemented screening programs result in efficiency in applicant processing, and cost- and time-savings for both the job seeker and employer. Savings will be greater the more the supply of talent exceeds demand.

What follows is a review of some of the more commonly used screening procedures, including biographical data, application forms, résumés, and reference checks. Chapter 8 reviews selection testing and Chapter 9 concludes with an in-depth discussion of the employment interview. These procedures, from the most basic to the most sophisticated, must satisfy both psychometric (Chapter 2) and legal requirements (Chapter 3).

After reading this chapter you should:

- know the difference between employee screening and employee selection;
- know the advantages and disadvantages of using common screening devices, including biographical data, application forms, résumés, interviews, and work experience and reference checks;
- understand the legal and psychometric status of each of these screening procedures; and
- be able to propose an effective multiphase screening program when given position requirements.

"Good morning, Aaron," said Tyler, the CEO, from the comfort of his office chair. "I do hope that you have some good news to start my day, as I need a boost beyond this coffee. You know, we're at the crossroads of growth and prosperity or decline and bankruptcy. With 38 CD retail outlets, we're in a highly competitive and volatile business." Aaron, his director of operations, positioned himself awkwardly on the chair opposite Tyler, fidgeting with his briefcase.

"Well Tyler, the good news is that we're ahead of the competition in being fast off the mark in securing the most desirable, high-visibility stores in the major shopping centres throughout the province. Our name recognition is high. Also, we've been able to renegotiate downward the leasing costs of seven of these outlets as these leases have come up for renewal."

"This is good," replied Tyler, as he put his cup to his lips for another reassuring sip. "Tell me more."

"OK," said Aaron, peering directly at Tyler with an expression of tension and serious concern. "I'll lay it on the line. Sales and profits have been in a steady decline over the past three quarters, customer complaints are at an all-time high, and we can't seem to keep our staff. Average tenure is only three months. As soon as we get these people trained, they leave."

"So what's the plan?" interjected Tyler impatiently.

"Well, I've just spoken with Patti, our new human resources specialist. She says we need to do a better job of screening the people we hire. She believes that implementing an aggressive recruitment campaign and an effective screening program will increase retention, service quality, and sales. You know, she may be on to something here."

"How do we go about doing this, Aaron? Seems like an overly simplistic diagnosis of the problem to me. Surely there is more to this than stepping up our recruitment and screening programs, don't you think?"

"Yes, I suppose there is more to the story. We need to attract 'good people' and then run them through an initial screen using standardized, uniform procedures for all of our stores. You see, our screening, in addition to being effective, must be legally sound. Beyond this initial screen, we must also sharpen our candidate assessment tools, and Patti has some very cost-effective recommendations to make here. Finally, we've been talking about improving the orientation and training of our staff, and introducing sales incentives and graduated salary and commission increases with length of service.

"So, yes," continued Aaron, there is more to this story, but the best place to start is with ensuring that the right people are being hired in the first place. People are such an important part of our business, so we must get this right! Frankly, to date, we have let the individual stores pretty much operate independently when recruiting and hiring. Patti provides a compelling argument that we can do much better."

"OK, Aaron, bring me a proposal and budget that will take us into the 21st century on this front. I'll admit, I'm strong in business acumen but frankly don't know much about the soft 'touchy-feely' aspects of people management."

"Actually, from what Patti tells me, there is not much that is 'soft' or 'touchy-feely' about what she is proposing. It is just the opposite—very analytical, systematic, and founded on statistical analyses and such. She has convinced me that this is more science than art. I'm confident that we can give you a cost-effective proposal, which will include an evaluation of program outcomes using both performance and financial indicators."

"OK, Aaron, I'm relying on you. The future of this business is in your hands. We've got to turn things around in fast order. What sorts of things are you thinking about?"

"We can set up a centralized Web-based system for receiving applications and résumés, with software that scans them and identifies candidates that fit our company profile on such things as background experience, interests, and education, and then sorts them by the preferences given for store location. Candidates who pass this initial screening could then be called into the local store for a screening interview, although we might be able to do that online, as well, and save the on-site visit for a more intense behaviourally focused selection interview."

"This sounds promising. Get going on the proposal."

"Sure thing; I'll have it to you by a week from today."

Applicant Screening

Screening begins after the HR department receives a job application. It is the first phase of selection, in which the first "rough cut" of the larger applicant pool is performed. Typically, it involves identifying candidates who meet the **minimum qualifications** (MQs) established for a position. MQs are often listed as statements of education, experience, and closely related personal attributes required to perform a job satisfactorily and are used as standards to screen applicants.[2]

Screening procedures, such as those presented in this chapter, are designed to reduce the number of job applicants. Candidates who fall short

Screening
The first step of the selection process; involves identifying individuals from the applicant pool who have the minimum qualifications for the target position(s). Candidates "passing" this first hurdle then undergo more extensive assessments.

Minimum qualifications
Knowledge, skills, abilities, experiences, and other attributes deemed necessary for minimally acceptable performance in one or more positions; designed for making the "first cut" in screening job applicants, and sometimes referred to as *selection criteria*.

Designated targeted groups

The four groups (women, Aboriginal people, visible minorities, and people with disabilities) designated in the federal government's Employment Equity Act that receive legal "protection" in employment policies and practices because of their underrepresentation in the workplace.

 7.1

of the minimum standards are eliminated at this point and receive no further consideration. Accordingly, MQs critically affect the entire selection process, and are often closely scrutinized for possible adverse impact against **designated targeted groups**. It is essential that these MQs be systematically and carefully established. Levine et al.[3] provide a clear, step-by-step description of how they developed and validated MQs to withstand legal challenge for selected jobs in a large mental health facility. Their procedure is a useful guide for establishing MQs in other situations.

Recruitment, Screening, and Selection

Figure 7.1 diagrams the relationship among recruitment, screening, and selection in terms of different questions that are asked at each of these steps. *Recruitment* seeks to find a sufficient number of qualified applicants; *screening*

FIGURE 7.1

The Relationship among Recruitment, Screening, and Selection

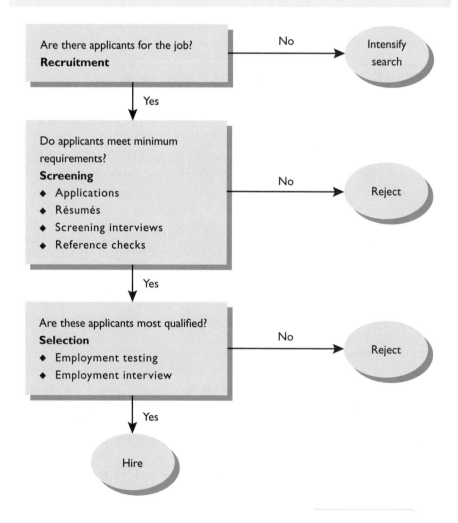

Recruitment and Selection in Canada

identifies whether those candidates who applied meet minimum requirements; and *selection* reviews each qualified candidate to find individuals who will be most successful in the job. The relationship between the actual number of people hired and the number who applied for a position is expressed in terms of a proportion, called the **selection ratio**. Two hundred applicants for 10 positions would yield a selection ratio of 0.05 (10/200 = 0.05, or one position for every 20 applicants).

Job applicants must be screened with great care. The screening devices are designed to quickly and inexpensively sort applicants into acceptable and unacceptable categories. Usually, the criteria on which these decisions are made are subjective; the decision maker often has to interpret what an applicant meant when he or she wrote a specific statement or what a person's job experience and training actually are. Screening procedures are susceptible to error, however, in the form of both **false positives** and **false negatives**. Over the complete selection process, applicants who pass through the initial screening as false positives are likely to be eliminated through more extensive testing. The false negatives—individuals who have the qualifications but are mistakenly eliminated—are gone forever. These may turn to the courts if they believe the initial screening procedures discriminated on grounds that were unrelated to job performance.

Screening instruments that are used without considering their psychometric properties and without regard for the legal environment leave employers open to litigation. False negatives can be a real concern for organizations, particularly in highly competitive industries. For example, it can be very costly to underestimate the creative potential of a research scientist, resulting in a no-hire decision, only to find this individual employed by a competing firm and responsible for new product lines that have taken away substantial market share.

Screening Methods

This chapter focuses on traditional approaches to employee screening, including application forms, résumés, interviews, reference letters, background checks, and work experience assessments. These procedures all seek to predict job performance from past life or work events. If the screening procedures are properly developed, they will identify individuals who meet minimum qualifications. The following sections examine these screening tools in more detail.

Application Forms

When individuals apply for a job with an employer, they are frequently asked to complete an employment application form (commonly referred to as an **application blank**). Practically all organizations use employment application forms to collect information that will allow them to assess whether the candidate is minimally suitable for the job in question. Application forms consist of a series of questions aimed at securing information on the general suitability

---

Selection ratio

The proportion of applicants for one or more positions who are hired.

 7.2

False positives

Individuals who are predicted to perform successfully for a given position (based on pre-selection assessment scores), but who do not perform at satisfactory levels when placed on the job.

False negatives

Individuals who are predicted to perform unsuccessfully for a given position (based on pre-selection assessment scores), but who would perform at satisfactory levels if hired.

Application blank

A form completed by job candidates to provide an employer with basic information about their knowledge, skills, education, or other job-related information.

of the applicants to the target position. Questions often ask about the applicant's educational background, job experience, special training, and other areas deemed relevant to performance of the job. For example, applicants for a security dispatcher position may be required to have passed a course on CPR (cardiopulmonary resuscitation). Applicants who do not have such training can be identified through a question on the application form and screened out of the competition.

Regardless of the exact format, application forms are used to provide a preliminary pre-employment screen, allowing the employer to determine whether the applicant is minimally qualified for the position. A standardized application form allows an employer to collect information in a consistent format. This information may then be used by the hiring team as a standardized reference guide for any subsequent screening interviews and to compare applicants when discussing the results of those interviews. If the applicant pool is large compared with the number of positions being filled, employers may choose to be more selective at this stage, assessing and comparing the relative strengths and weaknesses of each candidate. A standardized application form makes it easier to do these types of comparisons.

Employers often overlook the fact that before any information on an application form can be used for screening, its job-relatedness should be established through a job analysis. For example, in a court challenge, it must be shown that CPR training is related to the work of a security dispatcher. It is *not* sufficient to believe that applicants "ought" to have a particular level of education, or to have graduated from a specific type of training program. Where there is adverse impact against members of a designated minority group, whether intentional or otherwise, the standard used to screen applicants must be demonstrably job-related. Because information collected at this stage may be used to restrict or deny employment to women and members of minority groups, the human rights issues must be considered during the development and use of application forms.

Human Rights Considerations

Employers cannot ask for information that is prohibited on discriminatory grounds under human rights legislation unless it can be established that the information is a bona fide occupational requirement (BFOR). If challenged about any information being collected, an employer will have to show that the information constitutes a BFOR. Many employers routinely collect information through application forms as required by the human resources department should the employee be hired, but will not be used in making a hiring decision. The justification for collecting these data is expediency; if the applicant is hired, the HR office will already have the necessary personal information on file.

Frequently, employers unwittingly collect information on application forms that will leave them open to charges of discriminatory hiring practices; for example, applicants may be asked their social insurance number, date of birth, sex, marital status, number of dependants, name of next of kin, health status, and so on.[4,5] Having obtained this information before making a hiring decision, an employer may have to prove that it was not used in making the hiring decision. It is far better to collect this information from applicants only after they have been hired. Some employers now request the appropriate human rights commission to review their application forms to ensure that they are in compliance with relevant laws and then state on the application form that it was approved by the commission to forestall complaints from applicants.

Recruitment and Selection Today 7.1 presents an application form that is designed specifically for the position of security dispatcher. This form requests only the most minimal information. There is always the temptation to collect as much background data as possible about a candidate through the application form on the grounds that this may help the human resources

Recruitment and Selection Today 7.1

Job Application Form: Security Dispatcher

Application for Employment

The personal information on this form is collected under the Provincial Freedom of Information and Protection of Privacy Act and in accordance with the Provincial Human Rights Act. The information will be used to assess applicant qualifications as they pertain to appointments and/or employment in the position indicated below. If you have any questions about the collection of this information, contact Human Resource Services at 1-800-555-5555. The Provincial Human Rights Commission has approved this form.

Employment Data

Type of Employment: _____ Permanent _____ Temporary _____ Part-time

Competition No:_____   Date: _____

Position Applied For: _____

Where did you learn of this job? Newspaper_____   Company Posting _____   Web Site _____

Other (Identify) _____

Have you ever worked for us before? Yes ___ No ___ If yes, when? _____

If hired, when can you begin work? _____ Expected Salary _____

Hours of availability for work (place a checkmark in the applicable box to indicate you are available):

	Monday	Tuesday	Wednesday	Thursday	Friday	Saturday	Sunday
Days							
Evenings							

continued

Continued from previous page

Personal Information

Name: _____   _____
                    Last   First

Home Phone: _____   Alternative Phone: _____

E-Mail: _____

Mailing Address: _____
                         Street, City, Province, Postal Code

Are you legally entitled to work in Canada?   Yes ____ No ____

Have you ever been convicted of a criminal offence for which you
have not been pardoned?   Yes ____ No ____

Languages Spoken: <u>English</u> : Yes ____ No ____   <u>French</u>: Yes ____ No ____

Languages Read: <u>English</u> : Yes ____ No ____   <u>French</u>: Yes ____ No ____

Education and Training

Grade 12 Completed?   Yes ____ No ____   If No, indicate highest grade completed: _____

Post-Secondary:

Institution	Degree/Diploma/ Certificate	Date Completed

Program or areas studied (check all that apply to you):

Security ___ Computer ___ Clerical ___ Management ___ Communications ___ Electronics ___ Criminology ___

Public Relations ___ Other (please specify) _____

Do you currently possess a valid First-Aid Certificate? Yes ____ No ____

continued

Continued from previous page

Employment History

List all positions you have held, beginning with the most recent. Should you require more space, please attach a separate sheet to this application.

Employer:	Position:
Date of Employment:	From:	To:
Duties and Responsibilities:		
Supervisor's Name and Title:		
Reasons for Leaving		
May we contact this employer? Yes _____ No _____		

Employer:	Position:
Date of Employment:	From:	To:
Duties and Responsibilities:		
Supervisor's Name and Title:		
Reasons for Leaving		
May we contact this employer? Yes _____ No _____		

Employer:	Position:
Date of Employment:	From:	To:
Duties and Responsibilities:		
Supervisor's Name and Title:		
Reasons for Leaving		
May we contact this employer? Yes _____ No _____		

continued

Continued from previous page

Employer:		Position:	
Date of Employment	From:		To:

Duties and Responsibilities:

Supervisor's Name and Title:

Reasons for Leaving

May we contact this employer?   Yes _____   No _____

Declaration (Please read carefully)

I certify that the information provided in this application is true and complete to the best of my knowledge. I realize that you will rely on this information in engaging and in continuing my employment. I also realize that this information may be verified and that any misrepresentation of the facts and any false, misleading, or incomplete information may constitute grounds for immediate dismissal from employment.

Signature: _____

Date: _____

manager prepare to interview the candidate. However, with irrelevant information in hand, it can be tempting to use it in making a decision.

Before putting any item on an application form, the human resources manager should ask the following questions:

- What is the purpose of having the item on the form?
- Is there a better way to obtain the information elicited by the item?
- How will the information be used?
- Does the question conflict with provincial, territorial, or federal human rights guidelines on what can and cannot be asked on an application form? (See Chapter 3.)
- Are responses to the item, if used in making a selection decision, likely to have an adverse impact in screening out members of protected minority groups?

- Is it more appropriate to obtain the information only after making a job offer?
- Has the job-relatedness of the item been established?

Guidelines on what is legally inappropriate to ask on application forms are provided by the Canadian Human Rights Commission (http://www .chrc-ccdp.ca/pdf/screen.pdf; also see, for example, Chapter 3, Table 3.5 on pages 84–86) and by other jurisdictions throughout Canada. *The Canadian Human Rights Reporter* (http://www.cdn-hr-reporter.ca) is a useful source of information for human rights cases and legal guidelines for recruitment, screening, and assessment.

In addition to risking lawsuits, employers who include questions on application forms that potentially discriminate against members of designated minority groups are likely to disadvantage themselves, particularly in tight labour markets. Specifically, applicants who complete application forms containing discriminatory questions tend to view the organization as being less attractive. They perceive the organization as less just and express higher litigation intentions than do candidates completing legally advisable applications forms, especially where no explanation is provided for unfavourable hiring decisions.[6] Whether or not they are offered a position, candidates encountering application forms with discriminatory questions are less likely to pursue employment with the organization, less likely to accept an offer of employment, and less likely to recommend the organization to a friend.[7]

Where sensitive demographic information, such as designated group membership, must be collected for monitoring applicant flow data as prescribed by employment equity legislation, this information should be collected separately from the application form (or should be asked on a "tear-off" section of the form). Applicants should be assured that the information is being collected as per government requirements and will not be accessible to those making hiring decisions). Specific guidelines for collecting such sensitive information are available from government employment equity officers.

As well as ensuring that the rights and interests of job candidates are respected, employers must take measures to protect their own interests. Specifically, the credentials that the applicants claim to have should be verified. A case in point is Marilee Jones, Dean of Admissions at the Massachusetts Institute of Technology (MIT), who was forced to resign from her position for having falsely stated in her résumé that she had both bachelor's and master's degrees.[8] Similarly, the CEO of Radio Shack, David Edmondson, was forced to resign because of inaccuracies reported on his résumé with respect to his educational credentials.[9]

In anticipation that candidates may distort their actual credentials, employers should communicate explicitly and visibly on the application form that the accuracy of the data applicants provide will be thoroughly checked. A statement should accompany this to the effect: "I understand that providing any false, misleading, or incomplete information is grounds for immediate discharge from employment"[10] (see also Recruitment and Selection Today 7.1 on pages 295–98). This requirement should discourage misrepresentation and provide grounds for dismissal should the candidate be hired and subsequently found to have embellished his or her credentials.

Weighted Application Blanks

Each item on an application form provides information about the candidate. Only rarely is any one item sufficient to screen out a candidate. Candidates for a staff lawyer position that involves the actual practice of law would need to have passed the bar exam. That credential would be sufficient to screen out candidates who had graduated from law school but had not been called to the bar. However, an organization might consider hiring such a candidate if the position did not involve actual practice. Many organizations hire lawyers to provide advice or to do research, without expecting them to practice law.

How can information obtained from an application form be objectively combined to make a decision when there is no single item that screens out candidates? Can information from the application form be used to make a prediction about job success or failure? In many cases, the person responsible for making the decision examines the application and makes a subjective decision. Much like a clinical psychologist making a diagnosis, the recruiter or human resources manager examines all of the information and comes to a conclusion about a particular applicant based on personal experience and knowledge.

As an alternative to this subjective procedure, the manager develops a scoring key for applicant responses to items on the application form. In the case of lawyers applying for a job, those who have not passed the bar exam might be given a score of 0, while those who have passed are scored 1. Similarly, weights are assigned to the responses given to other items; adding all of the assigned weights together produces a total score on the application form for each job candidate. Weights are not assigned arbitrarily; they reflect the difference between successful and unsuccessful workers on a criterion measurement. This alternative is called a **weighted application blank (WAB)**.

Like any selection instrument, the WAB must exhibit good psychometric properties. WABs are developed in relation to a **criterion measure** of performance established for current and previous employees. If an employer were concerned with the level of absenteeism among security dispatchers, number of days absent could serve as a criterion measure. The human resources manager would define the acceptable number of days absent in a year, and then divide the current and previous security dispatchers into two groups: those who fall above and below that value. Then the applications on file for security dispatchers are reviewed and the frequency of responses for each item on the application form is recorded separately for the low- and high-absenteeism groups. For example, 80 percent of security dispatchers with only a high school education fall into the good attendance category while the remaining 20 percent fall into the poor attendance group. The difference between these two percentages, 60 percent (i.e., $80 - 20 = 60$), is used to derive a "net weight" for applicants with a "high school graduate" education level.

Weighted application blank (WAB)

A method for quantitatively combining information from application blank items by assigning weights that reflect each item's value in predicting job success.

Criterion measures

Measures of job performance or productivity that differentiate employees. These performance measurements, such as supervisory ratings or absenteeism rates, are used to establish the validity of screening or selection instruments.

Similarly, in the case of university graduates, if 60 percent have a low absenteeism rate, and 40 percent have a high rate, the difference between these two percentages, 20 percent (i.e., 60 − 40 = 20), is used to derive a "net weight" for applicants with a "university graduate" education level. The net weight derived for each education level is then transformed into a specific score. For instance, applicants with only a high school education would be given a higher score (e.g., "2") than university graduates (e.g., "1"). Because establishing weights and specific scores is a relatively complex task, researchers have developed specific tables to facilitate these steps. The specific weighting procedure described above is called the *vertical percentage method*, but other effective procedures are available.[11,12]

Benefits of WABs

Well-constructed WABs are good predictors of many types of work behaviour (e.g., absenteeism, accidents, and turnover, among others). WABs are also easy and economical to use. They are economical in the sense that virtually all organizations require job candidates to complete an employment application as part of their selection process, so the only additional costs are those associated with the scoring of the forms. Moreover, WABs are cost-effective. For example, they were shown to reduce employee turnover in the hotel industry[13] and among clerical employees.[14] If well-constructed, weighted application forms are unlikely to be seen as intrusive or threatening, as most job applicants expect to complete an application form when seeking employment.

Concerns about WABs

Some concerns are associated with the use of the WAB technique. First, criterion measures such as turnover, absenteeism, and accident rates that are typically used to validate weighted application forms may not adequately represent a job's complex performance domain. For example, WAB scoring keys are typically derived to predict one specific, often narrow, criterion (e.g., tenure), as opposed to a broader measure of performance. Ghiselli's analysis of validity data suggests that WABs can also predict training success and overall job proficiency.[15]

Second, the WAB procedure requires data from a large number of employees to obtain percentages that are good, stable estimates of the appropriate weights. This could require several years of data collection, and there is risk that changes in the job, the applicants, or the organization over time may produce weights that represent neither the first- nor last-hired employees. Also, the weights used for scoring, derived from an original sample, must be shown to hold up for a second independent sample from the same population of workers (i.e., cross-validated). Still, a meta-analysis suggests that weighted application forms that include biographical information may have greater stability than previously thought.[16]

Finally, while WABs provide the basis for good empirical predictions,[17] they do not offer any *understanding* of why these relationships exist.[18] This approach is sometimes referred to as *dust-bowl empiricism*. This criticism applies less where the application form items are *rationally* derived from a systematic analysis of the job.

When to Use WABs

WABs are often used as a means of doing rapid screening and may also be combined with other predictors (e.g., personality or cognitive ability) to improve selection decisions. The procedure is particularly appropriate when there is a large number of applicants for a single position or when organizations are hiring large numbers of employees for similar kinds of jobs. WABs are often used for positions requiring long and costly training, where turnover is high, and where large numbers of applicants are competing for few positions (i.e., there is a low selection ratio).[19]

Biographical Data

As presented in Recruitment and Selection Today 7.1 (pages 295–98), a typical application form requires job candidates to provide information about their knowledge, skills, education, and a narrow range of job-related information. Biographical data extends what is available from the application form by covering a variety of areas, including educational experiences, hobbies, family relationships, leisure-time pursuits, personal accomplishments, and early work experiences. Whereas an application form focuses on more limited, factual, and verifiable information on educational background, training, and work experience, biographical data covers an array of less verifiable information, such as personal interests, attitudes, and values.[20] As discussed later in this chapter ("Concerns over the Use of Biodata," page 306), some content areas of biographical data may run afoul of privacy and human rights legislation.

It is worth noting here that biographical data are synonymous with or frequently referred to as autobiographical data, personal or life history information, "background data," or more simply, "biodata." There are several ways in which biographical data can be collected, including interviews, life history essays, and self-report questionnaires, the latter of which is referred to as the **biographical information blank (BIB)**. The BIB requires job candidates to answer a series of multiple-choice or short-answer questions.[21,22] Recruitment and Selection Today 7.2 presents an example of a BIB that was developed for use with job candidates for a managerial position. The information obtained from the BIB is scored to produce either a total overall score or scores for specific sets of items or factors. Like the WAB, the BIB should be validated before being used to select from among job applicants. Compared with the WAB, the BIB provides greater insights into the type of individuals who experience job success, given the content and higher contextual richness of the items.

The life insurance industry has used **biodata** as part of its selection procedures since 1942. The Life Insurance Marketing Research Association (LIMRA), in its role as an industry trade association, has provided biodata selection instruments to the life insurance industry for selecting sales representatives. Since 1942, these biodata instruments have been widely used on literally millions of candidates throughout Canada and the United States. Life

Biographical information blank (BIB)

A pre-selection questionnaire that asks applicants to provide job-related information on their personal background and life experiences.

Biodata

Biographical data for job applicants that have been gathered from BIBs, application blanks, or other sources.

Example of a Biographical Information Blank

Personal Information

Name: _____   _____
                          Last   First

Mailing Address: _____
                          Street, City, Province, Postal Code

How long have you lived at your current address? _____

Do you consider your net worth to be low _____ moderate _____ or high _____?

Have you ever been turned down for a loan? Yes _____ No _____

How many credit cards do you have? _____

Education and Training

Highest level of education completed:

High School _____ Vocational _____ College _____ University _____ Postgraduate _____

What educational degrees do you have? Diploma/Certificate _____ B.A. _____ B.Sc. _____ B.Comm. _____ M.B.A. _____

Master's _____ Other (Identify) _____

What subjects did you major in? _____   _____

What was your grade-point average in college or university? A _____ B _____ C _____ D _____

Did you graduate with honours? Yes _____ No _____

Did you receive any awards for academic excellence? Yes _____ No _____

Did you receive any scholarships? Yes _____ No _____

List the extracurricular activities you participated in during school: _____

Information about You

Did you find school stimulating _____ boring _____ ?

Did you hold a job while attending school? Yes _____ No _____

How did you pay for your post–high-school training? (Check as many as appropriate)

Parents paid _____ Loans _____ Scholarships _____ Paid own way _____

Have you ever held a job where you earned commissions on sales? Yes _____ No _____

If "Yes," were your commissions low _____ moderate _____ high _____ ?

Five years from now, what do you expect your salary to be? _____

Do you enjoy meeting new people? Yes _____ No _____

How many social phone calls do you receive a week? _____

Do people count on you to "cheer up" others? Yes _____ No _____

How many parties do you go to in a year? _____

Do you enjoy talking to people? Yes _____ No _____

Rate your conversational skills:

Excellent _____ Very Good _____ Good _____ Fair _____ Poor _____

How often do you introduce yourself to other people you don't know?

Always _____ Sometimes _____ Never _____

continued

insurance sales positions are demanding. Sales agents are not normally provided with "leads," but rather are expected to prospect for customers among friends, family, and acquaintances. Rejection rates from among potential clients are high, requiring successful agents to be "thick-skinned" and persevering. First-year attrition rates are also high, at about 50 percent, and occur before the company can recoup its training costs. The current version of the LIMRA biodata instrument is the *Career Profile*, which provides scores on five primary dimensions for individuals with no previous life insurance sales experience:[23]

- *Insurance-related experiences—belief in the value and importance of insurance.* Question types include: "Do individuals own the product they will be selling?" and "Does the candidate have a personal insurance sales representative?" Individuals whose life experiences show a belief in the value of the product are more likely to be effective sales representatives.

- *Number of friends, relatives, and personal contacts in the industry.* Questions include: "Does the individual know any current sales representatives?" and "Does the candidate have any relatives or close friends working in the insurance industry?" Individuals who know people in the insurance industry are more likely to be effective sales agents because they tend to be more aware of the challenges of the position before committing to the job. They know what they are getting into and tend to show greater perseverance in the face of adversity.

- *Recruiting method—knowledge of the position.* This focuses on knowledge of the specific office to which the person is applying rather than general knowledge of the industry. People with greater knowledge of the specific office show lower turnover rates.

- *Establishment—financial and occupational stability.* Question types cover: "What is the candidate's financial situation?" and "How many jobs has the candidate held over the past five years?" Financial and occupational stability predict success in the life insurance industry. Past stability and success predict future stability and success.

- *Commitment to present situation—ties to current job situation.* Includes questions like: "What is your employment status?" and "How soon would you be available to accept a position?" Individuals with weak ties to their current employer show overall lower success rates as life insurance representatives.

LIMRA, on behalf of the Canadian insurance industry, has developed a BIB for use exclusively in Canada. This biodata instrument conforms to Canadian human rights legislation and is sensitive to the Canadian cultural context.

BIB Dimensions

The BIB, which is also known as a *life history* or *personal history inventory*, is based on the view that past behaviour is the best predictor of future behaviour. Understanding how a job applicant behaved in the past through examining related BIB items allows one to predict that applicant's future interests and capabilities. Statistical analyses of different BIBs suggest that the BIB items cluster on 13 to 15 major dimensions.[24] Although the comparability of dimensions across different BIBs may be questionable,[25] rational comparison of the different biodata factors suggests that the following eight dimensions may be common to many life event inventories:[26]

- School achievement (academic success and positive academic attitude).
- Higher educational achievement (holding a degree from a postsecondary school).
- Drive (motivation to be outstanding, to attain high goals, to achieve).
- Leadership and group participation (involvement in organized activities and membership in groups).
- Financial responsibility (financial status and handling of finances).
- Early family responsibility (an "own family" orientation).
- Parental family adjustment (happy parental home experience).
- Situational stability (mid-life occupational stability).

These dimensions appear relatively stable and explain why certain applicants are more successful than others. That is, a relationship between a particular item on the BIB and a criterion measure is not as important to predicting future behaviour as is the relationship of the dimension represented by the item and the criterion. Knowing that the applicant is high in *drive* and *financial responsibility* is more important than knowing an applicant's precise goals or financial status. Moreover, it is reasonable to expect that the magnitude of the relationships will vary depending on the BIB dimension and criterion measurement pairing, suggesting the use of differential weighting of dimensions based on the criterion being predicted.[27] More recently, BIB items have been written to reflect each of the five broad dimensions of personality and offered as an alternative to a direct self-report assessment of personality that could be subject to distortion (i.e., "faking" or "impression management").[28]

Concerns over the Use of Biodata

Despite the impressive predictive validity of biodata, concerns remain about its use for selection purposes. These issues include questions of legality, invasiveness, fakability, and generalizability. With respect to legality and invasiveness, many BIB items may request personally sensitive information on family background and experiences that borders on violation of human rights legislation.[29] A case can be made for these types of items provided they are job-related; however, the employer is responsible for establishing their worth as predictors.

Many other items on a BIB delve into areas that are not protected by legislation but do raise issues of privacy invasion. For example, job applicants may feel it inappropriate to share information pertaining to their financial status or the number of credit cards they carry. As we discussed earlier, job applicants form perceptions of the organization and its values, which influence their decisions to accept job offers. If a BIB includes items that give the appearance of unfair discrimination or invasion of privacy, it may deter highly qualified candidates. In one study, potential job applicants who completed application forms with discriminatory items reacted more negatively to the organization than others who completed forms with the discriminatory items removed. Applicants believed that the organization in the first instance was a less attractive place to work and reported that they were less likely to pursue a job in that organization and less likely to accept one if offered. They were also less inclined to recommend the organization to a friend and tended to view it as one that treated employees unfairly.[30]

Both professionals and nonprofessionals perceive certain types of biodata items to be invasive, specifically, those items that are less verifiable, less transparent in purpose, and more personal.[31] Four general topics generate the most apprehension toward biodata items: fear of stigmatization, concern about having applicants recall traumatic events, intimacy, and religion. Avoiding these types of attributes may help to reduce the perceived invasiveness of biodata items.

The perceived acceptability and fairness of BIBs might be context-specific—for example, asking applicants for information on home, spousal, and parental situations; recreation and hobbies; interest in travel and new experiences; and nonwork interests was perceived as more job-relevant, fair, and appropriate when used to select applicants for international postings rather than for domestic positions.[32] Personal history questions appear to be more acceptable to job applicants for international assignments because such assignments involve relocation and readjustment of the applicant's entire family. Personal interests, values, stability, and family relationships are seen as key to coping with the demands of international assignments.[33] Increasing the transparency of the purpose of biodata items increases their perceived acceptability.[34]

In the United States, each item on a BIB must be shown *not* to have an adverse impact on members of protected groups.[35] Canadian human rights legislation requires that any information used in the hiring process that adversely impacts one or more designated minority groups be bona fide (demonstrably job-related). Employers must decide whether the benefits of using a BIB outweigh the potential hazards, or whether it can be replaced by an equally valid but less intrusive selection instrument.

When carefully developed and systematically scored, however, biodata items have less adverse impact on women and other designated minority groups than many other traditional selection measures.[36] The Canadian insurance industry has shown that having a BIB comply with human rights legislation does not sacrifice its predictive validity. The biodata form developed by LIMRA has been the subject of extensive validation research. Criterion-related studies carried out by LIMRA show that the Canadian biodata form successfully predicts retention of life insurance agents and their sales.[37,38]

Managers often express concern that job applicants are less than honest in completing a BIB or life event history, particularly when it comes to reporting negative information. Evidence on the degree of accuracy in applications is mixed. Cascio reviewed over 100 biodata inventories completed by job applicants for positions with a Florida police department.[39] He compared the answers that applicants gave to 17 items on the BIB with the actual event. On average, he found an exceptionally high correlation (0.94) between the applicant's answer and the true state of affairs.

This research suggests that applicants who expect their answers to be verified are more likely to tell the truth. Obviously, this is more likely to happen when the BIB items ask for factual, objective information that can be checked. Indirect biodata items (those that ask respondents to report on others' opinions of them) show higher validities than items that ask respondents to directly report their past experiences and behaviours.[40] Perhaps higher validities of the former are due less to their indirect assessment and more to their personality-revealing factors. Specifically, the majority of these indirect items related to personality constructs, including supervisors' views of the respondents' conscientiousness, openness to new ideas, outgoing nature, anxiety, and "ability to catch on quickly."[41] Higher predictive validities have also been positively associated with more verifiable and job-relevant items.

Some distortion on BIBs should be expected. Specific types of information reported on traditional application forms may be inaccurate in up to 25 percent of cases.[42] This last figure is consistent with the degree of inaccuracy or misrepresentation (33 percent) found in application materials supplied by job candidates.[43] Reports of the prevalence and severity of "faking" or deception in assessments for entry-level positions are particularly pronounced where special measures are taken to ensure anonymity of responses. For example, where such provisions for anonymity are provided, approximately 50 percent of all respondents indicated that they had overstated their standing on such personal qualities as dependability and reliability; and more than 60 percent reportedly "downplayed" their negative attributes.[44] Unfortunately, accuracy of application forms and BIBs specifically has not been extensively examined, although distortion does not always lower predictive validities. For example, perhaps "impression management" is advantageous for front-line service positions and sales provided that it does not cross ethical boundaries (e.g., misrepresentation of services or products).

As with the WAB, the predictive validity of a BIB is typically established for a fairly large and specific pool of individuals applying for a particular job. A case in point is LIMRA, whose life history form has been validated on thousands of individuals throughout North America applying for the position of life insurance sales agent. With very few exceptions, employers cannot purchase a commercially available BIB that will suit their needs. Rather, they need to develop and validate one on their own. This requires large applicant pools and someone in the human resources department with the technical knowledge to spearhead the project. Accordingly, despite a respectable track record as a useful predictive tool that has minimal adverse impact, this may explain the infrequent use of BIBs by North American corporations.[45-47]

Sometimes a biodata instrument can be used outside of the specific organization for which it was developed.[48] The validity of a biodata instrument developed and keyed within a single organization may generalize to other organizations. Specifically, the biodata component of the *Managerial Performance Record* (MPR), which was developed within a single organization, predicted the rate of managerial progress (e.g., rate of promotion) in 24 other organizations. The MPR predicted the rate of promotional progress across *all* organizations and its validity did not vary much across organizations ($r = 0.53$, $SD = 0.05$). There were no differences in the validity of the MPR for males and females, or for managers of varying age groups, lengths of company service, and educational levels.[49]

Similarly, a biodata instrument improved the entry-level selection of graduate trainees in the accounting profession.[50] The biodata form remained valid for applicants selected by the company over the next five years and could be used across a wide range of different firms.

This generalizability of biodata forms advocates for a consortium approach to developing and keying biodata instruments that can be used across organizations.[51] Evidence for the generalizability of biodata also comes from the insurance industry; biodata scoring keys and factor structures remained stable across applicant pools drawn from the United States, the United Kingdom, and the Republic of Ireland.[52]

Predictive Validity of Biodata

Overall, a carefully developed and validated BIB can offer a very effective, non-invasive, and defensible means of improving human resources selection decisions. Moreover, BIBs can have similar levels of predictive validity for similar jobs *across* organizations. Validation research on biodata produces results similar to that for the WAB. Biodata predicts quite well certain types of job behaviours (e.g., absenteeism, turnover, job proficiency, supervisory effectiveness, and job training) in a wide range of occupations.[53-59]

Rothstein et al. place biodata second only to cognitive ability as a valid predictor of job proficiency.[60] On average, corrected correlations between scores on biodata instruments and job-relevant criteria range from 0.30 to 0.40.[61-63] Asher and Sciarrino reported that the **validity coefficients** for biodata exceeded 0.50 in 6 of the 11 studies they reviewed.[64] Hunter and Hunter

Validity coefficient

The correlation between assessment scores and job performance measurements.

reported the mean correlation between biodata and job proficiency as 0.37.[65] High predictive validity, high utility (e.g., cost-effectiveness), and no adverse impact (e.g., nondiscriminatory against minorities) has been shown for the BIB when administered via interactive voice-response technology, when candidates provide their responses to automated questions asked over the phone.[66]

When to Use BIBs

As with WABs, the BIB procedure is particularly appropriate for organizations hiring large numbers of employees for similar kinds of jobs and where large numbers of applicants are competing for a few positions (i.e., when there is a low selection ratio).[67]

Résumés

A résumé is another source of biographical information produced by job applicants. The intent of the résumé is to introduce the applicant to the organization through a brief, written self-description. The information contained on most résumés overlaps with information requested by the employer through application blanks or biographical inventories. Unlike these other assessments, however, applicants voluntarily provide autobiographical information in their résumés.

Employers presume that this information is job-related and that it will allow them to determine whether a candidate satisfies minimum job requirements and warrants further consideration. However, job applicants may include information on the résumé that the employer might rather not see. Although it is not as common as it was a few years ago, some job applicants still list information about their citizenship or national origin, height, weight, marital status, or other characteristics that, if used as part of selection, run afoul of employment legislation. It might be extremely difficult for an employer to prove that such prohibited information did not influence an employment decision.

The uniqueness of each applicant's résumé does not work well for standardized scoring. Yet, all of the psychometric and legal considerations that apply to application forms and biodata apply equally to using résumés for selection purposes. Information obtained from the résumé must be job-related and must not discriminate against designated minority groups. While many résumés are still presented in a paper format, use of electronic résumés, particularly standardized ones on Internet job boards, is becoming so prevalent that the paper résumé may soon be regarded as a curiosity sent by someone who is not computer literate.

First Impressions

In addition to providing specific biographical information, the résumé presents a first impression of the applicant. The recruiter or human resources manager may form an image of the applicant based on characteristics of the résumé itself. The résumé's style, neatness, organization, layout of information, and vocabulary and phrases used throughout convey information about the candidate, in addition to the facts presented in the résumé. Thoms and colleagues manipulated résumé and candidate characteristics in a policy-capturing study in which business professionals selected from among seven sets of four résumés the two individuals they would invite for interviews.

With respect to these interview invitations, one-page résumés fared better than two-page résumés; specific objective statements were better than general statements; listing a 3.00 GPA was better than not listing one at all; listing a 3.5 GPA was better than listing a 2.75 GPA; listing relevant course work was better than not listing any; and listing accomplishments was better than not listing them. The authors concluded that "when job candidates do not have previous professional experience and their part-time experience is similar to that of other candidates, businesspersons will use résumé characteristics of the sort they studied to distinguish between résumés" (p. 351).[68]

Knouse found that relevant job experience and education enhanced business managers' evaluations of résumés, as did "impression management," wherein candidates described *concrete* examples of their accomplishments.[69] However, general impression management tactics, employing self-descriptive adjectives such as "excellent," "extremely hard working," and "energetic" (e.g., not tied to specific accomplishments) lead to *negative* impressions.[70]

Studies also suggest that the human resources manager considers résumé characteristics to reflect different aspects of the applicant in much the same way as a projective personality test (see Chapter 8). For example, research suggests that applicants' résumé information as evaluated by recruiters may predict their cognitive ability and personality.[71,72] Perhaps not surprisingly, recruiters who infer from résumé characteristics that candidates are conscientious consider these candidates more suited to conventional jobs (e.g., accounting) whereas recruiters making inferences of extraversion consider these candidates more suited to "enterprising" jobs (e.g., marketing).[73]

To present a favourable first impression with a résumé, it should be accompanied by a well-written cover letter. In a survey of 100 senior executives from the largest companies in Canada, 93 percent indicated that cover letters are valuable when assessing job candidates. Executive director Dave Willmer of OfficeTeam, the firm that contracted this survey, commented: "Submitting a résumé without a cover letter is like not shaking hands when meeting someone for the first time." He notes that a cover letter should reveal the applicant's knowledge of the company, highlight relevant skills and work experience, and explain résumé anomalies (e.g., extended employment gaps).[74]

OfficeTeam (http://www.officeteam.com) is a staffing services agency that provides temporary replacement of highly skilled office and administrative support professionals. It provides seven tips to help job seekers develop strong cover letters:

1. Address your letter to the specific hiring manager rather than including a generalized introduction.
2. Research the company online and communicate (succinctly) how your knowledge and skills fit the job and could benefit the organization.

3. Explain anomalies in your résumé (e.g., employment gaps).
4. Limit your cover letter to one page, double-spaced.
5. Show your excitement for the position by concluding with "next steps" (e.g., "I'll follow up next week to discuss this in person").
6. Review (and have others review) your cover letter for typos and grammatical errors.
7. When applying through online job boards, always choose the option to add your cover letter to your résumé. Additionally, you should provide an e-mail address so that the recruiter can contact you, but it should be professional and easy to read and copy (i.e., not "cutesy and suggestive").[75]

Writing a Résumé

Many job applicants have difficulty writing a good résumé. Vocational guidance counsellors and employment counsellors often provide help in writing résumés as part of their services. As well, most libraries have many references on writing effective job résumés. There are a few basic points to consider in reviewing, or preparing, a résumé. It should include the applicant's name, address, and phone number(s), education and training, employment history, names of references and their contact information, and a brief statement of employment goals and objectives. Information on hobbies, interests, and other pursuits should be included only if it is relevant to the career goals. For example, a candidate for a forest ranger position may want to note an interest in hiking.

The résumé should be well organized and highlight key information. The typeface size (usually a 12-point font) and style (e.g., Arial) should make for easy and quick reading. It should be typed and printed with a laser-quality printer. Incorporating features such as unusual fonts, small type, excessive italics, or single-line spacing (all of which make the résumé congested and difficult to read) generally guarantees that it will not be read.

As electronic submission of résumés is becoming common, some career and employment counsellors recommend listing a key word summary at the beginning of the résumé and using appropriate nouns to match words that the recruiter's computer software is likely to search for (see Recruitment and Selection Today 7.3). Recruitment and Selection Notebook 7.1 presents a checklist of tips on writing an effective résumé and Recruitment and Selection Notebook 7.2 presents an example of a standard résumé.

Screening Résumés

In today's labour market, where many candidates are competing for a limited number of jobs, a voluminous number of résumés makes screening more difficult. Organizations have had to develop procedures for efficiently and systematically processing résumés. Wein reports the following pre-employment screening procedure:[76]

- Think of what the company needs for excellent job performance in terms of its job performance criteria.

In Chapter 6, we discussed the impact that the Internet has had on recruiting through online job sites such as Workopolis.com (http://workopolis.com) and Monster.ca (http://www.monster.ca). One disadvantage of such recruiting methods is dealing with the potential flood of applications and résumés. A company using such services may receive hundreds of applications daily. Fortunately, however, sophisticated software programs can be used to create and manage applicant databases and to screen candidates quickly.

With the appropriate software, client companies can access application service agencies for potential hires, such as Workstream Inc. (http://www.workstreaminc.com), which has an office in Ottawa. Clients using this software can screen online applications and spot an excellent prospect in a matter of minutes. In addition to submitting a résumé, a candidate may be asked to fill out a questionnaire that is specific to the recruiting company. The questionnaire typically solicits information not likely to be available in a general résumé. Some companies will accept an application and résumé only if the candidate provides the information requested on this questionnaire. Example questions for an international company might include "Can you travel immediately?" and "Do you have a passport?"

Questionnaires for screening candidates may include multiple-choice items related to skills or experience (e.g., "How much experience have you had using a programming language?") or short essays (e.g., "How would you handle a programming problem that you could not solve by yourself?"). Some software programs assign points to answers and only those candidates achieving a minimum score are invited to submit a résumé.

Source: A. Kerr. 2000. "Sophisticated Software Does the Job for On-Line Recruiters: The More Complex Programs Manage Everything from Posting Positions to Pre-Screening Applicants and Keeping Tabs on Future Prospects." *The Globe and Mail* (June 30). Reprinted with permission from The Globe and Mail.

- Read each résumé with reference to the organization's criteria of job performance.
- Check résumés for work experience, chronology, and history.
- Examine résumés for concrete accomplishments and identifiable skills.
- Look at résumés one more time for appearance.

Computer software is adding speed and accuracy to screening procedures.[77] As the use of job sites on the Internet to receive résumés increases, so too does the availability of tools for screening online applications and résumés. Video résumés are also becoming increasingly popular, wherein candidates send employers a video self-presentation of their skills, experiences, credentials, and accomplishments. A particular concern about video use, however, is that candidate information that could be used by recruiters to unfairly discriminate becomes obvious, such as age, gender, ethnicity, religion (e.g., wearing of a turban, hijab, sari, kippah), and handicap (e.g., a speech impediment).

Moreover, not all candidates may have access to the technology required to produce their own videos, and when they do, the quality of production may vary widely, regardless of the suitability of the candidate to the posted position. Likewise, there is no standardization of presentation structure, format, length, or content, making difficult a fair and objective comparison of job can-

Tips on Writing an Effective Business Résumé

1. Do a self-assessment—produce a first draft of your résumé by collecting all relevant information about yourself.

2. Analyze and sort out what should and should not be included on your résumé—it should fit comfortably on no more than two pages.

3. Choose a format and font style that is professional in appearance and easy to read.

4. Begin your résumé with your name, address, e-mail address, and phone number(s)—it is preferable not to include any personal information such as birth date, marital status, or health.

5. List your education—use reverse chronological order, that is, indicate the most recent first. High school can easily be left off unless it is of particular importance.

6. List work experience—Use point form (bullets work nicely) and begin each job description with an action verb that describes exactly what you did, for example, *analyzed, performed, directed, produced,* and so forth (try not to use the phrase "responsible for").

7. Be skills-oriented, not duty-oriented. Emphasize what you learned and achieved, and what new skills you gained.

8. Avoid unsubstantiated self-describing general statements, such as "I'm creative, dynamic, a quick learner, a hard worker," and so on. Qualify your statements with facts; for example, "Was commended for my creativity in developing a new marketing strategy."

9. Quantify your experience where possible; for example: "Increased sales by 10 percent"; "Handled cash up to $10 000 per shift"; "Supervised a five-member team."

10. Include any relevant summer, part-time, and/or volunteer experience, especially if it demonstrates leadership skills or other skills or attributes that may set you apart from others.

11. Highlight special awards, achievements, scholarships, professional affiliations, memberships, other languages spoken and/or written, and so forth. Emphasize your uniqueness.

12. Include extracurricular activities such as sports, hobbies, and organizations that you are involved with. This will give you a more "well-rounded" appearance.

13. Make sparing use of italics, boldface, and so on to highlight results, accomplishments, and successes.

14. Check and double-check for spelling and grammatical errors—a single mistake on a résumé can put you out of the running.

15. Choose a good-quality paper that will not overpower the résumé in either texture or colour—your best bets for colour are white, cream, buff, vanilla, light grey, and for texture, heavy bond, linen-look, or water-stained. As well, several appealing recycled papers are available in various colours and textures.

Source: Business Career Services, Michael G. DeGroote School of Business, McMaster University. Reprinted with permission.

didates. In addition, while search engines can quickly search out electronically submitted résumés for key words or passages, it is not clear how these video résumés can be scanned as quickly. Viewing video résumés is likely a very time-consuming exercise.

Concerns about video résumés have not stopped entrepreneurs from providing related services. For example, Vidres.net is a Philippine Internet company that makes video résumés available to employers (http://www.vidres .net). It reports having a database in excess of 2000 job seekers from across the Philippines. These résumés are accessible to local corporate clients, ranging from call centres to hospitals and maritime agencies. The chief executive of Vidres, Florante Cruz, notes: "Through a video presentation, job applicants

An Example of a Business Résumé

JANE SMITH

595 Main Street West

Halifax, NS

B3H 2N9

Phone: (902) 555-8000; E-mail: jsmith@smu.ca

OBJECTIVE

Recruiter in a Human Resources division of a large corporation

EDUCATION

Certificate in Human Resources   2002–2003
- Nova Scotia Community College, Halifax, NS

Bachelors of Arts, Major Psychology   1998–2002
- Saint Mary's University, Halifax, NS
- GPA 3.7/4.0

WORK HISTORY

Bluenose Shipbuilding, Ltd.—Halifax, NS

Associative Staffing Representative   2002–Present
- Recruit new employees; advertise for jobs on the intranet, Internet, job/college fairs, newspaper.
- Interview all internal and external applicants.
- Serve as the liaison between management and applicants.
- Coordinate relocation for new hires with Procurement Department.
- Audit recruiting efforts to ensure compliance with federal and provincial regulations and current corporate organizational procedures.
- Administration of company new hire paperwork, orientation for direct hires, and maintain applicant tracking.
- Advise management of employment law/policy/procedure change.
- Completed special projects as requested.
  Management Approach Survey
  - Developed Management Approach Survey under guidance of Company president and Marketing Director to measure knowledge and compliance of the organization's five primary management principles.
  - Electronically distributed to over 600 employees. Analyzed results and presented to senior staff.

Human Resources Assistant (Part-time 15 hrs/wk)   2000–2002
- Assisted in administration of corporate benefit programs and policies, including medical, dental and vision insurance coverage, group life and voluntary life insurance plans.

continued

Continued from previous page

- Administration of company new hire paperwork and orientations for both direct and subcontracted employees.
- Maintained subcontracted staffing service employee records. Served as a liaison for the employee with the staffing agencies along with recruiter.

COMPUTER SKILLS/LANGUAGE

- Proficient in Microsoft Office Applications, SPSS, ADP, and HR Perspective.
- Fully bilingual in oral and written English and French.

AWARDS & HONOURS

- Certified Human Resources Professional—Candidate, 2004
- Bluenose Shipbuilding New Employee of the Year Award—2003
- Nova Scotia Community College President's Gold Medal for Outstanding Contributions to the College and Community
- Saint Mary's University—Dean's Honour List, 2000–2002

MEMBERSHIPS & VOLUNTEER ACTIVITIES

- Human Resources Association of Nova Scotia
  - AGM Planning Committee
- Peninsula South Community Association
  - Heritage Building Preservation Committee
- United Way Campaign
  - Bluenose Shipbuilding HR Division Liaison

ACTIVITIES & INTERESTS

- Participate in jogging, in-line skating, and weight training to stay fit.
- Interests include reading, baking, and learning new computer programs.

References Available Upon Request

Source: Business Career Services, Michael G. DeGroote School of Business, McMaster University. Reprinted with permission.

can demonstrate their communication skills and personality and highlight their unique qualifications … it also makes hiring faster and cheaper as it lessens the time and cost, and eliminates the initial screening process."[78] Recently, for example, the Philippine Department of Labor and Employment asked for access to the search engine for its own Internet-based job and applicant matching system. Another site for posting and/or viewing video résumés is maintained by ResumeTube at http://www.resumetube.com.

Still, given the concern about potential bias, most firms appear reluctant to embrace the video résumé.[79] For example, the Royal Bank of Canada uses a computerized filtering tool on résumés it receives so that competencies can be viewed without seeing an applicant's name—which could signal ethnicity and gender. It is best that candidates check with targeted employers before sending any type of résumé or referring potential employers to personal blogs.[80]

InterviewStudio (http://www.interviewstudio.com) offers a Web-based service for screening executive-level candidates. It is designed to shorten hiring time and costs by enabling employers and recruiters to screen a database of prequalified candidates. The database is made up predominantly of senior-level candidates who are instructed to build online "showcases" in an easy step-by-step process. This system is more comprehensive and sophisticated than the typical résumé video in that it combines a candidate's résumé, video interviews, professional assessment test results, Web page portfolio, reference checks, colleague endorsements, and other personal data found in Internet search engines.[81] However, it still creates the potential for employers to screen out candidates based on prohibited grounds of discrimination that are not as accessible in more typical screening systems.

Honesty and the Résumé

Job applicants should customize their résumés to include their unique attributes or experiences. However, it is important to be honest and to avoid exaggeration in presenting qualifications or accomplishments. If facts are found to have been embellished, embarrassment and job loss is likely to follow. Drawing from various surveys across a number of occupational groups and conducted by various consulting firms, it appears that approximately one-third of job candidates fabricate or exaggerate information contained in their résumés; the most common fabrications are related to educational credentials, grade point averages, current or previous salaries, and past experiences and accomplishments.[82,83] Research also suggests that the likelihood of job candidates fabricating or embellishing their credentials is lessened considerably to the degree that they believe the employer will seek to verify the information provided.[84] Accordingly, a statement to this effect by employers will serve them well.

In a highly competitive labour market, job candidates may be most prone to "fudging" the truth about their credentials. There is often a fine line between presenting yourself in the "best possible light" and intentionally misrepresenting your background. Clearly, human resources managers must learn how to "read between the lines" of résumés (see Recruitment and Selection Today 7.4).

The characteristics identified in Recruitment and Selection Today 7.4 should serve as a "flag" to examine the résumé closely and to undertake a thorough references check before proceeding with the application. Moreover, even when candidates "pass" the screening, subsequent phases of selection provide for opportunities to probe the credibility of information provided by applicants.

Predictive Validity of Résumés

There are few validation studies on the résumé itself. Rather, studies report the validity of inferences based on information typically found in a résumé. Hunter and Hunter's meta-analysis showed that information of the type

What to Look for When Examining a Résumé

- Unexplained gaps in work or education chronology.
- Conflicting details or overlapping dates.
- Career regression, or "downward" trend.
- Use of qualifiers such as "knowledge of," "assisted in" to describe work experience.
- Listing of schools attended without indicating receipt of a degree or diploma.

- Failure to provide names of previous supervisors or references.
- Substantial periods in a candidate's work history listed as "self-employed" or "consultant."

included in a résumé had relatively low validity in predicting future job success.[85] Experience had the highest validity ($r = 0.18$), followed by academic achievement ($r = 0.11$) and education ($r = 0.10$). Nonetheless, a résumé and its accompanying cover letter remain the primary means by which many job applicants introduce themselves to an organization and create an impression of their fit to the job and to the company. It is usually a "ticket" to receiving further consideration.

Screening Interviews

In North America, the interview is the most popular selection device; it is used almost universally.[86,87] The interview, a face-to-face interaction between two people, is designed to allow the parties to obtain information about one another. In employment, the employer's representative is called the *interviewer*, while the job applicant is called the *interviewee* or *applicant*. This traditional terminology does not convey the complex, dynamic, interactive nature of the interview. It is used only as a matter of convenience to identify each of the parties involved in the interview, since both attempt to obtain information about the other through the interview process. Each, at times, is both an interviewer and an interviewee.

Screening for Organizational Fit

In our discussion of recruitment in Chapter 6, we described how job applicants use their initial interview with a recruiter to obtain information about the organization. The interviewer takes the opportunity of this interview to find out information about the applicant that is not apparent from an application form or résumé. The interview has considerable value as a recruiting device and as a means of initiating a social relationship between a job applicant and an organization.[88] A selection interview provides the applicant with information, mostly favourable, about the organization as an employer, in the hope of increasing the odds that a desired applicant will accept a forthcoming job offer. The job applicant uses the interview to learn more about the organization as an employer and to make inferences about its values and philosophy in deciding whether there is a fit.[89]

Without a doubt, interviewing that is done as part of the recruitment process serves as a screening mechanism. Job applicants who do not meet the recruiter's standards do not proceed further. Today, organizations such as Goodyear Canada are using the initial screening interview to determine whether job candidates possess competency in core performance areas related to corporate mission statements and strategic plans. Ford Motor Company selects students for sponsorship through universities and technical colleges on the basis of how well the students fit four competency dimensions related to successful job performance. These core competencies and performance areas are identified through procedures discussed in Chapters 4 and 5. This initial assessment also includes screening of values believed necessary to achieve the company's strategic goals.

Successful Canadian organizations recognize that selection and performance measurement go hand in hand. Moreover, the urgency to fill vacancies should not mean compromising rigour in screening and selection, as illustrated by Trevor Maurer, former executive director of sales for CIBA Vision, a U.S./Canadian contact lens and lens-care business, who had to hire 45 sales representatives within six weeks. Recruitment and Selection Today 7.5 outlines how he went about doing this.

Improving the Interview—A Preview

For almost as long as it has been used as a selection device, the interview has suffered criticism for poor reliability and validity. However, the seminal work by Latham[90] and Janz[91] shows that both the reliability and validity of

Recruitment and Selection Today 7.5

Hiring Smart and Fast at CIBA Vision

Trevor Maurer, former executive director of sales for CIBA Vision, a U.S./Canadian contact lens and lens-care business, set out to establish a sales force dedicated to selling a new product line that showed especially good promise. It was essential to get this new product to market as soon as possible, so he was given six weeks to hire 45 sales representatives. With help from his human resources group, he developed the "perfect candidate profile," and hired four dedicated recruiters with whom he developed a five-stage sequential recruitment and screening process.

Stage 1 solicited basic information on previous experience, education, and salary expectations. Stage 2 involved telephone interviews in which the recruiter asked behavioural-based questions, with structured guidelines for scoring candidate responses. Stage 3 involved written responses to behavioural questions transmitted by e-mail. In Stage 4, a profile of each candidate was written and

given to sales managers, who probed further in a telephone interview, using a structured template as their guide. Finally, in Stage 5 the remaining candidates were invited for an on-site structured interview.

The number of candidates was reduced in each sequential stage of the recruitment process, from an initial applicant pool of 2000. Given that time was of the essence, Maurer generated the original applicant pool through Thingamajob (http://www.thingamajob.com), an Internet-based sourcing program that placed the company's posting and searched other sites such as CareerBuilder (http://www.careerbuilder.ca), Hotjobs (http://hotjobs.yahoo.com), and Workopolis (http://www.workopolis.com).

Source: Adapted from T. Maurer. 2003. "Hiring Smart ... and Fast." *Sales and Marketing Management* 155(5): 63–64.

the interview can be substantially improved by structuring job analysis information into interview questions. The work of these two Canadian psychologists on the employment interview is described in more detail in Chapter 9. That chapter examines the use of the interview in the final stages of the selection process as part of deciding which candidates are the most qualified. The remainder of this section reviews the role of the interview in the earlier stages of the selection process as a screening device to decide whether a job applicant meets minimum requirements.

The Typical Screening Interview

Screening interviews typically consist of a series of freewheeling, unstructured questions designed to fill gaps left on the candidate's application form and résumé. Such traditional interviews take on the qualities of a conversation and often revolve around a set of common questions such as "What is your greatest accomplishment?" These questions cover the applicant's personal history, attitudes and expectations, and skills and abilities.

The information obtained from many of these questions is often better collected through a well-constructed application form. Skillful interviewees know how to give socially desirable answers to many of these frequently asked questions. While some distortion is to be expected in the answers, there is no reason to believe these inaccuracies, intentional or otherwise, occur with greater frequency than do inaccuracies in biodata and résumé information. There is very little direct evidence on the rate or percentage of misinformation that takes place over the course of an interview. As with application forms and biodata, when interview questions focus on verifiable events related to past work or educational experiences, accuracy will likely increase.

Screening Interview Format

The interviewer often obtains better information from a screening interview by following an interview guide. Following a set of preplanned questions or topics during the interview in addition to having reviewed the applicant's file before the interview begins will improve the reliability or consistency of information gathered.[92] The format for a screening interview begins with some opening remarks by the recruiter to put the applicant at ease. This generally involves an exchange of pleasantries and personal information, including information on the purpose of the interview and how the information will be used. The applicant is also advised whether any information presented during the interview will be held in confidence or shared with others. In addition, the interviewer informs the interviewee whether any notes or recordings will be made during the interview.

Following these clarifications, questions typically focus on the applicant's past work history, education and training, and general background. The interviewee is given an opportunity to ask questions about the job and company, as well as about issues raised during the interview. In closing, the interviewer outlines the timeline for the decision process and when applicants are likely to hear the outcome. After the applicant leaves, the interviewer prepares a

Computer-Assisted Interview Screening at Nike

Nike uses computer-assisted interviewing to hire employees for Niketowns, which are retail stores that showcase Nike products. For their Las Vegas store, Nike received 6000 responses to ads for 250 positions. The first cut was made by interactive voice-recognition (IVR) technology, with applicants responding to eight questions over the telephone. In this first stage, 3500 applicants were screened out for being unavailable when needed or for not having retail experience.

Candidates who passed this first assessment were then given a computer-assisted interview at the store, which identified individuals who had been in customer service environments, had a passion for sports, and would therefore probably be good Nike service representatives. They were then shown a video of three scenarios for helping a customer and asked to choose the "best one." A printout of applicant responses allowed interviewers to flag areas for further probing during the face-to-face interview that followed. The use of technology for screening interviews helped Nike speed up their staffing and reduce turnover in the retail division by 21 percent over two years.

Source: Adapted from L. Thornburg. 1998. "Computer-Assisted Interviewing Shortens Hiring Cycle." *HR Magazine* 43(2): 73–79.

summary of the interview by completing either a written narrative or a rating form. Today, an increasing number of organizations are turning to computer-assisted interviewing (see Recruitment and Selection Today 7.6).

Decisions Based on the Screening Interview

The interviewer is frequently required to make inferences about an applicant's personal qualities, motivation, overall ability, attitude toward work, and potential not only for doing the job but also for fitting into the organizational culture. Organizations that use screening interviews often require the interviewer to rate specific attributes or characteristics of the applicant either in addition to, or instead of, making an overall recommendation. Recruitment and Selection Notebook 7.3 presents a sample form used to rate applicants following a screening interview. The traits or attributes that interviewers are asked to rate vary among organizations. They range from the very specific (e.g., attitude toward working irregular hours) to the very general (e.g., initiative).

Microsoft Canada uses screening interviews to identify computer science graduates whose thinking is fast, flexible, and creative. The Microsoft interview includes questions related to computer science knowledge and brainteaser-type questions about balloons that move in mysterious ways. More than the right answer, Microsoft is looking for an ability to think creatively and an inquiring mind. Only about 25 percent of applicants from one of Canada's leading computer science programs made it through the final stages of one of these screening interviews.[93]

Impression Formation

Interviewers use both verbal and nonverbal behaviour of job applicants to form an impression of interviewees.[94,95] Similarly, applicants interpret the interviewer's verbal and nonverbal behaviours to form an impression of the

Example of a Post-Interview Summary

Applicant's Name _____   Date _____

Position _____   Interviewed By_____

Ratings: 0–Unacceptable; 1–Poor; 2–Satisfactory; 3–Good; 4–Excellent

	Rating	Comments
Previous Experience	0 1 2 3 4	
Neatness/Grooming	0 1 2 3 4	
Communicating	0 1 2 3 4	
Interpersonal Skills	0 1 2 3 4	
Adaptability	0 1 2 3 4	
Maturity	0 1 2 3 4	
Emotional Stability	0 1 2 3 4	
Leadership Potential	0 1 2 3 4	
Ability to Work with Others	0 1 2 3 4	
Planning/Organizing	0 1 2 3 4	
Attitude toward Work	0 1 2 3 4	
Realistic Expectations	0 1 2 3 4	
Overall Impression	0 1 2 3 4	

Total Score _____

Recommendation:_____Unacceptable/Notify applicant of rejection

_____Applicant is acceptable for position

If acceptable, arrange for the following:

_____Employment Testing

_____Selection Interview

Recruitment and Selection Today 7.7

Interviewee Behaviours That Influence Interviewer Impressions

Applicant Behaviours That Make a Favourable Impression

- Being on time for the interview.
- Being prepared for the interview by having done homework on the company and anticipating common interview questions.
- Making direct eye contact with the interviewer.
- Remaining confident and determined throughout the interview, regardless of how the interviewer's cues suggest the interview is going.
- Providing positive information about oneself when answering questions.
- Answering questions quickly and intelligently.
- Demonstrating interest in the position and organization.

Applicant Behaviours That Make a Negative Impression

- Presenting a poor personal appearance or grooming.
- Displaying an overly aggressive, know-it-all attitude.
- Failing to communicate clearly (e.g., mumbling, poor grammar, use of slang).
- Lacking career goals or career planning.
- Overemphasizing monetary issues.
- Evasiveness or not answering questions completely.
- Lacking maturity, tact, courtesy, or social skills.

organization and to judge whether they will accept any potentially forthcoming job offer. Recruitment and Selection Today 7.7 lists common behaviours of interviewees that leave the interviewer with either positive or negative impressions. While presenting all positive behaviours and avoiding the negative ones will not guarantee candidates that they will move on to the next step in the selection process, it should certainly improve their odds.

Value of the Screening Interview

Much research has investigated the effectiveness of the selection interview, but much less has examined the interview used for employment screening. This may be because traditional interviews are resource-intensive (considering the time and labour). Advanced technology enables automatic administration and scoring of interview questions (e.g., interactive voice-recognition), allowing for automatic assessment. There are, however, face-to-face screening interviews that can be cost-effective. For example, it is common for graduating Ph.D. students seeking employment as university professors to be invited for a screening interview at academic/professional conferences. This is ideal for the hiring universities in that they do not incur costs for candidates' travel and accommodation, plus (in addition to the screening interview) they often have the opportunity to view candidates publicly presenting and defending their research (often a doctoral thesis)—a work sample of sorts, where the presentation and analytic skills of the aspiring professor can be assessed. Based on the screening interview (and research presentation), recruiters are then better positioned to determine whether (at their expense) to invite the candidate for an on-campus interview. Such pre-screening is quite common for other professional groups as well.

"Speed interviewing" is now being used by recruiters who need to fill several positions as quickly and cost-effectively as possible. Likened to speed dating, speed interviewing typically consists of a series of short (5–15-minute), consecutive interviews. For example, the University of Windsor hosted a recruitment fair for 14 law firms seeking to fill internship/articling positions. Candidates were processed through a four-hour circuit of 15-minute mini-interviews with firm representatives.[96]

Speed interviews typically last less than 12 minutes. One of the largest forums for speed interviewing was held in Montreal in 2005, hosted by Videotron, a subsidiary of Quebecor Media Inc. Videotron held a job fair to hire 300 new employees, ranging from systems architects to technicians, analysts, and sales representatives for its new Internet telephone service. The event attracted more than 2000 applicants who had already been pre-screened on the basis of résumés that they had submitted online. Each candidate was assigned to a circuit of five 7-minute interviews with recruiters and company officials of different speciality backgrounds. About 1000 applicants were retained based on their interview performance and given a half-hour test. Those making the short list following this testing were then given a second interview, lasting 15 minutes to an hour. By the end of the day, 200 of the 300 positions posted had been filled.[97]

Critics of speed interviewing question whether a 5–15-minute interview is sufficient to ascertain a candidate's fit with position requirements, while advocates argue that the speed interview is typically only a screening process, used with other more extensive assessments. Still, the concern remains that potentially very capable candidates could be screened out early based on such a brief encounter. Unlike the job fair hosted by the University of Windsor for law firms, where each candidate was given a 15-minute interview with each firm, Videotron had each candidate assessed in a *circuit* of several separate speed interviews conducted by different company representatives. Accordingly, a total interview score could be calculated across the different interviewers.

It is argued that potential biases of any one interviewer are "cancelled" when scores are cumulated across assessors and interview questions, thereby providing a robust and accurate assessment of the candidate's job suitability. Another attractive attribute of the speed interview is that it enables recruiters to assess a large number of candidates efficiently and cost-effectively.

McMaster University uses a version of the speed interview, which it refers to as the "Multi-Mini-Interview" (MMI), to screen applicants to its medical school.[98] Each spring, candidates pre-screened on the basis of their GPA and autobiographical profile are invited to participate in a circuit of 12 eight-minute MMIs. These MMIs, some consisting of role-playing exercises and simulations, assess a variety of attributes deemed essential for Canadian physicians. Admission decisions are then made based on a combination of scores from the MMI, autobiographical profile, and GPA.

McMaster's MMI was developed to better assess noncognitive (e.g., interpersonal) skills and to augment predictions afforded by GPA and SAT scores. Previously, pre-screened applicants were given one-on-one interviews, but this proved too resource-intensive, requiring an unsustainable commitment of labour hours and causing logistical difficulties and inconvenience to both interviewers and candidates. With the MMI, McMaster University is able to evaluate 400 applicants over two days, with eight parallel circuits run twice daily on each of two consecutive days.[99]

Predictive Validity of Screening Interviews

There is considerable research on the validity of interviews in employee selection. Meta-analyses report the validity for unstructured employment interviews, which is the type mostly used in screening, as ranging from 0.14 to 0.20.[100,101] Even at 0.20, the validity of the screening interview is still low in comparison with other types of selection procedures. However, an interview will likely always play a role in hiring, regardless of its validity. Put simply, employers want to meet the prospective employee face to face before making a job offer.

Chapter 9 presents ways of improving the interview by developing it from job analysis information. The improvements to the interview discussed in Chapter 9 should be incorporated into screening interviews as well as selection interviews. Properly developed interview questions have the potential to provide value-added screening. The reality is that, as presently done (e.g., unstructured, ad hoc, not directly linked to position or organizational requirements), most screening interviews fall short of achieving their full potential value.

There are too few studies to speak confidently on the predictive validity of speed interviewing. The medical school at McMaster University, however, is at the forefront here. Over the past several years, the university has been collecting validation data that are looking quite promising. These data show that MMI scores uniquely predict performance in the noncognitive domain (interpersonal realm) of physician responsibilities.[102,103]

Cautions on Using Screening Interviews

Using the interview as a screening device brings with it the potential for introducing discriminatory practices into the hiring process. Interviews, including those that are highly structured, are conversations between individuals. Something is said that provokes a response. In opening an interview with small talk or chitchat, interviewers often delve into the personal background of the applicant. They may ask questions about marital status, childcare arrangements, birthplace or birth date, or the applicant's name that relate to proscribed personal information and national or ethnic origin. Information of this type is clearly prohibited. If a job applicant who has been asked these questions is turned down, the onus will be on the employing organization to show that the reason was a lack of job-related requirements and not discriminatory hiring practices. Interview questions should follow the same rule of thumb as application blanks: Is the information obtained from this question job-related? If the answer is "no," the question should not be asked.

Reference Checks

Job applicants are often asked to suggest the names of people who can provide personal references, including past supervisors. Generally, most candidates expect that these individuals will be contacted by the recruiter. Past supervisors may be asked to verify information presented by an applicant or comment on the candidate's traits, characteristics, and behaviours. Overall, however, the **reference check** may refer to vastly different procedures, with varying levels of reliability and validity.

Reference checks usually are done *last* in the screening process, as references are checked only for the applicants surviving previous screens. Mostly, this is to protect the confidentiality of candidates who may not have informed their current employers that they are looking for another job. In addition, reference checking can be quite expensive, so employers aim to reserve such expenditures for only the most promising candidates.

Employers attempt to screen out job applicants who have poor work behaviours or who have problematic backgrounds. Generally, however, reference checks with previous employers are quite ineffective, for good reason. Consider the following situation:

> An unproductive employee of yours has applied for a job with another company. You receive a call asking for your judgment of the employee. While you want to be honest and helpful, you do not want to say anything that will discourage the other company from taking the employee off your hands. Accordingly, while you answer the questions truthfully, you do not volunteer any negative information, hoping that your problem employee will be hired away. However, if you are asked specifically about problem behaviours and you intentionally mislead the reference checker or cover up the problems, you could be liable for economic losses or hardship suffered by the new employer attributable to the hiring of this problem employee.[104,105]

For reasons like this, many Canadian employers are hesitant to make strong, negative statements about current or former employees. For example, it is not uncommon for employers to have a policy of verifying only name, position, and length of service when speaking to callers about former employees.[106,107] Yet, this could be unfair to former employees who have favourable performance records, and, in the case of problematic employees, could result in harm to the future employer, its employees, and its clients. Also, in reality, it is extremely difficult in Canada for a former employer to be sued for libel or slander by a past employee as a result of a poor reference, even if that reference contains some inaccuracies. This is because Canadian courts have endowed employment references with the protection of the law of "qualified privilege." Under this law, employers cannot be sued if the comments are

Reference check

Information gathered about a job candidate from supervisors, co-workers, clients, or other people named as references by the candidate; The information is usually collected from the references through telephone interviews.

"honestly made"; the employee would have to prove that the referee did not believe the facts as asserted (e.g., that she or he *knowingly* fabricated information, acted maliciously, or in bad faith).[108]

While it is unlikely that Canadian employers will be sued for honestly providing unfavourable references, employers are quite vulnerable to being sued in cases where they knowingly hold back unfavourable information, particularly where the employee is subsequently hired and causes harm to the new employer or its clientele. In this case, the new employer could sue for damages for "negligent misrepresentation."[109] This legal right of prospective employers seems to be well placed. For example, Charles Cullen, a nurse, was able to move from hospital to hospital from one U.S. state to another, intentionally killing patients at each facility. This went on for 16 years, despite Cullen having been under investigation in seven of these hospitals and having been fired or forced to resign in several instances! This continued because none of these institutions was prepared to give a bad reference.[110]

On the other hand, failure to give a deserved favourable reference can also put an employer in a legally precarious situation, where this failure is seen by Canadian courts as having impeded a former employee's job search. For example, in a precedent-setting case, the Supreme Court of Canada ruled in 1977 that employers have an obligation to act in good faith when an employee is terminated. In this case, Jack Wallace, the plaintiff, was awarded 24 months of salary when it was found that his employer, United Grain Growers, neglected to provide a reference letter in time for him to secure a new job.[111]

Court awards such as this can be interpreted to suggest that employers are being encouraged to provide honest written and oral references for their former employees. AXiOM International Reference Checking Service (http://www.axiom-int.com) provides regular surveys of Canadian employers regarding their reference checking policies and practices, and employers are encouraged to access this site for the results of AXiOM's most recent survey results. The firm recommends that employers consider the following steps with respect to providing references on behalf of former employees:

1. On request, the employer should provide a substantive reference on behalf of a former employee, particularly in circumstances where the individual's performance and character were never in question.
2. The employer must act objectively and in good faith in preparation of the reference, assuming that it will be relied upon by third parties in determining the departing employee's future.
3. The employer must exercise reasonable skill and diligence in the preparation of the reference and must understand that such preparation is owed to the departing employee.

While, implicitly, job candidates grant permission to the prospective employer to collect references from past employers when they list these past employers as references, the prospective employer should explicitly (in writing) secure such permission. Moreover, the credibility of the reference will depend in part on the length of time the prospective employee worked for the supervisor providing the reference (i.e., the longer the better) and the amount of direct contact between these two parties in their employment relationship (the closer the contact, the better). It will also depend on the extent to which the job previously held by the applicant is similar to the target job.[112]

Telephone Reference Checks

Many employers are reluctant to provide references in writing, preferring instead to do so over the phone. The telephone reference is perhaps the most common way in which Canadian employers check references. Many have resorted to using a set list of questions designed to obtain standardized information on all potential employees. Regrettably, most of the questions asked as part of these reference checks ask for judgments on the part of the reference rather than focusing on objective information and, as a result, are as ineffective as more general letters of reference. Typical questions asked about the job applicant in telephone checks include some of the following:

- How long, and in what capacity, have you known the applicant?
- What sort of employee is the applicant?
- Does the applicant show initiative?
- How did the applicant get along with other employees, supervisors, clients?
- Did the applicant meet deadlines? Get work done on time?
- Was the applicant punctual? Were there attendance problems?
- Were you satisfied with the applicant's performance?
- Why did the applicant leave your company?
- Is there anything you feel I should know about this candidate?
- Would you rehire the applicant?

Asking the Right Questions

In many cases, the right questions are not asked, and many that are asked may not have any relevance to the job under consideration. Also, reference checks often fail to ask for confirmation of specific information provided by job candidates in their application materials. The reference should be asked to compare the candidate with other employees—for example, "If your worst employee is given a rating of 1 and your best a rating of 10, what rating would you give to this candidate?"

References should be probed for more information on the candidate when their answers are not forthcoming or appear to be too qualified or general. Ask for specifics and have them describe examples of the candidate's behaviour—for example, "Describe a situation in which the candidate performed exceptionally well or exceptionally poorly." Many of the techniques discussed in Chapter 9 for developing structured or behaviour-based interview questions can be adapted for use in reference checking. As in the case of interviewing, asking specific, behaviour-based questions related to job performance is likely to increase the accuracy of the information obtained through the reference check.

Is the Reference Competent to Provide an Assessment?

Implicit assumptions are made when a former supervisor or a personal reference is called on for information about a job candidate, namely, that the references themselves are competent to make the assessment and are sufficiently knowledgeable about the candidate to provide accurate information. These are not always well-founded assumptions. As noted earlier, a former supervisor may not have been in a position long enough to learn much about the employee's behaviour; there is also no guarantee that the supervisor is capable of discriminating between poor and excellent job behaviour. When the assumptions are true, however, the reference information is likely to have a higher degree of accuracy. In effect, the reference checker must also know something about the references themselves to establish the credibility of their statements. This is why greater value is placed on references from people who are known to the recruiter.

Background Checks

Reference checks are on safer ground when they concentrate on verifying information obtained from the applicant's biodata, résumé, or interview. Given the legal sensitivities of conducting background checks and the time-consuming nature of this activity, many organizations contract the work out to employment screening firms. The Society for Human Resource Management (http://www.shrm.org) found in a 2004 online survey of 373 HR professionals that 61 percent of respondents reported routinely finding résumé inaccuracies.[113]

Common inaccuracies include: candidates listing family members as former supervisors; gaps in employment that were not shown on the résumé; incorrectly stated start and end dates; false academic credentials; and incorrect job titles.[114] In conducting 2.6 million background checks in 2001, ADP Screening and Selection Services (https://www.adpselect.com) found that 44 percent of applicants lied about their work histories, 41 percent lied about their education, and 23 percent falsified credentials or licences.[115]

Clearly, an employer who does not conduct a background check is being negligent in his or her hiring practices. Recruitment and Selection Notebook 7.4 provides a checklist of guidelines for conducting a thorough and legally defensible background reference check to obtain maximum information of value. Recruitment and Selection Today 7.8 lists some of the most common misrepresentations made by job applicants.

Finally, because it is so easy today for employers to "Google" names of prospective employees, it is important for job candidates to also do this on a regular basis to check what information results from such searches. Candidates should ensure that any information posted on the Web (including information in a blog) is professional and in good taste, as this same information can be viewed by potential employers.

Field Investigations

In most cases, checking information is limited to phone calls to supervisors and personal references. However, a very extensive search of an applicant's background may occur for some occupations or positions. Applicants for sen-

Reference Checklist

- **Obtain Waivers:** Have candidates sign a comprehensive waiver granting the employer or its agents express permission to contact references and anyone else who might be familiar with the candidate's past job performance.
- **Check Three References:** Check at least three references. Multiple references are preferable, allowing prospective employers to look for consistency and to show that they exercised care in hiring.
- **Ask for Different Types of References:** Best references typically come from former supervisors. Peers and subordinates are also excellent references. Collecting references from supervisors, peers, and subordinates provides for varying perspectives on the candidate.
- **Ask about Past Job Performance:** Ask questions that relate directly to job performance.
- **Ask Questions on Recent Job Performance:** The reference check should cover the preceding five- to seven-year period.
- **Avoid Personal References:** References from personal friends and family tend to be a waste of time. Insist that candidates provide references who can comment on direct observation of past job performance.
- **Verify All Licences and Degrees:** One of the most common deceptions on résumés and job applications is claiming to hold a degree that was never conferred

or a licence never issued. Don't take a document or a copy of it at face value. Call the licensing bureau/board or the registrar's office of the university/college.
- **Check References by Telephone:** Thorough reference checking includes listening carefully to responses: A person's tone of voice can change the meaning of a response considerably. Talking directly to the reference also allows for follow-up questions.
- **Avoid "Closed" Questions:** Avoid questions that can be answered with a simple "yes" or "no."
- **Use Qualified Professionals or Trained Staff to Check References:** People who check references must be trained to listen for the underlying meaning of statements. Whether handled internally or by an outside agency, reference checking should be thorough, professional, and legal. Never be satisfied with a response such as "She was the best employee we ever had." Follow up with the question: "Could you give examples that show why her performance was so outstanding?"
- **Avoid Invasive/Discriminatory Questions:** Never ask questions about race, age, religion, or national origin.

Source: Adapted from P.W. Barada. 1996. "Reference Checking Is More Important Than Ever." *HR Magazine* 41(11): 49. Copyright © the Society for Human Resource Management, Alexandria, VA. Reprinted with permission of the Copyright Clearance Center (CCC).

sitive government jobs or with security services such as the RCMP undergo field investigations that involve interviews with people who know the applicant, including former employers and co-workers; credit checks; and a review of police files and court records, educational records, and any other available documentation.

Background checks of this sort are very expensive but, in most cases, they provide an accurate description of the applicant and identify any problem areas that might affect job performance. Corporations often use field investigations before they make top-level managerial appointments. Most organizations are not equipped to conduct such costly and elaborate investigations of potential new employees. Increasingly, Canadian corporations are turning to a growing number of firms such as Infocheck (http://www.infocheck.com) and AXiOM that specialize in this activity.

Recruitment and Selection Today 7.8

Misrepresentations by Job Applicants

The following misrepresentations by job applicants in the banking industry are considered "significant" and common, as reported by HR administrators:

- Length of time spent with prior employer and/or in a previous position
- Salary earned in last job
- Possession of a degree
- Name of school at which attendance has been claimed
- Name of past employer

- Grade point average
- Denial of police record
- Creditworthiness
- Academic field of concentration

Source: Adapted from A.A. Sloan. 1991. "Countering Résumé Fraud Within and Beyond Banking: No Excuse for Not Doing More." *Labor Law Journal* 42: 303–10. © 1991, CCH Incorporated. All rights reserved. Reprinted with permission from *Labor Law Journal*.

Predictive Validity of Personal References

Written references from an applicant's past supervisors do not predict well the performance ratings given by the applicant's current supervisor.[116,117] Indeed, information in reference letters often reflects more the attributes of the person writing the reference than attributes of the applicant. Canadian human resources consultants now routinely warn corporate clients to also be leery of making hiring decisions based on personal references.[118,119] Hunter and Hunter showed that the validity of personal references ranges from as low as 0.16 for promotion criteria to a high of 0.26 for supervisor rating criteria.[120] The predictive validity of written references is low relative to biodata and the types of employment tests discussed in Chapter 8. Personal references (and reference checks) are most useful for screening out especially weak or potentially problematic candidates.

Reasons for Poor Validity of Personal References

There appear to be several reasons for the low validity of reference checks. In the case of personal references, it is highly unlikely that a job applicant will knowingly offer the name of someone who will provide a bad reference. (Doing so might be more of a statement about the cognitive ability of the applicant!) Most applicants are fairly confident about the type of references they will provide. Applicants should not hesitate to ask intended references if they would provide positive comments before listing their names on an application form. It is in the applicant's best interests to do this.

The result, however, is a set of uniformly positive recommendations for each applicant. The lack of variability in the references limits their use in discriminating among candidates; this is an example of range restriction, discussed in Chapter 2, which leads to low validity coefficients. This is one reason why even the slightest negative information contained in a reference may be sufficient to eliminate an applicant from the job competition.[121]

However, predictive validities of reference information may be significantly improved if standardized reference forms are used. For example, McCarthy and Goffin (2001) found that a form that required references to indicate the relative percentile standing of candidates showed promising predictive validity among 520 recruits for the Canadian military. Specifically, this form, referred to as the *Relative Percentile Method* (see Chapter 5, page 201), contained a series of attributes that references rated on a 100-point scale, ranging from 0 (below average) to 100 (above average).[122]

Work Experience

Screening job applicants through review of résumés, preliminary interview, or reference checking emphasizes a candidate's credentials, including formal training and work experiences. Formal credentials (e.g., licence, diploma, or degree) and the work experiences of the candidate are identified and verified. Indeed, in many cases, candidates without some specified minimum level of formal training, education, or work experience do not get any further than the résumé review stage of the screening and selection process. While there are widely agreed-upon, easily verifiable indicators of formal training and educational achievements, this is not the case with work experience.

Work experience refers to events experienced by an individual that relate to job performance. There are many aspects to work experience, including length of time on a job, time with an organization, or number of times a specific task has been performed.[123–125] For example, in hiring a car salesperson, you might consider the time that candidates spent working for other car dealerships, the time spent specifically as a car salesperson, or the number of vehicles sold. The number of previous car sales is likely the most relevant measure of work experience in making a hiring decision in this instance. These are all *quantitative* measures.

On the other hand, *qualitative* measures allow for probing into the nature, level, diversity, and complexity of a candidate's work experiences. For example, what is the demographic profile of the customers served by the applicant (age, gender, ethnicity, socioeconomic background)? How much autonomy in negotiating car sales did the candidate have in the previous job? What was the complexity of the job (e.g., number of car models, amount of staff assistance, use of technology/computers, and so on)? Qualitative assessments of work experience are generally done during the screening interview but can also be inferred to a certain extent through the résumé.

Clearly, work experience has many dimensions. Consider two managers who have worked with their employer for 15 consecutive years. One may have acquired 15 years of experience of varied activities and responsibilities, while the other may have experienced the identical activities and responsibilities year in and year out for 15 years! The former manager may have worked in a challenging, dynamic, growth-oriented organization, while the other may have worked in a stable, predictable, unchallenging work environment. So, in assessing work experience, it is good practice to evaluate both quantitative and qualitative aspects of work experience.

In the initial sorting of résumés, however, the temptation still may be to simply make quick cuts of those with the fewest years of previous work experience. Remember, though, that those with fewer years of work experience may have had "richer" experiences and developed more competencies than the candidates with longer work histories. Ford, Quinones, Sego, and Speer-Sorra[126] demonstrated that two individuals with equal job and organizational tenure can differ considerably in the level of challenge and complexity encountered in their assignments and tasks. This is why, when conducting screening interviews and reference checks, the HR manager should probe with behavioural questions that tap job-relevant competencies. While work experience is typically measured in terms of tenure in a job or organization, this is a crude measure given the many different facets of work experience. The aspect of work experience considered in screening and selection should be aligned with the specific criterion measurement of performance that the employer wants to predict.

Predictive Validity of Work Experience

Several studies have shown a significant and positive relationship between work experience and work performance. Job tenure—the most widely used measure of experience—relates positively to job performance because it increases job knowledge and skill competencies.[127,128] For example, Vance, Coovert, MacCallum, and Hedge reported that the length of time spent as an engine mechanic predicted performance on three different sets of tasks.[129]

Three meta-analyses (quantitative reviews) of the relationship between work experience and job performance show mean correlations ranging from 0.18 to 0.32, with work experience defined in terms of job tenure.[130–132] These mean correlations were considerably higher ($r = 0.41$) when work experience was defined in terms such as "number of times performing a task" or "level of task difficulty." Finally, work experience has higher correlations with hard (e.g., work samples) as opposed to soft (e.g., ratings) measures of performance: Mean $r = 0.39$ versus mean $r = 0.24$.[133] This suggests that HR practitioners should carefully consider work experience when making screening or selection decisions. Specifically, they need to identify the kind (quantitative and qualitative) of work experience that is most relevant to the work to be performed in the new job and then fine-tune the screening and selection process to ensure that those aspects of work experience are adequately assessed.

Harnessing Technology in Employment Screening

This chapter has focused primarily on traditional approaches to employee screening, including application forms, résumés, interviews, reference letters, background checks, and work experience assessments. Increasingly, however, with advances in technology, we are seeing what has traditionally been part of post-screening assessments being incorporated into the early stages of screening. For example, as presented earlier in this chapter, Interview Studio (http://www.interviewstudio.com) offers a Web-based service for screening executive-level candidates. The "showcase" (profile) accessible for each executive on this site includes a video résumé, references checks, professional test results, Web page portfolio, colleague endorsements, and other personal data found in Internet search engines. As well, the site provides capabilities for online interviewing.

Recently, Select International (http://www.selectinternational.com) and Toyota Motor Engineering and Manufacturing of North America Incorporated partnered to create "virtual job auditions."[134] Applicants for jobs building Tundra trucks at the San Antonio plant in Texas must first engage in an online work simulation. This high-tech screening has candidates read dials and gauges, spot safety problems, and complete an interactive job simulation that assesses general problem-solving ability and learning capacity. Candidates who perform well enough in this virtual job audition are then invited for a hands-on tryout, lifting 23-kilogram car parts, bolting nuts with an airgun, and spray-painting vehicles. Moreover, Toyota is considering adapting this technology for administrative positions and introducing it in its newest Canadian plant.[135]

Perhaps because such simulations are obviously job-related, candidates who take part in such a virtual audition will be less inclined to legally challenge them. Quite likely, the extent and richness of the application of virtual reality technology to employee screening, selection, and development will grow exponentially over the next few years.

Legal Considerations

All of the selection tools reviewed in this chapter have the potential to run afoul of privacy and human rights legislation, leading to charges of discriminatory hiring practices. Before any of them are used, they should be reviewed carefully to eliminate questions prohibited under human rights legislation.

Summary

Organizations must be staffed with people capable not only of doing the work required, but of doing that work well. Although the role of recruiting is primarily to secure an adequate supply of qualified job applicants, the role of screening is typically to identify those individuals within the applicant pool possessing the basic required qualifications for the position. Individuals so identified are then referred for further assessment, using more resource-intensive procedures. If screening is to be successful, it must be embedded in organization and job analysis, predict relevant job performance criteria, be legally defensible, and be perceived as acceptable (fair) to job candidates.

Screening, which is often the first stage of the selection process, categorizes job applicants as either acceptable or unacceptable with respect to job requirements. Selection gives greater emphasis to identifying the *degree* to which applicants will be successful. In screening, organizations commonly rely on the application form or biodata, the résumé, the preliminary screening interview, and reference checks. Candidates who pass these screening assessments go on for further, more in-depth assessments. As part of the selection process, these screening devices must meet the same standards required of other, more extensive and expensive selection procedures; that is, they must be valid and reliable as well as meeting current legal requirements.

Screening devices yield predictions about future job performance based on past behaviour, interests, and experiences. When biodata and interview questions focus on *verifiable* information, their predictive validity is enhanced. Information gathered through application blanks or biodata forms can provide a good prediction of job performance if the instruments are rationally developed and derived systematically from the knowledge, skills, ability, and key competency requirements of the target position. Traditional unstructured screening interviews are poor predictors but can be substantially improved by the inclusion of structured questions derived from a job analysis. Reference checks appear to offer little value to the screening process other than in screening out the most undesirable candidates. As these screening devices all have the potential for violating human rights legislation, great care must be taken with their use.

One reason for the popularity of screening devices is their cost and ease of use. They are relatively inexpensive, administered quickly, and easy to interpret. With the exception of weighted application blanks and biographical inventories, there are few, if any, developmental costs associated with these devices. However, these low costs must be compared with the potential for inaccuracy. The cost of *false positives* screened into the organization through these procedures can be quite high, particularly in smaller firms where hiring a poor performer can be crippling to morale and overall productivity. Advanced technology is now rapidly spreading to enable quicker, cost-effective, comprehensive, in-depth virtual reality assessments as part of an increasingly seamless screening and selection process.

Key Terms

application blank, p. 293

biodata, p. 302

biographical information blank (BIB), p. 302

criterion measurements, p. 300

designated targeted group, p. 292

false negatives, p. 293

false positives, p. 293

minimum qualifications, p. 291

reference check, p. 325

screening, p. 291

selection ratio, p. 293

validity coefficient, p. 308

weighted application blank (WAB), p. 300

Web Links

To view updated news releases and a list of publications of the Canadian Human Rights Commission, visit **http://www.chrc-ccdp.ca**.

A useful source of information about human rights cases and legal guidelines for recruitment, screening, and assessment is the *Canadian Human Rights Reporter* at **http://www.cdn-hr-reporter.ca**.

Visit Internet-based recruitment and applicant screening service provider Workstream at http://www.workstreaminc.com.

For examples of firms that provide for applicant background checks, go to http://www.infocheck.com and http://www.axiom-int.com.

To view examples of sites for posting and/or viewing video résumés, visit Vidres (http://www.vidres.net), ResumeTube (http://www.resumetube.com), and InterviewStudio (http://www.interviewstudio.com).

Required Professional Capabilities (RPCs)

RPC 7.1 Forecasts HR supply and demand conditions.
- Use of business and HR software
- Assessment and forecasting techniques for HR requirements (including benefits and types of qualitative and quantitative forecasting methods
- Research methods and designs (including measurement of HR)
- HR planning concepts and techniques
- The organization's strategic business plan and the goals of the business unit

RPC 7.2 Maintains an inventory of people talent for the use of the organization.
- HR planning concepts and techniques
- Recruiting sources and techniques
- Use of business and HR software
- Measurement and assessment tools and techniques (and their limitations)

RPC 7.3 Contributes to development of an environment that fosters effective working relationships.
- Communication theories, tools, techniques, and processes
- Work processes, the interdependence of workers and their productivity
- General influences on human behaviour (e.g., motivation theory)
- Behaviour of individuals, groups, and organizational units
- Techniques in managing workforce diversity
- Methods of creating interpersonal effectiveness
- Employee recognition and reward strategies and practices

Discussion Questions

1. What are the differences between employee screening and employee selection?
2. What are the advantages and disadvantages of using the following screening devices?

    a. biographical data
    b. application forms

c. résumés

d. reference checks

3. What is the purpose of a screening interview? Does it differ from a selection interview? If so, how?

4. Are screening procedures exempt from legal challenges? If not, how would you defend them?

5. Describe an effective screening program that you could use to deal with a large number (over 1000) of job applications.

6. What are applicant behaviours that influence positive impressions on the part of an employer? Negative impressions?

Using the Internet

1. Identify three Canadian employers that have Web-based application systems. If possible, download copies of the application forms. Summarize the biodata items and discuss the potential usefulness of these biodata items given the nature of the job(s) for which the application is intended. Discuss whether the items on the application blank conform to the applicable federal or provincial legislation. Do you consider the items an invasion of your privacy? How do you feel about applying to an employer who collects data that you consider to be private?

Exercises

1. Prepare your own personal résumé using the résumé presented in this chapter as a model (see pages 314–15) Exchange your résumé with one of your classmates. Critique each other's document in terms of organization, clarity of information, style, and presentation. Write a short paragraph describing the impressions you formed from reading your classmate's résumé.

2. Develop an interview guide for doing a screening interview that lists the questions that *cannot* be asked because the information relates to prohibited grounds of discrimination (see Chapter 3, Table 3.1 on pages 72–74).

3. Develop a set of questions based on the security dispatcher's job description that can be used to screen applicants for that position.

4. Suppose that you are managing a Swiss Chalet franchise and need to recruit table servers for your store. List in priority order the three things you would be most inclined to screen for, how you would do the screening, and provide a rationale for each.

5. In reference to Exercise 4 above, develop a set of three questions that could be useful in your background reference checks on applicants for the Swiss Chalet table server position and explain their use.

6. Recruitment and Selection Today 7.5 (page 318) describes the screening process used by CIBA Vision to hire 45 sales associates in six weeks. Comment on how the job profiles of the "perfect" sales associate were likely to have been developed, and evaluate the five-stage screening process in light of the principles introduced in this chapter.
7. Think of the key activities of a job that you have held (part-time or full-time). From these key activities, list biodata items that could be helpful in predicting success in this job. A brief rationale should accompany each item. Develop a one-page biodata questionnaire by phrasing each item in question format.

Case

ABC Glass, a Canadian-based manufacturer of glass with a dominant share of the international market, seeks to fill the newly created position of "director of communications." This person will be responsible for both internal and external communications of the company, including writing corporate newsletters, communicating with the press in a public relations function, coaching senior officers on ways to improve their presentation skills, communicating orally and in writing the corporate directions (mission statements) and policies to employees, and soliciting news from employees for reporting in corporate newsletters to enhance cohesiveness and morale following the merger of French- and English-speaking companies.

The president of the merged company has hired you to recruit and screen for this position, referring to him the top three candidates. He, along with the human resources director, will select their top candidate from among these three, using one or more focused assessments. The position requirements for this appointment, developed from the job analysis workshop, include:

- Fluency in both written and spoken French and English
- Excellent oral and written communication skills
- Ability to manage interpersonal conflict
- Ability to work under tight timelines, with multiple conflicting demands
- Ability to plan and organize
- Ability to remain calm when demands considered unreasonable are being made by one's boss
- Ability to solicit information and cooperation from others and overcome personal obstacles
- Ability to extract relevant information from an abundance of reports and summarize it
- Ability to present relatively difficult material in an easily understandable way
- Ability to provide effective coaching to senior officers for improving their presentation skills
- Ability to motivate others to embrace and execute corporate policies
- Willingness to "go above and beyond the call of duty"

The president has contracted you to: (1) establish a recruitment plan, specifying the specific recruitment outlets; (2) propose a screening strategy, outlining each stage of screening and the tools to be used; (3) describe a post-screening selection assessment; and (4) speak to the merits of your proposal. Finally, develop biodata items that are likely to be useful for screening for this position and provide your rationale for each. (Of course, before using such items, you would need to determine empirically whether they are appropriate.)

Discussion Questions

1. Should background checks be mandatory for all jobs or only for certain jobs? Explain your reasoning.
2. Describe a procedure that could be used for doing background checks in a tight labour market.
3. Should background checks be made before a candidate receives a job offer? If so, how do you avoid obtaining information that may be used to discriminate against the candidate (see Chapter 3, Table 3.1 on pages 72–74)?
4. How can the Internet be used to do background checks and to speed up the process? Are there any risks in this process?
5. Explain why background checks may be an invasion of a job applicant's right to privacy.
6. If you discover that a job applicant has a criminal record, can you disqualify the candidate solely on that ground and without fear of violating the candidate's human rights?
7. What is the value of a degree from a prestigious university on a résumé? Would such a degree influence your hiring decision if everything else were equal among candidates? Should it? Why or why not?
8. What should you do if you discover someone has fudged his or her application form information or résumé or lied during the screening interview? Does it matter how big the lie is? Explain and argue your case.

Endnotes

1. Anastasi, A. 1988. *Psychological Testing*. 6th ed. New York: Macmillan.
2. Levine, E.L., D.M. Maye, A. Ulm, and T.R. Gordon. 1997. "A Methodology for Developing and Validating Minimum Qualifications (MQs)." *Personnel Psychology* 50: 1009–23.
3. Levine, E.L., D.M. Maye, A. Ulm, and T.R. Gordon. 1997.
4. Kethley, B.R., and D.E. Terpstra. 2005. "An Analysis of Litigation Associated with Use of the Application Form in the Selection Process." *Public Personnel Management* 34(4): 357–76.
5. Wallace, C.J., and S.J. Vodanovich. 2004. "Personnel Application Blanks: Persistence and Knowledge of Legally Inadvisable Application Blank Items." *Public Personnel Management* 33(3): 331–49.

6. Wallace, C.J., E.E. Page, and M. Lippstreu. 2006. "Applicant Reactions to Pre-Employment Application Blanks: A Legal and Procedural Justice Perspective." *Journal of Business and Psychology* 20(4): 467–88.

7. Saks, A.M., J.D. Leck, and D.M. Saunders. 1995. "Effects of Application Blanks and Employment Equity on Applicant Reactions and Job Pursuit Intentions." *Journal of Organizational Behavior* 16: 415–30.

8. Winstein, K.J., and D. Golden. 2007. "MIT Admissions Dean Lied on Résumé in 1979, Quits." *Wall Street Journal* (Eastern edition) (April 27): B1.

9. Heller, L. 2006. "RadioShack CEO Resigns amid Controversies." *DSN Retailing Today* 45(5): 2, 25.

10. Solomon, B. 1998. "Too Good to Be True?" *Management Review* 87(4) (April): 27.

11. Owens, W.A. 1976. "Biographical Data." In M.D. Dunnette, ed., *Handbook of Industrial and Organizational Psychology* (pp. 609–50). 1st ed. Chicago: Rand-McNally.

12. Telenson, P.A., R.A. Alexander, and G.V. Barrett. 1983. "Scoring the Biographical Information Blank: A Comparison of Three Weighting Techniques." *Applied Psychological Measurement* 7: 73–80.

13. Kaak, S.R., H.S. Feild, W.F. Giles, and D.R. Norris. 1998. "The Weighted Application Blank: A Cost Effective Tool That Can Reduce Employee Turnover." *Cornell Hotel and Restaurant Administration Quarterly* 39: 18.

14. Lee, R., and J.M. Booth. 1974. "A Utility Analysis of a Weighted Application Blank Designed to Predict Turnover for Clerical Employees." *Journal of Applied Psychology* 59: 516–18.

15. Ghiselli, E.E. 1966. *The Validity of Occupational Aptitude Tests*. New York: Wiley.

16. Rothstein, H.R., F.L. Schmidt, F.W. Erwin, W.A. Owens, and C.P. Sparks. 1990. "Biographical Data in Employment Selection: Can Validities Be Made Generalizable?" *Journal of Applied Psychology* 75: 175–84.

17. Mitchell, T.W., and R.J. Klimoski. 1982. "Is It Rational to Be Empirical? A Test of Methods for Scoring Biographical Data." *Journal of Applied Psychology* 67: 411–18.

18. Guion, R.M. 1998. *Assessment, Measurement and Prediction for Personnel Decisions*. London: Lawrence Erlbaum Associates.

19. England, G.W. 1971. *Development and Use of Weighted Application Blanks*. Rev. ed. Minneapolis: University of Minnesota Industrial Relations Center.

20. Gatewood, R.D., H.S. Field, and B. Murray. 2008. *Human Resource Selection*. 6th ed. Mason, Ohio: Thomson/South-Western.

21. Owens, W.A., and L.F. Schoenfeldt. 1979. "Toward a Classification of Persons." *Journal of Applied Psychology* 65: 569–607.

22. Owens, W.A. 1976.

23. McManus, M.A., and M.L. Kelly. 1999. "Personality Measures and Biodata: Evidence Regarding Their Incremental Predictive Value in the Life Insurance Industry." *Personnel Psychology* 52(1): 137–48.

24. Owens, W.A. 1976.

25. Klimoski, R.J. 1993. "Predictor Constructs and Their Measurement." In N. Schmitt and W.C. Borman, eds., *Personnel Selection in Organizations* (pp. 99–134). San Francisco: Jossey-Bass.

26. Owens, W.A. 1976.

27. Rynes, S.L. 1993. "Who's Selecting Whom? Effects of Selection Practices on Applicant Attitudes and Behavior." In N. Schmitt et al., eds., *Personnel Selection in Organizations* (pp. 240–74). San Francisco: Jossey-Bass.

28. Sisco, H., and R.R. Reilly. 2007. "Development and Validation of a Biodata Inventory as an Alternative Method to Measurement of the Five Factor Model of Personality." *The Social Science Journal* 44: 383–89.

29. Mael, F.A., M. Connerley, and R.A. Morath. 1996. "None of Your Business: Parameters of Biodata Invasiveness." *Personnel Psychology* 49: 613–50.

30. Saks, A.M., J.D. Leck, and D.M. Saunders. 1995.

31. Mael, F.A., M. Connerley, and R.A. Morath. 1996.

32. Elkins, T.J., and J.S. Phillips. 2000. "Job Context, Selection Decision Outcome, and Perceived Fairness of Selection Tests: Biodata as an Illustrative Case." *Journal of Applied Psychology* 85(3): 479–84.

33. Elkins, T.J., and J.S. Phillips. 2000.

34. Mael, F.A., M. Connerley, and R.A. Morath. 1996.

35. *State of Connecticut v. Teal.* 457 U.S. 440, 1981.

36. Mitchell, T.W. 1994. "The Utility of Biodata." In G.S. Stokes, M.D. Mumford, and W.A. Owens, eds., *Biodata Handbook* (pp. 492–93). Palo Alto, CA: CPP Books.

37. McManus, M.A., and M.L. Kelly. 2006. "Personality Measures and Biodata: Evidence Regarding Their Incremental Predictive Value in the Life Insurance Industry." *Personnel Psychology* 52(1): 137–48.

38. McManus, M.A., and S.H. Brown. 2006. "Adjusting Sales Results Measures for Use as Criteria." *Personnel Psychology* 48(2): 391–400.

39. Cascio, W.F. 1975. "Accuracy of Verifiable Biographical Information Blank Response." *Journal of Applied Psychology* 60: 767–69.

40. Lefkowitz, J., M.I. Gebbia, T. Balsam, and L. Dunn. 1999. "Dimensions of Biodata Items and Their Relationships to Item Validity." *Journal of Occupational and Organizational Psychology* 7(3): 331–50.

41. Lefkowitz, J., M.I. Gebbia, T. Balsam, and L. Dunn. 1999.

42. Goldstein, I.L. 1971. "The Application Blank: How Honest Are the Responses?" *Journal of Applied Psychology* 71: 3–8.

43. "Looking at Job Applications? Remember—It's Hirer Beware." 1994. *Canadian Banker* 101 (May/June): 10.

44. Donovan, J.J., S.A. Dwight, and G.M. Hurtz. 2003. "An Assessment of the Prevalence, Severity and Verifiability of Entry-Level Applicant Faking Using the Randomized Response Technique." *Human Performance* 16(1): 81–106.

45. Donovan, J.J., S.A. Dwight, and G.M. Hurtz. 2003.

46. Hammer, E.G., and L.S. Kleiman. 1988. "Getting to Know You." *Personnel Administrator* 34: 86–92.

47. Terpstra, D.E., and E.J. Rozell. 1993. "The Relationship of Staffing Practices to Organizational Level Measures of Performance." *Personnel Psychology* 46: 27–48.

48. Thacker, J.W., and R.J. Cattaneo. 1992. "Survey of Personnel Practices in Canadian Organizations: A Summary Report to Respondents." Working Paper W92-04, Faculty of Business, University of Windsor.

49. Carlson, K.D., S.E. Scullen, F.L. Schmidt, H. Rothstein, and F. Erwin. 1999. "Generalizable Biographical Data Validity Can Be Achieved without Multi-Organizational Development and Keying." *Personnel Psychology* 52(3): 731–55.

50. Harvey-Cook, J.E., and R.J. Taffler. 2000. "Biodata in Professional Entry-Level Selection: Statistical Scoring of Common Format Applications." *Journal of Occupational and Organizational Psychology* 73(1): 631–64.

51. Harvey-Cook, J.E., and R.J. Taffler. 2000.

52. Dalessio, A.T., M.M. Crosby, and M.A. McManus. 1996. "Stability of Biodata Keys and Dimensions across English-Speaking Countries: A Test of the Cross-Situational Hypothesis." *Journal of Business and Psychology* 10(3): 289–96.

53. Asher, J.J. 1972. "The Biographical Item: Can It Be Improved?" *Personnel Psychology* 25: 251–69.

54. Ghiselli, E.E. 1966.

55. Hunter, J.E., and R.F. Hunter. 1984. "Validity and Utility of Alternative Predictors of Job Performance." *Psychological Bulletin* 96: 72–98.

56. Maertz, C.P., Jr. 1999. "Biographical Predictors of Turnover among Mexican Workers: An Empirical Study." *International Journal of Management* 16(1): 112–19.

57. Rothstein, H.R., F.L. Schmidt, F.W. Erwin, W.A. Owens, and C.P. Sparks. 1990.

58. Stokes, G.S., and L.A. Cooper. 1994. "Selection Using Biodata: Old Notions Revisited." In G.S. Stokes, M.D. Mumford, and W.A. Owens, eds., *Biodata Handbook* (pp. 103–38). Mahwah, NJ: Erlbaum.

59. Vinchur, A.J., J.S. Schippmann, F.S. Switzer, III, and P.L. Roth. 1998. "A Meta-Analytic Review of Predictors of Job Performance for Salespeople." *Journal of Applied Psychology* 83(4): 586–97.

60. Rothstein, H.R., F.L. Schmidt, F.W. Erwin, W.A. Owens, and C.P. Sparks. 1990.

61. Reilly, R.R., and G.T. Chao. 1982. "Validity and Fairness of Some Alternative Employee Selection Procedures." *Personnel Psychology* 35: 1–62.

62. Hunter, J.E., and R.F. Hunter. 1984.

63. Schmitt, N., R.Z. Gooding, R.A. Noe, and M. Kirsch. 1984. "Meta-Analysis of Validity Studies Published between 1964 and 1982 and the Investigation of Study Characteristics." *Personnel Psychology* 37: 407–22.

64. Asher, J.J., and J.A. Sciarrino. 1974. "Realistic Work Samples Tests: A Review." *Personnel Psychology* 27: 519–23.

65. Hunter, J.E., and R.F. Hunter. 1984.

66. Van Iddekinge, C.H., C.E. Eidson, Jr., J.D. Kudisch, and A.M. Goldblatt. 2003. "A Biodata Inventory Administered Via Interactive Voice Response (IVR) Technology: Predictive Validity, Utility and Subgroup Differences." *Journal of Business and Psychology* 18(2): 145–56.

67. England, G.W. 1971.

68. Thoms, P., R. McMasters, M.R. Roberts, and D.A. Dombkowski. 1999. "Résumé Characteristics as Predictors of an Invitation to Interview." *Journal of Business and Psychology* 13(3): 339–56.

69. Knouse, S.B. 1994. "Impressions of the Résumé: The Effects of Applicant Education, Experience and Impression Management." *Journal of Business and Psychology* 9: 33–45.

70. Knouse, S.B., R.A. Giacalone, and P. Hinda. 1988. "Impression Management in the Résumé and Its Cover Letter." *Journal of Business and Psychology* 3: 242–49.

71. Cole, M.S., H.S. Feild, and W.F. Giles. 2003. "What Can We Uncover about Applicants Based on Their Résumés? A Field Study." *Applied HRM Research* 8(2): 51–62.

72. Cole, M.S., H.S. Feild, and W. Giles. 2003. "Using Recruiter Assessments of Applicants' Résumé Content to Predict Applicant Mental Ability and Big Five Personality Dimensions." *International Journal of Selection and Assessment* 11(1): 78–88.

73. Cole, M.S., H.S. Feild, W.F. Giles, and S.G. Harris. 2004. "Job Type and Recruiters' Inferences of Applicant Personality Drawn from Résumé Biodata: Their Relationships with Hiring Recommendations." *International Journal of Selection and Assessment* 12(4): 363–67.

74. "Cover Letters Still Play a Valuable Role in Hiring Decisions, Survey Suggests." 2008. *CNW Group* (June 26): http://www.newswire.ca/en/releases/archive/June2008/26/c8058.html.

75. "Cover Letters Still Play a Valuable Role in Hiring Decisions, Survey Suggests." 2008. *CNW Group* (June 26): http://www.newswire.ca/en/releases/archive/June2008/26/c8058.html.

76. Wein, J. 1994. "Rifling through Résumés." *Incentive* 168: 96–97.

77. Bachler, C. 1995. "Résumé Fraud: Lies, Omissions, and Exaggerations." *Personnel Journal*, 74(6): 50.

78. Pedrasa, I.M.J.P. 2008. "Filipino Video Résumés Set to Go Global." *BusinessWorld* (January 4): 1.

79. Cywinski, M. 2008 (August). "Video Résumés: To Use or Not to Use?" *CanadaOne*: http://www.canadaone.com/ezine/briefs.html?StoryID=08Aug16_1.

80. Roberts, J. 2006. "Didn't Get the Job? Could It Be Your Name?" *The Globe and Mail* (August 2): C1.

81. "InterviewStudio." 2007. *HRMagazine* 52(11): 113.

82. Akkad, O.E. 2006. "Confronting the Fib No Easy Task for Boards." *The Globe and Mail* (February 20): B12.

83. Luciw, R. 2007. "In Résumés, Cutting the Fiction Reduces the Friction: It's Okay to Sell Your Strengths (and Admit Your Weaknesses), But Recruiters Prefer You Back It Up with Hard Facts." *The Globe and Mail* (February 24): B10.

84. Donovan, J.J., S.A. Dwight, and Hurtz, G.M. 2003.

85. Hunter, J.E., and R.F. Hunter. 1984.

86. Catano, V.M., and A. Bissonnette. 2003. *Selection Practices and Organizational Performance.* Paper presented at the annual meeting of the Administrative Sciences Association of Canada, Halifax, NS.

87. Rowe, P.M., M.C. Williams, and A.L. Day. 1994. "Selection Procedures in North America." *International Journal of Selection and Assessment* 2: 74–79.

88. Rowe, P.M., M.C. Williams, and A.L. Day. 1994.

89. Gati, I. 1989. "Person–Environment Fit Research: Problems and Prospects." *Journal of Vocational Behavior* 35: 181–93.

90. Latham, G.P. 1989. "The Reliability, Validity, and Practicality of the Situational Interview." In R.W. Eder and G.R. Ferris, eds., *The Employment Interview: Theory, Research, and Practice* (pp. 169–82). Newbury Park, CA: Sage.

91. Janz, T. 1982. "Initial Comparisons of Patterned Behaviour Description Interviews versus Unstructured Interviews." *Journal of Applied Psychology* 67: 577–80.

92. Schwab, D.P., and G.G. Henneman, III. 1969. "Relationship between Interview Structure and Interviewer Reliability in an Employment Situation." *Journal of Applied Psychology* 53: 214–17.

93. Carpenter, R. 1995. "Geek Logic." *Canadian Business* 68: 57–58.

94. Dreher, G.F., and P.R. Sackett. 1983. *Perspectives on Selection and Staffing.* Homewood, IL: Irwin.

95. Webster, E.C. 1982. "The Employment Interview: A Social Judgment Process." Schomberg, ON: S.I.P. Publications.

96. Immen, W. 2006. "Quick Encounters of the Hiring Kind." *The Globe and Mail,* (February 8): C1.

97. Immen, W. 2006.

98. Reiter, H.I., J. Rosenfeld, and L. Giordano. 2004. "Selection of Medical Students at McMaster University: A Quarter Century Later." *McMaster University Medical Journal* 2: 41–45.

99. Rosenfeld, J.M., H.I. Reiter, K. Trinh, and K.W. Eva. 2008. "A Cost-Efficiency Comparison between the Multiple Mini-Interview and Traditional Admissions Interviews." *Advances in Health Sciences Education* 13(1) (Spring): 43–58.

100. Webster, E.C. 1982.

101. Harris, M.M. 1989. "Reconstructing the Employment Interview: A Review of Recent Literature and Suggestions for Future Research." *Personnel Psychology* 42: 691–726.

102. Reiter, H.I., K.W. Eva, J. Rosenfeld, and G.R. Norman. 2007. "Multiple Mini-Interviews Predict Clerkship and Licensing Examination Performance." *Medical Education* 41: 378–384.

103. Rosenfeld, J.M., H.I. Reiter, K. Trinh, and K.W. Eva. 2006. "A Cost Efficiency Comparison between the Multiple Mini-Interview and Traditional Admissions Interviews." *Advances in Health Sciences Education: Theory and Practice.*

104. Leavitt, H. 1992. "Should Companies Be Hesitant to Give Ex-Employees References?" *The Toronto Star* (July 20): C3.

105. Clark, L., and P. Snitzer. 2005. "'Speak No Evil' Is a Risky Policy; Reference Checks on Former Workers Can Be Tricky for Healthcare Employers." *Modern Healthcare* 35: 49.

106. Clark, L., and P. Snitzer. 2005.

107. Hutton, D. 2008. "Job Reference Chill Grows Icier; Employers' Growing Reluctance to Talk about Former Employees Frustrates Both Those Doing the Hiring and Those Trying to Get Hired." *The Globe and Mail* (June 18): C1.

108. Hutton, D. 2008.

109. "The Legalities of Providing a Reference Check on a Former Employee." 2007. *AXIOM International Reference Checking Service*: http://www.axiom-int.com/survey_legalities.htm.

110. Clark, L., and P. Snitzer. 2005.

111. Hutton, D. 2008.

112. Gatewood, R.D., H.S. Feild, and B. Murray. 2008.

113. *Résumé Inaccuracies Common, SHRM Survey Finds*. 2004 (August 31). SHRM press release: www.shrm.org/press.

114. Humber, T. 2003. "Name, Rank and Serial Number." *Canadian Human Rights Reporter* 16(10): G1, G7.

115. Babcock, P. 2003. "Spotting Lies: As a First-Line Defense, HR Can Take Steps to Weed Out Dishonest Applicants." *HR Magazine* 48(10): 46.

116. Mosel, J.N., and H.W. Goheen. 1958. "The Validity of the Employment Recommendation Questionnaire in Personnel Selection: I. Skilled Traders." *Personnel Psychology* 11: 481–90.

117. Mosel, J.N., and H.W. Goheen. 1959. "The Validity of the Employment Recommendation Questionnaire: III. Validity of Different Types of References." *Personnel Psychology* 12: 469–77.

118. Solomon, B. 1998.

119. Kabay, M. 1993. "It Pays to Be Paranoid When You're Hiring." *Computing Canada* (April 26): 21.

120. Hunter, J.E., and R.F. Hunter. 1984.

121. Knouse, S.B. 1983. "The Letter of Recommendation: Specificity and Favorability of Information." *Personnel Psychology* 36: 331–42.

122. McCarthy, J.M., and R.D. Goffin. 2001. "Improving the Validity of Letters of Recommendation: An Investigation of Three Standardized Reference Forms." *Military Psychology* 13(4): 199–222.

123. Quinones, M.A., J.K. Ford, and M.S. Teachout. 1995. "The Experience between Work Experience and Job Performance: A Conceptual and Meta-Analytic Review." *Personnel Psychology* 48: 887–910.

124. Rowe, P.M. 1988. "The Nature of Work Experience." *Canadian Psychology* 29: 109–15.

125. Tesluk, P.E., and R.R. Jacobs. 1998. "Toward an Integrated Model of Work Experience." *Personnel Psychology* 51: 321–55.

126. Ford, J.K., M.A. Quinones, D.J. Sego, and J. Speer-Sorra. 1992. "Factors Affecting the Opportunity to Perform Trained Tasks on the Job." *Personnel Psychology* 45: 511–27.

127. Schmidt, F.L., J.E. Hunter, and A.N. Outerbridge. 1986. "Impact of Job Experience and Ability on Job Knowledge, Work Sample Performance, and Supervisory Ratings of Job Performance." *Journal of Applied Psychology* 71: 432–39.

128. Borman, W.C., M.A. Hanson, S.H. Oppler, E.D. Pulakos, and L.A. Whilte. 1991. "Job Behavior, Performance, and Effectiveness." In M.D. Dunnette and L.M. Hough, eds., *Handbook of Industrial and Organizational Psychology*, Vol. 2 (pp. 271–326). 2nd ed. San Diego: Consulting Psychologists Press.

129. Vance, R.L., M.D. Coovert, R.C. MacCallum, and J.W. Hedge. 1989. "Construct Models of Task Performance." *Journal of Applied Psychology* 74: 447–55.

130. Hunter, J.E., and R.F. Hunter. 1984.

131. Quinones, M.A., J.K. Ford, and M.S. Teachout. 1995.
132. McDaniel, M.A., F.L. Schmidt, and J.E. Hunter. 1988. "Job Experience Correlates of Job Performance." *Journal of Applied Psychology* 73: 327–30.
133. Quinones, M.A., J.K. Ford, and M.S. Teachout. 1995.
134. Winkler, C. 2006. "Job Tryouts Go Virtual: Online Job Simulations Provide Sophisticated Candidate Assessments." *HRMagazine* 51(9): 131–33.
135. Winkler, C. 2006.

Chapter 8

Selection II: Testing

Chapter Learning Objectives

This chapter introduces the use of testing in personnel selection. It presents background material on the technical, ethical, and legal requirements governing the use of employment tests, along with a description of different testing procedures.

After reading this chapter you should:

- have a good understanding of psychological tests and their use in selection;
- be familiar with the professional and legal standards that govern the use of employment tests;
- know the advantages and disadvantages of using some of the more popular selection testing procedures, including personality and ability testing;
- understand the importance and limitations of cognitive ability testing;
- be able to understand the Five-Factor Model of Personality and its relationship to employment testing;
- be aware of controversial testing methods related to honesty or integrity, physical fitness, and drug use;
- appreciate the potential of work samples, simulations, and assessment centres as selection procedures;
- understand how both test validity and test utility can be used to evaluate testing effectiveness; and
- be aware of how job applicants may view the use of different employment tests.

LISTENING TO THE AIRPORT GURU

My name is Aaron. I was the HR director for a large CD retail operation. Tyler, the CEO, said he couldn't understand why we had to spend so much time and money on our selection procedures. He felt that the CD retail business had to hire people in the 19–34 age group, about the same demographic as most of our customers. He wanted us to hire people who knew "music" rather than sales.

He kept showing me all these articles he read on the airplane; you know the ones, where the newest management guru has the quick fix to all your problems (for a small fee). He brought in this one guy he read about to give us a seminar on the best way to hire people. The guru had a method that was guaranteed to work. It involved hiring only those applicants who had a high "developmental quotient." You brought the candidate in, sat the person down in a quiet room, and asked a series of questions about his or her childhood and adolescence.

The guru claimed that most people were stuck in the adolescent stage and your goal was to find candidates who had progressed to the adult level, which was difficult to do since very few people had attained that level. You could hire people who were at the pre-adult stage if you sent them to his training seminar to learn how to advance to the next stage. He trained people to identify a person's "developmental quotient" based on the person's answers to the interview questions.

After the seminar, Tyler pulled me aside and said he wanted to change our selection procedures to the "DQ" method. I laughed and told him what I thought of the procedure. He said I would either implement the "DQ" selection system and a training program to increase "DQ" levels or look for a new job. I knew I should have stood up for what was right and for what I believed in, but I couldn't afford to lose my job at my age with a mortgage to pay. I convinced myself that the new system met the selection standards outlined by my professional association and decided to give it a try.

I now spend most of my time preparing for court and tribunal hearings. Some of our job candidates found out we were only hiring people between 19 and 34 years old. They filed a complaint with the human rights tribunal that we were discriminating against them. We also had another problem with the "DQ" system when some female applicants thought some of the questions about their adolescent experiences were too intimate and suggestive. They filed a sexual harassment suit.

These cases became so costly we had to hire two lawyers to deal with them. We wound up paying these people hundreds of thousands of dollars when our lawyers brought in external consultants who told us there was no way we could legally defend the "DQ" test as a valid and reliable selection instrument. The lawyers told us to cut our losses and settle the suits. Of course, as the HR director, I took the fall for all these problems and was fired by Tyler.

What Do You Know about Employment Tests?

Many of you reading this book will seek work as human resources professionals. You will be responsible for improving the life of your organization or contributing to corporate business functions by implementing HR practices that lead to high performance. Yet, many organizations, like the one headed by Tyler, often fail to adopt practices that research has shown to be effective[1] or continue to use practices for which there is little empirical support.[2] In particular, many organizations lag behind research in their use of employment tests or use tests and procedures that do not meet professional standards.

One reason for this may be that HR practitioners do not have time to keep up with new developments. Rynes, Colbert, and Brown[3] surveyed 5000 HR professionals who were members of the Society for Human Resource Management (SHRM). Each HR professional was asked to make a true-or-false answer to 39 questions from different HR content areas, including staffing, which included personnel selection. How did the HR professionals do? Their average score was 57 percent. How would you have answered the following questions from the survey? If you are not sure, write down your answers anyway so you can review them as we go through this chapter.

1. Despite the popularity of drug testing, there is no clear evidence that applicants who score positive on drug tests are less reliable or productive employees.
2. Although people use many different terms to describe personalities, there are only four basic dimensions of personality as captured by the *Myers-Briggs Type Indicator* (MBTI).
3. Being very intelligent is actually a disadvantage in a low-skilled job.
4. There is very little difference among personality inventories in terms of how well they predict an applicant's job performance.
5. Integrity tests that try to predict whether employees will steal, be absent, or otherwise take advantage of an employer don't work very well in practice because so many people lie on them or fake their answers.
6. Employees of companies that screen job applicants for values have higher performance levels than employees of those that screen for intelligence.
7. On average, conscientiousness is a better predictor of job performance than is intelligence.

Don't feel bad if, after studying this chapter, you find out that some of your answers are wrong, or if you couldn't answer some of the questions. Less than 50 percent of HR professionals answered the questions on HR staffing correctly. Rynes and her colleagues discovered that very few HR professionals took time to read research articles and relied only on professional literature or colleagues for information. We will leave it to you to read the rest of this chapter to find out what the prevailing research suggests as the answers to these questions. Who knows, they may appear on an exam you take one day.

Applicant Testing

Psychological Testing

 **8.1**

We have all been tested at one time or another. You will most likely be tested on your knowledge of this chapter's contents. You may be given a set of questions related to material in this chapter, such as those you just read; based on your answers to those questions, your instructor will assign a number to your test, which reflects your knowledge and understanding of the chapter material. In preparing for the test, you probably read the material, attended lectures, took notes, discussed the material with classmates, went to the library to read material on reserve, and questioned your instructor on it. All of these activities or behaviours should lead to increased understanding of the material. The test you are given is simply a means of obtaining an assessment of the level of your understanding under controlled conditions.

A psychological test is nothing more than a standardized procedure used to obtain an assessment of a person's psychological construct and to describe that construct with the aid of some measurement scale.[4] Psychological testing is one of the oldest and most common methods used to quantify how individuals differ with respect to some variable of interest.

Use of Tests

Psychological tests are used for many different purposes in a variety of settings. In schools, psychological tests may be used to determine levels of academic ability, achievement, or interest. In counselling centres, tests may be used to assist in identifying different strengths and weaknesses of clients and may involve assessment of personality, attitudes, or values. In clinical settings, psychological tests are used to assist a psychologist in making a diagnosis of the suspected difficulty or problem being experienced by the client. In hospital settings, neuropsychological tests are often used to assess different types of brain damage. In business or organizational settings, psychological tests are used to hire people, to classify those selected into the most appropriate positions, to assist in promotion of people, and to identify needs for training. The focus of this chapter will be limited primarily to the use of psychological tests in organizational settings as part of the selection process.

Employment Testing

In most hiring situations, there are more applicants than there are positions to be filled. The employer's goal is to select those candidates who best possess the knowledge, skills, abilities, or other attributes and competencies (KSAOs) that lead to successful job performance. As we discussed in previous chapters, these KSAOs must be related to job performance criteria that have been identified through a job analysis. The employer believes that applicants differ with respect to essential KSAOs and wants to measure these individual differences to meet the goal of hiring the best-qualified people for the job. The central requirement for any selection tests or assessment procedures is that they accurately assess the individual's performance or capacity to perform the essential components of the job in question safely, efficiently, and reliably, without discriminating against protected group members except where the KSAO can be established as a bona fide occupational requirement (BFOR; see Chapter 3).[5]

In Chapter 2, we discussed the process of measurement and quantification of such individual characteristics. If "knowing how to get things done" is important for job success, the employer must be able to measure know-how in a reliable and valid manner that meets the requirements imposed by relevant labour legislation and wins approval from external agencies, such as the Canadian Human Rights Commission (CHRC), which may have jurisdiction over hiring decisions.

Testing Standards

Occasionally in newspapers, magazines, or on the Internet, you may come across an article that asks you to test or rate your career interests, personality, compatibility with a partner, or some other topic. You may be asked to complete a series of multiple-choice questions and, based on your score, you are placed into a particular category that defines your personality type or interest. Rarely, if ever, do these popular tests have any value. They are usually created for the purpose of an article and are mostly for entertainment. The development of a reliable and valid test takes considerable time and effort, which can be undermined by the widespread publication of the test in the popular media. The only tests with any value in terms of hiring decisions are those that meet accepted professional standards for their development and use.

In Chapter 2, we established some fundamental measurement principles. We expect tests to assign numbers to the construct that is being assessed in a *reliable* and *valid* manner. We also expect tests to be *fair and unbiased*, and to have *utility* (see Chapter 10 for a discussion of utility concepts). Psychological tests vary in the degree to which they meet these four standards. These technical or psychometric properties of a psychological test should be established before a test is used as a decision-making tool. The development and construction of a psychological test is a major undertaking, which is governed by several sets of technical guidelines.

Professional Guidelines

The Canadian Psychological Association[6] (CPA) has published *Guidelines for Educational and Psychological Testing.* Its U.S. counterpart is the *Standards for Educational and Psychological Testing,* published by the American Psychological Association in association with two other organizations (see Chapter 2). The *Standards* have been endorsed by the Canadian Society for Industrial and Organizational Psychology (CSIOP) for use in Canada. These documents present the professional consensus on the appropriate procedures for constructing and evaluating tests, for using and administering tests, and for interpreting test results. The *Guidelines* and *Standards* apply to all tests, including those used for personnel selection.

There are also supplementary guidelines that apply specifically to the use of tests as part of the personnel selection process; the most influential of these is the *Principles for the Validation and Use of Personnel Selection Procedures* (http://www.siop.org/_Principles/principlesdefault.aspx), published by the Society for Industrial and Organizational Psychology.[7] Another document, the *Uniform Guidelines on Employee Selection Procedures,*[8] was developed by the U.S. Equal Employment Opportunity Commission, the U.S. Department of Justice, and the U.S. Department of Labor for use in evaluating personnel selection programs that fall under the regulations of the U.S. federal government. The *Uniform Guidelines* have played a prominent role in court challenges that have alleged discrimination in the selection process.

While the U.S.-based *Uniform Guidelines, Standards,* and *Principles for Validation* have no legal standing in Canada, they are often cited as representing best practice and professional consensus; they are used by different provincial and federal agencies in assessing selection programs. Anyone using tests as part of a selection process must be familiar with these professional standards. Running afoul of these standards will jeopardize the defensibility of a selection system before any legal tribunal.

Code of Ethics

In addition to these documents, which regulate the technical aspects of test development and use, are ethical standards, which regulate the behaviour of psychologists using the tests. The CPA's *Canadian Code of Ethics for Psychologists*[9] specifies four principles on which ethical behaviour is based:

1. respect for dignity of persons;
2. responsible caring;
3. integrity in relationships; and
4. responsibility to society.

The ethical standards related to each of these principles apply to all testing carried out by psychologists. These ethical standards cover such issues as confidentiality of test results, informed consent, and the competence of those administering and interpreting the test results. The foremost concern is to protect the welfare and dignity of those being tested. A consumer or client may bring any concerns over a psychologist's use of tests, including selection tests, to appropriate regulatory bodies.

The Certified Human Resources Professional (CHRP) ethical code that applies to human resources practitioners specifies principles similar to those in the CPA code of ethics. Notably, CHRPs must:

- Support, promote, and apply the principles of human rights, equity, dignity, and respect in the workplace, within the profession, and in society as a whole.
- Adhere to any statutory Acts, regulations, or by-laws that relate to the field of human resources management, as well as all civil and criminal laws, regulations, and statutes that apply in one's jurisdiction.
- Not knowingly or otherwise engage in or condone any activity or attempt to circumvent the clear intention of the law.
- Strive to balance organizational and employee needs and interests in the practice of the profession.

Who Can Test?

The availability of standardized tests and computerized scoring and interpretation systems often tempts unqualified people to administer tests and to interpret results from them. Proficiency in psychological testing requires a considerable degree of training and experience. Reputable test publishers require purchasers to establish their expertise in using a test before allowing its purchase. These safeguards help protect the public against misuse of tests and information collected through testing.[10]

The CHRP National Code of Ethics requires human resources professionals to recognize their own limits and to practise within those limits of their competence, culture, and experience in providing services and advice. If a human resources professional wants or needs to provide services in an unfamiliar area, such as the administration and interpretation of employment tests, that person must obtain proper training or guidance from a professional who is qualified in employment testing.

Cautions

Well-designed tests provide information on different aspects of individuals, including their personality, thinking or reasoning ability, and motivation, among many others. The standards described in the preceding section were developed by professional associations to protect the welfare and rights of individuals who are being tested. These rights, which must be respected, include the following:

1. *Informed consent.* Job applicants must be told why they are being tested; they must be informed in clear language that the test results may be provided to the prospective employer and that those results may be used in making employment decisions. Applicants should also be given general information, preferably in advance, about the types of

tests that they will be asked to take, the testing process, the intended use of the test, scoring procedures, testing policy, and procedures for protecting the confidentiality of the test results. The extent of the general information provided should be consistent with any restrictions that are necessary to obtain valid responses and consistently applied to all candidates.

2. *Access to test results.* Whenever possible and feasible, job applicants should receive feedback on their test performance and on any decisions that are based on those tests, unless this right has been waived by the applicant or if it is prohibited by law or court order. This information should be provided in nontechnical language that can be understood by the job applicants. Such feedback must be put into a proper context by explaining the purpose of the test and the results of the test relative to other applicants. Care must be taken in providing this feedback as this information may contain negative implications about the applicant's ability, knowledge, or personality. Care must also be taken to avoid use of labels or terms that may stigmatize the applicant.[11] Providing feedback can create a very stressful situation and is best done by a qualified psychologist or a human resources specialist who is sensitive to the possible consequences of the feedback. As a matter of policy, many organizations do not provide job applicants with feedback about how they did on employment tests.[12]

3. *Privacy and confidentiality.* Job applicants reveal information about themselves during the job selection process, but there is no justification for obtaining any information that is not job-related. Applicants have a right to privacy, so information that is provided by job applicants must be held in confidence. As part of gathering information, whether through application forms, interviews, or tests, job applicants must be informed about how that information will be used and who will have access to it *before* they provide the information. The limits of confidentiality must be explained to the job applicants. Care must be taken to safeguard the use of any information collected during the selection process. This information should be released only to persons with a legitimate, professional interest in the applicant. Failure to respect the applicant's privacy may leave the employing organization open to legal action.

Workplace privacy is a significant and growing issue. Municipal and provincial employees in Ontario have a right of access to and protection of their own personal information, including that obtained through employment testing, under existing freedom-of-information and protection-of-privacy legislation.[13]

Selection of employees requires a balancing act for employers, who must weigh the concerns of job applicants about the fairness of the selection procedures being used, the rights of workers not to have co-workers who will be unproductive or pose a threat of violence to them, and the right of the organization to hire the most qualified personnel within the context of the law and the greater needs of society.[14]

4. *Language and culture.* Job applicants have the right to be tested in a language in which they are fluent. In Chapter 2, we discussed how bias can influence measurements. *Bias* refers to systematic measurement errors that are related to aspects of group membership. Language and culture are two important ways of identifying groups. Canada is both bilingual and multicultural.

There is no guarantee that a test developed in one language or in one culture will produce meaningful results when administered to people from different linguistic or cultural backgrounds. It is not sufficient simply to translate a test into another language. (Recruitment and Selection Today 8.1 illustrates some famous faux pas that occurred through literal translations from one language to another.) The construct that is being measured must be represented in both cultures and the translation must capture the cultural differences as well as language differences. The reliability and validity of the test in the new language must be established. The test must measure the same construct in the new language and culture.

Similarly, administering the test to applicants who do not have good command of the language in which the test is written will also lead to test bias; the test results will be confounded by their language incomprehension. Both the Public Service Commission of Canada's Personnel Psychology Centre (http://www.psc-cfp.gc.ca/ppc-cpp/index-eng.htm) and the Canadian Forces rely on various employment tests in making hiring decisions. Both of these organizations undertake extensive research to ensure that equivalent forms of all testing materials are available in both English and French.

In coming years, test translation will become more of an issue as businesses operate globally in many languages. Employment tests used in one culture cannot be used in others without establishing the

Recruitment and Selection Today 8.1

Translation Faux Pas

- In Chinese, Pepsi's "Come Alive with the Pepsi Generation" became "Pepsi Brings Your Ancestors Back from the Grave."
- American Airlines' "Fly in Leather" campaign for its first-class seats translated into "Fly Naked" in Mexico.
- The Dairy Association's "Got Milk?" campaign became "Are you lactating?" in Spanish.
- Coors' "Turn It Loose" slogan turned into "Suffer from Diarrhea" in Spanish.

- In the United States, a Scandinavian vacuum cleaner manufacturer stated, "Nothing sucks like an Electrolux."
- Gerber regretted selling food in Africa with a picture of a baby on the label, as pictures on labels there represent the container's contents.

Source: Adapted from D.W. Beauvais. 1999. *Just for Grins: Translations*: http://www.langa.com/newsletters/1999/apr-11-99.htm.

validity of the measurement in the new language and cultural environment, a task that is more complex than demonstrating the equivalency of a test in both English and French.

Other Considerations: Disability

Chapter 3 drew attention to the legal and human rights concerns that apply to selection procedures. A disabling condition cannot be used to screen out applicants unless it can be demonstrated that the ability in question is a bona fide occupational requirement. Employers are expected to make reasonable accommodation to meet the needs of employees or applicants with disabilities who meet job requirements. In Canada, the employment of people with disabilities falls under either provincial or federal human rights legislation. In the United States, this situation is covered by the Americans with Disabilities Act of 1990.

Disabling conditions must be considered as part of selection testing. For example, some paper-and-pencil ability tests have time limits; a person with limited mobility of the hands or arms might have difficulty completing the test in the allowed time, leading to an ability score that falls below the level set for the job. It is impossible to state whether the low score is a true reflection of the tested ability rather than a test of the disability. In this case, provision should be made for either using a test that is not time-based or allowing for verbal responses, which are recorded by machine. The guiding principle should be that the test is given to the applicant in a way that accommodates the disability, even at the expense of changing standardized testing procedures. We will explore the issue of accommodation in testing in more detail later in this chapter.

Testing Methods Used in Selection

The first large-scale use of tests to select or classify Canadian employees occurred during World War II. Tests were constructed to screen people for military service and for entry into different training programs (e.g., airplane pilots).[15] Over the years, thousands of Canadians have been tested for a variety of purposes. Unfortunately, many people remain skeptical about the benefits of testing. People often become upset over testing, particularly that done in the schools, and the decisions that are based on test results. These concerns also arise in the use of employment tests. Although it is quite easy to demonstrate the financial benefits that can be gained through the use of employment tests, only about 29 percent of Canadian companies use tests to select employees.[16]

Reliability and Validity Issues

The technical guidelines and professional standards described previously often deter companies from adopting employment tests. Many companies continue to rely on the application form, résumés, references checking, and interviews to select employees. Organizations may falsely believe that these selection procedures are exempt from requirements to demonstrate reliability, validity, and fairness. Human resources managers often justify not using employment tests by noting that the reliability of a test may be affected by items that may be misunderstood, by lack of uniform testing conditions, by variation in instructions, by lack of rapport between a candidate and the test administrator, and by improper test items. But how does this differ from a typical selection interview, where interview questions are misunderstood, where there is lack of uniformity and standardization in interviews, where there is variation in the introduction given to candidates at the start of the interview, where there is often a lack of rapport between the candidate and the interviewer, and where improper questions are often asked?

Using Tests Developed in the United States

There is no need for any organization to develop its own employment tests; unless the KSAOs required for the job are unique, one or more of the over 1000 commercially available tests are likely to be suitable for use in most situations. Usually these tests have well-known psychometric properties that are extensively documented in technical manuals. However, most of these tests have been developed and validated on workers in the United States, thereby raising the question of whether expensive validity studies must be done in Canada before those tests can be properly used to select Canadian workers. Fortunately, validity generalization procedures like those described in Chapter 2 have established that test validities from U.S. workers generalize across the border, lessening the need to re-establish their validity in Canada.[17] Tests that are valid for an occupational category in the United States should also be valid for the same occupational category in Canada.

Just as with any other selection device, the information obtained through tests should not be used in isolation. Any test, no matter how reliable and valid, may still provide inaccurate information about a job candidate. Again, this is no different from any other source used to gather information about a job candidate. In fact, well-designed employment tests will produce fewer errors than other selection procedures. Nonetheless, the information gained from employment tests should be compared with information obtained from other sources, and vice versa. Information obtained from several valid tests and measurements that are evaluating the same construct should converge and lead to accurate decisions about the job candidate.

Choosing a Test

Recruitment and Selection Notebook 8.1 presents some points that should be considered in selecting commercially available employment tests. These points reflect the technical considerations discussed above. Anyone who has the responsibility for choosing employment tests should be knowledgeable about the various standards and technical documents related to the use of tests. Goffin[18] states:

 8.3

> Often, because of flashy promotional materials or charismatic test-hawkers, there is a tendency for HR professionals to choose "the

Points to Consider in Selecting a Test

1. Do a job analysis to determine the knowledge, skills, abilities, or other qualities that have been related to job success.

2. Consult an information resource on testing to identify tests that are relevant to your job needs. Obtain information from several sources including test publishers or developers and human resources consultants knowledgeable about testing.

3. Obtain information on several tests related to what you want to measure. Read through the materials provided by the test developers. Reject out of hand any test for which the publisher or developer presents unclear or incomplete information.

4. Read the technical documentation to become familiar with how and when the test was developed and used. Does the technical documentation provide information on the test's reliability and validity? Does it address the issue of test fairness? Does it include normative data based on sex, age, and ethnicity that are comparable to your intended test takers? Does it include references for independent investigations of the test's psychometric properties? Eliminate from consideration any tests whose documentation does not allow you to answer "yes" to these questions.

5. Read independent evaluations of the tests that you are considering adopting. Does the independent evidence support the claims of the test developers? Is the test valid and reliable? Eliminate those tests that are not supported by this evidence.

6. Examine a specimen set from each of the remaining tests. Most publishers will sell a package that includes a copy of the test, instructions, test manual, answer sheets, and sample score report at a reasonable cost. Are the test format and reading level appropriate for the intended test-takers? Is the test available in languages other than English? Can the test accommodate test-takers with special needs? Is the content of the test appropriate for the intended test-takers? Eliminate those tests that you do not feel are appropriate.

7. Determine the skill level needed to purchase the test, to administer the test, and to interpret test scores correctly. Do you have the appropriate level of expertise? Does someone else in your organization meet the test's requirements? If not, can you contract out for the services of a qualified psychologist or human resources professional who does?

8. Select and use only those tests that are psychometrically sound, that meet the needs of your intended test-takers, and that you have the necessary skills to administer, score, and interpret correctly.

flavor of the month" when it comes to pre-employment tests rather than taking a serious look at what the job really requires. To be useful for hiring purposes, the test should measure attributes that are important for successful performance in the target job.

Information on thousands of psychological tests, including employment tests, can be found on the Internet. One of the best sites is the Buros Center for Testing: http://www.unl.edu/buros. This site presents reviews of an extensive list of tests by experts and information on their reliability and validity. The remainder of this chapter presents an introduction to the wide variety of employment tests used in Canadian organizations. Recruitment and Selection Notebook 8.2 lists some of the more common tests used to select employees. Examples of cognitive ability, personality, and emotional intelligence test items can be found at http://www.queendom.com, although the tests pre-

Examples of Psychological Tests Used to Select Employees

Personality Tests

California Psychological Inventory
Guilford-Zimmerman Temperament Survey
Hogan Personality Inventory
Jackson Personality Inventory
NEO-FFI and NEO-PI-R
Personal Characteristics Inventory (PCI)
Sixteen Personality Factor Questionnaire (16PF)
Work Personality Index (WPI)
Work Profile Questionnaire (WPQ)

Honesty/Integrity Tests

Hogan Personality Inventory–Reliability Scale
Inwald Personality Test
London House Personnel Selection Inventory
PDI Employment Inventory
Reid Report
Stanton Survey

Tests of Emotional Intelligence

Bar-On Emotional Quotient Inventory (EQi)
Emotional Competence Inventory (ECI)
Mayer, Salovey, Caruso Emotional Intelligence Test
   (MSCEIT)
Work Profile Questionnaire–emotional intelligence
   (WPQei)

Vocational Interest Inventories

Jackson Vocational Interest Survey
Kuder Preference and Interest Scales
Occupational Preference Inventory

Self-Directed Search
Strong Interest Inventory
Vocational Preference Inventory

Cognitive Ability Tests

Otis-Lennon Mental Ability Test
Stanford-Binet Intelligence Scale
Watson-Glaser Critical Thinking Appraisal
Wechsler Adult Intelligence Scale (WAIS)
Wonderlic Personnel Test

Aptitude Tests

Comprehensive Ability Battery (CAB)
Differential Aptitude Tests (DAT)
General Aptitude Test Battery (GATB)
Multidimensional Aptitude Battery–II

Psychomotor Tests

General Aptitude Test Battery (GATB)
- Subtest 8—Motor Coordination
- Subtests 9 and 10—Manual Dexterity
- Subtests 11 and 12—Finger Dexterity

O'Connor Tweezer Dexterity Test
Purdue Pegboard Test
Stromberg Dexterity Test

Physical Ability and Sensory/Perceptual Ability Tests

Dynamometer Grip Strength Test
Ishihara Test for Colour Blindness
Visual Skills Test

sented at this site may not meet the psychometric standards we would expect from tests used to make employment decisions.

Ability and Aptitude Tests

As we have seen in earlier chapters, job-related KSAOs, including competencies, play an important role in successful job performance. For example, applicants for the position of electronic repair technician might be expected to have a high degree of finger dexterity (to perform repairs on circuit boards), colour vision (to tell the difference between different wires), and a potential for acquiring knowledge related to electronics (to achieve an understanding of basic circuit theory).

Selection programs seek to predict the degree to which job applicants possess the KSAOs related to the job. Many different tests have been developed to measure specific human abilities and aptitudes. In the case of electronic repair technicians, we would seek to employ those applicants with the highest levels of finger dexterity and colour vision, and the most aptitude for learning electronics.

Ability Tests

Abilities

Enduring, general traits or characteristics on which people differ and which they bring to a work situation.

Abilities are attributes that an applicant brings to the employment situation—the enduring, general traits or characteristics on which people differ. It is of no importance whether an ability has been acquired through experience or inheritance. Abilities are simply general traits that people possess and bring with them to the new work situation. For example, finger dexterity is the ability to carry out quick, coordinated movements of fingers on one or both hands and to grasp, place, or move very small objects.[19]

An ability can underlie performance on a number of specific tasks; finger dexterity might be required to operate a computer keyboard and to assemble electronic components. One keyboard operator may have taken several months of practice to develop the finger dexterity needed to type 100 words per minute; another may have come by that ability naturally. Both have the same ability, regardless of how it was acquired. An ability exists in individuals at the time they first begin to perform a task, whether that task is operating a keyboard or assembling electronic components.

Skill

Refers to an individual's degree of proficiency or competency on a given task, which develops through performing the task.

Skill, on the other hand, refers to an individual's degree of proficiency or competency on a given task, based on both ability and practice, which has developed through performing the task. Two keyboard operators may have the same level of finger dexterity; however, one may have learned to type with hands raised at an inappropriate angle in relation to the keyboard. As a result, the two have different skill levels, or proficiencies, in using a keyboard despite having the same ability. Similarly, a keyboard operator and an electronics assembler might have the same level of finger dexterity but the keyboard operator might be more skilled at word processing than the assembler is at wiring circuit boards. An **aptitude** can be thought of as a specific, narrow ability or skill. Measures or tests of different aptitudes are used to predict whether an individual will do well in future job-related performance that requires the ability or skill being measured.

Aptitude

A specific, narrow ability or skill that may be used to predict job performance.

Based on a test of finger dexterity, a human resources manager might predict that a job applicant has an aptitude for operating a keyboard, or for assembling electronic components. Over the years, Fleishman and his associates[20] have identified 52 distinct human abilities, which can be grouped into four broad categories: cognitive, psychomotor, physical, and sensory/perceptual abilities. Over time, many psychometrically sound tests have been developed to assess these different abilities.

Cognitive Ability Tests

Cognitive abilities are related to intelligence or intellectual ability. These abilities include verbal and numerical ability, reasoning, memory, problem solving, and processing information, among others. The first wide-scale, systematic use of cognitive ability testing took place during World War I, when a group of industrial psychologists developed the U.S. Army Alpha Intelligence Test. This was a paper-and-pencil test that could be efficiently administered to groups of army recruits to determine how those recruits could best be employed. The Army Alpha test sought to measure intellectual or basic mental abilities that were thought to be essential to performing military duties.

Today, an extensive array of paper-and-pencil tests are available to measure specific cognitive abilities. Most likely you have taken one or more of these during your student career. The Public Service Commission's Personnel Psychology Centre uses many different types of tests to evaluate applicants and employees. These include "general competency tests," a form of cognitive ability testing that assesses verbal and quantitative abilities. Sample test questions from the General Competency Test: Level 1 (GCT 1) are available online (go to http://www.psc-cfp.gc.ca/ppc-cpp/index-eng.htm and click on "Practice Tests") and are reprinted in Recruitment and Selection Today 8.2.

Cognitive abilities

Refers to intelligence, general mental ability, or intellectual ability.

Recruitment and Selection Today 8.2

General Competency Test: Level 1

GCT I Sample Questions

The **General Competency Test: Level I** (GCT I) contains three types of questions: understanding written material, solving numerical problems, and drawing logical conclusions.

A sample question of each type is provided below.

Type I - Understanding Written Material

This type of question involves reading a short passage, which is usually in memorandum format, and answering a question about the information in the text.

Question I

Government of Canada MEMORANDUM	Gouvernement du Canada NOTE DE SERVICE
TO: All employees FROM: Manager Please note that the answer sheets currently being used will be replaced with new ones next year. The existing supply of answer sheets should be used from now until the end of the year. It is important that the new sheets are used next year because they will enable the collection of additional information that will be required at this time.	

continued

The main purpose of this memorandum is to:

(1) Indicate the need for new answer sheets.
(2) Notify employees that new answer sheets will replace the existing ones.
(3) Notify employees that the current answer sheets are inadequate.
(4) Indicate the need for additional information.

Type II - Solving Numerical Problems

This type of question involves choosing the correct answer to a practical numerical problem.

Question 2

You are in charge of financial services and must calculate overtime pay for employees in your division. Due to a heavy workload, an employee had to work 35 hours of overtime in two weeks. For 28 of these hours, the employee was paid at one and one-half times the hourly rate. For the remaining hours, the employee was paid at twice the usual hourly pay. The employee's hourly pay is $10. How much overtime money should the employee be paid for the two-week period?

(1) $340   (3) $560
(2) $420   (4) $760

Type III - Drawing Logical Conclusions

In this type of question, the task is to choose the correct answer to a practical problem.

Question 3

One of your duties is the selection and disposal of boxes of obsolete files. According to regulations, ordinary files become obsolete after 24 months, protected files after 36 months, and classified files after 48 months. Which of the following boxes of files can be discarded?

A. A box containing ordinary files dated 26 months ago and classified files dated 34 months ago.
B. A box containing ordinary files dated 38 months ago and protected files dated 28 months ago.

(1) A only
(2) B only
(3) Both A and B
(4) Neither A nor B

Answers

(2)
(3)
(4)

Source: *General Competency Test Level 1: A Practice Test and Guide.* http://www.psc-cfp.gc.ca/ppc-cpp/pract-test-examn-pract/gct1-ecg1-pratc-i-eng.htm. Reproduced with the permission of the Public Service Commission of Canada, October 2008.

More recently, there has been a move away from assessing many individual, specific abilities to a more general cognitive ability assessment. General cognitive ability, or general mental ability (abbreviated g, GCA, or GMA), is thought to be the primary ability among those abilities that make up intellectual capacity. General cognitive ability is believed to promote effective learning, efficient and accurate problem solving, and clear communications. General cognitive ability can be thought of as a manager of other, specific cognitive abilities, similar to a computer's operating system managing software programs. It is essentially the ability to learn.[21] General cognitive ability has been related to successful job performance in many different types of occupations.[22] It is related to how easily people may be trained to perform job tasks, how well they can adjust and solve problems on the job, and how well satisfied they are likely to be with the demands of the job.[23]

A test of general cognitive ability can provide a quick and efficient basis for selecting applicants for more extensive, and costly, testing. The National Football League (NFL) has given the *Wonderlic Personnel Test*, a test of general cognitive ability, to potential recruits since 1968. According to Charles Wonderlic, president of the testing company, "The test measures a person's ability to learn, solve problems and adapt to new situations."[24] Wonderlic test scores, along with information on the candidate's physical prowess and ability, are available to each NFL team for use in drafting players (i.e., making selection decisions). The Wonderlic has a maximum possible score of 50. The average score for factory workers is 17, for lawyers, 30, and for NFL prospects, 21, which is the overall average for the test. A low score on the test does not eliminate an NFL prospect but red-flags him as someone who may not be able to meet the demands of a game that is becoming ever more cognitively complex. The Wonderlic is used as part of a battery of tests to develop a psychological profile on each candidate. Recruitment and Selection Today 8.3 presents a case where an organization was actually looking for applicants with scores *below* a specific level on the Wonderlic!

Measures of general cognitive ability, which have an average validity coefficient of 0.50, are among the most powerful predictors of success in training and job performance for a variety of occupational groups, ranging from retail clerks to skilled workers to managers and executives.[25,26] Cognitive ability predicts job performance much better as the complexity of the job increases. Its validity ranges from about 0.20 in the simplest jobs to about 0.80 in the most complex.[27] Schmidt and Hunter[28] established, through meta-analyses, that the validity of a cognitive ability test was 0.23 for unskilled jobs, 0.40 for semiskilled jobs, and 0.58 for managerial/professional positions.

For all jobs, regardless of complexity or skill level, cognitive ability can be considered to be a primary predictor of job performance.[29] Schmidt[30] presents a comprehensive review of the major meta-analytic studies that conclusively demonstrates that general cognitive ability measures, as well as specific abilities tests, predict both training and job performance across many different occupations. Salgado, Anderson, Moscoso, Bertua, and de Fruyt[31] noted that previous conclusions about the potency of general cognitive ability were based on data gathered in North America. They examined data from 10 European Community countries that varied in terms of language, culture, religion, and social values. Their meta-analyses replicated the North American findings. One notable difference was that general cognitive ability was an even stronger predictor of job performance in the European countries.

What? I'm Too Smart for This Job?

When job applicants are asked to take a cognitive ability test, there is an underlying assumption that those with the best scores will qualify for a job offer. Job applicants do their best to achieve a high score on the test. What if the company or organization is actually looking for applicants whose cognitive ability falls *below* a specific level? The company may feel that people with high cognitive ability will become bored in the job, dissatisfied with the work, and soon leave. What are the likely consequences of adopting such a procedure?

The Boston Globe reported a case in which the Southeastern Connecticut Law Enforcement Consortium rejected a police force applicant, Robert Jordan, who scored 33 out of 50 points on the *Wonderlic Personnel Test*.* Jordan was disqualified from the competition along with 62 other high-scoring applicants. The Wonderlic test manual recommends that applicants for police officer positions have a score in the range of 20–27. The New London, Connecticut, police chief was quoted as saying, "Police work, believe it or not, is a boring job. What happens if you get certain people who can't accept being involved in that sort of occupation is it becomes very frustrating. Either the day they come in they want to be chief of police, or they become very frustrated and leave."

Jordan went to Federal Court but lost his case. After reviewing evidence about the validity of the Wonderlic and job analysis requirements for "police officer," the judge ruled that it was reasonable to reject people who

scored higher than the requirements set out for the position. Jordan may have had the last laugh, as the report quotes him as saying, "I made them the laughingstock of the country. Jay Leno made up this great song. The theme music was 'Dumb cops, dumb cops, whatcha gonna do, with a low IQ.' People can't get over it that they want to cultivate this kind of department."

Laughter and questions of legality aside, there is an important consideration here for practitioners. Is it ethical to seek applicants with average or less-than-average intelligence when applicants expect that doing well on a test will lead to a job offer? It may be, provided there is strong job analysis data to support that position. But then another problem arises: Applicants taking employment tests are to be fully informed of the purpose of the test and how it is going to be used. The applicants would have to be told that, contrary to expectations, those with high scores would be disqualified.[†] In that circumstance, how many applicants are likely to do well on the test? Furthermore, while a high IQ might predict high turnover in certain jobs, it also strongly predicts job performance: Higher cognitive ability, higher performance. Turnover may not be the most appropriate criterion in cases like this. So, maybe Jay Leno was right.

Sources: * E. Barry. 1999. "Smarter Than the Average Cop." *The Boston Globe* (September 10): B1. [†] R.L. Lowman, ed. 1998. *The Ethical Practice of Psychology in Organizations*. Bowling Green, OH: Society for Industrial and Organizational Psychology.

Similarly, Bertua, Anderson, and Salgado[32] reviewed 283 studies done in the United Kingdom that used cognitive ability as a predictor of job and training performance. Their results were very similar to those of Salgado et al. in that validities ranged from 0.50 to 0.60, with higher validities associated with more complex occupations. In the context of globalization, the Salgado et al. and Bertua, Anderson, and Salgado results suggest that cognitive ability transcends language and culture and can be used as a valid personnel selection test in many countries of the world.

The growing demands on workers to learn new tasks quickly as they move among assignments and encounter ever-changing technology will not diminish. Accordingly, the power of general cognitive ability measures to predict job success is likely to strengthen. Cognitive ability testing is extremely cost-effective and has withstood court challenges both in Canada and the United States, although it tends to be one of the more frequently challenged selection tools in U.S. courts.[33–35]

Murphy, Cronin, and Tan[36] surveyed members of the Society for Industrial and Organizational Psychology with respect to their views on testing for general cognitive ability. There was consensus among the SIOP members that cognitive ability tests are valid and fair and that they provide good but incomplete information, with a substantial number of respondents holding that different abilities are needed for different jobs. With very few exceptions, then, a measure of general cognitive ability can be used for selection in almost all occupations; however, it may need to be supplemented by other measures to make the most accurate assessments. Adding another valid predictor of performance to cognitive ability almost always provides a significant increase in the predictive validity associated with the combined measures.[37]

One issue must be given serious consideration before adopting a measure of general cognitive ability as part of a selection program, however. Cognitive ability tests have disparate impact on blacks compared to whites, with differences that are three to five times larger than other predictors; the disparate impact on Hispanics compared to whites is smaller but still substantial.[38] Indeed, Murphy, Cronin, and Tan[39] found that the SIOP members in their study could be grouped into two classes, based on their survey responses. One group believed that societal concerns about the consequences of cognitive ability testing on diversity took precedence, while the second group's responses reflected the unique status of g as an excellent predictor of job performance.

Outtz[40] offered a way out of this controversy by suggesting that the adverse impact of cognitive ability tests for blacks could be eliminated by replacing their use with structured interviews, biodata, and personality measures that have lower validities than cognitive ability tests but also considerably less adverse impact on blacks. Including measures with low adverse impact in a battery of selection tests can improve the validity based solely on g, while at the same time reducing adverse impact.[41, 42] This is a worthwhile strategy to consider when an applicant pool is likely to include members of different racial groups.

Another strategy that can be used is to first determine the nature of the job and then determine if verbal ability is a bona fide occupational requirement. Most measures of cognitive ability are verbal measures in that they require a fair degree of reading ability. If verbal ability is not essential, it may be appropriate to base employment decisions on nonverbal measurements of cognitive ability. Vanderpool and Catano[43] demonstrated that members of First Nations living in remote areas of Manitoba performed as well as predominantly white recruits undergoing military training on nonverbal cognitive tests such as *Raven's Standard Progressive Matrices*, but at a much lower level on verbal measures such as the *Wonderlic Personnel Test*.

If enrollment decisions for the Canadian Forces and subsequent occupational assignments were made solely on the basis of the verbal cognitive tests, adverse impact most likely would occur: First Nations members might not qualify for military enrollment or, if they did, they might be assigned to the lowest-status jobs. The study suggested that nonverbal tests of cognitive ability could be substituted for verbal cognitive ability tests with little loss in predictive ability for occupations involving a high degree of spatial ability.

Multiple Aptitude Test Batteries

Over the years, a number a specific cognitive abilities have been identified; for example, verbal and numerical ability and inductive and deductive reasoning (see Fleishmann and Reilly[44] for a comprehensive list). Psychometrically sound tests exist for these specific cognitive abilities. The question is whether assessing specific abilities provides improvement on predictions made from measurements of general mental ability. One line of research suggests that specific abilities add only marginally to predictions based on g.[45] On the other hand, specific ability tests do provide significant, although small, increases in predictive validity from those made solely on the basis of general mental ability.[46] As well, tests of specific abilities such as verbal and numerical ability and reasoning provide validity coefficients in the same range as g.[47] Proponents of g suggest that the validities of specific ability tests occur because they and g are measuring the same construct.[48]

There are different theories as to why measures of specific abilities may improve on predictions based on overall g. Carroll[49] proposed a hierarchical model in which g, at the apex, is the most general level of cognitive ability and underlies performance across a broad spectrum of cognitively demanding tasks. The next level down contains broad abilities that apply to performance on clusters of tasks. These broad abilities include broad visual perception, broad auditory perception, and cognitive speediness, among others. At the lowest level in the hierarchy are more specific abilities that are more homogeneous and narrower than those at the broad ability level. For example, spatial relations, sound discrimination, and perceptual speed, respectively, would relate to the noted broad abilities.

Job applicants who do well on g may not possess the narrower abilities related to successful job or task performance. If identifiable abilities are essential for successful performance, then inclusion of predictors related to those abilities in selection systems should lead to improved validity. In two recent studies, Catano and his colleagues[50,51] showed that a measure of a specific ability improved validity significantly beyond a measure of cognitive ability (the *Canadian Forces Aptitude Test* discussed below). In the first study, a measure of manual dexterity improved prediction of training success for military jobs that belonged to a mechanical occupational family that required the same underlying psychomotor ability.[52]

In the second study, a measure of auditory attention improved the prediction of training success for an operator occupational family that included jobs such as combat information officer and acoustic sonar operator. In both cases, the increases in validity brought about by measuring the specific abilities were of practical importance.

The Canadian Forces use cognitive ability testing as part of its selection process. Potential recruits into the Forces complete the *Canadian Forces Aptitude Test* (CFAT), which validly predicts performance in a wide range of military occupations. (For examples and practice questions, go to http://www.publicserviceprep.com/public/full_pkg_canadianforces.aspx. Click on "Sample Questions" at the bottom of the page to work through a sample aptitude test based on the CFAT.) The CFAT is an example of a multiple aptitude test battery. Tests like the CFAT include subtests related to specific cognitive abilities; as well, they may include tests of noncognitive abilities. The CFAT includes subtests related to problem solving, spatial ability, and verbal skills. It is a valid predictor for entry into the Canadian Forces, although as Catano and colleagues have shown, predictive validity of the CFAT for specific trades training can be improved by adding a measure of the specific ability underlying the trades.

The U.S. military also administers a test battery primarily based on cognitive abilities, the Armed Services Vocational Aptitude Battery (ASVAB), to over a million high school students each year, as well as to all applicants. (For sample questions, see http://www.baseops.net/militarybooks/asvab.) The ASVAB is the best overall predictor of U.S. military services applicant performance, particularly for performance on technical jobs.[53] The ASVAB is similar to the General Aptitude Test Battery (GATB), which is used as part of the selection process for jobs throughout the United States federal government.

Tests such as the GATB and the ASVAB take up to three hours to complete. The question that a practitioner must answer is whether the small increase in validity that testing specific abilities provides over g is worth the time and money spent in testing the specific abilities, particularly since the measurements of the specific abilities tend to be highly correlated with measurements of g.[54] Although the majority of evidence supports the view that "all you need is g,"[55] more recent research based on thorough job analyses that identified underlying abilities suggests that adding measures of specific abilities may be worthwhile.[56,57]

Drasgow[58] notes several methodological flaws in Ree and Carretta's[59] work that limit their "all you need is g" conclusion; among these is the argument that the ASVAB is not a reliable and valid measure of the lower-order, broad and specific abilities presented in Carroll's model.[60] Drasgow states that it is "premature to conclude unequivocally that there is 'not much more than g.'"[61] He points out that while g predicts task performance, the validity of predicting overall performance could be improved by searching for noncognitive predictors of other types of job behaviour. Murphy, Cronin, and Tan reported that most of the professionals in their survey believed that an assessment of different abilities was needed to predict success in different jobs.[62]

Practical Intelligence/Job Knowledge

Sternberg and his associates[63,64] distinguish practical intelligence from intellectual or academic ability and argue that while tests of cognitive ability predict intellectual performance, those tests are not as successful as they should be in predicting job success. To obtain that success, measures of cognitive ability need to be supplemented by measures of practical intelligence. The distinction between academic intelligence and **practical intelligence** is similar to the difference between declarative knowledge and procedural knowledge described in Chapter 5. Practical knowledge is related to knowing how to get things done without the help of others. It can be characterized as "street smarts" or "common sense" in contrast to academic intelligence or "book smarts."[65]

Consider two department managers competing to increase their respective budgets. Both have the intellectual ability to put together a rational proposal based on facts and figures to support their positions. The successful manager knows that the proposal alone will not succeed; the successful manager will know how to craft the report to demonstrate that the budget increase will also accomplish the goals of the decision makers and will know whom to lobby in the organization for support of the proposal. The successful manager knows how to get things done.

Tacit knowledge is an important component of practical knowledge or procedural knowledge that is used to solve practical, everyday problems. It is knowledge that is derived from experience when learning is not the primary objective. It is knowledge about how to perform tasks in different situations. It is knowledge that an individual uses to help attain specific goals.[66] Tacit knowledge is typically measured through situational judgment tests (SJTs, which are discussed later in this chapter) that consist of a series of questions that specify problems or situations with several response options, one of which is thought to reflect the best way to handle the problem.[67]

Tacit knowledge or practical intelligence has predicted performance of bank managers, salespeople, and military personnel.[68–70] Other evidence, however, does not provide support for practical intelligence as a predictor of job success. Taub[71] compared general mental ability and practical intelligence as predictors of real-world success among a sample of university students. Taub found that intellectual and practical intelligence were, indeed, independent constructs, but he could not find any evidence to support the proposition that practical intelligence was a better predictor of real-world success than general mental ability. Lobsenz[72] found results similar to Taub's when he used a measurement of practical intelligence to predict job performance of entry-level telecommunications managers. Practical intelligence did not improve on the predictions that could be made from general mental ability.

McDaniel and Whetzel[73] make the point that measurements of practical intelligence are SJTs that measure multiple constructs, mostly g and personality, and have a long history of predicting job performance in personnel selection. They argue that SJTs do not measure a general factor as suggested by Sternberg, whether that factor is called practical intelligence or something else. While practical intelligence remains an intriguing concept, it is premature to use only measurements of practical intelligence to make workplace decisions about job applicants or employees. Adding a measure of tacit intelligence to a measure of cognitive ability may increase the overall validity of

Practical intelligence

Knowing how to get things done without the help of others.

Tacit knowledge

Knowledge that is derived from experience when learning is not the primary objective.

the prediction being made, because SJTs improve on predictions of job performance made solely from *g*, not because there is such a thing as practical intelligence.[74]

A concept related to practical intelligence or tacit knowledge is **job knowledge**. In fact, Schmidt and Hunter[75] argue that practical intelligence is a narrow, specialized case of job knowledge, although Sternberg argues that unlike job knowledge, which is simply declarative knowledge, practical knowledge is broader in that it includes procedural knowledge.[76] Job knowledge tests examine the degree to which job applicants or employees are knowledgeable about issues or procedures that are deemed essential to successful job performance—in other words, whether they know how to do the job. Members of many professions must submit to an examination of their knowledge related to important professional practices and procedures before they are allowed entry into the profession. To practise law, a law school graduate must first have served a form of apprenticeship (articling) to gain knowledge and experience about legal procedures and then have passed a written "bar exam," which is a test of legal knowledge and procedures.

Job knowledge tests have validities that average 0.45 with job performance. These types of tests tend to have higher validity when used to select people for high-complexity jobs. Job knowledge tests are more effective when they are job-specific, that is, when a unique knowledge test is developed for each occupation or profession.[77]

Job knowledge

The degree to which a job applicant or employee is knowledgeable about issues or procedures that are essential for successful job performance.

Emotional Intelligence

Recently, the media, the business press, and Oprah Winfrey have discovered **emotional intelligence**. Daniel Goleman popularized this term in two books—*Emotional Intelligence*[78] and *Working with Emotional Intelligence*.[79] He defines emotional intelligence (EI) as:

> a set of abilities which include self-control, zeal and persistence, and the ability to motivate oneself.

He expresses this as the ability to "persist in the face of frustration; to control impulse and delay gratification, to regulate one's moods and keep distress from swamping the ability to think, to empathize and to hope."[80]

Olive[81] quotes Goleman as saying, "In top management posts, emotional intelligence abilities like initiative and self-confidence or collaboration matter twice as much as IQ. And the higher you go in the organization, the more EQ [emotional intelligence] matters. For the top leaders, it's about 85% of what characterizes the star performer." This is an alluring, although controversial, concept that has led consulting companies (e.g., the Hay Group—http://www.haygroup.com/TL) to offer services for identifying and selecting individuals with high levels of EI. Is there empirical support for Goleman's position? Are there measures of emotional intelligence that can validly predict job success?

The short answer to these questions is that there is scant evidence to justify the use of EI as part of a selection program.[82–84] Most of the evidence that

Emotional intelligence

The ability to perceive accurately, appraise, and express emotion.

does exist consists of opinion, anecdote, case studies, and unpublished proprietary surveys of test publishers.[85] There are two primary reasons for this conclusion. First, there is lack of clarity about what constitutes EI. Goleman based his ideas on the work of Salovey and Mayer,[86] who proposed that emotional intelligence represents a group of abilities that are distinct from the traditional verbal–propositional/spatial–performance dimensions of intelligence. Mayer and Salovey later defined EI as:

> the ability to perceive accurately, appraise and express emotion; the ability to access and/or generate feelings when they facilitate thought; the ability to understand emotions and emotional knowledge; and the ability to regulate emotions to promote emotional and intellectual growth.[87]

Goleman's[88] and Mayer and Salovey's[89] definitions are not the same. The version popularized by Goleman views emotional intelligence as a set of traits, instead of abilities. As well, people working in this area have a tendency to change the definition of EI to suit their purposes. There is also disagreement about whether emotional intelligence is more an inherent potential, or whether it is a set of learned "abilities," "competencies," or "skills." Others have argued that components of EI, as defined by Goleman, are simply aspects of the Big Five personality dimensions[90] (which we will discuss later in this chapter). This lack of agreement makes it difficult to know what is really meant by the construct and to identify it as a job requirement.

The second major impediment to using EI in selection systems is the lack of measurements that can provide us with valid inferences about the construct. At present, there are four measurements of EI (see Recruitment and Selection Notebook 8.2 on page 357); two of these, the *Bar-On Emotional Quotient Inventory* (EQi)[91] and the *Mayer, Salovey, Caruso Emotional Intelligence Test* (MSCEIT)[92] (see http://www.emotionaliq.com), appear to be the most frequently used measures. Trait based, Bar-On's EQi is the oldest of these; it has been in development the longest and is arguably the most commonly used measurement of EQ.

Many of the factors that EQi measures are not included in either Goleman's or Mayer and Salovey's conceptions of EQ, nor are they very different from traditional personality factors. Newsome, Day, and Catano,[93] in fact, showed that there were moderate to high correlations between the EQi subscales and the "Big Five" personality measurements that are described later in this chapter (see pages 392–94). They reported that the EQi did not predict academic success, whereas a Big Five factor, conscientiousness, did. The EQi did not improve on any predictions about success that could be made from measurements of cognitive ability and personality, lending support to Polednik and Greig's[94] position that a personality measure may be a more effective predictor of organizational performance.

These findings were recently confirmed by Grubb and McDaniel,[95] who showed that there was considerable overlap between the EQi measure and the Big Five personality variables, casting doubt on the concept of EI when operationalized by the EQi measure. They viewed the EQi as an aggregate of the Big Five measures. In addition, their study showed that the EQi was highly fakable and that individuals could raise their scores on the measure considerably.

Whether the newer measurements of EQ, which are based more closely on either Mayer and Salovey's or Goleman's conceptions of EQ, have more success remains to be determined. Day and Carroll[96] examined whether the MSCEIT, an ability-based measurement of EI, predicted work-related tasks on both an individual and group basis. Only the Emotional Perception scale correlated with individual task performance ($r = 0.17$). None of the other MSCEIT scales predicted individual performance or individual citizenship behaviour; as well, none of the scales, including Emotional Perception, predicted group performance on a decision-making task.

After examining measurements of EI, Davies, Stankov, and Roberts[97] concluded that "as presently postulated, little remains of emotional intelligence that is unique and psychometrically sound." More recently, Conte[98] reached much the same conclusion—that serious concerns remained with respect to the four prominent EI measurements he evaluated, although ability-based measurements appeared to be the most promising. Ashkanasy and Daus,[99] on the other hand, argue that emotional intelligence is an individual difference variable in organizational behaviour related to the way employees perceive, understand, and manage their emotions in the workplace.

On the whole, there are inadequate data to justify incorporating EI into a selection system, despite the claims of the popular press and test publishers who advocate the use of EI tests for personnel selection on the grounds that research shows a strong correlation between EI and job performance.[100] There is little, if any, published evidence that supports using EI as a decision-making tool in organizational settings. Additional research needs to be done on the EI construct; foremost is the need to come to an agreement on a definition of EI. Research to date suggests that there is evidence to support the construct validity of an ability-based definition of EI,[101] while trait-based definitions overlap considerably with personality.[102,103] EI, as an ability-based concept, remains promising, as emotions and moods may be better predictors of specific, short-term workplace behaviours than more stable personality traits.[104] Perhaps the last word on this topic is best left to Mayer and his associates:[105] "The applied use of EI tests must proceed with great caution" (p. 104).

Psychomotor Ability Tests

Psychomotor abilities involve controlled muscle movements that are necessary to complete a task. Examples of psychomotor abilities include finger dexterity, multi-limb coordination, reaction time, arm–hand steadiness, and manual dexterity. Many tasks, from simple to complex, require coordinated movements for their success. Psychomotor abilities are often overlooked in selecting people for jobs. Consider a drummer who must independently move all four limbs and exercise hand–wrist coordination, all in a controlled and coordinated fashion; imagine an orchestra whose drummer had an extensive knowledge of music theory but very little psychomotor ability. While a test of

Psychomotor abilities

Traits or characteristics that involve the control of muscle movements.

cognitive ability might predict ability to learn to read and understand music, it would not predict the level of motor coordination.

Tests of psychomotor ability tend to be very different from cognitive ability tests. They generally require the applicant to perform some standardized task on a testing apparatus that involves the psychomotor ability in question. Cognitive ability tests, on the other hand, are generally paper-and-pencil tests. For example, the *Purdue Pegboard Test*, which measures finger dexterity, requires applicants to insert as many pegs as possible into a pegboard in a given time.

This test has good predictive validity for many industrial jobs, including watch-making and electronics assembly. Canadian dental schools also use tests of finger and manual dexterity as part of their selection process; all applicants are required to carve a tooth from a block of soap, which is subsequently judged by a panel of dentists. The *General Aptitude Test Battery* (GATB) also includes tests that involve apparatus that validly measure psychomotor ability in addition to cognitive and perceptual aptitudes. The Manual Dexterity and Finger Dexterity scales of the GATB are among those that Fleishman and Reilly list as suitable measurements of those abilities.[106]

Although psychomotor tests can be quite successful in predicting performance in a number of jobs,[107–109] they are not as popular as cognitive tests. Psychomotor tests involve individual testing on a specialized piece of equipment, and require more time and expense to administer than paper-and-pencil cognitive tests. Nonetheless, they can improve predictions that are based only on cognitive ability. Johnston and Catano[110] showed that the addition of psychomotor measures from the GATB significantly improved predictions of training success for mechanical jobs in the Canadian Forces by 5 percent when added to a cognitive ability measure.

Physical and Sensory/Perceptual Ability Tests

Physical abilities

Traits or characteristics that involve the use or application of muscle force over varying periods of time, either alone or in conjunction with an ability to maintain balance or gross body coordination.

Physical abilities are those characteristics involved in the physical performance of a job or task. These abilities generally involve the use or application of muscle force over varying periods of time, either alone or in conjunction with an ability to maintain balance or gross body coordination. Physical abilities include both static and dynamic strength, body flexibility, balance, and stamina. Physical requirements for occupational tasks generally fall into three broad physical ability categories: strength, endurance, and quality of movement.[111]

Sensory/perceptual abilities

Traits or characteristics that involve different aspects of vision and audition, as well as the other senses.

Sensory/perceptual abilities involve different aspects of vision and audition. These abilities include near and far vision, colour discrimination, sound localization, and speech recognition, among others.[112] Although they focus on different sets of abilities, physical abilities and sensory/perceptual abilities are very similar in their relationship to job performance and in how they are assessed.

The performance of many jobs or tasks may require the worker to possess one or more physical or sensory/perceptual abilities. A firefighter may need the strength to carry a body out of a burning building; a pilot may need adequate near and far vision to fly a plane; a soldier may need the strength and stamina to carry 100 kg of equipment for a long period of time and still be ready for combat; a construction worker may need strength to lift material and balance to keep from falling off a roof. People who possess greater amounts of these sensory/perceptual abilities perform better in jobs where such abilities play an important role.[113] Physical tests of strength and endurance are routinely used in selecting police officer applicants and other protective services personnel such as firefighters.[114] As part of its comprehensive selection procedures, the Royal Canadian Mounted Police tests all applicants for physical ability.

Statistics from the National Institute of Occupational Safety and Health in the United States indicate that workers are three times more likely to be injured while performing jobs for which they have not demonstrated the required strength capabilities. Although medical and physical fitness exams (which are discussed later in this chapter) provide a measure of wellness, they do not give sufficient indication of whether the candidate can perform the task requirements safely. Thus, physical ability testing can aid employers in selecting workers who are capable of performing strenuous tasks, with such selections leading to a reduction in accidents, injuries, and associated costs, as well as potential increases in productivity.[115]

Tests of sensory/perceptual abilities generally require the use of specialized tests or equipment that have been designed to assess each sensory or perceptual ability. Almost everyone has had his or her vision examined through the use of a Snellen Chart, which contains letters of various sizes. This test assesses an individual's far-vision ability. Similarly, many people have experienced a test of their hearing sensitivity when they are asked to recognize a series of tones, which are presented at different levels of intensity and pitches to either or both ears through a headset.

Tests of physical ability are quite varied but involve physical activity on the part of the applicant. Only a few physical ability tests require equipment. For example, a hand dynamometer is used to measure static strength. The hand dynamometer resembles the handgrips used in most gyms. The applicant squeezes the grips with full strength and the resultant force is measured by an attached scale. Pull-ups or push-ups are used to measure dynamic strength, sit-ups are used to assess body trunk strength, while 1500-metre runs, step tests, and treadmill tests are used to measure stamina and endurance.

The performance of the applicants on these measures must be related to normative data, which compare the physical performance on the test with that obtained from actual job occupants. It is reasonable to expect applicants to run 1500 metres in under six minutes if 90 percent of all army recruits meet that performance standard; it would be unreasonable to select only those applicants for the army who could run the 1500 metres in under four minutes. The selection would be based on performance standards higher than those in force.

Establishing cut-off scores on physical tests often leads to litigation, with unsuccessful applicants challenging the appropriateness of the scores that were chosen. This was precisely the situation that led to the Supreme Court's *Meiorin* decision we discussed in Chapter 3, in which an employed forest firefighter lost her job because she failed to complete a 2.5-km run in the required time, even though she had passed the other physical ability tests. The Court upheld a labour arbitrator's decision to reinstate the dismissed firefighter. It held that the established cut-off had not taken into account differences in aerobic capacity between men and women and that most women could not raise their aerobic capacity to the required level even with training. The Court found that the employer had not shown that the cut-off adopted by the employer was reasonably necessary to identify individuals who could perform in a satisfactory manner as firefighters. Neither did the employer demonstrate that accommodating women would cause undue hardship.[116]

In some cases, physical standards, rather than physical ability or sensory/perceptual ability tests, are used for selection purposes. A police department may require all applicants to meet certain height and weight requirements and to have uncorrected 20/20 vision. The physical standards are being used as a substitute for actual physical testing. It is assumed that people who fall within the specified range will have the physical abilities required for successful job performance.

It is often very difficult to justify that the physical standards in use meet legitimate job requirements. Indeed, many physical standards were set in the past to exclude members of certain groups, particularly women. When physical standards are set in such an arbitrary fashion, they are open to challenge before human rights tribunals, with the employer subject to severe penalties. It is reasonable to set physical requirements for jobs as long as those standards are job-related and nondiscriminatory. The Supreme Court, in its decision involving the aerobic standard for firefighters, upheld this position and laid out a series of important questions that must be answered in establishing physical or sensory/perceptual standards (see Chapter 3, Recruitment and Selection Notebook 3.5 on page 97).

Physical Fitness and Medical Examinations

 8.4

Many employers routinely administer physical fitness tests as part of the hiring process. The intent of these physical fitness tests is not to identify job-related physical abilities, but rather to screen out unhealthy or unfit employees who may pose a liability to the employer. The employer is concerned that placing physically unfit employees in jobs that require some degree of physical effort may lead to injury or illness, or that the work will be carried out in an unsafe manner. From the employer's view, hiring physically unfit workers means lost productivity, replacement costs, and legal damages from co-workers and customers who have been injured through their actions.

The intent of physical fitness tests is to ensure that an applicant meets minimum standards of health to cope with the physical demands of the job. Canadian federal regulations also require physical or medical testing of applicants for certain dangerous occupations (e.g., deep-sea diver), or for jobs that may bring them into contact with dangerous chemical substances such as lead or asbestos. In addition to identifying any health problems, the examinations provide baseline data for comparison of any job-related changes in the applicant's health that may be covered through Workers' Compensation or other insurance programs.

When Should Physical/Medical Exams Be Given?

Fitness testing or physical or medical examinations should be administered only after the applicant has been given an offer of employment, which is made conditional on the applicant's passing the test or exam. The physical or medical exam is generally the last step in the selection process. The employer must demonstrate that the health or fitness requirement is related to carrying out the job in question safely, reliably, and efficiently. Physical fitness testing is no different from any other assessment procedure and must meet the same technical standards. In Canada, various human rights Acts require that medical or physical examinations of job candidates be job-related as established through a job analysis.

People with Disabilities

Requiring physical examinations before any offer of employment is made raises issues of privacy and also leaves the prospective employer open to charges of discrimination. This last concern is a major issue in hiring people who may have a disability. Canada was the first country to include equality rights for persons with mental or physical disabilities in its Constitution. Section 15.1 of the Canadian Charter of Rights and Freedoms provides for equal protection and equal benefit of the law without discrimination based on mental or physical disability. Every human rights Act in Canada now includes protection against discrimination on the grounds of disability or handicap.

In the United States, the Americans with Disabilities Act of 1990 prevents employers from excluding applicants who have disabilities that are not job-related solely on the grounds of that disability. The Act further requires employers to make accommodations in the workplace for people with disabilities. In Canada, the duty to accommodate people with disabilities in the workplace is much stronger. After the *Meiorin* decision, which we discussed in Chapter 3, there is a legal requirement for employers to work proactively, to the point of undue hardship, to eliminate policies, work rules, standards, or practices that discriminate against groups or individuals on the basis of physical or mental disability or handicap (there is no legal distinction between the terms "disability" and "handicap"). An employer could not refuse to hire an applicant who was the best computer programmer simply because the programmer used a wheelchair and the employer had no provision for such disabilities in the workplace. The employer would be required to make suitable accommodations.

The only exception would be if the employer could establish that the mobility of the employee was a bona fide occupational requirement under the stringent test laid out in the *Meiorin* decision. The legal precedent established in *Meiorin* has been reinforced through many decisions rendered by human rights tribunals and the judiciary since then. The *Meiorin* decision's criteria for establishing a bona fide occupational requirement was presented in Chapter 3, Recruitment and Selection Notebook 3.5. The Canadian Human Rights Commission's statement on the duty to accommodate can be found at http://www.chrc-ccdp.ca/pdf/dta_faq_en.pdf. The Treasury Board Secretariat, which is the employer for the federal government, also has policies on the accommodation of persons with disabilities, which can be found at http://www.tbs-sct.gc.ca/pol/doc-eng.aspx?id=12541.

HIV and AIDS Testing

Employers are becoming increasingly sensitive to hiring individuals who have acquired immune deficiency syndrome (AIDS) or the human immunodeficiency virus (HIV). The current Canadian Human Rights Commission (CHRC) policy, adopted in 1996, states, "The Commission will not accept being free from HIV/AIDS as a bona fide occupational requirement (BFOR) or a bona fide justification (BFJ) unless it can be proven that such a requirement is essential to the safe, efficient and reliable performance of the essential functions of a job or is a justified requirement for receiving programs or services."[117] The CHRC cited policy statements of the Canadian Medical Association in support of its position and believes that "in the employment setting, medical testing should occur only where determination of the condition being tested for is necessary for the safe, efficient and reliable performance of the essential components of the job." The CHRC does not support pre- or post-employment testing for HIV. Decisions from the Canadian Human Rights Tribunal with respect to HIV/AIDS complaints can be found at http://www.chrt-tcdp.gc.ca.

Genetic Testing

Genetic testing

The testing or monitoring of genetic material to determine a genetic propensity or susceptibility to illness resulting from various workplace chemicals or substances.

The Health Law Institute at the University of Alberta reported that 24 percent of genetic specialists believed employers should have access to an employee's confidential medical records to determine whether the employee is likely to develop a genetic disease that might be costly to the employer.[118] Undoubtedly, many employers agree. **Genetic testing** is a controversial issue that proposes that job applicants be screened or monitored for genetic propensity or susceptibility to illness resulting from various workplace chemicals or substances. Genetic monitoring is used to detect exposure to workplace toxins or as an alert to workplace hazards. Genetic screening is used to detect hereditary disease or susceptibility to workplace toxins. The genetic screen could be used as a pre-employment test to reduce the employer's risk.[119] For example, applicants who have an inherited sensitivity to lead would not be hired for work in a lead battery plant.

Genetic screening raises many ethical and legal considerations.[120] MacDonald and Williams-Jones[121] argue that it is morally problematic to require employees to submit to genetic testing, as this would be an invasion of privacy and subject employees to a range of poorly understood tests. They propose that it is permissible to offer employees, on a voluntary basis, the opportunity for genetic testing only when certain conditions are met (see Recruitment and Selection Notebook 8.3). They believe that no company should rush into genetic testing without considerable forethought because of the associated ethical problems. On the other hand, MacDonald and Williams-Jones argue that in some cases the employer has an obligation to offer genetic testing to its employees when the testing may be *beneficial* to the employees. In addition to meeting the requirements specified in Recruitment and Selection Notebook 8.3, the results of the genetic testing, the costs of which are reasonable, could influence employees' decisions to stay in their current positions.

The Human Genome Project, a $4 billion international effort to map all genetic material, has the potential to have a profound effect on how workers and their employers look at health hazards, privacy, and medical information. In the United States, where most health-care programs are privately funded by employers, there have been reports that applicants are being denied employment on the grounds that they are genetically more likely to develop cancer or environmentally related illnesses. In response to these concerns, the U.S. government amended the Americans with Disabilities Act to define genetic predisposition as a disability and to prohibit discrimination on the basis of genetic information. Over half of U.S. states have followed suit in banning the use of genetic information in making workplace decisions. There is less incentive for employers to do genetic screening in Canada to exclude potential employees with certain genetic predispositions because of publicly funded health care in Canada.[122]

Recruitment and Selection Notebook 8.3

Requirements That Must Be Met Before Offering Voluntary Genetic Testing to Employees

1. A genetic test is available that is highly specific and sensitive and has acceptably low false-positive and false-negative rates.

2. Tests must be carried out by an independent lab, with the results given directly to the worker by a genetic counsellor on a confidential basis and revealed to the employer only by the employee.

3. Pre-test and post-test genetic counselling must be provided to the employees at the employer's expense.

4. The test must not focus on a gene that is predominantly associated with an identifiable and historically disadvantaged group.

5. Where relevant, the employer must guarantee continued access to group insurance regardless of the test outcome.

6. The employer must ensure that those employees who disclose that they have tested positive will retain a reasonable degree of job security.

Additional sources on the ethics of genetic testing can be found at http://www.genethics.ca.

Source: Adapted from C. MacDonald and B. Williams-Jones. 2002. "Ethics and Genetics: Susceptibility Testing in the Workplace." *Journal of Business Ethics* 35: 235–41. Copyright Kluwer Academic Publishers Group, Feb. 2002. With the kind permission of Kluwer Academic Publishers.

At present, there is no ban on using genetic information to make employment decisions in Canada and it is probable that some use has occurred. It is very likely, however, that any workplace discrimination on the basis of genetic information would be excluded under existing provisions of the Charter of Rights and the various provincial human rights Acts. A genetic predisposition would likely be considered a disability that would have to be reasonably accommodated by an employer.

The Need for Accommodation

Canadian employers cannot discriminate on the basis of a medical, genetic, or physical condition unless that condition poses a serious and demonstrable impediment to the conduct of the work or poses serious threats to the health and safety of people. Employers have an obligation to accommodate workers with medical or physical conditions on an *individual* basis. As stated by the Supreme Court of Canada in its *Meiorin* decision, "The legislatures have determined that the standards governing the performance of work should be designed to reflect all members of society, in so far as this is reasonably possible." The Court reinforced the need for accommodation by noting:

> Courts and tribunals should be sensitive to the various ways in which individual capabilities may be accommodated. Apart from individual testing to determine whether the person has the aptitude or qualification that is necessary to perform the work, the possibility that there may be different ways to perform the job while still accomplishing the employer's legitimate work-related purpose should be considered in appropriate cases. The skills, capabilities and potential contributions of the individual claimant and others like him or her must be respected as much as possible. Employers, courts and tribunals should be innovative yet practical when considering how this may best be done in particular circumstances.

Drug and Alcohol Testing

Inevitably, societal changes find their way into the workplace. One of the most profound changes in North American society has been the increased use of drugs as a recreational activity that may carry over into the workplace. Employers often believe that workplace drug and alcohol use is an added expense through costs associated with employee accidents, absenteeism, turnover, and tardiness. Additionally, there may be costs associated with reduced product quality and productivity on the part of employees who use drugs and alcohol in the workplace. In some cases, drug or alcohol use by employees while working may result in threats to the safety of the public and co-workers. In the United States, where many workers receive health insurance through their employer, employers may face the escalating costs of health-care insurance due to the presence of a significant number of drug users.

For these reasons, many employers, with support from both their employees and the public, believe that they are justified in screening job applicants for drug and alcohol use. The screening programs generally apply to all employees and job applicants and not just those in safety-sensitive positions. The intent of pre-employment alcohol and drug testing programs is to scare off any individual who may have a substance abuse problem from applying for a position with the company.

Are these concerns justified? The empirical evidence in support of alcohol and drug testing is far from clear. The relationship between drug use and turnover is relatively small, with correlations ranging from 0.04 to 0.08. However, in a longitudinal study, employees who tested positive for drug use had a 59 percent higher absenteeism rate and a 47 percent higher involuntary turnover rate than those who tested negative.[123] While there are some links between drug and alcohol use and accidents and disciplinary measures,[124] the magnitude of the relationship is probably smaller than people have assumed. Self-reported drug use on the job does appear to be related to how workers behave in the workplace and interact with their co-workers, including antagonistic behaviours such as arguing with co-workers. In almost every workplace there is some expression of deviant behaviour that is not related to substance abuse. When that general deviant behaviour is taken into account, the relationship between substance abuse and job performance becomes insignificant.[125]

Notwithstanding the empirical evidence, workplace drug and alcohol testing programs have become quite common in the United States. The Americans with Disabilities Act (ADA) stipulates that pre-employment alcohol testing is a medical examination and may be required only after a conditional offer of employment has been made and in accordance with ADA regulations on pre-employment physicals. However, it allows drug tests to be performed before a conditional offer is made provided that the test:

1. accurately identifies only the use of illegal drugs;
2. is not given in conjunction with a pre-employment physical; and
3. does not require the applicant to disclose information about prescription drug use, unless a positive test result may be explained by use of a prescription drug.

Drug Testing in Canadian Organizations

Random or mandatory drug testing by Canadian companies is not common. Only 1.4 percent of nearly 25 000 employees who participated in a 1999 Statistics Canada survey reported that they received a pre-employment drug test; however, this figure grew significantly to 2.4 percent in the 2003 survey.[126] Based on recent Canadian court decisions, these percentages are not likely to increase. Canadian courts have taken the position that random drug testing, on its face, is discriminatory and must meet the standards of the *Meiorin* decision to qualify as a bona fide occupational requirement. Courts have ruled that random drug testing can meet the *Meiorin* standards for a BFOR when implemented in certain safety-sensitive positions, that is, in positions where incapacity due to drug or alcohol impairment could result in direct and significant risk of injury to the employees, others, or the environment.

Court and tribunal decisions limit drug and alcohol screening to the narrowest circumstances, where a direct link can be established with respect to job performance or to the safety and health of people. Even then, substance abuse on the part of employees is considered a disability that must be accommodated. The effect of these court decisions is to make drug and alcohol testing impractical in most work situations.

Canadian workers support the limitation of drug and alcohol testing in the workplace. Seijts, Skarlicki, and Gilliland[127] compared the reactions of Canadian and American truck drivers to workplace testing programs. The Canadian drivers perceived the testing as being less fair than their American counterparts did. Canadians were more inclined to file official protests over the implementation of drug and alcohol programs. This last finding is certainly supported by the large number of drug- and alcohol-related testing cases that have gone before various courts and tribunals in Canada.

Following the *Meiorin* decision, in the limited circumstances where drug and alcohol testing may be permissible, the primary obligation of the employer is to accommodate those employees to the point of undue hardship. The accommodation procedures should include provisions for the employee to undergo treatment or rehabilitation. Policies that allow for the automatic dismissal of employees who test positive, their reassignment, or imposition of impossible or inflexible reinstatement provisions will not meet accommodation standards. However, if the health or safety risks to workers or members of the public are so serious that they outweigh the benefits of providing accommodation to an individual with a drug or alcohol problem, accommodation may be waived.

The difference in Canadian and U.S. drug and alcohol testing policies leads to problems for some industries that operate in both countries, most notably cross-border trucking and bus services. In these cases, not being banned from driving in the United States because of testing positive for alcohol or drugs may be a bona fide occupational requirement for companies that drive exclusively or predominantly between Canada and the United States. The company still has the obligation to show that continuing the employment of a banned driver would constitute an undue hardship. Under Canadian regulations, the company would still have the obligation to accommodate the banned employee through alternative employment with the company, or reassigning a driver to Canada-only routes. These policies have the most impact on the truck or bus drivers themselves.

Work Samples and Simulation Tests

In Chapter 5, we discussed two types of testing that were used to develop criterion measures of work performance: work samples and simulations. Both of these procedures are more commonly used as part of the selection process. They tend to be used to assess skills and competencies that are less amenable to traditional cognitive ability and personality testing. For example, written communication skills are best assessed by obtaining a sample of the candidate's writing; oral communication skills are best assessed by watching the candidate give an oral presentation; leadership and influence within teams are best assessed by observing the candidate participate in a simulated unstructured group situation.

Work samples and simulations require the job candidate to produce behaviours related to job performance under controlled conditions that approximate those found in the real job. The candidate is not asked to perform the real job for several reasons. Actual job performance may be affected by many factors other than the applicant's proficiency or aptitude for the job; these factors could affect candidates differentially, so that two applicants with the same proficiency might perform differently. Placing the applicant in the job may also be extremely disruptive, costly, and time-consuming, if not outright dangerous in some situations.

The major difference between work samples and simulations is the degree of their approximation of the real work situation. The major difference between both of these tests and a job knowledge test is that work samples and simulations rely on the reproduction of job-related behaviours, whereas written responses to a job knowledge test are used to make inferences about the applicant's potential to perform required job behaviours.

Work sample tests include major tasks taken from the job under consideration; these tasks are organized into an assignment, which the applicant is asked to complete. The work sample and the scoring of an applicant's performance are standardized, allowing for comparisons of skill or aptitude across candidates. Work samples include both motor and verbal behaviours.[128] Motor work samples require the applicant to physically manipulate machinery or tools; verbal work samples require the applicant to solve problems that involve communication or interpersonal skills.

For example, a secretary's job might include using a computer and related software to type letters and reports, to manage the office budget, to track purchases, to send data files electronically to other people, together with operating the phone and voice-mail systems, scheduling appointments, and receiving people who visit the office. A work sample test given to applicants for this position might include both a motor work sample, using a computer to type and electronically transmit a standardized letter, and a verbal work sample, dealing with a message from the boss that asks the secretary to reschedule several important appointments to allow the boss to keep a dental appointment.

The work sample test would not seek to include every aspect of the job but only those deemed to be the most important. The work sample test could be given to the candidate in the actual place of employment or in an off-site setting. Regardless of where the testing takes place, it would be carried out using standardized instructions, conditions, and equipment. The results of the work sample test tell how well the applicant performed on the work sample tasks, but this is only an estimate, or prediction, of actual job performance.

Recall our discussion of typical versus maximum performance in Chapter 5; work sample performance is clearly a case of maximum performance, where the applicant's motivation may be quite different from that exhibited through typical, day-to-day job performance. Like any test, the

Work samples and simulations

Testing procedures that require job candidates to produce behaviours related to job performance under controlled conditions that approximate those found in the job.

validity of a work sample test must be established as part of the selection procedure; however, work sample tests, if developed properly, will predict job performance in a reliable and valid manner.[129] Because they incorporate aspects of the job into selection, work samples have the potential to attain relatively high levels of validity (mean validity = 0.54; see Table 8.3 on pages 403–404). At the same time, however, work samples may require expenditures on expensive equipment and personnel to administer the test to each applicant individually. As is the case with simulations, these costs may be more than offset by the increased benefits of improved selection.

Simulations, like work sample tests, attempt to duplicate salient features of the job under consideration. Candidates perform a set of designated tasks and are given an objective score based on their performance. The score is used to predict aptitude or proficiency for job performance. Unlike work samples, the tasks and the setting in which they are carried out represent less of an approximation of the actual job. That is, the simulation asks the candidate to carry out critical job tasks in a more artificial environment than work sample testing.

The most distinguishing feature of a simulation is its fidelity, the degree to which it represents the real environment. Simulations can range from those with lower fidelity (e.g., a computer simulation of an air traffic controller's function: http://www.atc-sim.com) to those with higher fidelity (e.g., a flight simulator that highly resembles a cockpit to predict pilot behaviour). High-fidelity simulations can be quite expensive, but in some cases, there may be no alternative. The simulation allows a type of hands-on performance in an environment that provides substantial safety and cost benefits compared with allowing the applicant to perform in the actual job. While a computer-controlled flight simulator may cost several million dollars to develop and construct, it is far preferable to having prospective pilots demonstrate their flying proficiency in an actual aircraft where a mistake can be deadly, as well as much more costly.

High-fidelity computer-assisted flight simulators are normally used as part of training programs by Air Canada and other Canadian airlines. The Canadian Forces, however, is one of the few organizations to use a simulator in selecting candidates for flight school; performance on the high-fidelity simulator is a much better predictor of the flying success of future pilots than a battery of cognitive and psychomotor tests.[130] Generally, the savings from reductions in training failures and training time more than offset the initial cost of the simulator.

Situational exercises

Assess aptitude or proficiency in performing important job tasks by using tasks that are abstract and less realistic than those performed on the actual job.

Situational exercises are a form of work sample testing used in selecting managers or professionals. Situational exercises attempt to assess aptitude or proficiency in performing important job tasks, but do so by using tasks that are more abstract and less realistic than those performed on the job. To a large extent, situational exercises are really a form of low-fidelity simulation. The situational exercise involves the types of skills that a manager or professional may be called on to use in the actual job.

Situational exercises have been designed to assess problem-solving ability, leadership potential, and communication skills. For example, at the women's prison in Kitchener, Ontario, a professional actor was hired to play the part of an inmate to assess a candidate's handling of difficult interpersonal situations.[131]

Situational judgment tests (SJTs), also known as *job situation exercises*, are a special type of situational exercise designed to measure an applicant's judgment in workplace or professional situations. They are normally paper-and-pencil tests that ask job candidates how they would respond in different workplace situations.[132,133] However, a variety of video-based SJTs have been developed for use in several occupations.[134–136] The situations are developed through interviews with subject-matter experts about critical incidents they have observed in their workplace. The critical incident technique, described in Chapter 4, is used to gather this information. The information is then transformed into items that constitute the SJT.

The number of items on a test may vary. Each situational question includes several response alternatives from which an applicant is asked to choose one. Generally, the candidate is asked to identify the "best" response that could be made in the situation; that is, what one "should do" in a situation. What constitutes the "best" course of action? Generally, after the questions have been developed, they are presented to a second panel of subject-matter experts, who identify what, in their collective judgment, constitutes the best approach to solving the problem. Recruitment and Selection Today 8.4 presents a sample item that might be found on an SJT given to candidates for a managerial position.

Situational judgment test

Type of situational exercise designed to measure an applicant's judgment in workplace or professional situations.

Recruitment and Selection Today 8.4

A Sample Situational Judgment Test Item

You are the new supervisor of a 22-member department. The department is organized into two working groups of 10 members, plus a group leader. You have been on the job for less than a month but members from one working group have been dropping by your office to complain about their leader, Jane. They claim that she has been absent, on average, almost two days a week for the last three months and is not there to provide advice and help when they need it. Even when she is physically present, they claim that she is "not there." As a result, they believe that their own work is suffering. They demand that you take action to ensure that their group leader is performing her job.

Of the following options, which is the best course of action to take?

A. Inform Jane of the complaints made against her and encourage her to meet with her work group to resolve the problems between them.

B. Call Jane to a meeting and inform her that you have reviewed her absence record and that she has been missing two days a week for the last three months. Tell her that this must stop immediately and that any further missed time must be accompanied by a doctor's medical excuse or else she will be suspended.

C. Consult with your boss on how to handle the problem. Find out if Jane is "well-connected" to minimize any problems for you in case you have to take action against her.

D. Review Jane's absence record to verify her work group's claims. Review her absence and performance record prior to the recent poor record of absence. Once you have completed the information, call Jane to a meeting, lay out your concerns, and try to determine the causes for her poor attendance. Help formulate a plan to help her overcome the obstacles to her attendance.

On an SJT, candidates could also be asked what they "would do" in the same situations. Ployhart and Erhart[137] showed that asking candidates to make "should do" or "would do" responses in SJTs alters both the reliability and validity of the test. They found that "should do" instructions produced outcomes with lower variability but also with lower reliabilities and criterion-related validities than "would do" instructions. However, one limitation of their study was that the SJT consisted of only five items developed for use with student samples, and the results may not apply to selecting employees in actual work situations. Nonetheless, the instructions used as part of the SJT must be carefully considered and match the purpose for which the test is being used.

On the whole, SJTs are very good predictors of job performance. McDaniel, Morgeson, Finnegan, Campion, and Braverman[138] reported results from a meta-analysis that placed their validity coefficient in the population at 0.34 for predicting job performance. SJTs' correlation with cognitive ability, $r = 0.36$, suggests that they are tapping into some aspect of general mental ability, which one would expect to see in a test of judgment. However, as Chan and Schmitt[139] showed when working with 164 civil service employees, SJTs measure a stable individual difference attribute that is distinct from cognitive ability and personality.

Chan and Schmitt also demonstrated that SJTs were not only a very good measure of overall job performance but also predicted both task and contextual performance. Their SJT was based on "task statement and work-related competencies derived from the job analysis"[140] and most likely included items relevant to both task and contextual performance.

Drasgow uses the results from the McDaniel et al. meta-analysis to distinguish between SJTs that are highly correlated with cognitive ability and those that are lowly correlated.[141,142] He proposes that "high-g" SJTs primarily predict task performance, while "low-g" SJTs may primarily predict contextual behaviour. SJTs appear to be a very promising assessment method.

Leaderless group discussion

A simulation exercise designed to assess leadership, organizational, and communication skills.

The two most prominent situational exercises are the leaderless group discussion and the in-basket test. In a **leaderless group discussion**, a group of candidates for a managerial position might be asked to talk about or develop a position or statement on a job-related topic. In the leaderless group discussion used by IBM, candidates must advocate the promotion of a staff member. In a leaderless group discussion, the group is not provided with any rules on how to conduct the discussion, nor is any structure imposed on the group. The primary purpose of the exercise is to see which of the candidates emerges as a leader by influencing other members of the group. Each candidate is assessed on a number of factors by a panel of judges; these factors might include communication and organizational skills, interpersonal skills, and leadership behaviour.

In-basket test

A simulation exercise designed to assess organizational and problem-solving skills.

The **in-basket test** seeks to assess the applicant's organizational and problem-solving skills. The Public Service Commission of Canada uses an in-basket test in selecting applicants for certain managerial and professional positions in the federal civil service (http://www.psc-cfp.gc.ca/ppc-cpp/psc-tests-cfp/in-basket-827-eng.htm). As part of an in-basket test, each candidate is given a standardized set of short reports, notes, telephone messages, and memos of the type that most managers have to deal with on a daily basis. The applicants must set priorities for the various tasks, determine which can be deferred or delegated, and which must be dealt with immediately. They must also indicate how they would approach the different problems the material suggests they will encounter as a manager. Each candidate's performance on the in-basket test is scored by a panel of judges.

The in-basket exercise has great intuitive appeal as a selection test for managers because it resembles what managers actually do; unfortunately, empirical evidence suggests that it does not have high validity as a selection instrument.[143] In part, this may be due to the lack of agreed-on scoring procedures for the in-basket test; successful managers who complete the in-basket do not always arrive at the same conclusions. Additionally, those judging the in-basket performance often fail to distinguish among various target abilities that are supposed to be measured by the in-basket exercise, calling into question the accuracy of inferences made about potential managerial performance that are based on in-basket scores.[144]

Most types of work samples and situational tests discussed here are labour-intensive and costly to develop and administer. However, the importance of making the right selection decision increases when organizations expect more from fewer employees. Particularly for small businesses, selecting the right individual is critical to their success. Additionally, because the relationship of work samples and situational tests to the job is so transparent, candidates from different gender and ethnic groups tend to perceive them as fair. This is most desirable, given the growing minority segment of the work force. For these reasons, the use of work samples and simulation tests is likely to increase in coming years. It will become even more important to ensure that scoring of candidates is done systematically and objectively.

Assessment Centres

Although situational exercises can be used as stand-alone selection tests, they generally play a prominent role in testing carried out as part of an **assessment centre**. The term *assessment centre* is somewhat misleading. It does not refer to a physical place but rather to a standardized assessment procedure that involves the use of multiple measurement techniques to evaluate candidates for selection, classification, and promotion purposes. Assessment centres had their origin during World War II, when they were used by both Germany and Britain to assess the military leadership potential of recruits. Following the war, the procedure was adapted by AT&T in the United States to assess managerial potential. Today, the procedure is mostly used to assess applicants for managerial or administrative positions.

The assessment centre may be used as a procedure to select external applicants; however, it is typically used by most organizations for internal selection, that is, promotion. While some assessment procedures (e.g., an interview) may involve only one candidate, the vast majority of assessment

Assessment centre

A standardized procedure that involves the use of multiple measurement techniques to evaluate candidates for selection, classification, and promotion.

Chapter 8: Selection II: Testing

Essential Elements of an Assessment Centre

According to the International Congress on Assessment Center Methods (http://www.assessmentcenters.org), assessment centres allow companies to meet their challenges by helping them:

- Identify, hire, and promote the most talented people.
- Improve bench strength and plan for succession.
- Provide candidates with realistic job previews.
- "Grow" their own leaders and accelerate leadership development.

Toward these goals, the International Congress has developed the following guidelines for effective assessment centres:

1. Job analysis is used to identify job dimensions, tasks, and attributes that are important to job success.
2. Behaviour displayed by candidates must be categorized by trained assessors and related to dimensions, aptitudes, attributes, or KSAOs.
3. Assessment techniques must provide information related to the dimensions and attributes identified in the job analysis.
4. Multiple assessment procedures are used to elicit a variety of behaviours and information relevant to the selected dimensions and attributes.

5. A sufficient number of job-related simulations must be included in the procedure to allow opportunities to observe behaviour on the selected dimensions.
6. Multiple assessors, diverse in ethnicity, age, gender, and functional work areas, are used to observe and assess each candidate.
7. Assessors must receive thorough training and meet performance standards before being allowed to evaluate candidates.
8. Systematic procedures must be used by assessors to record specific behavioural observations accurately at the time of their occurrence.
9. Assessors must prepare a report or record of observations made during each exercise in preparation for consolidating information across assessors.
10. Data from all assessor reports must be pooled or integrated either at a special meeting of assessors or through statistical methods.

Source: *Guidelines and Ethical Considerations for Assessment Center Operations.* 2000. International Task Force on Assessment Center Guidelines: http://www.assessmentcenters.org/pdf/00guidelines.pdf. © Development Dimensions International. Reprinted with permission.

centre procedures involve group activity. The candidates are evaluated in groups by a panel of trained assessors. The assessment centre is also unique in including managers along with psychologists and other human resources professionals on the assessment team. The managers are trained in the use of the assessment techniques and scoring procedures. The managers selected to be assessors are those who are familiar with the job for which the candidates are being selected.[145] The key features of an assessment centre are outlined in Recruitment and Selection Today 8.5.

Assessment Centre Testing

While the specific testing procedures may vary from one assessment centre to another, depending on the purpose of the assessment, assessment centres generally include tests or procedures from each of the following categories:

- ability and aptitude tests;
- personality tests, both objective and projective;
- situational exercises; and
- interviews.

Following completion of all of the assessment centre components, the team of assessors reviews each individual's performance on a number of variables. The variables represent different dimensions, including administrative skills, cognitive skills, human relations skills, decision-making ability, problem-solving skills, leadership potential, motivation, resistance to stress, and degree of flexibility, among others.[146] Based on the ratings and observations made over the period of the assessment, the team prepares a report summarizing the information obtained through the various techniques. Candidates are provided with feedback on their performance at the assessment centre.

Scoring Performance at the Assessment Centre

When the assessment is conducted for selection purposes, the various ratings are combined into an overall assessment centre score, which can be used to rank the applicants. Generally, some score is established as the minimum needed for consideration, with employment offers made to the highest-ranking applicant and proceeding downward until all of the positions have been filled. When the assessments are made for other purposes, the assessment centre score and report may be used to predict the candidate's long-range managerial potential and likelihood of promotion. Some organizations, like AT&T, require all managers at a particular level to attend an assessment centre as a means of identifying those with potential for advancement in the company. Also, the assessment centre information can be used to develop training programs for individuals in the organization, to increase their chances of future advancement.

Use of Assessment Centres in Canada

In Canada, assessment centre procedures are used by the Public Service Commission of Canada to select candidates for senior managerial positions in the federal civil service and as part of its executive development and education program. They are also used extensively by Ford Motor Company, General Motors, Nortel, and Weyerhaeuser Canada, as well as many other organizations. Assessment centres are also used by the Canadian Forces to select applicants for training as naval officers and military police.

Location and Cost of the Assessment Centre

The assessment centre procedure can be quite extensive and usually takes place over two or three days. The assessment centre may be located on the company's premises but is generally held at an off-site location. Given the length of time and the number of personnel involved in the procedure, it should not be surprising that assessment centres are an expensive proposition.

They require a substantial investment on the part of an organization both to develop and to operate. This cost factor generally limits their use to larger organizations that have ongoing selection and promotion programs.

Effectiveness of Assessment Centres

Do assessment centres improve on other selection techniques? Are they worth the cost? Both organizations and candidates who have gone through an assessment centre attest to their satisfaction with the procedure. The objective data supporting their effectiveness, however, are equivocal. For example, personality testing was used to predict job performance and promotability of forestry products managers as well as an assessment centre procedure; however, the predictive validity improved when both measures were used.[147]

While many research studies have confirmed the validity of the procedure, a troubling number have not shown any improvement in validity that can be attributed to the assessment centre, or have reported low validities. A meta-analytic evaluation of 50 assessment centres reported a validity coefficient of 0.37,[148] while a study of one assessment centre evaluated across 16 sites found a much lower validity of 0.08 to 0.16, depending on the criterion measure.[149] A more recent meta-analysis[150] that looked only at the ability of assessment centres to predict supervisory performance ratings found a corrected validity coefficient of 0.28.

In part, these mixed results may be due to the lack of standardization, wide variability in the exercises carried out at different assessment centres, and the constructs that different assessment centres purport to measure. A more recent meta-analysis first attempted to specify the constructs that were measured through the assessment centre process. Arthur, Day, McNelly, and Edens[151] identified six dimensions—consideration/awareness of others, communication, drive, influencing others, organizing and planning, and problem solving—before conducting their meta-analysis. Criterion-related validities in the population ranged across the dimensions from 0.25 to 0.39. A composite based on ratings of four of the dimensions explained more of the variance in job performance (20 percent) than did the overall assessment rating (14 percent) used by Gaugler et al.[152]

Collins and her colleagues[153] took a different approach to investigating the constructs underlying assessment centres. They reviewed the primary attributes of the different assessment centre measures, and argued that tests such as the in-basket test relied on cognitive ability, while leaderless group discussions favoured personality variables. They performed a meta-analysis comparing overall assessment ratings (OARs) to cognitive ability and personality dimensions. OARs correlated at 0.67 for cognitive ability. The correlations for the Big Five personality dimensions (see the discussion on the Big Five personality model on page 392) were 0.50 for extraversion, 0.35 for emotional stability, 0.25 for openness, and 0.17 for agreeableness. The results from the Collins study suggest that personality and cognitive ability substantially affect the overall assessment ratings given to individuals.

Another factor that may affect validity is the role played by the assessor. Considerable research has investigated how assessors rate candidates. There is some indication that assessors may base their ratings on a candidate's past job experience or performance rather than on how the candidate performs at the assessment centre.[154] First-hand experience with candidates through the extensive interaction at the assessment centre may allow assessors to identify and to weight important information from the candidate's previous experience.

The assessor's expertise, cognitive ability, and personality are all factors that may affect assessment centre validity. For example, assessors who are warm-hearted tend to rate candidates more leniently.[155] Furthermore, the interaction of the candidate and the assessor is likely affected by the personality of both the candidate and the assessor.[156]

The contradictory empirical results for assessment centres have led several researchers to try to identify the underlying constructs on which the assessment centres are based. The argument revolves around whether the competencies that the assessment centres are attempting to measure or the methods or tools used to assess the different competencies are the components that lead to whatever criterion-related validity they have. Several meta-analyses have attempted to identify those components.

The most recent review[157] that reanalyzed previous studies suggests that both the dimensions or competencies being assessed and the assessment centre exercises play a role, although some dimensions and exercises appear to be more important than others in producing an overall rating score that predicts subsequent job performance. These dimensions were communication, influencing others, organizing and planning, and problem solving. The exercises included in-baskets, interviews, role-plays, case analysis, leaderless group discussions, and presentations; these exercises, however, accounted for more variance than did the dimensions. These results suggest that careful attention should be paid to both the dimensions or competencies that are being measured in the assessment centre and the exercises used to measure them.

Assessment centres are likely to increase in popularity as a procedure for assessing potential for managerial or professional careers. The procedure produces a wealth of information that is useful throughout the candidate's career within the organization. It provides a comprehensive assessment of an individual and identifies strengths and weaknesses that form the basis of future development programs. Organizations have started to use assessment centres as a means of providing realistic job previews to job applicants and as a source of organizational and employee development.[158]

Cautions, however, are in order, and assessment procedures may not be the best selection method in all cases. The worth of an assessment centre, like any selection device, rests on an evaluation of its psychometric properties and its utility. An additional consideration is the adverse impact that may be associated with an assessment centre. Dean, Roth, and Bobko[159] assessed adverse impact of assessment centres through a meta-analysis of previous research.

They found that assessment centres had more adverse impact on blacks than previously thought, but that they had less adverse impact and were "diversity friendly" toward women and Hispanics.

Assessment centres are expensive propositions. Before establishing one, consideration should be given to whether the same decisions could be made simply by assessing candidates' cognitive ability and personality through inexpensive paper-and-pencil measures.

Personality Tests

In making hiring decisions, it is not unusual to hear a manager argue in support of one applicant over another because "she is the right type of aggressive person we're looking for to sell cars," or "he is a very pleasant, outgoing person, the type that will do well as a receptionist." Generally, these sorts of comments are made following a job interview, when the manager has formed an impression of what the applicant is like as a person. The manager is stating a personal opinion, or "gut feeling," that the individual's characteristics or traits qualify the applicant for the job. This is the belief that some aspects of what we call *personality* are related to job success. Indeed, given a choice, most managers would welcome employees who are hard-working and well-motivated, accept higher levels of initiative, fit into existing work groups, and are committed to the continuous development of their skills. Most managers and employees believe characteristics like these define the most effective employees.[160] Although these characteristics may be very appealing in an employee, more often than not managers may not succeed in hiring people with these characteristics, or if they do, the person may not turn out to be an effective employee.

There are two reasons for these failures. First, the specific personality traits or characteristics that formed the manager's opinion of the applicant may not be job-related; they may represent only the manager's opinion that they are necessary for effective job performance and may not have been derived through a job analysis. Personality traits or characteristics must be linked to a job or occupation through the same procedures that we use to link other knowledge, skills, abilities, and competencies. Second, the manager's assessment of the applicant's personality may not be objective, reliable, or valid; it is only an opinion. In the next sections, we define personality, examine several measurement issues, and review personality as a predictor of job performance. As we go through this material, keep in mind the information in Recruitment and Selection Today 8.6: A poor personality measure will not offer any more value than a gut feeling.

Defining Personality

One of the major difficulties in using personality tests for selection purposes is the lack of agreement about the definition of *personality*. **Personality** is generally defined as a set of characteristics or properties that influence, or help to explain, an individual's behaviour.[161]

Personality

A set of characteristics or properties that influence, or help to explain, an individual's behaviour.

Buyer Beware

Many personality tests are commercially available and have been used in personnel selection. We listed in Recruitment and Selection Notebook 8.2 (page 357) some of the more commonly used personality tests, without comment on their validity or reliability. Many commercially available tests do not have credible supporting material on their reliability or validity or on how they assess faking and social desirability responding. Often, employers do not know where to begin in evaluating the merits of a personality test and in many cases end up paying large sums of money for no return. Recruitment and Selection Notebook 8.1 (page 356) provides guidelines for choosing a test that should help an employer in making a choice among different personality tests.

Most important, before purchasing a personality test, have someone trained in testing issues review the test's technical manual. The lack of a technical manual tells you that there are no supporting data on the test's reliability and validity. It is not good enough to accept on faith testimonials from the test publisher that the supporting research has been done and is available. It is essential to ask for the technical manual.

Different personality theories may propose different ways in which people vary (e.g., aggressiveness, pleasantness). These variables are called **personality traits**. Personality traits are thought to be stable over time and measurable. Thus, if two people differ in aggressiveness or pleasantness, appropriate measurements can be developed to reflect those differences. Traits can be distinguished from personality *states*, which are more transitory or temporary characteristics. One applicant may be very nervous and anxious during a job interview but calm otherwise; another applicant may always be anxious. In the first case, anxiety is a state, but in the second it is a trait.

Personality traits
Stable, measurable characteristics that help explain ways in which people vary.

Sets, collections, or patterns of traits and states can be used to define a personality *type*. Personality tests attempt to measure traits and/or states and from these measures derive some indication of the type of individual being assessed. A person whose behaviour reflects traits of extreme competitiveness, achievement, aggressiveness, haste, impatience, restlessness, hyper-alertness, explosiveness of speech, tenseness of facial musculature, and feelings of being under the pressure of time and under the challenge of responsibility might be said to have a Type A personality.[162]

Self-report inventories are the most frequently used technique in assessing personality for selection purposes. A **self-report inventory** consists of sets of short, written statements related to various traits. For example, items such as "I constantly interrupt other people when they are speaking" or "I hate standing in lines" might be used as part of an objective, self-report inventory to assess *time urgency*, a trait related to a Type A personality. The individual answers by stating the extent to which they agree or disagree with each item, using a rating scale much like those presented in Chapter 5. Items included in the inventory relate to whatever trait is of interest and might include traits such as aggressiveness, competitiveness, and need for achievement, among others.

Self-report inventory
Short, written statements related to various personality traits.

A self-report inventory may measure only one trait or it may include subscales related to several different traits. A score for each trait included in the inventory is determined by combining the ratings for those items that belong to a specific trait. These scores can be compared with normative data that already exist for the inventory or to specific populations that might be of interest. Patterns of scores across the measured traits are often used to derive statements about personality types. Self-report inventories are also called *objective techniques* because of their scoring methodology.

One criticism of self-report inventories is that they are prone to *faking* and *social desirability responses*. Faking occurs when individuals respond to inventory questions with answers that do not reflect their true beliefs or feelings. Social desirability responding is a form of faking, where individuals choose responses they believe will present them in a socially desirable way or in a positive light. For example, a woman may believe that men and women are equally aggressive but states that men are more aggressive than females because she believes that this is what she is expected to say, and that not saying it may create a negative impression. There is no doubt that individuals can distort their responses on self-report inventories in desired directions.[163,164] What is less clear is the impact of such distortions on employment decisions based on personality inventories.

The major concern in using self-report inventories as part of personnel selection is that job applicants who do distort their responses in a socially desirable manner will improve their chances of being hired.[165–167] Response distortion may cause a change in the rank-ordering of applicants at the upper end of a distribution of personality scores, leading to a loss of the best-qualified candidates.[168] This is why some researchers[169,170] argue that examining the effects of faking on validity coefficients, which has been the predominant method of investigating the effects of faking, is an inappropriate way to measure its impact on hiring decisions.

Not everyone agrees that faking and socially desirable responding have an impact on personality-based selection.[171,172] Ones and Viswesvaran,[173] using meta-analytic data, argue that socially desirable responding does not affect the validity of personality inventories, including integrity tests, that are used in work settings and go so far as to call the whole issue a "red herring." They argue that individuals are responding to items to present an identity and that individuals behave in a manner that is consistent with that identity. That is, individuals who view themselves as conscientious will portray themselves in a manner consistent with their identity when asked to complete a personality inventory.

Recently, Alliger and Dwight[174] challenged the methodological soundness of the past meta-analyses leading to Ones and Viswesvaran's position. Their own meta-analysis showed that fakers could indeed fake their way through a selection process involving self-report measures. Their suggestion that it is premature to make any conclusions about the impact of response distortion on self-report measures without additional empirical evidence is perhaps good advice to follow.

There is no doubt that people can distort their responses on self-report measures in laboratory settings when instructed to do so. It is less certain what impact intentional distortion or faking may have in real-life settings, where most of the evidence, based on change in validity coefficients, suggests that faking takes place but that its impact is not as serious as shown in laboratory studies, particularly when applicants are warned that faking can be detected and that it will have negative consequences for them.[175] While strategies have been developed to "correct" for response distortion, adjusting individual scores may lead to different hiring decisions unless all scores are adjusted, including those where there is no evidence of faking. Such correction procedures may be difficult to defend in a courtroom.[176]

In addition, procedures that correct for faking have little, if any, impact on the validity of the selection test, but they may have a significant impact on individual selection decisions.[177] Recently, Hogan, Barrett, and Hogan[178] examined personality test data taken from over 5000 applicants who had been rejected for customer service positions with a large, national U.S. company. The applicants had reapplied for the position and were required to retake the selection tests. Hogan and her associates concluded that the applicants' scores did not significantly change on the retest and argued that it is reasonable to assume that the applicants would have tried to improve their performance on the second attempt and were unable to do so substantially.

Perhaps the best way to deal with faking is to warn job applicants that faking can be detected and that it will be taken into consideration when making hiring decisions. In addition, the results from a self-report inventory should not be viewed in isolation but in conjunction with a careful review of a candidate's complete file for evidence of distortion.[179]

Personality as a Predictor of Job Performance

Historically, personality tests were not thought to be good predictors of job performance. Guion[180,181] reviewed the technical and ethical problems associated with personality testing and concluded that there was insufficient evidence to justify the use of personality tests in most situations as a basis for making employment decisions about people. Guion was very concerned that personality testing invaded the privacy of job applicants and that such tests asked applicants to provide much information about themselves that was not clearly job-related.

With few exceptions, this view prevailed until the 1990s, when both meta-analytic and new empirical studies suggested that personality testing could predict certain aspects of job performance. These studies grouped related personality characteristics into a smaller number of personality dimensions and then linked those broader dimensions to job performance. Personality dimensions that were chosen on the basis of a job analysis were better predictors of job performance.[182–187] This body of research and more recent work[188] demonstrates convincingly that personality characteristics can be used successfully as part of a personnel selection system, provided that the personality measure meets acceptable standards and the personality dimensions are linked to job performance through a job analysis.

The Society for Human Resource Management reports that over 20 percent of its members use personality tests for new hires as well as for existing employees. Business and industry are increasingly concerned about whether their hires will fit into the organization in terms of such factors as being a team player, working well with little supervision, or being too controlling.[189] Personality is one of the "other" attributes often identified as a KSAO and included in competency dictionaries.

The Big Five

The more recent studies on personality tests, which led to the change in views on the usefulness of such tests in selection, have been heavily influenced by the argument that the many hundreds of different personality traits could be summarized under five categories or dimensions.[190] These "Big Five" dimensions are conscientiousness, emotional stability (also known as *neuroticism*), openness to experience, agreeableness, and extroversion. Recruitment and Selection Notebook 8.4 presents definitions for each of these dimensions and examples of the traits associated with them. While not everyone agrees with the Big Five model as the best way to categorize personality, it has become an important classification scheme in summarizing relationships between personality and job performance variables.[191]

Barrick and Mount found that each of the Big Five dimensions could predict at least one aspect of job performance with some degree of accuracy, while conscientiousness predicted several different aspects of job or training performance at moderate levels. Recall that Campbell[192] believed that "demonstrating effort" and "maintaining personal discipline" were major performance components of every job (see Chapter 5). It is quite easy to see, from the definition given in Recruitment and Selection Notebook 8.4, how conscientiousness could predict each of these two job dimensions. Of all the Big Five dimensions, conscientiousness correlates most strongly with job performance ($r = 0.31$).[193]

The other four Big Five personality dimensions vary in ability to predict job success by occupational group. For example, extroversion predicts performance in occupations involving social interaction, such as sales occupations,[194] while openness to experience and extroversion predict training readiness and training success.[195] Moreover, conscientiousness and extroversion together predict job performance for managers in highly autonomous positions.[196] Agreeableness and emotional stability, in addition to conscientiousness, play an important role in predicting performance in jobs that involve interpersonal interactions.[197]

Hough and Furnham[198] present exhaustive tables that report the validity coefficients, based on meta-analytic studies, for each of the Big Five measures and overall job performance, contextual performance, and counterproductive behaviours. The validities varied over the different criteria, with conscientiousness correlating most highly with overall job performance for many jobs, but extroversion, openness to experience, and emotional stability correlated most highly with leadership in business settings.

Personality measures do predict job performance but not as strongly as cognitive ability. Even conscientiousness (with $r = 0.31$) as a predictor falls

The Big Five Personality Dimensions

1. **Conscientiousness** is a general tendency to work hard and to be loyal, to give a full day's work each day, and to do one's best to perform well—following instructions and accepting organization goals, policies, and rules—even with little or no supervision. It is an approach to work characterized by industriousness, purposiveness, persistence, consistency, and punctuality. It also includes paying attention to every aspect of a task, including attention to details that might easily be overlooked.

2. **Emotional stability** reflects a calm, relaxed approach to situations, events, or people. It includes an emotionally controlled response to changes in the work environment or to emergency situations. It is an emotionally mature approach to potentially stressful situations, reflecting tolerance, optimism, and a general sense of challenge rather than of crisis, and maturity in considering advice or criticism from others. (Note: "Emotional stability" is used in place of the older term *neuroticism* to describe this factor.)

3. **Openness to experience** reflects a preference for situations in which one can develop new things, ideas, or solutions to problems through creativity or insight. It includes trying new or innovative approaches to tasks or situations. It is a preference for original or unique ways of thinking about things. It is concerned with newness, originality, or creativity.

4. **Agreeableness** reflects a desire or willingness to work with others to achieve a common purpose and to be part of a group. It also includes a tendency to be a caring person in relation to other people, to be considerate and understanding, and to have genuine concern for the well-being of others; it is an awareness of the feelings and interests of others. It is the ability to work cooperatively and collaboratively either as part of a group or in the service of others. It is involved in assisting clients and customers as a regular function of one's work, or assisting co-workers to meet deadlines or to achieve work goals.

5. **Extroversion** reflects a tendency to be outgoing in association with other people, to seek and enjoy the company of others, to be gregarious, to interact easily and well with others, and to be likable and warmly approachable. It involves enjoying the company of others and a concern for their interests; it implies sociableness whether work is involved or not. *Extroversion* refers to being comfortable and friendly in virtually any sort of situation involving others.

Sources: M.R. Barrick and M.K. Mount. 1991. "The Big Five Personality Dimensions and Job Performance: A Meta-Analysis." *Personnel Psychology* 44: 1–26; J.M. Digman. 1990. "Personality Structure: Emergence of the Five Factor Model." In M. Rosenzweig and L.W. Porter, eds., *Annual Review of Psychology*. Palo Alto, CA: Annual Reviews.

below the average predictive ability of cognitive ability ($r = 0.51$). The best use of a personality measurement may be as a supplement to cognitive ability testing. Conscientiousness added to cognitive ability will improve the accuracy of predicting job performance by 18 percent.[199] There may be another benefit to adding a personality measure. Unlike cognitive ability tests, personality measures have little, if any, adverse impact on protected groups.[200] Adding a personality measure to a cognitive ability–based selection system may moderate the adverse impact of the cognitive ability measure.[201]

A word of caution is in order with respect to personality measures, as well as other assessment instruments. Make sure that the personality measure has acceptable psychometric properties for its intended use and that the measure reports scores for the Big Five dimensions. The personality tests listed in Recruitment and Selection Notebook 8.2 (see page 357) are safe bets to use. For others, obtain their psychometric properties from sources such as Buros's *Mental Measurements Yearbook* (http://www.unl.edu/buros/bimm/index.html). One measure that purports to measure personality, and tends to be popular with HR people, is the *Myers-Briggs Type Indicator* (MBTI). It identifies four types of individuals; however, these types do not coincide with the Big Five and do not predict job performance.[202]

Selecting for Work Teams

In many Canadian organizations, employees are selected to be part of a work team, either on a permanent basis or as the demands of a project dictate. We need to know how to select members of teams to maximize team performance. Unfortunately, there is a paucity of research on this issue. Personality measures may have the potential to identify those individuals who are capable of working as part of a team and to identify the most desirable combination of people to ensure a good working relationship among team members, resulting in an optimal personality profile for the team.[203]

Kichuk and Wiesner[204] conducted one of the few studies to examine the relationship between the Big Five personality factors and team performance. They asked teams of engineering students to design and construct a model bridge using limited resources. Teams whose members were more homogeneous in conscientiousness tended to do better than those teams whose members differed more. Extroversion predicted team member satisfaction, which is necessary for team longevity. Successful teams had higher levels of extroversion, emotional stability, and agreeableness than did those judged to be unsuccessful. Openness to experience was not related to any aspect of team performance. While these results are preliminary, they do demonstrate the potential of using personality measures to construct work teams.

Halfhill and his associates[205] studied the personality of members of 47 intact military teams that were part of the U.S. Air National Guard. They assessed through self-reports the level of conscientiousness and agreeableness of individuals and the average ratings for groups to which the individuals were assigned. The mean personality ratings significantly correlated with the mean performance ratings of the groups. Both agreeableness and conscientiousness were related to supervisory ratings of group-level performance. Groups high on both personality variables received significantly higher supervisory ratings.

Broad versus Narrow Traits

Some researchers[206,207] argue that narrower, more specific personality traits are the best predictors of performance and that the reason previous research has not confirmed this is related to the lack of use of personality-related job analyses and psychometrically sound personality measures. For example, a measure of "achievement," a narrow facet of conscientiousness, might be more useful as a predictor of job performance than the broader trait. Paunonen and Nicol[208] argue that only one of the many facets of the broader Big

Five dimension could be entirely responsible for the relationship of the Big Five dimension to job performance. Others have been equally outspoken on behalf of the position that "broader and richer personality traits will have higher predictive validity than narrower traits."[209] Ones and Viswesvaran argue that the broad personality dimensions are better predictors of broad workplace criteria that are used in validation studies.

Hough and Furnham[210] point out that it need not be a case of either narrow or broad traits. They argue that the focus must be on the nature of the criteria that are of interest. If the criterion is narrow, then a narrow trait may be best; however, if the focus is on broad workplace behaviours, such as overall job performance, then broad personality traits may be best. The dilemma for practitioners is to know whether the relationship between the predictor and criterion is narrow or broad and when to use narrow or broad predictors. That is, the narrowness or broadness of the personality measure should match the narrowness or broadness of the criterion measure in order to maximize predictive validity.

Polygraph and Honesty (Integrity) Testing

The Big Five personality dimensions are also related to contextual performance and organizational citizenship behaviour. A manager's desire to find honest, hard-working team players may not be related so much to the specific job that individuals will do but rather to how well they will fit into the organization. Contextual performance involves activities that do not belong to a worker's specific job but are, nevertheless, activities that are considered important for organizational effectiveness.

In many cases, organizational effectiveness may be limited by employee theft or misuse of the organization's property or proprietary information, or other forms of dishonesty. The costs associated with such counterproductive behaviour were $2.3 billion in the Canadian retail sector for 1999, an increase of 21 percent from 1997. The average amount stolen by employees, $450, is now more than triple the average amount, $116, lost through customer theft. In 1999, Dylex Ltd., a major Canadian retail chain, was forced to take a $25 million write-down, partly because of employee theft.[211] In the United States, national retail surveys attribute 43 percent of inventory "shrinkage" to employee theft.[212] In response to this problem, many retailers have established "loss prevention" departments; they have emphasized employee training and workplace improvements as well as installing procedures for controlling inventory. Many organizations have also initiated programs designed to select people who are not only capable of doing the job but who, in addition, are honest, reliable, and of high integrity.

Honesty or integrity are personality traits and can be measured. Over the years, a number of techniques have been used in an attempt to identify these traits. Polygraph testing, otherwise known as using a lie detector, was once used extensively to check on employee honesty and to screen job applicants. The polygraph test is based on the assumption that measurable, physiological changes occur when people lie, and that no matter how hard they try to control their responses, changes take place in heart rate, breathing, blood pressure, and so on.

Although lie detectors enjoy a reputation among the public for actually being able to detect lies, the empirical evidence shows that there are many unresolved issues about their reliability and validity. Polygraph results are mostly related to the skill of the polygraph operator, many of whom are poorly trained. Relatively few jurisdictions in either Canada or the United States have any licensing requirements for polygraph operators. Polygraph results are generally not accepted as evidence in North American courtrooms unless the test-taker agrees to their admission. Many legislatures, including the U.S. Congress, which passed the 1988 Employee Polygraph Protection Act,[213] have banned the use of polygraph testing as part of most pre-employment screening procedures.[214] Subject to restrictions and strict standards for their use, the Act does allow employers to test applicants for security service firms and of pharmaceutical-related industries. The test can also be given to employees who are reasonably suspected of theft, embezzlement, or other economic crimes that result in economic loss or injury to an employer. In Canada, Ontario has taken the lead in prohibiting the use of mandatory polygraph tests under its Employment Standards Act. Polygraph testing has no place in any selection program.

Integrity or Honesty Testing

The restrictions placed on polygraph testing have led to an increase in the use of paper-and-pencil **honesty or integrity tests**. These tests are personality-based measures.[215] They can easily be incorporated into a selection system, and they are inexpensive and typically inoffensive to most applicants. There are no legislative restrictions on their use; however, they must meet the same professional and scientific standards as any other type of employment test.

There are two general types of integrity tests. *Covert tests* are subtests or scales that are included in a general personality inventory; for example, the Reliability Scale of the *Hogan Personality Inventory*[216] is commonly used to assess employee honesty and reliability. *Overt honesty tests*, such as the *Reid Report*, ask very direct questions about the individual's attitude toward theft and other forms of dishonesty, as well as the person's prior involvement in theft or other illegal activities. Applicants may not be aware that their integrity is being assessed with a covert honesty test when they complete a personality inventory. There is no doubt about the purpose of an overt test, and this is likely the reason that overt tests are more susceptible to faking than those embedded in personality inventories.[217]

Honesty tests are an increasingly popular method of screening out potentially dishonest employees. Dishonest applicants may be discouraged from applying for jobs when they know they will be tested for honesty. In the case of white-collar crime, personality-based integrity tests may be the best measure of psychological differences between white-collar criminals and honest employees.[218] After a chain of home improvement centres in Great Britain

Honesty or integrity tests
Self-report inventories designed to assess employee honesty and reliability.

started using an honesty test as part of its selection procedures, inventory shrinkage dropped from 4 percent to less than 2.5 percent.[219]

A review of over 180 studies that involved 25 different measures of honesty or integrity tests and a wide range of performance measures found integrity tests successfully predict a wide range of dysfunctional job behaviours, including absenteeism, tardiness, violence, and substance abuse.[220] There is no evidence that integrity tests produce adverse impact. Ones and Viswesvaran[221] found trivial differences on integrity test outcomes when comparisons were made between whites, Asians, Native Americans, and blacks. Table 8.1 presents a summary of criterion-related validity data for both overt and covert integrity tests.[222, 223]

A striking aspect of Table 8.1 is that integrity tests are more successful in predicting certain types of negative behaviours. They are much more successful at predicting property damage than detecting theft, one of the main reasons for administering integrity tests to employees and job applicants. A more recent and exhaustive review of psychological studies and law review articles on integrity tests, along with an examination of professional and legislative investigations of integrity tests, came to similar conclusions that honesty or integrity tests provide valid information about an applicant's potential to engage in certain types of dysfunctional job behaviours.[224]

TABLE 8.1

Summary of Meta-Analytic Integrity Test Criterion-Related Validities

Criterion	Type of Integrity Test	Mean Observed Validity Coefficient, r	Corrected Validity Coefficient, ρ^*
Detected theft	Overt	0.09	0.13
Admitted theft	Overt	0.30	0.42
Property damage	Overt and personality-based	0.50	0.69
Accidents on job	Overt and personality-based	0.37	0.52
Broad counterproductive behaviours	Overt	0.27	0.39
Broad counterproductive behaviours	Personality-based	0.20	0.29

* The mean observed validity coefficient, r, has been corrected for range restriction and unreliability in the criterion measure.

Source: Adapted from J.E. Wanek. 1999. "Integrity and Honesty Testing: What Do We Know? How Do We Use It?" Table 1. *International Journal of Selection and Assessment* 7: 183–95. Reprinted with permission from Wiley-Blackwell.

Nonetheless, honesty tests do have disadvantages (see Recruitment and Selection Today 8.7). Test scores from honesty tests, like those from any other personality measurement, are open to misinterpretation and may constitute an invasion of the applicant's privacy. There is some evidence that job applicants do not hold favourable views of personality measures as selection instruments.[225] Applicants may form a negative impression of the organization that uses integrity tests, although there is no evidence that this happens or that it affects the applicant's reaction to the company.[226] Existing data do suggest that honesty tests may have a high number of false positives; that is, they may tend to screen out a large number of applicants who are truly honest but do poorly on the test.[227] An applicant who is falsely rejected may feel stigmatized and take legal action.[228]

One procedure that might reduce the false negative problem would be to follow the practice used in drug testing, where a positive test is followed by an analysis of a holdout sample before any conclusions are drawn. In other

Recruitment and Selection Today 8.7

Integrity at the Checkout Counter

Sobeys (http://www.sobeys.com), with its head office in Stellarton, Nova Scotia, operates a chain of food stores throughout Canada under several names. Sobeys' use of the *Reid Report* illustrates some of the pitfalls and negative publicity that may accompany integrity testing. The case involves a job applicant who failed the *Reid Report*. This applicant had worked for Sobeys for six years and had resigned her job to stay home and take care of her children for a year.

When she applied for a position with the company again, she was required to take the *Reid Report*, which had been introduced during her absence. She failed the integrity test. Since Sobeys' policy was to hire only those applicants who passed the test, her job application was rejected. The applicant questioned how she could have been rejected for failing the integrity test when she had worked without complaint for Sobeys for six years. The incident made local and national headlines and was the subject of a television feature on the CBC. It also led to a great deal of discussion about the worth of integrity tests.

Sobeys was not alone in sharing the media spotlight over using integrity tests. A few years earlier, one of its main competitors, Loblaw's Real Canadian Superstore subsidiary, began using the *Reid Report* in its Vancouver operations. The British Columbia Civil Liberties Union became aware of the practice and publicly denounced the use of the test. It also called for legislation banning the practice as an invasion of privacy.

Even successful applicants may react negatively to an integrity test and the company using it. David Lindsay* wrote about his experience with an integrity test in *This Magazine*. He found the experience to be invasive and insulting, and failed to see the relevance of questions that involved such statements as "I like to take chances" and "I am afraid of fire." Neither did he see the value of answering questions such as "What drugs have you taken and how often?" He claims that he and his co-workers had all lied to achieve high "honesty" ratings: "Each of us had falsified a low-risk profile, feigning caution, docility, obedience, and inviolable, angelic truthfulness. We had denied all illegal activity, labour sympathies, and feelings of bitterness and alienation."

Lindsay doubts that a quality such as honesty can be measured quantitatively. Sobeys, on the other hand, continues to see the merit in integrity testing and has not been deterred by the negative publicity arising from its assessing the honesty of job applicants. Sobeys continues to use the *Reid Report* in its hiring process. What do you think?

Source: * D. Lindsay. 1998. "True Lies—An Applicant Writes an 'Integrity' Test." *This Magazine* 31: 4.

words, when an integrity test suggests that the job candidate may be prone to engaging in counterproductive work behaviours, the candidate should be given a second, and different, integrity test before any decision is made. Failing both integrity tests would reduce the probability that the results are false negatives. Although this procedure may be a bit more time-consuming and expensive, it may spare an employer bad publicity and legal fees.

There is also a practical problem with the use of integrity tests. Most publishers of integrity tests require the proprietary testing forms to be returned to the publisher, who releases only an overall total score and subscale scores. The publishers of the *Reid Report* have become more responsible about the administration and reporting of scores.[229] The HR specialist is not able to review the correctness of the responses and must rely on the publisher's interpretation of the scores in the context of the publisher's proprietary normative data, which cannot be inspected.[230]

Should integrity tests be used to select employees? Table 8.1 shows that integrity tests are valid with respect to a number of criteria. An HR practitioner must first decide on the negative behaviour that is of concern and then select an integrity test that predicts that behaviour with acceptable reliability and validity. These values can generally be found in Buros's *Mental Measurements Yearbook* or other sources of information on tests.

Catano and Prosser[231] reviewed some of the most popular integrity tests with respect to their psychometric properties. Table 8.2 summarizes this data, which should be considered when selecting an integrity test. Evaluate the test against the criteria presented in Recruitment and Selection Notebook 8.1 (see page 356). Never use an integrity test by itself, that is, as the sole selection test. The test should be used in conjunction with another test that is a valid predictor of job performance; for example, an integrity test added to a test of cognitive ability can raise the validity of the selection decisions from 0.51 to 0.65.[232] The integrity test should be given as the last hurdle in the selection procedure; that is, between two candidates who are equal in cognitive ability, selecting the candidate with the higher integrity test score will likely lead to a work force composed of employees who are more productive and who engage in fewer counterproductive behaviours.[233]

Graphology

There are several indirect methods for assessing personality. These methods require an individual to respond in some fashion to an ambiguous stimulus such as a drawing or picture. The inkblot, or Rorschach test, is an example of a projective technique that has been popularized through movies and television. The premise of such tests is that individuals project something about their personality into their responses. In the case of handwriting, the assumption is that the unique characteristics of the handwriting indirectly reflect something about personality traits, which a graphologist or graphoanalyst can interpret. While several projective techniques are useful diagnostic tools in clinical psychology, graphology does not fall into this category. There is little, if any, scientific evidence that supports the use of graphology in personnel selection. Whatever success graphologists appear to have had seems

TABLE 8.2

Comparison of Integrity Tests*

TEST	RELIABILITY	VALIDITY	FAKING POTENTIAL	AVAILABLE IN FRENCH	COMMENTS
London House Personnel Selection Inventory	0.85	Need for local validation studies	High	Yes	No technical data in manual. Only the Canadian version of the PSI that excludes drug avoidance scales can be used in Canada.
Reid Report	0.92	0.33 with return of money	High	Yes	Uses category scoring that violates APA recommendations. Arbitrary cut points used to establish categories. Confusion over how scores are generated. Includes drug-use scale but that can be deleted in the abbreviated form.
Stanton Survey New Edition	0.92	Weakness in validation data	High	No	New edition presents scores in percentiles grouped, however, in categories. Includes a Social Desirability check. Cannot be used with current employees, only applicants.
Employee Reliability Inventory	"Not technically well supported"	Need for local validation studies	Moderate	No	No compelling evidence of validity. Uses category scoring that violates APA recommendations.
Personnel Reaction Blank	0.73	0.25/0.40 with work quality	High	No	Not recommended for use as it does not meet *Standards for Educational and Psychological Testing*.
Personnel Decisions Incorporated Employment Inventory	0.74	0.20–0.40 job performance and turnover	Low	No	Social Desirability check. Evidence of dimensionality, reliability, and validity is weak. Many variables represented in the global score. Not good enough to warrant uncritical use.
Inwald Personality	0.92	0.41 with general performance	Moderate	No	Developed on obsolete procedures; no theoretical basis; does not measure conscientiousness.
Hogan Personality Inventory– Revised	0.80	0.40 (Prudence scale with Absence)	Low	Yes	Theoretically sound, carefully conceptualized, and well validated.

* All reliability and validity data were taken from reviews of the tests in Buros's *Mental Measurements Yearbook*.

    Almost all of these tests are available in a variety of formats: paper-and-pencil, computer-administered, telephone-administered, and Internet-administered. While the tests may be administered by anyone, all of the proprietary tests require scoring by the test publisher. The report from the publisher may vary considerably in detail; however, all of these tests require a master's degree–level person trained in assessment to score and/or interpret the results, even though some test manuals do not make this clear.

Source: Adapted from V.M. Catano and M.A. Prosser. 2007. "A Review of Integrity Tests and Their Implications for Selection of Security Personnel in a Canadian Context." *The Canadian Journal of Police & Security Services* 5: 1–18. Reprinted with permission of V.M. Catano.

to be based on inferences drawn from information contained in the content of the writing and not in the handwriting itself.[234]

Nonetheless, the lack of scientific support has not deterred companies from using graphology to select employees, particularly at the executive level. Graphology is most popular in Western Europe, with reports estimating its use as a selection tool in over 50 percent of companies in France and Germany. Despite its apparent widespread use, potential French job applicants ranked it ninth out of ten selection procedures in terms of effectiveness and fairness; the only procedure to receive lower ratings was honesty testing.[235]

Although there are no firm figures, a few Canadian companies and consultants are beginning to use graphology either by itself or in conjunction with other selection devices, although they are often ashamed to admit it, partly because of human rights issues that might be involved.[236] The shame is understandable; any company making hiring or placement decisions with the aid of graphology should be aware that there is no scientific evidence to support its use. They should also consider the negative impact that such a procedure may have on potential applicants.

Legal Considerations

Personality measures, particularly those based on the Big Five structure, effectively predict job performance; as well, integrity tests predict counterproductive work behaviours.[237] Both types of tests are legally defensible and can be used as part of selection systems. Of course, such tests are subject to the same legal standards as other selection measures. These include establishing that the personality traits or dimensions are related to job or contextual performance through job analysis procedures and that the traits or dimensions are required for effective job performance. Without this type of supporting documentation, a company will almost certainly lose any litigation involving use of the personality or integrity measures.[238] Adherence to professional guidelines, such as those presented earlier in this chapter, that are designed to protect the human rights of job applicants will also enhance the chances of winning any court challenges.

Fairness does not appear to be an issue with respect to personality or integrity testing. There is no evidence that psychometrically sound personality inventories and integrity tests have an adverse impact on any protected group.[239] In fact, it appears that adding personality or integrity tests to a selection system that includes measures of cognitive ability may reduce the bias in selection.[240] Personality measures may help persons with disabilities demonstrate their qualifications, as they do not differ significantly on personality from the remainder of the population.[241]

Privacy Issues

The concerns about privacy still remain and may prove troublesome to the point that they limit the use of personality tests. The U.S. Target department stores used two personality tests, the *Minnesota Multiphasic Personality Inventory* (MMPI) and the *California Psychological Inventory* (CPI), to assess aggressiveness in applicants for security guard positions. A job applicant filed suit in California alleging religious discrimination (the MMPI at that time contained the item "I believe in the second coming of Christ"), sexual orientation discrimination (the MMPI included the item "I am very strongly attracted to members of my own sex"), and invasion of privacy, a right under California's constitution. In *Soroka v. Dayton Hudson Corp.*,[242] the California courts upheld the complaint and awarded damages to Soroka.

The effect of the ruling was that every item on a personality test had to be free of discrimination and not just the scores provided by the test. Since then, most personality tests that are used in employment settings have been vetted for discriminatory items. The personality tests listed in Recruitment and Selection Notebook 8.2 (see page 357) are safe bets to meet legal standards; nonetheless, it is essential that, to avoid costly litigation, personality testing should be chosen and carried out by trained professionals guided by relevant legal and ethical standards.

EVALUATING TESTING EFFECTIVENESS Throughout this chapter, we have emphasized that tests used as part of selection procedures must exhibit sound psychometric properties, particularly reliability and validity. The tests must be constructed and used in accordance with accepted professional standards and must meet any legal requirements that govern their use. These selection procedures involve the expenditure of time and money; in the case of assessment centres, the time and cost involved can be considerable. Therefore, it is not sufficient to simply demonstrate that a selection test or procedure has acceptable psychometric properties. A more important question is whether the new selection tests improve on the outcomes that are expected from the existing selection system. Also at issue is whether the new selection system will produce benefits or advantages that exceed the cost of operating the selection system.

Utility analysis is a method that can be used to evaluate the performance of different selection systems by comparing the net gains that accrue to the organization through their use. We present an introduction to utility analysis in Chapter 10 and illustrate that discussion with several examples. You may wish to read ahead and review that section now.

Comparing Selection Predictors

With the exception of the employment interview, which will be discussed in the next chapter, we have reviewed the most commonly used predictors that are used in personnel selection. Which, if any of these, are the better predictors? Which should be considered for adoption as part of a selection system? In large part, the answers to these questions depend on the specific information that is being sought, as determined through a job analysis. Each of these predictors has different strengths and weaknesses and may be more suited to specific uses. Most of all, the selection measure must provide information that is related to the specific job, or class of jobs, that is being staffed. Consideration must also be given to the type of criterion measure that will be used. The validity of predictors may vary among criteria such as training performance, job tenure, performance ratings, and promotion.

Selection measures must meet prevailing psychometric and professional standards. They must also be reviewed in the context of fairness and legal and organizational policies. Table 8.3 has been compiled from meta-analytic studies that have reviewed the validity of different selection measures. The validities reported here are averaged across job performance criteria and

continued

TABLE 8.3

Mean Validities for Predictors Used in Selection with Overall Job Performance as the Criterion

PREDICTOR	MEAN VALIDITY WHEN USED BY ITSELF	MEAN VALIDITY WHEN USED TO SUPPLEMENT COGNITIVE ABILITY TEST*	SUBGROUP DIFFERENCES (d)**
Cognitive ability*	0.51	—	
White–Black			0.99
White–Asian			−0.20
Male–Female			0.00
Work samples/SJTs*	0.54	0.63	
White–Black			0.40
White–Asian			0.49
Male–Female			−0.12
Interview—structured*	0.51	0.63	
White–Black			0.23
Job knowledge tests	0.48	0.58	
White–Black			0.48
Integrity tests*	0.41	0.65	
White–Black			
White–Asian			
Male–Female			
Interview—unstructured*	0.38	0.55	
Assessment centre*	0.37	0.53	
White–Black			0.37
Biographical data*	0.35	0.52	
White–Black			0.33
Psychomotor ability[†]	0.35	—	
White–Black			−0.72
Male–Female			−1.06
Perceptual ability[†]	0.34	—	
White–Black			0.66
Physical ability[‡]	0.32	—	
Male–Female			1.02 to 2.10

continued

Continued from previous page

Predictor	Mean Validity When Used by Itself	Mean Validity When Used to Supplement Cognitive Ability Test*	Subgroup Differences (d)**
Conscientiousness*	0.31	0.60	
White–Black			0.06
White–Asian			0.08
Male–Female			−0.08
Reference checks*	0.26	0.57	
Emotional stability§	0.12	—	
White–Black			−0.04
White–Asian			−0.01
Male–Female			0.24
Extroversion§	0.12	—	
White–Black			0.10
White–Asian			0.08
Male–Female			0.09
Agreeableness§	0.10	—	
White–Black			0.02
White–Asian			0.01
Male–Female			−0.39
Openness to experience§	0.05	—	
White–Black			0.21
White–Asian			0.18
Male–Female			0.07
Résumé components			
Grade point average#	0.32	—	
Job experience*	0.18	—	
Years of education*	0.10	0.52	
Graphology*	0.02	0.51	

Sources: *F.L. Schmidt and J.E. Hunter. 1998. "The Validity and Utility of Selection Methods in Personnel Psychology: Practical and Theoretical Implications of 85 Years of Research Findings." *Psychological Bulletin* 124: 262–74; ** R.E. Ployhart and B.C. Holtz. 2008. "The Diversity–Validity Dilemma: Strategies for Reducing Racioethnic and Sex Subgroup Differences and Adverse Impact in Selection." *Personnel Psychology* 6: 153–72; † J.E. Hunter and R.F. Hunter. 1984. "Validity and Utility of Alternative Predictors of Job Performance." *Psychological Bulletin* 96: 72–98; ‡ N.A. Schmitt, R.Z. Gooding, R.D. Noe, and M. Kirsch. 1984. "Meta-Analyses of Validity Studies Published between 1964 and 1982 and Investigation of Study Characteristics." *Personnel Psychology* 37: 407–22; § M.R. Barrick and M.K. Mount. 1991. "The Big Five Personality Dimensions and Job Performance: A Meta-Analysis." *Personnel Psychology* 44: 1–26; # P.L. Roth, C.A. BeVier, F.S. Switzer, III, and J.S. Schippmann. 1996. "Meta-Analyzing the Relationship between Grades and Job Performance." *Journal of Applied Psychology* 81: 548–56.

Note: The validity coefficients have been corrected for range restriction and unreliability in the criterion measures. The *d* values are uncorrected.

are presented in descending order based on their mean, corrected validity coefficient. Table 8.3 also presents data on the increase in validity that can be expected from adding a second predictor to cognitive ability. As well, information is provided on the degree to which the selection tool may have adverse impact, noted by the index d, on minority groups and women. (The greater the positive value of d, the greater the likely adverse impact on the group; a negative value of d means the targeted group has an advantage over the majority group on the selection device.)[243]

Data are not available for all of the selection instruments that we have discussed. As can be seen, adding a second predictor can provide a substantial increase in validity. While these validities may be influential, the difference in utility provided by different predictors may also influence choice of a measure. The potential net gains from using different predictors in the hiring situation should be compared before making any final decision on which predictor to use. As a rule of thumb, replacing a low-validity predictor with one of higher validity, at little or no cost, will lead to substantial benefits in terms of productivity for an organization.

The second point to note from Table 8.3 is that some of the most valid predictors, such as cognitive ability, have the most adverse impact on minorities. These data argue that HR specialists must balance validity and diversity to obtain qualified employees who are representative of the general population. Recruitment and Selection Notebook 8.5 provides some guidelines for how organizations can minimize the validity–diversity dilemma.

Recruitment and Selection Notebook 8.5

Guidelines for Balancing Validity and Diversity in Selection

1. Use job analysis to carefully define the nature of performance on the job, being sure to recognize both technical and nontechnical aspects of performance.

2. Use cognitive and noncognitive predictors to measure the full range of relevant cognitive and noncognitive KSAOs, as much as is practically realistic.

3. Use alternative predictor measurement methods (interviews, SJTs, biodata, accomplishment record, assessment centres) when feasible. Supplementing a cognitive predictor with alternative predictor measurement methods can produce sizable reductions of adverse impact (if they are not too highly correlated), but the specific reductions are variable.

   Using alternative predictor measurement methods is costly but effective because they measure multiple KSAOs, reduce reading requirements, and have higher

face validity. Among the best alternative predictor measures are interviews, SJTs, and assessment centres. Nevertheless, the data are unclear about work samples, which may have less validity and larger racioethnic subgroup differences than prior research indicated.

4. Decrease the cognitive loading of predictors and minimize verbal ability and reading requirements to the extent supported by a job analysis. For example, if a job analysis indicates the need for a high school reading level, ensure the predictors do not require a college reading level. Doing so may involve lowering the reading level of instructions and items, allowing constructed response options, or using video formats (but again, only if consistent with the job analysis findings).

continued

Continued from previous page

5. Enhance applicant reactions. Although this strategy has only a minimal effect on subgroup differences, it does not reduce validity and is almost invariably beneficial from a public relations perspective. Simply using face valid predictors (such as interviews and assessment centres) goes a long way toward enhancing these perceptions. And some approaches are free (e.g., giving explanations for why the selection procedure is being used). Sensitivity review panels may help ensure content validity and legal defensibility.

6. *Consider* banding. We emphasize the word "consider" because this remains a controversial strategy among IO psychologists and will substantially reduce subgroup differences only when there is explicit racioethnic minority or female preference in final hiring decisions. (See Chapter 10.)

Source: R.E. Ployhart and B.C. Holtz. 2008. "The Diversity–Validity Dilemma: Strategies for Reducing Racioethnic and Sex Subgroup Differences and Adverse Impact in Selection." *Personnel Psychology* 6: 153–72. Reprinted with permission from Wiley-Blackwell.

Rynes, Colbert, and Brown[244] noted that many U.S. organizations have not made use of the best HR practices. The same can be said for Canadian companies with respect to the use of selection tests. Catano and Bissonnette[245] examined data from Statistics Canada's *Workplace Environment Survey* (WES) of over 5000 organizations and 25 000 employees in relation to selection practices. In 1999, 22 percent of employees reported not receiving any type of pre-hiring assessment; however, this decreased to 17 percent by 2003. A selection interview (75 percent) was the most commonly used method in each of the three years the survey was administered. (The WES did not explore the nature of the selection interview that was used.) Table 8.4 presents the percentage of employees who reported having received a specific type of selection test prior to employment in each year. Another notable change is the significant increase in the use of pre-hire security checks, increasing from almost 9 percent in 1999 to almost 13 percent in 2003. This increase probably reflects increased concerns with security issues following the 9/11 terrorist attacks.

There is variability in use of pre-hire selection tools over different economic sectors, with the financial and insurance industries being the most likely to use some type of pre-employment selection testing. The construction industry was the most likely to hire employees without any type of assessment, with retail and service industries falling in the middle.

Canadian firms, particularly small and medium-sized ones, are more likely to use traditional selection instruments, which have lower validity,[246] or no pre-employment assessment.[247] Larger companies are more open to using employment testing and are benefiting from the higher returns from improved selection procedures. Analysis of the WES data with respect to outcome variables showed that firms who used more structured selection procedures had significantly higher revenues and more productive employees. Overall, improved selection practices were related to improved employee and organizational performance when measured by several indicators.[248]

 8.5 Given the advances in selection technology, there is no economic reason why any Canadian firm, no matter what its size, cannot make use of newer

Table 8.4

SELECTION TOOLS	1999 (%)	2001 (%)	2003 (%)
Reported Use of Pre-Employment Assessment Procedures in Canadian Organizations			

Reported Use of Pre-Employment Assessment Procedures in Canadian Organizations

SELECTION TOOLS	1999 (%)	2001 (%)	2003 (%)
No pre-hiring assessment	22.6	21.9	17.4
Pre-hiring personal interview	74.5	75.3	78.7
One selection tool used in pre-hire assessment	49.8	51.9	50.8
Two or more selection tools used in pre-hire assessment	28.0	26.3	31.8
Skills test	10.7	9.4	10.7
Aptitude or personality test	7.5	7.1	8.6
Test of job knowledge	5.7	5.8	8.3
Test of general knowledge or literacy skills	2.6	3.1	5.6
Medical examination	12.8	11.5	13.6
Security check	8.9	7.8	12.7
Drug test	1.4	1.6	2.4

Source: V.M. Catano and A. Bissonnette. 2008. *Evolution of Selection Tools Used by Canadian Employers*. Unpublished manuscript. Halifax, NS. Reprinted with permission of V.M. Catano.

selection procedures. Their economic survival may depend on their ability to do so. It is the function of Canadian HR personnel to be knowledgeable about selection procedures and to call for the implementation of improved selection procedures in their organizations. The frequency of use of valid selection procedures must increase if economic benefits are to accrue to Canadian organizations and to Canada.

Recall from Chapter 2 that test fairness includes the reaction of applicants to selection procedures. Adverse reactions to selection tests and procedures may impair the ability of an organization to recruit and hire the best applicants. It may also lead to costly litigation. Table 8.5 presents reactions of potential job applicants in the United States and France toward several different selection methods. The job applicants rated the effectiveness and fairness of the personnel selection methods, which were converted to a favourability rating for each method.[249] Despite differences in language and culture, both groups gave good to moderate favourability ratings to interviews, résumés, work samples, biographical data, ability tests, reference checking, and personality tests.

The U.S. group rated both ability tests and personality tests slightly lower than French job applicants did. Both groups gave poor ratings to personal contacts (selection based on the influence of a connection in the company), honesty testing, and graphology. French-speaking job applicants in Belgium also reacted very positively to selection interviews and less so, but positively, to personality, ability, and work sample tests. Graphology provoked strong negative reactions. The applicants' reactions to the selection procedures influenced their intentions to recommend the organization to others as a place to

TABLE 8.5

Applicant Favourability Perceptions of Selection Methods

	RATING BY APPLICANTS	
SELECTION METHOD	U.S.	FRENCH
Interview	Good	Good
Résumé	Good	Good
Work samples	Good	Good
Biodata	Good	Medium
Ability tests	Medium	Medium–good
Reference checking	Medium	Medium
Personality tests	Medium	Medium–good
Honesty/integrity tests	Poor	Poor
Personal contacts	Poor	Poor
Graphology	Poor	Poor

Source: Adapted from D.D. Steiner and S.W. Gilliland. 2001. "Procedural Justice in Personnel Selection: International and Cross-Cultural Perspectives." *International Journal of Selection and Assessment* 9: 124–37. Reprinted with permission from Wiley-Blackwell.

work and their intentions to buy its products.[250] Job applicants in Germany, Spain, and Portugal reported similar reactions, but there were a few major differences in these cultural groups: German applicants gave poor ratings to biodata and medium ratings to integrity testing, and Portuguese students gave a medium favourability rating to integrity testing.

Most recently, Anderson and Witvliet[251] extended the data on applicant reactions to the Netherlands, as part of reanalyzing the previous data sets they had obtained from Steiner and Gilliland. Their findings were very similar to past research. They concluded that applicant reactions were quite similar across countries and outweighed cross-cultural differences. They suggested that organizations engaged in international and expatriate selection should expect similar reactions from candidates to selection tools as reported in Table 8.5. While data for Canadian applicants are not available, there is no reason to believe that they would be substantially different from those summarized in Table 8.5. Canadian organizations that are considering using integrity tests, graphology, and personal contacts in their hiring process should consider the possible negative consequences for their ability to recruit and hire the best available people.

Summary

 8.6

Psychological testing can be carried out for many purposes, including selection of personnel. Employment testing must meet acceptable professional and legal standards and should be carried out by professionals who are knowledgeable about tests and testing procedures. Only those tests that are psychometrically sound should be used for employment purposes. The rights of job applicants asked to take employment tests, including the right to privacy, must be respected at all times and balanced against the needs of the organization. A fundamental issue is whether the test provides information that is related to those dimensions identified through job analysis.

A variety of tests can be used for selection purposes. Ability tests, both general cognitive ability and more specialized tests, consistently provide highly valid information about future job performance for a broad class of occupations. Cognitive ability tests are the primary predictor for almost every job. The addition of specific ability tests to a general cognitive ability test may increase the overall validity of the selection system. Cognitive ability tests may disadvantage members of some minority groups and should be used with caution or supplemented with assessments that are known not to have adverse impact on protected groups.

Work samples and simulations, particularly situational judgment tests, attempt to base selection on the ability of job applicants to perform actual job components either directly or in some abstract form. Work samples have validity coefficients in the same range as cognitive ability tests and may be very appropriate to use in cases where cognitive ability testing might provoke a negative reaction, for example, in the selection of senior management and executives. Assessment centres appear to be well suited for the selection of managers and professionals and provide a wealth of information, although some evidence suggests that these are elaborate means of assessing both cognitive ability and personality.

All of these approaches are alternatives to more traditional selection procedures. Some of these new selection tools are expensive, and their costs may offset the benefits they provide. Before adopting specific selection techniques, consideration must be given to their perceived fairness and utility.

Personality tests have not had a good reputation as selection predictors, although more recent studies suggest a Big Five construction of personality may improve prediction of certain job performance dimensions. Adding personality tests to a selection system can improve overall validity and reduce adverse impact from testing for cognitive ability. Personality tests are also increasingly being used to assess honesty or integrity, with a considerable degree of predictive accuracy; however, their use may run the risk of inducing unfavourable reactions among job candidates, to the point where they will not consider employment with a company that uses honesty or integrity testing as part of selection.

Employers are increasingly seeking information on applicant physical fitness and drug use. Collection of this type of information may pose a threat to the applicant's privacy, and the use of such tests must conform to appropriate human rights guidelines and professional and ethical standards.

On the whole, the use of selection tools, other than the employment interview, is not extensive in Canada. Most Canadian organizations continue to use selection procedures that have low validity and result in less productive employees and organizations than would be the case if they had adopted selection tools with higher validities for predicting job performance.

Hopefully, HR professionals who are exposed to the benefits of using valid selection tests will have an impact on their company's future bottom line.

Key Terms

ability, p. 358

aptitude, p. 358

assessment centre, p. 383

cognitive ability, p. 359

emotional intelligence, p. 367

genetic testing, p. 374

honesty or integrity tests, p. 396

in-basket test, p. 382

job knowledge, p. 367

leaderless group discussion, p. 382

personality, p. 388

personality traits, p. 389

physical abilities, p. 370

practical intelligence, p. 366

psychomotor abilities, p. 369

self-report inventory, p. 389

sensory/perceptual abilities, p. 370

situational exercises, p. 380

situational judgment tests, p. 381

skill, p. 358

tacit knowledge, p. 366

work samples and simulations, p. 379

Web Links

The *Principles for the Validation and Use of Personnel Selection Procedures*, 4th ed., is available at **http://www.siop.org/_Principles/principlesdefault .aspx.**

The U.S. government's *Uniform Guidelines on Employee Selection Procedures* can be found at **http://www.dol.gov/dol/allcfr/Title_41/Part_60-3/toc.htm.**

The Personnel Psychology Centre's testing information and sample tests are at **http://www.psc-cfp.gc.ca/ppc-cpp/index-eng.htm.**

You will find a wide variety of sample tests at **http://www.queendom .com.**

For Buros's *Mental Measurements Yearbook*, go to **http://www.unl.edu/buros.**

Canadian Forces Aptitude Test (CFAT) examples and practice questions can be accessed at **http://www.publicserviceprep.com/public/full_pkg _canadianforces.aspx.**

Sample questions from the ASVAB can be found at **http://www.baseops .net/ militarybooks/asvab.**

The Hay Group statement on emotional intelligence is at **http://www .haygroup.com/TL.**

For more information on the *Mayer, Salovey, Caruso Emotional Intelligence Test* (MSCEIT), go to **http://www.emotionaliq.com.**

The Treasury Board Secretariat's guidelines on the duty to accommodate persons with disabilities can be found at **http://www.tbs-sct.gc.ca/pol/ doc-eng.aspx?id=12541.**

The complete Canadian Human Rights Commission (CHRC) policy on AIDS/HIV is at http://www.chrc-ccdp.ca/legislation_policies/aids-en.asp.

For the complete CHRC policy on drug and alcohol testing, go to http://www.chrc-ccdp.ca/pdf/poldrgalceng.pdf.

Additional sources on the ethics of genetic testing can be found at http://www.genethics.ca.

A computer simulation of an air traffic controller's function is at http://www.atc-sim.com.

The International Congress on Assessment Center Methods website is located at http://www.assessmentcenters.org.

Required Professional Capabilities (RPCs)

RPC 8.1 Determines the appropriate selection tools and develops new tools as required.
- Selection concepts, and assessment techniques (e.g., interviews, tests, and other widely used selection procedures)
- Human Rights legislation
- Employment Equity legislation
- Organization policies and procedures
- Validity and reliability (conceptual definitions and assessment techniques)
- Statistical analyses and evaluation
- Current and future business plans

RPC 8.2 Administers a variety of selection tools, including tests, interviews, reference checks, etc.
- Selection concepts and assessment techniques (e.g., interviews, tests, and other widely used selection procedures)
- Human Rights legislation
- Employment Equity legislation
- Corporate policies and procedures
- Validity and reliability (conceptual definitions and assessment techniques)

RPC 8.3 Evaluates the effectiveness of selection processes, tools and outcomes.
- Benchmarking techniques
- Relevant legislation and regulations
- Recruiting sources and techniques (both internal and external)
- Selection concepts and assessment techniques (e.g., interviews, tests, and other widely used selection procedures)
- Orientation and career development needs of new employees
- Validity and reliability (conceptual definitions and assessment techniques)

- Techniques to evaluate effectiveness of HR programs (e.g. selection, training, and compensation, etc.)
- Current and future business plans

RPC 8.4 Ensures that policies for required medical testing fall within the limits of statute & contract.
- Industry best practices
- Relevant legislation, regulations and jurisprudence
- Organization goals and culture
- Program and policy development
- Internal and external resources
- Reliability and validity concepts related to common medical tests for substance abuse
- Collective agreements and other contractual requirements
- The legal, ethical, financial, and health and safety issues of employee substance abuse

RPC 8.5 Establishes appointment procedures for candidates selected through the recruitment process, ensuring that conditions of employment are documented and consistent with established policies.
- Human Rights legislation
- Employment Equity legislation
- Organization policies and procedures
- Industry best practices
- Relevant legislation and regulations
- Selection concepts and assessment techniques (e.g., interviews, tests, and other widely used selection procedures)

RPC 8.6 Supports managers in the selection of candidates.
- Criteria for selection
- Human Rights legislation
- Selection concepts and assessment techniques (e.g., interviews, tests, and other widely used selection procedures)
- Communication theories, tools, techniques, and processes
- Methods of creating interpersonal effectiveness
- Employment equity legislation
- Organization policies and procedures
- Current and future business plans

Discussion Questions

1. Why must anyone working in the area of HR be familiar with the professional and legal standards that govern the use of employment tests?
2. What are the limitations of cognitive ability testing? Do these limitations outweigh the advantages of selecting employees based on cognitive ability?
3. What is the Big Five model of personality and what is its relationship to employment testing?

4. If you were going to use a personality test as part of a selection program, what characteristics should the test have?
5. Why is honesty or integrity testing controversial? When and how should these tests be used?
6. Is an employer free to test for physical fitness or drug use before making a job offer? Explain your answer.
7. What is an assessment centre?
8. What is more important: the reliability and validity of a test or the applicant's perception of the test?

Using the Internet

Recruitment and Selection Notebook 8.2 (page 357) identified a number of tests for cognitive ability, personality, integrity, and so on. We also identified several Internet resources that could be used to obtain more information about a particular test. There are many more resources available on the Web from which you could obtain this information. All you need to do is enter the name of the test into your favourite search engine to find them. In the course of this chapter, we identified two measures of emotional intelligence: the MSCEIT and the Bar-On EQi measure. As well, we mentioned the MBTI in relation to personality measures listed in Research and Selection Notebook 8.2.

Choose either the two emotional intelligence measures or the MBTI and a personality test from Recruitment and Selection Notebook 8.2 and answer the following questions:

1. What is the reliability and validity of your two measures?
2. What is known about the use of your two measures in making employment decisions?
3. Have the tests ever been the focus of legal proceedings?
4. Are the tests defensible with respect to human rights issues?
5. Evaluate the two tests against the criteria listed in Recruitment and Selection Notebook 8.1 (page 356) and at the Human Resources Professionals Association website: http://www.hrpa.ca/HRPA/HRResourceCentre/KnowledgeCentre.
6. If you were an HR manager and were asked to choose one or the other of your two tests for use in selecting employees, which one would you recommend, and why?

Exercises

1. Consult the government agency responsible for monitoring the use of selection tests, including physical fitness and drug testing, in your locality. This may be a human rights agency or other government body. Determine whether that agency has a policy on the use of selection tests. Compare that policy with the principles and standards identified in this chapter.

2. Survey 10 companies or organizations in your community to determine whether they use selection tests as part of their hiring procedures. List the tests that are used. Did any organization report using honesty, fitness, or drug tests? If the company did not use any type of testing, report the procedures it used and its reasons, if any, for not using selection tests.

3. Recruitment and Selection Today 8.4 (page 381) presented a sample item from a situational judgment test for use in hiring a manager. We intentionally did not indicate which of the responses was the "best" course of action. Assume that you and some of your classmates are a group of subject-matter experts who have been brought together to develop the responses to items on an SJT, including the "best" option. In conjunction with your other SMEs, identify which of the four options a manager "should do" in the Recruitment and Selection Today 8.4 example. What do you think a manager "would do" in that situation? What do you think would be the "worst" thing for the manager to do in the situation?

4. Design an assessment centre that could be used to select teachers. Describe the rationale for selecting the various procedures that would be included in the centre. Could your centre be replaced by a cognitive ability test and a personality measure?

5. Your workplace, by the nature of the work, has a high level of airborne dust particles. You are concerned about hiring people with environmental sensitivities. Assume that there is an accurate genetic screening device to identify people who might be susceptible to the dust particles. Under what circumstances should you institute the test as part of your hiring procedures? Should it be voluntary or mandatory? How would you implement the test? Who would have access to the results? What would you tell applicants who tested positive?

Case

Applicants to the Royal Canadian Mounted Police must pass a written examination, an interview, and a physical ability test before being accepted for basic training at the RCMP's training centre in Regina. As a federally regulated agency, the RCMP falls under the jurisdiction of the Employment Equity Act, designed to further the employment of women, visible minorities, and other designated groups. The RCMP has had difficulty meeting recruiting targets of 20 percent women, 4.5 percent Aboriginals, and 8.3 percent visible minorities that were set in compliance with the objectives of the Act. A review of testing data showed that Aboriginals and visible minorities scored slightly lower than other groups on the written tests and that 40–50 percent of women applicants fail the physical ability test, a rate considerably higher than that for men.

In response to concerns over failing to meet its recruiting objectives, the RCMP undertook a revision of the examination, which assesses cognitive ability. The revised test retains "academic" items related to composition and computation, but it also has additional items in the form of scenarios that are directed at problem solving. The revised questions are more job-directed and operational in nature. Test items were rewritten to minimize the impact of different regional language styles to ensure that the questions are fair and equitable for all applicants.

With respect to the physical ability test, women had particular difficulty with the upper-body strength requirements. To deal with this problem, the RCMP instituted a six-week pre-training fitness program to help women prepare for the fitness test. It also eased the physical standards for women.

These changes did not meet with unanimous approval, even from groups the changes were designed to help. A lawyer for the Federation of Saskatchewan Indian Nations is quoted as saying, "Instead of watering down their exams, the RCMP should try and change their relationship with Native people. The RCMP is trying to send the message that they want more Natives in the force, but the message to non-Natives is that the Indians are getting an easier ride. Indian people aren't stupid." An MP in Saskatchewan added that "the RCMP should set high physical standards and even higher intellectual standards for their recruits. Public safety should not be compromised for political correctness."

The changes, however, were applauded by members of Nova Scotia's black community, which sees more minority officers as necessary to preventing racial strife. A black leader said that while math may have clear-cut answers, "everyone's general knowledge is not exactly the same.... [General knowledge] is based on experience and exposure to certain things. I think our experiences are different in many respects." He noted that the black community was very different from the Aboriginal community.

Sources: *Alberta Report* (January 19, 1998); *Canadian Press* Newswire (August 11, 1996; January 4, 1998); *The Globe and Mail* (October 14, 1997).

Discussion Questions

1. Did the RCMP do the right thing in revising its written examination and fitness test? Did the RCMP reduce its entrance requirements? Base your response on what you have learned in this chapter.
2. It appears that the RCMP is trying to incorporate a "practical intelligence" component into its examinations. Is this appropriate? What type of "job knowledge" should applicants be tested on?
3. If physical ability is a job requirement for police officers, is it appropriate to have different standards for male and female applicants to the RCMP?
4. Is the existing test fair and equitable for all candidates? Will the new procedures discriminate against white males?

5. Can you design a recruiting campaign to attract more women and visible-minority applicants to the RCMP? What would it look like?
6. Chapter 10 looks at another method that can be used to improve the number of minority applicants: banding (see pages 502–506). This procedure is also controversial. You may want to read that section now and discuss this as an option. How would the public likely react to using banding?

Endnotes

1. Johns, G. 1993. "Constraints on the Adoption of Psychology-Based Personnel Practices, Lessons from Organizational Innovation." *Personnel Psychology* 46: 569–92.
2. Catano, V.M. 2001. "Empirically Supported Interventions and HR Practice." *HRM Research Quarterly* 5: 1–5.
3. Rynes, S.L., A.E. Colbert, and K.G. Brown. 2003. "HR Professionals' Beliefs about Effective Human Resource Practices: Correspondence between Research and Practice." *Human Resource Management* 41: 149–74.
4. Cronbach, L.J. 1990. *Essentials of Psychological Testing.* 5th ed. New York: Harper and Row.
5. Canadian Human Rights Commission. 2007. *Bona Fide Occupational Requirement and Bona Fide Justification under the Canadian Human Rights Act: Implications of Meiorin and Grissmer.* Ottawa: Minister of Pubic Works and Government Services.
6. Canadian Psychological Association. 1987. *Guidelines for Educational and Psychological Testing.* Ottawa.
7. Society for Industrial and Organizational Psychology, Inc. 2003. *Principles for the Validation and Use of Personnel Selection Procedures.* 4th ed. Bowling Green, OH: http://www.siop.org.
8. "Uniform Guidelines on Employee Selection Procedures." 1978. *Federal Register* 43: 38290–315.5.
9. Canadian Psychological Association. 1986.
10. Simner, M.L. 1994. *Recommendations by the Canadian Psychological Association for Improving the Safeguards That Help Protect the Public against Test Misuse.* Ottawa: Canadian Psychological Association.
11. Society for Industrial and Organizational Psychology, Inc. 2003.
12. Camara, W.J., and D.L. Schneider. 1994. "Integrity Tests: Facts and Unresolved Issues." *American Psychologist* 49: 112–19.
13. Ontario Commissioner's Report. 1994. "Workplace Privacy." *Worklife Report* 9: 8–9.
14. Connerly, M.L., R.D. Arvey, S.W. Gilliland, F.A. Mael, R.L. Paetzoid, and P.R. Sackett. 2001. "Selection in the Workplace: Whose Rights Prevail?" *Employee Responsibilities and Rights Journal* 13: 1–13.
15. Prociuk, T.J. 1988. "Applied Psychology in the Canadian Forces: An Overview of Current Research." *Canadian Psychology* 29: 94–102.
16. Catano, V.M., and Bissonnette, A. 2003. *Selection Practices and Organizational Performance.* Paper presented at the annual meeting of the Administrative Sciences Association of Canada, Halifax, NS.
17. Getkake, M., P. Hausdorf, and S.F. Cronshaw. 1992. "Transnational Validity Generalization of Employment Tests from the United States to Canada." *Canadian Journal of Administrative Sciences* 9: 324–35.
18. Goffin, R.D. 2003. "Pre-Employment Tests: Choosing the Best and Avoiding the Rest." Unpublished manuscript. University of Western Ontario.

19. Fleishman, E.A., and M.E. Reilly. 1992. *Handbook of Human Abilities*. Palo Alto, CA: Consulting Psychologists Press.

20. Fleishman, E.A., and M.K. Quaintance. 1984. *Taxonomies of Human Performance: The Description of Human Tasks*. Orlando, FL: Academic Press.

21. Schmidt, F.L. 2002. "The Role of General Cognitive Ability and Job Performance: Why There Cannot Be a Debate." *Human Performance* 15: 187–210.

22. Ree, M.J., and T.R. Carretta. 1998. "General Cognitive Ability and Occupational Performance." In C.L. Cooper and I.T. Robertson, eds., *International Review of Industrial and Organizational Psychology*, Vol. 13 (pp. 159–84). London: John Wiley and Sons.

23. Gottfredson, L. 1986. "Societal Consequences of the *g* Factor in Employment." *Journal of Vocational Behavior* 29: 379–411.

24. Bell, J. 1996. "Brain Power Counts, Too, When Evaluating Prospects." *USA Today* (April 10): 3C.

25. Ree, M.J., and T.R. Carretta. 1998.

26. Gottfredson, L. 1997. "Why *g* Matters: The Complexity of Everyday Life." *Intelligence* 24: 79–132.

27. Gottfredson, L. 2002. "Where and Why *g* Matters: Not a Mystery." *Human Performance* 15: 25–46.

28. Schmidt, F.L., and J.E. Hunter. 1998. "The Validity and Utility of Selection Methods in Personnel Psychology: Practical and Theoretical Implications of 85 Years of Research Findings." *Psychological Bulletin* 124: 262–74.

29. Schmidt, F.L., and J.E. Hunter. 1998.

30. Schmidt, F.L. 2002.

31. Salgado, J.F., N. Anderson, S. Moscoso, C. Bertua, and F. de Fruyt. 2003. "International Validity Generalization of GMA and Cognitive Abilities: A European Communities Meta-Analysis." *Personnel Psychology* 56: 573–605.

32. Bertua, C., N. Anderson, and J. F. Salgado. 2005. "The Predictive Ability of Cognitive Ability Tests: A UK Meta-Analysis." *Journal of Occupational and Organizational Psychology* 78: 387–409.

33. Gottfredson, L. 1986.

34. Cronshaw, 1986.

35. Terpstra, D.E., A.A. Mohammed, and R.B. Kethley. 1999. "An Analysis of Federal Court Cases Involving Nine Selection Devices." *International Journal of Selection and Assessment* 7: 26–34.

36. Murphy, K.R., B.E. Cronin, and A.P. Tan. 2003. "Controversy and Consensus Regarding the Use of Cognitive Ability Testing in Organizations." *Journal of Applied Psychology* 88: 660–71.

37. Schmidt, F.L., and J.E. Hunter. 1998.

38. Outtz, J.L. 2002. "The Role of Cognitive Ability Tests in Selection." *Human Performance* 15: 161–71.

39. Murphy, K.R., B.E. Cronin, and A.P. Tan. 2003.

40. Outtz, J.L. 2002.

41. Schmitt, N.A., W. Rogers, D. Chan, L. Sheppard, and D. Jennings. 1997. "Adverse Impact and Predictive Efficiency of Various Predictor Combinations." *Journal of Applied Psychology* 82: 719–30.

42. Cortina, J.M., N.B. Goldstein, S.C. Payne, H.K. Davison, and S.W. Gilliland. 2000. "The Incremental Validity of Interview Scores over and above Cognitive Ability and Conscientiousness Measures." *Personnel Psychology* 53: 325–51.

43. Vanderpool, M., and V.M. Catano. 2008. "Comparing the Performance of Native North American and Predominantly White Military Recruits on Verbal and Nonverbal Measures of Cognitive Ability." *International Journal of Selection and Assessment* 16: 239–48.

44. Fleishman, E.A., and M.E. Reilly. 1992.

45. Ree, M.J., and T.R. Carretta. 1998.

46. McHenry, J.J., L.M. Hough, J.L. Toquam, M.A. Hanson, and S. Ashworth. 1990. "Project A Validity Results: The Relationship between Predictor and Criterion Domains." *Personnel Psychology* 43: 335–54.

47. Levine, E.L., P.E. Spector, S. Menon, S. Narayanan, and J. Cannon-Bowers. 1996. "Validity Generalization for Cognitive, Psychomotor, and Perceptual Tests for Craft Jobs in the Utility Industry." *Human Performance* 9: 1–22.

48. Ree, M.J., and T.R. Carretta. 1998.

49. Carroll, J.B. 1993. *Human Cognitive Abilities: A Survey of Factor-Analytic Studies*. New York: Cambridge University Press.

50. Campbell, S., and V.M. Catano. 2004. "Using Measures of Specific Abilities to Predict Training Performance in Canadian Forces Operator Occupations." *Military Psychology* 16: 183–201.

51. Johnston, P.J., and V.M. Catano. 2002. "Psychomotor Abilities Tests as Predictors of Training Performance." *Canadian Journal of Behavioural Science* 34: 75–83.

52. Johnston, P.J., and V.M. Catano. 2002.

53. Campbell, J.P. 1990b. "An Overview: The Army Selection and Classification Project (Project A)." *Personnel Psychology* 43: 231–41.

54. Ree, M.J., and T.R. Carretta. 1998.

55. Ree, M.J., and T.R. Carretta. 2002. "g2K." *Human Performance* 15: 2–23.

56. Johnston, P.J., and Catano, V.M. 2002.

57. Campbell, S., and V.M. Catano. 2004.

58. Drasgow, F. 2003. "Intelligence and the Workplace." In W.C. Borman, D.R. Ilgen, and R. Klimoski, eds., *Handbook of Psychology: Industrial and Organizational Psychology* 12: 107–30. New York: John Wiley and Sons.

59. Ree, M.J., and T.R. Carretta. 2002.

60. Carroll, J.B. 1993.

61. Drasgow (p. 123). 2003.

62. Murphy, K.R., B.E. Cronin, and A.P. Tan. 2003.

63. Sternberg, R.J., G.B. Forsythe, J. Hedlund, J.A. Horvath, R.K. Wagner, W.M. Williams et al. 2000. *Practical Intelligence in Everyday Life*. New York: Cambridge University Press.

64. Sternberg, R.J. 2002. "Practical Intelligence, g, and Work Psychology." *Human Performance* 15: 142–60.

65. Sternberg, R.J. 2002.

66. Sternberg, R.J. 2002.

67. McDaniel, M.A., and D.L. Whetzel. 2005. "Situational Judgment Test Research: Informing the Debate on Practical Intelligence Theory." *Intelligence* 33: 515–25.

68. Wagner, R.K., and R.J. Sternberg. 1985. "Practical Intelligence in Real-World Pursuits: The Role of Tacit Knowledge." *Journal of Personality and Social Psychology* 49: 436–58.

69. Wagner, R.K., H. Sujan, M. Sujan, C.A. Rashotte, and R.J. Sternberg. 1999. "Tacit Knowledge in Sales." In R.J. Sternberg and J.A. Horvath, eds., *Tacit Knowledge in Professional Practice* (pp. 155–82). Mahwah, NJ: Lawrence Erlbaum Associates, Inc.

70. Hedlund, J., R.J. Sternberg, and J. Psotka. 2000. *Tacit Knowledge for Military Leadership: Seeking Insight into the Acquisition and Use of Practical Knowledge* (Tech. Rep. No. ARI TR 1105). Alexandria, VA: U.S. Army Research Institute.

71. Taub, G.E. 1999. "Predicting Success: A Critical Analysis of R.J. Sternberg and R.K. Wagner's Theory of Practical Intelligence: Is This an Ability beyond g?" *Dissertation Abstracts International: Section B—The Sciences and Engineering* 60: 0863.

72. Lobsenz, R.E. 1999. "Do Measures of Tacit Knowledge Assess Psychological Phenomena Distinct from General Ability, Personality, and Social Knowledge?" *Dissertation Abstracts International: Section B—The Sciences and Engineering* 59: 05147.

73. McDaniel, M.A., and D.L. Whetzel. 2005.

74. McDaniel, M.A., and D.L. Whetzel. 2005.

75. Schmidt, F.L., and J.E. Hunter. 1993. "Tacit Knowledge, Practical Intelligence, General Mental Ability, and Job Knowledge." *Current Directions of Psychological Science* 2: 8–9.

76. Sternberg, R.J. 2002.

77. Dye, D.A., M. Reck, and M.A. McDaniel. 1993. "The Validity of Job Knowledge Measures." *International Journal of Selection and Assessment* 1: 153–57.

78. Goleman, D. 1995. *Emotional Intelligence*. New York: Bantam Books.

79. Goleman, D. 1998. *Working with Emotional Intelligence*. New York: Bantam Books.

80. Goleman, D. 1995.

81. Olive, D. 1998. "EQ, Not IQ, Is Ticket to Top for Psych Guru." *Financial Post/National Post* (November 23): C12.

82. Day, A.L., and S.S. Carroll. 2004. "Using an Ability-Based Measure of Emotional Intelligence to Predict Individual Performance, Group Performance and Group Citizenship Behaviours." *Personality and Individual Differences* 36: 1443–58.

83. Mayer, J.D., P. Salovey, and D.R. Caruso. 2000. "Emotional Intelligence as Zeitgeist, as Personality, and as a Mental Ability." In R. Bar-On and R.J. Parker, eds., *The Handbook of Emotional Intelligence: Theory, Development, Assessment, and Application at Home, School, and in the Workplace* (pp. 92–117). San Francisco: Jossey-Bass.

84. Barrett, G.V., R.F. Miguel, J.A. Tan, and J.M. Hurd. 2001. *Emotional Intelligence: The Madison Avenue Approach to Science and Professional Practice*. Paper presented at the 16th annual conference of the Society for Industrial and Organizational Psychology, San Diego.

85. Zeidner, M., G. Matthews, and R.D. Roberts. 2004. "Emotional Intelligence in the Workplace: A Critical Review." *Applied Psychology: An International Review* 53: 371–99.

86. Salovey, P., and J.D. Mayer. 1990. "Emotional Intelligence." *Imagination, Cognition, and Personality* 9: 185–211.

87. Mayer, J.D., and P. Salovey. 1997. "What Is Emotional Intelligence?" In P. Salovey and D. Sluyter, eds., *Emotional Development and Emotional Intelligence: Implications for Educators*. New York: Basic Books.

88. Goleman, D. 1995.

89. Mayer, J.D., and P. Salovey. 1997.

90. Polednik, L., and E. Greig. 2000. "Personality and Emotional Intelligence." *The British Journal of Administrative Management* 19: 9.

91. Bar-On, R. 1997. *Emotional Quotient Inventory: Technical Manual*. Toronto: Multi-Health Systems.

92. Mayer, J.D., P. Salovey, and D.R. Caruso. 2000. *Test Manual for the Mayer, Salovey, Caruso Emotional Intelligence Test: Research Version 1.1*. 3rd ed. Toronto: Multi-Health Systems.

93. Newsome, S., A.L. Day, and V.M. Catano. 2000. "Assessing the Predictive Validity of Emotional Intelligence." *Personality and Individual Differences* 29: 1005–16.

94. Polednik, L., and E. Greig. 2000.

95. Grubb, W.L., III, and M.A. McDaniel. 2007. "The Fakability of Bar-On's Emotional Quotient Inventory Short Form: Catch Me If You Can." *Human Performance* 20: 43–50.

96. Day, A.L., and S.A. Carroll. 2004.

97. Davies, M., L. Stankov, and R.D. Roberts. 1998. "Emotional Intelligence: In Search of an Elusive Construct." *Journal of Personality and Social Psychology* 75: 989–1015.

98. Conte, J.M. 2005. "A Review and Critique of Emotional Intelligence Measures." *Journal of Organizational Behavior* 26: 433–40.

99. Ashkanasy, N.M, and C.S. Daus. 2005. "Rumors of the Death of Emotional Intelligence in Organizational Behavior Are Vastly Exaggerated." *Journal of Organizational Behavior* 26: 441–52.

100. "Emotional Intelligence: A Collection of New Measures and Industry-Leading Solutions." 2001. *Multi-Health Systems*. Toronto: Multi-Health Systems.

101. Day, A.L., and S.A. Carroll. 2004.

102. Davies, M., L. Stankov, and R.D. Roberts. 1998.

103. Newsome, S., A.L. Day, and V.M. Catano. 2000.

104. Arvey, R.D., G.L. Renz, and T.W. Watson. 1998. "Emotionality and Job Performance: Implications for Personnel Selection." In G.R. Ferris, ed., *Research in Personnel and Human Resource Management*, Vol. 16 (pp. 103–47). Stamford, CT: JAI Press.

105. Mayer, J.D., P. Salovey, D.R. Caruso, and G. Sitarenios. 2003. Measuring Emotional Intelligence with the MSCEIT V2.0. *Emotion* 3: 97–105.

106. Fleishman, E.A., and M.E. Reilly. 1992.

107. Levine, E.L., P.E. Spector, S. Menon, S. Narayanan, and J. Cannon-Bowers. 1996.

108. Johnston, P.J., and V.M. Catano. 2002.

109. Alderton, D.L., J.H. Wolfe, and G.E. Larson. 1997. "The eCAT Battery." *Military Psychology* 9(1): 5–37.

110. Johnston, P.J., and V.M. Catano. 2002.

111. Hogan, J. 1991. "Structure of Physical Performance in Occupational Tasks." *Journal of Applied Psychology* 76: 495–507.

112. Fleishman, E.A., and M.E. Reilly. 1992.

113. Campion, M.A. 1983. "Personnel Selection for Physically Demanding Jobs: Review and Recommendation." *Personnel Psychology* 36: 527–50.

114. Arvey, R.D., T.E. Landon, S.M. Nutting, and S.E. Maxwell. 1992. "Development of Physical Ability Tests for Police Officers: A Construct Validation Approach." *Journal of Applied Psychology* 77: 996–1009.

115. Dunn, K., and E. Dawson. 1994. "The Right Person for the Right Job." *Occupational Health and Safety Canada* 10: 28–31.

116. *British Columbia (Public Service Employee Relations Commission) v. BCGSEU.* Supreme Court of Canada decision rendered September 9, 1999.

117. Canadian Human Rights Commission. *Policy on HIV/AIDS*: http://www.chrc-ccdp.ca/legislation_policies/aids-en.asp.

118. "Specialists Back Genetic Testing—Study." 1995. *Halifax Daily News* (December 23): 10.

119. MacDonald, C., and Williams-Jones, B. 2002. "Ethics and Genetics: Susceptibility Testing in the Workplace." *Journal of Business Ethics* 35: 235–241. (Summary online: http://www.bioethics.ca/wgt).

120. Yanchinski, S. 1990. "Employees under a Microscope." *The Globe and Mail* (January 3): D3.

121. MacDonald, C., and B. Williams-Jones. 2002.

122. Sabourin, M. 1999. "Bad Blood: Issues Surrounding Workplace Genetic Testing." *Occupational Health and Safety* 15: 34–41.

123. Normand, J., S.D. Salyards, and J.J. Mahoney. 1990. "An Evaluation of Pre-Employment Drug Testing." *Journal of Applied Psychology* 75: 629–39.

124. Parish, D.C. 1989. "Relation of the Pre-employment Drug Testing Result to Employment Status: A One-Year Follow-Up." *Journal of General Internal Medicine* 4: 44–47.

125. Harris, M.M., and M.L. Trusty. 1997. "Drug and Alcohol Programs in the Workplace: A Review of Recent Literature." In C.L. Cooper and I.T. Robertson, eds., *International Review of Industrial and Organizational Psychology*, Vol. 12 (pp. 289–315). London: John Wiley and Sons.

126. Catano, V.M., and A. Bissonnette. 2008. *Evolution of Selection Tools Used by Canadian Employers*. Unpublished manuscript. Halifax, NS.

127. Seijts, G.H., D.P. Skarlicki, and S.W. Gilliland. 2003. "Canadian and American Reactions to Drug and Alcohol Testing Programs in the Workplace." *Employee Responsibilities and Rights Journal* 15: 191–208.

128. Asher, J.J., and J.A. Sciarrino. 1974. "Realistic Work Sample Tests." *Personnel Psychology* 27: 519–33.

129. Asher, J.J., and J.A. Sciarrino. 1974.

130. Spinner, B. 1990. *Predicting Success in Basic Flying Training from the Canadian Automated Pilot Selection System* (Working Paper 90-6). Willowdale, ON: Canadian Forces Personnel Applied Research Unit.

131. Thompson, C.T. 1995. "Actress to Help Test Applicants for Jobs at Prison." *Kitchener Record* (July 13): B1.

132. McDaniel, M.A., and N.T. Nguyen. 2001. "Situational Judgment Tests: A Review of Practice and Constructs Assessed." *International Journal of Selection and Assessment* 9: 103–13.

133. Weekley, J., and R. Ployhart (eds.). 2006. *Situational Judgment Tests: Theory, Measurement, and Application.* Mahwah, NJ: Lawrence Erlbaum Associates.

134. Richman-Hirsch, W.L., J.B. Olson-Buchanan, and F. Drasgow. 2000. "Examining the Impact of Administration Medium on Examinee Perceptions and Attitudes. *Journal of Applied Psychology* 85: 880–87.

135. Weekly, J.A., and C. Jones. 1997. "Video-Based Situational Testing." *Personnel Psychology* 50: 25–49.

136. Chan, D., and N. Schmitt. 1997.

137. Ployhart, R.E., and M.G. Ehrhart. 2003. "Be Careful What You Ask For: Effects of Response Instructions on the Construct Validity and Reliability of Situational Judgment Tests." *International Journal of Selection and Assessment* 11: 1–16.

138. McDaniel, M.A., F.P. Morgeson, E.B. Finnegan, M.A. Campion, and E.P. Braverman. 2001. "Use of Situational Judgment Tests to Predict Job Performance: A Clarification of the Literature." *Journal of Applied Psychology* 86: 730–40.

139. Chan, D., and N. Schmitt. 2002. "Situational Judgment and Job Performance." *Human Performance* 15: 233–54.

140. Chan, D., and N. Schmitt (p. 240). 2002.

141. McDaniel, M.A., F.P. Morgeson, E.B. Finnegan, M.A. Campion, and E.P. Braverman. 2001.

142. Drasgow, F. 2003.

143. Schippmann, J.S., E.P. Prien, and J.A. Katz. 1990. "Reliability and Validity of In-Basket Performance." *Personnel Psychology* 43: 837–59.

144. Rolland, J.P. 1999. "Construct Validity of In-Basket Dimensions." *European Revue of Applied Psychology* 49: 251–59.

145. Finkle, R.B. 1976. "Managerial Assessment Centers." In M.D. Dunnette, ed., *Handbook of Industrial and Organizational Psychology.* Chicago: Rand McNally.

146. Bray, D.W., R.J. Campbell, and D.L. Grant. 1974. *Formative Years in Business: A Long-Term AT&T Study of Managerial Lives.* New York: Wiley.

147. Goffin, R.D., M.G. Rothstein, and N.G. Johnston. 1996. "Personality Testing and the Assessment Center: Incremental Validity for Managerial Selection." *Journal of Applied Psychology* 81: 746–56.

148. Gaugler, B.B., D.B. Rosenthal, G.C. Thornton, and C. Bentson. 1987. "Meta-Analysis of Assessment Center Validity." *Journal of Applied Psychology* 72: 493–511.

149. Schmitt, N.A., J.R. Schneider, and S.A. Cohen. 1990. "Factors Affecting Validity of a Regionally Administered Assessment Center." *Personnel Psychology* 43: 2–11.

150. Hermelin, E., F. Lievens, and I.T. Robertson. 2007. "The Validity of Assessment Centers for the Prediction of Supervisory Performance Ratings: A Meta-Analysis." *International Journal of Selection and Assessment* 15: 405–11.

151. Arthur, W., Jr., E.A. Day, T.L. McNelley, and P.S. Edens. 2003. "A Meta-Analysis of the Criterion-Related Validity of Assessment Center Dimensions." *Personnel Psychology* 56: 125–54.

152. Gaugler, B.B., D.B. Rosenthal, G.C. Thornton, and C. Bentson. 1987.

153. Collins, J.D., F.L. Schmidt, M. Sanchez-Ku, L. Thomas, M.A. McDaniel, and H. Le. 2003. "Can Basic Individual Differences Shed Light on the Construct Meaning of Assessment Center Evaluations?" *International Journal of Selection and Assessment* 11: 17–29.

154. Klimoski, R.J., and M. Brickner. 1987. "Why Do Assessment Centers Work? The Puzzle of Assessment Center Validity." *Personnel Psychology* 40: 243–60.

155. Bartels, L.K., and D. Doverspike. 1997. "Assessing the Assessor: The Relationship of Assessor Personality to Leniency in Assessment Center Ratings." *Journal of Social Behavior and Personality* 12: 179–90.

156. Collins, J.D., F.L. Schmidt, M. Sanchez-Ku, L. Thomas, M.A. McDaniel, and H. Le. 2003.

157. Bowler, M.C., and D.J. Woehr. 2006. "A Meta-Analytic Evaluation of the Impact of Dimension and Exercise Factors on Assessment Center Ratings." *Journal of Applied Psychology* 91: 1114–24.

158. Howard, A. 1997. "A Reassessment of Assessment Centers: Challenges for the 21st Century." *Journal of Social Behavior and Personality* 12: 13–52.

159. Dean, M.E., P.L. Roth, and P. Bobko. 2008. "Ethnic and Subgroup Differences in Assessment Center Ratings: A Meta-Analysis." *Journal of Applied Psychology* 93: 685–91.

160. Hogan, R., J. Hogan, and B.W. Roberts. 1996. "Personality Measurement and Employment Decisions: Questions and Answers." *American Psychologist* 51: 469–77.

161. Hall, C.S., and G. Lindzey. 1970. *Theories of Personality.* New York: Wiley.

162. Jenkins, C.D., S.J. Zyzanski, and R.H. Rosenman. 1979. *Jenkins Activity Survey Manual.* New York: Psychological Corporation.

163. Hough, L.M. 1998. "Effects of Intentional Distortion in Personality Measurement and Evaluation of Suggested Palliatives." *Human Performance* 11: 209–44.

164. Ones, D., and C. Viswesvaran. 1998a. "The Effects of Social Desirability and Faking on Personality and Integrity Testing for Personnel Selection." *Human Performance* 11: 245–69.

165. Hough, L.M. 1998.

166. Rosse, J.G., M.D. Steecher, J.L. Miller, and R.A. Levin. 1998. "The Impact of Response Distortion on Preemployment Personality Testing and Hiring Decisions." *Journal of Applied Psychology* 83: 634–44.

167. Ellington, J.E., P.R. Sackett, and L.M. Hough. 1999. "Social Desirability Corrections in Personality Measurement: Issues of Applicant Comparison and Construct Validity." *Journal of Applied Psychology* 84: 155–66.

168. Zickar, M.J., and F. Drasgow. 1996. "Detecting Faking on a Personality Instrument Using Appropriateness Measurement." *Applied Psychological Measurement* 20: 71–87.

169. Zickar, M.J. 2001. "Conquering the Next Frontier: Modeling Personality Data with Item Response Theory." In B. Roberts and R.T. Hogan, eds., *Personality Psychology in the Workplace* (pp. 141–60). Washington, DC: American Psychological Association.

170. Zickar, M.J., and F. Drasgow. 1996.

171. Barrick, M.R., and M.K. Mount. 1991. "The Big Five Personality Dimensions and Job Performance: A Meta-Analysis." *Personnel Psychology* 44: 1–26.

172. Ones, D., and C. Viswesvaran. 1998a.

173. Ones, D., and C. Viswesvaran. 1998a.

174. Alliger, G.M., and S.A. Dwight. 2000. "A Meta-Analytic Investigation of the Susceptibility of Integrity Tests to Faking and Coaching." *Educational and Psychological Measurement* 60: 59–73.

175. Hough, L.M., and A. Furnham. 2003. "Use of Personality Variables in Work Settings." In W.C. Borman, D.R. Ilgen, and R. Klimoski, eds., *Handbook of Psychology: Industrial and Organizational Psychology* 12: 131–69. New York: John Wiley and Sons.

176. Rosse, J.G., M.D. Steecher, J.L. Miller, and R.A Levin. 1998.

177. Schmitt, N., and F.L. Oswald. 2006. "The Impact of Corrections for Faking on the Validity of Noncognitive Measures in Selection Settings." *Journal of Applied Psychology* 91: 613–21.

178. Hogan, J., P. Barrett, and R. Hogan. 2007. "Personality Measurement, Faking, and Employment Selection." *Journal of Applied Psychology* 92: 1270–85.

179. Rosse, J.G., M.D. Steecher, J.L. Miller, and R.A Levin. 1998.

180. Guion, R.M. 1965. *Personnel Testing.* New York: McGraw Hill.

181. Guion, R.M., and R.F. Gottier. 1965. "Validity of Personality Measures in Personnel Selection." *Personnel Psychology* 18: 135–64.

182. Tett, R.P., D.N. Jackson, and M. Rothstein. 1991. "Personality Measures as Predictors of Job Performance: A Meta-Analytic Review." *Personnel Psychology* 44: 703–42.

183. Salgado, J.F. 1997. "The Five Factor Model of Personality and Job Performance in the European Community." *Journal of Applied Psychology* 82: 30–43.

184. Salgado, J.F. 1998. "Big Five Personality Dimensions and Job Performance in Army and Civil Occupations: A European Perspective." *Human Performance* 11: 271–88.

185. McHenry, J.J., L.M. Hough, J.L. Toquam, M.A. Hanson, and S. Ashworth. 1990.

186. Hough, L.M., N.K. Eaton, M.D. Dunnette, J.D. Kamp, and R.A. McCloy. 1990. "Criterion-Related Validities of Personality Constructs and the Effect of Response Distortion on Those Validities." Monograph. *Journal of Applied Psychology* 75: 581–95.

187. Barrick, M.R., and M.K. Mount. 1991.

188. Hough, L.M., and A. Furnham. 2003.

189. "Personality Tests Flourishing as Employers Try to Weed Out Problem Hires." 1999. *Financial Post/National Post* (August 5): C7.

190. Digman, J.M. 1990. "Personality Structure: Emergence of the Five Factor Model." In M. Rosenzweig and L.W. Porter, eds., *Annual Review of Psychology.* Palo Alto, CA: Annual Reviews.

191. Hough, L.M., and A. Furnham. 2003.

192. Campbell, J.P. 1990a. "Modeling the Performance Prediction Problem in Industrial and Organizational Psychology." In M.D. Dunnette and L.M. Hough, eds., *The Handbook of Industrial and Organizational Psychology,* Vol. 1 (pp. 687–32). 2nd ed. San Diego: Consulting Psychologists Press.

193. Mount, M.K., and M.R. Barrick. 1995. "The Big Five Personality Dimensions: Implications for Research and Practice in Human Resources Management." In G.R. Ferris, ed., *Research in Personnel and Human Resources Management,* Vol. 13 (pp. 153–200). Greenwich, CT: JAI Press.

194. McManus, M.A., and M.L. Kelly. 1999. "Personality Measures and Biodata: Evidence Regarding Their Incremental Predictive Value in the Life Insurance Industry." *Personnel Psychology* 52: 137–48.

195. Barrick, M.R., and M.K. Mount. 1991.

196. Barrick, M.R., and M.K. Mount. 1991.

197. Mount, M.K., M.R. Barrick, and G.L. Stewart. 1998. "Five-Factor Model of Personality and Performance in Jobs Involving Interpersonal Interactions." *Human Performance* 11: 145–65.

198. Hough, L.M., and A. Furnham. 2003.

199. Schmidt, F.L., and J.E. Hunter. 1998. "The Validity and Utility of Selection Methods in Personnel Psychology: Practical and Theoretical Implications of 85 Years of Research Findings." *Psychological Bulletin* 124: 262–74.

200. Hogan, R., J. Hogan, and B.W. Roberts. 1996.

201. Outtz, J.L. 2002.

202. Gardner, W.L., and M.J. Martinko. 1996. "Using the Myers-Briggs-Type Indicator to Study Managers: A Literature Review and Research Agenda." *Journal of Management* 22: 45–83.

203. Kichuk, S.L., and W.H. Wiesner. 1998. "Work Teams: Selecting Members for Optimal Performance." *Canadian Psychology* 39: 23–32.

204. Kichuk, S.L., and W.H. Wiesner. 1996. *The Effect of the "Big Five" Personality Factors on Team Performance: Implications for Selecting Optimal Performance.* Paper presented at the Fourth Annual Advanced Concepts Conference on Work Teams, Dallas, TX.

205. Halfhill, T., T.M. Nielson, E. Sundstrom, and A. Weilbaecher. 2005. "Group Personality Composition and Performance in Military Service Teams." *Military Psychology* 17: 41–54.

206. Tett, R.P., D.N. Jackson, and M. Rothstein. 1991.

207. Paunonen, S.V., M.G. Rothstein, and D.N. Jackson. 1999. "Narrow Reasoning about the Use of Broad Personality Measures for Personnel Selection." *Journal of Organizational Behavior* 20: 389–405.

208. Paunonen, S.V., and A.A.A.M. Nicol. 2001. "The Personality Hierarchy and the Prediction of Work Behaviors." In B. Roberts and R.T. Hogan, eds., *Personality Psychology in the Workplace* (pp. 161–91). Washington, DC: American Psychological Association.

209. Ones, D., and C. Viswesvaran. 1996. "Bandwidth-Fidelity Dilemma in Personality Measurement for Personnel Selection." *Journal of Organizational Behavior* 17: 609–26.

210. Hough, L.M., and A. Furnham. 2003.

211. Strauss, M. 2000. "Retailers Plagued by Thieving Employees." *The Globe and Mail* (March 28): A1.

212. Fortman, K., C. Leslie, and M. Cunningham. 2002. "Cross-Cultural Comparisons of the Reid Integrity Scales in Latin America and South Africa." *International Journal of Selection and Assessment* 10: 98–108.

213. Employee Polygraph Protection Act (29 USC §2001 et seq.; 29 CFR 801).

214. Jones, J., ed. 1991. *Pre-Employment Honesty Testing: Current Research and Future Directions.* New York: Quorum Books.

215. Sackett, P.R., L.R. Burris, and C. Callahan. 1989. "Integrity Testing for Personnel Selection: An Update." *Personnel Psychology* 42: 491–529.

216. Hogan, J., and R. Hogan. 1989. "How to Measure Employee Reliability." *Journal of Applied Psychology* 74: 273–79.

217. Alliger, G.M., S.O. Lilienfeld, and K.E. Mitchell. 1996. "The Susceptibility of Overt and Covert Integrity Tests to Coaching and Faking." *Psychological Science* 7: 32–39.

218. Collins, J.D., and F.L. Schmidt. 1993. "Personality, Integrity, and White-Collar Crime: A Construct Validity Study." *Personnel Psychology* 46: 295–311.

219. Temple, W. 1992. "Counterproductive Behaviour Costs Millions." *British Journal of Administrative Management* (April/May): 20–21.

220. Ones, D., C. Viswesvaran, and F.L. Schmidt. 1993. "Comprehensive Meta-Analysis of Integrity Test Validities: Findings and Implications for Personnel Selection and Theories of Job Performance." *Journal of Applied Psychology* 78: 679–703.

221. Ones, D., and C. Viswesvaran. 1998a.

222. Ones, D., C. Viswesvaran, and F.L. Schmidt. 1993.

223. Ones, D.S., and C. Viswesvaran. 1998b. "Integrity Testing in Organizations." In R.W. Griffin, A. O'Leary, and J.M. Collins, eds., *Dysfunctional Behavior in Organizations:* Vol. 2, *Nonviolent Behaviors in Organizations.* Greenwich, CT: JAI Press.

224. Sackett, P.R., and J.E. Wanek. 1996. "New Developments in the Use of Measures of Honesty, Integrity, Conscientiousness, Dependability, Trustworthiness, and Reliability for Personnel Selection." *Personnel Psychology* 49: 787–827.

225. Steiner, D.D., and S.W. Gilliland. 1996. "Fairness Reactions to Personnel Selection Techniques in France and the United States." *Journal of Applied Psychology* 81: 131–41.

226. Dwight, S.A., and G.M. Alliger. 1997. "Reactions to Overt Integrity Testing Items." *Educational and Psychological Measurement* 50: 587–99.

227. Camara, W.J., and D.L. Schneider. 1994.

228. Arnold, D.W. 1991. "To Test or Not to Test: Legal Issues in Integrity Testing." *Forensic Psychology* 4: 62–67.

229. Neuman, G.A., and R. Baudoun. 1998. "An Empirical Examination of Overt and Covert Integrity Tests." *Journal of Business and Psychology* 13: 65–79.

230. Camara, W.J., and D.L. Schneider. 1994.

231. Catano, V.M., and M.A. Prosser. 2007. "A Review of Integrity Tests and Their Implications for Selection of Security Personnel in a Canadian Context." *The Canadian Journal of Police & Security Services* 5: 1–18.

232. Ones, D.S., and C. Viswesvaran. 1998b.

233. Wanek, J.E. 1999. "Integrity and Honesty Testing: What Do We Know? How Do We Use It?" *International Journal of Selection and Assessment* 7: 183–95.

234. Ben-Shukhar, G., M. Bar-Hillel, Y. Bilu, E. Ben-Abba, and A. Flug. 1986. "Can Graphology Predict Occupational Success? Two Empirical Studies and Some Methodological Ruminations." *Journal of Applied Psychology* 71: 645–53.

235. Steiner, D.D., and S.W. Gilliland. 2001. "Procedural Justice in Personnel Selection: International and Cross-Cultural Perspectives." *International Journal of Selection and Assessment* 9: 124–37.

236. "A New Slant on Job Applicants: How Grapho-Analysis, the Study of Handwriting, Can Play a Role in the Management Hiring Process." 1994. *This Week in Business* (August 1): F3–F4.

237. Goodstein, L.D., and R.I. Lanyon. 1999. "Applications of Personality Assessment to the Workplace: A Review." *Journal of Business and Psychology* 13: 291–322.

238. Hogan, R., J. Hogan, and B.W. Roberts. 1996.

239. Hogan, R., J. Hogan, and B.W. Roberts. 1996.

240. Ones, D., C. Viswesvaran, and F.L. Schmidt. 1993.

241. Hogan, R., J. Hogan, and B.W. Roberts. 1996.

242. *Soroka v. Dayton Hudson Corp.*, 1 Cal. Rptr. 2nd 77 (Cal. App. 1st Dist. 1991).

243. Ployhart, R.E., and B.C. Holtz. 2008. "The Diversity–Validity Dilemma: Strategies for Reducing Racioethnic and Sex Subgroup Differences and Adverse Impact in Selection." *Personnel Psychology* 6: 153–72.

244. Rynes, S.L., A.E. Colbert, and K.G. Brown. 2003.

245. Catano, V.M., and A. Bissonnette. 2008. *Evolution of Selection Tools Used by Canadian Employers.* Unpublished manuscript.

246. Thacker, J.W., and R.J. Cattaneo. 1987. "The Canadian Personnel Function: Status and Practices." *Proceedings of the Administrative Sciences Association of Canada Annual Meeting,* 56–66.

247. Catano, V.M., and A. Bissonnette. 2003. *Selection Practices and Organizational Performance.* Paper presented at the annual meeting of the Administrative Sciences Association of Canada, Halifax, NS.

248. Catano, V.M., and A. Bissonnette. 2003.

249. Steiner, D.D., and S.W. Gilliland. 1996.

250. Stinglhamber, F., C. Vandenberghe, and S. Brancart. 1999. "Les réactions des candidats envers les techniques de sélection de personnel: Une étude dans un contexte francophone." *Travail Humain* 62: 347–61.

251. Anderson, N., and C. Witvliet. 2008. "Fairness Reactions to Personnel Selection Methods: An International Comparison between the Netherlands, the United States, France, Spain, Portugal, and Singapore." *International Journal of Selection and Assessment* 16: 1–13.

Chapter 9

Selection III: Interviewing

Chapter Learning Objectives

This chapter presents new and more effective alternatives to the traditional approaches to employment interviewing.

After reading this chapter you should:

- understand the purposes and uses of employment interviews;
- know the multiple phases of the employment interview and the factors affecting employment interview decisions;
- appreciate the selection errors associated with traditional approaches to employment interviewing;
- understand the elements of employment interview structuring;
- be aware of different structured interviewing techniques and their relative advantages and disadvantages;
- appreciate the legal and predictive advantages of structured employment interviewing methods;
- begin developing competence in the design of effective interview questions and scoring guides;
- know about innovations and future directions in interview research and practice; and
- appreciate the role of employment interviews in the changing organizational environment.

The dean of the faculty at a university decided to create the position of academic advisor for undergraduate students. The associate dean had done much of this advising in the past. The work consisted mostly of meeting with students and reviewing their transcripts and records to determine if they were fulfilling their degree and major course requirements. Both the students and advisors had access to an online reporting system that contained all of the necessary information, although it was not presented in the most user-friendly manner. The advisor, when he or she spotted difficulties in a student's record, would have to arrange for the student to take corrective action, which meant liaising with heads of departments within the faculty. The advisor was also to provide career information to students and to make them aware of resources within the university that they could use to improve their academic performance and to prepare for postgraduate programs.

The dean created a Search Committee consisting of the dean and associate dean and two department heads. The committee met and developed an ad for the position, along the lines presented above. The advertisement was posted both internally and externally. The position drew a fairly large number of applicants, who were requested to submit a résumé along with their application letter.

The Search Committee reviewed the applications to develop a shortlist. A number of the applicants had experience in academic advising; several others did not have this experience but had experience in a university environment. One internal applicant, in particular, drew the attention of the Search Committee. She did not have advising experience but had worked in the Registrar's Office, where she dealt with student records and was familiar with the online reporting system. The committee was divided over whether this internal candidate should even be considered for the position because of her lack of relevant work experience, but in the end they decided to interview her.

Each member of the committee developed a few questions that they would ask candidates. No forethought was given to the nature of the questions, nor were all candidates asked the same set of questions. In some cases, the questions were made up as the interview progressed. With respect to the internal candidate, most of the questions focused on the online reporting system and the candidate's knowledge of statistics regarding the numbers of students in different programs and other information she had developed through her job in the Registrar's Office. The candidate was very personable and had a good interaction with the committee. She had known several of the members through her work in the Registrar's Office. The Search Committee was extremely impressed by her knowledge of student statistics and her demeanour. Through the interview, they developed a picture of the candidate as someone who was very familiar with the university's academic rules and regulations. They felt she would be just the right person for the position and unanimously recommended her hiring.

The applicant was placed on a year's probationary appointment. During the first month, the dean and associate dean began to have doubts about the wisdom of their choice. The new hire had difficulty interacting with students and faculty, a primary requirement of the position. Increasingly, she would refer students to others for the advice that she was supposed to be giving them. Often, the advice she gave was wrong and led to students dropping or adding courses without justification. In some cases, these decisions caused the university to refund tuitions to students. Complaints about her performance continued throughout the year, with suggestions given to her for remedial action not having led to any improvements. Finally, at the end of the probationary period, the advisor was let go.

The dean learned from the experience. Before initiating a new search for the academic advisor's replacement, the dean decided that the Search Committee needed to understand what the position really involved and the requirements for doing it. The dean also realized that in the next round of interviews, the committee had to ask questions that were most relevant to the tasks and duties that the advisor would perform. It takes more than a "gut feeling" to find the right person.

The kind of interview used by the Search Committee in the opening vignette was not unusual. Neither was the manner in which it was constructed and used. The goal of this chapter is to provide insights into interviewing best practices that permit interviewers to be much more effective than the Search Committee was in selecting the best candidate for a position.

The employment interview is one of the oldest and most widely used of all selection procedures.[1,2] Data from Statistics Canada's *Workplace and Employee Survey* show that 75 percent of the firms that used pre-hiring selection relied on some type of interview.[3] Moreover, when making selection decisions, recruiters tend to have more confidence in the interview than in information provided from application forms, references, test results, or any other source of information about the applicant.[4,5] This was the case in the vignette, when the Search Committee went with information it obtained through the interview rather than the information in the candidate's résumé that suggested she did not have the required experience for the position.

Chapter 9: Selection III: Interviewing

Given the interview's importance in the employee selection process, it is worth devoting close attention to this selection technique, particularly to relatively recent improvements in interview methods. Modern interview techniques, if used properly, can significantly improve the effectiveness of the traditional interview as a selection tool.

Purposes and Uses of the Interview

Although interviews, as discussed in Chapter 7, are often used as preliminary screening devices (e.g., in recruitment centres), they are most frequently used as one of the last stages in the selection process. Leaving the interview until the end allows the other selection instruments, such as tests, to screen out unqualified applicants and reduces the number of people who must be interviewed. It is usually desirable to reduce the number of interviewees because interviews are relatively expensive, compared with other selection instruments such as tests or the screening of résumés.

The interview is often used to collect information that has not been provided in the résumé or application form. Interviews are typically conducted by HR staff or by supervisors or line managers (who usually have little interview training).[6] They tend to have little time available for preparing interview questions and often use standard questions, which they hear others using or which they remember having been asked when they were interviewees. In many organizations, applicants are interviewed by several interviewers, either simultaneously as part of panel or board interviews or in sequential or serial interviews.[7,8]

Although interviews can be and have been used to assess job knowledge and cognitive ability, they are probably best suited to the assessment of non-cognitive attributes such as interpersonal relationships or social skills, initiative, dependability, perseverance, teamwork, leadership skills, adaptability or flexibility, organizational citizenship behaviour, and organizational fit.[9–15] As you may recognize from our discussion of personality in Chapter 8, several of these attributes are also measured by different personality inventories.

Interviews are also used to sell the job to the applicant. They provide applicants with an opportunity to ask questions about the job and the organization and to decide whether the job and the organization provide an appropriate fit. In fact, an interviewer's friendliness, warmth, and humour, as well as job knowledge and general competence, seem to increase applicant attraction to the organization and the likelihood that an applicant will accept a job offer.[16] However, interviewers' effects on applicant job choice are not as strong as factors such as pay, the job itself, promotion opportunities, or geographical location.[17,18] Moreover, when recruiters put too much effort into selling the job, rather than focusing on the selection function, they actually reduce the attractiveness of the job for applicants.[19] It is possible that applicants become suspicious and back away when they perceive the recruiter trying too hard to convince them of the merits of the job or organization.

Recently, interviews have also been used in the termination of employees. As organizations downsize or "rightsize," jobs are eliminated and employees must compete for a smaller number of redesigned jobs. The interview serves to assist in identifying employees who have the necessary knowledge, skills, abilities, and other attributes (KSAOs) to perform well in the redesigned jobs and who therefore should remain employed by the organization. Although there is considerable debate about the merits of downsizing as a cure for ailing organizations, such interviews have become commonplace.[20]

A Model of Information Processing and Decision Making in the Interview

Employment interviews are complex interactions between applicants and interviewers, which occur in the context of a larger selection system. That is, in addition to conducting interviews, employers collect information about the applicant from other sources, such as application forms, résumés, reference checks, and tests. This information from other sources creates pre-interview impressions, which may influence the interview process and interview outcomes.[21-23] Moreover, the interviewee and interviewer generally have different objectives. The interviewee is motivated to create a positive impression with the objective of receiving a job offer. The interviewer, on the other hand, is motivated to get an accurate assessment of the interviewee in order to select the best candidate and avoid making a hiring mistake. In order to do this, the interviewer needs to process and make sense of a large amount of complex and often inconsistent or contradictory information.

Several models have been developed to help us better understand the information-processing and decision-making challenges faced by the interviewer. One such model, developed by Dipboye, is presented in Figure 9.1.[24] The model describes in detail the interaction between applicant and interviewer during the interview, as well as the information processing and decision making engaged in by both interviewer and applicant before, during, and after the interview. However, it is important to keep in mind that these processes occur in the context of an organization and its environment. Factors such as organizational culture, norms, strategy, market (e.g., supply of and demand for applicants), and government legislation will influence the interaction between the applicant and the interviewer and may affect the outcome of this interaction.[25]

For example, in some organizations interviews are conducted by human resources staff; in others, interviews are conducted by supervisors and/or line managers; and in still others, interviews are conducted by both. In some organizations, HR staff make the final hiring decision, while in others, the supervisor or line manager has the final say. Thus, the interview can involve interactions among members of the organization as well as interactions between the applicant and the interviewer(s) and can sometimes be affected by authority structures, interdepartmental politics, and power games.[26] On the other hand, the interview process and decisions can be affected by the supply of and demand for applicants. When unemployment rates are low and it is more difficult to find suitable applicants, interviewers tend to be more lenient, whereas when applicants are plentiful, they can be more selective.[27]

FIGURE 9.1

A Model of Information Processing and Decision Making in the Interview

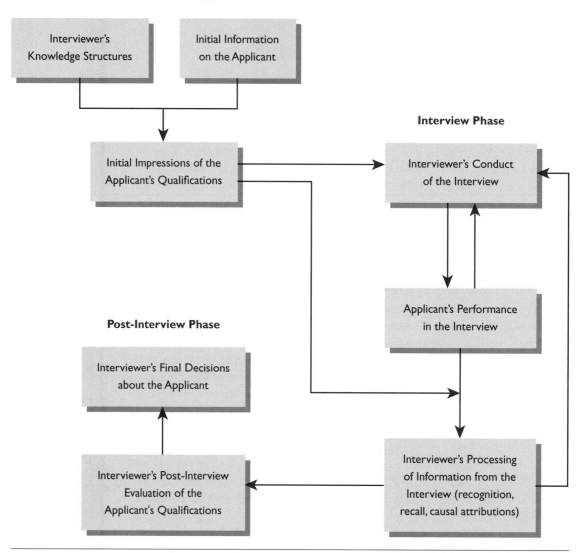

Source: R. Dipboye. 1992. *Selection Interviews: Process Perspective*s. 1st ed. © 1992. Reprinted with permission of South-Western, a part of Cengage Learning, Inc. http://www.cengage.com/permissions.

Knowledge structures

Interviewers' beliefs about the requirements of the job and the characteristics of applicants.

According to Dipboye's model, the interviewer comes to the interview with certain **knowledge structures**. These knowledge structures are the beliefs the interviewer holds about the requirements of the job and about the characteristics that applicants need to have in order to do the job. The interviewer develops such knowledge structures through formal training and previous experience. With respect to applicant characteristics, an interviewer might believe that good grades in school reflect hard work and conscientiousness, or that a firm handshake reveals assertiveness and confidence. Sometimes such beliefs can be reasonably accurate but, all too often, they are misleading and contribute to error in interviewer judgment.

The information that an interviewer has about the job can also vary in detail and accuracy. The interviewer might know some jobs well, particularly if he or she has worked at the job. However, for most jobs, interviewers are likely to rely, at least to some extent, on personal beliefs (e.g., this is a "male" job or this is a "female" job, or this job is tedious) and these beliefs might or might not be accurate.

Interviewers usually have access to *initial information* on the applicant before the interview. This information usually comes from the application form or résumé; sometimes, interviewers also have access to references, test scores, and other information. This information, in combination with the interviewer's knowledge structures, contributes to the interviewer's *initial impressions of the applicant's qualifications*. That is, before the interview has begun, the interviewer already has an impression of the applicant and the degree to which the applicant appears to be suitable or unsuitable for the position.

These pre-interview impressions can influence the *interviewer's conduct in the interview*.[28,29] An interviewer may be more attentive and supportive with applicants evaluated more positively than with applicants deemed to be unsuitable. Moreover, interviewers tend to seek information that will confirm their initial impressions; they will shape the interview with the kinds of questions they ask and how these questions are phrased. Thus, while interviewers' initial impressions may be supplemented or modified by impressions gained during the interview, there is a strong tendency for interviewers to seek and to find support for their initial impressions. In addition, factors such as the applicant's physical appearance and nonverbal behaviours during the interview, as well as responses to the interview questions, can affect the interviewer's evaluation of the applicant and the interviewer's responses to the applicant.

How the interviewer behaves can affect the applicant's performance in the interview.[30] Applicants who sense that the interview is not going well or that the interviewer has developed a negative impression of them may experience greater anxiety, which might negatively affect their performance. The applicants might come to believe that there is little likelihood of obtaining a job offer and, therefore, reduce their efforts in the interview. Conversely, an applicant who senses that things are going well or that the interviewer is interested and supportive is likely to respond in a more positive manner, with greater composure, enthusiasm, and effort. Thus, the applicant and interviewer continue to influence each other throughout the interview, so that there is a tendency to perpetuate, if not intensify, initial negative or positive impressions.

The *interviewer's processing of data from the interview* is very much influenced by the knowledge structures, as well as by the initial impressions he or she has of the applicant. The knowledge structures assist the interviewer in categorizing or stereotyping applicants (e.g., as highly motivated but lacking common sense, as a housewife who wishes to resume her career, as an elderly person who needs the money, etc.). Through the course of the interview, the interviewer may recategorize an applicant several times. The interviewer's knowledge structures also influence the interviewer's attributions of applicant behaviour. That is, the interviewer makes determinations as to the extent to which the behaviours described or exhibited by the applicant are caused by stable personal traits or by situational circumstances. For example, an interviewer might regard an applicant's description of a successful accomplishment as indicative of the applicant's capabilities and perseverance, while a similar description from another applicant might be attributed to an easy task or luck or exaggeration on the part of the applicant. Interviewers may adjust their attributions several times during the interview as more information is obtained. Thus, the interviewer's knowledge structures guide the interviewer in both shaping and interpreting the data collected in the interview.[31]

In the last part of the interview, the *post-interview phase*, the interviewer evaluates the applicant's qualifications and then makes a final decision about the applicant. The *evaluation of the applicant's qualifications* is dominated by global impressions obtained in the interview. These global impressions are also influenced by the interviewer's knowledge structures in at least three ways. First, knowledge structures provide the interviewer with a prototype or image of the ideal applicant. The interviewer compares applicants with his or her own prototype of the ideal applicant and evaluates the applicants based on a perceived match or mismatch.

Secondly, the knowledge structures influence the interactions between the interviewer and the applicant during the interview, and these interactions contribute to the emotions or mood the interviewer experiences during and after the interview (e.g., "I feel good about this applicant"). The interviewer's emotions or mood affect the evaluation of the applicant's qualifications after the interview. Thirdly, the knowledge structures contribute to the initial impressions the interviewer has of the applicant. Interviewers seek to confirm their initial impressions during the interview and these impressions tend to persist and affect the interviewer's evaluation of the applicant after the interview.

The *interviewer's final decision about the applicant* is influenced by various factors, such as pressure to hire quickly, hiring quotas, and interdepartmental or intradepartmental politics. Sometimes personal motivations influence an interviewer's decisions, particularly when he or she knows one of the applicants (or one of the applicant's references), or has something in common with an applicant. Contrast effects also come into play in that the interviewer usually compares several applicants in order to decide which one to hire. Applicants may benefit or suffer in these comparisons, depending on whether their competitors are deemed more or less qualified than they are.

In making comparisons, the interviewer may rely to some degree on a memory of what was said in the interview. Unfortunately, the interviewer's memory can be faulty or biased.[32] In fact, we have witnessed interviewers becoming confused as to which applicant said what after interviewing a series of applicants. This is not surprising, given the large amount of complex information interviewers must process and make sense of in making a selection decision. Thus, interviewers often rely on their knowledge structures and stereotypes to organize and simplify the information they have collected. As noted above, however, the interviewer's evaluations and decisions are likely to be in error if the interviewer's knowledge structures are inaccurate or biased.[33]

The model described in this section presents the difficult challenges faced by interviewers in trying to make accurate assessments of applicants in the interview. It very much reflects the processes taking place in traditional, unstructured approaches to employment interviewing. Recent efforts to structure employment interviews have substantially reduced the effects of the idiosyncratic interview processes described in this model and have improved the accuracy of interview assessments.[34] Because many employers continue to use unstructured interviews, it is worth examining these traditional interviews before turning to the more valid structured interviewing techniques.

Unstructured Interviews

The traditional approach to employment interviewing is one that has become known as an **unstructured interview**. In such interviews, the interviewer typically engages in an open-ended conversation with the interviewee. There are few constraints on the kinds of questions that may be asked, and furthermore, many of the questions used in the interview may not occur to the interviewer until partway through the interview. Most interviewers, however, appear to rely on a common set of questions, often ones that they have heard others use. Recruitment and Selection Today 9.1 presents a list of questions often used by interviewers. These types of questions invite applicants to evaluate themselves or to describe the evaluations of others. Naturally, applicants who want to create a positive impression are likely to evaluate themselves much more favourably than perhaps they should.

Unstructured interview
A traditional method of interviewing that involves no constraints on the questions asked, no requirements for standardization, and a subjective assessment of the candidate.

Recruitment and Selection Today 9.1

Commonly Used Interview Questions

1. Why did you leave your last job? (Why do you want to leave your current job?)
2. What do you consider to be your strengths? What are your weaknesses?
3. What were your strongest/weakest subjects at school? (What did you learn in school that you could use in this job?)
4. How would other people (or someone who knows you or has worked with you) describe you as an individual?
5. What is your greatest accomplishment (or most meaningful work experience)?
6. What were the most enjoyable aspects of your last job? What were the least enjoyable aspects?
7. Why do you want this job? What are you looking for from this job (or from us)?
8. Why should we hire you? (What can you do for us? or Why are you the best candidate for this position?)
9. What are your long-range plans or goals? (Where do you plan to be five years from now?)
10. Tell me about yourself.

Moreover, many interviewees have learned to respond to such questions with standard answers. For example, common responses to the question, "What are your weaknesses?" include "I get too involved in my work" and "I'm too much of a perfectionist." Answers to such questions reveal very little useful information about the applicant. The interviewer is forced to take on the role of an amateur psychologist trying to read meaning into vague self-evaluations, verbal expressiveness, or body language. Sometimes, as Recruitment and Selection Today 9.2 shows, the questions that interviewers ask suggest that they may need to see a clinical psychologist for help!

Impression management

Attempts by applicants to create a favourable impression by monitoring interviewer reactions and responding accordingly.

Some interviewees are particularly skilled at **impression management**, that is, creating a favourable impression of themselves by picking up cues from the interviewer concerning what answers the interviewer wishes to hear. They are able to monitor and change their own responses and behaviours in order to align them with those they perceive to be desired by the interviewer. By artfully guiding the conversation and making effective use of

---

Recruitment and Selection Today 9.2

Excerpts from *Don't Get Stumped by Off-the-Wall Job Interview Questions*

Although not as common as the interview questions listed in Recruitment and Selection Today 9.1, the questions or comments listed below must certainly rank among the most off-the-wall questions used in employment interviews:

- If you could be any character in fiction, who would you be?
- If Hollywood made a movie about your life, who would you like to see play the lead role as you?
- If you could be a superhero, what would you want your superpowers to be?
- If someone wrote a biography about you, what do you think the title should be?
- If you were shipwrecked on a deserted island, but all your human needs—such as food and water—were taken care of, what two items would you want to have with you?
- If you had six months with no obligations or financial constraints, what would you do with your time?
- If you had only six months left to live, what would you do with your time?
- If you could have dinner with anyone in history, who would it be and why?

- If you could compare yourself to any animal, which would it be and why?
- If you were a type of food, what type of food would you be?
- If you won $20 million in a lottery, what would you do with the money?
- If you were a salad, what kind of dressing would you have?
- How do I rate as an interviewer?
- If you were a car, what kind would you be?
- Whom do you admire the most and why?
- In the news story of your life, what would the headline say?
- If aliens landed in front of you and, in exchange for anything you desire, offered you any position on their planet, what would you want?
- What would I find in your refrigerator?
- If you had the opportunity to switch to the opposite gender for just a week, would you do it? Why or why not?

Source: Adapted from Katherine Hansen, Ph.D. 2008. "Don't Get Stumped by Off-the-Wall Job Interview Questions." *Quintessential Careers*: http://www.quintcareers.com/wild_card_interview_questions.html. For more terrible interview questions and incidents, see *Interview Horrors*: http://www.garywill.com/worksearch/worst.htm.

nonverbal behaviours, the polished interviewee is able to impress the interviewer and obfuscate the true purpose of the interview.[35,36] Thus, instead of hiring the best *candidate*, the interviewer is likely to hire the most skillful *interviewee*.

In fact, skillful interviewees can divert the conversation from relevant and important interview topics to topics that result in pleasant but uninformative conversations that cast themselves in a more favourable light. For example, on noticing the golf trophy in an interviewer's office, such an interviewee may engage the interviewer in an amiable conversation about the game of golf that lasts most of the interview. The interviewer, left with a good feeling about the applicant, is likely to hire the applicant without actually having obtained any job-relevant information during the interview.

Research suggests that more than 90 percent of applicants make use of impression management tactics or "faking" during the interview but most of them do not resort to outright invention or lying.[37] Rather, most exaggerate slightly or tailor their answers to make their experiences seem more positive or relevant to the job. Many also try to ingratiate themselves with the interviewer by appearing to agree with the interviewer's views or complimenting the interviewer or the organization. Unfortunately, good impression managers or fakers are somewhat more likely to get a job offer than non-fakers.[38] Nevertheless, faking is not necessary to gain a job offer, and it is better for applicants to answer questions honestly, in a way that will get a job offer that fits their true personality and ability.

As Recruitment and Selection Today 9.3 shows, however, not all job candidates are skilled at impression management and some behave in ways that guarantee that they will not receive a job offer. Several websites provide interviewing tips for applicants, including http://www.careercc.com/interv3.shtml, http://www.quintcareers.com/intvres.html, and http://www.ctdol.state.ct.us/progsupt/jobsrvce/intervie.htm.

Another characteristic typical of unstructured interviews is that no systematic rating procedure is used. Interviewers are free to interpret interviewee responses in any manner they choose, as there are no guidelines for evaluating the responses. Rather than evaluating responses or answers to interview questions, the interviewer, in fact, uses the interview to get a "feeling" or a "hunch" about the applicant. The interviewer emerges from the interview with a global, subjective evaluation of the applicant, which is biased by personal views and preferences and likely to be inaccurate. In fact, many interviewers report that they rely on such "gut feelings" in making their hiring decisions. Worse yet, some writers are still recommending such practices.[39]

Webster[40,41] and his colleagues at McGill University, along with Dipboye,[42] Jelf,[43] Posthuma,[44] and others, have documented the numerous biases and perceptual and information-processing errors that have plagued the unstructured employment interview (see Recruitment and Selection Notebook 9.1). For example, interviewers rate applicants more favourably if the applicants are perceived as being similar to themselves.[45] Moreover, interview ratings are susceptible to first impressions.[46,47] That is, an interviewer's initial impression

Job Interviews That Didn't Go Well

Interviewers are not the only ones who mishandle interviews—applicants do their share of bungling as well. A survey conducted by a Canadian recruitment firm, Office Team, asked 150 executives and HR managers about unusual interview experiences. Below are some of the responses.

- After answering the first few questions, the candidate picked up his cellphone and called his parents to tell them that the interview was going well.
- At the end of the interview, the candidate expressed her interest in getting the position, but only if her boyfriend liked the company and the hiring manager. She then said, "He's waiting outside. Can I bring him in to say hello?"
- When asked why he wanted to work for the company, the applicant responded, "That's a good question. I really haven't given it much thought."
- When asked how the candidate would improve sales if hired for the position, he replied, "I'll have to think about that and get back to you." He then stood up, walked out, and never came back.
- When asked by the hiring manager why she was leaving her current job, the applicant said, "My manager is a jerk. All managers are jerks."
- A candidate disparaged his former boss during the interview, not realizing the boss and the interviewer had the same last name—and were related.
- When asked what he liked least in his current job, the applicant replied, "Staff management." He was interviewing for a management position.
- After being complimented on his choice of college and the grade point average he achieved, the candidate replied, "I'm glad that got your attention. I didn't really go there."
- When asked by the hiring manager if he had any questions, the candidate replied by telling a knock-knock joke.
- When asked by the manager about his goals, the job seeker said, "To work in this position for the least amount of time possible until I can get your job."

Source: Adapted from Anonymous. 2002. "Candidates Say the Darndest Things." *Canadian HR Reporter* 15(19): 4. Reprinted with permission from *Canadian HR Reporter*. For other interview blunders made by applicants, go to *The Stupidest Job Interview Blunders*: http://www.citynews.ca/news/news_23215.aspx.

of an applicant, such as might be formed upon reading the résumé, affects the way the interview is conducted, the questions asked, and the evaluation of the candidate's answers.

In addition, interview ratings are influenced by visual cues such as physical attractiveness of the applicant, eye contact, body orientation, smiling, and hand gestures, as well as vocal cues such as rate of speaking, number and duration of pauses, variability in loudness, and pitch (e.g., lower voices tend to be rated more positively than higher voices for management positions).[48] Recruitment and Selection Notebook 9.1 summarizes some of the research findings pertaining to the unstructured employment interview. (Descriptions of additional interview biases can be found at http://www.indiana.edu/~uhrs/employment/best.html.) Such biases and errors contribute to the poor reliability and validity of unstructured interviews.

Some Research Findings on the Unstructured Interview

Interview Decisions

- Interviewers tend to make a hire/not hire decision before completing the interview (i.e., before all the information has been collected).[49,50]
- Unfavourable information provided by the applicant tends to have greater impact on interview ratings than favourable information.[51,52]
- Once interviewers have formed an impression of an applicant, they tend to look for information that will confirm their impression.[53,54]

Order Effects

- Interviewers tend to remember information provided at the beginning of the interview better than information provided in the middle (primacy effect).[55,56]
- Information provided at the end of the interview tends to be remembered better than information provided in the middle (recency effect).[57,58]
- An applicant's interview rating can be affected by the preceding applicant (contrast effects)—the applicant tends to benefit if the preceding applicant was relatively poor but suffer if the preceding applicant was relatively good.[59,60]

Effects of Information

- Impressions formed by the interviewer as a result of information obtained about the applicant prior to the interview (e.g., by reading the résumé) affect how the applicant is treated and rated in the interview.[61,62]

- Interviewers who have more information about the job tend to have a more accurate perception (template) of what the "ideal" applicant should look like.[63,64]

Demographic Characteristics

- Minority applicants tend to receive lower interview ratings than nonminority applicants.[65]
- Interviewers tend to give higher ratings to applicants who are most like themselves (similar-to-me effect) in terms of demographic characteristics or in terms of attitudes.[66,67]

Verbal/Nonverbal Behaviour

- An applicant's verbal skills and expressiveness and attractiveness of voice can affect interview ratings.[68,69]
- An applicant's mannerisms can affect interview ratings.[70,71]
- An applicant's appearance (e.g., physical attractiveness, posture, age, clothing) can affect interview ratings.[72]

Reliability and Validity

- Agreement on ratings among interviewers interviewing the same applicants tends to be quite low (low reliability).[73,74]
- Correlations between interview scores and job performance ratings (for those hired) tend to be fairly low (low criterion validity).[75–77]

Attempts to Improve Interview Effectiveness

Given the research on the biases and errors inherent in the unstructured interview, past reviews of employment interview research have, understandably, been rather pessimistic concerning the reliability and validity of the interview as a selection instrument.[78] Nevertheless, the interview has remained popular among employers, who seem to have considerable confidence in its

RPC 9.1

Structured interview

An interview consisting of a standardized set of job-relevant questions; a scoring guide is used.

W W W

usefulness for employee selection. Now, exciting developments in interview research over the last two decades will give those employers even more reason for confidence. In the early 1980s, a number of researchers began working on new approaches to employment interviewing, which have become known as **structured interviews.**[79–81]

Reviews of the employment interview literature some 20 years ago indicated that structuring an interview appeared to contribute to increased interview reliability and validity.[82–84] In fact, today, meta-analytic investigations of interview validity reveal that structured selection interviews do indeed have significantly greater reliability and predictive validity than traditional, unstructured interviews.[85–88] Among the variables investigated, interview structure is by far the strongest moderator of interview validity. The effects of interview structure are displayed in Figures 9.2 and 9.3. Figure 9.2 summarizes the results of Wiesner and Cronshaw's meta-analysis,[89] while Figure 9.3 summarizes the results of Huffcutt and Arthur's meta-analysis.[90] Note the similarity of the findings in these two meta-analyses.

References to interview structure in selection interview literature tend to give the impression that structure is a dichotomous variable (i.e., that interviews are either structured or unstructured). Interview structure, however, is a function of several factors and it can vary along a continuum, ranging from very unstructured to highly structured. In fact, Huffcutt and Arthur found that interview validity increases as the degree of interview structure

FIGURE 9.2

Criterion-Related Validity of Selection Interview: Wiesner and Cronshaw's Meta-Analysis

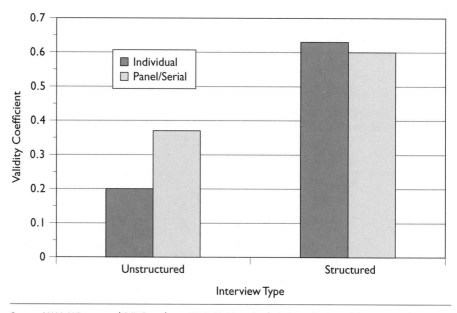

Source: W.H. Wiesner and S.F. Cronshaw. 1988. "A Meta-Analytic Investigation of the Impact of Interview Format and Degree of Structure on the Validity of the Employment Interview." *Journal of Occupational Psychology* 61: 275–90. Reprinted with permission.

FIGURE 9.3

Criterion-Related Validity of Selection Interview: Huffcutt and Arthur's Meta-Analysis

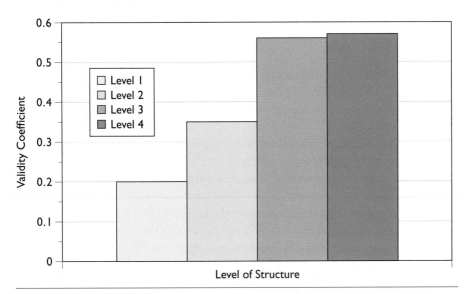

Source: Adapted from A.I. Huffcutt and W. Arthur, Jr. 1994. "Hunter and Hunter (1984) Revisited: Interview Validity for Entry-Level Jobs." *Journal of Applied Psychology* 79: 184–90. Copyright © 1994 by the American Psychological Association. Adapted with permission.

increases.[91] It is useful to gain an understanding of what is meant by interview "structure."

Structuring Employment Interviews

Although there has been an apparently sudden discovery of structured employment interview techniques in recent years, their development is actually due to the contributions of numerous researchers over more than half a century. These researchers sought to address what were perceived as the shortcomings of the traditional, unstructured interview by applying psychometric principles to employment interview design. Over time, these researchers uncovered a number of structuring elements that seemed to contribute to interview reliability and validity. Although not all interviews referred to as "structured" make use of all elements, the more of these elements that are part of the interview, the more structured it is. In other words, employment interviews can be structured in a number of ways and to varying degrees. Below is a summary of components that can contribute to employment interview structure, extracted from a detailed review provided by Campion, Palmer, and Campion:[92]

1. Interview questions are derived from a job analysis (they are job-related).
2. Interview questions are standardized (all applicants are asked the same questions).

3. Prompting, follow-up questioning, probing, and/or elaboration on questions are limited.
4. Interview questions focus on behaviours or work samples rather than opinions or self-evaluations.
5. Interviewer access to ancillary information (e.g., résumés, letters of reference, test scores, transcripts) is controlled.
6. Questions from the candidate are not allowed until after the interview.
7. Each answer is rated during the interview using a rating scale tailored to the question (this is preferable to rating dimensions at the end of the interview and certainly preferable to making an overall rating or ranking at the end).
8. Rating scales are "anchored" with behavioural examples to illustrate scale points (e.g., examples of a "1," "3," or "5" answer).
9. Total interview score is obtained by summing across scores for each of the questions.
10. Detailed notes are taken during the interview (such notes should be a record of applicants' actual words and behaviours as related in the interview rather than evaluations of applicants).[93]

In addition, Campion and his colleagues recommend using the same interviewer(s) across all candidates for greater standardization, not permitting interviewers to discuss candidates or answers between interviews, and providing interviewers with extensive training.[94] Recruitment and Selection Notebook 9.2 provides some guidelines for building more structure into an interview.

It is worth noting that Huffcutt and Arthur found no significant difference between validity coefficients for structure Level 3 and structure Level 4 (see Figure 9.3).[95] Their Level 3 structure is characterized by partial standardization of questions. That is, interviewers may use probes or follow-up questions and, in some instances, select from a set of questions.[96] Level 4 involves complete standardization of questions, and applicant responses to individual questions are rated during the interview using a behaviourally anchored scale.[97,98] Huffcutt and Arthur's results suggest that even moderate levels of structure (i.e., Level 3) can contribute to high interview validity.[99]

Panel and Serial Interviews

Among their recommendations, Campion and his colleagues[100] advocate using panel or serial interviews. **Panel interviews**, also known as *board interviews*, are interviews conducted by two or more interviewers together at the same time. Although panel or board interviews appear to be most common in the public sector, notably for civil service jobs, police, and military positions,[101] a recent survey of Canadian HR practitioners suggests that almost two-thirds of Canadian organizations use panel interviews.[102] These interview panels operate in various ways. One member of the panel may ask all the questions or panel members may take turns asking questions. In some

Panel interview

An interview conducted by two or more interviewers together at one time.

The Structured Interviewing Process

Preparing for the Interview

1. Determine the amount of time available for the interview and how many questions you will be able to ask, without rushing, in that length of time.
2. Make a standardized list of interview questions so that all applicants are asked the same questions, in the same order. If possible, develop a scoring guide with benchmark or sample answers. Allow space in the guide or have a notepad for taking notes.
3. Use an office or arrange for an interview room where you can have privacy, freedom from distractions, and quiet. Ensure good lighting and ventilation, a comfortable temperature, and comfortable seating for yourself and the applicant (as well as any other interviewers who may be present).
4. Schedule the interviews with sufficient time for a brief break between interviews and to allow for some interviews to run a little overtime.
5. Arrange to hold all calls and prevent interruptions during the interview. If you are interrupted to attend to a critical matter, apologize to the applicant and resolve the matter as quickly as possible, delegating it if you can.

Conducting the Interview

1. Spend a few minutes at the beginning of the interview putting the applicant at ease. Greet the applicant by name. Introduce yourself and other interview panel members (if there are others). Indicate where the applicant is to sit. Provide the applicant with an overview of the interview process.
2. Ask each question in turn without omitting or skipping any. Let the candidate know he or she has lots of time to answer and you don't mind his or her taking time to think. Allow silence. If the applicant seems confused or stuck, rephrase the question but don't do so too quickly. If the applicant still has difficulty, indicate you will come back to the question later.

3. Take detailed notes of the applicant's responses, focusing on behaviours described by the applicant. Your notes should not be evaluative. Use the scoring guide, if you have one, to score the answers to interview questions as soon as possible.
4. Allow the applicant to ask questions at the end of the interview and answer them to the best of your ability without committing to a decision or indicating any kind of preference.
5. Follow the same procedures for each applicant and retain interview documentation for future reference.

Closing the Interview

1. Tell the candidate when he or she should expect to hear from you, or someone else in your organization, and how you will communicate your decision (e.g., telephone, e-mail, letter).
2. If you are likely to contact references or call the applicant back for a second interview, inform the applicant.
3. Thank the applicant for coming in for the interview. Escort him or her to the door and take your leave.
4. Review your notes and make your ratings (if you have not already done so). If the interview was conducted by a panel, briefly meet with the panel and compare your ratings. Discuss and resolve large discrepancies. Either average the ratings (if discrepancies are not large) or arrive at a consensus rating.
5. Make sure you inform all candidates of your decision when you have made it. It's a common practice to hold back on informing second- or third-choice candidates in case the first- and/or second-choice candidates turn down the offer. If you do so, inform the remaining candidates as soon as the offer has been accepted. Thank the candidates who were not accepted for their interest in the job and the organization.

panels, one member is assigned the task of taking notes, while in other panels several or all members take notes. Some panels consist of only two members, while others may have many members.

Unfortunately, there has not been much research on the relative effectiveness of these different approaches and the little research that has been done has provided largely inconclusive results.[103,104] While panel interviews offer an efficient way for several interviewers to interview applicants, they require considerable coordination of schedules to permit all interviewers to attend, particularly as the number of interviewers increases. Moreover, panel interviews can be quite intimidating to applicants and may negatively affect their performance in the interview.

Serial interviews

A series of interviews where the applicant is interviewed separately by each of two or more interviewers.

Serial interviews, also known as *sequential interviews*, are interviews conducted by two or more interviewers separately or in sequence. That is, the applicant is usually interviewed individually by the first interviewer, then by the second interviewer, and so on until all interviewers have interviewed the applicant. The applicant may move from office to office for each interview or stay in one interview room while each interviewer visits in turn. The interviewers usually get together, either after they have all interviewed each applicant or after they have interviewed all applicants, in order to discuss and evaluate the applicant(s) and make a decision.

Scheduling interviewers is less of a problem with serial interviews than with panel interviews as there is greater flexibility in scheduling a particular interviewer. Also, serial interviews are not as intimidating as panel interviews[105] but they can be quite exhausting, as the applicant may spend many hours in a series of interviews. Moreover, the questions and answers can become somewhat repetitive from one interview to the next, and applicants may lose track of what they have or have not said by the fifth or sixth interview.

Despite their problems, panel and serial interviews should reduce the impact of biases held by an individual interviewer because interviewers are accountable to each other and provide a check on each other to ensure irrelevant information does not enter the decision. Each interviewer contributes a different perspective that should increase accuracy, and the aggregation of multiple judgments should cancel out random errors. The recall of information should also be better with multiple interviewers.[106]

Conway, Jako, and Goodman[107] found that panel interviews are more reliable than individual interviews, and Wiesner and Cronshaw[108] found that panel interviews have greater validity than individual interviews when the interview is unstructured, but did not find a difference for structured interviews. However, other meta-analyses have produced inconsistent results with respect to the reliability and validity of panel versus individual interviews.[109] These inconsistencies could be the result of factors such as inadequate controls for structure in the analyses, the fact that most panel interviews occur in public-sector settings, the possibility of group process losses in interview panels (e.g., conformity, conflict, loafing), differences in training of interviewers, and the type of interview questions used, all of which might reduce the advantages in some applications.[110,111]

Nevertheless, the use of panel or serial interviews appears to be viewed favourably by courts and, therefore, gives some measure of protection from discrimination suits.[112,113] In addition, interview panels can include representation from different gender or ethnic groups, thus contributing to perceptions of fairness. More information on panel interviews can be found at http://www.liscareer.com/peters_interviews.htm and http://sciencecareers .sciencemag.org (at the latter, click on "Career Magazine Previous Issues" at the bottom of the page, then on "2000," then on "December 15," and finally on "How to Prepare for and Succeed at Panel Interviews").

Structured Employment Interview Techniques

The Situational Interview

One of the approaches to structured interviewing is the **situational interview** (SI) developed by Latham and his colleagues.[114,115] The interviewer describes to the applicant hypothetical situations that are likely to be encountered on the job and asks the applicant what he or she would do in the situations. The interviewer then uses a **scoring guide** consisting of sample answers to each question to evaluate and score the applicant's answers. The scoring guide is designed using the critical incidents technique,[116] in which examples of actual job-related behaviours that varied in effectiveness in particular situations are collected and refined to serve as sample answers. Thus, numerical values on the scale are illustrated with examples of answers that would be worth a 1 or a 3 or a 5. An example of an SI question is provided in Table 9.1. Please note that the scoring guide is visible only to the interviewer(s), not to the interviewee. Cover up the scoring guide in Table 9.1 with your hand and try answering the question. Once you have answered the question, compare your answer with the scoring guide.

The scoring guide for an SI question should be based on behaviours that have been shown to be either effective or ineffective in that situation in the past. However, because organizations differ, what is an effective response in one organization might not be effective in another. Thus, the scoring guide might differ from one company to another. In the example in Table 9.1, applicants who indicate that they would ignore the supervisor's suggestion and insist on following through on the initial decision would be ignoring potentially important information. The result might be a serious mistake, which could cost the company considerable money. Such a response would not score well. Doing what the supervisor suggests or openly discussing the merits of the supervisor's suggestion might result in a good decision being made. However, this course of action would likely undermine the new manager's authority.

The ideal answer does not have to be given exactly as written in the scoring guide. However, the interviewer would be looking for evidence that the applicant recognizes the dynamics at play in the situation and understands basic principles of human behaviour. First, it is important to recognize that there is the potential for a serious mistake if the manager persists in

Situational interview

A highly structured interview in which hypothetical situations are described and applicants are asked what they would do.

Scoring guide

A behavioural rating scale consisting of sample answers to each question that is used by the interviewer to evaluate and score the applicant's answers.

TABLE 9.1

Example of a Situational Interview Question

You have just been hired as the manager of our purchasing department and it's your first day on the job. After carefully reviewing product and price information, you make a decision to purchase parts from a particular supplier. Your immediate subordinate, an experienced supervisor who is considerably older than you, questions your judgment in front of other employees and suggests that another supplier would be better. He seems quite convinced that you are making a mistake. The employees look to you for a response, some of them smirking. What would you do?

Scoring Guide

1—I would tell the supervisor that I'm in charge and I am going with my initial decision.

3—I would do what the supervisor suggests, as he knows the suppliers and materials better than I do, *or* I would openly discuss the merits of his suggestion versus my own judgment.

5—I would take the supervisor to a private place, thank him for the information, but instruct him never to question me in front of the employees again. Then, after asking him for information on the best supplier and dismissing him, I would think about the options again and after a brief period announce *my* decision to go with the supplier suggested in our private conversation.

---

the original course of action. Second, the applicant should recognize that the manager's authority is being undermined, whether intentionally or not. The fact that the supervisor raises the issue in front of the employees and some of them are smirking suggests that there might be a test of leadership going on. So, the manager needs to determine the validity of the supervisor's suggestion but also to assert authority. Recognizing that these objectives would best be accomplished in a private conversation reveals an understanding of human nature. Confronting the supervisor in public might make the supervisor defensive and evoke a need for him to "save face" in front of the employees. As much as possible, the manager needs to claim the final decision as his or her own.

The interviewer's task is to compare the applicant's answers with the examples on the scoring guides and to score the answers accordingly. There may be instances where an answer falls somewhere between two scoring guide examples (e.g., better than a 3 answer but not as good as a 5 answer). Under such circumstances, the interviewer has the discretion of assigning an intermediate score (e.g., a 4 or even a 4.5).

The assumption underlying the SI approach is that intentions are related to subsequent behaviours.[117] Critics of this approach have argued that what applicants say they would do in a given situation and what they actually do may be quite different. However, a convincing counterargument is that just *knowing* what the appropriate response should be can differentiate effective from ineffective performers. Latham and Sue-Chan conducted a meta-analysis of the SI based on 20 coefficients and obtained a mean criterion validity coefficient of 0.29 (0.39 corrected for criterion unreliability and range restriction).[118] The mean validity coefficient increased to 0.35 (0.47 corrected) when they removed one very large study and one "outlier" (i.e., a study with extremely different results from the remaining studies) from their analysis.

Two more recent meta-analyses both obtained a mean criterion validity coefficient of 0.26 (between 0.43 and 0.47 with corrections for criterion unreliability and range restriction) based on 29 and 32 coefficients, respectively, for the situational interview.[119,120] One of these meta-analyses reported a mean inter-rater reliability of 0.79 for the SI. Although there is some disagreement among these meta-analyses as to the precise validity coefficient attributable to the SI, it is clear that the SI is a valid predictor of job performance. Additional information on situational interviews can be found at http://www.careertalk .com/itips02-left.html.

The Comprehensive Structured Interview

Campion, Pursell, and Brown,[121] in what has become known as the **comprehensive structured interview** (CSI),[122] combine situational interview questions with questions assessing job knowledge, job simulation questions, and worker characteristic or willingness questions. The job knowledge questions assess the degree to which the applicant possesses relevant job knowledge (e.g., "When putting a piece of machinery back together after repairing it, why would you clean all the parts first?"). The job simulation questions assess job-relevant verbal skills (e.g., "Many jobs require the operation of a forklift. Please read this [90-word] forklift procedure aloud."). Finally, the worker willingness questions assess the applicant's willingness to engage in particular activities (e.g., "Some jobs require climbing ladders to a height of a five-storey building and going out on a catwalk to work. Give us your feeling about performing a task such as this.").

Comprehensive structured interview

A highly structured interview consisting of a combination of situational interview, job knowledge, job simulation, and worker characteristic or willingness questions.

Campion and his associates were able to predict job performance as well using this approach ($r = 0.56$ with corrections for criterion unreliability and range restriction, $r = 0.34$, uncorrected; reliability is estimated at 0.88).[123] For more information on the comprehensive structured interview, see http:// www.mmsearch.com/html/interview_prep.html.

The Behaviour Description Interview

Finally, Janz,[124,125] following up on a suggestion made by Latham et al.[126] and based on Ghiselli's findings,[127] used another approach, which he refers to as the *patterned behaviour description interview* (PBDI). More recent variations of this approach are simply called **behaviour description interviews** (BDIs) or *behavioural interviews*. The interviewer is asked to predict the interviewee's behaviours in a given job situation based on the interviewee's descriptions of his or her behaviours in similar situations in the past.

Behaviour description interview

A structured interview in which the applicant is asked to describe what he or she did in given situations in the past.

Table 9.2 provides an example of a BDI question based on the same critical incidents, and thus the same dynamics, as were used in the development of the SI question in Table 9.1. However, because BDI questions are

TABLE 9.2

Example of a Patterned Behaviour Description Interview Question

We all encounter situations in which our judgment is challenged. Tell me about a time when you were not certain you had made the right decision and then someone openly challenged your decision. What did you do?

Probes: What aspect of your decision were you uncertain about?

Did the person who challenged you have essential information that you did not possess?

Could anyone overhear the person's challenge?

What issues and possible consequences did you consider in responding to this person's challenge?

What was your final decision and what was the outcome?

Scoring Guide

1—I told the person that I was in charge and I was sticking with my decision.

3—I changed my mind and did what the person suggested *or* I openly discussed the merits of his/her suggestion (in front of others).

5—I took the person to a private place and thanked him or her for the advice but asked not to be questioned in front of other people. Then, after asking the person for suggestions, I took some time to reconsider the options and consequences. I made the decision that had the greatest probability of success, regardless of where the ideas came from, but made it clear it was *my* decision.

concerned with past behaviours in a potentially wide variety of settings, their inquiry must be more general. Therefore, the goal in designing BDI questions is to make the questions apply to a wide variety of previous experiences or situations.

Comparison of the questions in Tables 9.1 and 9.2 suggests that the BDI question is likely to generate responses with considerably broader scope than the SI question. Whereas the SI question relates to a very specific situation, the BDI could elicit descriptions of a wide variety of situations, depending on the applicants' experiences. One applicant might relate an experience as the chair on the board of directors of an organization, whereas another applicant might discuss his or her experience as a member of a group working on an assignment at school.

The broad nature of BDI questions and probable responses makes it likely that the interviewer will need to clarify the applicant's answers in order to allow them to be scored accurately. Follow-up questions or **probes** are used to guide the applicant's descriptions of situations or events until sufficient information is obtained to permit scoring. Some probes are written in advance, as in the example in Table 9.2, in anticipation of probable responses and with consideration of the information that will be required for scoring. However, the interviewer is permitted to supplement the list of probes with additional

Probes

Follow-up questions or prompts used by the interviewer to guide the applicant's descriptions of situations or events or to provide elaboration of answers.

probes during the interview if the information obtained is insufficient to make a rating. Probing to obtain required information without giving away the content of the ideal answer requires considerable skill on the part of the interviewer.

The example in Table 9.2 contains a scoring guide similar to the one used for the SI question. Initial approaches to BDI did not include the use of scoring guides but, rather, had interviewers rate applicants on various dimensions or traits (e.g., motivation) based on their responses to interview questions.[128] The process of translating answers to dimension ratings was a rather subjective one, for scores would be derived on the basis of impressions gained by interviewers listening to answers to various questions. There was no direct correspondence between any one question and any one dimension. Such an approach would be expected to compromise interview reliability and validity (this is discussed in the next section). More recent approaches to the BDI have incorporated scoring guides.[129,130]

Note that the BDI question in Table 9.2 requests information that the applicant might construe as negative and might thus be reluctant to provide. When asking questions that might be viewed as requesting negative information, it is helpful to begin the question with what is called a *disarming statement*. In the example, the disarming statement communicates to the applicant that it is normal and perfectly acceptable to have had one's judgment challenged. The disarming statement is intended to reduce the likelihood that the applicant will deny having experienced this situation and to set the applicant at ease about discussing it freely. Table 9.3 provides additional examples of BDI questions that request both positive and negative information.

Like the SI and CSI, the BDI is an attempt to apply Wernimont and Campbell's suggestion that the predictor should sample behaviours that are representative of criterion behaviours (i.e., a work sample).[131] However, in contrast to the SI, the BDI approach is based on the premise that the best predictor of future behaviour is past behaviour. Critics of this approach have argued that people learn from past mistakes and that situational factors (e.g., relationships with supervisors, tasks, organizational norms) constrain behaviour; therefore, past behaviours will not necessarily be repeated in the future, particularly if the situation is somewhat different or if learning has taken place. After describing negative experiences, applicants can be asked, however, to indicate if they would repeat the behaviour next time or to relate an experience where they were successful in a similar situation.

Taylor and Small report a mean criterion validity coefficient of 0.26 (0.47 with corrections for criterion unreliability and range restriction) for the BDI when no descriptively anchored scoring guides were used (across 8 coefficients), but a mean criterion validity coefficient of 0.35 (0.63 with corrections for criterion unreliability and range restriction) when scoring guides were used (across 11 coefficients).[132] Inter-rater reliability was 0.73 without scoring guides and 0.77 with scoring guides. Clearly, the use of scoring guides has improved the reliability and validity of the BDI. Huffcutt et al. obtained similar results for the BDI (based on 22 coefficients), with a mean criterion validity coefficient of 0.31 (0.51 corrected).[133] For more information on

TABLE 9.3

Additional Examples of Behaviour Description Interview Questions

1. Sometimes we encounter individuals who seem to avoid us when we try to conduct personal or corporate business with them. Tell me about a time you were trying to contact an individual who seemed to be avoiding you or not answering your calls.

   Probes: What efforts did you make to contact this person?
   How long did you keep trying?
   Were you successful? What happened?
   If you were not successful, what did you do?
   What was the outcome?

   1—I stopped calling or trying to make contact. There was no point in continuing because the individual was clearly not interested.

   3—I continued trying to contact the individual. I left messages until I was successful.

   5—I tried to contact the individual in person. I tried to discover what the problem was and why the individual was avoiding me. I tried to rectify the situation, if possible.

2. Sometimes we find ourselves in situations where something is wrong or out of place, which nobody else seems to notice, and which could have serious consequences or hurt someone if not corrected. Tell me about a time where you experienced such a situation and tell me what you did.

   Probes: What about the situation seemed dangerous or potentially harmful?
   What steps did you take to ensure those nearby would be safe?
   What did you do to reduce the danger or resolve the situation?
   What was the outcome?

   1—I left things well enough alone. Nobody else seemed concerned, so I wasn't going to get involved.

   3—I took some steps to fix the situation *or* I reported the situation to someone in authority.

   5—I reported the situation to those nearby as well as to someone in authority. I recommended that appropriate action be taken to keep everyone safe. I tried to fix the problem or assisted in trying to fix it to the extent possible.

3. Sometimes we are asked to settle disputes between conflicting parties concerning limited resources. In fact, sometimes the settlement has a personal cost for us. Tell me about a time when you were asked to help resolve a conflict over resources between two other individuals, especially one where there was some potential cost to you.

   Probes: Who were the participants in the conflict and what was the conflict about?
   What did you do to facilitate the discussion?
   How did you help the parties resolve the conflict?
   What potential cost was there to you in the process or the resolution?
   What was the outcome?

   continued

1—I refused to get involved.

3—I supported one of the sides (based on friendship, my sense of who had the stronger case, etc.) *or* I told them to work it out between themselves.

5—I tried to help them resolve the issue by seeking a compromise. I tried to discover what the factors were and to consider them as objectively as possible. If no solution was reached, I arbitrated based on the merits of each position.

different aspects of the BDI approach to interviewing, see http://careerplanning.about.com/library/weekly/aa080900a.htm and http://www.brockport.edu/career/behave.htm.

Comparison of the Structured Interview Approaches

According to the research evidence available to date (see above), validity coefficients for the situational interview, comprehensive structured interview, and behaviour description interview seem to be reasonably similar. However, these comparisons are indirect because, in most studies, researchers examined either the SI or the BDI (there are very few studies of the CSI). A few competitive tests of the BDI and SI approaches have been conducted.[134] Unfortunately, the results of these studies are conflicting and inconclusive and, taken together, do not suggest that either approach has an advantage in terms of predictive validity.[135] There is some evidence that the BDI might be a bit better than the SI for highly complex jobs (e.g., management positions).[136] However, there are also conflicting findings in this regard. That is, if the SI is properly designed with questions that contain a dilemma (see the section on designing interview questions later in this chapter) and are pilot-tested to reduce the effects of impression management, it appears to be at least as effective as the BDI for complex jobs.[137]

The conclusion that the SI and BDI are equally effective is evident in a recent comparative study. Day and Carroll used critical incidents to generate related SI and BDI questions like those in Tables 9.1 and 9.3, with accompanying scoring guides.[138] The resultant questions were then used to interview undergraduate students for admission into a fictitious academic program. Two trained interviewers conducted the interviews. In some cases, the applicants had been given the interview questions to study prior to the interview. Day and Carroll also obtained the students' grade point averages, their past academic experience, a measurement of cognitive ability, and their perceptions of the fairness of the questions.

Both types of structured interview questions predicted academic success and accounted for incremental validity over and above that provided by cognitive ability and experience. They also found that knowing the interview questions beforehand led to significantly higher interview scores. Neither the SI nor BDI elicited differing perceptions of fairness; however, interviews were perceived as more fair when the interview questions had been provided ahead of time to participants. Overall, Day and Carroll concluded that neither the SI nor the BDI produced significantly different results in their ability to predict performance.[139]

Other research has addressed the question of whether there are differences in the constructs measured by SI and BDI interviews. Berry, Sackett, and Landers found that BDIs have a lower correlation with cognitive ability than SIs (0.12 for the BDI and 0.26 for the SI, uncorrected).[140] In fact, they found that interviews generally have lower correlations with cognitive ability than previously thought, which means that interviews have greater potential to predict components of job performance that are not predicted by cognitive ability than previously thought and, therefore, increase the accuracy of our predictions of job performance (i.e., they have incremental validity—see Chapter 10).

Correlations between structured interviews and personality measurements are also quite modest.[141-144] Both the BDI and the SI have modest correlations with Conscientiousness (0.12 and 0.10, respectively), but the BDI appears to also correlate with Extroversion (0.12), while the SI seems to correlate negatively with Neuroticism (−0.12).[145]

In fact, the constructs best measured by structured interviews, whether SI or BDI, seem to be job experience, job knowledge, situational judgment, social skills, and organizational fit.[146,147] These constructs are multidimensional and it is likely that good interview questions are multidimensional as well. For example, answering the question in Table 9.1 (and behaving appropriately in such a situation) likely involves not just one but several constructs, such as motivation to lead, understanding human motivation and behaviour, situational judgment, rational and analytical thinking, social skills, self-control, and self-confidence. Thus, it should not be surprising that interview questions often do not correlate highly with other measurements of the single constructs they are supposed to assess or with other interview questions ostensibly measuring the same single construct.[148]

Some researchers have explored how applicants use impression management tactics in the SI and BDI. They found that applicants tend to use more ingratiation tactics (e.g., complimenting the interviewer or organization) in the SI, while they tend to use more self-focused and defensive tactics (e.g., self-promotion, explaining mistakes or failures) in the BDI.[149,150] The latter finding should not be surprising, given that the BDI requires applicants to discuss past situations where they have either been successful or where they have encountered difficulty or failure.

Other researchers have compared BDI questions with SI questions in terms of how much effect applicant impression management tactics actually have on interview ratings. Van Iddekinge, McFarland, and Raymark[151] found that SI questions are less susceptible to impression management behaviour, while Levashina and Campion[152] found that BDI questions are more resistant to faking. Thus, again, the evidence is inconclusive. Nevertheless, regardless of the type of questions, it is clear that using structured interviews reduces the effects of impression management tactics on interview ratings.[153]

Validity and other issues notwithstanding, the BDI appears to be more appropriate in some selection situations, whereas the SI and CSI appear to be more appropriate in others. In particular, the BDI seems best suited to the selection of candidates who have had prior work experience (especially in related areas of work) or have been engaged in relevant volunteer activities or hobbies. The job knowledge questions, and possibly the job simulation and worker characteristics questions, of the CSI also appear better suited to applicants with related experience. However, the situational questions of the CSI and the SI are useful with both experienced and inexperienced applicants. Experienced applicants may still have some advantage over inexperienced applicants competing for the same job when situational questions are asked, but the difference would likely be reduced.

As noted above, interviewers appear to require a fair degree of skill in order to conduct the BDI effectively. The SI or CSI might therefore be more foolproof in the hands of supervisors and line managers when they do the interviewing. The SI and CSI seem to require less skill or training because the interviewer simply reads the questions and compares the answers given with the scoring guide examples. Probing is not permitted. If the BDI is to be used, a thorough training program is highly recommended.

It is important to recognize that the above discussion of the relative merits of the two approaches is somewhat speculative. More research is needed to investigate the relative merits of the BDI and the SI in various situations and with varying degrees of interviewer training and experience. In addition to addressing the theoretical questions surrounding the relationships of past behaviour and behavioural intentions with subsequent behaviour, such research would provide highly useful information for improving the design of structured interviews.

It may well be that both SI and BDI approaches could be used effectively in tandem within one interview session. Applicants who have difficulty answering a BDI question because of a lack of relevant work experience could be asked a corresponding SI question. Alternatively, SI questions could be followed by corresponding BDI questions in order to determine whether the behavioural intentions are consistent with past behaviours. For more information on situational, comprehensive, and behaviour description interviews, visit http://www.mmsearch.com/html/interview_prep.html.

Structured Interviews in Practice

Employer Reactions to Interview Structure

When employers were first exposed to structured interview methods a couple of decades ago, they tended to be somewhat suspicious of them. Most felt more comfortable with unstructured approaches that relied to a large extent on "gut feelings." Moreover, many interviewers prefer the greater discretion, personal contact, and ease of preparation provided by unstructured interviews.[154] However, it appears that most employers have begun using interviews with at least moderate levels of structure.[155–158]

In the most recent survey by Simola, Tagger, and Smith, more than 48.2 percent of Canadian HR practitioners reported always using Behaviour Description questions, while another 37.5 percent reported using them most of the time. Situational questions were used less frequently, with 17.6 percent reporting always using them and another 26.6 percent reporting using them most of the time.[159] However, it is not clear whether these interviews are being used appropriately. The survey suggests that most HR practitioners do not have a strong understanding of best practices concerning employment interviewing. Only 34.6 percent reported basing interview questions on a job analysis and more than 75 percent reported that they add questions during the interview.

These disturbing findings are supported by those of Chapman and Zweig, who found that interviewers tend not to use formal rating systems to rate applicant answers and generally do not even have an ideal response in mind with which to compare applicant answers. Moreover, they tend to use their global impressions of the applicant rather than combining scores statistically to come to a selection decision (see the following section and Chapter 10).[160] Providing interviewers with training concerning structured interviewing techniques and strong organization support for the use of structured interviews seem to be effective ways of increasing the likelihood that structured interviews will be used correctly.[161–163]

Applicant Reactions to Interview Structure

Applicants seem to like interviews more than any other selection devices such as cognitive ability tests, personality tests, biodata inventories, or work samples, and consistently rate interviews very favourably.[164–165] They perceive them to be fairer and more valid than other selection methods, and minority applicants in particular seem to prefer interviews to other selection methods.[166] However, applicant reactions to structured interviewing techniques have been mixed. Wagner found that using structured techniques did not affect applicants' impressions of the company or the likelihood of accepting a job offer.[167] Chapman and Zweig found that applicants perceive structured interview questions as more difficult than typical questions, but interview structure is not related to perceptions of interview fairness nor is it related to whether applicants are likely to accept a job offer.[168]

On the other hand, Chapman and Rowe[169] and Kohn and Dipboye[170] found that applicants are most attracted to organizations that use less structured interviews. Kohn and Dipboye found that, when structured interviews were used, participants were less likely to accept a job offer and rated the organization as less attractive, less social, and more authoritarian, and the interviewer as less fair and less likable than when unstructured interviews were used.[171] Structuring an interview may reduce applicants' perceptions of rapport with the interviewer and provide less opportunity to develop positive feelings about the interviewer and the organization. It also provides less opportunity for applicants to use impression management tactics and may, therefore, be frustrating for some applicants.[172]

Interviews serve both a recruitment and a selection function. Unfortunately, these two purposes may conflict in that factors related to improved validity (e.g., interview structure) might result in negative applicant reactions. Kohn and Dipboye found that the negative effect of structure on applicant attraction to the organization could be reduced if the interviewer provided more information about the job and organization in the interview.[173]

Moreover, as pointed out at the beginning of this chapter, compared with factors such as pay, promotion opportunities, or geographical location, interviewers' effects on applicant job choice are minimal.[174] Nevertheless, some time should be taken during the interview to put the applicants at ease and build rapport. The nature of the questions and the interview process can be explained and opportunities should be given for the applicants to ask questions. These steps should not only reduce possible negative reactions but also contribute to a less stressful interview situation, which should allow interviewees to perform at their best when answering the questions.

Interview Practice and Employment Equity

As noted above, one of the hallmarks of structured interviews is the standardization of interview questions. When interviews are standardized, applicants can be compared on the basis of the same criteria and the interviewer obtains a better picture of the merits of each applicant relative to other applicants. In fact, a number of researchers have suggested that standardization may contribute to increased interview reliability and validity.[175]

Equally, if not more important, the standardized treatment of applicants is perceived as being fairer than nonstandardized treatment in today's society. The likelihood of organizations that use standardized interview questions becoming embroiled in selection-related litigation is therefore reduced. Moreover, when such organizations do go to court, the courts tend to rule in their favour.[176–178] Standardization therefore gives the interviewer and organization some measure of protection from discrimination suits.

Another aspect of structured interviews that appears to have a strong impact on the organization's ability to defend itself against litigation is the exclusive use of job-related questions (i.e., questions based on a formal job analysis). Questions that probe areas not directly relevant to the job run the risk of being interpreted as having discriminatory intent by the applicant and by the courts.[179–181] A question such as "Do you plan to have children?" which is frequently posed to female but not to male applicants, is not only unrelated to job requirements but treats male and female applicants differently (i.e., is not standardized). Such questions are particularly troublesome from a human rights perspective. Such questions also result in negative applicant reactions to the interview and the interviewer and a decreased likelihood that they will accept a job offer or recommend the organization to others.[182]

The job relevance of interview questions has a significant impact on interview validity as well.[183] Structured interviews may have greater predictive validity, in part, because structuring an interview increases its reliability and accuracy in differentiating between applicant competencies on job-relevant dimensions. Moreover, the greater job relevance of structured interview questions may direct the interviewer's attention away from irrelevant information and focus it on job-relevant information. This focusing of interviewer attention may reduce the potential effects of the biases and processing errors inherent in the unstructured interview. Therefore, the degree to which structured interview questions are job-relevant and interview ratings are reliable appears to contribute to the validity of the interview.

However, the job relevance of interview questions does not, by itself, guarantee the reliability of interview ratings. Interviewers often disagree in their ratings of the same dimensions or characteristics for a given applicant and even give different ratings for the same answer to an interview question. Therefore, some kind of job-relevant rating or scoring guide is essential if high reliability among raters is to be achieved and if the interview ratings are to be based on job-relevant criteria. In fact, such scoring guides appear to reduce the effects of bias and increase interview reliability, and therefore validity, particularly when they are used to assess the answers given by interviewees rather than trait dimensions.[184–186]

The use of a standardized, job-relevant scoring system for assessing and comparing candidates may also contribute to an effective defence against litigation.[187,188] The courts have been particularly concerned when there is evidence that applicants giving the same responses are treated differently on the basis of gender or race or any other grounds on which discrimination is forbidden. To build on a previous example, it is insufficient for an employer to standardize the interview by asking both male and female applicants whether they intend to have children if a male's response to the question is irrelevant to the selection decision whereas a female's response might determine whether or not she is offered the job (i.e., the *scoring* of responses is not standardized).

Latham and his colleagues' approach requires interviewers to sum the scores given for each individual question to give an overall interview score, rather than permitting interviewers to make global judgments.[189] The final score can then be used to make the selection decision by ranking candidates or by determining cut-off scores, which must be exceeded by candidates if they are to qualify for the job. In essence, this approach relieves the interviewer of much of the decision-making function and isolates the selection decision from the interviewer's biases and stereotypes.[190] The selection decision, then, is a statistical or actuarial process that has greater criterion-related validity than the error-prone judgmental processes typically engaged in by interviewers when they make overall ratings or recommendations.[191]

This advantage for the statistical combination of scores does not appear to hold, however, when interview questions with low job-relevance are used. Rather than evaluating behaviours, interviewers using such questions make subjective judgments with respect to each answer given.[192] The total interview score for such questions therefore represents the sum of several subjective judgments, which does not differ significantly from a single overall subjective rating.

Day and Carroll's study also raises an important point about access to the interview questions.[193] Knowing the questions in advance, whether they are SI or BDI, will lead to higher interview scores. Strict control must be maintained of all questions or the interview questions must be given to all candidates beforehand to remove the possibility of some candidates having an advantage through prior knowledge of the questions. As Day and Carroll show, knowing the questions beforehand does not lead to every applicant giving brilliant answers; there is still a distribution of scores. All applicants must be treated fairly with respect to access to the interview questions.

It should be emphasized, with respect to the discussion above, that interview validity and reliability issues are very much related, in that reliability can place an upper limit on validity.[194] In fact, Wiesner and Cronshaw found that interview validity and reliability were correlated at 0.48 in the studies they examined.[195] Conditions that serve to make interviews more reliable should therefore be the same as those that make them more valid.[196]

Although unstructured interviews are vulnerable targets of potential litigation, there is comparatively little evidence of bias in structured interviews. Arvey and Campion found no evidence of age or gender bias in their semistructured interviews.[197] Similarly, in their investigation of over 27 000 structured interviews for 18 different jobs, Blankenship and Cesare found no evidence of bias on the basis of age.[198] Although Lin, Dobbins, and Farh also found no evidence of age bias in their structured interview, they found a very small effect for a same-race bias.[199]

More recent studies have also found no evidence of age or gender bias, although there continues to be a very small same-race bias.[200,201] In particular, interview panels or boards consisting of all black or mostly black interviewers tend to give slightly higher scores to black applicants than do panels or boards made up of all white or mostly white interviewers (ratings do not differ for white or Hispanic applicants).[202] However, Lin, Dobbins, and Farh found less evidence of race bias when structured interviews were used than when unstructured interviews were used.[203] Moreover, they note that the true performance levels of the applicants are unknown. Nevertheless, they recommended the use of mixed-race interview boards to reduce the potential for bias.

Paullin[204] reviews seven studies, including four conducted by Motowidlo et al.,[205] and finds no consistent trends for bias with respect to gender or race or ethnic group. Any differences that do exist tend to be less than half a standard deviation and do not consistently favour any group. Finally, Huffcutt and Roth conducted a meta-analysis of 31 studies to assess racial group differences in employment interview scores.[206] Like Lin, Dobbins, and Farh,[207] they found differences in ratings were quite small for structured interviews and much less than for unstructured interviews. The studies represent a variety of jobs including marketing, entry-level management, nonmanagerial telecommunications jobs, and firefighting.

Brecher, Bragger, and Kutcher found that, compared to unstructured interviews, structured interviews reduce bias with respect to physical disability.[208] In addition, Reilly and her colleagues found that using behaviourally anchored scoring guides is effective in removing bias with respect to disability in structured interviews.[209] Not only are structured interviews less vulnerable to bias than unstructured interviews, but applicants perceive them as more job-related and, thus, fairer.[210,211] Consequently, applicants are less likely to be concerned about decisions made on the basis of structured interviews.

There is an important caveat that we have to make with respect to the defensibility of structured interviews. The improved reliability, validity, and lack of bias occur in structured interviews that have been developed from the principles presented in this chapter. Too often we have seen HR practitioners use shortcuts to develop a set of structured interview questions or to simply choose questions off the shelf from books on structured interviews. In our practice, we have seen HR practitioners fail to ensure that questions were job-related, to develop appropriate scoring keys, to screen out candidates on answers to one question rather than the total score, and to fail to properly train those who will be doing the interviews. As with any tool, to get the best results, interviews must be properly used. Failure to follow the "best practices" with respect to structured interviews will undermine their defensibility. Information on structured interviewing and human rights concerns can be found at http://www.canadavisa.com/canada-immigration-employment-interviews.html.

Designing Interview Questions

Although a variety of job analysis methods can be used to develop structured interview questions, the most common is the critical incidents technique.[212] The critical incidents technique has been the basis of both the SI and the BDI. Examples of effective and ineffective as well as typical behaviours that contributed to the success or failure of employees in particular job-related situations or tasks should be collected. Each important task or situation should thus be linked with several examples of typical, effective, and ineffective behaviours. This information can be obtained from incumbents and their supervisors through interviews, focus group sessions, and questionnaires.

Once the critical incidents have been collected, the situations on which they are based can be turned into CSI, BDI, or SI questions. For SI questions, the situation should be described in sufficient detail to allow an applicant to visualize it accurately and should be followed by a "What would you do?" question. For each situation, the best critical incidents (i.e., most representative and most likely to be used as answers by interviewees) demonstrating effective, typical, and ineffective behaviours can serve as behavioural anchors for the scoring guide (i.e., poor, average, and good answer, respectively). Scores are typically assigned so that 1 represents the poor answer, 3 an average answer, and 5 a good answer.

Care should be taken to select situations and to phrase questions in a way that does not make the best answer readily apparent to the applicant. Situations where there is tension between competing demands or options are ideal if the options appear equally aversive or attractive to inexperienced individuals (i.e., there is a dilemma). Questions and scoring guides should be pre-tested on a group of applicants or recently hired employees to ensure that the questions are clear and elicit a range of responses. For example, if the poor answer is never given, the answers that are given should be examined to determine whether some of them reflect an alternative critical incident representing ineffective performance. Alternatively, the question should be reworked to create more tension.

BDI questions are designed by examining each task or situation in order to identify the behavioural dimension underlying the situation (e.g., meeting deadlines). The dimensions are turned into BDI questions, which retain the essence rather than the details of the original situation. In other words, the BDI question applies to a variety of situations that share the underlying behavioural dimension (e.g., meeting deadlines in a job, at school, when sending birthday cards, etc.). As with the SI, critical incidents are used to develop a scoring guide. However, the scoring guide anchors also need to be rephrased to make them more generally applicable to a variety of situations. The underlying behavioural dimensions rather than the actual incidents serve as anchors (e.g., "planning ahead, setting up contingency plans, monitoring progress" instead of "working long hours at the last minute, asking for extensions, missing the deadline").

Probes are developed by anticipating the kinds of responses that applicants from different backgrounds or with different levels of experience are likely to give to a BDI question. For example, applicants with limited work experience might never have been in a situation where they disagreed with a superior. A probe might then focus on responses to a disagreement with parents or friends in a situation similar to the one of relevance to the job. The probes should provide a clear understanding of the situation, the behaviour, and the outcome so that the applicant's response can be accurately scored. General probes like "What led up to the situation?" "What did you do?" "What happened?" "What was your reason for ... ?" or "Can you tell me more about ... ?" seem to apply in most circumstances.

Job knowledge or job simulation questions can also be derived from critical incidents. The situations that lead to ineffective or effective behaviours can be simulated during the interview. For example, if problems have occurred on the job because solvents have been mixed or used inappropriately and if a contributing factor is functional illiteracy, applicants could be asked to read the directions on a solvent container aloud and then to explain in their own words what the directions mean. Similarly, an applicant could be asked to "sell" a product to interviewers playing the roles of the kinds of customers who have been challenging for salespeople in the past. Additional information on the development of structured interview questions and scoring guides can be found at http://www.spb.ca.gov/WorkArea/show content.aspx?id=1208.

Interviewer Training

Interviewer training has tended to focus on reducing common sources of bias and inaccuracy such as halo error, similar-to-me effects, contrast effects, and leniency and severity errors. Interviewers are also taught to put the applicant at ease, ask open-ended questions, develop good listening skills, maintain control of the interview, take appropriate notes, and ignore or interpret correctly the nonverbal behaviours occurring in the interview. Unfortunately, such training efforts have achieved mixed results at best.[213,214] Most studies report that interviewer training designed to eliminate halo and other rating biases has minimal effect on interviewer behaviour and interview outcomes, particularly when shorter training programs are examined.

Training interviewers to administer a structured interview is a considerably different endeavour than training them to avoid errors and biases or develop good listening skills. Although rapport building is an important skill, interviewers using structured interviews need to learn how to ask questions, evaluate answers, and use scoring guides, as well as how to take notes.[215] For example, interviewers require training on how to score an answer when it does not match the examples in the scoring guide. The training should provide interviewers with decision rules to use in such circumstances.

Interviewers using techniques that allow more discretion, such as the BDI, might require more extensive training than those using more standardized approaches, such as the SI. When using their discretion, interviewers need to learn how to select questions or probes and when to probe. They need to learn how to use probes effectively without giving away the ideal answer. Demonstrations, behavioural role modelling, and opportunities for active practice are likely to be essential training techniques in any such training program.[216,217] Training that focuses on the evaluation and scoring of applicant answers has been found to contribute to higher interview reliability and validity.[218,219]

Interview Coaching for Applicants

Being interviewed for a job can be an anxiety-arousing situation for applicants.[220,221] Interview anxiety is negatively related to interview performance and, as a result, anxious applicants are less likely to be hired, even though their interview anxiety might be unrelated to job performance.[222] Such applicants can benefit from coaching to help them handle employment interviews more effectively. In fact, most applicants can benefit from some interview coaching but those who have not been interviewed for a long time, those who have not experienced structured approaches to interviewing, and those who have experienced ongoing difficulty doing well in interviews stand to gain the most from such coaching.

Coaching applicants for structured employment interviews generally involves explaining the purpose of the interview, suggestions and advice on how to do well in the interview, exposing applicants to different kinds of questions, discussing the nature of responses interviewers are looking for with illustrations of how to perform, providing opportunities for role-play or practice, providing feedback to applicants, and providing reinforcement for appropriate interview behaviours.[223] Providing applicants with interview coaching increases their interview self-efficacy (reducing their anxiety) and improves their performance in interviews.[224,225]

Coaching applicants to improve their interview performance might seem counterintuitive, given the interviewer's objective of selecting the best job candidates rather than the most polished interviewees. However, the interview coaching described here appears to actually increase the validity of structured interviews.[226] This may be because coaching helps applicants to focus their answers, describing more job-relevant behaviours more clearly, thus helping the interviewer obtain a more accurate perspective of the applicant's capabilities. Additional information and tips about preparing for interviews as an applicant can be found at http://www.careercc.com/interv3 .shtml, http://www.quintcareers.com/intvres.html, and http://www.ctdol .state.ct.us/progsupt/jobsrvce/intervie.htm.

Future Directions for Interview Research and Practice

The Behavioural Sample Interview

A relatively new concept in selection interviewing is what might be referred to as the *work sample interview* or **behavioural sample interview** (BSI). Whereas the SI focuses on future behaviours (behavioural intentions) and the BDI focuses on past behaviours, the BSI is concerned with behaviour in the present. It could be argued that a sampling of an applicant's current behaviour should be a better predictor of job performance than either behavioural intentions or past behaviours. What applicants say or even believe they will do and what they actually do in a given situation can be quite different. Similarly, because applicants can learn from mistakes and change over time, a past behaviour may not be repeated in the future.

Several approaches have been taken to behavioural sample interviewing, but they are all concerned with current behaviour. Campion, Pursell, and Brown[227] used job knowledge questions as well as work sample questions in their comprehensive structured interview, and Wright, Lichtenfels, and Pursell[228] describe the use of similar questions by themselves and by Kennedy.[229] Examples of these job knowledge and work sample questions are provided in the section on comprehensive structured interviews. Essentially, work sample questions require the applicant to demonstrate a skill or competence (i.e., provide a work sample) during the interview (e.g., "If this item costs $5.67 and I give you $10, how much change should I get?" or "Show me how to wire these two 3-way switches").

A related approach to work sample interviewing involves role-playing. One of the interviewers or an assistant plays a foil to the role played by the applicant, while the interviewer or others observe and evaluate. The Edmonton Police Service uses such role-play to assess assertiveness in candidates. The applicant is to assume he or she has just set up a chair to watch a parade. The chair happens to be similar to ones set up by the city for public use. The applicant is told to assume that he or she has left the chair unattended in order to get a drink and returns to find the chair occupied (by the

Behavioural sample interview

One of several structured interview techniques, including job knowledge interviews, work sample interviews, and walk-through interviews, that require the demonstration of behaviours in the present.

foil). The applicant's task is to convince the foil to vacate the chair without resorting to aggressive behaviour (physical or verbal).

Another approach to the BSI is the walk-through interview used by Hedge and Teachout and also by Ree, Earles, and Teachout to select U.S. Air Force enlistees.[230,231] The walk-through interview involves asking the interviewees to describe in detail, step by step, how they perform a job-related task while visualizing themselves performing the task.

Like the SI and BDI, the behavioural sample interview can be derived from critical incidents through focused group sessions. Scoring guides should also be developed using the procedures described for the SI and BDI. However, in some respects, the BSI may be a little more difficult to construct than either the SI or BDI. Care must be taken when simulating situations in the interview setting to ensure fidelity to the actual situation. Due to the length of time required to administer some of the BSI questions, fewer of them are likely to be usable in one session. They should therefore be selected judiciously to assess the most important performance domains. Nevertheless, the behavioural sample interview offers yet-unexplored potential for predicting job performance.

Long-Distance Interviews

Many organizations recruit candidates across the country or internationally. However, the costs of flying candidates in for interviews and paying for their accommodations or, conversely, flying recruiters across the country or overseas can be prohibitive. Moreover, there have been recent concerns about the safety of air travel. As a result, some organizations have turned to telephone interviews, videoconference interviews, Internet interviews, or computerized interviews as alternatives to face-to-face interviews.[232]

Although preliminary evidence suggests that long-distance, structured interviews can be valid predictors of job performance,[233] there is also evidence that the use of technology can, in some circumstances, make the interview an unsatisfying, or even unpleasant, experience for both the applicant and the interviewer.[234,235] Moreover, there are a number of obstacles, such as limited access to videoconferencing facilities, high costs, and technical limitations (e.g., picture and sound quality) that need to be overcome if such technology is to be used effectively.[236]

Some preliminary research suggests that applicants interviewed using videoconference technology receive higher ratings than those interviewed face to face.[237,238] The implications of this finding are of considerable concern if an organization interviews some applicants in face-to-face situations, while interview technology is used to interview others. Applicants interviewed face to face would be at a disadvantage. There is also some evidence that interview technology interacts with interview structure in complex ways.[239,240] Clearly, more research is needed on applicant and interviewer reactions to interview technology, as well as on the validity of such technology-dependent interviews compared with face-to-face interviews.

Other Research Issues

Although there is indisputable evidence that structured interviews are good predictors of job performance, we still do not have a clear understanding of why they predict.[241] More research based on good theoretical models of the structured interview is needed to provide a better understanding of the mechanisms responsible for interview effectiveness. Such research would contribute greatly to improvements in interview design and performance.

Despite the predictive validity of structured interviews, many employers and applicants have responded negatively to them. Some employers resist using structured interviews or modify them, possibly because they don't fully understand how to use structured interviews or because they want more control of the interview process. Likewise, some applicants do not like structured interviews, possibly because they find them more difficult or because they have less influence on the interview process. Research is needed to find ways of improving user reactions to structured interviews and making them easier to use.

Summary

Employment interviews are the most popular selection procedure among employers and employees. Over the past two decades, many Canadian employers have abandoned traditional, unstructured approaches to interviewing in favour of structured interviews, notably behavioural interviews. However, most do not seem to be following best practices in implementing structured interview techniques. Moreover, many employers continue to use unstructured interviews, which have been plagued by poor reliability and validity and have placed the employers in a legally vulnerable position.

Dipboye's model of information processing and decision making in the interview was presented in this chapter.[242] This model is particularly relevant to unstructured interviews, although it applies, to a lesser degree, to structured interviews as well. According to the model, interviewers bring knowledge structures and initial information to the interview situation, both of which can be biased. These knowledge structures and the preliminary information contribute to pre-interview impressions that can influence the interviewer's attributions and behaviour in the interview. The interviewer's behaviour, in turn, influences the applicant's behaviour. The interviewer emerges from the interaction with global impressions of the applicant that are influenced by his or her stereotype of the ideal applicant, an emotional response to the applicant (e.g., liking the applicant), and the first impressions carried through the interview and sometimes intensified by the interview experience. Various factors, including time pressures, quotas, and politics, affect the final decision.

Structured approaches to employment interviewing were developed to address the shortcomings of the unstructured interview. Structuring factors include standardization, job-relatedness of interview questions, and standardized scoring systems. Such interviews need to be based on a job analysis so that they assess only job-relevant attributes. Interview questions should be nontransparent and tend to be most effective when they centre on situations involving dilemmas or tension between competing demands. Appropriate scoring guides and rater training are essential to maintaining high rating accuracy.

Various approaches to constructing structured interviews are available, including situational interviews, comprehensive structured interviews, behaviour description interviews, and recent innovations such as behavioural sample interviews. Structured interviews provide improved reliability and predictive validity and are more legally defensible than unstructured interviews. However, interviewers should be trained in the proper administration and scoring of the interview. Although the evidence is not clear on whether panel or serial interviews contribute to interview reliability and validity, they do appear to provide some degree of protection from discrimination suits.

As job requirements change in response to the ever-changing workplace, organizations are beginning to shift the focus of selection from specific job skills to organizational fit, transferable skills, and personality attributes. Structured employment interviews are well suited to assessing such attributes and will continue to play an important role in selection for the workplace of tomorrow. New approaches to interviewing involving the use of technology, such as videoconferencing and Internet interviews, are also being adopted by employers. However, considerable research remains to be done to determine the effects of such technology on interview validity, as well as on interviewer and applicant responses.

Key Terms

behavioural sample interview, p. 461

behaviour description interview, p. 447

comprehensive structured interview, p. 447

impression management, p. 436

knowledge structures, p. 432

panel interview, p. 442

probes, p. 448

scoring guide, p. 445

serial interviews, p. 444

situational interview, p. 445

structured interview, p. 440

unstructured interview, p. 435

Web Links

Examples of bad interviews as well as links for interviewees can be found at http://www.quintcareers.com/wild_card_interview_questions.html, http://www.garywill.com/worksearch/worst.htm, and http://www.citynews.ca/news/news_23215.aspx.

For interviewing tips for applicants, go to http://www.careercc.com/interv3.shtml, http://www.ctdol.state.ct.us/progsupt/jobsrvce/intervie.htm, and http://www.quintcareers.com/intvres.html.

A summary of common biases in the unstructured interview is at http://www.indiana.edu/~uhrs/employment/best.html.

More panel interview information can be found at http://www.liscareer.com/peters_interviews.htm and http://sciencecareers.sciencemag.org/career_magazine. At the latter site, click on "Tooling Up: 15 Minutes to a Better Interview."

For more information on situational interviews, visit http://www.theiia.org/download.cfm?file=81429.

Situational, comprehensive, and behaviour description interview information can be found at http://www.mmsearch.com/html/interview_prep.html.

Behavioural interviews are discussed at http://careerplanning.about.com/library/weekly/aa080900a.htm and http://www.brockport.edu/career/behave.htm.

For more information on employment interviewing and human rights in Canada, visit http://canadavisa.com/documents/career/interview.htm.

Required Professional Capabilities (RPCs)

RPC 9.1 Stays current with professional knowledge.
- HR issues, trends, and developments
- Business issues, trends, and developments
- Information sources for professional development
- Expectations and professional requirements for CHRP designation

RPC 9.2 Fosters and promotes advancement of the profession.
- HR best practices
- Standards of professional practice
- Professional association activities
- The history of HRM
- Communication theories, tools, techniques, and processes

Discussion Questions

1. Describe the multiple phases of the employment interview.
2. What factors affect employment interview decisions?
3. What are the different errors or biases that commonly occur as part of a traditional employment interview?
4. What is a situational interview? What role does a critical incident play in formulating situational questions?
5. What is a behaviour description interview? What does it have in common with a situational interview? How does it differ?
6. How do structured interviews compare to traditional interviews in terms of reliability and validity?
7. Why is a scoring guide crucial to the success of a structured interview?

8. Why is a structured employment interview likely to be more defensible than other types of employment interviews?
9. Which is more effective—a situational interview or a behaviour description interview?

Using the Internet

Interview Construction

Several of the websites mentioned in this chapter provide guidance on how to write SI and BDI questions (e.g., http://www.spb.ca.gov/WorkArea/showcontent.aspx?id=1208). Use these sites to assist you in doing the following exercises.

1. Select a job you have done or know well. Identify the five most important tasks for this job. If you are having difficulty, go to the O*NET website (see Chapter 4) and find the five top-rated tasks for your job.
2. For each of the five tasks, think of examples of both effective and ineffective performance that you have observed or have been a part of (i.e., critical incidents).
3. For each task, write an SI or a BDI question. Use the critical incidents to develop a three-point scoring guide (example of a poor answer, a typical answer, and a good answer).

This exercise can be completed individually or in small groups of three to five. The product of the exercise is used in the role-play that follows in the exercises below. An alternative to selecting a job with which the group participants are familiar is to have the participants develop an interview for the job of "course instructor."

Exercises

Interview Question Writing

1. Are the following good interview questions? If not, how would you change them?

   a. "How did you get along with your supervisor?"
   b. "Do you follow policies, rules, and procedures carefully?"

2. "Are you an organized worker?" is obviously not a good interview question because it is transparent and requests a self-evaluation. Is the following wording satisfactory? If not, why not, and how would you change it?

   "Can you give me an example of how organized you are?"

3. Rewrite the following questions to make them more effective.

   a. Are you able to handle stress?
   b. How are you at meeting deadlines?

c. Do you have problems working closely with others?

d. When you make a mistake, what do you do to fix it?

e. How are you at solving problems?

f. Do have any problems communicating with people?

g. How do you feel about staying late to finish a project?

h. Are you a good leader? Can you motivate others?

i. What do you do when you encounter obstacles to meeting your goals?

j. Are you a good planner?

Personality Characteristics Assessment

4. Organizations exist in an increasingly dynamic environment. As a result, jobs change and employees are required to move around the organization, to do a variety of tasks, to develop multiple skills, and to "retool" or upgrade themselves on an ongoing basis. Employees are being hired less for specific job skills and more for their abilities to fit themselves to the needs of the organization. Organizations are looking for employees who are innovative, flexible, willing to learn, and conscientious, and who fit into the organizational culture—in other words, those who are good organizational citizens. (You may want to review the sections in Chapters 4 and 5 that cover these issues.)

a. Can the employment interview be used to assess such personality characteristics effectively? How?

b. Are there better selection tools than the interview for assessing these characteristics? If so, what are they and why are they superior? If not, why not?

c. Does the assessment of organizational fit and relevant personality attributes pose a danger to human rights? If so, how? If not, why not? How might you reduce the dangers of human rights violations while still pursuing employees who fit into the organizational culture?

Interview Role-Play

5. Form small groups of between three and five. Assign the role of applicant to one group member and the role of interviewer to another. The remaining members of the group serve as observers. The applicant is to be interviewed for one of the jobs selected for the interview construction exercise in the Using the Internet section.

a. As a group, select five self-evaluation questions from the list in Recruitment and Selection Today 9.1 (page 435). The interviewer is to use these questions to begin interviewing the applicant for the job.

b. Next, the interviewer is to use the five job-relevant questions developed in the Using the Internet exercise.

c. While the interviewer is conducting the interview, the observers should record their answers to the following questions:

    i.   How do the answers to the first five questions differ from the answers to the second five questions?

   ii.   Does one set of questions provide better information on which to base a selection decision? If so, which one?

  iii.   Is there a difference between the two question sets in terms of how much time the applicant spends talking? If so, which takes more time and why?

  iv.   Of the second set of questions, are there any questions that don't seem to work as well as they should? If so, why? How would you improve these questions?

   v.   How useful is the scoring guide? Would you recommend any modifications to the scoring guide? If so, how would you change it?

e. After the interview, the observers are to debrief the interviewer and the applicant. How did they perceive the relative effectiveness of the two sets of questions? Where did they experience difficulties? The observers should also provide feedback to both the interviewer and the applicant as to how they might improve their interview performance.

This role-play can be conducted as a class demonstration with one interviewer and one applicant as role-players and the remainder of the class as observers. A discussion of the relative effectiveness of the two question sets and the effectiveness of the interviewer and applicant can be held with the entire class.

Case

Cuts in health-care funding have led to restructuring of the health-care delivery system across Canada. In Kitchener, Ontario, the operations and administration of Kitchener-Waterloo General Hospital and Freeport Hospital were merged under the new name of Grand River Hospital Corporation. The duplication of services was eliminated by moving some services completely to one facility and all other services to the other facility.

Similarly, duplication of administration was eliminated by merging jobs across the two hospitals, so that where there were once two positions, there was now only one. For example, prior to restructuring, each hospital had its own director of human resources. However, there was room for only one director of human resources in the restructured Grand River Hospital. Thus, as jobs were merged, positions were eliminated. In some cases, due to funding cuts, as many as three or four jobs were merged into one. As a consequence, incumbents in most administrative jobs lost their original jobs and had to compete for the new, restructured positions.

Two of the authors of this text were asked by Grand River Hospital to assist in designing structured employment interviews for the new positions. They met with teams of subject-matter experts (SMEs—employees who knew the job well) for each of the new positions in order to conduct job analyses and develop interview questions and scoring guides. The two merging hospitals were represented by roughly equal numbers of SMEs on each of the teams. Importantly, the authors acted only as consultants and facilitators—it was the teams of SMEs who developed the questions and scoring guides.

Clearly, the SMEs had the best understanding of the relevant jobs and the peculiarities of each hospital, but having them develop the questions and scoring guides also ensured their acceptance of the interview process and the outcome. In addition to developing the interview questions and scoring guides, the teams or panels of SMEs were responsible for interviewing the candidates for the new positions. The authors participated in the interviews as observers and in the post-interview discussions as facilitators and consultants.

As the interviews progressed, an interesting phenomenon emerged. Not surprisingly, interview panel members from Freeport Hospital tended to favour candidates from Freeport Hospital, whereas interview panel members from Kitchener-Waterloo General Hospital tended to favour candidates from their home hospital. What was unexpected was the degree to which many argued for changes to the scoring guide or wanted to disregard the scoring system when the results were not favourable for their preferred candidate. Remember that all interview panel members had agreed on the questions and the scoring guides when they developed the interviews.

Now some claimed that their preferred candidate knew more than was reflected in his or her answer. Some argued that their preferred candidate was too nervous to think clearly. Others claimed that the interview questions or scoring guides reflected the working conditions at the other hospital more than those at their own hospital. Some argued that the range of opportunities to gain work experience was greater at the other hospital and that their preferred candidate was disadvantaged as a result. Still others felt the questions were not clear enough or that the scoring guide was too rigid. Yet the panel members who expressed such concerns when their preferred candidates did not do well tended to argue strongly in support of the interview process and scoring system when their preferred candidates did well. Needless to say, the authors were called on to mediate some lively discussions.

Discussion Questions

1. How is this situation different from that of the typical selection interview?
2. What factors need to be taken into consideration in this situation that don't normally apply in a selection interview?
3. Why do you think some of the interview panel members sought to sidestep the interview scoring process that they had helped develop in the first place? (Review the section "A Model of Information Processing and Decision Making in the Interview" on pages 431–35 if you're not sure.)
4. If you had been one of the consultants on this project, how would you have responded to the concerns expressed by some of the interview

panel members? Given the strong disagreements among interview panel members, what would you have done to facilitate agreement on an interview score for each candidate?

5. Is there anything the consultants on this project could have done to strengthen the acceptance of and adherence to the scoring process and minimize the potential for conflict? If so, what should they have done? If not, why not?

Endnotes

1. Rowe, P.M., M.C. Williams, and A.L. Day. 1994. "Selection Procedures in North America." *International Journal of Selection and Assessment* 2: 74–79.

2. Posthuma, R.A., F.P. Morgeson, and M.A. Campion. 2002. "Beyond Employment Interview Validity: A Comprehensive Narrative Review of Recent Research and Trends over Time." *Personnel Psychology* 55: 1–81.

3. Catano, V.M., and A. Bissonnette. 2003. *Selection Practices and Organizational Performance*, Table 8.3. Paper presented at the annual meeting of the Administrative Sciences Association of Canada, Halifax, NS.

4. Kinicki, A.J., C.A. Lockwood, P.W. Hom, and R.W. Griffeth. 1990. "Interviewer Predictions of Applicant Qualifications and Interviewer Validity: Aggregate and Individual Analysis." *Journal of Applied Psychology* 75: 477–86.

5. Sanyal, R., and T. Guvenli. 2004. "Personnel Selection in a Comparative Setting: Evidence from Israel, Slovenia, and the USA." *Journal of East–West Business* 10: 5–27.

6. Di Milia, L. 2004. "Australian Management Selection Practices: Closing the Gap between Research Findings and Practice." *Asia Pacific Journal of Human Resources* 42: 214–28.

7. Simola, S.K., S. Taggar, and G.W. Smith. 2007. "The Employment Selection Interview: Disparity among Research-Based Recommendation, Current Practices and What Matters to Human Rights Tribunals." *Canadian Journal of Administrative Sciences* 24: 30–44.

8. Dixon, M., S. Wang, J. Calvin, B. Dineen, and E. Tomlinson. 2002. "The Panel Interview: A Review of Empirical Research and Guidelines for Practice." *Public Personnel Management* 31: 397–428.

9. Motowidlo, S.J., G.W. Carter, M.D. Dunnette, N. Tippins, S. Werner, J.R. Burnett, and M.J. Vaughan. 1992. "Studies of the Structured Behavioral Interview." *Journal of Applied Psychology* 77: 571–87.

10. Latham, G.P., and D.P. Skarlicki. 1995. "Criterion-Related Validity of the Situational and Patterned Behavior Description Interviews with Organizational Citizenship Behavior." *Human Performance* 8: 67–80.

11. Pulakos, E.D., and N. Schmitt. 1995. "Experience-Based and Situational Interview Questions: Studies of Validity." *Personnel Psychology* 48: 289–308.

12. Huffcutt, A., J.M. Conway, P.L. Roth, and N.S. Stone. 2001. "Identification and Meta-Analytic Assessment of Psychological Constructs Measured in Employment Interviews." *Journal of Applied Psychology* 86: 897–913.

13. Posthuma, R.A., F.P. Morgeson, and M.A. Campion. 2002.

14. Sue-Chan, C., and G.P. Latham. 2004. "The Situational Interview as a Predictor of Academic and Team Performance: A Study of the Mediating Effects of Cognitive Ability and Emotional Intelligence." *International Journal of Selection and Assessment* 12: 312–20.

15. Maurer, S.D. 2006. "Using Situational Interviews to Assess Engineering Applicant Fit to Work Group, Job, and Organizational Requirements." *Engineering Management Journal* 18: 27–35.

16. Carless, S.A., and A. Imber. 2007. "The Influence of Perceived Interviewer and Job and Organizational Characteristics on Applicant Attraction and Job Choice Intentions: The Role of Applicant Anxiety." *International Journal of Selection and Assessment* 15: 359–71.

17. Posthuma, R.A., F.P. Morgeson, and M.A. Campion. 2002.

18. Rynes, S.L., and D. Cable. 2003. "Recruitment Research in the Twenty-First Century." In W.C. Borman, D.R. Ilgen, and R.J. Klimoski, eds., *Industrial–Organizational Psychology*; I.B. Weiner, ed., *Handbook of Psychology* 12: 55–76. Hoboken, NJ: John Wiley and Sons.

19. Rynes, S.L., and D. Cable. 2003.

20. Cascio, W.F. 2005. "Strategies for Responsible Restructuring." *The Academy of Management Executive* 19: 39–50.

21. Dougherty, T.W., D.B. Turban, and J.C. Callender. 1994. "Confirming First Impressions in the Employment Interview: A Field Study of Interviewer Behavior." *Journal of Applied Psychology* 79: 659–65.

22. Macan, T.H., and R.L. Dipboye. 1990. "The Relationship of Pre-Interview Impressions to Selection and Recruitment Outcomes." *Personnel Psychology* 43: 745–68.

23. Reilly, N.P., S.P. Bocketti, S.A. Maser, and C.L. Wennet. 2006. "Benchmarks Affect Perceptions of Prior Disability in a Structured Interview." *Journal of Business and Psychology* 20: 489–500.

24. Dipboye, R.L. 1992. *Selection Interviews: Process Perspectives*. Cincinnati, OH: South-Western Publishing.

25. Dipboye, R.L. 2005. "The Selection Interview: Core Processes and Contexts." In A. Evers, N. Anderson, and O. Voskuijl, eds., *The Blackwell Handbook of Personnel Selection*. Malden, MA: Blackwell Publishing.

26. Bozionelos, N. 2005. "When the Inferior Candidate Is Offered the Job: The Selection Interview as a Political and Power Game." *Human Relations* 58: 1605–31.

27. Latham, G.P., and Z. Millman. 2001. "Context and the Employment Interview." In J.F. Gubrium and J.A. Holstein, eds., *Handbook of Interview Research: Context and Method*. Thousand Oaks, CA: Sage Publications.

28. Macan, T.H., and R.L. Dipboye. 1990.

29. Dougherty, T.W., D.B. Turban, and J.C. Callender. 1994.

30. Liden, R.C., C.L. Martin, and C.K. Parsons. 1993. "Interviewer and Applicant Behaviors in Employment Interviews." *Academy of Management Journal* 36: 372–86.

31. Dipboye, R.L. 1992.

32. Middendorf, C.H., and T.H. Macan. 2002. "Note-Taking in the Employment Interview: Effects on Recall and Judgments." *Journal of Applied Psychology* 87: 293–303.

33. Dipboye, R.L. 1992.

34. Campion, M.A., D.K. Palmer, and J.E. Campion. 1997. "A Review of Structure in the Selection Interview." *Personnel Psychology* 50: 655–702.

35. Goldberg, C., and D.J. Cohen. 2004. "Walking the Walk and Talking the Talk: Gender Differences in the Impact of Interviewing Skills on Applicant Assessments." *Group & Organization Management* 29: 369–84.

36. Levashina, J., and M.A. Campion. 2007. "Measuring Faking in the Employment Interview: Development and Validation on an Interview Faking Behavior Scale." *Journal of Applied Psychology* 92: 1638–56.

37. Levashina, J., and M.A. Campion. 2007.

38. Levashina, J., and M.A. Campion. 2007.

39. Buhler, P. 2007. "Managing in the New Millennium: Ten Keys to Better Hiring." *SuperVision* 68 (November): 17–20.

40. Webster, E.C. 1964. *Decision Making in the Employment Interview*. Montreal: Industrial Relations Centre, McGill University.

41. Webster, E.C. 1982. *The Employment Interview: A Social Judgement Process*. Schomberg, ON: S.I.P. Publications.

42. Dipboye, R.L. 1992.

43. Jelf, G.S. 1999. "A Narrative Review of Post-1989 Employment Interview Research." *Journal of Business and Psychology* 14: 25–58.

44. Posthuma, R.A., F.P. Morgeson, and M.A. Campion. 2002.

45. Garcia, M.F., R.A. Posthuma, and A. Colella. 2008. "Fit Perceptions in the Employment Interview: The Role of Similarity, Liking, and Expectations." *Journal of Occupational and Organizational Psychology* 81: 173–89.

46. Dougherty, T.W., D.B. Turban, and J.C. Callender. 1994.

47. Macan, T.H., and R.L. Dipboye. 1990.

48. DeGroot, T., and S.J. Motowidlo. 1999.

49. Tucker, D.H., and P.M. Rowe. 1977. "Consulting the Application Form Prior to the Interview: An Essential Step in the Selection Process." *Journal of Applied Psychology* 62: 283–88.

50. Tullar, W.L., T.W. Mullins, and S.A. Caldwell. 1979. "Relational Control in the Employment Interview." *Journal of Applied Psychology* 64: 669–74.

51. Dipboye, R.L., C. Stramler, and G.A. Fontenelle. 1984. "The Effects of Application on Recall of Information from the Interview." *Academy of Management Journal* 27: 561–75.

52. Rowe, P.M. 1963. "Individual Differences in Selection Decisions." *Journal of Applied Psychology* 47: 986–93.

53. Dougherty, T.W., D.B. Turban, and J.C. Callender. 1994.

54. Macan, T.H., and R.L. Dipboye. 1990.

55. Dipboye, R.L., C. Stramler, and G.A. Fontenelle. 1984.

56. Farr, J.L., and C.M. York. 1975. "The Amount of Information and Primacy–Recency Effects in Recruitment Decisions." *Personnel Psychology* 28: 233–38.

57. Dipboye, R.L., C. Stramler, and G.A. Fontenelle. 1984.

58. Farr, J.L., and C.M. York. 1975.

59. Rowe, 1963.

60. Wexley, K.N., G.A. Yukl, S.Z. Kovacs, and R.E. Saunders. 1972. "Importance of Contrast Effects in Employment Interviews." *Journal of Applied Psychology* 56: 45–48.

61. Dougherty, T.W., D.B. Turban, and J.C. Callender. 1994.

62. Macan, T.H., and R.L. Dipboye. 1990.

63. Dipboye, R.L. 1992.

64. Rowe, P.M. 1984. "Decision Processes in Personnel Selection." *Canadian Journal of Behavioural Science* 16: 326–37.

65. Huffcutt, A.I., and P.L. Roth. 1998. "Racial Group Differences in Employment Interview Evaluations." *Journal of Applied Psychology* 83: 179–89.

66. Graves, L.M., and G.N. Powell. 1996. "Sex Similarity, Quality of the Employment Interview and Recruiters' Evaluation of Actual Applicants." *Journal of Occupational and Organizational Psychology* 69: 243–61.

67. Howard, J.L., and G.R. Ferris. 1996. "The Employment Interview Context: Social and Situational Influences on Interviewer Decisions." *Journal of Applied Social Psychology* 26: 112–36.

68. DeGroot, T., and S.J. Motowidlo. 1999. "Why Visual and Vocal Interview Cues Can Affect Interviewers' Judgments and Predict Job Performance." *Journal of Applied Psychology* 84: 986–93.

69. DeGroot, T., and D. Kluemper. 2007. "Evidence of Predictive and Incremental Validity of Personality Factors, Vocal Attractiveness and the Situational Interview." *International Journal of Selection and Assessment* 15: 30–39.

70. Liden, R.C., C.L. Martin, and C.K. Parsons. 1993.

71. Wiesner, W.H., and S.F. Cronshaw. 1988. "A Meta-Analytic Investigation of the Impact of Interview Format and Degree of Structure on the Validity of the Employment Interview." *Journal of Occupational Psychology* 61: 275–90.

72. Morrow, P.C. 1990. "Physical Attractiveness and Selection Decision Making." *Journal of Management* 16(1): 45–60.

73. McDaniel, M.A., D.L. Whetzel, F.L. Schmidt, and S.D. Maurer. 1994. "The Validity of Employment Interviews: A Comprehensive Review and Meta-Analysis." *Journal of Applied Psychology* 79: 599–616.

74. Wiesner, W.H., and S.F. Cronshaw. 1988.

75. Huffcutt, A.I., and W. Arthur, Jr. 1994. "Hunter and Hunter (1984) Revisited: Interview Validity for Entry-Level Jobs." *Journal of Applied Psychology* 79: 184–90.

76. McDaniel, M.A., D.L. Whetzel, F.L. Schmidt, and S.D. Maurer. 1994.

77. Wiesner, W.H., and S.F. Cronshaw. 1988.

78. Schmitt, N. 1976. "Social and Situational Determinants of Interview Decisions: Implications for the Employment Interview." *Personnel Psychology* 29: 79–101.

79. Janz, T. 1982. "Initial Comparisons of Patterned Behavior Description Interviews versus Unstructured Interviews." *Journal of Applied Psychology* 67: 577–80.

80. Latham, G.P., L.M. Saari, E.D. Pursell, and M.A. Campion. 1980. "The Situational Interview." *Journal of Applied Psychology* 65: 422–27.

81. Latham, G.P., and L.M. Saari. 1984. "Do People Do What They Say? Further Studies on the Situational Interview." *Journal of Applied Psychology* 69: 569–73.

82. Arvey, R.D., and J.E. Campion. 1982. "The Employment Interview: A Summary and Review of Recent Research." *Personnel Psychology* 35: 281–322.

83. Harris, M.M. 1989. "Reconsidering the Employment Interview: A Review of Recent Literature and Suggestions for Future Research." *Personnel Psychology* 42: 691–726.

84. Webster, E.C. 1964.

85. Conway, J.M., R.A. Jako, and D.F. Goodman. 1995. "A Meta-Analysis of Inter-Rater and Internal Consistency Reliability of Selection Interviews." *Journal of Applied Psychology* 80: 565–79.

86. McDaniel, M.A., D.L. Whetzel, F.L. Schmidt, and S.D. Maurer. 1994.

87. Huffcutt, A.I., and W. Arthur, Jr. 1994.

88. Wiesner, W.H., and S.F. Cronshaw. 1988.

89. Wiesner, W.H., and S.F. Cronshaw. 1988.

90. Huffcutt, A.I., and W. Arthur, Jr. 1994.

91. Huffcutt, A.I., and W. Arthur, Jr. 1994.

92. Campion, M.A., D.K. Palmer, and J.E. Campion. 1997.

93. Burnett, J.R., C. Fan, S.J. Motowidlo, and T. DeGroot. 1998. "Interview Notes and Validity." *Personnel Psychology* 51: 375–96.

94. Campion, M.A., D.K. Palmer, and J.E. Campion. 1997.

95. Huffcutt, A.I., and W. Arthur, Jr. 1994.

96. Janz, T. 1982.

97. Green, P.C., P. Alter, and A.F. Carr. 1993. "Development of Standard Anchors for Scoring Generic Past-Behaviour Questions in Structured Interviews." *International Journal of Selection and Assessment* 1: 203–12.

98. Latham, G.P., L.M. Saari, E.D. Pursell, and M.A. Campion. 1980.

99. Huffcutt, A.I., and W. Arthur, Jr. 1994.

100. Campion, M.A., D.K. Palmer, and J.E. Campion. 1997.

101. Dixon, M., S. Wang, J. Calvin, B. Dineen, and E. Tomlinson. 2002.

102. Simola, S.K., S. Taggar, and G.W. Smith. 2007.

103. Dixon, M., S. Wang, J. Calvin, B. Dineen, and E. Tomlinson. 2002.

104. Van Iddekinge, C.H., C.E. Sager, J.L. Burnfield, and T.S. Heffener. 2006. "The Variability of Criterion-Related Validity Estimates among Interviewers and Interview Panels." *International Journal of Selection and Assessment* 14: 193–205.

105. Bayne, R., C. Fletcher, and J. Colwell. 1983. "Board and Sequential Interviews in Selection: An Experimental Study of Their Comparative Effectiveness." *Personnel Review* 12: 14–19.

106. Arvey, R.D., and J.E. Campion. 1982.

107. Conway, J.M., R.A. Jako, and D.F. Goodman. 1995.

108. Wiesner, W.H., and S.F. Cronshaw. 1988.

109. Dixon, M., S. Wang, J. Calvin, B. Dineen, and E. Tomlinson. 2002.

110. Campion, M.A., D.K. Palmer, and J.E. Campion. 1997.

111. Dixon, M., S. Wang, J. Calvin, B. Dineen, and E. Tomlinson. 2002.

112. Hackett, R.D., L.M. Lapierre, and H.P. Gardiner. 2004. "A Review of Canadian Human Rights Cases Involving the Employment Interview." *Canadian Journal of Administrative Sciences* 21: 215–28.

113. Hackett, R.D., J.B. Rose, and J. Pyper. 2000. "The Employment Interview: An Analysis of Canadian Labour Arbitration Decisions." In K. Whitaker, J. Sack, M. Gunderson, R. Filion, and B. Bohuslawsy, eds., *Labour Arbitration Yearbook 1999–2000*, Vol. 1. Toronto: Lancaster House.

114. Latham, G.P., L.M. Saari, E.D. Purcell, and M.A. Campion. 1980.

115. Latham, G.P., and L.M. Saari. 1984.

116. Flanagan, J.C. 1954. "The Critical Incident Technique." *Psychological Bulletin* 51: 327–58.

117. Fishbein, M., and I. Ajzen. 1975. *Belief, Attitude, Intention, and Behavior: An Introduction to Theory and Research*. Reading, MA: Addison-Wesley.

118. Latham, G.P., and C. Sue-Chan. 1999. "A Meta-Analysis of the Situational Interview: An Enumerative Review of Reasons for Its Validity." *Canadian Psychology* 40: 56–67.

119. Taylor, P.J., and B. Small. 2002. "Asking Applicants What They Would Do versus What They Did Do: A Meta-Analytic Comparison of Situational and Past Behaviour Employment Interview Questions." *Journal of Occupational and Organizational Psychology* 75: 277–94.

120. Huffcutt, A.I., J.M. Conway, P.L. Roth, and U.C. Klehe. 2004. "The Impact of Job Complexity and Study Design on Situational and Behavior Description Interview Validity." *International Journal of Selection and Assessment* 12: 262–73.

121. Campion, M.A., E.D. Pursell, and B.K. Brown. 1988. "Structured Interviewing: Raising the Psychometric Properties of the Employment Interview." *Personnel Psychology* 41: 25–42.

122. Harris, M.M. 1989.

123. Campion, M.A., E.D. Pursell, and B.K. Brown. 1988.

124. Janz, T. 1982.

125. Janz, T. 1989. "The Patterned Behavior Description Interview: The Best Prophet of the Future Is the Past." In R.W. Eder and G.R. Ferris, eds., *The Employment Interview: Theory, Research, and Practice*. Newbury Park, CA: Sage Publications, Inc.

126. Latham, G.P., L.M. Saari, E.D. Pursell, and M.A. Campion. 1980.

127. Ghiselli, E.E. 1966. "The Validity of the Personnel Interview." *Personnel Psychology* 19: 389–94.

128. Janz, T., L. Hellervik, and D.C. Gilmore. 1986. *Behavior Description Interviewing: New, Accurate, Cost-Effective*. Boston, MA: Allyn and Bacon.

129. Campion, M.A., D.K. Palmer, and J.E. Campion. 1997.

130. Taylor, P.J., and B. Small. 2002.

131. Wernimont, P.F., and J.P. Campbell. 1968. "Signs, Samples, and Criteria." *Journal of Applied Psychology* 52: 372–76.

132. Taylor, P.J., and B. Small. 2002.

133. Huffcutt, A.I., J.M. Conway, P.L. Roth, and U.C. Klehe. 2004.

134. Taylor, P.J., and B. Small. 2002.

135. Taylor, P.J., and B. Small. 2002.

136. Huffcutt, A.I., J.M. Conway, P.L. Roth, and U.C. Klehe. 2004.

137. Klehe, U.C., and G.P. Latham. 2005. "The Predictive and Incremental Validity of the Situational and Patterned Behavior Description Interviews for Teamplaying Behavior." *International Journal of Selection and Assessment* 13: 108–15.

138. Day, A.L., and S.A. Carroll. 2003.

139. Day, A.L., and S.A. Carroll. 2003.

140. Berry, C.M., P.R. Sackett, and R.N. Landers. 2007. "Revisiting Interview–Cognitive Ability Relationships: Attending to Specific Range Restriction Mechanism in Meta-Analysis." *Personnel Psychology* 60: 837–74.

141. Huffcutt, A., J.M. Conway, P.L. Roth, and N.S. Stone. 2001.

142. Salgado, J.S., and S. Moscoso. 2002. "Comprehensive Meta-Analysis of the Construct Validity of the Employment Interview." *European Journal of Work and Organizational Psychology* 11: 299–324.

143. Roth, P.L., C.H. Van Iddekinge, A.I. Huffcutt, and M.J. Schmit. 2005. "Personality Saturation in Structured Interviews." *International Journal of Selection and Assessment* 13: 261–73.

144. Van Iddekinge, C.H., P.H. Raymark, and P.L. Roth. 2005. "Assessing Personality with a Structured Employment Interview: Construct-Related Validity and Susceptibility to Response Inflation." *Journal of Applied Psychology* 90: 536–52.

145. Roth, P.L., C.H. Van Iddekinge, A.I. Huffcutt, and M.J. Schmit. 2005.

146. Huffcutt, A., J.M. Conway, P.L. Roth, and N.S. Stone. 2001.

147. Salgado, J.S., and S. Moscoso. 2002.

148. Huffcutt, A.I., J. Weekley, W.H. Wiesner, T. DeGroot, and C. Jones. 2001. "Comparison of Situational and Behavior Description Interview Questions for Higher Level Positions." *Personnel Psychology* 54: 619–44.

149. Ellis, A.P.J., B.J. West, A.M. Ryan, and R.P DeShon. 2002. "The Use of Impression Management Tactics in Structured Interviews: A Function of Question Type." *Journal of Applied Psychology* 87: 1200–1208.

150. Peeters, H., and F. Lievens. 2006. "Verbal and Nonverbal Impression Management Tactics in Behavior Description and Situational Interviews." *International Journal of Selection and Assessment* 14: 206–22.

151. Van Iddekinge, C.H., L.A. McFarland, and P.H. Raymark. 2007. "Antecedents of Impression Management Use and Effectiveness in a Structured Interview." *Journal of Management* 33: 752–73.

152. Levashina, J., and M.A. Campion. 2007.

153. Tsai, W.C., C.C. Chen, and S.F. Chiu. 2005. "Exploring Boundaries of the Effects of Applicant Impression Management Tactics in Job Interviews." *Journal of Management* 31: 108–25.

154. Lievens, F., and A. De Paepe. 2004. "An Empirical Investigation of Interviewer-Related Factors That Discourage the Use of High Structure Interviews." *Journal of Organizational Behavior* 25: 29–46.

155. Simola, S.K., S. Taggar, and G.W. Smith. 2007.

156. Lievens, F., and A. De Paepe. 2004.

157. Simola, S.K., S. Taggar, and G.W. Smith. 2007.

158. Way, S.A., and J.W. Thacker. 1999. "Selection Practices: Where Are Canadian Organizations?" *HR Professional* 16: 33–37.

159. Simola, S.K., S. Taggar, and G.W. Smith. 2007.

160. Chapman, D.S., and D.I. Zweig. 2005. "Developing a Nomological Network for Interview Structure: Antecedents and Consequences of the Structured Selection Interview." *Personnel Psychology* 58: 673–702.

161. Chapman, D.S., and D.I. Zweig. 2005.

162. Chen, Y.C., W.C. Tsai, and C. Hu. 2008. "The Influences of Interviewer-Related and Situational Factors on Interviewer Reactions to High Structured Job Interviews." *The International Journal of Human Resource Management* 19: 1056–71.

163. Lievens, F., and A. De Paepe. 2004.

164. Posthuma, R.A., F.P. Morgeson, and M.A. Campion. 2002.

165. Hausknecht, J.P., D.V. Day, and S.C. Thomas. 2004. "Applicant Reactions to Selection Procedures: An Updated Model and Meta-Analysis." *Personnel Psychology* 57: 639–83.

166. Becton, J.B., H.S. Feild, W.F. Giles, and A. Jones-Farmer. 2008. "Racial Differences in Promotion Candidate Performance and Reactions to Selection Procedures: A Field Study in a Diverse Top-Management Context." *Journal of Organizational Behavior* 29: 265–85.

167. Cited in Posthuma, R.A., F.P. Morgeson, and M.A. Campion. 2002.

168. Chapman, D.S., and D.I. Zweig. 2005.

169. Chapman, D.S., and P.M. Rowe. 2001. "The Impact of Videoconference Technology, Interview Structure, and Interviewer Gender on Interviewer Evaluations in the Employment Interview: A Field Experiment." *Journal of Occupational and Organizational Psychology* 74: 279–98.

170. Kohn, L.S., and R.L. Dipboye. 1998. "The Effects of Interview Structure on Recruiting Outcomes." *Journal of Applied Social Psychology* 28: 821–43.

171. Kohn, L.S., and R.L. Dipboye. 1998.

172. Tsai, W.C., C.C. Chen, and S.F. Chiu. 2005.

173. Kohn, L.S., and R.L. Dipboye. 1998.

174. Posthuma, R.A., F.P. Morgeson, and M.A. Campion. 2002.

175. Campion, M.A., D.K. Palmer, and J.E. Campion. 1997.

176. Hackett, R.D., L.M. Lapierre, and H.P. Gardiner. 2004.

177. Hackett, R.D., J.B. Rose, and J. Pyper. 2000.

178. Williamson, L.G., J.E. Campion, S.B. Malos, M.V. Roehling, and M.A. Campion. 1997. "Employment Interview on Trial: Linking Interview Structure with Litigation Outcomes." *Journal of Applied Psychology* 82: 900–912.

179. Hackett, R.D., L.M. Lapierre, and H.P. Gardiner. 2004.

180. Hackett, R.D., J.B. Rose, and J. Pyper. 2000.

181. Williamson, L.G., J.E. Campion, S.B. Malos, M.V. Roehling, and M.A. Campion. 1997.

182. Saks, A.M., and J.M. McCarthy. 2006. "Effects of Discriminatory Interview Questions and Gender on Applicant Reactions." *Journal of Business and Psychology* 21: 175–91.

183. Campion, M.A., D.K. Palmer, and J.E. Campion. 1997.

184. Campion, M.A., D.K. Palmer, and J.E. Campion. 1997.

185. Maurer, S.D. 2002. "A Practitioner-Based Analysis of Interviewer Job Expertise and Scale Format as Contextual Factors in Situational Interviews." *Personnel Psychology* 55: 307–27.

186. Reilly, N.P., S.P. Bocketti, S.A. Maser, and C.L. Wennet. 2006. "Benchmarks Affect Perceptions of Prior Disability in a Structured Interview." *Journal of Business and Psychology* 20: 489–500.

187. Hackett, R.D., L.M. Lapierre, and H.P. Gardiner. 2004.

188. Hackett, R.D., J.B. Rose, and J. Pyper. 2000.

189. Latham, G.P., L.M. Saari, E.D. Pursell, and M.A. Campion. 1980.

190. Webster, E.C. 1964.

191. Campion, M.A., D.K. Palmer, and J.E. Campion. 1997.

192. Wiesner, W.H. 1989. "The Contributions of Job Relevance, Timing, and Rating Scale to the Validity of the Employment Interview." In S.F. Cronshaw, chair, *Improving Interview Validity and Legal Defensibility through Structuring.* Symposium conducted at the 50th Annual Convention of the Canadian Psychological Association.

193. Day, A.L., and S.A. Carroll. 2003.

194. Nunnally, J.C., and I.H. Bernstein. 1994. *Psychometric Theory.* 3rd ed. New York: McGraw-Hill.

195. Wiesner, W.H., and S.F. Cronshaw. 1988.

196. Schmidt, F.L., and R.D. Zimmerman. 2004. "A Counterintuitive Hypothesis about Employment Interview Validity and Some Supporting Evidence." *Journal of Applied Psychology* 89: 553–61.

197. Arvey, R.D., and J.E. Campion. 1982.

198. Blankenship, M.H., and S.J. Cesare. 1993. "Age Fairness in the Employment Interview: A Field Study." In R.D. Arvey, chair, *Perceptions, Theories, and Issues of Fairness in the Employment Interview*. Symposium presented at the 101st Annual Convention of the Psychological Association, Toronto.

199. Lin, T.R., G.H. Dobbins, and J.L. Farh. 1992. "A Field Study of Age and Race Similarity Effects on Interview Ratings in Conventional and Situational Interviews." *Journal of Applied Psychology* 77: 363–71.

200. Buckley, M.R., K.A. Jackson, M.C. Bolino, J.G. Veres, III, and H.S. Feild. 2007. "The Influence of Relational Demography on Panel Interview Ratings: A Field Experiment." *Personnel Psychology* 60: 627–46.

201. McFarland, L.A., A.M. Ryan, J.M. Sacco, and S.D. Kriska. 2004. "Examination of Structured Interview Ratings across Time: The Effects of Applicant Race, Rater Race, and Panel Composition." *Journal of Management* 30: 435–52.

202. McFarland, L.A., A.M. Ryan, J.M. Sacco, and S.D. Kriska. 2004.

203. Lin, T.R., G.H. Dobbins, and J.L. Farh. 1992.

204. Paullin, C. 1993. "Features of Structured Interviews Which Enhance Perceptions of Fairness." In R.D. Arvey, chair, *Perceptions, Theories, and Issues of Fairness in the Employment Interview*. Symposium presented at the 101st Annual Convention of the American Psychological Association, Toronto.

205. Motowidlo, S.J., G.W. Carter, M.D. Dunnette, N. Tippins, S. Werner, J.R. Burnett, and M.J. Vaughan. 1992.

206. Huffcutt, A.I., and P.L. Roth. 1998. "Racial and Group Differences in Employment Interview Evaluations." *Journal of Applied Psychology* 83: 179–89.

207. Lin, T.R., G.H. Dobbins, and J.L. Farh. 1992.

208. Brecher, E., J. Bragger, and E. Kutcher. 2006. "The Structured Interview: Reducing Bias toward Applicants with Disabilities." *Employee Responsibilities and Rights Journal* 18: 155–70.

209. Reilly, N.P., S.P. Bocketti, S.A. Maser, and C.L. Wennet. 2006.

210. Harris, M.M. 1993. "Fair or Foul: How Interview Questions Are Perceived." In R.D. Arvey, chair, *Perceptions, Theories, and Issues of Fairness in the Employment Interview*. Symposium presented at the 101st Annual Convention of the American Psychological Association, Toronto.

211. Williamson, L.G., J.E. Campion, S.B. Malos, M.V. Roehling, and M.A. Campion. 1997.

212. Campion, M.A., D.K. Palmer, and J.E. Campion. 1997.

213. Dipboye, R.L. 1992.

214. Posthuma, R.A., F.P. Morgeson, and M.A. Campion. 2002.

215. Campion, M.A., D.K. Palmer, and J.E. Campion. 1997.

216. Campion, M.A., D.K. Palmer, and J.E. Campion. 1997.

217. Dipboye, R.L. 1992.

218. Conway, J.M., R.A. Jako, and D.F. Goodman. 1995.

219. Huffcutt, A.I., and D.J. Woehr. 1999. "Further Analysis of Employment Interview Validity: A Quantitative Evaluation of Interviewer-Related Structuring Methods." *Journal of Organizational Behavior* 20: 549–60.

220. Carless, S.A., and A. Imber. 2007.

221. McCarthy, J., and R. Goffin. 2004. "Measuring Job Interview Anxiety: Beyond Weak Knees and Sweaty Palms." *Personnel Psychology* 57: 607–37.

222. McCarthy, J., and R. Goffin. 2004.

223. Maurer, T.J., and J.M. Solamon. 2006. "The Science and Practice of a Structured Employment Interview Coaching Program." *Personnel Psychology* 59: 433–56.

224. Latham, G.P., and M.H. Budworth. 2006. "The Effect of Training in Verbal Self-Guidance on the Self-Efficacy and Performance of Native North Americans in the Selection Interview." *Journal of Vocational Behavior* 68: 516–23.

225. Maurer, T.J., J.M. Solamon, and M. Lippstreu. 2008. "How Does Coaching Interviewees Affect the Validity of a Structured Interview?" *Journal of Organizational Behavior* 29: 355–71.

226. Maurer, T.J., J.M. Solamon, and M. Lippstreu. 2008.

227. Campion, M.A., E.D. Pursell, and B.K. Brown. 1988.

228. Wright, P.M., P.A. Lichtenfels, and E.D. Pursell. 1989. "The Structured Interview: Additional Studies and a Meta-Analysis." *Journal of Occupational Psychology* 62: 191–99.

229. Kennedy, R. 1985. "Validation of Five Structured Interviews." Unpublished master's thesis. East Carolina University.

230. Hedge, J.W., and M.S. Teachout. 1992. "An Interview Approach to Work Sample Criterion Measurement." *Journal of Applied Psychology* 77: 453–61.

231. Ree, M.J., J.A. Earles, and M.S. Teachout. 1994. "Predicting Job Performance: Not Much More Than g." *Journal of Applied Psychology* 79: 518–24.

232. Chapman, D.S., and P.M. Rowe. 2001.

233. Schmidt, F.L., and M. Rader. 1999. "Exploring the Boundary Conditions for Interview Validity: Meta-Analytic Validity Findings for a New Interview Type." *Personnel Psychology* 52: 445–64.

234. Chapman, D.S., and P.M. Rowe. 2002.

235. Martin, C.L., and D.H. Nagao. 1989. "Some Effects of Computerized Interviews on Job Applicant Responses." *Journal of Applied Psychology* 74: 72–80.

236. Meckenbach, G. 1997. "Your Next Job Interview Might Be at Home." *Computing Canada* 16: 1–4.

237. Chapman, D.S., and P.M. Rowe. 2001.

238. Van Iddekinge, C.H., P.H. Raymark, P.L. Roth, and H.S. Payne. 2006. "Comparing the Psychometric Characteristics of Ratings of Face-to-Face and Videotaped Structured Interviews." *International Journal of Selection and Assessment* 14: 347–59.

239. Chapman, D.S., and P.M. Rowe. 2002.

240. Chapman, D.S., and P.M. Rowe. 2001.

241. Campion, M.A., D.K. Palmer, and J.E. Campion. 1997.

242. Dipboye, R.L. 1992.

Chapter 10

Decision Making

Chapter Learning Objectives

This chapter considers ways of reducing subjectivity and error in making selection decisions by using scientific methods that maximize selection effectiveness and efficiency. It also discusses utility analysis—decision-making procedures that can be used to evaluate the overall performance of selection systems.

After reading this chapter you should:

- appreciate the complexity of decision making in the employee selection context;
- be familiar with the sources of common decision-making errors in employee selection;
- understand the distinction between judgmental and statistical approaches to the *collection* and combination of applicant information;
- understand the advantages and disadvantages of various decision-making models;
- appreciate issues involved with group decision making;
- know the basic principles in the application of cut-off scores, banding, and top-down selection;
- be familiar with utility analysis as one way to evaluate personnel selection systems; and
- be able to discuss the benefits of using best practices in recruitment and selection.

CHOOSING THE RIGHT APPLICANT

Walter looked at the stack of files in front of him. He couldn't believe it. All these applications for one position! How was he going decide on whom to hire? So many of them looked just like the others. Walter was thinking he might as well pull names out of a hat. Just then, Helen, the director of human resources, appeared in his doorway. "You sure look bewildered," she observed. "What's wrong?"

"Oh, hiring my new executive assistant isn't going to be as easy as I thought. I don't know how I'm going to get through all of these files, never mind finding the right person."

"Walter, I wish you had called me before you started your search," replied Helen. "I could have helped you save a lot of time and made your job much easier. I can still help now, but it's going to be more work than it needed to be and we'll have less information than I would like to make a good selection decision."

"What do you mean?" asked Walter. "How could I have done this differently?"

"Well, for starters, you could have reduced your pile of applications significantly by testing your applicants," answered Helen. "There are some very good, valid tests available that are well suited to testing for this position."

Walter was skeptical: "How would testing the applicants have helped me whittle down this pile? Anyway, wouldn't it be too expensive to test all these people?"

"I'll admit there is some cost involved in testing but it's a lot cheaper than paying you to sort through résumés," Helen explained. "I'm sure you have better things to do with your time."

Walter grinned and nodded. "You're right about that."

Helen went on, "What the tests do is help identify those applicants who posses the strongest attributes or qualities necessary to do well on the job. You can then interview those applicants with the highest test scores, using the behavioural-based interviewing techniques I presented in our recent in-house seminar. In other words, the tests can do the job of sorting out your applicants and deciding who should be interviewed."

"I see," mused Walter, "but tests can't tell you everything you need to know about the applicant."

"You're right," replied Helen. "That's why you also review the résumés, conduct interviews, check references, and get any other information you can about the applicants who have the top test scores—not everyone who applied."

"All right, I can buy that," Walter agreed, "but what do you do if some of the information doesn't agree? I once interviewed a candidate who had outstanding recommendations, but she did horribly in the interview. I wasn't sure what to do but, in the end, I decided not to hire her. I've always wondered if I made a mistake. Jenn Hill hired her and seems to be very pleased with her."

"Well, all the information you collect is important and needs to be taken into consideration," explained Helen, "but no matter how good your information is, mistakes happen. Sometimes you'll hire the wrong person; another time you'll let a good candidate get away. All we can hope to do is decrease the errors you make by putting in place a very good system that helps you to make the best decisions. You need to have a system where each bit of information is given appropriate weight and added to the other bits of information to arrive at a total score."

"You mean like in a regression equation?" asked Walter.

"I see you still remember your statistics," Helen laughed. "Yes, that's one approach we can use, but there are other procedures we can use to combine all of these data."

Walter looked at her pleadingly. "Could you help me develop such a system?"

"I'd be happy to," replied Helen. "That's what I'm here for. Having a valid selection system in place not only helps us to fulfill our human rights mandate but also will provide a return to the company through the increased productivity of the people we hire. But first, we need to tackle this stack on your desk. Unfortunately, we don't have test scores for these applicants. Let's discuss what criteria you can use to evaluate these résumés and make the job a bit easier."

The purpose of selection is to discriminate. This statement may sound strange in the context of our discussion of employment equity in Chapter 3. Unfortunately, the term *discrimination* has acquired a negative connotation because of its frequent association with the word *unfair*. In fact, we do not want to discriminate illegally or unfairly, but we do want to differentiate on the basis of applicants' abilities to do the work. Just as we differentiate in the grocery store between the desirable fruit or vegetables and those we do not want, our task in employee selection is to differentiate between those applicants we believe will become effective employees and those who will not. Thus, selection involves making decisions about which applicants to hire and which not to hire, based on the information available.

Unfortunately, humans are imperfect decision makers.[1] The use of phrases such as "I'm only human" as justification for having made mistakes reflects our common understanding of this principle. Factors other than logic typically enter into our HR decisions—emotional reactions to applicants, pressures to hire, political motives, and a variety of constraints.[2-4] Decision makers often make decisions based on inadequate or erroneous information. As a result, employers frequently make poor hiring decisions. The purpose of this chapter is to provide information and tools that can assist employers in making better selection decisions.

The vignette at the beginning of this chapter illustrates some of the issues that we will discuss here. It is not simply a case of using proper selection tools. HR professionals must know how to integrate data from the different assessments that they have obtained from job candidates. They must understand the advantages and limitations of the different procedures that they might use and recognize that the recommended list of candidates may change, depending on the method they used to integrate the information.

In our vignette, Walter thought he had to use a judgmental procedure that relied on his subjective interpretation of the data—the application forms. He was concerned that he might make a mistake, as he suspected had happened previously. In this chapter, we advocate the use of statistically based decision-making models and illustrate how they are used to make selection decisions.

The Context of Selection Decisions

Employers typically have to contend with a number of constraints and competing demands when making selection decisions. Often, time pressures prevent them from making logical or objective choices. If they need to fill vacant positions quickly, they tend to *satisfice*.[5] That is, rather than searching for the best candidates, they will select the first applicants they encounter who meet the minimum qualifications or levels of acceptability. Similarly, if an insufficient number of suitable applicants are available or if the level of applicant qualifications is quite low, employers' standards of acceptability tend to drop.[6] They will often accept less-qualified applicants rather than continue their recruitment efforts in order to generate applications from better-qualified candidates.

Sometimes, rather than selecting for a specific job, employers select applicants for the organization. Their selection decisions are based on perceptions of the applicants' overall suitability for the organization, or *organizational fit*, particularly during the interview stages of the selection process.[7] They do not concern themselves with which job a candidate should be placed in until after the hiring decision has been made. Such organizations tend to have *promote-from-within* policies, flexible job descriptions, or jobs that change quickly, or they tend to practise job rotation or rapid promotion.

Another form of selection involves promotion or transfer. Although promotions or transfers are often made on the basis of seniority or merit, they are most effective if treated as selection decisions. The candidates selected should be those most qualified for the vacant positions. When candidates are selected on the basis of merit or good job performance, the selection decision is based on the assumption that good performance in one job is indicative of good performance in another. However, the best salesperson or machinist will not necessarily make the best sales manager or shop supervisor. In fact, that person might be quite incompetent in the new job.

On the other hand, promotions based on seniority are based on the assumption that the most experienced employee would be most effective. But the most experienced salesperson might not even be the best salesperson, let alone the best sales manager. Therefore, just as in other selection decisions, candidates for promotion or transfer should be assessed in terms of the knowledge, skills, abilities, and other attributes (KSAOs) they possess relevant to the positions for which they are being considered.

Selection Errors

Many employers believe they have a knack for making good selection decisions. Some look for a firm handshake, unwavering eye contact, or upright posture in an applicant. Others look for confidence, enthusiasm, or personality (see Recruitment and Selection Today 10.1). Most employers hold *implicit*

Recruitment and Selection Today 10.1

What Do Employers Look for in an Applicant?

Employers have long hired applicants for a variety of reasons that do not appear to be job-related. You be the judge as to the merits of the selection techniques described below.

- One employer asked applicants to lunch in order to observe them eating. The employer believed that those who eat quickly are energetic workers, that they eat quickly in order to be able to get on with their work. Conversely, those who eat slowly are expected to take longer at lunch and coffee breaks, as well as to work more slowly. It appears the employer believed in a variation of the well-known maxim: "You are *how* you eat."
- Another employer looked for the same characteristic by observing how applicants walked into the office for their interviews. Those who had a spry, determined step were more likely to be hired than those who ambled into the office or those who seemed hesitant as they entered. The employer believed that an energetic, determined walk is indicative of an energetic, determined worker.
- Yet another employer didn't like to hire applicants who have a lot of hobbies or who are involved in a lot of extracurricular activities. The employer reasoned that people who are active outside of work or who have a lot of nonwork interests will be too distracted by their hobbies to sufficiently devote themselves to their work and that they might use some of their work time to pursue their own interests.
- Finally, one employer had a tendency to hire applicants who seemed to desperately need the job. It appears the applicants' needs triggered the employer's sense of social responsibility and compassion. The employer felt good about being able to help these needy individuals and reasoned that the more capable applicants could easily find employment elsewhere.

What advice would you have for each of these employers?

Chapter 10: Decision Making

theories about how certain behaviours, mannerisms, or personality characteristics go together. *Implicit theories* are personal beliefs that are held about how people or things function, without objective evidence and often without conscious awareness. For example, an employer might believe that unwavering eye contact reveals honesty, directness, and confidence. However, such an assumption is not necessarily warranted. Maintaining eye contact could be an interview tactic learned by the applicant or it could even reflect hostility. Moreover, in some cultures maintaining direct eye contact is considered rude and inappropriate behaviour. Applicants from these cultures would be disadvantaged if eye contact was a factor in the selection decision.

Many other employers make subjective decisions based on gut feelings about the applicant. They hire applicants simply because they like them or seem to get along well with them, at least based on the few minutes they spend together in the interview. Invariably, such gut feelings, as well as implicit theories, lead to poor selection decisions, as we discussed in Chapter 2.

Although employers assess a considerable amount of often complex information about each candidate, they must simplify this information to produce a dichotomous decision. Candidates are classified as either acceptable or unacceptable and hired or not hired on the basis of this assessment. Sometimes these decisions turn out to be correct, and the applicant who is hired becomes a productive and valued employee. Other times (more often than many employers care to admit), employers make mistakes by hiring individuals who turn out to be unsuitable. The four possible outcomes of a selection decision are presented in Figure 10.1.

Two of the outcomes in Figure 10.1, the true positive and the true negative, are correct decisions, or "hits." In the *true positive* outcome, the employer

FIGURE 10.1

Outcomes of the Selection Process

		Not Hired	Hired
Criterion Measures of Job Performance	Success	False Negative (Miss)	True Positive (Hit)
	Failure	True Negative (Hit)	False Positive (Miss)
		Not Hired	Hired
		Selection Decision	

has hired an applicant who turns out to be a successful employee. In the *true negative* outcome, the employer did not hire an applicant who would have been considered a failure as an employee if hired. Obviously, an employer would want to maximize both these "hits" or correct predictions but, as we will demonstrate later in this chapter, that can be quite difficult to accomplish. The two other outcomes represent selection errors or "misses."

A **false positive error** occurs when an applicant is assessed favourably and is hired, but proves to be unsuccessful on the job. This is a costly error and may even be disastrous in some jobs. Productivity, profits, and the company's reputation may suffer when such errors are made. It may be difficult to terminate the employees once hired, termination can be costly, and grievance proceedings could result from the termination. Moreover, a replacement for the unsuccessful employee must be recruited, selected, and trained, all at additional cost. Some organizations use probationary periods (e.g., between one and six months) for new employees in order to reduce the costs of false positive errors. In fact, tenure for professors is really a probationary system—in this case, the probationary period is five or six years.

A **false negative error** is one in which the applicant is assessed unfavourably and is not hired but would have been successful if hired. Such errors tend to go unnoticed because there are usually no obvious negative consequences for the employer as there are with false positive errors. The employer rarely finds out about the quality of the applicant who was not hired. Only in high-profile occupations such as professional sports does a false negative error become readily apparent. When an athlete who is turned down by one team becomes a star pitcher, goalie, or fullback with a competing team, the first team is constantly faced with its mistake.

Even though false negative errors are rarely that obvious in most organizations, they can be costly. Applicants for key jobs (e.g., software designer) might develop highly successful products for the competing organization that did hire them. Furthermore, when an organization turns down a number of good candidates who are then hired by a competitor, even for non-key jobs, the competitor could gain a significant advantage in productivity. In addition, false negative errors might adversely affect minority applicants and could result in human rights litigation.

Although it is not possible to entirely avoid or even recognize all errors when making selection decisions, they can be minimized. Valid selection methods and systematic procedures will serve to improve the probability of making correct selection decisions. One particular challenge faced by employers is how to make sense of the various, and sometimes conflicting, sources of information about applicants in order to make an informed decision. The next section considers different ways of combining complex information and suggests some systematic procedures for making selection decisions.

False positive error
Occurs when an applicant who is assessed favourably turns out to be a poor choice.

False negative error
Occurs when an applicant who is rejected would have been a good choice.

Collection and Combination of Information

Before a selection decision can be made, information about the applicants must be collected from various sources and combined in an effective way. Typically, employers collect this information on application forms or from résumés, in employment interviews, and through reference checks. Many employers also administer ability, personality, and/or other tests; collect and score biographical information; or make use of assessment centres. These methods of collecting applicant information are discussed in detail in Chapters 7, 8, and 9.

Sometimes all information is in agreement and the decision can be straightforward. Other times, the information is contradictory and the decision is more difficult. For example, if one applicant looks very good on paper (i.e., in the application form or résumé), has a high score on a cognitive ability test, and receives glowing recommendations from the references, but does poorly in the interview, while another applicant does well on everything except the cognitive ability test, what is the appropriate decision? The employer must find some way of making sense of this information so that the best possible selection decision can be made.

Information collected from some sources, such as test scores, tends to be more objective. A good test result provides a reliable and valid measurement of some attribute, which can be readily used to compare applicants on a numerical or statistical basis. That is, no (or very little) human judgment is involved in collecting this score. We will refer to these methods of collecting applicant information or data as *statistical*. Information collected from more subjective sources, such as unstructured interviews, relies much more, or even exclusively, on human judgment. We will refer to these methods of collecting applicant information or data as *judgmental* (some authors refer to these as "clinical" methods).

Just as applicant data can be collected statistically or judgmentally, the data can be *combined* using statistical and judgmental methods. Data combined mathematically, using a formula, have been synthesized in a more objective fashion, which we will call *statistical* combination. Combining data through human judgment or an overall impression is a more subjective process, which we will refer to as *judgmental* combination. So, a number of permutations are possible. Judgmentally collected data can be combined in either a judgmental or a statistical manner, and statistically collected data can be combined in either a judgmental or a statistical manner. Moreover, it is possible that some of the data are collected judgmentally (e.g., an unstructured interview), whereas other data are collected statistically (e.g., test scores). This composite of judgmental and statistical data can also be combined in either a judgmental or statistical manner. The possible permutations of methods of data collection and combination are presented in Table 10.1.

Pure judgment approach

An approach in which judgmental data are combined in a judgmental manner.

In the **pure judgment approach**, judgmental data are collected and combined in a judgmental manner. The decision maker forms an overall impression of the applicant based on gut feeling or implicit theories rather than explicit, objective criteria. In this approach, the decision maker both collects information and makes a decision about the applicant. An employer making a selection decision based on an unstructured interview is representative of this approach. The employer who hires applicants because he feels sorry for them is using intuition or pure judgment to make his decisions.

Trait rating approach

An approach in which judgmental data are combined statistically.

The **trait rating approach** is one in which judgmental data are combined statistically. A number of judgmental ratings are made (e.g., based on inter-

TABLE 10.1

Methods of Collecting and Combining Applicant Information		
Method of Collecting Data	**Method of Combining Data**	
	JUDGMENTAL	STATISTICAL
Judgmental	Pure judgment	Trait ratings
Statistical	Profile interpretation	Pure statistical
Both	Judgmental composite	Statistical composite

Source: Adapted from J. Sawyer. 1966. "Measurement and Prediction, Clinical and Statistical." *Psychological Bulletin* 66: 178–200. Copyright © 1966 by the American Psychological Association.

views, application forms or résumés, or reference checks). The ratings are combined using a mathematical formula, which produces an overall score for each applicant. Although the decision makers collect the information and make ratings on each of the components, the decision is based on the overall score generated by the mathematical formula.

The **profile interpretation** strategy involves combining statistical data in a judgmental manner. Data are collected from objective sources such as tests or biographical inventories. The decision maker examines these data to form an overall, subjective impression of the applicant's suitability for the job. The selection decision is based on this overall impression or gut feeling.

In the **pure statistical approach**, statistically collected data are combined statistically. Test scores or scores from other objective sources such as biographical inventories or weighted application blanks are fed into a formula or regression equation, which produces an overall combined score. Applicants are then selected in order of their scores (i.e., the top scorer, then the second-highest, and so on, until the desired number of applicants has been selected).

The **judgmental composite** involves collecting both judgmental and statistical data and then combining them judgmentally. A decision maker might conduct unstructured interviews and reference checks (judgmental data) and have access to test scores (statistical data). The decision maker then examines the test scores and considers the impressions of the applicants gained from the interviews and reference checks in order to form an overall impression and make a decision concerning who should be hired. This is probably the most common method used by employers to make selection decisions.

The **statistical composite** also involves collecting both judgmental and statistical data, but the data are combined statistically. Ratings or scores are given or obtained from each component, such as an interview, a reference check, a personality test, and a mental ability test. The ratings or scores are combined in a formula or regression equation to produce an overall score for each applicant. Selection decisions are thus based on the applicants' scores.

Although all six of the basic decision-making approaches described above have been used in employee selection, they are not equally effective. A considerable body of research indicates that the pure statistical and the

Profile interpretation

An approach in which statistical data are combined in a judgmental manner.

Pure statistical approach

An approach in which data are combined statistically.

Judgmental composite

An approach in which judgmental and statistical data are combined in a judgmental manner.

Statistical composite

An approach in which judgmental and statistical data are combined statistically.

statistical composite approaches are generally superior to the other methods in predicting performance.[8,9] Both of these approaches involve combining information in a statistical manner.

There are several possible explanations for the superiority of statistical methods over judgmental methods of combining information.[10] First, as noted previously, implicit theories are more likely to bias evaluations and contribute to error when judgmental methods are used. Irrelevant factors such as the applicant's appearance or mannerisms are likely to unduly influence the decision. Second, it is difficult for decision makers to take into account the complexity of all of the information available to them when they use judgmental processes to make decisions. Because the ability to remember and process information is easily overloaded, decision makers tend to oversimplify or inappropriately simplify information to create applicant summaries that are inaccurate.

Third, it is virtually impossible to assign appropriate weights to all of the selection instruments when judgmental procedures are used. How important should reference checks be in comparison to ability tests or interviews? It is difficult to give even equal weighting to all selection information in a subjective manner. Sometimes particular applicant data, such as test scores, are largely ignored in favour of impressions based on other sources, such as the interview. Statistical approaches are likely to provide better decisions, even when scores from all of the selection instruments are weighted equally, because all applicant information is taken into consideration in a systematic manner.[11]

It is worth noting that statistical approaches are compromised when poor-quality information goes into the selection equation. The maxim "garbage in, garbage out" applies just as well to employee selection methods as it does to computer programming. Erroneous or irrelevant information, such as might be obtained from bad interview questions, invalid tests, or inaccurate references, will contribute error variance to the equation and reduce the likelihood of making good selection decisions. It is therefore important to ensure that only data coming from reliable and valid selection measures are combined to yield an overall score for each applicant.

Why Do Employers Resist Using Statistical Approaches?

 10.1

Although statistical approaches to decision making are clearly superior to judgmental approaches, employers tend to resist them.[12] They prefer relying on gut feelings or instinct. There are probably several reasons why employers cling to judgmental approaches. Employers might find it difficult to give up the personal control that judgmental approaches give them. They can choose to ignore or discount information that is at odds with gut feelings and they can emphasize or rely solely on information that is in accord with their feelings. When they use statistical approaches, their role becomes simply that of information collectors rather than judgmental decision makers.

Employers also tend to be overconfident in their decision-making abilities.[13,14] They generally believe that they are quite successful in selecting good job candidates. Unfortunately, few employers bother to keep track of their success or "hit" rates by reviewing the job performance of those they hired. If they did, they would become much more concerned about their abilities to judge applicant competence. Granted, there might be a very small minority of employers who are be able to assess job applicants with reasonable accuracy, but even they are outperformed by statistical models based on their own decision rules (known as *bootstrapping*).[15] Unfortunately, most employers are not very good judges of job applicant potential.

Finally, some employers use judgmental approaches because they feel they can't afford the time or money required to develop a statistical selection model. However, statistical models can be quite simple and need not be expensive. Moreover, as discussed in the utility analysis section of this chapter, any costs incurred can be more than recouped in savings generated by an effective selection system.

HR professionals are responsible for collection, management, protection, and disposition of all HR information within the parameters of professional practice, organizational policy, and the applicable legislative and regulatory framework. They are responsible for the effective and efficient provision of HR information systems for the benefit of the organization or any other party that is legally entitled to that information. This involves the development, maintenance, and use of manual and/or automated systems.

Most organizations, even small businesses, have the capability to collect and integrate data through specialized or enterprise software. PeopleSoft, one of the more ubiquitous systems, has the capability for storing competency or other KSAO data for use in selection and promotion decisions. HR-Guide .com lists many software packages and consultants that can provide specialized selection software. These systems can assist in the efficient collection and integration of assessment data for statistical decision-making purposes.

One method we have used quite effectively in workshops to demonstrate to managers the inaccuracy of their judgments is to show them videotapes of actual employment interviews. In fact, the applicants appearing on the videotapes had been hired and we had obtained job performance ratings from their supervisors after they had been working at least half a year. We asked the managers attending the workshops to rate the applicants and predict their job performance. We were then able to compare the managers' ratings and predictions with the applicants' actual job performance ratings. It was quite a surprise for most of the managers at the workshops to discover how badly they had misjudged the applicants. The experience made them much more receptive to a statistical approach to decision making.

Group Decision Making

Although most employee selection research has explored individual models of decision making, several surveys indicate that in most organizations, selection decisions are made by groups. Some researchers suggest that groups can be poor decision makers. Power motives, politics, conformity to the group, and lack of information sharing serve to reduce the objectivity of group decisions.[16,17] However, in spite of all of the potential problems encountered in group decision making, many researchers conclude that groups are generally better at problem solving and decision making than the average individual.[18] As indicated in Chapter 9, selection interview boards or panels are better at predicting job performance than individual interviewers when the interview is unstructured and as good as individual interviewers when the interview is structured (see Chapter 9, Figure 9.2, on page 440).

In most organizations, there appears to be an intuitive understanding that groups might make better selection decisions than individuals; thus, selection teams or panels are commonplace. For example, in a large company, the immediate supervisor, a member from the HR department, and a support staff person might all be involved in the hiring of a data entry clerk. In hiring the data entry clerk's supervisor, the group charged with making the decision might include the supervisor's manager, a more senior HR person, and an experienced data entry clerk.

Having two or more individuals make the selection decision can reduce the effects of the biases that any one individual might have. Selection team or panel members are more likely to be careful in their assessments when they have to justify their ratings to other team members. The fact that differences of opinion concerning an applicant must be resolved to everyone's satisfaction will tend to reduce the impact of biases. Also, with more individuals examining applicant information, it is less likely that particular information will be overlooked or distorted.

A less commendable reason for organizations to use selection teams or panels is that such teams make it easier to share the blame for poor decisions. Individual members might be somewhat less conscientious than they should be because they can evade personal responsibility and consequences for their decisions. Nevertheless, based on the research evidence, it is advisable that any judgmental information be collected by a selection team or panel. In fact, numerous Canadian human rights tribunals have cited the use of selection panels as an important factor in defending against discrimination suits.[19,20]

One recent development in the Canadian workplace is the increasing use of teams to do work. Selecting appropriate team members has thus become an important challenge and research focus.[21-23] Not only job-related abilities but also personality and interpersonal factors must be taken into consideration when selecting for a team.

When teams make selection decisions (see Recruitment and Selection Today 10.2 for an example of team decision making at SC Johnson, Ltd.), there are often disagreements among team members as to appropriate ratings or who should be hired. It is important that such differences be resolved as objectively as possible. The easiest way to resolve differences is to average the team members' individual scores to arrive at a combined score for each applicant (this is analogous to statistical combination).

However, as noted when we discussed the collection and combination of information, such combinations can be misleading if some of the team mem-

Team Decision Making at SC Johnson Ltd.

SC Johnson Ltd. (http://www.scjohnson.ca) produces a wide variety of products, including Pledge furniture polishes, Glade air fresheners, Windex glass and surface cleaners, Raid insecticides, Off insect repellents, Edge shaving gels, Ziploc bags, Saran Wrap, Shout stain remover, and Scrubbing Bubbles bathroom cleaners. The Canadian plant, located in Brantford, Ontario, was at one time one of the poorest-producing plants in the Johnson family. However, management and employees at the plant were able to turn the plant into one of Johnson's star performers. They attribute much of their success to the implementation of a team-based manufacturing process.

Teams at the Brantford plant construct and take apart assembly lines as needed to manufacture seasonal products such as insect repellents and citronella candles. The team members may choose who does what tasks on the assembly line, may rotate tasks, may elect their team leader, and may also interview and select new members. The teams use a semistructured interview focusing primarily on assessing factors that have to do with working in a team environment, such as cooperation, conscientiousness, and other aspects of contextual performance.

While they do make occasional hiring errors, for the most part the teams seem to enjoy good success in selecting individuals who fit well into the team environment. The existing team members seem to have a good sense of the personal qualities that will contribute to effective team membership. Moreover, given that the team is responsible for selecting a new member, the team members all tend to take responsibility for ensuring that the new member receives sufficient direction, correction, and encouragement to become an effective team member and productive employee.

---

bers submit erroneous or biased ratings. As a general rule, when there is close agreement among team members' ratings, the individual ratings can be safely averaged. But when there is disagreement (e.g., a range of two or more points), team members should discuss the reasons for their ratings until they arrive at a consensus. By discussing their rationales for the ratings, team members are likely to uncover some of the misperceptions, biases, and errors in recollection that can contribute to differences in scores.

Incremental Validity

As pointed out earlier in this chapter, employers typically rely on various sources of information about applicants in making selection decisions. Sometimes each source of information (e.g., test score, interview, reference check) provides unique information, which gives a more complete picture of the applicant's capabilities. Often, different sources provide considerable redundant information and, therefore, do not add value to the selection process. For example, if an interview collected only information about where the applicant had worked, how long he or she worked for each employer, and what education he or she had received, the interview would be useless because all of this information could be found in the résumé or application form.

Predictors that are highly correlated with each other (e.g., measurements of cognitive ability and university admission test scores) provide considerable redundant information and, therefore, there is little value in using both. Instead, employers benefit by using predictors that have low intercorrelations. When predictors are used that are relatively uncorrelated with each other but that are correlated with the criterion (e.g., job performance), they assess different aspects of the KSAOs needed for the job and, therefore, each predictor provides incremental validity. That is, each predictor adds value to the selection system, and the validity of the system increases.

Figure 10.2 provides an illustration of incremental validity using hypothetical data. Each predictor is represented by a circle (P1 and P2, respectively) and the criterion is also represented by a circle (C). In Figure 10.2(a), the correlation between the two predictors is 0.8 and the correlation between each predictor and the criterion is 0.5. As the figure demonstrates, there is considerable overlap between the parts of the predictors (P1 and P2) that overlap with the criterion (C) and there is a relatively small area of unique overlap between P2 and C once the overlap between P1 and C is taken into account. As you can see, the second predictor provides relatively little incremental validity when two predictors are highly correlated.

In Figure 10.2(b), there is a zero correlation between the two predictors and the correlation between each predictor and the criterion is 0.5. Each predictor (P1 and P2) overlaps with a completely different part of the criterion (C) and provides incremental validity over the other predictor. In the example in Figure 10.2(b), P1 accounts for 25 percent of the variance in C and P2 accounts for an additional 25 percent of the variance in C (variance is the square of the correlation). Thus, P1 and P2 together account for 50 percent of the variance in C.

When employers use selection instruments (predictors) that are uncorrelated or have low intercorrelations with each other but are correlated with job performance (the criterion), these selection instruments provide better prediction as a group than each instrument provides on its own (i.e., they have incremental validity). Often, scores are collected from each selection instrument and entered into a regression equation to provide a composite score for each applicant that reflects the information provided by each of the components of the selection system (see the section on decision-making models in this chapter).

Setting Cut-off Scores

In the next section we will consider different models of decision making. Several of these models make use of a *cut-off score*, so it is necessary to understand cut-off scores before we discuss the models. Cut-off scores serve as criteria or thresholds in selection decisions. Applicants who score below the cut-off on a given predictor (e.g., test, interview) are rejected. Thus, cut-off scores ensure that applicants meet some minimum level of ability or qualification to be considered for a job. In college or university, a grade of 50 percent often serves as a cut-off. A student whose grade is lower than 50 percent fails the course. This cut-off has been established by convention. In most organizations, cut-offs are established based on the predictor scores of individuals who are

Incremental validity

The value in terms of increased validity of adding a particular predictor to an existing selection system.

Cut-off score

A threshold; those scoring at or above the cut-off score pass, those scoring below fail.

FIGURE 10.2

An Illustration of Incremental Validity: Correlated and Uncorrelated Predictors

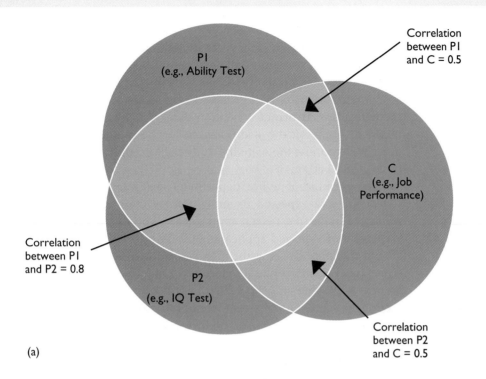

(a)

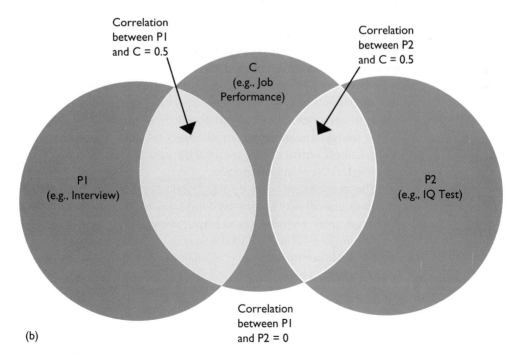

(b)

successful in the job being selected for, or based on expert judgments concerning the difficulty of the predictor items.[24]

One method of establishing cut-off scores involves identifying the proportion of applicants who are to be hired and determining how stringent the cut-off score should be to select only the desired number of applicants. First, the expected **selection ratio** is calculated (number of individuals to be hired divided by the expected number of applicants). Next, the distribution of the applicants' scores on the predictor is estimated by examining the predictor score distributions of past groups of applicants or of current employees (i.e., predictive or concurrent validation data). Finally, the cut-off score is established by applying the selection ratio to the predictor score distribution in order to determine the score that only the top applicants (the proportion to be hired) would attain.

For example, if a fire department seeks to hire five firefighters and 150 people are expected to apply, the selection ratio will be 0.03 (5/150). About 3 percent of expected applicants will be accepted, or, conversely, about 97 percent of expected applicants will have to be rejected. The cut-off score should therefore be set at the 97th percentile of the distribution of predictor scores (plus or minus one standard error of measurement). That is, the cut-off score is set so that only 3 percent of applicants would be expected to meet or exceed the score (or 97 percent would fall below it). This approach is limited to setting cut-offs for a single predictor. When more than one predictor is to be used, it is common to use expert judges, although computational methods have been developed recently to facilitate the setting of multiple cut-offs.[25]

There are several ways in which expert judges can be used to establish cut-offs, but they differ only slightly in their methods. We will consider the general approach; consult Cascio and Aguinis[26] or Gatewood, Feild, and Barrick[27] for more detailed treatments of the various methods. Experienced employees, supervisors, or managers who know the job well or industrial psychologists typically serve as expert judges. Essentially, the expert judges are asked to rate the difficulty of test items (or interview questions) and to indicate what score on each item should be attained by a minimally competent applicant. These ratings are summed for all items to yield a pass threshold or cut-off score. Cut-off scores can be established in this manner for each of the predictors used in the selection process.

The procedures used by the Public Service Commission of Canada to establish cut-off scores can be found on the commission's Personnel Psychology Centre website. Go to http://www.psc-cfp.gc.ca/ppc-cpp/index-eng.htm, enter "cut-off scores" in the Search window, and select "Setting Cut-Off Scores: A Matter of Judgment." General information on setting cut-off scores is also provided here.

Decision-Making Models

Several different decision-making models involve combining applicant information statistically (regardless of how that information was collected). These models are *multiple regression*, *multiple cut-offs*, *multiple hurdle*, *combination*, and

Selection ratio
The proportion of applicants for one or more positions who are hired.

profile matching.[28] We will consider the models in terms of their usefulness for different purposes and under different conditions.

Multiple Regression Model

In the multiple regression model, the applicant's scores on each predictor (e.g., tests, interviews, reference checks) are weighted and summed to yield a total score (e.g., predicted job performance). The appropriate regression weights or *b* values are determined through prior research, where the unique contributions of each predictor (*X*) to predicting job performance (*Y*) are investigated.

Table 10.2 provides the hypothetical scores of four applicants on each of four predictors—the maximum scores, regression weights, cut-off scores, and mean or average scores for each predictor. Applicants for a retail sales position wrote a cognitive ability test, completed an extroversion personality scale, were interviewed, and provided references, which were scored. The maximum score on the cognitive ability test (X_1) is 50 and the regression weight (b_1) is 1. The maximum score on the extroversion scale (X_2) is 40 and the regression weight (b_2) is 0.5 (i.e., the extroversion score contributes only half as much as the cognitive ability score to the prediction of job performance). The maximum interview score (X_3) is 30 and the weighting for the interview score (b_3) is 0.7, while the maximum reference check score (X_4) is 15 and the score for the reference check is given a weight (b_4) of 0.6. The regression equation for predicting job performance in this case is:

$$Y = b_1 X_1 + b_2 X_2 + b_3 X_3 + b_4 X_4$$

TABLE 10.2

Examples of Sales Applicant Data

| | Predictor Scores | | | |
APPLICANT	COGNITIVE ABILITY TEST	EXTROVERSION SCALE	STRUCTURED INTERVIEW	REFERENCE CHECK
Mr. A	36	30	27	11
Ms. B	32	37	16	10
Mr. C	44	22	24	13
Ms. D	37	27	28	14
Maximum Possible Scores	50	40	30	15
Regression Weights	1.0	0.5	0.7	0.6
Cutoff Scores	30	24	18	10
Mean Scores	35	27	23	11

Predicted job performance = Cognitive ability score + 0.5 Extroversion score + 0.7 Interview score + 0.6 Reference check score. A predicted job performance score can thus be calculated for each applicant.

Chapter 10: Decision Making

Applying the regression equation to the data in Table 10.2 yields a total predicted score of 76.5 for Mr. A, 67.7 for Ms. B, 79.6 for Mr. C, and 78.5 for Ms. D. The applicants can now be ranked based on their total predicted scores: (1) Mr. C, (2) Ms. D, (3) Mr. A, and (4) Ms. B (see Table 10.3). They can be selected on a top-down basis until the desired number of candidates has been obtained. If two candidates are needed, Mr. C and Ms. D would be selected.

The multiple regression model assumes that the predictors are linearly related to the criterion and that a low score on one predictor can be compensated for by a high score on another predictor. Applicants could do very poorly in the interview (e.g., receive a score of zero) and still do well if they received high scores on the tests and the reference check. However, the assumptions made by the multiple regression model are not necessarily warranted. First, very high scores on some predictors might be as undesirable as very low scores. For example, while an extreme introvert might have difficulty relating to customers in a retail sales position, an extreme extrovert might annoy them and drive them away.

Second, there might be a minimum level of competence required on each of the predictors for the individual to perform acceptably in the job. For example, a very low interview score might indicate that the applicant has such poor interpersonal and communication skills that the applicant cannot function acceptably in retail sales, regardless of high cognitive ability and extroversion scores. The multiple regression approach also has the disadvantage of being expensive, particularly for large applicant pools, because all applicants must be assessed on all predictors.

Nevertheless, the multiple regression approach does have several advantages. It is an efficient method of combining multiple predictors in an optimal manner and it minimizes errors in prediction. Moreover, different regression equations can be produced for different jobs, even if the same predictors are used for all jobs. So, if applicants are being selected for more than one job, they can be placed in the job for which their total score is the highest or they can be placed in the job where their total score is the farthest above the minimum score necessary for acceptable job performance. The multiple regression approach is probably the most efficient decision-making approach if the assumptions underlying the model are not violated.[29]

Multiple Cut-Off Model

In the multiple cut-off model, scores on all predictors are obtained for all applicants, just as in the multiple regression model. Using the data in Table 10.2, all applicants would write the cognitive ability and extroversion tests, all would be interviewed, and reference check information would be scored for all. However, in this model, applicants are rejected if their scores on any of the predictors fall below the cut-off scores. In our example, both Mr. A and Ms. D score above the cut-offs on all four predictors. Ms. B's score falls below the cut-off on the structured interview, and Mr. C's score falls below the cut-off on the extroversion scale. Ms. B and Mr. C would thus be rejected. Note that this is quite a different result from the multiple regression approach,

TABLE 10.3

Examples of Results for Sales Applicant Data in Table 10.2

Multiple Regression Model

APPLICANT		RANK
Mr. A	$Y = 36 + (0.5)30 + (0.7)27 + (0.6)11 = 76.5$	3
Ms. B	$Y = 32 + (0.5)37 + (0.7)16 + (0.6)10 = 67.7$	4
Mr. C	$Y = 44 + (0.5)22 + (0.7)24 + (0.6)13 = 79.6$	1
Ms. D	$Y = 37 + (0.5)27 + (0.7)28 + (0.6)14 = 78.5$	2

Multiple Cut-Off Model

APPLICANT	COGNITIVE ABILITY TEST (CUT-OFF = 30)	EXTROVERSION SCALE (CUT-OFF = 24)	STRUCTURED INTERVIEW (CUT-OFF = 18)	REFERENCE CHECK (CUT-OFF = 10)	DECISION
Mr. A	36 (above)	30 (above)	27 (above)	11 (above)	accept
Ms. B	32 (above)	37 (above)	16 (below)	10 (at cut-off)	reject
Mr. C	44 (above)	22 (below)	24 (above)	13 (above)	reject
Ms. D	37 (above)	27 (above)	28 (above)	14 (above)	accept

Multiple Hurdle Model

APPLICANT	STAGE 1 COGNITIVE ABILITY TEST (CUT-OFF = 30)	STAGE 2 EXTROVERSION SCALE (CUT-OFF = 24)	STAGE 3 STRUCTURED INTERVIEW (CUT-OFF = 18)	STAGE 4 REFERENCE CHECK (CUT-OFF = 10)	RESULT
Mr. A	36 (pass)	30 (pass)	27 (pass)	11 (pass)	pass
Ms. B	32 (pass)	37 (pass)	16 (fail)		fail
Mr. C	44 (pass)	22 (fail)			fail
Ms. D	37 (pass)	27 (pass)	28 (pass)	14 (pass)	pass

Combination Model

Only Mr. A and Ms. D meet all cut-off requirements (see results for Multiple Hurdle Model above). So, Mr. B and Ms. C are rejected.

APPLICANT		RANK
Mr. A	$Y = 36 + (0.5)30 + (0.7)27 + (0.6)11 = 76.5$	2
Ms. D	$Y = 37 + (0.5)27 + (0.7)28 + (0.6)14 = 78.5$	1

Profile Matching

APPLICANT		RANK
Mr. A	$D^2 = (36 - 35)^2 + (30 - 27)^2 + (27 - 23)^2 + (11 - 11)^2 = 26$	1
Ms. B	$D^2 = (32 - 35)^2 + (37 - 27)^2 + (16 - 23)^2 + (10 - 11)^2 = 159$	4
Mr. C	$D^2 = (44 - 35)^2 + (22 - 27)^2 + (24 - 23)^2 + (13 - 11)^2 = 111$	3
Ms. D	$D^2 = (37 - 35)^2 + (27 - 27)^2 + (28 - 23)^2 + (14 - 11)^2 = 38$	2

where Mr. C obtained the highest score and would have been selected (see Table 10.3).

The multiple cut-off model assumes that a minimum level is required on each of the attributes measured by the predictors for successful job performance (i.e., there is a nonlinear relationship among the predictors and job performance). The model also assumes that the predictors are not compensatory—it is not possible to compensate for a low score on one predictor with a high score on another predictor.

A disadvantage of the multiple cut-off model is that, just like the multiple regression approach, it requires that all applicants be assessed on all procedures. This requirement makes it expensive to administer. Another disadvantage is that the model identifies only those applicants who have minimum qualifications for the job. There is no way of distinguishing among those who have surpassed the minimum cut-offs. If 10 applicants have passed the cut-offs but the employer wants to select only five candidates, how is the employer to decide which ones to select?

In spite of its disadvantages, the multiple cut-off model does serve to narrow the pool of applicants to a smaller set of minimally qualified candidates and it is an easy model for managers to understand. It is probably most useful when minimum levels of certain physical abilities are required for job performance.[30] For example, some occupations such as law enforcement, firefighting, or heavy manufacturing have minimum specifications for eyesight, colour vision, or strength.

 ## Multiple Hurdle Model

In the multiple hurdle model, applicants must pass the minimum cut-off for each predictor, in turn, before being assessed on the next predictor. As soon as an applicant has failed to meet the cut-off on a given predictor, the applicant ceases to be a candidate for the job and is not assessed on any of the remaining predictors. In Chapter 2, Recruitment and Selection Today 2.1 (page 26) described the selection procedures used to hire Winnipeg police constables; this was an example of a multiple hurdle procedure. Applicants had to pass the current step in the process before moving on to the next; those applicants who failed a step are screened out of the process (see http://www .winnipeg.ca/police/HumanResources/selection_process.stm).

In our example in Table 10.2, all four applicants pass the cognitive ability test and go on to write the extroversion scale. Mr. C fails to meet the cut-off on the extroversion scale and is dropped from further consideration. Only Mr. A, Ms. B, and Ms. D go on to the structured interview, where Ms. B fails to meet the cut-off and is rejected. Reference checks are performed only for Mr. A and Ms. D, who both pass and become candidates for the job (see Table 10.3).

The result is identical to the one for the multiple cut-off model but the approach is less expensive because fewer applicants need to be assessed at each stage of the selection process. Both models make the same assumptions but differ in the procedure used for collecting predictor information. The multiple cut-off approach uses a nonsequential procedure, whereas the multiple hurdle procedure is sequential (i.e., applicants must pass each predictor cut-off, in sequence, before going on to the next predictor). Like the multiple cut-off approach, the multiple hurdle model narrows the pool of applicants to a smaller set of candidates who meet minimum qualifications and is also an easy model to understand.

The multiple hurdle approach has the disadvantage of being more time-consuming than the multiple regression or multiple cut-off approaches. Applicants need to be assessed and scored on each predictor before a decision can be made on whether to assess them on the next predictor. It also makes it difficult to estimate the validity of each procedure, particularly in later stages of the selection process. Relatively fewer applicants are being assessed on predictors toward the end of the sequence (e.g., interview and reference check, in our example), so restriction of range becomes a problem for estimating the validity of these predictors. One other disadvantage is that, like the multiple cut-off model, this model identifies only those applicants who have minimum qualifications for the job and does not distinguish among those who have surpassed all of the cut-offs.

Like the multiple cut-off approach, the multiple hurdle approach is most appropriate when minimum levels of particular KSAOs are necessary for job performance and cannot be compensated for by higher levels on other KSAOs. Moreover, the multiple hurdle approach is most useful when the applicant pool is large and some of the selection procedures are expensive.[31] In such circumstances, the less expensive procedures (e.g., tests) can be used as hurdles at the beginning in order to screen out inappropriate applicants and reduce the applicant pool. Thus, the more expensive procedures (e.g., interviews) are used on a smaller pool of select applicants. More information on the multiple hurdle approach, as well as other methods for integrating selection data, can be found at http://www.hr-guide.com/data/G366.htm.

Combination Model

In the combination model, all applicants are measured on all predictors and those falling below the cut-off on any of the predictors are rejected, just as in the multiple cut-off model. Then, multiple regression is used to calculate the total scores of those applicants who surpass the cut-off scores. The applicants are ranked by total score and selected on a top-down basis, as in the multiple regression method. The combination model is therefore a mixture of the multiple cut-off and multiple regression approaches.

If we apply this model to the data in Table 10.2, Ms. B and Mr. C would be rejected because they do not surpass all the cut-off scores. So far, this result is identical to the result for the multiple cut-off model. Now the regression equation is applied to the remaining applicants, Mr. A and Ms. D. Recall from our discussion of the multiple regression model that Mr. A's total score is 76.5 and Ms. D's total score is 78.5. Ms. D is therefore ranked first and Mr. A ranked second. If we were hiring only one candidate, Ms. D would be selected (see Table 10.3).

Like the multiple cut-off model, the combination model assumes that a minimum level of each of the KSAOs is required for effective job performance. A further assumption is that, once minimum levels have been reached, high scores on one predictor can compensate for low scores on another predictor. As might be expected, the combination model has the same advantages as the multiple cut-off model but has the additional advantage of providing a means of selecting from among those candidates who surpass all of the cut-off scores. However, the combination approach is just as expensive as the multiple cut-off approach because all applicants are assessed on all predictors.

Obviously, the combination model is useful as long as the assumptions underlying the approach hold. It is an appropriate model when selection instruments do not vary greatly in cost and is particularly useful when a considerable number of applicants tend to surpass all of the cut-offs. When more applicants than can be hired surpass the cut-off scores, the combination model facilitates selection among those applicants.

Profile Matching

In the profile matching model, current employees who are considered successful on the job are assessed on several predictors. Their average scores on each predictor are used to form an *ideal* profile of scores required for successful job performance. One should also try to obtain average predictor scores for current employees who are considered poor or marginal performers. Obtaining scores for poor or marginal employees is not always easy because such employees are often dismissed or leave of their own accord soon after being hired or, if a valid selection system is used, tend not to be hired in the first place. If it is possible to obtain scores for poor performers, their average predictor scores should be compared with the average predictor scores of good performers to ensure that the predictors differentiate between good and poor performers. Those predictors that do not differentiate should not be included in the ideal profile of scores.

Once an ideal profile of scores has been established, applicants' predictor scores can be compared with the ideal profile. Those applicants whose profiles are most similar to the ideal profile can then be selected. One of two methods can be used to determine the degree of similarity between applicant profiles and the ideal profile: the correlation method and the D^2 method. The correlation method involves correlating an applicant's scores on the predictors with the predictor scores of the ideal profile. The higher the correlation, the greater the similarity between the applicant's profile and the ideal profile.

The D^2 method involves calculating differences between an applicant's scores and ideal profile scores on each predictor, squaring the differences, and summing the squared differences to yield D^2. The larger D^2 is, the poorer the match is between the applicant's profile and the ideal profile. The D^2 method is preferred because it considers the magnitude of applicants' mean scores across the predictors, the degree to which applicant scores differ from the ideal scores, and the pattern or shape of applicant scores relative to the ideal profile. The correlation method considers only the pattern or shape of the scores.[32]

In our example in Table 10.2, let's assume the mean scores across the predictors represent the ideal profile. These can be correlated with the applicants' scores across the predictors to produce a correlation coefficient for each of the applicants. The resulting correlation coefficients are as follows: Mr. A ($r = 0.987$), Ms. B ($r = 0.825$), Mr. C ($r = 0.910$), and Ms. D ($r = 0.979$). Using the D^2 method requires the subtraction of the mean score for each predictor from each applicant's score on that predictor to obtain a difference. The resulting differences are squared and the squares summed across predictors for each applicant to obtain a D^2 score. Our applicants in Table 10.2 obtained the following D^2 scores: Mr. A ($D^2 = 26$), Ms. B ($D^2 = 159$), Mr. C ($D^2 = 111$), and Ms. D ($D^2 = 38$). Recall that the smaller the D^2 score is, the better the match. Thus, in this example, the rank orders for the correlation and the D^2 method are the same: (1) Mr. A, (2) Ms. D, (3) Mr. C, and (4) Ms. B (see Table 10.3).

Although the two methods produced identical rank orders in this example, the resulting rank orders are not always the same. Moreover, the correlation method often yields very high correlation coefficients, which barely differentiate applicants from each other. The D^2 method can also produce misleading results. An applicant whose scores substantially *exceed* the mean scores will have a high D^2 score and rank below an applicant whose scores fall close to the mean scores (whether slightly above or even below the means). Thus, this model is based on the assumption that scores that are higher than the ideal are as undesirable as scores that are lower than the ideal. In fact, the model assumes that there is one best profile, whereas there could be several profiles that predict success just as well.

As noted previously, the profile matching model cannot be implemented if the predictors do not differentiate between employees who are poor performers and those who are good performers. Moreover, restriction of range can be a problem because truly poor performers are often difficult to find (i.e., they are asked to leave or are not hired in the first place). Also, because the profiles of successful employees could change over time, ideal profiles need to be checked periodically.

Profile matching does have the advantage of permitting the ranking of applicants based on their similarities to the ideal profile. It is an appropriate method to use when there is clearly a best type of employee for the job and when it is known that poor employees tend to score higher as well as lower on the predictors than good employees (i.e., there is a curvilinear relationship between predictor scores and job performance). As these conditions rarely apply, multiple regression remains a more appropriate approach in virtually all circumstances.[33]

Making Selection Decisions

Regardless of which decision-making model is used, the eventual aim of the selection process is to decide which applicants to hire. The models described in the previous sections lend themselves to one of two basic approaches: *top-down*

selection and *banding*. Each method is based on particular assumptions and has certain advantages and disadvantages.

Top-Down Selection

Top-down selection involves ranking applicants on the basis of their total scores and selecting from the top down until the desired number of candidates has been selected. This approach is based on the assumption that individuals scoring higher on the predictors will be better performers on the job than individuals scoring lower on the predictors (i.e., there is a linear relationship between predictor scores and job performance). As long as this assumption is not violated, top-down selection is considered the best approach for maximizing organizational performance.[34] Only those who are likely to be the top performers are hired.

One difficulty with using top-down selection is that it can have an adverse impact on certain minority groups. For example, black applicants tend to have slightly lower average scores than white applicants on certain tests. Selecting from the top down could therefore result in disproportionately more white than black applicants being hired. *Race norming* or *within-group scoring* has been suggested as a method of preventing such adverse impact. Applicants can be ranked on their predictor scores within their relevant minority groups. For example, white applicants could be ranked on their predictor scores relative to other white applicants, and black applicants could be rank-ordered on their predictor scores relative to other black applicants. Then the top-ranking black candidate and the top-ranking white candidate could be selected, followed by the black and white candidates ranking second, and so on until the desired number of candidates is selected. Although top-down selection across all groups would result in the best-quality candidates being hired, on average, ranking within groups permits employers to achieve employment equity goals while still hiring high-quality applicants.[35]

Although the American Civil Rights Act of 1991 prohibits race norming (the adjustment of scores, or the use of different cut-off scores for different minority groups in the United States), there is no such legislation in Canada. Nevertheless, employment equity initiatives can be difficult to implement, as one Canadian fire department discovered. In Ontario, the Kitchener Fire Department attempted to increase minority representation in the department by reducing the cut-off score for women. Whereas male applicants needed a score of 85 to pass, the cut-off score for females was set at 70. The public outcry was so great that the department had to abandon this approach. Many individuals perceived this method as an example of reverse discrimination—discrimination against the white male applicants.

Banding

Banding

Grouping applicants based on ranges of scores.

An alternative approach to accomplishing employment equity is banding. **Banding** involves grouping applicants based on ranges of scores. In fact, cut-off scores are actually a form of banding where there are two bands (i.e., those above the cut-off score are in one band and those below the cut-off score are in another band). Sometimes bands are devised in a subjective manner through expert or managerial judgment. For example, applicants can be grouped into "Top Choice," "Very Good," "Acceptable," and "Unacceptable" candidates. However, the term *banding* usually refers to a grouping process that takes into account the concept of *standard error of measurement* (from classical test theory).

Essentially, the standard error of measurement (SEM) reflects the fact that almost any measurement contains an error as well as a true score component. For example, if you obtain a score of 83 percent on an exam, part of that score reflects your true knowledge of the material tested but part of it reflects other factors such as your level of alertness during testing, level of stress, distractions, and luck. Not sleeping well the night before the test, experiencing personal problems, or spending considerable time studying material that turns out to be a very small component of the exam can reduce your test score so that it under-represents your true knowledge. On the other hand, if you study only some of the course material but, as luck would have it, that very material constitutes most of the test, or if you obtain some advance knowledge of test content, or if you simply make some lucky guesses, your test score over-represents your true knowledge. Such errors of measurement are taken into account by the SEM, a statistic that reflects the reliability of an individual's score. In banding, SEM is used to calculate the *standard error of difference* (SED) using the formula SED = $\sqrt{2}$ SEM. SED is the standard deviation associated with the difference in two independent scores.[36]

Bands around a given score are calculated as 1.96 × the standard error of difference (i.e., ±1.96$\sqrt{2}$ SEM). Assuming that the error is randomly distributed, we would be correct 95 percent of the time in asserting that an individual's true score lies within the band defined by ±1.96 SED. If the SEM in our example above is 2.03, we can establish a band of 5.63 points (1.96 × $\sqrt{2}$ × 2.03) around your score of 83. That is, there is a 95 percent probability that your true score is somewhere between 77.37 and 88.63 (i.e., 83 ± 5.63).

Now, let's assume you have a friend who wrote the same exam and scored 80 percent. Before you belittle your friend's lower grade, consider the effects of measurement error. If we construct a band around your friend's score of 80, we discover that her true score is somewhere between 74.37 and 85.63 (with a 95 percent probability). It is therefore possible that your friend's true score is higher than yours! Because there is an overlap in the bands around your scores, we can assert that you and your friend's scores are not statistically different from each other. From a measurement perspective, both of you can be viewed as being at the same level of proficiency with respect to the course material. In fact, in this example, both of you would receive a grade of A−. Of course, SED is not used to differentiate grades of A− from B+, or B+ from B, but such grades are a form of banding.

Banding is applied to selection decisions by calculating a band from the top score downward. If the top score on a test is 96 and the 1.96 × SED is 5, then the band extends from 96 down to 91 (96 − 5). There is no need to extend the band above 96, as 96 is the top score. Any scores falling within the band from 91 to 96 are considered equal because the differences among them are not statistically significant. We are therefore free to select any applicants we wish within the band. In fact, as long as their scores fall within the same band, we could select minority applicants ahead of nonminority applicants in order to accomplish employment equity objectives.

Bands can be constructed in one of two ways: fixed or sliding. *Fixed bands* are calculated starting at the top score, as described above. All of the applicants within the band must be selected before a new band can be calculated. A new band is calculated starting from the highest score among those applicants who were not included in the first band. This process continues until the desired number of applicants has been hired.

Figure 10.3 illustrates both fixed and sliding bands with hypothetical data. The scores of 19 applicants have been ranked and some of them have been identified as minority applicants. If we assume that the 1.96 × SED is 5, then the first band ranges from 91 to 96 (as described above). Using the fixed band approach, we would select the applicants scoring 93 and 96 and then construct a second fixed band from 89 (the new highest score) down to 84.

FIGURE 10.3

Fixed versus Sliding Bands for the Selection of Minority Applicants

Fixed Bands	Applicant Scores and Minority Status		Sliding Bands						
Band 1	96		1						
	93	Minority							
Band 2	89			2					
	89	Minority							
	87								
	86				3				
	85								
	85	Minority							
	85	Minority							
	84					4			
Band 3	82	Minority					5		
	82								
	81							6	
	80								
	80								7
	79	Minority							
	78	Minority							
	78								
	77								

Recruitment and Selection in Canada

Within the second fixed band, we would select the minority applicants first and then the remainder of the applicants until all of the required applicants who scored within the band have been selected. If we required additional candidates, we would construct a third fixed band from 82 down to 77.

With *sliding bands*, not every applicant in the band needs to be selected before the next band is constructed. Once the top scorer in the band has been selected, a new band is constructed from the next highest score. In this manner, the band slides down each time the top scorer within the band is selected. Applying the sliding band approach to the data in Figure 10.3, we would first select the minority applicant scoring 93 and then the applicant scoring 96. Once we've selected the top scorer (96), we would construct the second sliding band from 84 to 89. Within this band we would select the three minority applicants and then the highest remaining scorer (89). Once the highest scorer has been selected, we would construct the third sliding band from 82 to 87 and so on.

The sliding band approach provides a larger number of applicants to select from than does the fixed band approach and therefore provides greater likelihood of selecting minority applicants. To illustrate, assume we want to select seven candidates from among the applicants represented in Figure 10.3. Using the traditional top-down approach, we would select as few as two and at the most three minority applicants. The fixed band approach would result in the selection of four minority candidates, whereas the sliding band approach would result in the selection of five minority applicants. Of course, the number of minority applicants selected in any particular situation depends on a number of factors such as the proportion of applicants who are minority group members, the distribution of minority scores, and selection ratios.[37] Nevertheless, on average, banding should contribute to the hiring of a greater proportion of minority applicants, provided minority status is used as the criterion of selection within bands.

The principle of banding has survived legal scrutiny in the United States. Nevertheless, U.S. courts have ruled that it is not permissible to use minority status as a primary criterion for selection within bands because they consider that a form of race norming (see http://www.siop.org/tip/backissues/tipjul97/Gutman.aspx).[38–40] Employers may select within bands on the basis of secondary criteria such as education, experience, or professional conduct. However, minority status may be used only as a tie-breaker among individuals with the same scores. Under such circumstances, banding is not likely to significantly reduce adverse impact.[41,42] In Canada, there is no legislation prohibiting preferential selection of minority applicants. As a result, banding could be a workable means of achieving employment equity objectives in a manner that might be more acceptable to nonminority applicants and employees than race norming, particularly if the principles behind banding are explained to them.[43]

Although banding appears to be permissible in Canada, there has been considerable debate concerning the logic and psychometric soundness of SED-based banding.[44–47] Critics have argued that there are logical inconsistencies in banding (e.g., in a band ranging from 84 to 96, 84 and 96 are considered equivalent while 83 and 84 are not equivalent), that the SED approach leads to very wide bands (i.e., the first band can include up to 38 percent of applicants), and that banding negatively affects the validity and utility of selection instruments.[48,49]

A particularly troubling criticism involves the fact that the SEM is derived from all the scores in an applicant group but is applied to the top scoring individual(s). Critics point out that the SEM is usually much smaller for top-scoring individuals than it is for individuals in the middle of the distribution. Therefore, if bands are calculated from the top score down, using the group-based SEM is inappropriate. However, if bands are calculated using the SEM of top-scoring individuals, the bands become so narrow that they are not likely to be of much help for employment equity purposes.[50,51]

Given these concerns about banding, many researchers recommend other approaches to help achieve employment equity objectives.[52-54] For example, greater effort can be made to recruit members of minority groups or to better prepare minority applicants for testing (e.g., through training on test-taking). Also, selection tools, such as structured interviews, personality scales, or biodata inventories, that have less adverse impact on minority applicants should be used for this purpose.

Practical Considerations

A variety of decision-making models and methods are available for making selection decisions. Which model or method is best in a given situation depends on a number of factors. The number of applicants expected, the amount of time available before selection decisions have to be made, and the costs associated with the selection instruments all have to be considered in making a choice. However, whenever they are feasible, linear models appear to outperform other approaches to decision making.

Many of the models discussed in this chapter assume large applicant pools or frequent and regular selection activity. Yet small businesses, which constitute a growing proportion of the Canadian economy, often hire small numbers of applicants on an infrequent basis. How can selection decisions in such small businesses be made more effectively?

Most of the rating procedures described in this chapter can be simplified to serve the needs of a small-business owner or manager.[55] The owner or manager can conduct an "armchair" job analysis by considering what tasks the employee would be expected to perform and how job performance would be assessed. As well, the owner or manager could consult the NOC or O*NET (see Chapter 4) for tasks related to similar jobs and the stated job requirements for those jobs.

Next the owner or manager should determine what behaviours related to these tasks could best be assessed in an interview and/or in simulations. Subjective weights could be attached, in advance, to each of the behaviours assessed, and the owner or manager should ensure that all applicants are evaluated systematically and fairly on the same criteria. Thus, although applicant information may be collected in a judgmental fashion or in a judgmental

Making the Selection Decision

1. Identify all of the sources of information about the applicant available to you (résumés, references, tests, interviews, etc.).
2. Use reliable, valid selection instruments whenever possible (e.g., structured interviews, reliable tests). Apply standardized criteria to the assessment of résumés, references, and other nonstandardized instruments so that they can be scored.
3. Determine which decision-making model you will use (taking into account the number of applicants, number and nature of predictors, cost factors, etc.).
4. If using the regression or combination model, collect and save data over a period of time for all predictors as well as job performance data for those applicants who are hired. When sufficient data have been collected, compute a regression equation, regressing job performance on the predictors. Determine the appropriate weights for each predictor.
5. If using the multiple cut-off or multiple hurdle model, determine appropriate cut-off scores for each predictor.
6. Combine data from different predictors statistically to yield an overall score.
7. Offer the position(s) to the candidate(s) with the highest overall score(s).

and statistical fashion, the information is combined statistically (i.e., trait rating or statistical composite) to yield a total score for each applicant. This total score can then be used to make the selection decisions.

Increasingly, small businesses are recognizing that they need to improve their human resources. Small-business associations have started to provide information on a vast array of topics, including the latest developments in human resources and how they can be adapted to a small-business environment. Many HR personnel now see the provision of HR services to small businesses on a consulting basis as a viable alternative to working in the HR department of a large firm.

Recruitment and Selection Notebook 10.1 provides guidelines that should help the HR professional in making a selection decision. Although the processes outlined here may seem intimidating, use of these procedures, with some practice, should lead to the selection of the best candidates who will, in turn, be more productive and effective.

Making Selection Decisions: Conclusions

Although valid selection instruments are necessary for making good selection decisions, they are not sufficient. Good selection procedures must be used as well. Selection systems can be made more effective if some of the following recommendations are followed:[56]

1. Use valid selection instruments.
2. Dissuade managers from making selection decisions based on gut feelings or intuition.

3. Encourage managers to keep track of their own selection "hits" and "misses."
4. Train managers to make systematic selection decisions using one of the approaches described in this chapter.
5. Periodically evaluate or audit selection decisions in order to identify areas needing improvement.

Utility Analysis

At this point, you may be asking yourself whether the cost of developing a valid selection system is worth all of the aggravation and actually produces any benefits. Utility analysis is a procedure that may allow you to come up with answers to this question. If you review the selection model presented in Chapter 2 (see Figure 2.1 on page 24), you will see that one of the last steps in developing and implementing a selection system is to conduct a utility analysis.

A selection system takes time and money to develop and implement, with no guarantee that it will be free of bias or that it will be perceived as fair. Furthermore, validity coefficients that have not been adjusted to account for range restriction, attenuation, and sampling error mostly fall in the range from 0.30 to 0.60, accounting for 36 percent or less of the variability in outcome measures. Decisions based on the selection system have important implications for both applicants and the company. HR managers must be able to demonstrate that a selection system produces benefits or advantages for the organization that exceed the cost of operating the selection system. HR managers must know if the cost of implementing a new selection system will produce benefits that exceed those produced by the old system. **Utility analysis** is a decision-making procedure that is used to evaluate selection systems by determining the net gains that accrue to the organization from their use.

Utility analysis

A decision-making procedure used to evaluate selection systems.

Taylor-Russell Utility Model

Taylor and Russell developed a procedure to demonstrate the practical effectiveness of selection systems.[57] The procedure relied not only on the validity coefficient but also on two other conditions that influenced the worth of the system: the selection ratio and base rate. The selection ratio is the proportion of job applicants selected for positions in the company. The **base rate** is the proportion of applicants who would be successful if all of the applicants had been hired.

Base rate

The proportion of applicants who would be successful if all of the applicants for a position had been hired.

The base rate can be estimated from available employment data. For the performance data presented in Table 2.2 (see page 33), a company considers any employee who obtains a score of 6 or above to be a success. Figure 10.4 shows that five of the employees are at or above this level of performance; therefore, the base rate is 0.50, meaning that half of the workers hired through the current selection system are satisfactory. What if only four positions were open when these people originally applied for work, and selection had been based on cognitive ability? The selection ratio would be 0.40 (i.e., 4 out of 10

FIGURE 10.4

Cognitive Ability and Job Performance

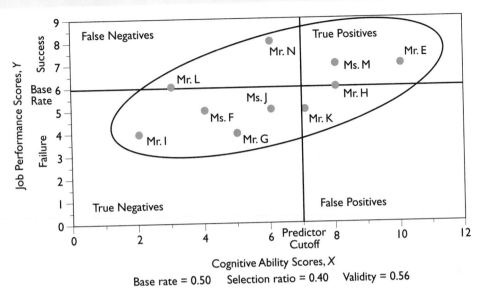

Base rate = 0.50   Selection ratio = 0.40   Validity = 0.56

applicants are hired). Using the regression line previously established for this group in Chapter 2, cognitive ability scores equal to or greater than 7 predict performance scores that are equal to or greater than 6. Selecting the four applicants with the highest cognitive ability scores would lead to the employment of Mr. E, Ms. M, Mr. H, and Mr. K.

The intersection of the lines representing the base rate and selection ratio divide the scatterplot into four quadrants, representing the four different outcomes of the selection process described in Table 10.1 (page 487). Mr. E, Ms. M, and Mr. H represent applicants who are true positives (those predicted to be successful and who turn out to be successful). Mr. K. is an example of a false positive (predicted to be successful but would fail if hired). Mr. L and Mr. N are false negatives (predicted to be unsatisfactory but would be successful if hired). Ms. F, Mr. G, Mr. I, and Ms. J. are true negatives (those predicted to be unsatisfactory and would be so if hired). Taylor and Russell defined the success rate as the proportion of applicants hired through the selection system who are judged satisfactory. Three of the four people hired fall into this category, producing a success rate of 0.75. If the success rate is greater than the base rate, as it is here (0.75 versus 0.50), the selection system is considered to be useful since it leads to a greater proportion of successful hires than would otherwise be the case.

The success rate is determined by the specific base rate, selection ratio, and validity that apply in any given situation. Changing the selection ratio (effectively moving the cut-off line to the left or right in Figure 10.4) or the base rate (moving the base rate line up or down) would alter the number of people falling into each quadrant and would have an impact on the success rate. A different validity, changing the orientation or shape of the oval, would

Success rate

The proportion of applicants hired through the selection system who are judged satisfactory.

also affect the success rate. Taylor and Russell produced a series of tables that estimate the success rate for any given combination of validity, base rate, and selection ratio.

Brogden-Cronbach-Gleser Utility Model

The Taylor-Russell model evaluates the worth of a selection system in terms of an increase in the percentage of successful workers who are hired through the system. It assumes that workers fall into only two categories: successful or unsuccessful. However, most workers vary in the degree of success they exhibit in doing their jobs. Those who are more successful are more valuable employees because they increase the overall productivity of an organization. Can this overall increase in productivity, or utility, be established for selection systems? If so, then comparison of the utility figures reflects the relative worth of different selection systems. Higher utility values indicate that the selection process has added well-qualified, more productive workers to the organization.

Over the years, several researchers have developed a formula for calculating the utility of a selection test or system:[58,59]

$$u = nr_{xy}sd_y\bar{z}_x - c$$

where
u = the increase in utility or productivity in one year from hiring n employees through the selection system;

n = the number of employees hired with the selection system;

r_{xy} = the criterion-related validity coefficient;

sd_y = the standard deviation of job performance;

$\bar{z}_x$ = the average, standardized predictor score of the employees hired through the selection system; and

c = the total costs involved in obtaining the new employees, including prorated costs associated with development of the system.

This formula shows that the benefit that accrues from each person hired through the selection system is related not only to the size of the validity coefficient but also to the standard deviation of job performance of the employees and the average predictor score of the hired employees. A large standard deviation suggests that there is great variability in job performance among the workers. For any validity coefficient, a selection system will be more valuable in this situation, since the outcome of the selection process may result in hiring someone who is either exceptionally good or exceptionally bad. If all of the workers, once hired, perform at relatively the same level, the selection system will have less impact on productivity.

The average standardized score on the predictor, which is related to the selection ratio, indicates the extent to which top candidates were hired. Average z scores closer to zero suggest that people of average ability were hired, while average z scores greater than 1.0 suggest that on average the best candidates were selected. The best candidates should add more value to the organization. The net benefit is obtained by subtracting the cost of developing and operating the selection system. Costs can be quite variable, ranging from a few dollars to administer a paper-and-pencil test to several million to develop a system to select jet pilots.

Different estimation procedures can be used to express sd_y as a dollar value, which then allows a dollar figure to be placed on the actual productivity gain,[60] although not everyone agrees on the appropriateness or need to do this.[61] The dollar-value gain in productivity can be considerable when a large number of employees are being hired, giving rise to questions about the credibility of such values to managers, and may lead to less support for valid selection procedures.[62] For example, Cronshaw showed that the use of a selection test battery by the Canadian Forces resulted in a gain of close to $3 million per year for the 417 people selected for a clerical/administrative trade group.[63] If this figure is multiplied by the number of years an average person remains in this job category, the utility increases to over $51 million.

It is not clear whether the large values or how the utility analysis is "sold" to management leads to the loss of credibility.[64] Managers with less understanding of utility information do seem to react more favourably when utility information is presented as an opportunity cost rather than as a monetary gain.[65] Nevertheless, the utility formula, either in dollar or nondollar form, allows a comparison of different selection systems in terms of the productivity they bring to an organization. If nothing else, the Brogden-Cronbach-Gleser model demonstrates the significant gains that may accrue through a scientifically based selection system. Holling presents a more detailed presentation of the Brogden-Cronbach-Gleser model online at http://www .dgps.de/fachgruppen/methoden/mpr-online/issue4/art2/holling.pdf.[66] Utility analysis information has a small, positive influence on managers' decisions to implement HR interventions. Utility analysis information is highly influential, compared to other types of data, in helping them to make a decision.[67]

An Illustration of Utility Analysis

In Canada, the federal government offers second-language training to selected employees. Suppose that 50 percent of all applicants for second-language training are accepted and that of those accepted, only 20 percent become fully bilingual. That is, the program has a selection ratio of 0.50 and a base rate of 0.20. In an attempt to improve the outcome, a second-language aptitude test (SLAT) is developed to select applicants for training. The validity of the SLAT turns out to be 0.35.

From the tables developed by Taylor and Russell, for these values of validity, selection ratio, and base rate, the success rate will be 0.36, or an increase of 16 percent in utility.[68] That is, for every 100 applicants, 18 out of the 50 candidates (0.36 × 50) selected for language training with the SLAT should succeed at becoming bilingual. This change represents an increase of

8 over the 10 (0.20 × 50) who would be successful under the old system. If some effort were put into improving the SLAT so that its validity reached 0.50, the success rate would increase to 0.44, representing a gain of 8 percent over the older version of the SLAT and a 24 percent increase over the base rate. Both versions of the SLAT could be considered successful in that they increased the number of successful candidates selected in every group of 50 applicants.

While the improved SLAT produced an 8 percent gain over the older version, it is difficult to say whether that increase offsets the costs of the improvement. The Taylor-Russell utility model does not provide an easy means of integrating costs and benefits. The Brogden-Cronbach-Gleser model allows such cost–benefit comparisons. We would need to assemble some additional information before we could use this model. First, we would need to calculate the cost of improving the SLAT validity; let's set this cost at $100 000. Next, we need to determine the average score, in standardized form, of all those selected with the improved SLAT; let $\bar{z}_x = 1.25$. The value of both of these variables would be obtained from data associated with the test development and with the testing. Finally, we need to estimate sd_y, the standard deviation of performance in dollars. Several estimation techniques can be used to do this and, according to managers, they produce estimates that are accurate enough for decision-making purposes.[69]

One procedure, which seems to produce conservative estimates, is simply to let this value equal 40 percent of the salary and benefits of the position. For our example, let salary and benefits total $40 000; we would then use $16 000 as an estimate of sd_y. The utility of selecting 50 employees with the improved SLAT would be:

$$U_{New} = (50)[(0.50)(1.25)(\$16\ 000)] - \$100\ 000 = \$500\ 000 - \$100\ 000 = \$400\ 000$$

However, this figure assumes that the utility of the old selection system is zero. We know that this is not the case, as the validity of the old SLAT was 0.35. If we assume that the old SLAT had long since paid for itself and that the only costs were the cost of purchasing and administering the test, let's say $10 per selected applicant, then its utility was:

$$U_{Old} = (50)[(0.35)(1.25)(\$16\ 000)] - \$500 = \$350\ 000 - \$500 = \$349\ 500$$

The net gain would be the difference between the two utility values:

$$U_{Net} = U_{New} - U_{Old} = \$400\ 000 - \$349\ 500 = \$50\ 500$$

Of course, if we had decided to amortize the cost of development over the life span of the test, the utility would appear to be much greater. For example, having "paid" the development costs up front, the next 50 candidates selected (and every other group of 50 selected applicants), would return a net benefit of $150 000, compared with using the old SLAT, assuming the same administration costs of $10 per selected applicant. Over time, the return on the investment to improve the test could be quite substantial. The net utility represents the benefits associated with the improved productivity that is obtained from

Recruitment and Selection in Canada

hiring better-qualified applicants through use of the selection system, minus the costs of that system.

Evaluating testing programs through utility analysis is more complicated than the simple illustrations presented here. Often, many assumptions have to be made about the appropriate way to calculate costs and to estimate the other parameters needed by the models. However, utility analysis does provide the kind of information that managers want when making human resources decisions,[70] providing a means of comparing different selection systems in addition to yielding quite useful information for the human resources specialist. Utility models can demonstrate, in quite convincing fashion, whether the implementation of personnel testing programs will produce productivity gains for the organization.

The Utility of Best Practices in Staffing

Organizations are undergoing change at an accelerating rate. They must adapt to unanticipated innovations in technology, global competition, changing labour force demographics, and increasing government regulation and societal pressures for conformity to ethical, environmental, and human rights standards if they are to survive. Best practices in recruitment and selection are part of an organization's survival tools. We conclude by presenting some of the major challenges that confront HR specialists with respect to recruitment and staffing.[71] We believe that the procedures we have outlined in this text address the need for reliable, valid, and legally defensible staffing procedures that provide a return on their investment and enhance a firm's productivity.

RPC 10.3

RPC 10.4

Global Competition

Foreign trade has always been vital to the Canadian economy, dating as far back as the trading of beaver pelts. As more than half of what is now produced in Canada is exported, we are extremely vulnerable to foreign market conditions. What has changed is the *level of competition*, as new players enter international markets and trade barriers between countries are softened. In the retail sector, large U.S.-owned discount chains such as Costco and Wal-Mart are serious threats to the survival of smaller, Canadian-owned retailers, who must scramble to increase efficiencies and lower their operating costs. Canadian businesses must continually work on improving their competitiveness in providing goods and services domestically and internationally. Within the context of higher costs for human resources in Canada, companies and organizations must find ways to become more efficient. One of the important ways is to find the best, most productive employees through the use of best practices in staffing.

Rapid Advances in Technology

Technology is affecting every aspect of our lives, from the way we do our banking to the way we study and pursue our education. Employers now expect new hires to be computer-literate. Employers are also using technology to a greater extent than ever before to recruit and select the best employees, including use of the Internet.

Changing Work Force Demographics

The demographic makeup of the Canadian labour force is also undergoing significant transformations. The work force is older, more gender-balanced, more culturally diverse, and more highly educated than at any other time in Canadian history. Today, women and nonwhites make up 70 to 80 percent of new entrants into the Canadian labour force. Ethnic groups in Canada possess expertise, skills, knowledge of foreign cultures and business practices, and natural trade links with overseas markets that are of value to employers in today's global economy.

Special challenges, but tremendous opportunities, emerge from having a workplace that is increasingly diverse in functional expertise, gender, and culture. Additionally, there is a growing population of people who have physical or mental challenges. Employers cannot discriminate against existing or potential employees with respect to characteristics that are not job-related. They must hire on the basis of an applicant possessing the knowledge, skills, and abilities or other characteristics that are necessary to perform a job. Best practices in staffing will not only find the best employees but will also help to establish recruitment and selection systems that are legally defensible.

The Economic Context

The state of the economy has a profound effect on staffing. Economic booms bring with them skilled labour shortages, so recruitment and retention are taking on strategic importance and are given high priority. Economic slowdowns or recessions generally lead to cutbacks in jobs or hiring freezes. In a slowdown, a glut of qualified people are looking for jobs, so recruitment may be easier for companies that are hiring; however, there are also more unqualified applications to review. The number of people in the applicant pool has a major impact on the quality of those people who are selected for employment. If there are critical shortages of skilled labour or professionals, more emphasis must be placed on recruitment, and companies may become less selective. On the other hand, employers can take advantage of an oversupply of labour by placing less emphasis on recruitment and becoming more selective in hiring people.

Type of Organization

The public sector, both federal and provincial, tends to have more formalized recruitment and selection systems. Governments are accountable to their electorates for managing public employees and, with the exception of political appointees, have established fair recruitment and selection procedures that in most cases follow accepted professional standards. Public services tend to be highly unionized and to follow negotiated processes for recruitment and selection.

In the private sector, recruitment and selection procedures may vary by the type and size of the business or industry. A large segment of the Canadian economy is based on small or family-run enterprises. The selection procedures in these types of business may be more informal, as the owners may not have the resources to implement sophisticated selection systems. This is one reason why we use more examples from the public sector in this book. In general, larger organizations, public or private, are more likely to use formal recruitment and selection procedures. The challenge for HR is to increase the use of best practices regardless of sector or the size of an organization.

Organizational Restructuring

At the same time that technology is reducing the need for labour, organizations must cope with a large segment of their work force that is approaching retirement. To cope with these changes, employers have implemented layoffs and early-retirement incentive packages, and have restructured or downsized their enterprises. Most notably, the traditional organizational structure of a pyramid, with a broad base of employees at entry-level positions and fewer employees at each of several higher levels, is being flattened. In the coming years, as aging "boomers" retire, will there be an adequate labour supply to replace them? In a seller's market, more emphasis will have to be placed on recruiting, as more organizations compete to hire fewer qualified candidates. In times of recession or slowdowns when there are many people looking for jobs, organizations will have even more difficulty in choosing the right person from among all that are available. Best practices in recruiting and selection will be essential in finding the right employees for an organization.

Redefining Jobs

In today's information era, workers are required to apply a wider range of skills to an ever-changing series of tasks. Individuals just entering the work force may face at least three to four career changes in their lifetime. Employers will expect workers to possess the skills and knowledge of two or three traditional employees. On the factory floor, jobs are moving targets, as they change rapidly. Workers themselves may be asked to move or rotate among positions; to do so they will need to have or be able to acquire multiple generic skills. This poses special challenges when trying to match people to jobs. Does it make sense to select people on the basis of very specific skills and abilities required by one job? Should employers redefine recruitment and selection in terms of finding people with broader skills or competencies that are of value to the organization and cut across many jobs? Using the procedures outlined in this text will help to answer these questions.

Summary

Employers face a difficult task in trying to combine and make sense of complex applicant information in order to make selection decisions. They are vulnerable to numerous biases and errors and they often oversimplify information because their information processing abilities are overloaded. Unfortunately, many employers prefer to rely on their gut instincts rather than on more objective sources of information.

In many organizations, selection decisions are made by groups rather than by individuals. There is some evidence that groups can make better decisions and the use of selection panels has been supported in Canadian human rights tribunals.

Although several approaches to making selection decisions can be used, methods that involve combining applicant information in a statistical manner are generally superior to other methods in reducing errors and predicting job performance.

Various decision-making models, such as multiple regression, multiple cut-off, multiple hurdle, combination, and profile matching, can help in making effective selection decisions when used under appropriate conditions. The multiple regression approach is probably the most efficient decision-making model if the assumptions underlying the model are not violated. Generally, the models produce a total score, which can be used to rank candidates and select them from the top down until the desired number of candidates have been selected. However, banding is suggested as an alternative to conventional top-down selection because banding satisfies employment equity objectives, while still enabling the hiring of top-quality applicants. Finally, utility analysis is presented as a means to evaluate the effectiveness of selection systems.

Today's organizations are undergoing rapid change and, to survive, must adapt to unanticipated innovations in technology, global competition, changing labour force demographics, and increasing government regulation and societal pressures for conformity to ethical, environmental, and human rights standards. Best practices in recruitment and selection are part of an organization's survival tools. The procedures we have outlined in this text address the need for reliable, valid, and legally defensible staffing procedures that provide a return on their investment and enhance a firm's productivity.

Key Terms

banding, p. 502

base rate, p. 508

cut-off score, p. 492

false negative error, p. 485

false positive error, p. 485

incremental validity, p. 492

judgmental composite, p. 487

profile interpretation, p. 487

pure judgment approach, p. 485

pure statistical approach, p. 487

selection ratio, p. 494

statistical composite, p. 487

success rate, p. 509

trait rating approach, p. 487

utility analysis, p. 508

Web Links

Information on setting cut-off scores for tests, as developed by the Public Service Commission of Canada, is available on the commission's Personnel

Psychology Centre website: Go to **http://www.psc-cfp.gc.ca/ppc-cpp/index-eng.htm**, enter "cut-off scores" in the Search window, and select "Setting Cut-Off Scores: A Matter of Judgment."

An example of a multiple hurdle approach can be found at the Winnipeg Police Service website at **http://www.winnipeg.ca/police/HumanResources/selection_process.stm**.

For more information on the multiple hurdle approach, as well as other methods for integrating selection data, go to **http://www.hr-guide.com/data/G366.htm**.

The status of banding is discussed at **http://www.siop.org/tip/backissues/tipjul97/Gutman.aspx**.

A more detailed presentation of the Brogden-Cronbach-Gleser model is available online at **http://www.dgps.de/fachgruppen/methoden/mpr-online/issue4/art2/holling.pdf**.

Required Professional Capabilities (RPCs)

RPC 10.1 Assesses the effectiveness of people and talent management plans.
- Training and development program evaluation methods
- Rationale and process of program evaluation
- Research methods and designs (including measurement of HR)
- Measurement and assessment tools and techniques (and their limitations)
- Statistical analyses and evaluation
- HR functions and activities
- Needs analysis
- The organization's strategic business plan and the goals of the business unit
- Industry best practices

RPC 10.2 Provides the information necessary for organization to effectively manage its people practices.
- Career and succession planning and management
- Nature of internal working procedures and information flows
- Contract administration
- HR planning techniques
- Trends in human resources information management
- HRMS concepts and techniques
- Procedures for collection, manipulation, and analysis of information
- The organization's strategic business plan and the goals of the business unit
- Use of business software
- Statistical analyses and evaluation
- HRMS project planning and management

RPC 10.3 **Keeps current with emerging HR trends.**
- HR issues, trends, developments, and best practices
- Business issues, trends, and developments
- The importance/benefits of HR Planning
- Trends in all functional areas of HR practice
- Trends in labour force characteristics (e.g., labour force growth, employment trends and rates, unemployment, participation rates, occupational distribution of the workforce, and compensation)
- Trends and issues affecting the particular industry
- Global trends and issues in business/industry
- Organizational behaviour, leadership, and management practices in an international context

RPC 10.4 **Gathers, analyzes, and reports relevant business and industry information (including global trends) to influence the development of strategic business HR plans.**
- Sources of business/industry information
- Global trends in business/industry
- Analytical techniques/tools
- Data validation techniques/tools
- Procedures for collection, manipulation, and analysis of information
- Organizational behaviour, leadership, and management practices in an international context
- Strategic HR management

Discussion Questions

1. What are the common decision-making errors made in employee selection? Can these be eliminated? If so, how? If not, can they be reduced? If so, how?
2. What is the difference between judgmental and statistical approaches to the collection and combination of applicant information?
3. What are the advantages and disadvantages of the following decision-making models?

   a. Regression models
   b. Multiple hurdle
   c. Multiple cut-off
   d. Profile matching

4. Are there benefits in group decision making? If so, what are they?
5. Discuss the differences among cut-off scores, banding, and top-down selection. Is any one of these more advantageous to use than the others? If so, under what circumstances?
6. Discuss how utility analysis can be used to evaluate personnel selection systems.
7. Discuss the benefits of using best practices in recruitment and selection.

Using the Internet

1. Table 10.2 (page 495) presented hypothetical data for four predictors used to hire sales representatives. For the purpose of the illustration, arbitrary cut-offs were set for each of the predictors. For this exercise, we want you to develop actual cut-off scores that you might assign to each of the four measures. Retain the maximum possible score stated in Table 10.2 for each measure.

   First, obtain the requirements for a sales representative by going to the National Occupational Classification or other job analysis procedure discussed in Chapter 4. Next, follow the Public Service of Canada guidelines to develop cut-off scores for each measure. The cognitive ability and extroversion measures are generic; however, you may want to use the resources identified in Chapter 8 (e.g., Buros's *Mental Measurements Yearbook*) to select specific cognitive ability and personality measures. Use the information from these specific tests, such as any normative data that is provided, to help set your cut-offs.

   a. What are your new cut-offs for each of the tests?
   b. Using your new cut-offs, reanalyze the data in Table 10.2, following the procedures in Table 10.3 (page 497), for each of the decision-making models. Compare your rank-ordering of the four candidates under each model to that obtained from using the Table 10.2 cut-offs. Are there differences in who would be hired?
   c. Discuss the importance of setting cut-offs with respect to hiring decisions.

Exercises

1. Assume that you occasionally hire cashiers for a small store. You generally do not hire more than two or three at a time. You have five applicants for two positions. You have obtained information from all of the applicants on a set of five predictors, as follows:

Predictor Scores

APPLICANT	COGNITIVE TEST	CONSCIENTIOUS-NESS SCALE	BIODATA FORM	STRUCTURED INTERVIEW	REFERENCE CHECK
Ms. Z	47	26	18	47	6
Mr. Y	36	36	15	45	8
Ms. W	46	36	16	32	9
Ms. V	44	30	10	36	7
Mr. U	39	38	14	41	10
Maximum Possible Scores	50	40	20	50	10

continued

Continued from previous page

Predictor Scores

Applicant	Cognitive Test	Conscientious- ness Scale	Biodata Form	Structured Interview	Reference Check
Regression weights	1.4	0.4	0.5	0.9	0.4
Cut-off scores	36	27	12	35	7
Mean scores	40	35	16	39	8

a. Using the information presented in the table, determine which of the applicants would be selected and, where appropriate, what their rank would be under each of the following decision-making models:

  i.   Multiple regression
  ii. Multiple cut-off
  iii. Combination
  iv. Profile matching (D^2 only)

b. Which of the selection models discussed do you believe is best suited to this situation? Why?

2. If the regression weights were 1.2, 0.7, 0.3, 1.5, and 0.5 for the five measures, respectively, who would now be selected (the cut-off scores remain unchanged from the original)? What would be the rank-order under each of the four decision-making models?

3. If the cut-offs were 30, 30, 15, 40, and 6, respectively, for the five measures, who would now be selected (the regression weights remain unchanged from the originals)? What would be the rank-order under each of the four decision-making models?

4. Discuss the impact that both cut-off scores and regression weights may have on selection decisions.

5. You are a human resources specialist trying to improve selection procedures in your organization. Under the current system, application forms are screened by relevant department managers to determine who should be interviewed. References are also collected. The managers do their own interviewing using individual, unstructured interviews and base their selection decisions almost exclusively on these interviews. They tend to have a lot of confidence in their gut feelings about candidates and believe they've been doing a pretty good job of selecting the right applicants.

a. How would you go about trying to convince them that they should adopt a more structured, objective (i.e., statistical) decision-making system?

b. What objections to your suggestion do you anticipate would be raised by the managers?

c. How would you address these objections?

Case

Dofasco (http://www.dofasco.ca) is one of Canada's largest and most successful steel producers. Headquartered in Hamilton, Ontario, since 1912, the company has wholly owned subsidiaries in Ohio and Mexico, and has also been engaged in strategic joint ventures with various steel mills and mines in Ontario, Quebec, and the United States. Some 7,400 employees are engaged in these operations. Dofasco was recognized as one of Canada's "Top 100 Employers" in 2007 for the fourth consecutive year by *Maclean's* magazine in its annual ranking of Canadian employers.

Steel making has become an increasingly sophisticated activity and, as a result, the levels of skills required have been rising. Not surprisingly, training and development have become vital elements of Dofasco's success. Dofasco has always prided itself on its relationship with employees. In fact, the company slogan, "Our product is steel, our strength is people," reflects Dofasco's commitment to developing and motivating its work force. One of the ways Dofasco motivates employees is through its promote-from-within policy. As a result, when Dofasco hires employees, the company not only is concerned with their ability to do entry-level jobs but is also looking for evidence of promotion potential (e.g., leadership potential) and organizational fit.

Given Dofasco's commitment to employee relations and development, the company has one of the lowest turnover rates in the manufacturing sector. In fact, the extremely low turnover rate has created a bit of a problem for Dofasco. Over the next 10 years, about one-half of Dofasco's work force (including management) will be retiring. The challenge for Dofasco in the meantime will be to fill the many vacated entry-level positions with employees who have the potential to quickly acquire the skills necessary to promote them into various technical and leadership positions that will also need to be filled. In particular, Dofasco will need new team leaders for work teams and project teams, new supervisors, and new managers.

Historically such leaders at Dofasco have been drawn from employee ranks and have been promoted on the basis of job performance and demonstration of leadership attributes such as initiative, decision-making ability, ability to communicate, ability to influence and motivate others, and conscientiousness. These attributes became apparent over a period of time and were developed through training, special assignments, and other developmental opportunities. However, as Dofasco faces the need to fill leadership positions quickly, the amount of time that employees spend in entry-level positions will likely be greatly reduced and many will find themselves in leadership positions shortly after joining the company. Thus, Dofasco will need to identify leadership potential at the selection stage and fast-track individuals identified as potential leaders through special training and developmental initiatives. An alternative would be to abandon the promote-from-within policy and hire experienced leaders, supervisors, and managers from outside the organization.

Discussion Questions

Pretend you have been put in charge of staffing at Dofasco. Your job is to plan and execute a selection strategy for Dofasco over the next 10 years. Assume that the number of retirements will be fairly evenly distributed over the next 10 years.

1. What steps can you take now, in preparation for the large-scale selection task that lies ahead? What information will you need to collect? How can this information be used? What strategy will you put in place to deal with the large number of employees who will need to be hired each year? Will you maintain a promote-from-within policy? If so, how? If not, what consequences do you anticipate and how will you deal with them?

2. What selection tools might be appropriate to assess the potential of applicants to acquire knowledge and skills quickly? How might you assess leadership potential? How about organizational fit? Justify your choices.

3. Design a selection system for entry-level employees, specifying the various selection tools you will use (e.g., structured interviews, personality tests, reference checks, etc.), the order in which you will apply them, and the weight you will assign to each of the selection tools. What decision-making model will you use?

   How will you determine whether your selection system is working (i.e., the best possible employees are being selected)? If you find that your system is not working as well as it should, how might you go about improving it? How will you determine whether your selection system has adverse impact on minority applicants? If you discover that your system does adversely affect minorities, what steps will you take to address the problem? Provide a detailed rationale for your design.

Endnotes

1. Simon, H.A. 1957. *Administrative Behavior.* 2nd ed. New York: Free Press.
2. Bazerman, M.H. 1986. *Judgment in Managerial Decision Making.* New York: Wiley.
3. Janis, I.L., and L. Mann. 1977. *Decision Making: A Psychological Analysis of Conflict, Choice, and Commitment.* New York: Free Press.
4. Huber, V.L, M.A. Neale, and G.B. Northcraft. 1987. "Decision Bias and Personnel Selection Strategies." *Organizational Behavior and Human Decision Processes* 40: 136–47.
5. Simon, H.A. 1957.
6. Ross, M., and J.H. Ellard. 1986. "On Winnowing: The Impact of Scarcity on Allocators' Evaluations of Candidates for a Resource." *Journal of Experimental Social Psychology* 22: 374–88.
7. Chuang, A. 2001. *The Perceived Importance of Person–Job Fit and Person–Organization Fit between and within Interview Stages.* Unpublished doctoral dissertation, University of Minnesota, Minneapolis, MN. UMI No. 3010543.
8. Meehl, P.E. 1954. *Clinical versus Statistical Prediction: A Theoretical Analysis and a Review of the Evidence.* Minneapolis, MN: University of Minnesota Press.